MW01702029

MATH

Smith

CENGAGE Learning™

Australia • Brazil • Japan • Korea • Mexico • Singapore • Spain • United Kingdom • United States

CENGAGE Learning

MATH

Executive Editors:
Maureen Staudt
Michael Stranz

Senior Project Development Manager:
Linda deStefano

Marketing Specialist:
Courtney Sheldon

Senior Production/Manufacturing Manager:
Donna M. Brown

PreMedia Manager:
Joel Brennecke

Sr. Rights Acquisition Account Manager:
Todd Osborne

Cover Image:
Getty Images*

*Unless otherwise noted, all cover images used by Custom Solutions, a part of Cengage Learning, have been supplied courtesy of Getty Images with the exception of the Earthview cover image, which has been supplied by the National Aeronautics and Space Administration (NASA).

MATH for Liberal Arts, 1st Edition
Karl Smith

For product information and technology assistance, contact us at
Cengage Learning Customer & Sales Support, 1-800-354-9706
For permission to use material from this text or product,
submit all requests online at **cengage.com/permissions**
Further permissions questions can be emailed to
permissionrequest@cengage.com

This book contains select works from existing Cengage Learning resources and was produced by Cengage Learning Custom Solutions for collegiate use. As such, those adopting and/or contributing to this work are responsible for editorial content accuracy, continuity and completeness.

Compilation © 2011 Cengage Learning
ISBN-13: 978-1-133-22754-0

ISBN-10: 1-133-22754-6

Cengage Learning
5191 Natorp Boulevard
Mason, Ohio 45040
USA
Cengage Learning is a leading provider of customized learning solutions with office locations around the globe, including Singapore, the United Kingdom, Australia, Mexico, Brazil, and Japan. Locate your local office at:
international.cengage.com/region.

Cengage Learning products are represented in Canada by Nelson Education, Ltd.
For your lifelong learning solutions, visit **www.cengage.com/custom.**
Visit our corporate website at **www.cengage.com.**

Printed in the United States of America

Brief Contents

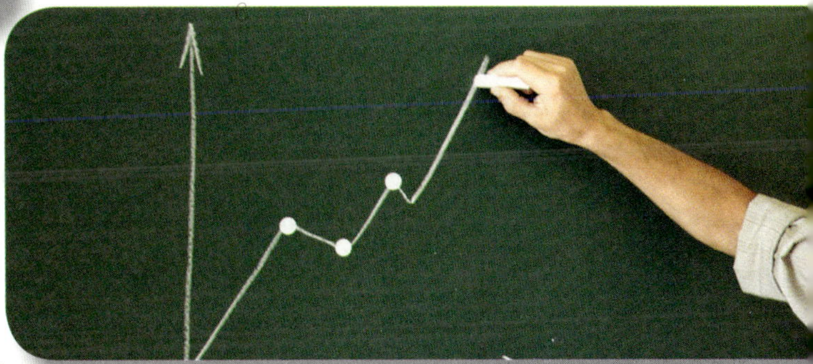

Remember

The portable cards at the back of the book are designed to help you with the course!

Contents

WHY MATH?

There are many reasons for reading a book, but the best reason is because you want to read it. Although you probably are reading this book because you were required to do so by your instructor, it is my hope that in a short while you will be reading this book because you *want* to read it. I wrote this book for people who think they can't work math problems, or people who think they are never going to use math. Take it as a challenge, but I'm guessing that by the time you finish this course you will be able to solve problems—not just the classroom-type problems, but those problems you encounter outside the classroom. You will more easily be able to make intelligent decisions about money, credit cards, purchases, as well as voting. You will be able to think critically about what you see and hear in your everyday life. As you begin your trip through this book I wish you BON VOYAGE!

K J Smith

math

Contents

MULTI-LINE PLAYBACK
ON/C
2ndF
DEL
MATH
sin
cos
tan
log
ln
CNST
CONV
Exp
RCL
STO
M+
ENT

Contents

Contents

The Nature of Numeration Systems

1.1 Math Anxiety

THERE ARE MANY REASONS FOR READING A BOOK, BUT THE BEST REASON IS BECAUSE YOU WANT TO READ IT. ALTHOUGH YOU ARE PROBABLY READING THIS FIRST PAGE BECAUSE YOU WERE REQUESTED TO DO SO BY YOUR INSTRUCTOR, IT IS MY HOPE THAT IN A SHORT WHILE YOU WILL BE READING THIS BOOK BECAUSE YOU WANT TO READ IT.

topics

Do you think that you are reasonably successful in other subjects but are unable to do math? Do you make career choices based on avoidance of mathematics courses? If so, you have *math anxiety*. If you

5 TOOLS FOR EXPRESSING NUMERALS

1. Order of operations agreement
2. Scientific notation
3. Expanded notation
4. Decimal notation
5. Base conversions

reexamine your negative feelings toward mathematics, you can overcome them. In this book, I'll constantly try to help you overcome these feelings.

This book was written for people who are math-avoiders, people who think they can't work math problems, and people who think they are never going to use math. Do you see yourself making any of these statements shown in Figure 1.1?

Sheila Tobias, an educator, feminist, and founder of an organization called Overcoming Math Anxiety, has become one of our nation's leading spokespersons on math anxiety. She is not a mathematician,

Figure 1.1

and in fact she describes herself as a math-avoider. She has written a book titled *Overcoming Math Anxiety* (New York: W. W. Norton & Company, 1978; available in paperback). I recommend this book to anyone who has ever said "I'm no good at numbers." In this book, she describes a situation that characterizes anxiety (p. 45):

> *Paranoia comes quickly on the heels of the anxiety attack. "Everyone knows," the victim believes, "that I don't understand this. The teacher knows. Friends know. I'd better not make it worse by asking questions. Then everyone will find out how dumb I really am." This paranoid reaction is particularly disabling because fear of exposure keeps us from constructive action. We feel guilty and ashamed, not only because our minds seem to have deserted us but because we believe that our failure to comprehend this one new idea is proof that we have been "faking math" for years.*

The reaction described in this paragraph sets up a vicious cycle. The more we avoid math, the less able we feel; and the less able we feel, the more we avoid it. The cycle can also work in the other direction. What do you like to do? Chances are, if you like it, you do it. The more you do something, the better you become at it. In fact, you've probably thought, "I like to do it, but I don't get to do it as often as I'd like to." This is the normal reaction toward something you like to do. In this book, I attempt to break the negative cycle concerning math and replace it with a positive cycle. However, I will need your help and willingness to try.

The central theme in this book is problem solving. Through problem solving, I'll try to dispel your feelings of panic. Once you find that you are capable of doing mathematics, we'll look at some of its foundations and uses. There are no prerequisites for this book; and as we progress through the book, I'll include a review of the math you never quite learned in school—from fractions, decimals, percents, and metrics to algebra and geometry. I hope to answer the questions that, perhaps, you were embarrassed to ask.

Math Anxiety Bill of Rights

By Sandra L. Davis

1. **I have the right to learn at my own pace and not feel put down or stupid if I'm slower than someone else.**
2. **I have the right to ask whatever questions I have.**
3. **I have the right to need extra help.**
4. **I have the right to ask a teacher or TA for help.**
5. **I have the right to say I don't understand.**
6. **I have the right not to understand.**
7. **I have the right to feel good about myself regardless of my abilities in math.**
8. **I have the right not to base my self-worth on my math skills.**
9. **I have the right to view myself as capable of learning math.**
10. **I have the right to evaluate my math instructors and how they teach.**
11. **I have the right to relax.**
12. **I have the right to be treated as a competent adult.**
13. **I have the right to dislike math.**
14. **I have the right to define success in my own terms.**

Sheila Tobias, *Overcoming Math Anxiety* (W.W. Norton & Co., 1995), 236–237.

Hints for Success

Mathematics is different from other subjects. One topic builds on another, and you need to make sure that you understand *each* topic before progressing to the next one.

You must make a commitment to attend each class. Obviously, unforeseen circumstances can come up, but you must plan to attend class regularly. Pay attention to what your teacher says and does, and take notes. If you must miss class, write an outline of the text corresponding to the missed material, including working out each text example on your notebook paper.

You must make a commitment to daily work. Do not expect to save up and do your mathematics work once or twice a week. It will take a daily commitment on your part, and you will find mathematics difficult if you try to "get it done" in spurts. You could not expect to become proficient in tennis, soccer, or playing the piano by practicing once a week, and the same is true of mathematics. Try to schedule a regular time to study mathematics each day.

You must read the text carefully. Many students expect to get through a mathematics course by beginning with the homework problems, then reading some examples, and reading the text only as a desperate attempt to find an answer. This procedure is backward; do your homework only *after* reading the text.

You must ask questions. Part of learning mathematics involves frustration. Don't put off asking questions when you don't understand something, or if you feel an anxiety attack coming. STOP and put this book aside for a while. Talk to your instructor, or call me. My telephone number is

(707) 829-0606.

I care about your progress with the course, and I'd like to hear your reactions to this book. I can be reached by e-mail at

smithkjs@mathnature.com.

Direct Your Focus

Read the following story. No questions are asked, but try to imagine yourself sitting in a living room with several others who share your feelings about math. Your job is to read the story and make up a problem you know how to solve from any part of the story. You should have a pencil and paper, and you can have as much time as you want; nobody will look at what you are doing, but I want you to keep track of your feelings as you read the story and follow the directions.

> *On the way to the market, which is 12 miles from home, I stopped at the drugstore to pick up a get-well card. I selected a series of cards with puzzles on them. The first one said, "A bottle and a cork cost $1.10 and the bottle is a dollar more than the cork. How much is the bottle and how much is the cork?" I thought that would be a good card for Joe, so I purchased it for $1.75, along with a six-pack of cola for $2.79. The total bill was $4.81, which included 6% sales tax. My next stop was the market, which was exactly 3.4 miles from the drugstore. I bought $15.65 worth of groceries and paid with a $20 bill. I deposited the change in a charity bank on the counter and left the store. On the way home I bought 8.5 gallons of gas for $22.10. Because I had gone 238 miles since my last fill-up, I was happy with the mileage on my new car. I returned home and made myself a ham and cheese sandwich.*

Have you spent enough time on the story? Take time to reread it (spend at least 10 minutes with this exercise). Now, write down a math question, based on this story, that you could answer without difficulty. Can you summarize your feelings? If my experiences in doing this exercise with my students apply to you, I would guess that you encountered some difficulty, some discomfort, perhaps despair or anger, or even indifference. Most students tend to focus on the more difficult questions (perhaps a miles-per-gallon problem) instead of following the directions to formulate a problem that will give them no difficulty.

How about the question: What is the round-trip distance from home to market and back?

Answer:

$$2 \times 12 \text{ miles} = 24 \text{ miles}$$

You say, "What does this have to do with mathematics?" The point is that you need to learn to *focus on what you know*, rather than what you do not know. You may surprise yourself with the amount that you do know, and what *you* can bring to the problem-solving process.

Navigating the Book

Throughout this book, I will take off my author hat and put on my teacher hat to write you notes about the material in the book. These notes will explain steps or give you hints on what to look for as you are reading the book. These notes are printed in this font.

I have included road signs throughout this book to help you successfully get through it.

When you see the stop sign, you should stop for a few moments and study the material next to the stop sign. It is a good idea to memorize this material.

When you see the caution sign, you should make a special note of the material next to the caution sign because it will be used throughout the rest of the book.

When you see the yield sign, it means that you need to remember only the stated result and that the derivation is optional.

When you see the bump sign, some unexpected or difficult material follows, and you will need to slow down to understand the discussion.

Math anxiety builds on focusing on what you can't do rather than on what you can do. This leads to anxiety and frustration. Do you know what is the most common fear in our society? It is the fear of speaking in public. And the fear of letting others know you are having trouble with this problem is related to that fear of speaking in public.

If you focus on a problem that is too difficult, you will be facing a blank wall. This applies to all hobbies or subjects. If you play tennis or golf, has your game improved since you started? If you don't play these games, how do you think you would feel trying to learn in front of all your friends? Do you think you would feel foolish?

Mathematicians don't start with complicated problems. If a mathematician runs into a problem that she can't solve, she will probably rephrase the problem as a simpler related problem that she can't solve. This problem is, in turn, rephrased as yet a simpler problem, and the process continues until the problem is manageable and she has a problem that she *can* solve.

Writing Mathematics

The fundamental objective of education always has been to prepare students for life. A measure of your success with this book is a measure of its usefulness to you in your life. What are the basics for your knowledge "in life"? In this information age with access to a world of knowledge on the Internet, we still would respond by saying that the basics remain "reading, 'riting, and 'rithmetic." As you progress through the material in this book, we will give you opportunities to read mathematics and to consider some of the great ideas in the history of civilization, to develop your problem-solving skills ('rithmetic), and to communicate mathematical ideas to others ('riting). Perhaps you think of mathematics as "working problems" and "getting answers," but it is so much more. Mathematics is a way of thought that includes all three Rs, and to strengthen your skills you will be asked to communicate your knowledge in written form.

Journals

To begin building your skills in writing mathematics, you might keep a journal summarizing each day's work. Keep a record of your feelings and perceptions about what happened in class. How long did the homework take? What time of the day or night did I spend working and studying mathematics? What is the most important idea from the day's lesson?

Journal ideas

Write in your journal every day.

Include important ideas.

Include new words, ideas, formulas, or concepts.

Include questions that you want to ask later.

If possible, carry your journal with you so you can write in it any time you get an idea.

Reasons for keeping a journal

It will record ideas you might otherwise forget.

It will keep a record of your progress.

If you have trouble later, it may help you diagnose areas for change or improvement.

It will build your writing skills.

1.2 What's the Problem?

IN MATHEMATICS, WE GENERALLY FOCUS OUR ATTENTION ON SOME PARTICULAR SETS OF NUMBERS.

The simplest of these sets is the set we use to count objects and the first set that a child learns. It is called the set of **counting numbers** or **natural numbers**.*

> The set of numbers {1, 2, 3, 4, . . .} is called the set of **counting numbers** or the set of **natural numbers**. If the number zero is included, then the set {0, 1, 2, 3, 4, . . .} is called the set of **whole numbers**.

* In mathematics, we use the word *set* as an undefined term. Although sets are discussed in Chapter 2, we assume that you have an intuitive idea of the word *set*. It is used to mean a collection of objects or numbers. Braces are used to enclose the elements of a set, and three dots (called ellipses) are used to indicate that some elements are not listed. We use three dots only if the elements not listed are clear from the given numbers.

Order of Operations

Addition, subtraction, multiplication, and division are called the **elementary operations** for the whole numbers, and it is assumed that you understand these operations. However, certain agreements in dealing with these operations are necessary. Consider this arithmetic example:

Find: $2 + 3 \times 4$

There are two possible approaches to solve this problem:

$$\textit{Left to right: } 2 + 3 \times 4 = 5 \times 4 = 20$$

$$\textit{Multiplication first: } 2 + 3 \times 4 = 2 + 12 = 14$$

Because there are different results to this arithmetic example, it is necessary for us all to agree on one method or the other. At this point, you might be thinking, "Why on earth would I start at the right and do the multiplication first?"

Consider the following example. Suppose that you sold a \$2 benefit ticket on Monday and three \$4 tickets on Tuesday. What is the total amount collected?

(SALES ON MONDAY) + (SALES ON TUESDAY) = (TOTAL SALES)

\$2 + 3 × \$4 = (TOTAL SALES)

CORRECT	NOT CORRECT
Multiplication first:	Left to right:
$2 + 3 \times 4 = 2 + 12$	$2 + 3 \times 4 = 5 \times 4$
$= 14$	$= 20$

Do you see why the correct result requires multiplication before addition?

Many of you may use a calculator to help you work problems in this book. If you do use a calculator, it is important that you use a calculator that carries out the correct order of operations. The correct simplification of the arithmetic problem

$2 + 3 \times 4$

is 14. If you intend on using a calculator, you should press these buttons as a calculator test:

[2] [+] [3] [×] [4] [=]

If you are using a calculator with this book, be sure you actually check out this answer.

Some calculators use a key labeled [ENTER] instead of the equal sign. The correct answer is 14, but some calculators will display the incorrect answer of 20. What is going on with a calculator that gives the answer 20? Such a calculator works from left to right without regard to the order of operations. For this book, you want to have a calculator that has been programmed to use the order of operations correctly.

If the operations are mixed, we agree to do multiplication and division *first* (from left to right) and *then* addition and subtraction from left to right. If the order of operations is to be changed from this agreement, then parentheses are used to indicate this change.

We can now summarize the correct **order of operations**, including the use of parentheses.

PROCEDURE: Order of Operations

In doing arithmetic with mixed operations, we agree to proceed by following these three steps:

STEP 1 Parentheses first

STEP 2 Multiplications and divisions, reading from left to right

STEP 3 Additions and subtractions, reading from left to right

*You should memorize these three steps.

You can remember this by using the mnemonic "**P**lease **M**ind **D**ear **A**unt **S**ally." The first letters will remind you of "**P**arentheses, **M**ultiplication and **D**ivision, **A**ddition and **S**ubtraction." However, if you use this mnemonic, remember that the order is *left to right* for pairs of operations:

multiplication and division (as they occur) and *then* addition and subtraction (as they occur).

Simplify a Numerical Expression

A **numerical expression** is one or more numbers connected by valid mathematical operations (such as *addition, subtraction, multiplication,* or *division*). To **simplify a numerical expression** means to carry out all the operations, according to the order of operations, and to write the answer as a single number.

Suppose we wish to simplify $2[56 - 4(2 + 8)] + 5 - 4(2 + 1)$. If there are parentheses inside parentheses (or brackets), the order of operations directs us to begin with the interior set of parentheses (shown in color):

$2[56 - 4(2 + 8)] + 5 - 4(2 + 1)$	Interior parentheses first
$= 2[56 - 4(10)] + 5 - 4(2 + 1)$	Parentheses next
$= 2[56 - 40] + 5 - 4(3)$	All parentheses should be completed before continuing; note that the brackets are used as parentheses.
$= 2[16] + 5 - 12$	
$= 32 + 5 - 12$	Multiplications/divisions next
$= 25$	Additions/subtractions

Pólya's Problem-Solving Method

The model for problem solving that we will use was first published in 1945 by the great, charismatic mathematician George Pólya. His book *How to Solve It* (Princeton University Press, 1973) has become a classic. In Pólya's book, you will find this problem-solving model as well as a treasure trove of strategy, know-how, rules of thumb, good advice, anecdotes, history, and problems at all levels of mathematics. His problem-solving model is shown in the Procedure box.

We will use this procedure as we develop the problem-solving idea throughout the book. However, we are not ready to tackle real problem solving, but need to start at the beginning with small steps. One of these small steps is developing skill in **translating** from English into math symbolism. The term **sum** is used to indicate the result obtained from addition, **difference** for the result from subtraction, **product** for the result of a multiplication, and **quotient** for the result of a division. When a problem involves mixed operations, it is classified as a sum, difference, product, or quotient according to the *last* operation performed, when using the order of operations agreement.

Verbal descriptions, such as "The product of 5 and the sum of 2 and 4," can be written using mathematical symbols in the form $5 \times (2 + 4)$. In this book we will generally write such a calculation as $5(2 + 4)$. The multiplication written this way is called **juxtaposition**, with the multiplication between the 5 and the parentheses understood.

PROCEDURE: Problem Solving

The problem solving guidelines known as **Pólya's method** set forth the following steps:

STEP 1 *Understand the problem.* Ask questions, experiment, or otherwise rephrase the question in your own words.

STEP 2 *Devise a plan.* Find the connection between the data and the unknown. Look for patterns, relate to a previously solved problem or a known formula, or simplify the given information to give you an easier problem.

STEP 3 *Carry out the plan.* Check the steps as you go.

STEP 4 *Look back.* Examine the solution obtained. In other words, check your answer.

A combined property of addition and multiplication is called the **distributive property for multiplication over addition**:

$$4 \times (3 + 2) = 4 \times 3 + 4 \times 2$$

Number outside parentheses (↑ under the first 4)

Number outside parentheses is **distributed** to **each** number inside parentheses. (↑ under the other two 4s)

This property holds for all whole numbers.

Exponents

We often encounter numbers that are made by repeated multiplication of the same numbers. For example,

$10 \times 10 \times 10 \qquad 6 \times 6 \times 6 \times 6 \times 6$

$15 \times 15 \times 15 \times 15 \times 15 \times 15 \times 15 \times 15 \times 15 \times 15 \times 15$

These numbers can be written more simply by inventing a new notation:

$$10^3 = \underbrace{10 \times 10 \times 10}_{\text{3 factors}}$$

$$6^5 = \underbrace{6 \times 6 \times 6 \times 6 \times 6}_{\text{5 factors}}$$

$$15^{11} = \underbrace{15 \times 15 \times \ldots \times 15}_{\text{11 factors}}$$

We call this **power** or **exponential notation**. The number that is multiplied as a repeated factor is called the **base**, and the number of times the base is used as a factor is called the **exponent**.

We now use this notation to observe a pattern for **powers of 10**:

$10^1 = 10$
$10^2 = 10 \times 10 = 100$
$10^3 = 10 \times 10 \times 10 = 1{,}000$
$10^4 = 10 \times 10 \times 10 \times 10 = 10{,}000$

Do you see a relationship between the exponent and the number?

$$10^5 = \underbrace{100{,}000}_{\text{5 zeros}}$$

Exponent is 5.

Notice that the exponent and the number of zeros are the same.

Could you write 10^{12} without actually multiplying?*

There is a similar pattern for multiplication of any number by a power of 10. Consider the following examples, and notice what happens to the decimal point:

$9.42 \times 10^1 = 94.2$
$9.42 \times 10^2 = 942$
$9.42 \times 10^3 = 9{,}420$
$9.42 \times 10^4 = 94{,}200$

We find these answers by direct multiplication.

Do you see a pattern? If we multiply 9.42×10^5, how many places to the right will the decimal point be moved?

$9.42 \times 10^5 = 9\ 42{,}000$

5 places →

* Answer: 1,000,000,000,000

This answer is found by observing the pattern, not by directly multiplying.

Using this pattern, can you multiply the following *without direct calculation*?†

9.42×10^{12}

We will investigate one final pattern of 10s, this time looking at smaller values in this pattern.

$\vdots$
$100{,}000 = 10^5$
$10{,}000 = 10^4$
$1{,}000 = 10^3$
$100 = 10^2$
$10 = 10^1$

Continuing with the same pattern, we have

$1 = 10^0$ — We interpret the zero exponent as "decimal point moves 0 places."
$0.1 = 10^{-1}$ — We will define negative numbers in Chapter 2.
$0.01 = 10^{-2}$ — For now, we use the symbols $-1, -2, -3, \ldots$ as exponents to show the position of the decimal point.
$0.001 = 10^{-3}$
$0.0001 = 10^{-4}$
$0.00001 = 10^{-5}$
$\vdots$

When we multiply some number by a power of 10, a pattern emerges:

$9.42 \times 10^2 = 942.$
$9.42 \times 10^1 = 94.2$
$9.42 \times 10^0 = 9.42$ — Decimal moves 0 places.
$9.42 \times 10^{-1} = 0.942$ — The answer by direct multiplying is: $9.42 \times 0.1 = 0.942$.
$9.42 \times 10^{-2} = 0.0942$
$9.42 \times 10^{-3} = 0.00942$

Do you see that the same pattern holds for multiplying by a negative exponent? Can you multiply 9.42×10^{-6} *without direct calculation*? The solution is as follows:

$9.42 \times 10^{-6} = 0.000009\ 42$

← Moved 6 places to the left.

These patterns lead to a useful way of writing large and small numbers, called **scientific notation**.

> The **scientific notation** of a number is that number written as a power of 10 or as a decimal number between 1 and 10 times a power of 10.

† Answer: 9,420,000,000,000

When working with very large or very small numbers, it is customary to use scientific notation. For example, suppose we wish to expand 2^{63}. A calculator can help us with this calculation:

2 ^ 63 =

The result is larger than can be handled with a calculator display, so your calculator will automatically output the answer in scientific notation, using one of the following formats:

9.223372037E18
9.223372037 18
$9.223372037 \times 10^{18}$

If you wish to enter a very large (or small) number into a calculator, you can enter these numbers using the scientific notation button on most calculators. Use the key labeled EE, EXP, or SCI. Whenever we show the EE key, we mean press the scientific notation key on your brand of calculator.

WATCH YOUR STEP *Do not confuse the exponent key* y^x *with scientific notation* EE*; they are NOT the same.*

Number

468,000
93,000,000,000

Scientific Notation

4.68×10^5
9.3×10^{10}

Calculator Input

4.68 EE 5
9.3 EE 10

Calculator Display

4.68 05 or 4.68 E5
9.3 10 or 9.3 E10

When you multiply numbers, the numbers being multiplied are called **factors**. The process of taking a given number and writing it as the product of two or more other numbers is called **factoring**, with the result called a **factorization** of the given number. We will consider this process in Chapter 2.

1.3 Early Numeration Systems

"DO YOU KNOW YOUR NUMBERS?" IS A QUESTION YOU MIGHT HEAR ONE CHILD ASKING ANOTHER. AT AN EARLY AGE, WE LEARN OUR NUMBERS AS WE LEARN TO COUNT, BUT IF WE ARE ASKED TO DEFINE WHAT WE MEAN BY *NUMBER*, WE ARE GENERALLY AT A LOSS.

There are many different kinds of numbers, and one type of number is usually defined in terms of more primitive types of numbers. The word *number* is taken as one of our primitive (or undefined) words, but the following definition will help us distinguish between a number and the symbol that we use to represent a number.

Number/Numeral

A **number** is used to answer the question "How many?" and usually refers to numbers used to count objects:

$\{0, 1, 2, 3, 4, 5, 6, 7, 8, 9, 10, \ldots\}$

A **numeral** is a symbol used to represent a number, and a **numeration system** consists of a set of basic symbols and some rules for making other symbols from them, the purpose being the identification of all numbers.

There is a story of a woman who decided she wanted to write to a prisoner in a nearby state penitentiary. However, she was puzzled over how to address him, since she knew him only by a string of numerals. She solved her dilemma by beginning her letter: "Dear 5944930, may I call you 594?"

The invention of a precise and "workable" numeration system is one of the greatest inventions of humanity. It is certainly equal to the invention of the alphabet, which enabled humans to carry the knowledge of one generation to the next. It is simple for us to use the symbol 17 to represent the amount of objects found in the grouping at the top of the next page.

However, this is not the first and probably will not be the last numeration system to be developed; it took centuries to arrive at this stage of symbolic representation. Here are some of the ways that 17 has been written:

The concept represented by each of these symbols is the same, but the symbols differ. The concept or idea of "seventeenness" is called a *number*; the symbol used to represent the concept is called a *numeral*.

Three of the earliest civilizations known to use numerals were the Egyptian, Babylonian, and Roman. We shall examine these systems for two reasons. First, it will help us to more fully understand our own numeration (decimal) system; second, it will help us to see how the ideas of these other systems have been incorporated into our system.

Egyptian Numeration System

Perhaps the earliest type of written numeration system developed was a **simple grouping system**. The Egyptians used such a system by the time of the first dynasty, around 2850 BC. The symbols of the Egyptian system were part of their *hieroglyphics* and are shown in Table 1.1.

Table 1.1 Egyptian Hieroglyphic Numerals

Usual Numeral (decimal)	Egyptian Numeral	Descriptive Name
1	𓏺	Stroke
10	𓎆	Heel bone
100	𓍢	Scroll
1,000	𓆼	Lotus flower
10,000	𓂭	Pointing finger
100,000	𓆐	Polliwog
1,000,000	𓁨	Astonished man

Any number is expressed by using these symbols *additively*; each symbol is repeated the required number of times, but with no more than nine repetitions. This additively is called the **addition principle**.

The Egyptians had a simple **repetitive-type** numeration system. Addition and subtraction were performed by repeating the symbols and regrouping.

In Egyptian arithmetic, multiplication and division were performed by successions of additions that did not require the memorization of a multiplication table and could easily be done on an abacus-type device. The Egyptians also used unit fractions (that is, fractions of the form $1/n$, for some counting number n). These were indicated by placing an oval over the numeral for the denominator. Thus,

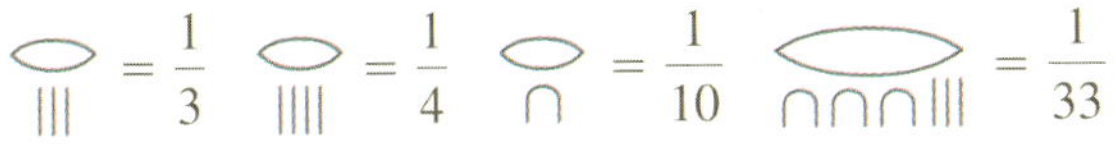
$= \frac{1}{3}$, $= \frac{1}{4}$, $= \frac{1}{10}$, $= \frac{1}{33}$

The fractions $\frac{1}{2}$ and $\frac{2}{3}$ were exceptions:

or $= \frac{1}{2}$; or $= \frac{2}{3}$

Fractions that were not unit fractions (with the exception of $\frac{2}{3}$ just mentioned) were represented as sums of unit fractions. For example,

$$\frac{2}{7} \text{ could be expressed as } \frac{1}{4} + \frac{1}{28}$$

Repetitions were not allowed, so $\frac{2}{7}$ would not be written as $\frac{1}{7} + \frac{1}{7}$. Why so difficult? We don't know, but the Rhind papyrus (see Figure 1.2) includes a table for all such decompositions for odd denominators from 5 to 101.

Figure 1.2 Rhind papyrus. The top portion is part of the actual papyrus, and the bottom portion is a translation. Look for the Egyptian symbols; can you see the polliwog and the astonished man?

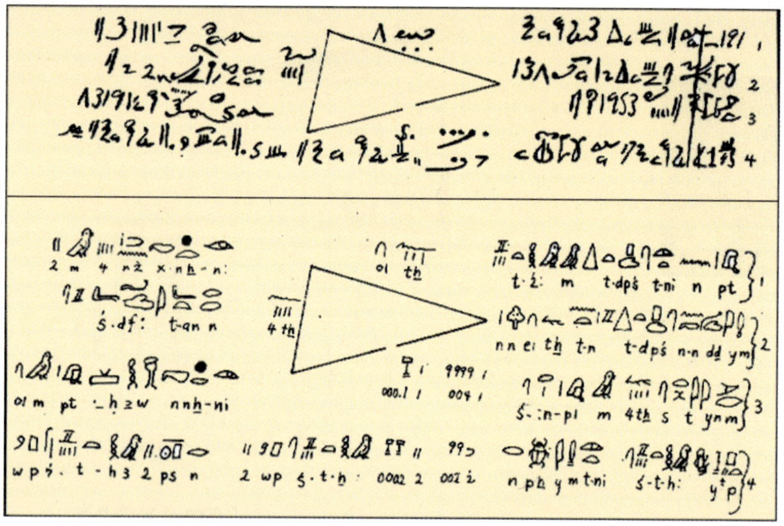

Roman Numeration System

The Roman numeration system was used in Europe until the 18th century, and is still used today in outlining, in numbering certain pages in books, and for certain copyright dates. The Roman numerals were selected letters from the Roman alphabet, as shown in Table 1.2.

Table 1.2 Roman Numerals

Decimal Numeral	1	5	10	50	100	500	1,000
Roman Numeral	I	V	X	L	C	D	M

The Roman numeration system is *repetitive*, like the Egyptian system, but has two additional properties, called the *subtraction principle* and the *multiplication principle*.

Subtraction Principle

One property of the Roman numeration system is based on the **subtraction principle**. Reading from the left, we add the value of each numeral unless its value is smaller than the value of the numeral to its right, in which case we subtract it from that number. Only the numbers 1, 10, 100, . . . , can be subtracted, and only from the next two higher numbers. For example,

I, II, III, IIII

or

IV, V, VI, VII, VIII, VIIII

or

IX, X, XI…

are the successive counting numbers. Instead of IIII we write IV, which (using the subtraction principle) means $5 - 1 = 4$. The I can be subtracted from V or X, and the X can be subtracted from L or C; thus

XL means $50 - 10 = 40$

The C can be subtracted only from D or M. For example,

DC means $500 + 100 = 600$ but

CD means $500 - 100 = 400$

Multiplication Principle

A bar is placed over a Roman numeral or a group of numerals to mean 1,000 times the value of the Roman numerals themselves. When one symbol (such as a bar) is used to multiply the value of an associated symbol, it is called the **multiplication principle**. For example,

$\overline{\text{V}}$ means $5 \times 1{,}000 = 5{,}000$ and

$\overline{\text{XL}}$ means $40 \times 1{,}000 = 40{,}000$

Babylonian Numeration System

The Babylonian numeration system differed from the Egyptian in several respects. Whereas the Egyptian system was a simple grouping system, the Babylonians employed a much more useful **positional system**. Since they lacked papyrus, they used clay as a writing medium, and thus the Babylonian cuneiform was much less pictorial than the Egyptian system. They employed only two wedge-shaped characters, which date from 2000 BC and are shown in Table 1.3.

Table 1.3 Babylonian Cuneiform Numerals

Decimal Numeral	Babylonian Numeral
1	▼
2	▼▼
9	▼▼▼▼▼▼▼▼▼
10	◁
59	◁◁◁◁◁ ▼▼▼▼▼▼▼▼▼

Notice from the table that, for numbers 1 through 59, the system is *repetitive*. However, unlike in the Egyptian system, the position of the symbols is important. The ◁ symbol *must* appear to the left of any ▼s to represent numbers smaller than 60. For numbers larger than 60, the symbols ◁ and ▼ are written to the left of ◁ (as in a positional system), and now take on a new value that is 60 times larger than the original value. That is,

▼ ◁◁◁ ▼▼▼▼▼ means $(1 \times 60) + 35$

The Babylonian numeration system is called a *sexagesimal system* and uses the principle of position. However, the system is not fully positional, because only numbers larger than 60 use the position principle; numbers within each basic 60-group are written by a simple grouping system. A true positional sexagesimal system would require 60 different symbols.

The Babylonians carried their positional system a step further. If any numerals were to the left of the second 60-group, they had the value of 60 × 60 or 60^2. Thus,

▼▼ ◁◁◁◁ ▼▼▼▼▼ ◁◁ ▼▼▼▼ $= (2 \times 60^2) + (45 \times 60) + 24$
$= 7{,}200 + 2{,}700 + 24$
$= 9{,}924$

The Babylonians also made use of a *subtractive symbol*, ⌈ . That is, 38 could be written

◁◁◁ ▼▼▼▼▼▼▼▼ or ◁◁◁◁ ⌈▼▼

Although this positional numeration system was in many ways superior to the Egyptian system, it suffered from the lack of a zero or placeholder symbol. For example, how is the number 60 represented? Does ▼▼ mean 2 or 61? Generally, the value of the number had to be found from the context. (Scholars tell us that such ambiguity can be resolved only by a careful study of the context.) However, in later Babylon, around 300 BC, records show that there is a zero symbol, an idea that was later used by the Hindus.

Arithmetic with the Babylonian numerals is quite simple, since there are only two symbols. A study of the Babylonian arithmetic will be left for the reader.

PROPERTIES OF NUMERATION SYSTEMS

A *numeration system* consists of a set of basic symbols. Because the set of counting numbers is infinite and the set of symbols in any numeration system is finite, some rules for using the set of symbols are necessary. Different historical systems use one or more of these properties:

A *simple grouping* system invents a symbol to represent the number of objects in a predeterminate group of objects. For example, the symbol

3 is used to represent ●●●

V is used to represent ●●●●●

and ∩ is used to represent ●●●●●●●●●●

A *positional system* reuses a symbol to represent different numbers of objects by changing the position in its symbolic (numerical) representation. For example, in 35 the "3" is used to represent

●●●●●●●●●●
●●●●●●●●●●
●●●●●●●●●●

whereas in 53 the "3" is used to represent

●●●

The *addition principle* means that the various values of individual symbols (numerals) are added, as in ∩∩∩|||, meaning

10 + 10 + 10 + 1 + 1 + 1

The *subtraction principle* means that certain values are subtracted, as in IX meaning 10 − 1 = 9. The *multiplication principle* means that certain symbolic values are multiplied, as in $\overline{\text{V}}$ meaning 1,000 × 5.

A *repetitive system* reuses the same number over and over in an additive manner, as in XXX meaning 10 + 10 + 10.

© Image Source Black/Jupiterimages

Table 1.4 Historical Numeration Systems

Numeration System	Classification	Selected Numerals							
Decimal system	positional (10s)	1	2	5	10	50	100	500	1,000
Egyptian system	grouping	|	||	|||||	∩	∩∩∩ ∩∩	𓍢	𓍢𓍢𓍢 𓍢𓍢	𓆼
Roman system	grouping	I	II	V	X	L	C	D	M
Babylonian (Sumerian)	positional (60s)	▼	▼▼	▼▼▼ ▼▼	◁	◁◁◁ ◁◁	▼ ◁◁ ◁◁	▼▼▼▼◁ ▼▼▼▼◁	◁ ▼▼▼◁◁ ▼▼▼◁◁
Greek	grouping								
Mayan	positional (vertical)	•	••	—	=	•• =	— ⊜	• — ⊜	•• = ⊜
Chinese	positional (vertical)	一	二	五	十	五 十	百	五 百	千

Other Historical Systems

One of the richest areas in the history of mathematics is the study of historical numeration systems. In this book, we discuss the Egyptian numeration system because it illustrates a simple grouping system, the Babylonian numeration system because it illustrates a positional numeration system, and the Roman system because it is still in limited use today.

Other numeration systems of interest from a historical point of view are the Mayan, Greek, and Chinese numeration systems. These are summarized in Table 1.4.

1.4 Hindu-Arabic Numeration Systems

THE NUMERATION SYSTEM IN COMMON USE TODAY (THE ONE WE HAVE BEEN CALLING THE DECIMAL SYSTEM) HAS TEN SYMBOLS—NAMELY, 0, 1, 2, 3, 4, 5, 6, 7, 8, AND 9.

The selection of ten digits was no doubt a result of our having ten fingers (digits).

The symbols originated in India in about 300 BC. However, because the early specimens do not contain a zero or use a positional system, this numeration system offered no advantage over other systems then in use in India.

The date of the invention of the zero symbol is not known. The symbol did not originate in India but probably came from the late Babylonian period via the Greek world.

By the year AD 750 the zero symbol and the idea of a positional system had been brought to Baghdad and translated into Arabic. We are not certain how these numerals were introduced into Europe, but it is likely that they came via Spain in the 8th century. Gerbert, who later became Pope Sylvester II in 999, studied in Spain and was the first European scholar known to have taught these numerals. Because of their origins, these numerals are called the **Hindu-Arabic numerals**. Since ten basic symbols are used, the Hindu-Arabic numeration system is also called the *decimal numeration system*, from the Latin word *decem*, meaning "ten."

Although we now know that the decimal system is very efficient, its introduction met with considerable controversy. Two opposing factions, the "algorists" and the "abacists," arose. Those favoring the Hindu-Arabic system were called algorists, since the symbols were introduced into Europe in a book called (in Latin) *Liber Algorismi de Numero Indorum*, by the Arab mathematician al-Khowârizmî. The word *algorismi* is the origin of our word *algorithm*. The abacists favored the status quo—using Roman numerals and doing arithmetic on an abacus. The battle between the abacists and the algorists lasted for 400 years. The Roman Catholic Church exerted great influence in commerce, science, and theology. The church criticized those using the "heathen" Hindu-Arabic numerals and consequently kept Europe using Roman numerals until 1500. Roman numerals were easy to write and learn, and addition and subtraction with them were easier than with the "new" Hindu-Arabic numerals. It seems incredible that our decimal system has been in general use only since about the year 1500.

Decimal System—Grouping by Tens

Let's examine the Hindu-Arabic or **decimal numeration system** a little more closely:

1. It uses ten symbols, called digits.

2. Larger numbers are expressed in terms of powers of 10.

3. It is positional.

Consider how we count objects:

At this point we could invent another symbol as the Egyptians did (you might suggest 0, but remember that 0 represents no objects), or we could reuse the digit symbols by repeating them or by altering their positions. We agree to use 10 to mean 1 group of

We call this group a **ten**. The symbol 0 was invented as a placeholder to show that the 1 here is in a different position from the 1 representing ■. We continue to count:

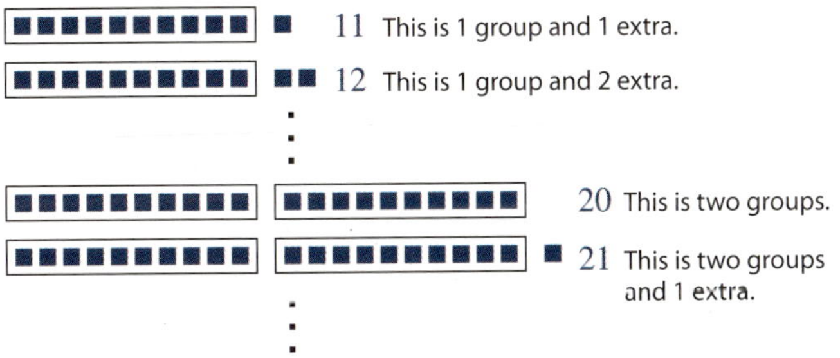

We continue in the same fashion until we have 9 groups and 9 extra. What's next? It is 10 groups or a group of groups:

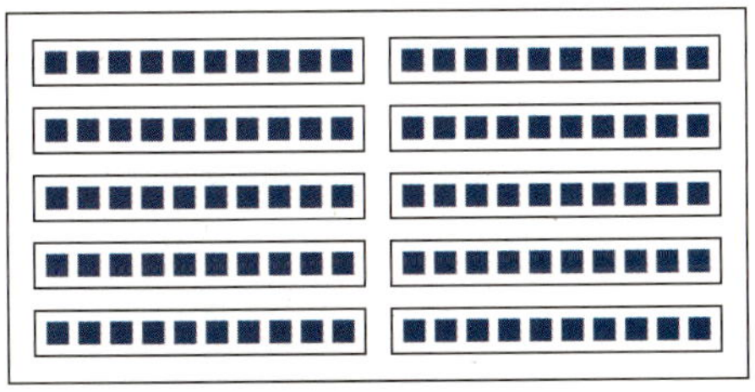

We call this group of groups a $10 \cdot 10$ or 10^2 or a **hundred**. We again use position and repeat the symbol 1 with yet a different meaning: 100.

Expanded Notation

The representation, or the meaning, of a number is called **expanded notation**. For example, if we ask, "What does 52,613 mean?," what can we say?

$$\begin{aligned} 52{,}613 &= 50{,}000 + 2{,}000 + 600 + 10 + 3 \\ &= 5 \times 10^4 + 2 \times 10^3 + 6 \times 10^2 + 1 \times 10 + 3 \end{aligned}$$

To reverse the procedure, write

$$4 \times 10^8 + 9 \times 10^7 + 6 \times 10^4 + 3 \times 10 + 7$$

in decimal form. You can use the order of operations and multiply out the digits, but you should be able to go directly to decimal form if you remember what place value means:

$$49\ 00600\ 37 = 490{,}060{,}037$$

Notice that there were no powers of 10^6, 10^5, 10^3, or 10^2.

A period, called a **decimal point** in the decimal system, is used to separate the fractional parts from the whole parts. The positions to the right of the decimal point are fractions:

$$\frac{1}{10} = 10^{-1}, \quad \frac{1}{100} = 10^{-2}, \quad \frac{1}{1{,}000} = 10^{-3}$$

To complete the pattern, we also sometimes write $10 = 10^1$ and $1 = 10^0$.

Write 479.352 using expanded notation.

$$\begin{aligned} 479.352 &= 400 + 70 + 9 + 0.3 + 0.05 + 0.002 \\ &= 400 + 70 + 9 + \frac{3}{10} + \frac{5}{100} + \frac{2}{1{,}000} \\ &= 4 \times 10^2 + 7 \times 10^1 + 9 \times 10^0 + 3 \times \\ &\quad 10^{-1} + 5 \times 10^{-2} + 2 \times 10^{-3} \end{aligned}$$

1.5 Different Numeration Systems

IN THE PREVIOUS SECTION, WE DISCUSSED THE HINDU-ARABIC NUMERATION SYSTEM AND GROUPING BY TENS.

However, we could group by twos, fives, twelves, or any other counting number. In this section, we summarize numeration systems with bases other than ten. This not only will help you understand our own numeration system, but will give you insight into the numeration systems used with computers, namely, base 2 (**binary**), base 8 (**octal**), and base 16 (**hexadecimal**).

Number of Symbols

The number of symbols used in a particular base depends on the method of grouping for that base. For example, in base ten the grouping is by tens, and in base five the grouping is by fives. Suppose we wish to count ■■■■■■■■■■■ in various bases. Let's look for patterns in Table 1.5. Note the use of the subscript following the numeral to keep track of the base in which we are working.

Table 1.5 Grouping in Various Bases

Base	Symbols	Method of Grouping	Notation
two	0, 1	[[(■■)(■■)] [(■■)(■■)]] (■■) ■	1011_{two}
three	0, 1, 2	[[■■■] [■■■] [■■■]] ■■	102_{three}
four	0, 1, 2, 3	[■■■■] [■■■■] ■■■	23_{four}
five	0, 1, 2, 3, 4	[■■■■■] [■■■■■] ■	21_{five}
six	0, 1, 2, 3, 4, 5	[■■■■■■] ■■■■■	15_{six}
seven	0, 1, 2, 3, 4, 5, 6	[■■■■■■■] ■■■■	14_{seven}
eight	0, 1, 2, 3, 4, 5, 6, 7	[■■■■■■■■] ■■■	13_{eight}
nine	0, 1, 2, 3, 4, 5, 6, 7, 8	[■■■■■■■■■] ■■	12_{nine}
ten	0, 1, 2, 3, 4, 5, 6, 7, 8, 9	[■■■■■■■■■■] ■	11_{ten}

Do you see any patterns? Suppose we wish to continue this pattern. Can we group by elevens or twelves? We can, provided new symbols are "invented." For base eleven (or higher bases), we use the symbol *T* to represent ■■■■■■■■■■. For base twelve (or higher bases), we use *E* to stand for ■■■■■■■■■■■. For bases larger than twelve, other symbols can be invented.

For example, $2T_{twelve}$ means that there are two groupings of twelve and *T* (ten) extra:

[■■■■■■■■■■■■] [■■■■■■■■■■■■] ■■■■■■■■■■

We continue with the pattern from Table 1.5 by continuing beyond base ten in Table 1.6.

Do you see more patterns? Can you determine the number of symbols in the **base *b* system**? Remember that *b* stands for some counting number greater than 1. Base two has two symbols, base three has three symbols, and so on.

Table 1.6 Grouping in Various Bases

Base	Symbols	Method of Grouping	Notation
eleven	0, 1, 2, 3, 4, 5, 6, 7, 8, 9, *T*	[■■■■■■■■■■■]	10_{eleven}
twelve	0, 1, 2, 3, 4, 5, 6, 7, 8, 9, *T*, *E*	■■■■■■■■■■■	E_{twelve}
thirteen	0, 1, 2, 3, 4, 5, 6, 7, 8, 9, *T*, *E*, *U*	■■■■■■■■■■■	$E_{thirteen}$
fourteen	0, 1, 2, 3, 4, 5, 6, 7, 8, 9, *T*, *E*, *U*, *V*	■■■■■■■■■■■	$E_{fourteen}$

Change from Base b to Base 10

To change from base b to base ten, we write the numerals in expanded notation. The resulting number is in base ten.

$$\begin{aligned}1011.01_{five} &= 1 \times 5^3 + 0 \times 5^2 + 1 \times 5^1 + 1 \times 5^0 + \\ &\quad 0 \times 5^{-1} + 1 \times 5^{-2} \\ &= 125 + 0 + 5 + 1 + 0 + 0.04 \\ &= 131.04\end{aligned}$$

Change from Base 10 to Base b

To see how to change from base ten to any other valid base, let's again look for a pattern:

To change from base ten to base two, group by twos.
To change from base ten to base three, group by threes.
To change from base ten to base four, group by fours.
To change from base ten to base five, group by fives.
⋮

© iStockphoto.com

The groupings from this pattern are summarized in Table 1.7.

To see how we can interpret this grouping process in terms of a simple division we convert 42 to base two.

Understand the Problem. Using Table 1.7, we see that the largest power of two smaller than 42 is 2^5, so we begin with $2^5 = 32$:

$$\begin{aligned}42 &= 1 \times 2^5 + 10 \\ 10 &= 0 \times 2^4 + \mathbf{10} \\ \mathbf{10} &= 1 \times 2^3 + \mathbf{2} \\ \mathbf{2} &= 0 \times 2^2 + 2 \\ 2 &= 1 \times 2^1 + \mathbf{0} \\ \mathbf{0} &= 0 \times 2^0\end{aligned}$$

We could now write out 42 in expanded notation.

Devise a Plan. Instead of carrying out the steps by using Table 1.7, we will begin with 42 and carry out repeated division, saving each remainder as we go.

Carry Out the Plan. We are changing to base 2, so we do repeated division by 2:

```
  21  r. 0 ← Save remainder.
2)42
```

Next we need to divide 21 by 2, but instead of rewriting our work we work our way up:

```
  10  r. 1 ← Save all remainders.
2)21  r. 0 ← Save remainder.
2)42
```

Continue by doing repeated division.

```
Stop when you get a zero here.
  ↓
  0  r. 1   Answer is found by reading down.
2) 1  r. 0   |
2) 2  r. 1   |
2) 5  r. 0   |
2)10  r. 1   |
2)21  r. 0   |
2)42         ↓
```

Thus, $42 = 101010_{two}$.

Look Back. You can check by using expanded notation:

$$\begin{aligned}101010_{two} &= 1 \times 2^5 + 1 \times 2^3 + 1 \times 2^1 \\ &= 32 + 8 + 2 \\ &= 42\end{aligned}$$

How would you change from base ten to base seven? To base eight? To base b? We see from the above pattern that we group by b's or perform repeated division by b.

Table 1.7 Place-Value Chart

Base	Place Value					
2	$2^5 = 32$	$2^4 = 16$	$2^3 = 8$	$2^2 = 4$	$2^1 = 2$	$2^0 = 1$
3	$3^5 = 243$	$3^4 = 81$	$3^3 = 27$	$3^2 = 9$	$3^1 = 3$	$3^0 = 1$
4	$4^5 = 1{,}024$	$4^4 = 256$	$4^3 = 64$	$4^2 = 16$	$4^1 = 4$	$4^0 = 1$
5	$5^5 = 3{,}125$	$5^4 = 625$	$5^3 = 125$	$5^2 = 25$	$5^1 = 5$	$5^0 = 1$
8	$8^5 = 32{,}768$	$8^4 = 4{,}096$	$8^3 = 512$	$8^2 = 64$	$8^1 = 8$	$8^0 = 1$
10	$10^5 = 100{,}000$	$10^4 = 10{,}000$	$10^3 = 1{,}000$	$10^2 = 100$	$10^1 = 10$	$10^0 = 1$
12	$12^5 = 248{,}832$	$12^4 = 20{,}736$	$12^3 = 1{,}728$	$12^2 = 144$	$12^1 = 12$	$12^0 = 1$

1.6 Binary Numeration Systems

ONE OF THE BIGGEST SURPRISES OF OUR TIME HAS BEEN THE IMPACT OF THE PERSONAL COMPUTER ON EVERYONE'S LIFE.

We have just completed a section on different numeration systems, and it is this study that enables us to understand how computers work (see Section 1.5). In this section, we focus on one of those systems—namely, the one that uses only two symbols (*binary numerals*), called the **binary numeration system**.

Base Two

For a computer to be of use in calculating, the human mind had to invent a way of representing numbers and other symbols in terms of electronic devices. In fact, it is the simplest of electronic devices, the switch, that is at the heart of communication between machines and human beings. A switch can be only "on" or "off". For example, a light bulb can either be on or off, not both at the same time. Therefore, light bulbs are an example of a two-state device.

We can see that it would be easy to represent the numbers "one" and "zero" by "on" and "off," but that won't get us very far. Binary numerals represent the numbers 1, 2, 3, … using only the symbols 1 and 0, as shown in Table 1.8. Can you see the pattern?

Recall that expanded notation provides the link between the binary numeration and decimal numeration systems, and that for a binary numeration system the grouping is by twos.

Lightbulbs serve as a good example of two-state devices. The 1 is symbolized by "on," and the 0 is symbolized by "off."

Table 1.8 Binary Numerals

Decimal		Binary
0	↔	0
1	↔	1
2	↔	10
3	↔	11
4	↔	100
5	↔	101
⋮		⋮
8	↔	1000
9	↔	1001
⋮		⋮
15	↔	1111
16	↔	10000
⋮		⋮
31	↔	11111
32	↔	100000
⋮		⋮

What does 1110_{two} mean? Change it to base 10.

fours column ↓ (second digit)
units column ↓ (fourth digit)

1 1 1 0

↑ twos column (third digit)
↑ eights column (first digit)

We see this means:

$$1 \times 8 + 1 \times 4 + 1 \times 2 + 0 = 8 + 4 + 2 = 14.$$

To change a number from binary to decimal, we write it in expanded notation and then carry out the arithmetic. To change a number from decimal to binary, it is necessary to find how many units (1 if odd, 0 if even), how many twos, how many fours, and so on are contained in that given number. This can be accomplished by repeated division by 2.

ASCII Code

In a computer, each switch, called a **bit** (from binary digit), represents a 1 or 0, depending on whether it is on or off. A group of eight of these switches is lined up to form a **byte**, which can represent any number from 0 to $11111111_{two} = 255_{ten}$.

Of course, when we use computers we need to represent more than numerals. There must be a representation

Table 1.9 Partial Listing of ASCII Code. The entire ASCII code has 127 symbols.

ASCII Code	Symbol	ASCII Code	Symbol	ASCII Code	Symbol	ASCII Code	Symbol
32	Space	53	5	67	C	95	-
33	!	54	6	68	D	96	‘
34	"	55	7	69	E	97	a
35	#	56	8	70	F	98	b
⋮	⋮	57	9	⋮	⋮	⋮	⋮
48	0	58	:	90	Z	119	w
49	1	59	;	91	[	120	x
50	2	⋮	⋮	92	\	121	y
51	3	65	A	93	]	122	z
52	4	66	B	94	^	⋮	⋮

for every letter and symbol that we wish to use. For example, we will need to represent statements such as

$$x = 3.45 - y$$

The code that has been most commonly used is the American Standard Code for Information Interchange, developed in 1964 and called **ASCII** (pronounced "ask-key") **code**. A partial list of this code is shown in Table 1.9.

From this table you can see that the word ***cat*** would be represented by the ASCII code

99 97 116

In the machine, this would be represented by binary numerals, each one in a different byte. Thus, ***cat*** is represented as shown:

Symbol	*ASCII Code*	*Binary*	*Byte*
c	99	01100011	off on on off off off on on
a	97	01100001	off on on off off off off on
t	116	01110100	off on on on off on off off

Each of these bytes is stored at some location in the computer called its *address.* Each address (billions of them) stores one byte of information. To store the information 3 *cats* would require six addresses:

Address	*Information*	
1000	00110011	← **Code for 3**
1001	00100000	← **Code for space**
1010	01100011	← **Code for *c***
1011	01100001	← **Code for *a***
1100	01110100	← **Code for *t***
1101	01110011	← **Code for *s***

During the process of solving a problem, the storage unit will contain not only the set of instructions that specify the sequence of operations required to complete the problem, but also the input data. Notice that an address number has nothing to do with the contents of that address. The early computers stored these individual bits with switches, vacuum tubes, or cathode ray tubes, but computers today use much more sophisticated means for storing bits of information. These advances in storing information have enabled computers to use codes that use many more than eight bits. For example, a location might look like the following:

Address 00101 | 00011111000110110110000000001101 |

Binary Arithmetic

The binary numeration system has only two symbols, 0 and 1, which makes counting in the system simple. Arithmetic is particularly easy in the binary system, since the only arithmetic "facts" one needs are the following:

Addition			Multiplication		
+	0	1	×	0	1
0	0	1	0	0	0
1	1	10	1	0	1

You simply must remember when adding 1 + 1 in binary that you put down 0 and "carry" the 1.

1.7 History of Calculating Devices

FEW PEOPLE FORESAW THAT COMPUTERS WOULD JUMP THE BOUNDARIES OF SCIENTIFIC AND ENGINEERING COMMUNITIES AND CREATE A REVOLUTION IN OUR WAY OF LIFE IN THE LAST HALF OF THE 20TH CENTURY.

No one expected to see a computer sitting on a desk, much less on desks in every type of business, large and small, and even in our homes. Today no one is ready to face the world without some knowledge of computers. What has created this change in our lives is not only the advances in technology that have made computers small and affordable, but the tremendous imagination shown in developing ways to use them. In this section we will consider the historical achievements leading to the easy availability of calculators and computers.

First Calculating Tool

The first "device" for arithmetic computations is finger counting. It has the advantages of low cost and instant availability. You are familiar with addition and subtraction on your fingers, but here is a method for multiplication by 9. Place both hands as shown at the left. To multiply 4×9, simply bend the fourth finger from the left as shown:

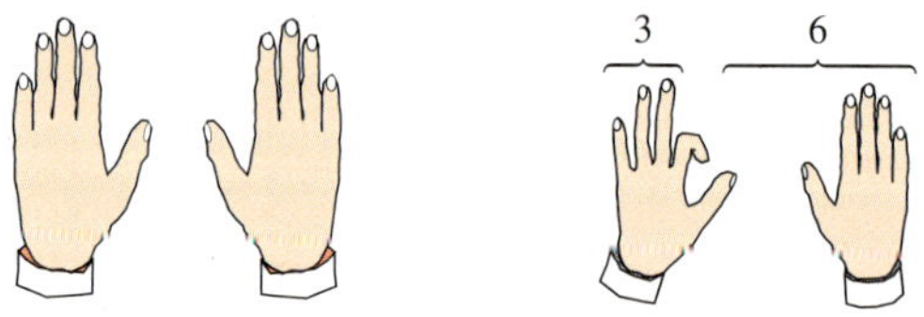

The answer is read as 36, the bent finger serving to distinguish between the first and second digits in the answer.

What about 36×9? Separate the third and fourth fingers from the left (as shown at the top of the next column), since 36 has 3 tens. Next, bend the sixth finger from the left, since 36 has 6 units. Now the answer can be read directly from the fingers:

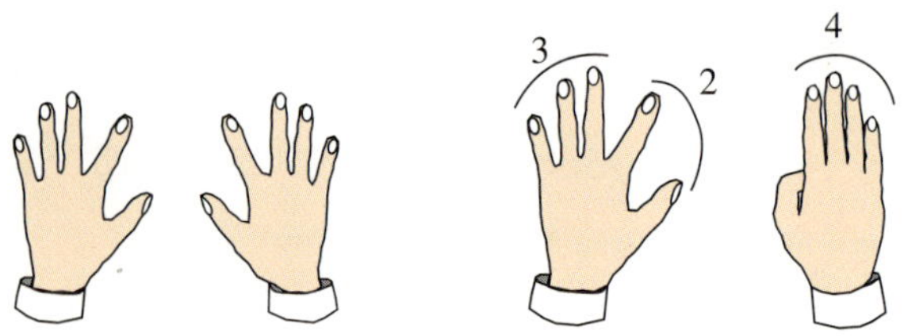

The answer is 324.

Aristophanes devised a complicated finger-calculating system in about 500 BC, but it was very difficult to learn. Figure 1.3 shows an illustration from a manual published about two thousand years later, in 1520.

Early Calculating Devices

Numbers can be represented by stones, slip knots, or beads on a string. These devices evolved into the abacus, as shown in Figure 1.4.

Figure 1.3 Finger calculation was important in the Middle Ages.

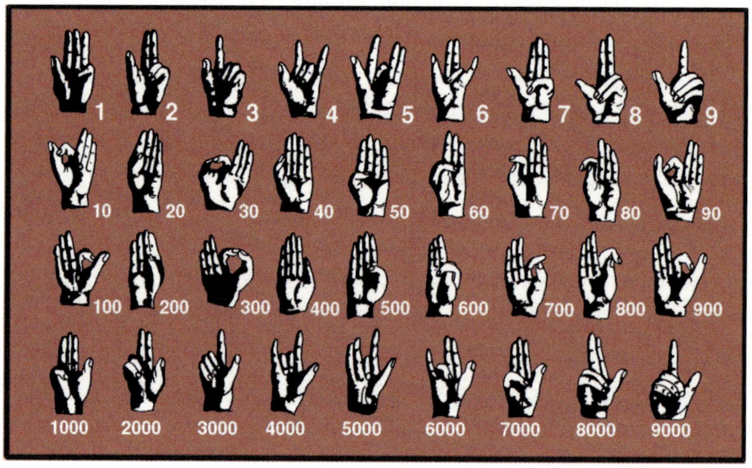

Figure 1.4 Abacus: The number shown is 31.

Abaci (plural of abacus) were used thousands of years ago, and are still used today. In the hands of an expert, they even rival calculators for speed in performing certain calculations. An abacus consists of rods that contain sliding beads, four or five in the lower section, and two in the upper that equal one in the lower section of the next higher denomination. The abacus is useful today for teaching mathematics to youngsters. One can actually see the "carry" in addition and the "borrowing" in subtraction.

In the early 1600s, Jhone Neper (John Napier, using the modern spelling) invented a device similar to a multiplication table with movable parts, as shown in Figure 1.5. These rods are known as Napier's rods or Napier's bones.

Figure 1.5 Napier's rods (1617)

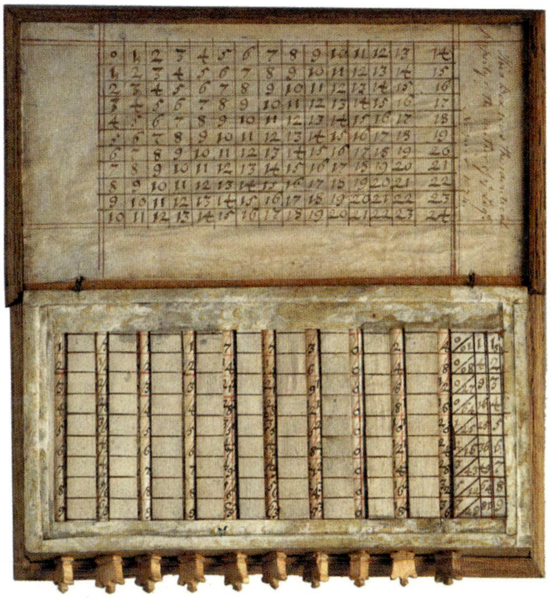

A device used for many years was a slide rule (see Figure 1.6), which was also invented by Napier. The answers given by a slide rule are only visual approximations and do not have the precision that is often required.

Figure 1.6 Slide rule

Mechanical Calculators

The 17th century saw the beginnings of calculating machines. When Blaise Pascal (1623–1662) was 19, he began to develop a machine to add long columns of figures (see Figure 1.7a). He built several versions, and since all proved to be unreliable, he considered this project a failure; but the machine introduced basic principles that are used in modern calculators.

Figure 1.7 Early mechanical calculators

a. Pascal's calculator (1642)

b. Babbage's calculating machine

The next advance in mechanical calculators came from Germany in about 1672, when the great mathematician Gottfried Leibniz studied Pascal's calculators, improved them, and drew up plans for a mechanical calculator. In 1695 a machine was finally built, but this calculator also proved to be unreliable.

In the 19th century, an eccentric Englishman, Charles Babbage, developed plans for a grandiose calculating machine, called a "difference engine," with thousands of gears, ratchets, and counters (see Figure 1.7b).

Four years later in 1826, even though Babbage had still not built his difference engine, he began an even more elaborate project—the building of what he called an "analytic engine." This machine was capable of an accuracy to 20 decimal places, but it, too, could not be built because the technical knowledge to build it was not far enough advanced. Much later, International Business Machines (IBM) built both the difference and analytic engines based on Babbage's design but using modern technology, and they worked perfectly.

Hand-Held Calculators

In the past few years, pocket calculators have been one of the fastest-growing items in the United States. There are probably two reasons for this increase in popularity. Most people (including mathematicians!) don't like to do arithmetic, and a good calculator is very inexpensive. It is assumed that you have access to a calculator to use with this book.

First Computers

The devices discussed thus far in this section would all be classified as calculators. With some of the new programmable calculators, the distinction between a calculator and a computer is less well defined than it was in the past. Stimulated by the need to make ballistics calculations and to break secret codes during World War II, researchers made great advances in calculating machines. During the late 1930s and early 1940s, John Vincent Atanasoff, a physics professor at Iowa State University, and his graduate student Clifford E. Berry built an electronic digital computer, but could not get it to work properly. The first working electronic computers were invented by J. Presper Eckert and John W. Mauchly at the University of Pennsylvania. All computers now in use derive from the original work they did between 1942 and 1946. They built the first fully electronic digital computer called ENIAC (Electronic Numerical Integrator and Calculator), as shown in the related article "And the Winner Is..."

The ENIAC filled 30 feet $\times$ 50 feet of floor space, weighed 30 tons, had 18,000 vacuum tubes, cost $487,000 to build, and used enough electricity to operate three 150-kilowatt radio stations. Vacuum tubes generated a lot of heat and the room where computers were installed had to be kept in a carefully controlled atmosphere; still, the tubes had a substantial failure rate, and in order to "program" the computer, many switches and wires had to be adjusted.

The UNIVAC I, built in 1951 by the builders of the ENIAC, became the first commercially available computer. Unlike the ENIAC, it could handle alphabetic data as well as numeric data. The invention of the transistor in 1947 and solid-state devices in the 1950s provided the technology for smaller, faster, more reliable machines.

Present-Day Computers

In 1958, Seymour Cray developed the first **supercomputer**, sometimes called the Cray computer, which could handle at least 10 million instructions per second. It is used in major scientific research and military defense installations. The newest version of this computer, the X-1, operates a million times faster than the first supercomputer. It is difficult to keep track of the world's fastest computer, so if you want up-to-date information, you should check the *Top500 Supercomputer Sites* (**www.top500.org/lists**). One of the fastest, "The Earth Simulator," was put into service in Tokyo, Japan, in 2002 (see facing page). It is reported that it can perform at a speed in excess of 40TFLOPS (40 trillion operations per second).

ENIAC computer (1946)

And the Winner Is...

There is some controversy over who actually invented the first computer. In the early 1970s there was a lengthy court case over a patent dispute between Sperry Rand (who had acquired the ENIAC patent) and Honeywell, who represented those who originally worked on the ENIAC project. The judge in that case ruled that "between 1937 and 1942, Atanasoff . . . developed and built an automatic electronic digital computer themselves for solving large systems of linear equations. . . . Eckert and Mauchly did not invent the automatic electronic digital computer themselves, but instead derived that subject matter from one Dr. John Vincent Atanasoff." On the other hand, others believe that a court of law is not the place for deciding questions about the history of science and give Eckert and Mauchly the honor of inventing the first computer. In 1980, the Association for Computing Machinery honored them as founders of the computer industry.

Computers Are Not *Always* Correct

Keep in mind some of the deception that goes on in the name of technology. People sometimes think that "if a calculator or computer did it, then it must be correct." This is false, and the fact that a "machine" is involved has no effect on the validity of the results. Have you ever been told that "The computer requires...," or "There is nothing we can do; it is done by the computer," or "The computer won't permit it"? What they really mean is they don't want to instruct the *programmer* to do it.

Throughout the 1960s and early 1970s, computers continued to become faster and more powerful; they became a part of the business world. The "user" often never saw the machines. A "job" would be submitted to be "batch processed" by someone trained to run the computer. The notion of "time sharing" developed, so that the computer could handle more than one job, apparently simultaneously, by switching quickly from one job to another. Using a computer at this time was often frustrating; an incomplete job would be returned because of an error and the user would have to resubmit the job. It often took days to complete the project.

The large computers, known as mainframes, were followed by the **minicomputers**, which took up less than 3 cubic feet of space and no longer required a controlled atmosphere. These were still used by many people at the same time, though often directly through the use of terminals.

The term **personal computer** was first used by Stewart Brand in *The Whole Earth Catalog* (1968), which, oddly enough, was before any such computers existed. In 1976, Steven Jobs and Stephen Wozniak designed and built the Apple II, the first personal computer to be commercially successful. This computer proved extremely popular. Small businesses could afford to purchase these machines that, with a printer attached, took up only about twice the space of a typewriter. Technology "buffs" could purchase their own computers. This computer was designed so that innovations that would improve or enlarge the scope of performance of the machine could be added with relatively little difficulty. Owners could open up their machines and install new devices. One such device, the **mouse**, was introduced to the world by Douglas Engelbart in 1968. This increased contact between the user and the machine produced an atmosphere of tremendous creativity and innovation. In many cases, individual owners brought their own machines to work to introduce their superiors to the potential usefulness of the personal computer.

In the fast-moving technology of the computer world, the invention of language to describe it changes as fast as teenage slang. Today there are battery-powered **laptops**, weighing about 4 pounds, that are more powerful than the huge ENIAC. In 1989 a pocket computer weighing only 1 pound was introduced.

The most recent trend has been to link together several personal computers so that they can share software and different users can easily access the same documents. Such arrangements are called LANs, or **local area networks**. The most widely known **networks** are the **Internet**, which was first described by Paul Baran of the RAND Corp. in 1962, and the **World Wide Web** (www), developed by Tim Berners-Lee based on Baran's ideas and released in 1992. The growth of the Internet and the World Wide Web could not have been predicted.

"The Earth Simulator" supercomputer

Computer Hardware

The machine, or computer itself, is referred to as **hardware**. A personal computer might sell for under $500, but many extras, called **peripherals**, can increase the price by several thousand dollars. In this section we will familiarize you with the various components of a typical personal computer system that you might find in a home, classroom, or office. We will also discuss the link between the electronic signals of the computer and the human mind that enables us to harness the power and speed of the computer. The basic parts of a computer are shown in Figure 1.8.

We will focus our attention in this section on the terminology you will need to know to purchase a computer. The central unit of a computer contains a small microchip, called the central processing unit, where all processing takes place, and the computer memory, where the information is stored while the computer is completing a given task. The microchip and the unit that contains this chip are collectively referred to as the CPU. Almost daily, new and more popular chips are announced.

Although you do not need to understand electronic circuitry, a simple conceptual model of the inside of a computer can be very useful. The memory of a computer can be thought of as rows and rows of little storage boxes, each one with an address—yes, an address, just like your address. These boxes are of two types: **ROM** (read-only memory) and **RAM** (random access memory). ROM is very special: You can never change what is in it and it is not erased when the computer is turned off. It is programmed by the manufacturer to contain routines for certain processes that the computer must always use. The CPU can fetch information from it but cannot send new results back. It is well protected because it is at the heart of the machine's capabilities. On the other hand, programs and data are stored in RAM while the computer is completing a task. If the power to the computer is interrupted for any time, however brief, everything in RAM is lost forever.

Your computer will also have memory. When referring to memory, we used to talk in terms of a thousand bytes, called a *kilobyte* (KB or K), or in terms of a thousand kilobytes, called a *megabyte* (MB or MEG). However, today, we refer to *gigabytes* (GB; one gigabyte is about one billion bytes) or *terabytes* (TB; one trillion bytes). Your computer will come with 2, 4, or 8 GB (or even more) of RAM.

You will also need a device that reads and stores data, called a **hard drive**, which is used as additional memory to store the programs you purchase. Hard drives in sizes of 500, 750, 1000, or more gigabytes are commonly installed in **microcomputers**.

To use a computer, you will need **input** and **output** devices. A **keyboard** and a mouse are the most commonly used input devices. The most common output devices are a **monitor** and a **printer**. One of the monitor's main functions is to enable you to keep track of what is going on in the computer. The letters or pictures seen on a monitor are displayed by little dots called **pixels**, just as they are on a television. As the number of dots is increased, we say that the **resolution** of the monitor increases. The better the resolution, the easier on your eyes.

Computer Software

Communication with computers has become more sophisticated, and when a computer is purchased it often comes with several *programs* that allow the user to communicate with the computer. A **computer program** is a set of step-by-step directions that instruct a computer how to carry out a certain task. Programs that allow the user to carry out particular tasks on a computer are referred to as **software**.

The business world has welcomed the advances made possible by the use of personal computers and powerful programs, known as **software packages**, that enable the computer to do many diverse tasks. The most widely used computer applications are **word processing**, **database management**, and **spreadsheets**.

There are several sources for obtaining software. You can buy it in a store or you can download *shareware*

Figure 1.8 Input and output with a computer

which is try-before-you-buy software. Some software is available on the Internet free of charge (*freeware* or *public domain software*). The most widely used software is from Microsoft, which owns *Windows*®, *Word*®, *Internet Explorer*®, and *Excel*®. Bill Gates (1956–   ) is the cofounder of Microsoft and is known as the world's wealthiest person. In 1975, Ed Roberts built the first personal computer (the Altair 8800) in Albuquerque, New Mexico; it was featured on the cover of *Popular Electronics*, and was named because the word *Altair* was used in an episode of *Star Trek.* Bill Gates and his partner, Paul Allen, were students at Harvard at the time and traveled to New Mexico to look at this new machine. The story about the beginning of the huge Microsoft empire is told by Stephen Segaller in *Nerds 2.0.1*:

> *He [Bill Gates] kept postponing and postponing actually writing the code [for the Altair]. He said, "I know how to write it, I have a design in my head, I'll get it done, don't worry about it, Paul." Four days before he was due to go back to Harvard he checked into a hotel and he was incommunicado for three days. Bill came back three or four days later with this huge sheet of paper. He'd written 4K of code in three days, and typed the whole thing in, got it working, and went back to school, just barely. It was really one of the most amazing displays of programming I've ever seen.*

Uses of Computers

Today, computers are used for a variety of purposes. **Data processing** involves large collections of data on which relatively few calculations need to be made. For example, a credit card company could use the system to keep track of the balances of its customers' accounts. **Information retrieval** involves locating and displaying material from a description of its content. For example, a police department may want information about a suspect, or a realtor may want listings that meet the criteria of a client. **Pattern recognition** is the identification and classification of shapes, forms, or relationships. For example, a chess-playing program will examine the chessboard carefully to determine a good next move. The computer carries out these tasks by accepting information, performing mathematical and logical operations with the information, and then supplying the results of the operations as new information. Finally, a computer can be used for **simulation** of a real situation. For example, a prototype of a new airplane can be tested under various circumstances to determine its limitations. Figure 1.9 illustrates these activities.

Misuses of Computers

Most companies and bulletin boards require a **password** or special procedures to be able to go online with their computers. A major problem for certain computer installations has been to make sure that it is impossible for the wrong person to get into their computer. There have been many instances where people have "broken into" computers just as a safecracker breaks into a safe. They have been clever enough to discover how to access the system. A few of these people have been caught and prosecuted. A security break of this nature can be very serious. By transferring funds in a bank computer, someone can steal money. By breaking into a military installation, a spy could steal secrets or commit sabotage. By breaking into a university's computers, one could change

Figure 1.9 Common computer uses

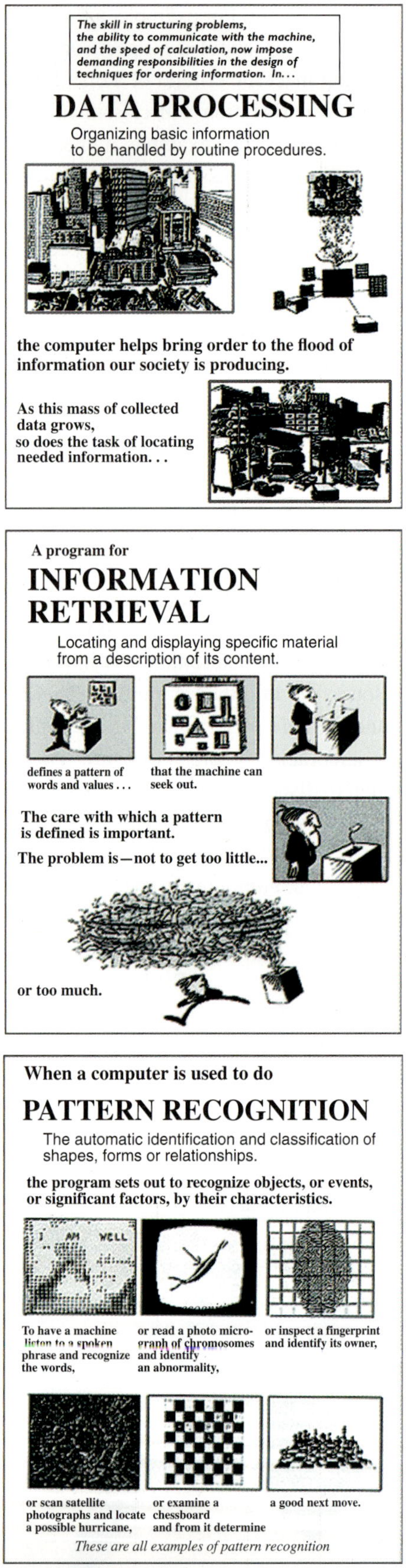

grades or records. **Computer abuse** includes *illegal use* (as described above, but also includes illegal copying of programs, called *pirating*) and abuse caused by *ignorance.* Ignorance of computers leads to the assumption that the output data are always correct or that the use of a computer is beyond one's comprehension.

The Future of Computers

With the tremendous advances in computer technology, financial investors and analysts can simulate various possible outcomes and select strategies that best suit their goals. Designers and engineers use computer-aided design, known as CAD. Using computer graphics, sculptors can model their work on a computer that will rotate the image so that the proposed work can be viewed from all sides. Computers have been used to help the handicapped with learning certain skills and by taking over certain functions. Computers can be used to "talk" for those without speech. For those without sight, there are artificial vision systems that translate a visual image to a tactile "image" that can be "seen" on their back. A person who has never seen a candle burn can learn the shape and dynamic quality of a flame.

Along with the advances in computer technology came new courses, and even new departments, in colleges and universities. New specialties developed involving the design, use, and impact of computers on our society. The feats of the computer captured the imagination of some who thought that a computer could be designed to be as intelligent as a human mind, and the field known as **artificial intelligence** was born. Many researchers worked on natural language translation with very high hopes initially, but the progress has been slow. Progress continues in "expert systems," programs that involve the sophisticated strategy of pushing the computer ever closer to human-like capabilities. The quest has produced powerful uses for computers.

What does the future hold? Earlier editions of this book attempted to make predictions of the future, and in every case those predictions became outdated during the life of the edition. Instead of making a prediction, we invite you to visit a computer store.

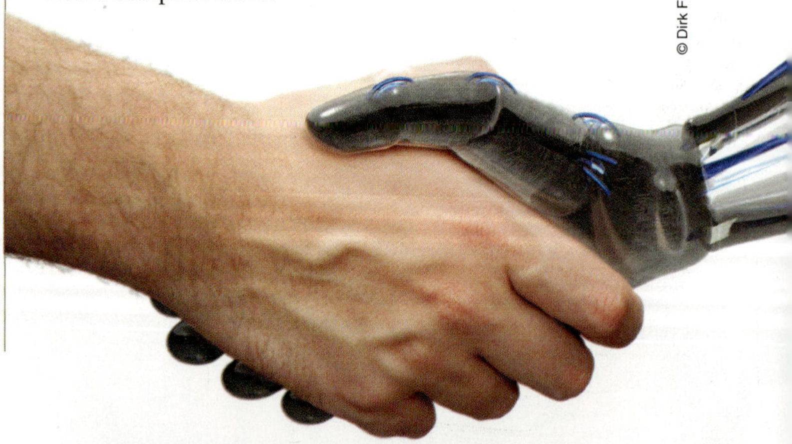

MORE AND MORE PROBLEM SETS

MATH puts a multitude of study aids at your fingertips. After reading the chapters, check out these resources for further help.

- Downloadable problem sets per chapter and chapter section that allow you to apply the math concepts you learned in the text.
- Online printable flashcards give you two additional ways to check your comprehension of key mathematics concepts.

Other great ways to help you study include **Watch It** video tutorials, **Practice It** worked-out examples, **Solve It** downloadable homework problem sets, an online glossary, and **Quiz It** interactive quizzing.

You can find all of the above at **4ltrpress.cengage.com/math.**

The Nature of Numbers

topics

2.1 It's Natural

THE MOST BASIC SET OF NUMBERS USED BY ANY SOCIETY IS THE SET OF NUMBERS USED FOR COUNTING:

$$\mathbb{N} = \{1, 2, 3, 4, 5, 6, 7, 8, 9, 10, 11, \ldots\}$$

This set of numbers is called the set of **counting numbers** or **natural numbers**. Let's assume that you understand what the numbers in this set represent, and you understand the operation of **addition**, +. That is, we assume, without definition, knowledge of the operation of addition of natural numbers, and we call the result of an addition a **sum**.

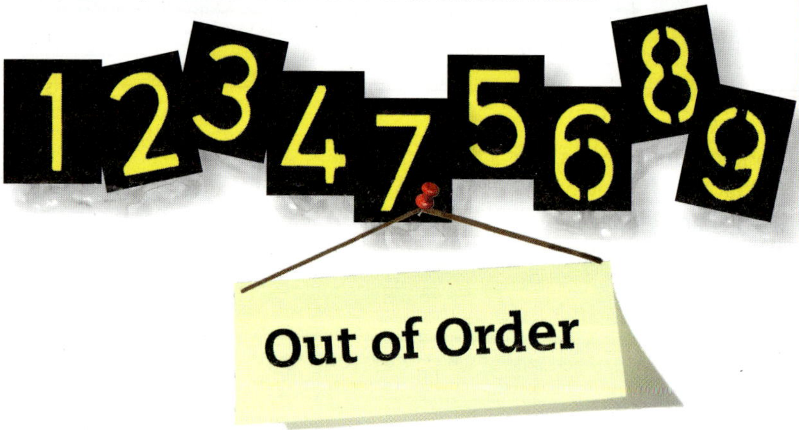

There are a few self-evident properties of addition for this set of natural numbers. They are called "self-evident" because they almost seem too obvious to be stated explicitly. For example, if you jump into the air, you expect to come back down. That assumption is well founded in experience and is also based on an assumption that jumping has certain undeniable properties. But astronauts have found that some very basic assumptions are valid on earth and false in space. Recognizing these assumptions (properties, axioms, laws, or postulates) is important.

Closure Property

When we add or multiply any two natural numbers, we know that we obtain a natural number. This "knowing" is an assumption based on experiences (inductive reasoning), but we have actually experienced only a small number of cases for all the possible sums and products of numbers. The scientist—and the mathematician in particular—is very skeptical about making assumptions too quickly. The assumption that the sum or product of two natural numbers is a natural number is given the name *closure* and is referred to as the **closure property**. The property is phrased in terms of sets and operations.

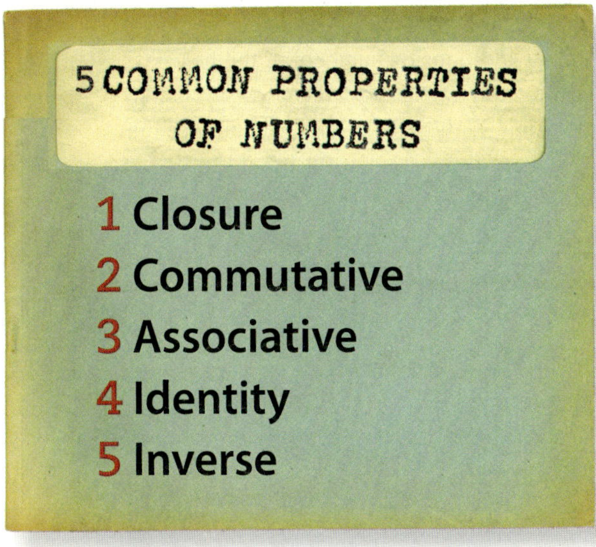

Think of a set as a "box"; there is a label on the box—say, addition. If *all* additions of numbers in the box have answers that are already *in* the box, then we say the set is **closed** for addition. If there is at least one answer that is not contained in the box, then the set is said to be **not closed** for that operation.

A closed box

A box that is not closed

Closure for + in ℕ

Let ℕ be the set of natural (or counting) numbers. Let a and b be any natural numbers. Then

$a + b$ is a natural number

We say ℕ is closed for addition.

Commutative and Associative Properties

The word *commute* can mean to travel back and forth from home to work. This back-and-forth idea can help you remember that the commutative property applies if you read from left to right or from right to left.

The word *associate* can mean connect, join, or unite. With this property, you associate two of the added numbers.

You need find only one *counterexample* to show that a property does not hold.

Another self-evident property of the natural numbers concerns the order in which they are added. It is called the **commutative property for addition** and states that the *order* in which two numbers are added makes no difference; that is (if we read from left to right),

$$a + b = b + a$$

for any two natural numbers a and b. The commutative property allows us to rearrange numbers; it is called a *property of order*. Together with another property, called the *associative property*, it is used in calculation and simplification.

The **associative property for addition** allows us to group numbers for addition. Suppose you wish to add three numbers—say, 2, 3, and 8:

$$2 + 3 + 8$$

To add these numbers you must first add two of them and then add this sum to the third. The associative property tells us that, no matter which two numbers are added first, the final result is the same. If parentheses are used to indicate the numbers to be added first, then this property can be symbolized by

$$(2 + 3) + 8 = 2 + (3 + 8)$$

This associative property for addition holds for *any* three or more natural numbers.

Add the column of numbers in the box to the right. How long does it take? Five seconds is long enough if you use the associative and commutative properties for addition:

9
8
7
6
5
4
3
2
+1

$$(9 + 1) + (8 + 2) + (7 + 3) + (6 + 4) + 5 = 10 + 10 + 10 + 10 + 5 = 45$$

However, it takes much longer if you don't rearrange (commute) and regroup (associate) the numbers:

$$
\begin{aligned}
(9 + 8) + (7 + 6 + 5 + 4 + 3 + 2 + 1) &= (17 + 7) + (6 + 5 + 4 + 3 + 2 + 1) \\
&= (24 + 6) + (5 + 4 + 3 + 2 + 1) \\
&= (30 + 5) + (4 + 3 + 2 + 1) \\
&= (35 + 4) + (3 + 2 + 1) \\
&= (39 + 3) + (2 + 1) \\
&= (42 + 2) + 1 \\
&= 44 + 1 \\
&= 45
\end{aligned}
$$

The properties of associativity and commutativity are not restricted to the operation of addition. For example, these properties also hold for $\mathbb{N}$ and multiplication, as we will now discuss.

Multiplication is defined as repeated addition.

the operation of multiplication

For $a \neq 0$, multiplication is defined as follows:

$a \times b$ means $\underbrace{b + b + b + \ldots + b}_{a \text{ addends}}$

If $a = 0$, then $0 \times b = 0$.

© Greg Nicholas/iStockphoto.com / © Jussi Santaniemi/iStockphoto.com

We now consider the **property of closure for multiplication**.

Closure for × in ℕ

Let $\mathbb{N}$ be the set of natural (or counting) numbers. Let a and b be any natural numbers. Then

ab is a natural number

We say $\mathbb{N}$ is closed for multiplication.

We can now consider commutativity and associativity for multiplication in the set $\mathbb{N}$ of natural numbers:

Commutativity: $2 \times 3 \stackrel{?}{=} 3 \times 2$

Associativity: $(2 \times 3) \times 4 \stackrel{?}{=} 2 \times (3 \times 4)$

The question mark above the equal sign signifies that we should not assume the conclusion (namely, that the expressions on both sides are equal) until we check the arithmetic. Even though we can check these properties for particular natural numbers, it is impossible to check them for all natural numbers, so we accept the following axioms.

COMMUTATIVE AND ASSOCIATIVE PROPERTIES

For any natural numbers a, b, and c:

Commutative properties	*Associative properties*
Addition: $a + b = b + a$	Addition: $(a + b) + c = a + (b + c)$
Multiplication: $ab = ba$	Multiplication: $(ab)c = a(bc)$

© rackerman/iStockphoto.com

To distinguish between the commutative and associative properties, remember the following:

1. When the *commutative property* is used, the *order* in which the elements appear from left to right is changed, but the grouping is not changed.
2. When the *associative property* is used, the elements are *grouped* differently, but the order in which they appear is not changed.
3. If *both* the order and the grouping have been changed, then both the commutative and associative properties have been used.

© iStockphoto.com

THERE STILL REMAIN THREE STUDIES SUITABLE FOR FREE MAN. ARITHMETIC IS ONE OF THEM.

— PLATO

We are not confined to ℕ when discussing the associative and commutative properties (or any of the properties, for that matter). Nor are we restricted to addition and multiplication for our operations. Indeed, it is often fun to form your own "group" of numbers and see whether the properties hold for your group under your designated operation.

Distributive Property

Are there properties in ℕ that involve both operations? Consider an example. Suppose you are selling tickets for a raffle, and the tickets cost $2 each. You sell three tickets on Monday and four tickets on Tuesday. How much money did you collect?

Solution I You sold a total of $3 + 4 = 7$ tickets, which cost $2 each, so you collected $2 \times 7 = 14$ dollars. That is,

$$2 \times (3 + 4) = 14$$

Solution II You collected $2 \times 3 = 6$ dollars on Monday and $2 \times 4 = 8$ dollars on Tuesday for a total of $6 + 8 = 14$ dollars. That is,

$$(2 \times 3) + (2 \times 4) = 14$$

Since these solutions are equal, we see

$$2 \times (3 + 4) = (2 \times 3) + (2 \times 4)$$

Do you suppose this would be true if the tickets cost a dollars and you sold b tickets on Monday and c tickets on Tuesday? Then the equation would be

$$a \times (b + c) = (a \times b) + (a \times c)$$

or simply

$$a(b + c) = ab + ac$$

This example illustrates the **distributive property for multiplication over addition**.

DISTRIBUTIVE PROPERTY

$$a(b + c) = ab + ac$$

* Memorize this—you'll use it a lot!

In the set ℕ of natural numbers, is addition distributive over multiplication? We wish to check

$$3 + (4 \times 5) \stackrel{?}{=} (3 + 4) \times (3 + 5)$$

Checking:

$$3 + (4 \times 5) = 3 + 20 = 23$$

and

$$(3 + 4) \times (3 + 5) = 7 \times 8 = 56$$

Thus, addition is not distributive over multiplication in the set of natural numbers.

The distributive property can also help to simplify arithmetic. Suppose you wish to multiply 9 by 71. You can use the distributive property to do the following mental multiplication:

$$\begin{aligned} 9 \times 71 &= 9 \times (70 + 1) \\ &= (9 \times 70) + (9 \times 1) \\ &= 630 + 9 = 639 \end{aligned}$$

This allows you to do the problem quickly and simply in your head.

Definition of Subtraction

Since these properties hold for the operations of addition and multiplication, we might reasonably ask whether they hold for other operations. **Subtraction** is defined as the opposite of addition, and the result of a subtraction is called a **difference**.

the operation of subtraction

is defined in terms of addition:

$a - b = x$ means $a = b + x$

* From the definition of subtraction, $2 - 3 = \square$ means $2 = \square + 3$ so we need to find a number that, when added to 3, gives the result 2.

To test the commutative property for subtraction, we check a particular example:

$$3 - 2 \stackrel{?}{=} 2 - 3$$

Now, $3 - 2 = 1$, but $2 - 3$ doesn't even exist in the set of natural numbers. Therefore, the commutative property does not hold for subtraction in ℕ.

Furthermore, to provide the result of the operation of subtraction for $2 - 3$, we must find a number that when added to 3 gives the result 2. But there is *no such natural number*. Thus, the set of natural numbers is *closed* for addition and multiplication, but is *not closed* for subtraction. In Section 2.3, we will add elements to the set of natural numbers to create the set of *integers*, which will be closed for subtraction as well as for addition and multiplication.

2.2 Prime Numbers

A SET OF NUMBERS THAT IS IMPORTANT, NOT ONLY IN ALGEBRA BUT IN ALL OF MATHEMATICS, IS THE SET OF PRIME NUMBERS.

To understand prime numbers, you must first understand the idea of divisibility, along with some new terminology and notation.

Divisibility

The natural number 10 is divisible by 2, since there is a natural number 5 so that $10 = 2 \cdot 5$; it is not divisible by 3, since there is no natural number k such that $10 = 3 \cdot k$. This leads us to the following definition of **divisibility**.

Divisibility means that if m and d are natural numbers, and if there is a natural number k so that $m = d \cdot k$, we say that d is a *divisor* of m, d is a *factor* of m, *d divides m*, and m is a *multiple* of d. We denote this relationship by $d|m$.

WATCH YOUR STEP

Do not confuse this notation with the notation sometimes used for fractions: "5/30" means 5 divided by 30, which is a fraction; "5|30" means "5 divides 30," which is a statement.

That is, $5|30$ is read "5 divides 30" and means that there exists some natural number k—namely, 6—such that $30 = 5 \cdot k$. The result of a division is called a **quotient**.

It is easy to see that 1 divides every natural number m, since $m = 1 \cdot m$. Also, by the commutative property of multiplication, $m = m \cdot 1$; thus every natural number m divides itself. We have proved the following theorem.

Number of Divisors

Every natural (counting) number greater than 1 has at least two distinct divisors, itself and 1.

The theorem of the number of divisors is basic to understanding what follows. Consider the number 341,592. Is this number divisible by 2? By 3? By 4? By 5? You may know some ways of answering these questions without the necessity of actually doing the division. We can formulate various rules of divisibility as shown in Table 2.1.

Table 2.1 Rules of Divisibility for a Natural Number N

N is divisible by	Test
1	all N
2	if the last digit is divisible by 2.
3	if the sum of the digits is divisible by 3.
4	if the number formed by the last two digits is divisible by 4.
5	if the last digit is 0 or 5.
6	if the number is divisible by 2 and by 3.
8	if the number formed by the last three digits is divisible by 8.
9	if the sum of the digits is divisible by 9.
10	if the last digit is 0.
12	if the number is divisible by 3 and by 4.

Finding Primes

Since every natural number greater than 1 has at least two divisors, can any number have more than two?

Checking:

- ✔ 2 has exactly two divisors: 1, 2
- ✔ 3 has exactly two divisors: 1, 3
- ✔ 4 has more than two divisors: 1, 2, and 4

Thus, some numbers (such as 2 and 3) have exactly two divisors, and some (such as 4 and 6) have more than two divisors. Do any natural numbers have fewer than two divisors?

We now state a definition that classifies each natural number according to the number of divisors it has.

> A **prime number** is a natural number that has exactly two divisors. A natural number that has more than two divisors is called a **composite number**.

We see that 2 is prime, 3 is prime, 4 is composite (since it is divisible by three natural numbers), 5 is prime, 6 is composite (since it is divisible by 1, 2, 3, and 6). Note that every natural number greater than 1 is either prime or composite. The number 1 is neither prime nor composite.

One method for finding primes smaller than some given number was first used by a Greek mathematician, Eratosthenes, more than 2,000 years ago.

The technique is known as the **sieve of Eratosthenes**. Suppose we wish to find the primes less than 100. We prepare a table of natural numbers 1-100 (Table 2.2) using the procedure below.

PROCEDURE:
Sieve of Eratosthenes

STEP 1 Write down a list of numbers from 1 to 100 (see Table 2.2).

STEP 2 Cross out 1, since it is not classified as a prime number.

STEP 3 Draw a circle around 2, the smallest prime number. Then cross out every following multiple of 2, since each is divisible by 2 and thus is not prime.

STEP 4 Draw a circle around 3, the next prime number. Then cross out each succeeding multiple of 3. Some of these numbers, such as 6 and 12, will already have been crossed out because they are also multiples of 2.

STEP 5 Circle the next open prime, 5, and cross out all subsequent multiples of 5.

STEP 6 The next prime number is 7; circle 7 and cross out multiples of 7.

STEP 7 Since 7 is the largest prime less than $\sqrt{100} = 10$, we now know that all the remaining numbers are prime.

Table 2.2 Finding Primes Using the Sieve of Eratosthenes

1	2	3	4	5	6	7	8	9	10
11	12	13	14	15	16	17	18	19	20
21	22	23	24	25	26	27	28	29	30
31	32	33	34	35	36	37	38	39	40
41	42	43	44	45	46	47	48	49	50
51	52	53	54	55	56	57	58	59	60
61	62	63	64	65	66	67	68	69	70
71	72	73	74	75	76	77	78	79	80
81	82	83	84	85	86	87	88	89	90
91	92	93	94	95	96	97	98	99	100

The process is a simple one, since you do not have to cross out the multiples of 3 (for example) by checking for divisibility by 3 but can simply cross out every third number. Thus, anyone who can count can find primes by this method. Also, notice that in finding the primes under 100, we had crossed out all the composite numbers by the time we crossed out the multiples of 7. That is, to find all primes less than 100: (1) Find the largest prime smaller than or equal to $\sqrt{100} = 10$ (7 in this case); (2) cross out multiples of primes up to and including 7; and (3) all the remaining numbers in the chart are primes.

This result generalizes. If you wish to find all primes smaller than n:

1. Find the *largest* prime less than or equal to $\sqrt{n}$.

2. Cross out the multiples of primes less than or equal to $\sqrt{n}$.

3. All the remaining numbers in the chart are primes.

Phrasing this another way, if n is composite, then one of its factors must be less than or equal to $\sqrt{n}$. That is, if $n = ab$, then it can't be true that *both a and b* are greater than $\sqrt{n}$ (otherwise $ab > \sqrt{n}\sqrt{n} = n = ab$, so $ab > ab$ is a contradiction). Thus, one of the factors must be less than or equal to $\sqrt{n}$.

Prime Factorization

Prime numbers are fundamental to many mathematical processes. In particular, we use prime numbers in working with rational numbers later in this chapter. You will need to understand *prime factorization, greatest common factor,* and *least common multiple.*

The operation of **factoring** is the reverse of the operation of multiplying. For example, multiplying 3 by 6 yields $3 \cdot 6 = 18$, and this answer is unique (only one answer is possible). In the reverse process, called factoring, you are given the number 18 and asked for numbers that can be multiplied together to give 18. This process is *not* unique; we list several different factorizations of 18:

$$18 = 1 \cdot 18 = 18 \cdot 1 = 2 \cdot 9 = 9 \cdot 2 = 1 \cdot 1 \cdot 2 \cdot 9 = 3 \cdot 6 = 2 \cdot 3 \cdot 3 = \ldots$$

There are, in fact, infinitely many possibilities. We make some agreements, so the process gives a unique answer:

1. We will not consider the order in which the factors are listed as important. That is, $2 \cdot 9$ and $9 \cdot 2$ are considered the same factorization.

2. We will not consider 1 as a factor when writing out any factorizations. That is, prime numbers do not have factorizations.

3. Recall that we are working in the set of natural numbers; thus, $18 = 36 \cdot \frac{1}{2}$ and $18 = (-2)(-9)$ are *not* considered factorizations of 18.

With these agreements, we have greatly reduced the possibilities:

$$18 = 2 \cdot 9 = 3 \cdot 6 = 2 \cdot 3^2$$

These are the only three possible factorizations. Notice that the last factorization contains only prime factors; thus it is called the **prime factorization** of 18. *Finding prime factorizations is a process that is used in a multitude of mathematical applications.*

It should be clear that, if a number is composite, it can be factored as the product of two natural numbers greater than 1. Each of these two numbers will be prime or composite. If both are prime, then we have a prime factorization. If one or more is composite, we repeat the process and continue until we have written the original number as a product of primes. It is also true that this representation is unique. This is one of the most important results in arithmetic, and it carries the impressive title **fundamental theorem of arithmetic**.

Fundamental Theorem of Arithmetic

Every natural number greater than 1 is either a prime or a product of primes, and its prime factorization is unique (except for the order in which the factors appear).

A *prime factorization* of a number is a factorization that consists exclusively of prime numbers. Suppose we wish to find the prime factorization of 36.

STEP 1 From your knowledge of the basic multiplication facts, write any two numbers whose product is the given number. Circle any prime factor.

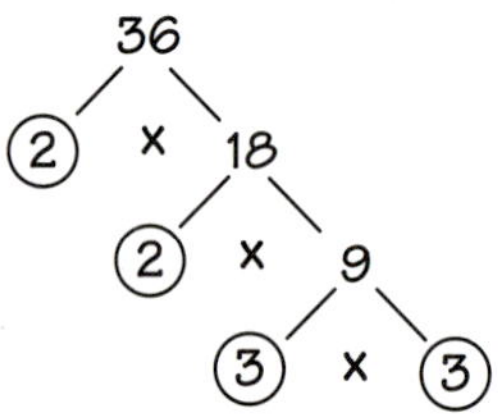

This process for finding a prime factorization is called a **factor tree**.

STEP 2 Repeat the process for uncircled numbers.

STEP 3 When all the factors are circled, their product is the *prime factorization*.

$36 = 2 \times 2 \times 3 \times 3 = 2^2 \times 3^2$

If you cannot readily find the prime factors of a number, you should look at the list of prime factors from the smallest to the larger numbers, as illustrated for 34,153.

First, try 2; you might notice that 34,153 is not an even number, so 2 is not a factor. Next, try 3 (the next prime after 2); 3 does not divide evenly into 34,153, so 3 is not a factor. Next, try 5; it is also not a factor.

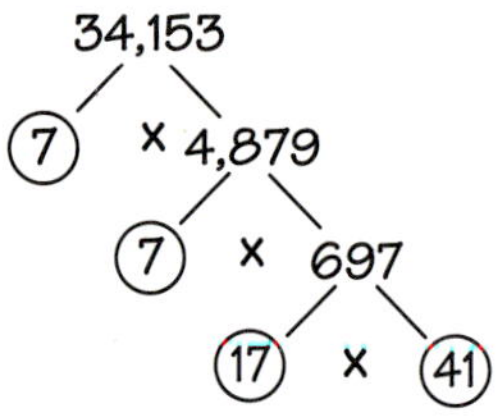

The next prime to try is 7 (by calculator or long division; calculator display is 4879). Now, focus on 4,879. Previously tried numbers cannot be factors, but since 7 *was* a factor, it might be again: $4{,}879 = 7 \times 697$.

Continue this process: 697 is not divisible (evenly) by 7, so try 11 (doesn't divide evenly), 13 (doesn't divide evenly), and 17 (does). The remaining number, 41, is a prime, so the process is complete:

$34{,}153 = 7^2 \times 17 \times 41$

Greatest Common Factor

Suppose we look at the set of factors common to a given set of numbers:

Factors of 18: {1, 2, 3, 6, 9, 18}
↕ ↕ ↕ ↕ Common factors: {1, 2, 3, 6}
Factors of 12: {1, 2, 3, 4, 6, 12}

The **greatest common factor** is the largest number in the set of common factors.

> The **greatest common factor** (g.c.f.) of a set of numbers is the largest number that divides (evenly) into each of the numbers in the given set.

The procedure for finding the greatest common factor involves the canonical form of the given numbers. For example, suppose we want to find the greatest common factor of 24 and 30. We first find all factors, then the intersection (common factors), and finally the greatest one in that set:

Factors of 24:	{1, 2, 3, 4, 6, 8, 12, 24}
Factors of 30:	{1, 2, 3, 5, 6, 10, 15, 30}
Common factors:	{1, 2, 3, 6}
g.c.f. = 6	

This process can be rather tedious, so we outline a more refined procedure:

PROCEDURE:
For Finding the g.c.f.

STEP 1 Write the factorizations in canonical form.

STEP 2 Select the representative of each factor with the SMALLEST exponent.

STEP 3 Multiply the representatives to find the greatest common factor (g.c.f.).

We illustrate this procedure for the numbers 24 and 30. First, find the canonical representation of each:

$$24 = 2^3 \cdot 3 \quad = 2^3 \cdot 3^1 \cdot 5^0$$
$$30 = 2 \cdot 3 \cdot 5 = 2^1 \cdot 3^1 \cdot 5^1$$

Select one representative from each of the columns in the factorizations. The representative we select when finding the g.c.f. is the one with the smallest exponent. The g.c.f. is the product of these representatives.

$$\text{g.c.f.} = 2^1 \cdot 3^1 \cdot 5^0 = 6$$

The procedure for finding the g.c.f. is summarized in Figure 2.1.

Figure 2.1 Flowchart for finding the greatest common factor (g.c.f.)

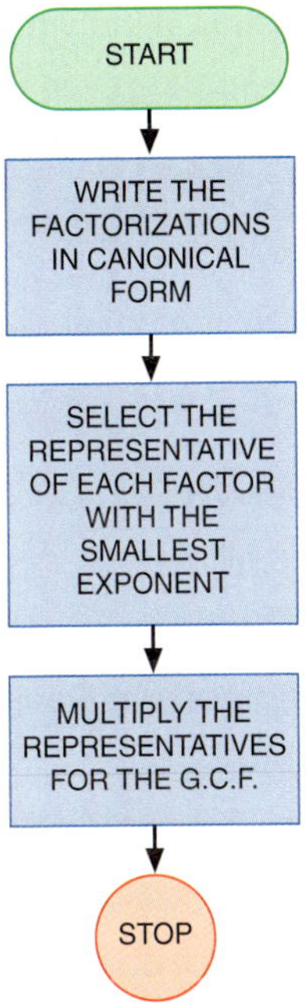

Figure 2.2 Procedure for finding the least common multiple (l.c.m.)

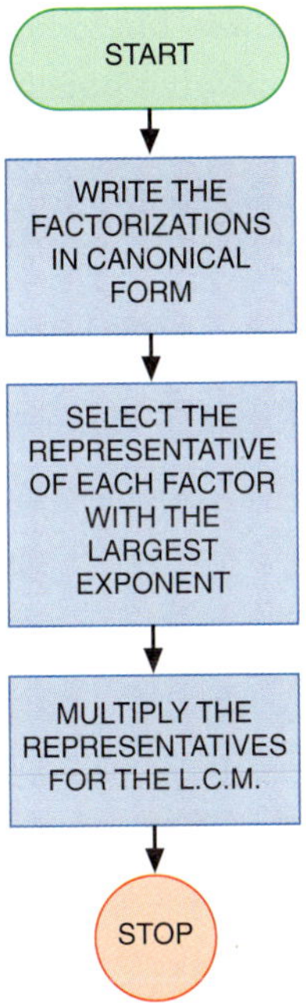

If the greatest common factor of two numbers is 1, we say that the numbers are **relatively prime**. Notice that 15 and 28 are relatively prime, but they themselves are not prime. It is possible for relatively prime numbers to be composite numbers.

Least Common Multiple

The greatest common factor is the largest number in the intersection of the factors of a set of given numbers. On the other hand, the **least common multiple** is the smallest number in the intersection of the multiples of a set of given numbers.

The **least common multiple** (l.c.m.) of a set of numbers is the smallest number that each of the numbers in the set divides into evenly.

For example, suppose we want to find the least common multiple of 24 and 30.

Multiples of 24:	{24, 48, 72, 96, 120, . . .}
Multiples of 30:	{30, 60, 90, 120, . . .}
Common multiples:	{120, 240, . . .}
l.c.m. = 120	

An algorithm for finding the least common multiple is very much like the one for finding the g.c.f.

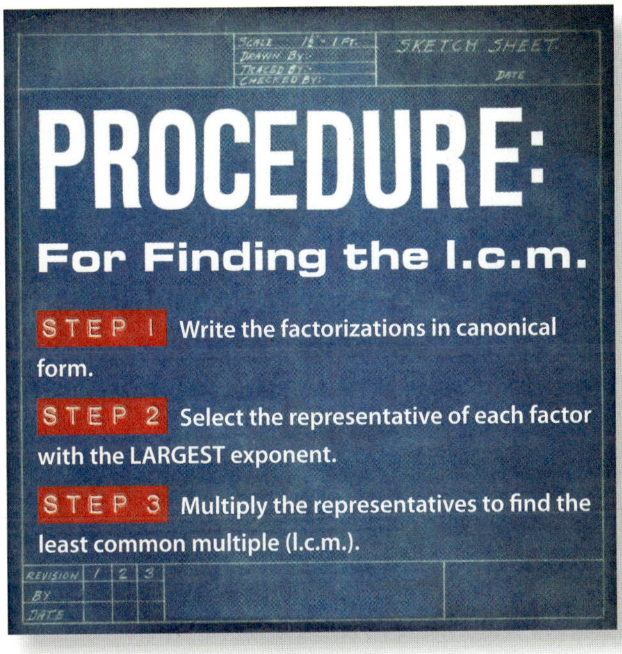

© Nicholas Belton/iStockphoto.com

The process, as before, begins by finding the canonical representations of the numbers involved. For example, to obtain the l.c.m. of the numbers 24 and 30, write each in canonical form:

$$24 = 2^3 \cdot 3^1 \cdot 5^0 \qquad 30 = 2^1 \cdot 3^1 \cdot 5^1$$

For the l.c.m., we choose the representative of each factor with the largest exponent. The l.c.m. is the product of these representatives.

$$\text{l.c.m.} = \mathbf{2^3 \cdot 3^1 \cdot 5^1 = 120}$$

The procedure for finding the least common multiple is shown in Figure 2.2.

in pursuit of primes

The method of Eratosthenes gives a finite list of primes, but it is not very satisfactory to use if we wish to determine whether a given number n is a prime. For centuries, mathematicians have tried to find a formula that would yield *every* prime. Let's try to find a formula that results in giving only primes. A possible candidate is

$$n^2 - n + 41$$

If we try this formula for $n = 1$, we obtain $1^2 - 1 + 41 = 41$.

For $n = 2$: $2^2 - 2 + 41 = 43$, a prime

For $n = 3$: $3^2 - 3 + 41 = 47$, a prime

So far, so good; that is, we are obtaining only primes. Continuing, we keep finding only primes for n up to 40:

For $n = 40$: $40^2 - 40 + 41 = 1{,}601$, a prime

Inductively, we might conclude that the formula yields only primes, but the next value provides a counterexample:

For $n = 41$: $41^2 - 41 + 41 = 41^2 = 1{,}681$, not a prime!

A more serious attempt to find a prime number formula was made by Pierre de Fermat, who tried the formula

$2^{2^n} + 1$ For $n = 1$: $2^{2^1} + 1 = 5$, a prime

For $n = 2$: $2^{2^2} + 1 = 2^4 + 1 = 17$, a prime

For $n = 3$: $2^{2^3} + 1 = 2^8 + 1 = 257$, a prime

For $n = 4$: $2^{2^4} + 1 = 2^{16} + 1 = 65{,}537$, a prime

For $n = 5$: $2^{2^5} + 1 = 2^{32} + 1 = 4{,}294{,}967{,}297$

Is 4,294,967,297 a prime?

The answer is not easy. It turns out this number is not prime! It is divisible by 641. Whether this formula generates any other primes is unknown.

In 1644, the French priest and number theorist Marin Mersenne (1588–1648) stated without proof that

$$2^{251} - 1$$

is composite. In the 19th century, mathematicians finally proved Mersenne correct when they discovered that this number was divisible by both 503 and 54,217. Mersenne did discover, however, that

$$2^{257} - 1$$

is a prime number.

In 1970, a young Russian named Yuri Matiyasevich discovered several explicit polynomials (such as $n^2 - n + 41$) of this sort that generate only prime numbers, but all of those he discovered are too complicated to reproduce here. The largest known prime number at that time was

$$2^{11{,}213} - 1$$

which was discovered at the University of Illinois through the use of number theory and computers. The mathematicians were so proud of this discovery that the university used the postmark above on their postage meter. Some other large prime numbers and the dates of their discovery are shown in Table 2.3.

If you are interested in finding out more about the search for large primes such as these, you might wish to check the Great Internet Mersenne Prime Search, or as it is usually known, GIMPS. GIMPS is a worldwide project coordinated by George Woltman, who wrote a program for the PC to find primes. The hunt for record prime numbers used to be the exclusive domain of supercomputers, but today by using thousands of individual machines, it is possible to collectively surpass even the most powerful computers. You can visit their website at www.mersenne.org.

Table 2.3 Some Large Primes

Prime Number	Date of Discovery	Source
$2^{257} - 1$	1644	Marin Mersenne
$2^{11,213} - 1$	1963	Donald B. Gillies
$2^{19,937} - 1$	1971	Bryant Tuckerman
$2^{21,701} - 1$	1978	L. Curt Noll and Laura Nickel
$2^{86,243} - 1$	1982	David Slowinski
$2^{216,091} - 1$	1985	David Slowinski
$2^{859,433} - 1$	1994	David Slowinski and Paul Gage
$2^{1,398,269} - 1$	1996	Armengaud, Woltman, et al. GIMPS
$2^{3,021,377} - 1$	1998	Clarkson, Woltman, Kurowski, et al. GIMPS
$2^{6,972,593} - 1$	1999	Hajratwala, Woltman, Kurowski, et al. GIMPS
$2^{13,466,917} - 1$	2001	Cameron, Woltman, Kurowski, et al. GIMPS
$2^{30,402,457} - 1$	2005	Cooper, Boone, Woltman, Kurowski, et al. GIMPS
$2^{32,582,657} - 1$	2006	Cooper, Boone, Woltman, Kurowski, et al. GIMPS
$2^{37,156,667} - 1$	2008	Elvenich, Woltman, et al. GIMPS
$2^{43,112,609} - 1$	2008	Smith, Woltman, et al. GIMPS

B.C. cartoon reprinted by permission of Johnny Hart and Creators Syndicate.

2.3 Numbers—Up and Down

HISTORICALLY, AN AGRICULTURAL-TYPE SOCIETY WOULD NEED ONLY NATURAL NUMBERS, BUT WHAT ABOUT A SUBTRACTION SUCH AS

$$5 - 5 = ?$$

Certainly society would have a need for a number representing $5 - 5$, so a new number, called **zero**, was invented, so that $5 = 5 + 0$ (remember the definition of subtraction). If this new number is annexed to the set of natural numbers, a set called the set of **whole numbers** is formed:

$$\mathbb{W} = \{0, 1, 2, 3, 4, \ldots\}$$

This one annexation to the existing numbers satisfied society's needs for several thousand years.

However, as society evolved, the need for bookkeeping advanced, and eventually the need to answer this: Can we annex new numbers to the set $\mathbb{W}$ so that it is possible to carry out *all* subtractions? The numbers that need to be annexed are the **opposites** of the natural numbers. The opposite of 3, which is denoted by -3, is the number that when added to 3 gives 0. If we annex these opposites to the set $\mathbb{W}$ we have the following set:

$$\mathbb{Z} = \{\ldots, -3, -2, -1, 0, 1, 2, 3, \ldots\}$$

This set is known as the set of **integers**. It is customary to refer to certain subsets of $\mathbb{Z}$ as follows:

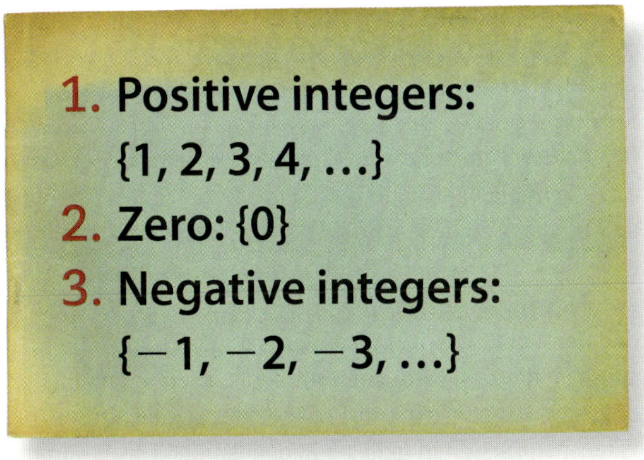

© Mike Bentley/iStockphoto.com / © Stefan Klein/iStockphoto.com

Now with this new enlarged set of numbers, are we able to carry out all possible additions, subtractions, and multiplications? Before we answer this question, let's review the process by which we operate within the set of integers. It is assumed that you have had an algebra course, so the following summary is intended only as a review.

You might recall that the process for describing the operations with integers requires the notion of **absolute value**, which represents the distance of a number from the origin when plotted on a number line. We give an algebraic definition.

The **absolute value** of x, denoted by $|x|$, is defined as

$$|x| = \begin{cases} x, & \text{if } x \geq 0 \\ -x, & \text{if } x < 0 \end{cases}$$

STOP *This definition may be difficult to understand; stop for a few moments to make sure you understand what it says.*

Using this definition we find $|5| = 5$, $|-5| = -(-5) = 5$, and $|-(-3)| = |3| = 3$.

LET'S REVIEW THE PROCESS BY WHICH WE OPERATE WITHIN THE SET OF INTEGERS.

Addition of Integers

If one (or both) of the integers is 0, then we use the identity property to write $x + 0 = 0 + x = x$, for all x. We could introduce the addition of nonzero integers in terms of number lines, and we note that if the numbers we're adding have the same sign, the result is the same as the sum of the absolute values, except for a plus or a minus sign (since their directions on a number line are the same). If we're adding numbers with different signs, their directions are opposite, so the net result is the difference of the absolute values with a sign to indicate final position. This is summarized by the procedure for adding integers to the right.

Multiplication of Integers

For whole numbers, multiplication is defined as repeated addition, since we say that $5 \cdot 4$ means

$$\underbrace{4 + 4 + 4 + 4 + 4}_{\text{5 addends}}$$

However, we cannot do this for the integers, since $(-5) \cdot 4$ or

$$\underbrace{4 + 4 + 4 + \ldots + 4}_{-5 \text{ addends does not make sense.}}$$

PROCEDURE:

Addition of Integers

To add integers *x* and *y*, look at the signs of *x* and *y*.

STEP 1 Check to see if at least one of the integers is 0; if so, then

$x + 0 = 0 + x = x$.

STEP 2 Check to see if the signs are the same. If so, then

$$\left.\begin{array}{l} \text{POSITIVE} + \text{POSITIVE} = \text{POSITIVE} \\ \text{NEGATIVE} + \text{NEGATIVE} = \underbrace{\text{NEGATIVE}}_{\text{Sign part}} \end{array}\right\} \underbrace{|x| + |y|}_{\text{Whole-number part}}$$

STEP 4 Check to see if the signs are different. If so, then

$$\begin{array}{l} \text{POSITIVE} + \text{NEGATIVE} = \\ \text{NEGATIVE} + \text{POSITIVE} = \end{array} \underbrace{\left\{\begin{array}{l}\text{Sign of the larger} \\ \text{absolute value}\end{array}\right.}_{\text{Sign part}} \underbrace{\left\{\begin{array}{l}\text{Subtract smaller absolute} \\ \text{value from larger one}\end{array}\right.}_{\text{Whole-number part}}$$

Notice that all integers consist of two parts: a sign part and a whole-number part.

WATCH YOUR STEP *You may feel you already know how to add integers, but this is one of the fundamental ideas of mathematics.*

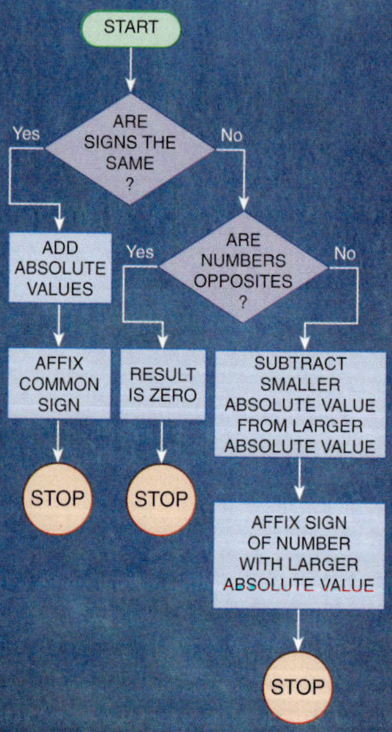

Addition of nonzero integers

Even though you may remember how to multiply integers, we consider four patterns.

POSITIVE · POSITIVE We know how to multiply positive numbers since these are natural numbers. *The product of two positive numbers is a positive number.*

POSITIVE · NEGATIVE Consider, for example, $3 \cdot (-4)$. We look at the pattern:

$$3 \cdot 4 = 12$$
$$3 \cdot 3 = 9$$
$$3 \cdot 2 = 6$$
$$3 \cdot 1 = 3$$
$$3 \cdot 0 = 0$$

What comes next? **Answer this question before reading further.**

$$3 \cdot (-1) = -3$$
$$3 \cdot (-2) = -6$$
$$3 \cdot (-3) = -9$$
$$3 \cdot (-4) = -12$$

Do you know how to continue? Try building a few more such patterns using different numbers. What did you discover about the product of a positive number and a negative number? *The product of a positive number and a negative number is a negative number.*

NEGATIVE · POSITIVE Since we now know how to multiply a positive by a negative, and if we assume the commutative property holds, the result here must be the same for a negative times a positive. *The product of a negative number and a positive number is a negative number.*

NEGATIVE · NEGATIVE Consider the example $-3 \cdot (-4)$. Let's build another pattern.

$$-3 \cdot 4 = -12$$
$$-3 \cdot 3 = -9$$
$$-3 \cdot 2 = -6$$
$$-3 \cdot 1 = -3$$
$$-3 \cdot 0 = 0$$

What comes next? **Answer this question before reading further.**

$$-3 \cdot (-1) = 3$$
$$-3 \cdot (-2) = 6$$
$$-3 \cdot (-3) = 9$$
$$-3 \cdot (-4) = 12$$

Thus, as the pattern indicates: *The product of two negative numbers is a positive number.* We summarize our discussion in the following box:

PROCEDURE:

Multiplication of Integers

To multiply integers x and y, look at the signs of x and y.

STEP 1 Check to see if at least one of the integers is 0; if so, then $x \cdot 0 = 0 \cdot x = 0$.

STEP 2

Sign part	Whole-number part
POSITIVE · POSITIVE = POSITIVE	$\lvert x \rvert \cdot \lvert y \rvert$
POSITIVE · NEGATIVE = NEGATIVE	
NEGATIVE · POSITIVE = NEGATIVE	
NEGATIVE · NEGATIVE = POSITIVE	

WATCH YOUR STEP *Take a few moments with this idea and make sure you know how to multiply integers. Can you explain this idea to someone else?*

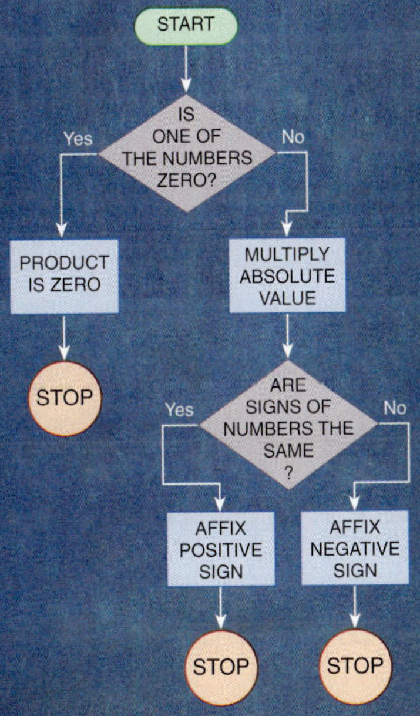

Multiplication of integers

Subtraction of Integers

What about subtracting negative numbers? Negative already indicates "going back." Does subtraction of a negative indicate "going ahead"? Consider the following pattern:

$$4 - 4 = 0$$
$$4 - 3 = 1$$
$$4 - 2 = 2$$
$$4 - 1 = 3$$
$$4 - 0 = 4$$

Stop and look for patterns:

$$4 - (-1) = 5$$
$$4 - (-2) = 6$$
$$4 - (-3) = 7$$

Guided by these results, we make the following procedure for subtraction of integers.

PROCEDURE: Subtraction of Integers

To subtract, add the opposite (of the number being subtracted). In symbols,

$$x - y = x + (-y)$$

STOP *This is saying that we do not actually subtract integers. Rather, we change subtraction problems to addition problems by adding the opposite.*

Division of Integers

Let's take an overview of what has been done in this chapter. We began with the *natural numbers*, which are closed for addition and multiplication. Next, we defined subtraction and created a situation where it was impossible to subtract some numbers from others. After looking at the prime numbers and factorization, we then "created" another set (called the *integers*) that includes not only the natural numbers, but also zero and the opposite of each of its members.

Since the subtraction of integers is defined in terms of addition, we can easily show that the integers are closed for subtraction. We now will define division and then ask the question, "Is the set of integers closed for division?"

Division is defined as the opposite operation of multiplication.

the operation of division

If a, b, and z are integers, where $b \neq 0$, then division $a \div b$ is written as $\frac{a}{b}$ and is defined in terms of multiplication.

$$\frac{a}{b} = z \quad \text{means} \quad a = bz$$

Since division is defined in terms of multiplication, the rules for dividing integers are identical to those for multiplication. We summarize the procedure for $x \div y$, but first we must make sure $y \neq 0$, because division by zero is not defined.

PROCEDURE: Division of Integers

To divide integers x and y, look at the signs of x and y.

STEP 1 $0 \div x = 0$ for all numbers x.
$x \div 0$ is not permitted.

STEP 2 If $y \neq 0$,

POSITIVE ÷ POSITIVE = POSITIVE
POSITIVE ÷ NEGATIVE = NEGATIVE
NEGATIVE ÷ POSITIVE = NEGATIVE
NEGATIVE ÷ NEGATIVE = POSITIVE

Sign part: the result above; Whole-number part: $\frac{|x|}{|y|}$

***NEVER DIVIDE BY 0.**

Abraham Lincoln used a biblical reference (Mark 3:25) to initiate his campaign in 1858. He said, "A house divided against itself cannot stand." I offer a corollary to Lincoln's statement: "A house divided by itself is one (provided, of course, that the house is not zero)."

Notice that for $\frac{a}{b}$, we require $b \neq 0$. Why do we not allow **division by zero**? We consider two possibilities.

1. Division of a nonzero number by zero:

$a \div 0 \quad \text{or} \quad \frac{a}{0} = x$

What does this mean? Is there such a number x so that this makes sense? We see that any number x would have to be such that $a = 0 \cdot x$. But $0 \cdot x = 0$ for all x, and since $a \neq 0$, we see that such a situation is impossible. That is, $a \div 0$ does not exist.

2. Division of zero by zero:

$0 \div 0 \quad \text{or} \quad \frac{0}{0} = x$

What does this mean? Is there such a number x? We see that *any* x makes this true, since $0 \cdot x = 0$ for all x. But this leads to certain absurdities, for example:

If $\frac{0}{0} = 2$, then this checks since $0 \cdot 2 = 0$; also

if $\frac{0}{0} = 5$, then this checks since $0 \cdot 5 = 0$.

But since both 2 and 5 are equal to the *same* number, we would conclude that $2 = 5$. This is absurd, so we say that division of zero by zero is excluded (or that it is *indeterminate*).

Is the set of integers closed for division? Certainly we can find many examples in which an integer divided by an integer is an integer. Does this mean that the set of integers is closed? What about $1 \div 2$ or $4 \div 5$? These numbers do not exist in the set of integers; thus, the set is *not* closed for division. Now, as long as society has no need for such division problems, the question of inventing new numbers will not arise. However, as the need to divide 1 into two or more parts arises, some new numbers will have to be invented so that the set will be closed for division. We'll do this in the next section. The problem with inventing such new numbers is that it must be done in such a way that the properties of the existing numbers are left unchanged. That is, closure for addition, subtraction, and multiplication must be retained.

2.4 It's a Long Way from Zero to One

HISTORICALLY, THE NEED FOR A CLOSED SET FOR DIVISION CAME BEFORE THE NEED FOR CLOSURE FOR SUBTRACTION. WE NEED TO FIND SOME NUMBER k SO THAT

$$1 \div 2 = k$$

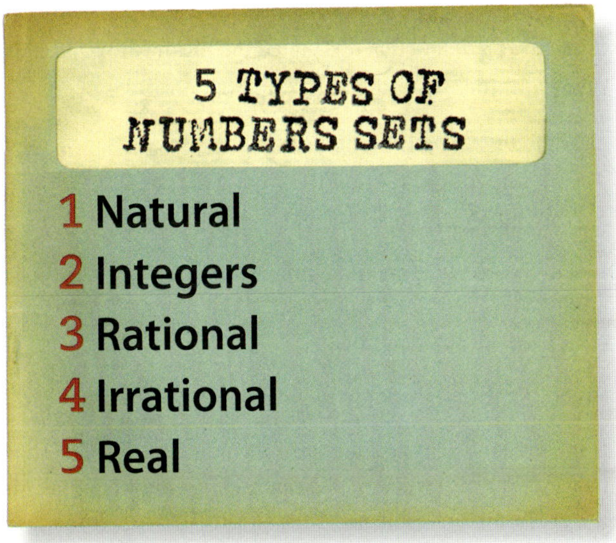

The ancient Egyptians limited their fractions by requiring the numerators to be 1. The Romans avoided fractions by the use of subunits; feet were divided into inches and pounds into ounces, and a twelfth part of the Roman unit was called an *uncia*.

Rational Numbers

However, people soon felt the practical need to obtain greater accuracy in measurement and the theoretical need to close the number system with respect to the operation of division. In the set $\mathbb{Z}$ of integers, some divisions are possible:

$$\frac{10}{-2}, \frac{-4}{2}, \frac{-16}{-8}, \ldots$$

However, certain others are not:

$$\frac{1}{2}, \frac{-16}{5}, \frac{5}{12}, \ldots$$

Just as we extended the set of natural numbers by creating the concept of opposites, we can extend the set of integers. That is, the number $\frac{5}{12}$ is defined to be that number obtained when 5 is divided by 12. This new set, consisting of the integers as well as the quotients of integers, is called the set of **rational numbers**.

> The set of **rational numbers**, denoted by $\mathbb{Q}$, is the set of all numbers of the form
>
> $$\frac{a}{b}$$
>
> where a and b are integers, and $b \neq 0$.

Notice that a rational number has fractional form. In arithmetic you learned that if a number is written in the form $\frac{a}{b}$ it means $a \div b$ and that a is called the **numerator** and b the **denominator**. Also, if a and b are both positive, $\frac{a}{b}$ is called

a **proper fraction** if $a < b$;
an **improper fraction** if $a > b$; and
a **whole number** if b divides evenly into a.

It is assumed that you know how to perform the basic operations with fractions, but we will spend the next few pages reviewing those operations.

Fundamental Property

If the greatest common factor of the numerator and denominator of a given fraction is 1, then we say the fraction is in lowest terms or **reduced**. If the greatest common factor is not 1, then divide both the numerator and denominator by this greatest common factor using the **fundamental property of fractions**.

FUNDAMENTAL PROPERTY OF FRACTIONS

If $\frac{a}{b}$ is any rational number and x is any nonzero integer, then

$$\frac{a \cdot x}{b \cdot x} = \frac{x \cdot a}{x \cdot b} = \frac{a}{b}$$

The fundamental property works only for products and not for sums. That is, given some fraction that you wish to simplify:

1. Find the g.c.f. of the numerator and denominator (this is x in the fundamental property).
2. Use the fundamental property to simplify the fraction.

Suppose we want to reduce $\frac{300}{144}$. First, find the greatest common factor:

$$300 = 2^2 \cdot 3^1 \cdot 5^2$$
$$144 = 2^4 \cdot 3^2 \cdot 5^0$$
$$\text{g.c.f} = 2^2 \cdot 3^1 \cdot 5^0 = 12$$
$$\frac{300}{144} = \frac{12 \cdot 5^2}{12 \cdot 2^2 \cdot 3} = \frac{5^2}{2^2 \cdot 3} = \frac{25}{12}$$

↑ g.c.f.

Note that $\frac{25}{12}$ is reduced because the g.c.f. of the numerator and denominator is 1. Notice that a reduced fraction may be an improper fraction. *In this book, we agree to leave all fractional answers in reduced form.*

Operations with Rationals

Now that we have defined rational numbers, we need to review how to add, subtract, multiply, and divide them. The procedure for each of these operations is given in algebraic form.

Operations with Rational Numbers

If $\frac{a}{b}$ and $\frac{c}{d}$ are rational numbers, then

Addition $\quad \frac{a}{b} + \frac{c}{d} = \frac{ad}{bd} + \frac{bc}{bd} = \frac{ad + bc}{bd}$

Subtraction $\quad \frac{a}{b} - \frac{c}{d} = \frac{ad}{bd} - \frac{bc}{bd} = \frac{ad - bc}{bd}$

Multiplication $\quad \frac{a}{b} \times \frac{c}{d} = \frac{ac}{bd}$

Division $\quad \frac{a}{b} \div \frac{c}{d} = \frac{ad}{bc} \quad (c \neq 0)$

You will note that both addition and subtraction require that we first obtain *common denominators*. That process requires a multiplication of fractions.

To carry out addition or subtraction of fractions, you must find the **least common denominator**. The least common denominator is the same as the least common multiple.

The set $\mathbb{Q}$ is closed for the operations of addition, subtraction, multiplication, and nonzero division. As an example, we will show that the rationals are closed for addition. We need to show that, given any two elements of $\mathbb{Q}$, their sum is also an element of $\mathbb{Q}$. Suppose

$$\frac{x}{y} \text{ and } \frac{w}{z}$$

are any two rational numbers. By definition of addition,

$$\frac{x}{y} + \frac{w}{z} = \frac{xz + wy}{yz}$$

We now need to show that $\frac{xz + wy}{yz}$ is a rational number. Since x and w are integers and y and z are nonzero integers, we know from closure of the integers for multiplication that xz and wy are also integers. Since the set of integers is closed for addition, we know that $xz + wy$ is also an integer. This means that, since yz is a nonzero integer,

$$\frac{xz + wy}{yz}$$

is a rational number. Thus, the rational numbers are closed for addition.

2.5 It's Irrational

WE HAVE BEEN CONSIDERING NUMBERS AS THEY RELATE TO PRACTICAL PROBLEMS.

However, numbers can be appreciated for their beauty and interrelationships. The Pythagoreans were a Hellenic group of astronomers, musicians, mathematicians, and philosophers who believed that all things are essentially numeric. To our knowledge, they were among the first to investigate numbers for their own sake.

Pythagorean Theorem

Much of the Pythagoreans' lifestyle was embodied in their beliefs about numbers. They considered the number 1 the essence of reason; the number 2 was identified with opinion; and 4 was associated with justice because it is the first number that is the product of equals (the first perfect squared number, other than 1). Of the numbers greater than 1, odd numbers were masculine and even numbers were feminine; thus, 5 represented marriage, since it was the union of the first masculine and feminine numbers $(2 + 3 = 5)$.

The students of Pythagoras were interested in numbers like primes and perfect squares, which they believed had mystical significance.

The Pythagoreans were also interested in special types of numbers that had mystical meanings: perfect numbers, friendly numbers, deficient numbers, abundant numbers, prime numbers, triangular numbers, square numbers, and pentagonal numbers. Other than the prime numbers we have already considered, the perfect square numbers are probably the most interesting. They are called **perfect squares** because they can be arranged into squares (see Figure 2.3). They are found by squaring the natural numbers.

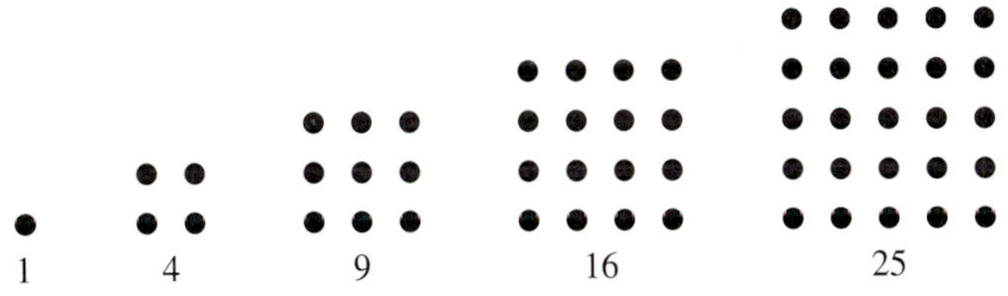

Figure 2.3 Square numbers 1, 4, 9, 16, and 25. Other square numbers (not pictured) are 36, 49, 64, 81, 100, 121, 144, 169, ...

The Pythagoreans discovered the famous **property of square numbers** that today bears Pythagoras' name. They found that if they constructed any right triangle and then constructed squares on each of the legs of the triangle, the area of the larger square was equal to the sum of the areas of the smaller squares (see Figure 2.4).

Figure 2.4 Relationships of sides of right triangles

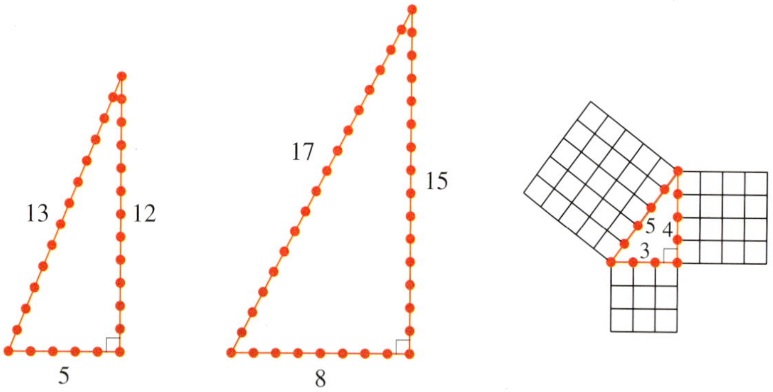

Today we state the **Pythagorean theorem** algebraically by saying that, if a and b are the lengths of the **legs** (or sides) of a right triangle and c is the length of the **hypotenuse** (the longest side), then the square of the length of the hypotenuse is equal to the sum of the squares of the lengths of the other two sides. The following result, called the Pythagorean theorem, is one of the most famous (and important) results in all of mathematics.

Pythagorean theorem

For a right triangle *ABC*, with sides of length *a*, *b*, and hypotenuse *c*,

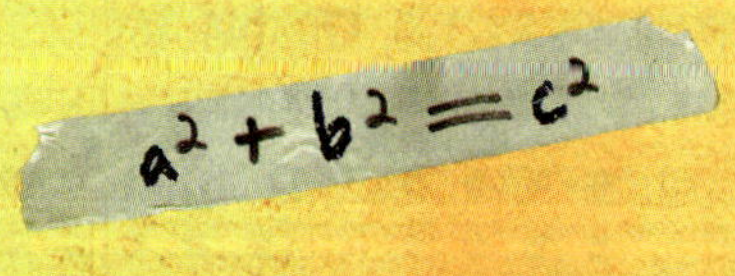

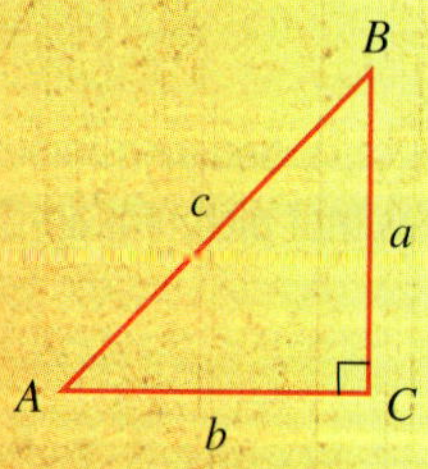

Also, if $a^2 + b^2 = c^2$ for a triangle with sides *a*, *b*, and *c*, then $\triangle ABC$ is a right triangle.

Square Roots

The Pythagoreans were overjoyed with this discovery, but it led to a revolutionary idea in mathematics—one that caused the Pythagoreans many problems.

Legend tells us that one day while the Pythagoreans were at sea, one of their group came up with the following argument. Suppose each leg of a right triangle is 1, then

$$a^2 + b^2 = c^2$$
$$1^2 + 1^2 = c^2$$
$$2 = c^2$$

If we denote the number whose square is 2 by $\sqrt{2}$, we have $\sqrt{2} = c$. The symbol $\sqrt{2}$ is read "square root of two." This means that $\sqrt{2}$ is that number such that, if multiplied by itself, is exactly equal to 2; i.e.,

$$\sqrt{2} \times \sqrt{2} = 2$$

The **square root** of a nonnegative number n is a number so that its square is equal to n. In symbols, the **positive square root of n**, denoted by $\sqrt{n}$, is defined as that number for which

$$\sqrt{n}\sqrt{n} = n$$

Some square roots are rational. For example, $\sqrt{4} \times \sqrt{4} = 4$ and we also know $2 \times 2 = 4$, so it seems that $\sqrt{4} = 2$. But wait! We also know $(-2) \times (-2) = 4$, so isn't it just as reasonable to say $\sqrt{4} = -2$? Mathematicians have agreed that the square root symbol may be used only to denote positive numbers, so that $\sqrt{4} = 2$ and NOT -2.

What about square roots of numbers that are not perfect squares? Is $\sqrt{2}$, for example, a rational number? Remember, if $\sqrt{2} = \frac{a}{b}$ where $\frac{a}{b}$ is some fraction so that

$$\frac{a}{b} \cdot \frac{a}{b} = 2$$

then it is *rational*. The Pythagoreans were among the first to investigate this question. Now remember that, for the Pythagoreans, mathematics and religion were one; they asserted that all natural phenomena could be expressed by whole numbers or ratios of whole numbers. Thus, they believed that $\sqrt{2}$ must be some whole number or fraction (ratio of two whole numbers). Suppose we try to find such a rational number:

$$\frac{7}{5} \times \frac{7}{5} = \frac{49}{25} = 1.96$$

or, try again:

$$\frac{707}{500} \times \frac{707}{500} = \frac{499{,}849}{250{,}000} = 1.999396$$

We are "getting closer" to 2, but we are still not quite there, so we really get down to business and use a calculator:

[2] [√] *Display:* 1.414213562

If you square this number, do you obtain 2? Notice that the last digit of this multiplication will be 4; what should it be if it were the square root of 2? Even if we use a computer to find the following possibility for $\sqrt{2}$, we see that its square is still not 2:

1.4142135623730950488016887242096980785696718753769480731766797379907324784

Can you give a brief argument showing why that can't be $\sqrt{2}$? Such a number is called an *irrational number*. The set of **irrational numbers** is the set of numbers whose decimal representations do not terminate nor do they repeat.

It can be shown that not only $\sqrt{2}$ is irrational, but also $\sqrt{3}, \sqrt{5}, \sqrt{6}, \sqrt{7}, \sqrt{8}, \sqrt{10}$; in fact, the square root of any whole number that is not a perfect square is irrational. Also the cube root of any whole number that is not a perfect cube, and so on, is an irrational number. The **number π**, which is the ratio of the circumference of any circle to its diameter, is also not rational. The number π cannot be written in exact decimal form (which is why we use the symbol "π"), but if you press the [π] key on your calculator, you will see the approximation 3.141592654. In everyday work, you will use irrational numbers when finding the circumference and area of a circle.

> One of the most famous irrational numbers is π. You are, of course, familiar with this number used to find the area or circumference of a circle. Technically, it is defined as the ratio of the circumference of a circle to its diameter. You may remember its decimal approximation of 3.1416. As an irrational number, it cannot be written as a terminating or repeating decimal. This number was featured in Leslie Nielsen's spoof *Spy Hard*, where Nicollette Sheridan plays Russian agent 3.14.

We also use irrational numbers when applying the Pythagorean theorem. Since the Pythagorean theorem asserts $a^2 + b^2 = c^2$, then

$$c = \sqrt{a^2 + b^2}$$

Also, if you wish to find the length of one of the legs of a right triangle, say a, when you know both b and c, you can use the formula

$$a = \sqrt{c^2 - b^2}$$

The Pythagorean theorem is of value only when dealing with a right triangle. Carpenters often make use of this property when they want to construct a right angle. That is, if $a^2 + b^2 = c^2$, then an angle of the triangle must be a right angle.

A carpenter wants to make sure that the corner of a room is square (is a right angle). If she measures out sides (legs) of 3 ft and 4 ft, how long should she make the diagonal (hypotenuse) in order to make sure the corner is square?

The triangle (corner of the room) is shown in Figure 2.5.

Figure 2.5 Building a right angle

The hypotenuse is the unknown, so use the formula

$$c = \sqrt{a^2 + b^2}$$

Thus,

$$c = \sqrt{3^2 + 4^2} = \sqrt{9 + 16} = \sqrt{25} = 5$$

If she makes the diagonal 5 ft long, then by the Pythagorean theorem, the angle is a right angle, which forces the corner of the room to be square.

Suppose that the result does not simplify so easily. That is, suppose the result were irrational. You can either leave your result in **radical form** or estimate your result.

Suppose that you need to attach several support wires to your volleyball net, as shown in Figure 2.6. If one support wire is attached 4-ft away from an 8-ft pole, what is the exact length of that support wire, and what is the length to the nearest foot?

The length of the support wire is the length of the hypotenuse of a right triangle:

$$\begin{aligned} c &= \sqrt{a^2 + b^2} \\ &= \sqrt{4^2 + 8^2} \\ &= \sqrt{80} \end{aligned}$$

The exact length of the support wire is $\sqrt{80}$; it is irrational, since 80 is not a perfect square. We can use a calculator for an approximation:

[80] [√] *Display:* 8.94427191

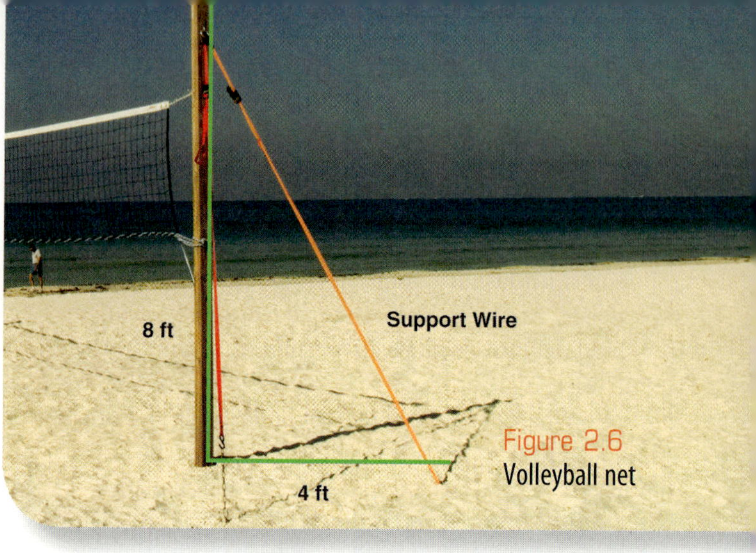

Figure 2.6 Volleyball net

The support wire is 9 ft long (to the nearest ft). *Note*: Make sure when you are rounding not to end up with a wire that is too short. For instance, if your net required a support wire of 8.43 ft, rounding down would create a wire that was too short. In that case you should round to the *next larger* foot—namely, 9 ft.

Operations with Square Roots

There are times when a square root is irrational and yet we do not want a rational approximation. In such cases, we will need to know certain **laws of square roots** and when a square root is simplified.

You will not be able to deal properly with radicals if you do not understand this law.

Laws of Square Roots

Let a and b be positive numbers. Then:

1. $\sqrt{0} = 0$
2. $\sqrt{a^2} = a$
3. $\sqrt{ab} = \sqrt{a}\sqrt{b}$
4. $\sqrt{\dfrac{a}{b}} = \dfrac{\sqrt{a}}{\sqrt{b}}$
5. A square root is *simplified* if:
   - The radicand (the number under the radical sign) has no factor with an exponent larger than 1 when it is written in factored form.
   - The radicand is not written as a fraction or by using negative exponents.
   - There are no square root symbols used in the denominators of fractions.

Suppose we wish to simplify $\sqrt{8}$. First, factor the radicand: $\sqrt{8} = \sqrt{2^3}$, and then write the radicand as a product of as many factors with exponents of 2 as possible; if there is a remaining factor, it will have an exponent of 1: $\sqrt{2^3} = \sqrt{2^2 \cdot 2^1}$.

Use Law 3 for square roots: $\sqrt{2^2 \cdot 2^1} = \sqrt{2^2} \cdot \sqrt{2^1}$
Use Law 2 for square roots: $\sqrt{2^2} \cdot \sqrt{2^1} = 2\sqrt{2}$

Notice that the simplified form $\sqrt{8}$ contains a radical, so it is an irrational number. We call $2\sqrt{2}$ the *exact* simplified representation for $\sqrt{8}$ and the calculator representation 2.828427125 is an *approximation*. The whole process of simplifying radicals depends on factoring the radicand and separating out the square factors, and is usually condensed as shown in the *Peanuts* cartoon below.

2.6 Be Real

YOU ARE FAMILIAR WITH THE RATIONAL NUMBERS (FRACTIONS, FOR EXAMPLE) AND THE IRRATIONAL NUMBERS (π OR SQUARE ROOTS OF CERTAIN NUMBERS, FOR EXAMPLE).

Now we wish to consider the most general set of numbers to be used in elementary mathematics. This set consists of the annexation of the irrational numbers to the set of rational numbers. The combined set is called the set of **real numbers** and is the most common set used in elementary math.

> The set of **real numbers**, denoted by $\mathbb{R}$, is defined as the union of the set of rationals and the set of irrationals.

Decimal Representation

Let's consider the decimal representation of a real number. If a number is *rational*, then its decimal representation is either **terminating** or **repeating**.

When a decimal repeats, we sometimes use an overbar to indicate the numerals that repeat. For example,

One digit repeats: $\frac{2}{3} = 0.\overline{6}$, $\quad \frac{1}{6} = 0.1\overline{6}$

Two digits repeat: $\frac{5}{11} = 0.\overline{45}$

Six digits repeat: $\frac{1}{7} = 0.\overline{142857}$

Real numbers that are *irrational* have decimal representations that are *nonterminating* and *nonrepeating*:

$$\sqrt{2} = 1.414213\ldots \qquad \pi = 3.141592\ldots$$

In each of these examples, the numbers exhibit no repeating pattern and are irrational. Other decimals that do not terminate or repeat are also irrational:

0.12345678910111213 . . .
0.101101110111101111110 . . .

We now have some different ways to classify real numbers:

1. Positive, negative, or zero
2. A rational number or an irrational number
   a. If the decimal representation terminates, it is rational.
   b. If the decimal representation repeats, it is rational.
   c. If it has a nonterminating and nonrepeating decimal, it is irrational.

We have illustrated the procedure for changing from a fraction to a decimal: Divide the numerator by the denominator. To reverse the procedure and to change from a terminating decimal representation of a rational number to a fractional representation, use expanded notation. Recall that $10^{-1} = \frac{1}{10}, 10^{-2} = \frac{1}{100}, 10^{-3} = \frac{1}{1000}, \ldots, 10^{-n} = \frac{1}{10^n}$. Thus 0.5 means $5 \times 10^{-1} = 5 \cdot \frac{1}{10} = \frac{5}{10} = \frac{1}{2}$.

Change 0.123 to fractional form.

$$0.123 = 1 \times 10^{-1} + 2 \times 10^{-2} + 3 \times 10^{-3}$$

$$= \frac{1}{10} + \frac{2}{100} + \frac{3}{1{,}000} = \frac{123}{1{,}000}$$

It is assumed that you can carry out the basic operations with real numbers written in decimal form. You are asked to carry out the basic operations of addition, subtraction, multiplication, and division of decimal fractions.

Figure 2.7 A number line

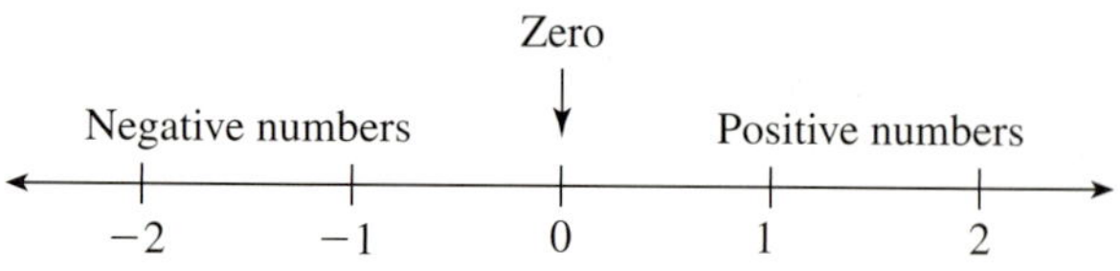

Figure 2.8 A number line with rationals

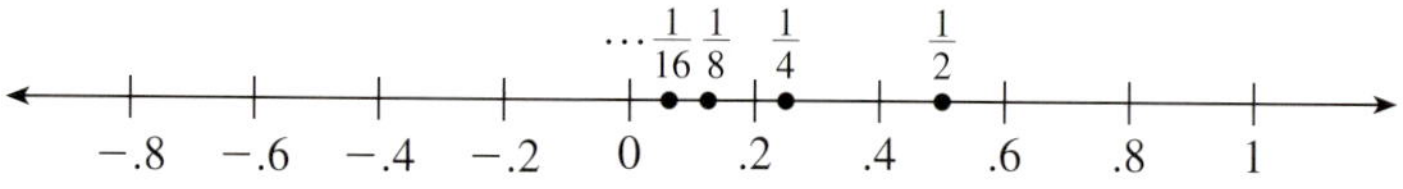

Real Number Line

If we consider a line and associate the numbers 0 and 1 with two points situated so that the 1 is to the right of 0, we call the distance between these points a **unit distance**. Next, if we mark off equal distances to the right and associate the successive points with the natural numbers, and mark equal distances to the left and associate those points successively with the opposites of the natural numbers, we have drawn a **number line**, as shown in Figure 2.7.

If we now associate points on the number line with rational numbers, it appears that the number line is just about "filled up" by the rationals. The reason for this feeling of "fullness" is that the rationals form what is termed a **dense set**. That is, between every two rationals we can find another rational (see Figure 2.8).

If we plot *all* the points of this dense set called the rationals, are there still any "holes"? In other words, is there any room left for any of the irrationals? We have shown that $\sqrt{2}$ is irrational. We can show that there is a place on the number line representing this length by using the Pythagorean theorem, as shown in Figure 2.9.

Figure 2.9 Finding an irrational "hole" on a dense number line with rationals plotted

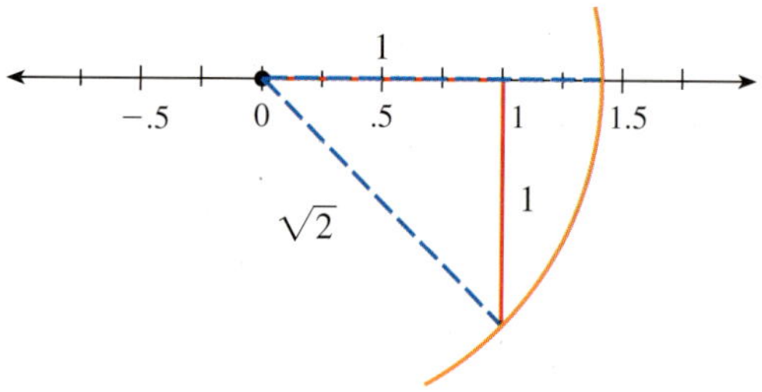

We could show that other irrationals have their places on the number line. These points (corresponding to both the rational and irrational numbers), when plotted on a line, form what is known as the **real number line**, as shown in Figure 2.10.

Figure 2.10 Real number line showing some rationals and some irrationals

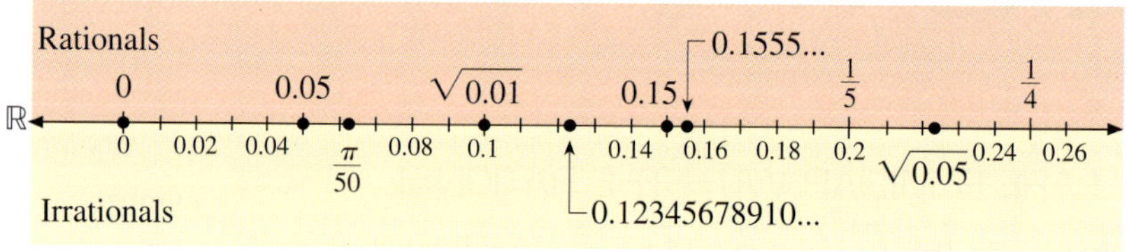

The relationships among the various sets of numbers we have been discussing are shown in Figure 2.11.

Figure 2.11 Classifications within the set of real numbers, $\mathbb{R}$

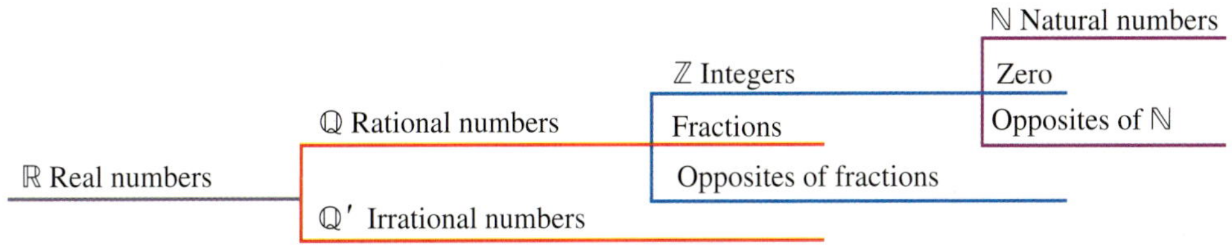

Identity and Inverse Properties

At the beginning of this chapter, we stated some properties of natural numbers that apply to sets of real numbers as well. We repeat them here for easy reference. Let *a*, *b*, and *c* be real numbers; we denote this by $a, b, c \in \mathbb{R}$.

	Addition	*Multiplication*
Closure:	$(a + b) \in \mathbb{R}$	$ab \in \mathbb{R}$
Associative:	$(a + b) + c = a + (b + c)$	$(ab)c = a(bc)$
Commutative:	$a + b = b + a$	$ab = ba$
Distributive for multiplication over addition:	$a(b + c) = ab + ac$	

There are two additional properties that are important in the set of real numbers: the identity and inverse properties.

The number 0 (zero) has a special property for addition that allows it to be added to any real number without changing the value of that number. This property is called the **identity property for addition** of real numbers.

Identity for Addition

There exists in $\mathbb{R}$ a number 0, called zero, so that

$$0 + a = a + 0 = a$$

for any $a \in \mathbb{R}$. The number zero is called the identity for addition or the additive identity.

Remember that when you are studying algebra, you are studying ideas and not just rules about specific numbers. A mathematician would attempt to isolate the *concept* of an identity. First, does an identity property apply for other operations?

Multiplication	*Subtraction*	*Division*
$\square \times a = a \times \square$	$\square - a = a - \square$	$\square \div a = a \div \square$
Same number	Same number	Same number

Is there a real number that will satisfy any of the blanks for multiplication, subtraction, or division?

The second property involves another special, important number in $\mathbb{R}$, namely the number 1 (one). This number has the property that it can multiply any real number without changing the value of that number. This property is called the **identity property for multiplication** of real numbers.

Identity for Multiplication

There exists in $\mathbb{R}$ a number 1, called one, so that

$$1 \times a = a \times 1 = a$$

for any $a \in \mathbb{R}$. The number one is called the identity for multiplication or the multiplicative identity.

Notice that there is no real number that satisfies the identity property for subtraction or division. There may be identities for other operations or for sets other than the set of real numbers.

In the last chapter we also spoke of opposites when we were adding and subtracting integers. Recall the property of opposites:

$$5 + (-5) = 0 \qquad -128 + 128 = 0 \qquad a + (-a) = 0$$

When opposites are added, the result is zero, the identity for addition. This idea, which can be generalized, is called the **inverse property for addition**.

INVERSE PROPERTY FOR ADDITION

For each $a \in \mathbb{R}$, there is a unique number $(-a) \in \mathbb{R}$, called the **opposite** (or **additive inverse**) of a, so that

$$a + (-a) = -a + a = 0$$

Recall that the product of a number and its reciprocal is 1, the identity for multiplication. The reciprocal of a number, then, is the multiplicative inverse of the number, as we will now show.

Inverse for multiplication ↓

$$5 \times \boxed{} = \boxed{} \times 5 = 1$$

$$5 \times \boxed{\tfrac{1}{5}} = \frac{1}{5} \times 5 = 1$$

↑ Since $\frac{1}{5} \in \mathbb{R}$, $\frac{1}{5}$ is an inverse of 5 for multiplication.

Inverse for multiplication ↓

$$-128 \times \boxed{} = \boxed{} \times (-128) = 1$$

$$-128 \times \boxed{\tfrac{1}{-128}} = \frac{1}{-128} \times (-128) = 1$$

↑ Since $\frac{1}{-128} \in \mathbb{R}$, $\frac{1}{-128}$ is an inverse of -128 for multiplication.

To show this inverse property for multiplication in a general way, we seek to find a replacement for the box for each and every real number a:

$$a \times \boxed{} = \boxed{} \times a = 1$$

Does the inverse property for multiplication hold for every real number a? No, because if $a = 0$, then

$$0 \times \boxed{} = \boxed{} \times 0 = 1$$

does not have a replacement for the box in $\mathbb{R}$. However, the inverse property for multiplication holds for all *nonzero* replacements of a, and we adopt this condition as part of the inverse property for multiplication of real numbers.

INVERSE PROPERTY FOR MULTIPLICATION

For *each* number $a \in \mathbb{R}$, $a \neq 0$, there exists a number $a^{-1} \in \mathbb{R}$, called the **reciprocal** (or **multiplicative inverse**) of a, so that

$$a \times a^{-1} = a^{-1} \times a = 1$$

2.7 Mathematical Modeling

A REAL-LIFE SITUATION IS USUALLY FAR TOO COMPLICATED TO BE PRECISELY AND MATHEMATICALLY DEFINED.

When confronted with a problem in the real world, therefore, it is usually necessary to develop a mathematical framework based on certain assumptions about the real world. This framework can then be used to find a solution to the real-world problem. The process of developing this body of mathematics is referred to as **mathematical modeling**. Most mathematical models are dynamic (not static), but are continually being revised (modified) as additional relevant information becomes known.

Some mathematical models are quite accurate, particularly those used in the physical sciences, such as the calculus model for the path of a projectile. Other rather precise models predict such things as the time of sunrise and sunset, or the speed at which an object falls in a vacuum. Some mathematical models, however, are less accurate, especially those that involve examples from the life sciences and social sciences.

What, precisely, is a mathematical model? Sometimes, mathematical modeling can mean nothing more than a textbook word problem. But mathematical modeling can also mean choosing appropriate mathematics to solve a problem that has not yet been solved. In this book, we use the term *mathematical modeling* to mean something between these two extremes. That is, it is a process we will apply to some real-life problem that does not have an obvious solution. It usually cannot be solved by applying a single formula.

The diagram in Figure 2.12 shows the four step process for creating a mathematical model. Let's take a look.

Figure 2.12 The process of mathematical modeling

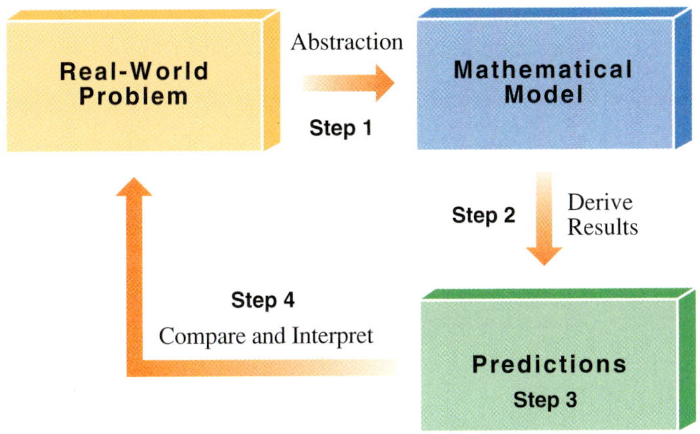

STEP 1 *Abstraction*
With the method of abstraction, certain assumptions about the real world are made, variables are defined, and an appropriate mathematics is developed to create a mathematical model.

STEP 2 *Deriving Results*
The next step is to simplify the mathematics or derive related mathematical facts from the mathematical model.

STEP 3 *Make Predications*
The results derived from the mathematical model should lead us to some predictions about the real world.

STEP 4 *Gather and Compare Data*
The next step is to gather data from the situation being modeled, and then to compare those data with the predictions. If the two do not agree, then the gathered data are used to modify the model's current assumptions.

Mathematical modeling is an ongoing process. As long as the predictions match the real world, the assumptions made about the real world are regarded as correct, as are the defined variables. On the other hand, as discrepancies are noticed, it is necessary to construct a closer and a more dependable mathematical model.

Mathematical Modeling: Creating a budget

Let's consider an example that illustrates mathematical modeling. Consider the task of developing a monthly budget for your personal expenses. You can assume any family situation (for example, number of people and amount of income and expenses), but this budget requires that you are self-sufficient and that income and expenses must always be equal.

***remember**

This example is not about budgets, but about the process of modeling.

Round 1

The first step in modeling is to understand the problem. Let us assume that we are budgeting for one person living at home with his or her parents. We begin by setting up a mathematical model to describe this person's income and expenses.

This budget satisfies the condition that income equals expenses.

Now we need to test whether our prediction is correct by comparing and interpreting the results of this budget with reality. What about taxes and FICA? As we can see there are certain factors which our model hasn't accounted for. Thus, our model does not reflect the real world.

Let us make a second attempt at abstraction.

Round 2

Take a minute to look over the revised budget below and think about how the mathematical modeling process was used to create it. After that, we'll consider the real world situation again compared to our new model.

Careful: You'll want to read over this next budget slowly to make sure you understand how the first budget was revised to create it.

First, we can see that the budget below is a rough estimate of actual real-world spending, but it is not quite balanced (which it needs to be) and does not include "hidden" income and expenses, such as the value of room and board at home. Even though "cash" is not exchanged for room and board, "value" is given and must be taken into account. What about income or expenses that do not occur monthly? How about clothes, car repairs, or a vacation? Once again, the modeling process compares and interprets, and then refines with another abstraction.

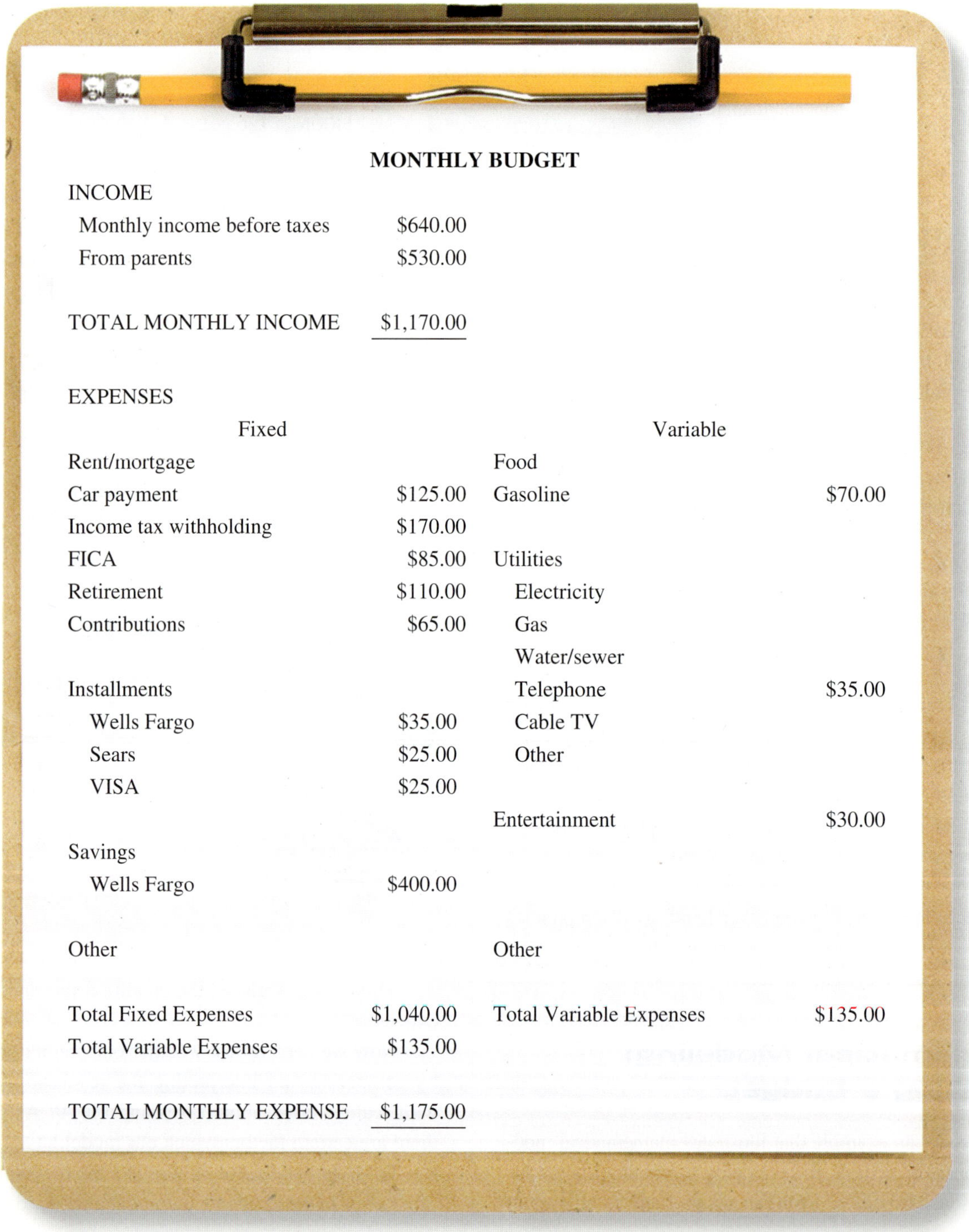

MONTHLY BUDGET

INCOME			
Monthly income before taxes	$640.00		
From parents	$530.00		
TOTAL MONTHLY INCOME	$1,170.00		
EXPENSES			
Fixed		Variable	
Rent/mortgage		Food	
Car payment	$125.00	Gasoline	$70.00
Income tax withholding	$170.00		
FICA	$85.00	Utilities	
Retirement	$110.00	Electricity	
Contributions	$65.00	Gas	
		Water/sewer	
Installments		Telephone	$35.00
Wells Fargo	$35.00	Cable TV	
Sears	$25.00	Other	
VISA	$25.00		
		Entertainment	$30.00
Savings			
Wells Fargo	$400.00		
Other		Other	
Total Fixed Expenses	$1,040.00	Total Variable Expenses	$135.00
Total Variable Expenses	$135.00		
TOTAL MONTHLY EXPENSE	$1,175.00		

Round 3 and Beyond

Now this iteration of the budget is much more realistic, but it still does not "balance." Each successive iteration should more closely model the real world, and to complicate the process, the real-world situation of income and expenses is always changing, which may require further revisions of the model shown below. For instance, what if our person gets a second job? What if this person decides they can't afford that vacation? As we can see, the process of modeling is ongoing and may never be "complete."

MONTHLY BUDGET

INCOME			
Monthly income before taxes	$640.00	Other nonmonthly income	$500.00
From parents	$530.00		$215.00
Credit cards	$125.00		
Total other/12	$59.58	Total other	$715.00
TOTAL MONTHLY INCOME	$1,354.58		

EXPENSES					
Fixed		Variable		Nonmonthly	
Rent/mortgage	$350.00	Food	$280.00	Car repairs	$290.00
Car payments	$125.00	Gasoline	$70.00	Home repairs	
Income tax withholding	$170.00			Car license	$85.00
FICA	$85.00	Utilities		Medical	
Retirement	$110.00	Electricity	$25.00	Dental	
Contributions	$65.00	Gas	$15.00	Clothing	$350.00
Insurance	$105.00	Water/sewer		Gifts	$400.00
Installments		Telephone	$35.00	Contributions	
Wells Fargo	$35.00	Cable TV	$20.00	Vacation	$800.00
Sears	$25.00	Other		Professional	
VISA	$25.00				
		Entertainment	$30.00	Insurance	
Savings					
Wells Fargo	$65.00				
Other		Other		Other	
Total Fixed Expenses	$1,160.00	Total Variable Expense	$475.00	Total Nonmonthly	$1,925.00
Total Variable Expenses	$475.00				
1/12 Nonmonthly	$160.42				
TOTAL MONTHLY EXPENSE	$1,795.42				

The final example below shows how these and other new factors are considered to create a balanced budget. As we can see, however, the process of modeling is ongoing and may never be "complete."

MONTHLY BUDGET

INCOME

Monthly income before taxes	$640.00	Other nonmonthly income	$500.00
From parents	$580.00		$215.00
Credit cards	$125.00		
Second job	$240.00		
Total other/12	$59.58	Total other	$715.00
TOTAL MONTHLY INCOME	$1,644.58		

EXPENSES

Fixed		Variable		Nonmonthly	
Rent/mortgage	$350.00	Food	$250.00	Car repairs	$290.00
Car payments	$125.00	Gasoline	$70.00	Home repairs	
Income tax withholding	$170.00			Car license	$85.00
FICA	$85.00	Utilities		Medical	
Retirement	$110.00	Electricity	$25.00	Dental	
Contributions	$65.00	Gas	$15.00	Clothing	$350.00
Insurance	$105.00	Water/sewer		Gifts	$300.00
Installments		Telephone	$35.00	Contributions	
Wells Fargo	$35.00	Cable TV	$20.00	Vacation	
Sears	$25.00	Other		Professional	
VISA	$25.00				
		Entertainment	$30.00	Insurance	
Savings					
Wells Fargo	$19.16				
Other		Other		Other	
Total Fixed Expenses	$1,114.16	Total Variable Expenses	$445.00	Total Nonmonthly	$1,025.00
Total Variable Expenses	$445.00				
1/12 Nonmonthly	$85.42				
TOTAL MONTHLY EXPENSE	$1,644.58				

The Nature of Algebra

4 ESSENTIAL ALGEBRAIC PROCESSES

1. Simplify
2. Factor
3. Evaluate
4. Solve

3.1 Polynomials

MANY PEOPLE THINK OF ALGEBRA AS SIMPLY A HIGH SCHOOL MATHEMATICS COURSE IN WHICH **VARIABLES** (SYMBOLS USED TO REPRESENT AN UNSPECIFIED MEMBER OF SOME SET) ARE MANIPULATED.

This chapter reviews many of these procedures; however, the word **algebra** refers to a structure, or a set of axioms that forms the basis for what is accepted and what is not. As you study the ordinary algebra presented in this chapter, you should remember this is only one of many possible algebras. Additional algebras are often studied in more advanced mathematics courses.

In this chapter we will review much of the algebra you have previously studied.

Terminology

You may think this terminology is not very important, but be careful! It is essential that you know how to correctly use the math vocabulary. Recall that a **term** is a number, a variable, or the product of numbers and variables. Thus, $10x$ is one term, but $10 + x$ is not (because the terms 10 and x are connected by addition and not by multiplication). A fundamental notion in algebra is that of a **polynomial**, which is a term or the sum (or difference) of terms. We classify polynomials by the number of terms and by degree:

A polynomial with one term is called a **monomial**.
A polynomial with two terms is called a **binomial**.
A polynomial with three terms is called a **trinomial**.

There are other words that could be used for polynomials with more than three terms, but this classification is sufficient. To classify by degree, we recall that the **degree of a term** is the number of *variable* factors in that term. Thus, 10 is zero-degree, $3x$ is first-degree, $5xy$ is second-degree, $2x^2$ is second-degree, and $9x^2y^3$ is fifth-degree. The **degree of a polynomial** is the largest degree of any of its terms. A first-degree term is sometimes called **linear**, and a second-degree term is sometimes referred to as **quadratic**. The numerical part of a term, usually written before the variable part, is called the **numerical coefficient**. In $3x$, it is the number 3, in $5xy$ it is the number 5, and in $9x^2y^3$ it is the number 9.

When writing polynomials, it is customary to arrange the terms from the highest-degree to the lowest-degree term. If terms have the same degree they are usually listed in alphabetical order.

Simplification

When working with polynomials, it is necessary to simplify algebraic expressions. The key ideas of simplification are *similar terms* and the *distributive property*. Terms that differ only in the numerical coefficients are called **like terms** or **similar terms**.

Simplify Polynomials

1. to simplify a polynomial means to carry out all operations* (according to the order-of-operations agreement) and to write the answer in a form with the highest-degree term first, with the rest of the terms arranged by decreasing degree. If there are two terms of the same degree, arrange those terms alphabetically.

*This is the first of the four main algebraic processes.

When the algebraic expressions that we are simplifying are polynomials, we specify the form of the simplified expression.

Remember from beginning algebra that $-x = (-1)x$, so to subtract a polynomial you can do it as shown by subtracting *each* term, or you can think of it as an application of the distributive property:

$$\begin{aligned}&(4x - 5) - (5x^2 + 2x - 3)\\&\quad = 4x - 5 + (-1)(5x^2 + 2x - 3)\\&\quad = 4x - 5 + (-1)(5x^2) + (-1)(2x) + (-1)(-3)\\&\quad = -5x^2 + 2x - 2\end{aligned}$$

BASIC TERMS

VARIABLE A symbol that represents unspecified elements of a given set. On a calculator, it refers to the name given to a location in the memory that can be assigned a value.

ALGEBRA A generalization of arithmetic. Letters called variables are used to denote numbers, which are related by laws that hold (or are assumed) for any of the numbers in the set. The four main processes of algebra are (1) simplify, (2) evaluate, (3) factor, and (4) solve.

MONOMIAL A polynomial with one and only one term.

BINOMIAL A polynomial with exactly two terms.

TRINOMIAL A polynomial with exactly three terms.

DEGREE (1) The degree of a term is the number of variable factors in the term. If the term has one variable, the degree is the exponent of the variable, or it is the sum of the exponents of the variables if there is more than one variable. (2) The degree of a polynomial is the degree of its highest-degree term. (3) A unit of measurement of an angle that is equal to 1/360 of a revolution.

POLYNOMIAL An algebraic expression that may be written as a sum (or difference) of terms. Each term of a polynomial contains multiplication only.

LINEAR (1) A first-degree polynomial. (2) In one variable, a set of points satisfying the equation $Ax + B = 0, A \neq 0$. (3) In two variables, a set of points satisfying the equation $Ax + By + C = 0$.

QUADRATIC (1) A second-degree polynomial. (2) In one variable, a set of points satisfying the equation $Ax^2 + Bx + C = 0, A \neq 0$.

NUMERICAL COEFFICIENT Any numerical factor of a term is said to be the coefficient of the remaining factors. The *numerical coefficient* is the numerical part of the term, usually written before the variable part. In $3x$, it is the number 3, in $9x^2y^3$, it is the number 9. Generally, the word coefficient is taken to be the numerical coefficient of the variable factors.

LIKE TERMS Terms that differ only in their numerical coefficients. Also called *similar terms*.

The distributive property is also important in multiplying polynomials.

Shortcuts with Products

It is frequently necessary to multiply binomials, and even though we use the distributive property, we want to be able to perform the calculations quickly and efficiently in our heads.

To help you remember the process, we sometimes call this binomial multiplication Ⓕ Ⓞ Ⓘ Ⓛ to remind you:

Ⓕirst terms + Ⓞuter terms +

Ⓘnner terms + Ⓛast terms

FOIL Binomial Product

To multiply two binomials, carry out this mental step.

$$(ax + b)(cx + d) = \underbrace{acx^2}_{\text{First terms}} + \underbrace{(ad + bc)x}_{\text{Outer + Inner}} + \underbrace{bd}_{\text{Last terms}}$$

Simplify (mentally): $(2x-3)(x+3)$

$$(2x - 3)(x + 3) = \underbrace{2x^2}_{\text{F}} + \underbrace{3x}_{\text{O + I}} - \underbrace{9}_{\text{L}}$$

Polynomials and Areas

We assume that you know the area formulas for squares and rectangles:

Area of a square: $A = s^2$
Area of a rectangle: $A = \ell w$

Areas of squares and rectangles are often represented as trinomials. Consider the area represented by the trinomial $x^2 + 3x + 2$. This expression is made up of three terms: x^2, $3x$, and 2. Translate each of these terms into an area:

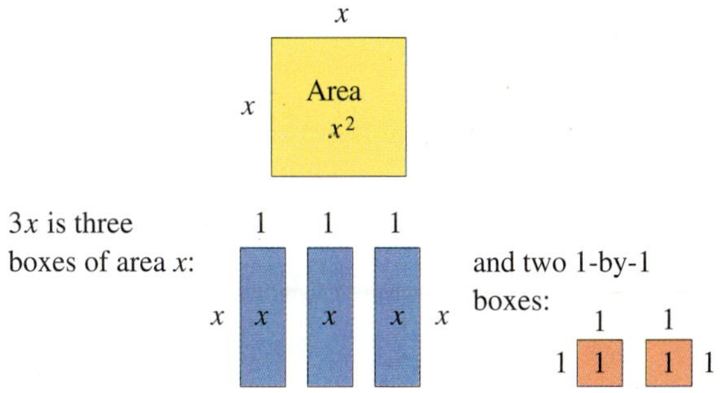

Now you must rearrange these pieces into a rectangle. Think of them as cutouts and move them around. There is only one way (not counting order) to fit them into a rectangle:

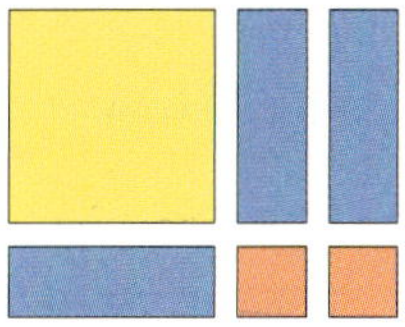

or put together it looks like:

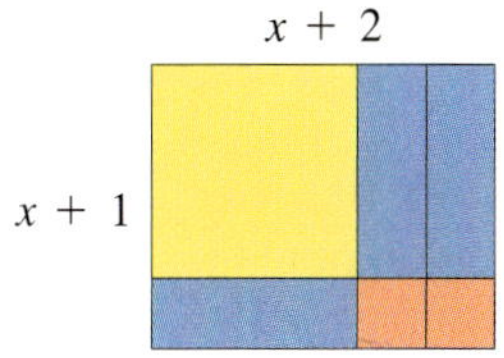

This is EASY if you cut out these figures and use them as manipulatives. Rearrangement of strips is hard to show in a book, but if you try it with cutout pieces, you will like it!

Note: The rectangle with dimensions $x + 2$ by $x + 1$ has the same area as one with dimensions $x + 1$ by $x + 2$.

Thus, $(x + 2)(x + 1) = x^2 + 3x + 2$. These observations provide another way (besides the distributive property) for verifying the shortcut method of FOIL.

3.2 Factoring

TO FACTOR AN EXPRESSION MEANS TO WRITE IT IN FACTORED FORM. THAT IS, THE WORD "FACTOR" IS SOMETIMES A NOUN AND SOMETIMES A VERB.

We have called numbers that are multiplied *factors.* In this section, we look at the process of *factoring,* and we will complete discussion of this topic in Section 3.4 when we use factoring to solve quadratic equations. Factoring is also used extensively in algebra, so to understand some of the algebraic processes, it is necessary to understand factoring.

The approach we take in this section is different from that you will normally see in an algebra course. So often algebra is learned by brute force and memorization or sym-

2. to factor an expression means to write it in factored form. The word "factor" can be a noun or a verb.

***This is the second of the four main algebraic processes.**

bol manipulation, but our development uses a geometric visualization that may help in your understanding not only of algebraic processes, but of geometric ones as well.

Using Areas to Factor

In the previous section, we showed how areas can be used to understand multiplication of binomials. We now use areas to factor polynomials. Factor $2x^2 + 7x + 6$ using areas. First draw the areas for the terms:

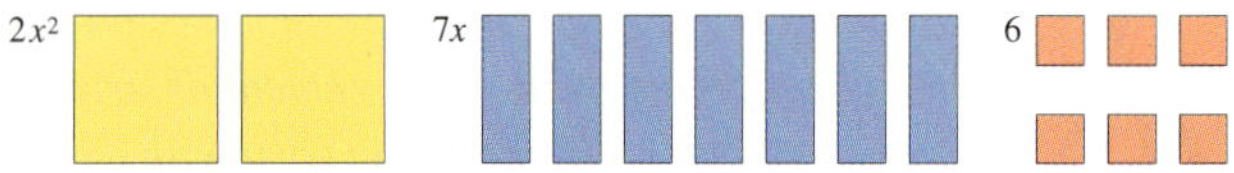

Rearrange to form a rectangle:

Push these pieces together to form a single rectangle:

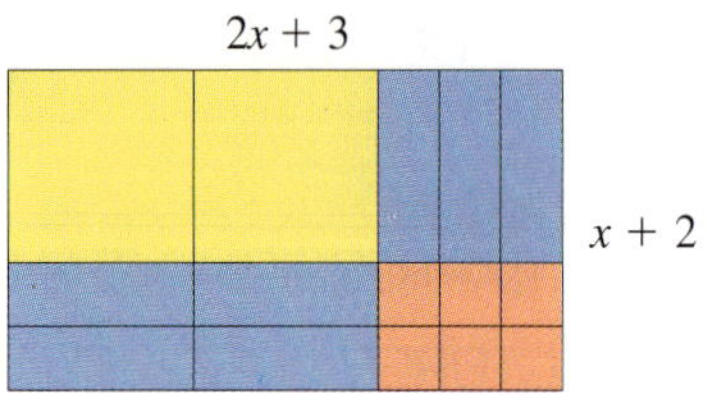

Thus, $2x^2 + 7x + 6 = (2x + 3)(x + 2)$.

Using Algebra to Factor

By thinking through the steps for factoring trinomials by using areas, we can develop a process for algebraic factoring. Consider $x^2 + 3x + 2$ and compare the process below with the discussion at the beginning of this section. We consider the first term and the last term of the given trinomial.

First term: Area of the large square with side x

$$x^2 + 3x + 2 = (x \quad 2)(x \quad 1)$$

Last term: Area of two squares with sides of length 1

There may be several ways of rearranging the areas for these first two steps (first term and last term). What you want to do is to rearrange them so that they form a rectangle. By looking at the binomial product and recalling the process we called FOIL, you see that the sum of the outer product and the inner product, which gives the middle term of the trinomial, will be the factorization that gives a rectangular area:

outer + inner; outer product + inner product

$$x^2 + 3x + 2 = (x + 2)(x + 1)$$

This method of factorization is called FOIL.

PROCEDURE:

Factoring Trinomials

To factor a trinomial:

STEP 1 Find the factors of the second-degree term, and set up the binomials.

STEP 2 Find the factors of the constant term, and consider all possible binomials (mentally). Think of the factors that will form a rectangle.

STEP 3 Determine the factors that yield the correct middle term. If no pair of factors produces the correct full product, then the trinomial is not factorable using integers.

This factoring approach is called FOIL.

***MAKE SURE YOU UNDERSTAND FACTORING TRINOMIALS.**

Common Factoring

If several terms share a factor, then that factor is called a **common factor**. For example, the binomial $5x^2 + 10x$ has three common factors: 5, x, and $5x$. To factor this sum of two terms, we must change it to a product, and this can be done several ways:

$$5x^2 + 10x = 5(x^2 + 2x)$$
$$5x^2 + 10x = x(5x + 10)$$
$$5x^2 + 10x = 5x(x + 2)$$

The last of these possibilities has the greatest common factor as a factor, and is said to be **completely factored**.

When combining common factoring with trinomial factoring, the procedure will be easiest if you look for common factors first.

Difference of Squares

The last type of factorization we will consider is called a **difference of squares**. Suppose we start with one square, a^2:

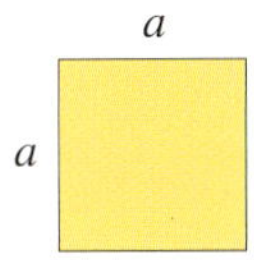

From this square, we wish to subtract another square, b^2: 

This gray square should be smaller than the first ($a^2 > b^2$). Place this square (since it is gray) on top of the larger square:

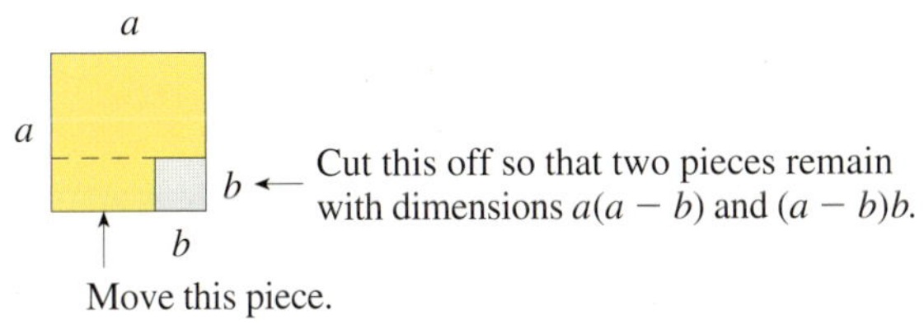

> A **common factor** is a factor that two or more terms of a polynomial have in common.
>
> An expression is **completely factored** if it is a product and there are no common factors and no difference of squares—that is, if no further factoring is possible.

Rearrange these two pieces by moving the smaller one from the bottom and positioning it vertically at the right:

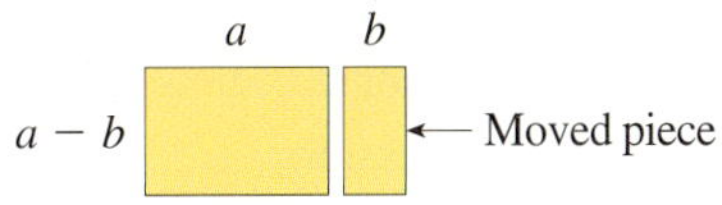

The dimensions of this new arrangement are $(a - b)$ by $(a + b)$. Thus,

$$a^2 - b^2 = (a - b)(a + b)$$

Difference of Squares

$$a^2 - b^2 = (a - b)(a + b)$$

STOP *You need to remember this formula.*

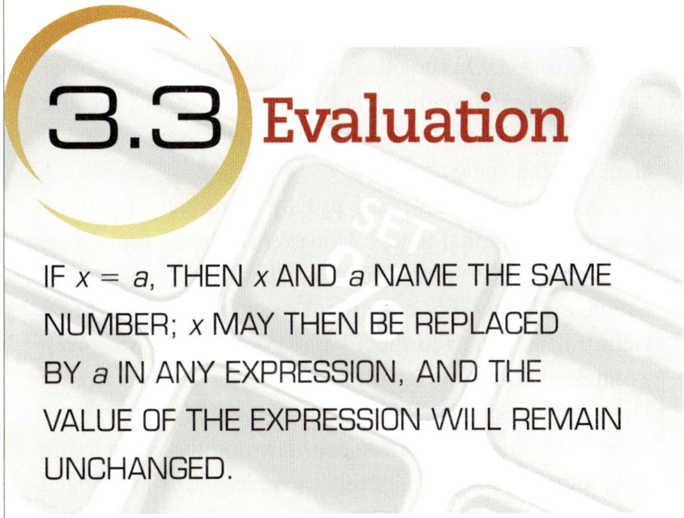

3.3 Evaluation

IF $x = a$, THEN x AND a NAME THE SAME NUMBER; x MAY THEN BE REPLACED BY a IN ANY EXPRESSION, AND THE VALUE OF THE EXPRESSION WILL REMAIN UNCHANGED.

When you replace variables by given numerical values and then simplify the resulting numerical expression, the process is called *evaluating an expression.*

Evaluate

To **evaluate** an expression means to replace the variable (or variables) with given values, and then to simplify the resulting numerical expression.

Evaluate $a + cb$, where $a = 2$, $b = 11$, and $c = 3$. Remember, cb means c ***times*** b.

STEP 1 Replace each variable with the corresponding numerical value. You may need additional parentheses to make sure you don't change the order of operations.

$$\begin{array}{ccccc} a & + & c & \cdot & b \\ \downarrow & \downarrow & \downarrow & \downarrow & \downarrow \\ 2 & + & 3 & (& 11) \end{array}$$

2 + 3(11) Parentheses are necessary so that the product cb is not changed to 311.

3. to evaluate an expression means to replace the variable (or variables) with given values, and then to simplify the resulting numerical expression.

*This is the third of the four main algebraic processes.

STEP 2 Simplify:

$$\begin{aligned} 2 + 3(11) &= 2 + 33 \quad \text{Multiplication before addition} \\ &= 35 \end{aligned}$$

Remember that a particular variable is replaced by a single value when an expression is evaluated. You should also be careful to write capital letters differently from lowercase letters, because they often represent different values. This means that you should not assume that $A = 3$ just because $a = 3$. On the other hand, it is possible that other variables *might* have the value 3. For example, just because $a = 3$, do not assume that another variable—say, t—cannot also have the value $t = 3$.

In algebra, variables are usually represented by either lowercase or capital letters. However, in other disciplines, variables are often represented by other symbols or combinations of letters. For example, I recently took a flight on Delta Airlines and a formula $VM = \sqrt{A} \times 3.56$ was given as an approximation for the distance you can see from a Delta jet (or presumably any other plane). The article defined VM as the distance you can view in miles when flying at an altitude of A feet. For this example, VM is interpreted as a single variable, and not as V *times* M as it normally would be in algebra.

An Application from Genetics

This application is based on the work of Gregor Mendel (1822–1884), an Austrian monk, who formulated the laws of heredity and genetics. Mendel's work was later amplified and explained by a mathematician, G. H. Hardy (1877–1947), and a physician, Wilhelm Weinberg (1862–1937). For years Mendel taught science without any teaching credentials because he had failed the biology portion of the licensing examination! His work, however, laid the foundation for the very important branch of biology known today as genetic science.

Assume that traits are determined by *genes,* which are passed from parents to their offspring. Each parent has a pair of genes, and the basic assumption is that each offspring inherits one gene from each parent to form the

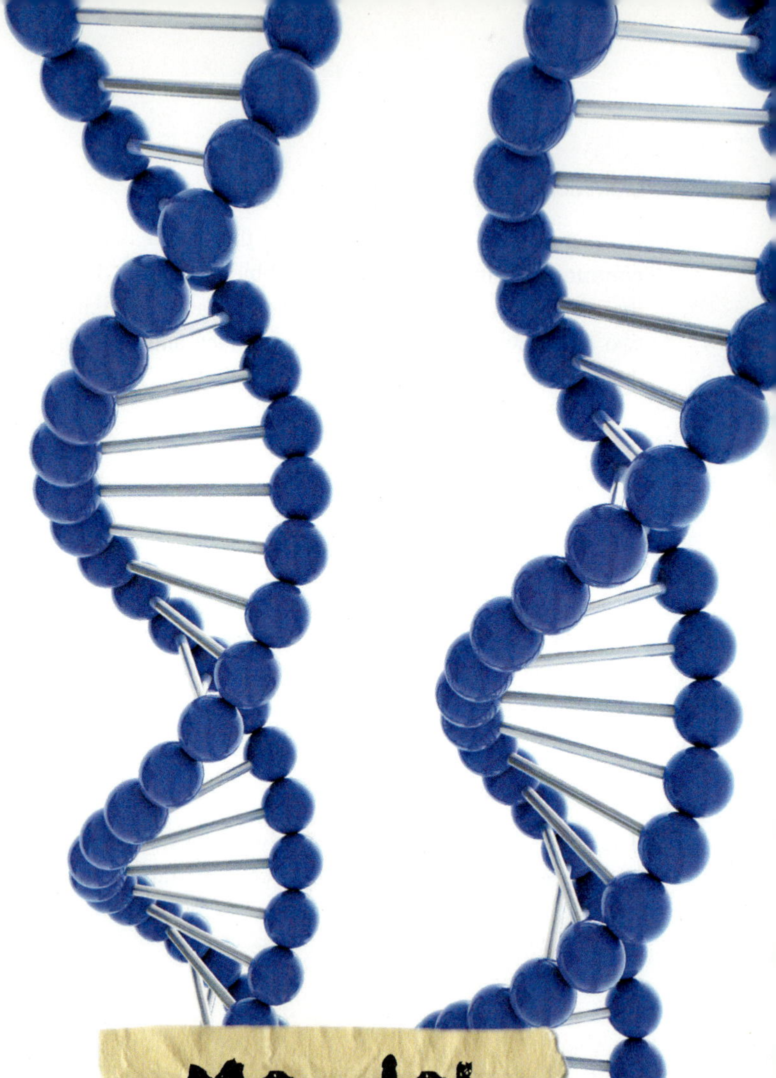

offspring's own pair. The genes are selected in a random, independent way. In our examples, we will assume that the researcher is studying a trait that is both easily identifiable (such as color of a rat's fur) and determined by a pair of genes consisting of a *dominant* gene, denoted by A, and a *recessive* gene, denoted by a.

The possible pairings are called *genotypes:*

AA is called *dominant,* or homozygous.

Aa is called *hybrid,* or heterozygous; genetically, the genotype aA is the same as Aa.

aa is called *recessive*.

The physical appearance is called the *phenotype:*

Genotype AA has phenotype A.

Genotype Aa has phenotype A (since A is dominant).

Genotype aA has phenotype A.

Genotype aa has phenotype a.

In genetics, a square called a *Punnett square* is used to display genotype. For example, suppose two individuals with genotypes Aa are mated, as represented by the following Punnett square:

		Parent 2	
		A	a
Parent 1	A	AA	Aa
	a	aA	aa

We see the result is $AA + Aa + aA + aa = AA + 2Aa + aa$. This reminds us of the binomial product

$$(p + q)^2 = p^2 + 2pq + q^2$$

Let's use binomial multiplication to find the genotypes and phenotypes of a particular example. In population genetics, we are interested in the percent, or relative frequency, of genes of a certain type in the entire population under study. In other words, imagine taking the two genes from each person in the population and putting them into an imaginary pot. This pot is called the *gene pool* for the population. Geneticists study the gene pool to draw conclusions about the population.

Mendel used experiments with pea plants to determine how genetic traits were passed from one generation to the next.

Spreadsheets

A spreadsheet is a computer program used to manipulate data and carry out calculations or chains of calculations. If you have access to a computer and software such as Excel, Lotus 1-2-3, or Quattro Pro, you might use that software in conjunction with this section. However, it is not necessary to have this software (or even access to a computer) to be able to study variables and the evaluation of formulas using the ideas of a spreadsheet. In fact, your first inclination when reading this might be to skip over this and say to yourself, "I don't know anything about a spreadsheet, so I will not read this. Besides, my instructor is not requiring this anyway." However, regardless of whether this is assigned, chances are that sooner or later you will be using a spreadsheet.

One of the most interesting, and important, new ways of representing variables is as a **cell**, or a "box."

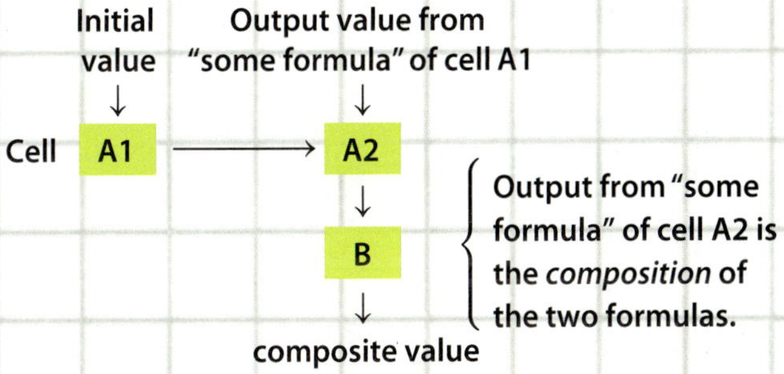

The information in a spreadsheet is stored in a rectangular array of *cells*. The content of each cell can be a number, text, or a formula. The power of a spreadsheet is that a cell's numeric value can be linked to the content of another cell. For example, it is possible to define the content of one cell as the sum of the contents of two other cells. Furthermore, if the value of a cell is changed anywhere in the spreadsheet, all values dependent on it are recalculated, and the new values are displayed immediately.

Instead of designating variables as letters (such as $x, y, z, \ldots$) as we do in algebra, a spreadsheet designates variables as cells (such as B2, A5, Z146, . . .). If you type something into a cell, the spreadsheet program will recognize it as text if it begins with a letter, and as a number if it begins with a numeral. It also recognizes the usual mathematical symbols of +, −, * (for ×), / (for ÷), and ^ (for raising to a power). Parentheses are used in the usual fashion as grouping symbols. To enter a formula, you must begin with +, @, or =, depending on the spreadsheet application. Compare some algebraic and spreadsheet evaluations:

Algebra	Comment	Spreadsheet	Comment
$3(x+y)$	Variables are x and y.	$+3{*}(A1+A2)$	Variables are in contents of cells A1 and A2.
x^2+2x-5	Variable is x.	$+B3\text{^}2+2{*}B3-5$	Variable is the content of cell B3. Begins with "+" to indicate that it is a formula.
$\frac{A+B}{2}$	Formula for the average of the variables A and B.	$+(A3+A4)/2$	Variables are the contents of cells A3 and A4.

For our purposes, we will assume that a spreadsheet program has an almost unlimited number of rows and columns. We will represent a typical spreadsheet as follows:

Spreadsheet Application

	A	B	C	D	E	F	G	H	I	J	K
1											
2											
3											
4											
5											

As an example, we will consider the way in which a spreadsheet program could be used to set up an electronic check-book. We might fill in the spreadsheet as follows:

Spreadsheet Application

	A	B	C	D	E	F
1	DESCRIPTION	DEBIT	DEPOSIT	BALANCE		
2	Beginning balance					
3				+D2-B3+C3		
4				+D3-B4+C4		
5				+D4-B5+C5		

After some entries are filled in, the spreadsheet might look like the following:

Spreadsheet Application

	A	B	C	D	E	F
1	DESCRIPTION	DEBIT	DEPOSIT	BALANCE		
2	Beginning balance			1000.00		
3	School bookstore	250.00		750.00		
4	Paper route		100.00	850.00		
5	Ski trip	300.00		550.00		

The power of a spreadsheet derives from the way variables are referenced by cells. For example, if you go back to the spreadsheet and enter a beginning balance of $2,500 in cell D2, *all* the other entries *automatically* change:

Spreadsheet Application

	A	B	C	D	E	F
1	DESCRIPTION	DEBIT	DEPOSIT	BALANCE		
2	Beginning balance			2500.00		
3	School bookstore	250.00		2250.00		
4	Paper route		100.00	2350.00		
5	Ski trip	300.00		2050.00		

Once the spreadsheet has been set up, the user will enter information in column A and, depending on whether a check has been written or a deposit made, make an entry in either column B or column C. The entries in column D (beginning with cell D3) are automatically calculated by the spreadsheet program. Empty cells are assumed to have the value 0.

It should be clear that each cell from D3 downward needs to contain a different formula. In this example, the column letters and operations of the formula remain unchanged, but each row number is increased by 1 from the cell above. If each of these formulas had to be entered by hand, one by one, it is obvious that setting up a spreadsheet would be very time-consuming. This is not the case, however, and a typical spreadsheet program allows the user to copy the formula from one cell into another cell and at the same time *automatically* change its formula references. Thus, with a single command, each cell in column D is given the correct formula. We will call this command **replicating** a formula or cell. Formulas replicated down a column have their row numbers incremented, and formulas replicated across a row have the column letters incremented.

We might once again remind you of the power of a computer spreadsheet. Note that the *entire* answer would *immediately* be filled in as soon as you fill in the number 12 in cell A2. If you now go back and reenter another number into cell A2, the entire spreadsheet would *immediately* change because every cell is ultimately defined in terms of the content of cell A2 in this example spreadsheet.

The real power of a spreadsheet program lies not in its ability to perform calculations, but rather in its ability to answer "what-if" types of questions.

To take advantage of the "what-if" power of a spreadsheet, the previous example could be set up to allow for any interest rate. This could be done in the following way:

Spreadsheet Application

	A	B	C	D	E	F	G	H	I	J	K
1	Interest rate =										
2	YEAR NUMBER	BALANCE									
3	0										
4	+A3+1	+B3+B1*B3									
5											

Note that when a number is inserted into cell B1, that number will act as the interest rate, and the number inserted into cell B3 will act as the amount of deposit. Therefore, we see that B1 is the variable representing the interest rate, and B3 is the variable representing the beginning balance. If row 4 is *replicated* into rows 5 to 10, we will then obtain the data for the next 7 years. The problem with this replication, however, is that the reference to cell B1 will change as the replication takes place down column B. This difficulty is overcome by using a special character that holds a column or a row constant. The symbol we will use for this purpose is \$. (Some spreadsheets use the symbol # for this purpose.) Thus, we would change the formula in cell B4 above to

+B3+\$B\$1*B3

to mean that we want not only column B to remain constant, but also we want row 1 to remain unchanged when this entry is replicated. Note that \$ applies only to the character directly following its placement. We show the first 7 rows (4 years) of such a spreadsheet for which the rate is 4% and the initial deposit is \$1,000.

Spreadsheet Application

	A	B	C	D	E
1	Interest rate =	0.04			
2	YEAR NUMBER	BALANCE			
3	0	1000.00			
4	1	1040.00			
5	2	1081.60			
6	3	1124.86			
7	4	1169.86			

3.4 Equations

EVEN THOUGH THERE ARE MANY ASPECTS OF ALGEBRA THAT ARE IMPORTANT TO THE SCIENTIST AND MATHEMATICIAN, THE ABILITY TO SOLVE SIMPLE EQUATIONS IS IMPORTANT TO THE LAYPERSON AND CAN BE USED IN A VARIETY OF EVERYDAY APPLICATIONS.

Terminology

An **equation** is a statement of equality. There are three types of equations: *true, false,* and *open*.

SOLVE

≠

SIMPLIFY

An *open equation* is one with a variable. A *true equation* is an equation without a variable, such as

$$2 + 3 = 5$$

A *false equation* is an equation without a variable, such as

$$2 + 3 = 15$$

Our focus is on *open equations,* those equations with a variable, or unknown. The values that make an open equation true are said to **satisfy** the equation and are called the **solutions** or **roots** of the equation.

There are three types of open equations. Those that are always true, as in

$$x + 3 = 3 + x$$

are called *identities.* Those that are always false, as in

$$x + 3 = 4 + x$$

An **equation** is a statement of equality.

4. to solve an open equation is to find all replacements for the variable(s) that make the equation true.

* This is the fourth of the four main algebraic processes.
** To solve is NOT the same as to simplify.

are called *contradictions.* Most open equations are true for some replacements of the variable and false for other replacements, as in

$$2 + x = 15$$

These are called *conditional equations.* Usually, when we speak of equations we mean conditional equations. Our concern when solving equations is to find the numbers that satisfy a given equation, so we look for things to do to equations to make the solutions or roots more obvious. Two equations with the same solutions are called **equivalent equations**. An equivalent equation may be easier to solve than the original equation, so we try to get successively simpler equivalent equations until the solution is obvious. There are certain procedures you can use to create equivalent equations. In this section, we will discuss solving the two most common types of equations you will encounter: *linear* and *quadratic*.

Linear equations: $ax + b = 0 \quad (a \neq 0)$

Quadratic equations: $ax^2 + bx + c = 0 \quad (a \neq 0)$

Linear Equations

To solve a linear equation, you can use one or more of the following **equation properties**.

EQUATION PROPERTIES

Addition property Adding the same number to both sides of an equation results in an equivalent equation.

Subtraction property Subtracting the same number from both sides of an equation results in an equivalent equation.

Multiplication property Multiplying both sides of a given equation by the same nonzero number results in an equivalent equation.

Division property Dividing both sides of a given equation by the same nonzero number results in an equivalent equation.

When the equation properties are used to obtain equivalent equations, ***the goal is to isolate the variable on one side of the equation***, as shown:

ADDITION PROPERTY: Solve $x - 36 = 42$.

$x - 36 = 42$	Given equation
$x - 36 + 36 = 42 + 36$	Add 36 to both sides.
$x = 78$	Simplify.

SUBTRACTION PROPERTY: Solve $x + 15 = 25$.

$x + 15 = 25$	Given equation
$x + 15 - 15 = 25 - 15$	Subtract 15 from both sides.
$x = 10$	Carry out the simplification.

The root (solution) of this simpler equivalent equation is now obvious (it is 10). We often display the answer in the form of this simpler equation, $x = 10$, with the variable isolated on one side.

MULTIPLICATION PROPERTY: Solve $\frac{x}{5} = -12$.

$\frac{x}{5} = -12$	Given equation
$5\left(\frac{x}{5}\right) = 5(-12)$	Multiply both sides by 5.
$x = -60$	Simplify.

DIVISION PROPERTY: Solve $3x = 75$.

$3x = 75$	Given equation
$\frac{3x}{3} = \frac{75}{3}$	Divide both sides by 3.
$x = 25$	Simplify.

You can always check the solution to see whether it is correct; substituting the solution into the original equation will verify that it satisfies the equation. Notice how the equation properties are used when solving these equations.

The equation $15 = x$ is the same as $x = 15$. This is a general property of equality called the **symmetric property of equality**: If $a = b$, then $b = a$.

Sometimes you will need to solve more complicated equations:

$3(m + 4) + 5 = 5(m - 1) - 2$	Given equation
$3m + 12 + 5 = 5m - 5 - 2$	Simplify (distributive property).
$3m + 17 = 5m - 7$	Simplify.
$17 = 2m - 7$	Subtract $3m$ from both sides.
$24 = 2m$	Add 7 to both sides.
$12 = m$	Divide both sides by 2.

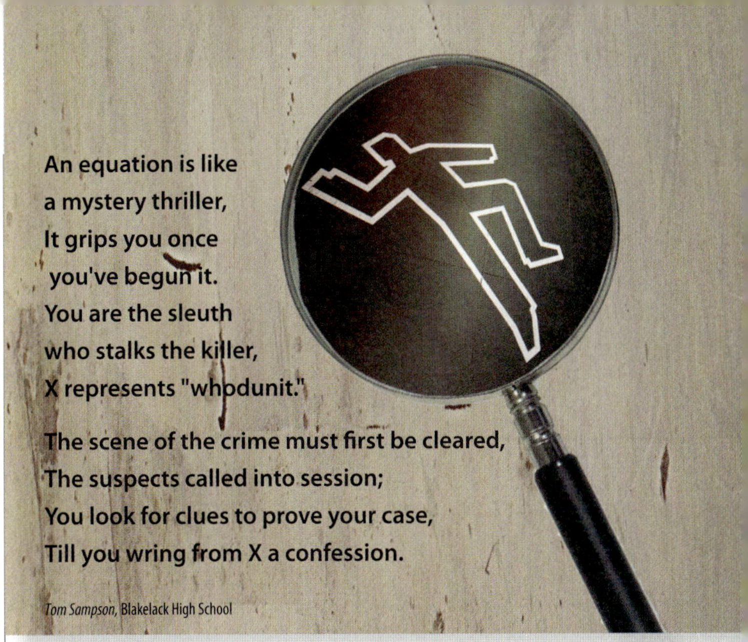

Quadratic Equations

To solve quadratic equations, you must first use the equation properties to write the equation in the form

$$ax^2 + bx + c = 0, (a \neq 0)$$

There are two commonly used methods for solving quadratic equations. The first uses factoring, and the second uses the quadratic formula. Both of these methods require that you apply the linear equation properties to obtain a 0 on one side. Next, look to see whether the polynomial is factorable. If so, use the **zero-product rule** to set each factor equal to 0, and then solve each of those equations. If the polynomial is not factorable, then use the quadratic formula.

Zero-Product Rule

If $A \cdot B = 0$, then $A = 0$ or $B = 0$, or $A = B = 0$.

If the product of two numbers is 0, then at least one of the factors must be 0.

***Note that you must first have a zero on one side.**

Solve $x^2 = x$.

$x^2 = x$	Given equation
$x^2 - x = 0$	Subtract x from both sides. First obtain a 0 on one side.
$x(x - 1) = 0$	Factor, if possible.
$x = 0, \quad x - 1 = 0$	Zero-product rule; set each factor equal to 0.
$x = 0, \; x = 1$	Solve each of the resulting equations.

The equation has two roots, $x = 0$ and $x = 1$. Usually you will set each factor equal to 0 and solve mentally.

Sometimes when equations are factored, there will be two factors that are the same so there is only one root. In such a case we say the root has **multiplicity** of two. Suppose you wish to solve $x(x - 8) = 4(x - 9)$.

$x(x-8) = 4(x-9)$	Given equation
$x^2 - 8x = 4x - 36$	Simplify.
$x^2 - 12x + 36 = 0$	Subtract 4*x* from both sides and add 36 to both sides.
$(x-6)(x-6) = 0$	Factor.
$x = 6$	Set each factor equal to 0 and mentally solve.

If the quadratic expression is not easily factorable (after you obtain a 0 on one side), then you can use the **quadratic formula**, which is derived in most high school algebra books.

Quadratic Formula

If $ax^2 + bx + c = 0$, and $a \neq 0$, then

$$x = \frac{-b \pm \sqrt{b^2 - 4ac}}{2a}$$

*This is one of the all-time "BIGGIES" in algebra. You should remember it.

Solve $2x^2 + 6x + 1 = 0$. Note that $2x^2 + 6x + 1 = 0$ has a 0 on one side and also that the left-hand side does not easily factor, so we will use the quadratic formula. We begin by (mentally) identifying $a = 2$, $b = 6$, and $c = 1$.

$2x^2 + 6x + 1 = 0$	Given equation
$x = \dfrac{-(6) \pm \sqrt{6^2 - 4(2)(1)}}{2(2)}$	Substitute for *a*, *b*, and *c* in the quadratic formula.
$= \dfrac{-6 \pm \sqrt{28}}{4}$	Simplify under the square root.
$= \dfrac{-6 \pm 2\sqrt{7}}{4}$	Simplify radical.
$= \dfrac{2(-3 \pm \sqrt{7})}{4}$	Factor a 2 out of the numerator so that we can reduce the fraction. This step is usually done mentally.
$= \dfrac{-3 \pm \sqrt{7}}{2}$	Reduce the fraction.

Sometimes the number under the radical symbol is negative. Since the square root of a negative number is not defined in the set of real numbers and since we are working in the set of real numbers, we say there is no real value.

3.5 Inequalities

THE TECHNIQUES OF THE PREVIOUS SECTION CAN ALSO BE APPLIED TO QUANTITIES THAT ARE NOT EQUAL.

Comparison Property

If we are given any two numbers x and y, then obviously either

$$x = y \quad \text{or} \quad x \neq y$$

If $x \neq y$, then either

$$x < y \quad \text{or} \quad x > y$$

This property is called the **comparison property**.*

COMPARISON PROPERTY

For any two numbers x and y, exactly one of the following is true:

1. $x = y$ *x* is equal to (the same as) *y*
2. $x > y$ *x* is greater than (larger than) *y*
3. $x < y$ *x* is less than (smaller than) *y*

Solving Linear Inequalities

The comparison property tells us that if two quantities are not exactly equal, we can relate them with a greater-than or a less-than symbol (called an **inequality symbol**). The solution of

$$x < 3$$

has more than one value, and it becomes very impractical to write "The answers are 2, 1, -110, 0, $2\frac{1}{2}$, 2.99, ..." Instead, we relate the answer to a number

* Sometimes this is called the *trichotomy property*.

The Calculator and the Quadratic

Solve $5x^2 + 2x - 2 = 0$ using an *algebraic calculator*. To approximate these roots:

(labels: b over the first 2; a over 5; c over 2 +/−)

[2] [x^2] [−] [4] [×] [5] [×] [2] [+/−] [=] This is $b^2 - 4ac$.

[√] [STO] Find the square root and store for later use.

(labels: $-b$ over 2 +/−; a over 5)

[+] [2] [+/−] [=] [÷] [2] [÷] [5] [=] This gives the first root.

(labels: $-b$ over 2 +/−; a over 5)

[2] [+/−] [−] [RCL] [=] [÷] [2] [÷] [5] [=] This gives the second root.

Some of the steps shown here could be combined because these are simple numbers. These steps give the numerical approximation for a quadratic equation with real roots. For this quadratic equation the roots are (to four decimal places) 0.4633 and −0.8633.

Since you will have occasion to use the quadratic formula over and over again, and since many calculators have programming capabilities, this is a good time to consider writing a simple program to give the real roots for a quadratic equation. First write the equation in the form $ax^2 + bx + c = 0$, input the a, b, and c values into the calculator as A, B, and C. The program will then output the two real values (if they exist). Each brand of *graphing calculator* is somewhat different, but it is instructive to illustrate the general process. Press the [PRGM] key. You will then be asked to name the program; we call our program QUAD. Next, input the formula for the two roots (from the quadratic formula). Finally, display the answer:

$:(-B+\sqrt{}(B^2 - 4AC))/(2A)$

:Disp Ans

$:(-B-\sqrt{}(B^2 - 4AC))/(2A)$

:Disp Ans

Continuing, input the A, B, and C values as follows:

[5] [STO→] [A] [2] [STO→] [B] [−2] [STO→] [C] [PRGM] QUAD

Then run the program for the DISPLAY: .4633249581
−.8633249581

Finally, today many calculators have a [SOLVE] key and the only requirement for solving the equation is to check your owner's manual for the correct format. For example, input

$$\text{solve}\,(5x^2 + 2x - 2 = 0, x)$$

which gives the solution as

$$x = \frac{-(\sqrt{11} + 1)}{5} \quad \text{or} \quad x = \frac{\sqrt{11} - 1}{5}$$

Note that the form here is equivalent to (but not the same as) $x = \dfrac{-1 \pm \sqrt{11}}{5}$.

line, as shown in Figure 3.1. The fact that 3 is not included (3 is not less than 3) in the solution set is indicated by an open circle at the point 3. A closed circle indicates that the endpoint $x = 3$ is included.

Figure 3.1 Graph of $x < 3$

If we want to include the endpoint $x = 3$ with the inequality $x < 3$, we write $x \le 3$ and say "x is less than or equal to 3." We define two additional inequality symbols:

$x \ge y$ means $x > y$ or $x = y$

$x \le y$ means $x < y$ or $x = y$

A *statement of order,* called an **inequality**, refers to statements that include one or more of the following relationships:

less than (<)	less than or equal to (≤)
greater than (>)	greater than or equal to (≥)

On a number line, if $x < y$, then x is to the left of y. Suppose the coordinates x and y are plotted as shown in Figure 3.2.

Figure 3.2 Number line showing two coordinates, x and y

If you add 2 to both x and y, you obtain $x + 2$ and $y + 2$. From Figure 3.3, you see that $x + 2 < y + 2$.

Figure 3.3 Number line with 2 added to both x and y

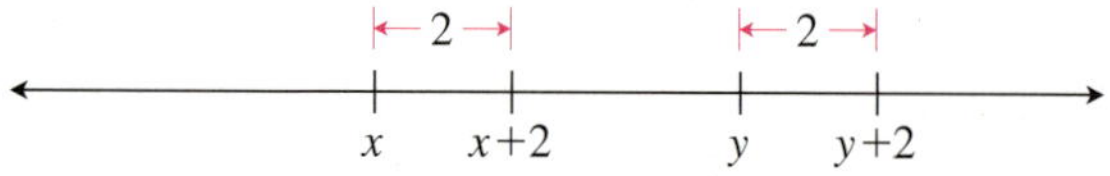

If you add some number c, there are two possibilities.

$c > 0$ ($c > 0$ is read "c is positive")

$c < 0$ ($c < 0$ is read "c is negative")

If $c > 0$, then $x + c$ is still to the left of $y + c$, as shown in Figure 3.4.

Figure 3.4 Adding positive and negative values to x and y

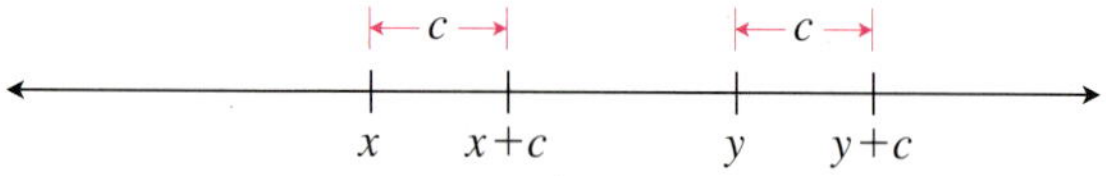

If $c < 0$, then $x + c$ is still to the left of $y + c$. In both cases, $x < y$, which justifies the addition property of inequality. (See bottom of this page.)

Because the **addition property of inequality** is essentially the same as the addition property of equality, you might expect that there is also a multiplication property of inequality. We would hope that we could multiply both sides of an inequality by some number c without upsetting the inequality. Consider some examples. Let $x = 5$ and $y = 10$, so that $5 < 10$.

Let $c = 2$: $5 \cdot 2 < 10 \cdot 2$

$10 < 20$ True

PROPERTIES OF INEQUALITIES

Addition Property of Inequality

If $x < y$, then

$x + c < y + c$

Also,

if $x \le y$, then $x + c \le y + c$

if $x > y$, then $x + c > y + c$

if $x \ge y$, then $x + c \ge y + c$

Multiplication Property of Inequality

Positive multiplication ($c > 0$)

If $x < y$, then

$cx < cy$

↑ Order unchanged

Also, for $c > 0$,

if $x \le y$, then $cx \le cy$

if $x > y$, then $cx > cy$

if $x \ge y$, then $cx \ge cy$

Negative multiplication ($c < 0$)

If $x < y$, then

$cx > cy$

↑ Order reversed

Also, for $c < 0$,

if $x \le y$, then $cx \ge cy$

if $x > y$, then $cx < cy$

if $x \ge y$, then $cx \le cy$

Let $c = 0$: $\quad 5 \cdot 0 < 10 \cdot 0$

$\qquad\qquad\quad 0 < 0$ False

Let $c = -2$: $\quad 5(-2) < 10(-2)$

$\qquad\qquad\quad -10 < -20$ False

You can see that you cannot multiply both sides of an inequality by a constant and be sure that the result is still true. However, if you restrict c to a positive value, then you can multiply both sides of an inequality by c. On the other hand, if c is a negative number, then the order of the inequality should be reversed. This is summarized by the **multiplication property of inequality**.

The same properties hold for positive and negative division. We can summarize with the following statement, which tells us how to **solve an inequality**.

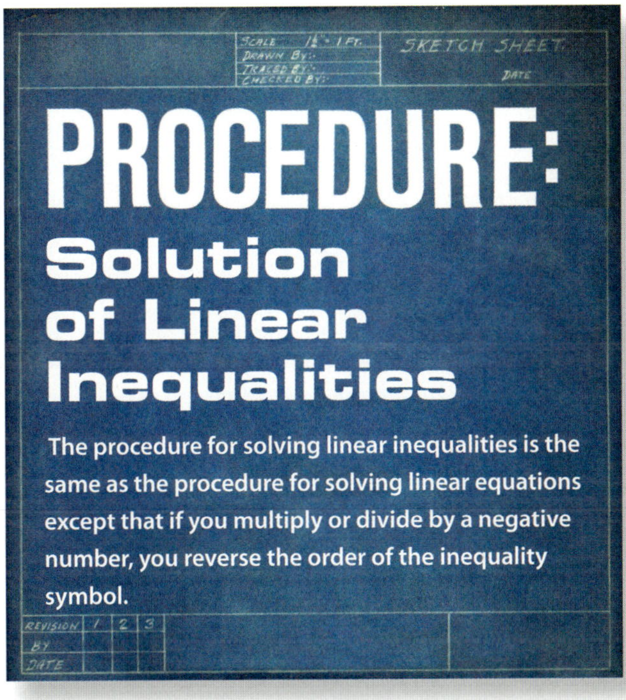

PROCEDURE:
Solution of Linear Inequalities

The procedure for solving linear inequalities is the same as the procedure for solving linear equations except that if you multiply or divide by a negative number, you reverse the order of the inequality symbol.

In summary, given $x < y$, $x \le y$, $x > y$, or $x \ge y$:

The **inequality symbols are the *same* if you**

1. Add the same number to both sides.
2. Subtract the same number from both sides.
3. Multiply both sides by a positive number.
4. Divide both sides by a positive number.

} This works the same as with equations.

The **inequality symbols are *reversed* if you**

1. Multiply both sides by a negative number.
2. Divide both sides by a negative number.
3. Interchange the x and the y.

} *This is where inequalities and equations differ.

Positive Multiplication Property: $5x - 3 \ge 7$

$$\begin{aligned} 5x - 3 &\ge 7 \\ 5x - 3 + 3 &\ge 7 + 3 \\ 5x &\ge 10 \\ \frac{5x}{5} &\ge \frac{10}{5} \\ x &\ge 2 \end{aligned}$$

Divide both sides by 5 and note that the inequality does not reverse.

The closed circle indicates that the endpoint $x = 2$ is included.

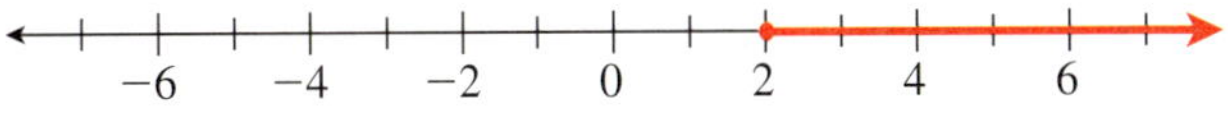

Negative Multiplication Property: $-x \ge 2$

$$\begin{aligned} -x &\ge 2 \\ x &\le -2 \end{aligned}$$

Multiply both sides by -1 and remember to reverse the order of the inequality.

Now, with the variable on the left of the inequality, we graph the solution on a number line:

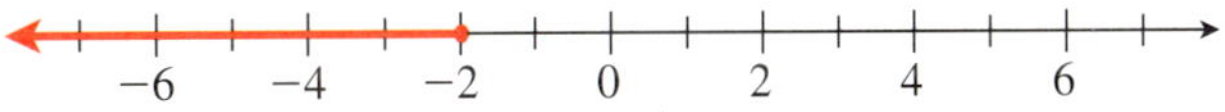

3.6 Problem Solving

ONE OF THE GOALS OF PROBLEM SOLVING IS TO BE ABLE TO APPLY TECHNIQUES THAT YOU LEARN IN THE CLASSROOM TO SITUATIONS OUTSIDE THE CLASSROOM.

However, a first step is to learn to solve contrived textbook-type word problems to develop the problem-solving skills you will need outside the classroom.

In this section, we will focus on common types of word problems that are found in most textbooks. You might say, "I want to learn how to become a problem solver, and textbook problems are not what I have in mind; I want to do *real* problem solving." But to become a problem solver, you must first learn the basics, and there is good reason why word problems are part of a textbook. We start with these problems *to build a problem-solving procedure that can be expanded to apply to problem solving in general.*

The most useful axiom in problem solving is the **principle of substitution**: If two quantities are equal, one may be substituted for the other without changing the truth or falsity of the statement.

SUBSTITUTION PROPERTY

If $a = b$, then a may be substituted for b in any mathematical statement without affecting the truth or falsity of the given mathematical statement.

The simplest way to illustrate the substitution property is to use it in evaluating a formula. A billiard table is 4 ft. by 8 ft. Find the perimeter.

"For a minute I thought we had him stymied!"

Use an appropriate formula, $P = 2\ell + 2w$, where P = PERIMETER, ℓ = LENGTH, and w = WIDTH. Substitute the known values into the formula:

$$\begin{aligned} &\quad\ \ \ell = 8 \qquad w = 4 \\ &\qquad \downarrow \qquad\quad \downarrow \\ P &= 2(8) + 2(4) \\ &= 16 + 8 \\ &= 24 \end{aligned}$$

These arrows mean substitution.

The perimeter is 24 ft.

A procedure for solving word problems is summarized in the box on the next page.

Problem solving depends not only on the substitution property, but also on translating statements from English to mathematical symbols, using *variables* as necessary. On a much more advanced level, this process is called *mathematical modeling*. (We will consider some mathematical modeling later in this book.) However, for now, we will simply call it **translating**. Note that we use the word **sum** to indicate the result obtained from addition, **difference** for the result from subtraction, **product** for the result of a multiplication, and **quotient** for the result of a division.

Number Relationships

The first type of word problem we consider involves number relationships. These are designed to allow you to begin thinking about the *procedure* to use when solving word problems. For example, if you add 10 to twice a number, the result is 22. What is the number?

Read the problem carefully. Make sure you know what is given and what is wanted. Next, write a verbal description (without using variables), using operation signs and an equal sign, but still using the key words. This is called *translating* the problem.

$$10 + 2(\text{A NUMBER}) = 22$$

When there is a single unknown, choose a variable.

IMPORTANT: DO NOT BEGIN BY CHOOSING A VARIABLE; CHOOSE A VARIABLE ONLY AFTER YOU HAVE TRANSLATED THE PROBLEM.

With more complicated problems you will not know at the start what the variable should be.

Let n = A NUMBER. Use the substitution property:

$$\begin{aligned} 10 + 2(\text{A NUMBER}) &= 22 \\ \downarrow \quad & \\ 10 + 2n \quad &= 22 \end{aligned}$$

Solve the equation and check the solution in the original problem to see if it makes sense.

$$\begin{aligned} 10 + 2n &= 22 \\ 2n &= 12 \\ n &= 6 \end{aligned}$$

Check: Add 10 to twice 6 and the result is 22. State the solution to a word problem in words: The number is 6.

The second type of number problem involves **consecutive integers**. If n = AN INTEGER, then

THE SECOND CONSECUTIVE INTEGER $= n + 1$, and

THE THIRD CONSECUTIVE INTEGER $= n + 2$

PROCEDURE: Problem Solving in Algebra

STEP 1 You have to *understand the problem.* This means you must read the problem and note what it is about. Focus on processes rather than numbers. You cannot work a problem you do not understand. A sketch may help in understanding the problem.

STEP 2 *Devise a plan.* **Write down a verbal description of the problem using operation signs and an equal or inequality sign.** Note the following common translations.

Symbol	*Verbal Description*
$=$	is equal to; equals; is the same as; is; was; becomes; will be; results in
$+$	plus; the sum of; added to; more than; greater than; increased by; combined; total
$-$	minus; the difference of; the difference between; is subtracted from; less than; smaller than; decreased by; is diminished by
$\times$	times; product; is multiplied by; twice ($2\times$); triple ($3\times$); of (as in 40% of 300)
$\div$	divided by; quotient of; ratio of; proportional to

STEP 3 *Carry out the plan.* In the context of word problems, we need to proceed deductively by carrying out the following steps.

Choose a variable. If there is a single unknown, choose a variable. If there are several unknowns, you can use the substitution property to reduce the number of unknowns to a single variable. Later we will consider word problems with more than one unknown.

Substitute. Replace the verbal phrase for the unknown with the variable.

Solve the equation. This is generally the easiest step. Translate the symbolic statement (such as $x = 3$) into a verbal statement. Probably no variables were given as part of the word problem, so $x = 3$ is not an answer. Generally, word problems require an answer stated in words. Pay attention to units of measure and other details of the problem.

STEP 4 *Look back.* Be sure your answer makes sense by checking it with the original question in the problem. **Remember to answer the question that was asked.**

Also, if E = AN EVEN INTEGER and if F = AN ODD INTEGER, then

$E + 2$ = THE NEXT CONSECUTIVE EVEN INTEGER, and

$F + 2$ = THE NEXT CONSECUTIVE ODD INTEGER

Notice that you add 2 when you are writing down consecutive evens or consecutive odds.

Distance Relationships

The first example of a problem with several variables that we will consider involves distances. The relationships may seem complicated, but if you draw a figure and remember that the total distance is the sum of the separate parts, you will easily be able to analyze this type of problem.

The drive from Buffalo to Albany is 210 miles across northern New York State. On this route, you pass Rochester and then Syracuse before reaching the capital city of Albany. It is 20 miles less from Buffalo to Rochester than from Syracuse to Albany, and 10 miles farther from Rochester to Syracuse than from Buffalo to Rochester. How far is it from Rochester to Syracuse?

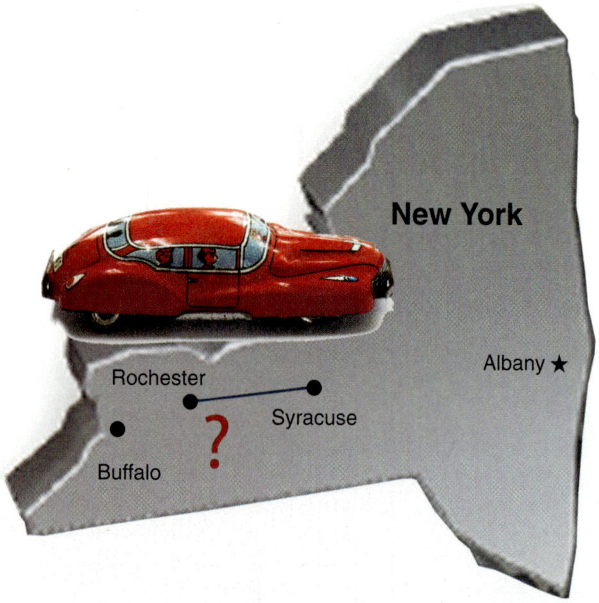

STEP 1 ***Understand the Problem.*** First, you should begin by examining the problem. Remember that you cannot solve a problem you do not understand. It must make sense before mathematics can be applied to it. All too often poor problem solvers try to begin solving the problem too soon. Take your time when trying to understand the problem. Start at the beginning of the problem, and make a sketch of the situation, as shown in Figure 3.5. The cities are located in the order sketched on the line.

Figure 3.5 Distance problem

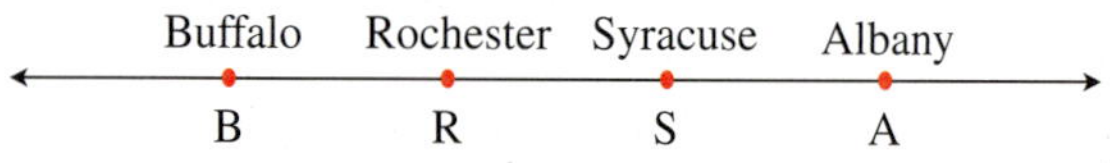

STEP 2 ***Devise a Plan.*** The cities are located in the order sketched in Figure 3.5, but how can that fact give us an equation? To have an equation, you must find an equality. Which quantities are equal? The distances from Buffalo to Rochester, from Rochester to Syracuse, and from Syracuse to Albany must add up to the distance from Buffalo to Albany. That is, the sum of the parts must equal the whole distance—so start there. This is what we mean when we say *translate.*

TRANSLATE

$$(\text{DIST. B TO R}) + (\text{DIST. R TO S}) + (\text{DIST. S TO A}) = (\text{DIST. B TO A})$$

Notice that there appear to be four variables. We now use the substitution property to *evolve.*

EVOLVE

With this step we ask whether we know the value of any quantity in the equation. The first sentence of the problem tells us that the total distance is 210 miles, so

$$(\text{DIST. B TO R}) + (\text{DIST. R TO S}) + (\text{DIST. S TO A}) = (\text{DIST. B TO A})$$

↓ Buffalo to Albany

$$(\text{DIST. B TO R}) + (\text{DIST. R TO S}) + (\text{DIST. S TO A}) = 210$$

Also, part of evolving the equation is to use substitution for the relationships that are given as part of the problem. We now translate the other pieces of given information by adding to the smaller distance in each case.

$$(\text{DIST. B TO R}) + 20 = (\text{DIST. S TO A})$$
$$(\text{DIST. R TO S}) = (\text{DIST. B TO R}) + 10$$

We now use substitution to let the equation evolve into one with a single unknown.

STEP 3 ***Carry Out the Plan.*** Pólya's method now tells us to carry out the plan. We use substitution on the above equations:

$$(\text{DIST. B TO R}) + (\text{DIST. R TO S}) + (\text{DIST. S TO A}) = 210$$

↑ (DIST. B TO R) + 10 ↑ (DIST. B TO R) + 20

$$(\text{DIST. B TO R}) + [(\text{DIST. B TO R}) + 10] + [(\text{DIST. B TO R}) + 20] = 210$$

This equation now has a single variable, so we let d = DIST. B TO R and substitute into the equation:

$$d + [d + 10] + [d + 20] = 210$$

SOLVE

$$3d + 30 = 210$$
$$3d = 180$$
$$d = 60$$

The equation is solved. Does that mean that the answer to the problem is "$d = 60$"? No, the question asks for the distance from Rochester to Syracuse, which is $d + 10$.

Answer

So now interpret the solution and answer the question: The distance from Rochester to Syracuse is 70 miles.

Notice that the steps we used above can be summarized as **translate**, **evolve**, **solve**, and **answer**.

STEP 4 ***Look Back.*** Pólya's procedure requires that we look back. To be certain that the answer makes sense in the original problem, you should always check the solution.

$$60 + 70 + 80 \stackrel{?}{=} 210$$
$$210 = 210 \quad ✓$$

Pythagorean Relationships

Many word problems are concerned with relationships involving a right triangle. If two sides of a right triangle are known, the third can be found by using the Pythagorean theorem. Remember, if a right triangle has sides a and b and hypotenuse c, then

$$a^2 + b^2 = c^2$$

Have you ever wondered why sidewalks, pipes, and tracks have expansion joints every few feet? The next example may help you to understand why; it considers the unlikely situation in which 1-mile sections of pipe are connected together.

A 1-mile-long pipeline connects two pumping stations. Special joints must be used along the line to provide for expansion and contraction due to changes in temperature. However, if the pipeline were actually one continuous length of pipe fixed at each end by the stations, then expansion would cause the pipe to bow. Approximately how high would the middle of the pipe rise if the expansion were just 1 inch over the mile?

STEP 1 ***Understand the Problem.*** First, understand the problem. Draw a picture as shown in Figure 3.6.

Figure 3.6 Pipeline problem

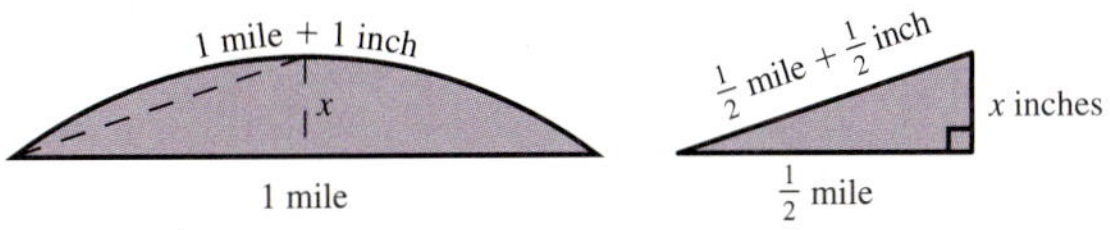

Before beginning the solution to this example, try to guess the answer. Consider the following choices for the rise in pipe:

A. 1 inch
B. 1 foot
C. 1 yard
D. 5 yards
E. 1 mile

Go ahead, choose one of these. This is one problem for which the answer was not intuitive for the author. I guessed incorrectly when I first considered this problem.

STEP 2 ***Devise a Plan.*** For purposes of solution, notice from Figure 3.6 that we are assuming that the pipe bows in a circular arc. A triangle would produce a reasonable approximation since the distance x should be quite small compared to the total length. Since a right triangle is used to model this situation, the Pythagorean theorem may be used. Remember: to carry out the plan, we'll use the method *translate, evolve, solve,* and *answer.*

STEP 3 ***Carry Out the Plan.***

Translate

$$(\text{SIDE})^2 + (\text{HEIGHT})^2 = (\text{HYPOTENUSE})^2$$

Once upon a time (about 450 BC), a Greek named Zeno made up several word problems that became known as Zeno's paradoxes. This problem is not a paradox, but was inspired by one of Zeno's problems. Consider a race between Achilles and a tortoise. The tortoise has a 100-meter head start. Achilles runs at a rate of 10 meters per second, whereas the tortoise runs 1 meter per second (it is an extraordinarily swift tortoise). How long does it take Achilles to catch up with the tortoise?

STEP 1 **Understand the Problem.** Before you begin, make sure you understand the problem. It is often helpful to draw a figure or diagram to help you understand the problem. The situation for this problem is shown in Figure 3.7.

STEP 2 **Devise a Plan.** The plan we will use is *translate, evolve, solve,* and *answer.*

STEP 3 **Carry Out the Plan.**

Translate. (ACHILLES' DISTANCE TO RENDEZVOUS) = (TORTOISE'S DISTANCE TO RENDEZVOUS) + (HEAD START)

Evolve. The equation we wrote has three unknowns. Our goal is to evolve this equation into one with a single unknown so that we can choose that as our variable. The evolution of the equation requires that we use the substitution property to replace the unknowns with known numbers or with other expressions that, in turn, will lead to an equation with one unknown. We will begin this problem by substituting the known number.

(ACHILLES' DISTANCE TO RENDEZVOUS) = (TORTOISE'S DISTANCE TO RENDEZVOUS) + (HEAD START)

↓

(ACHILLES' DISTANCE TO RENDEZVOUS) = (TORTOISE'S DISTANCE TO RENDEZVOUS) + 100

There are still two unknowns, which we can change by using the following distance = rate × time formulas:

(ACHILLES' DISTANCE TO RENDEZVOUS) = (ACHILLES' RATE)(TIME TO RENDEZVOUS)
(TORTOISE'S DISTANCE TO RENDEZVOUS) = (TORTOISE'S RATE)(TIME TO RENDEZVOUS)

These values are now substituted into the equations:

(ACHILLES' DISTANCE TO RENDEZVOUS) = (TORTOISE'S DISTANCE TO RENDEZVOUS) + 100

↓ ↓

(ACHILLES' RATE)(TIME TO RENDEZVOUS) = (TORTOISE'S RATE)(TIME TO RENDEZVOUS) + 100

There are now three unknowns, but the values for two of *these* unknowns are given in the problem.

(ACHILLES' RATE)(TIME TO RENDEZVOUS) = (TORTOISE'S RATE)(TIME TO RENDEZVOUS) + 100

↓ ↓

10 (TIME TO RENDEZVOUS) = 1 (TIME TO RENDEZVOUS) + 100

The equation now has a single unknown, so let

t = TIME TO RENDEZVOUS

The last step in the evolution of this equation is to substitute the variable:

$$10t = t + 100$$

Solve.

$$10t = t + 100$$
$$9t = 100$$
$$t = \frac{100}{9}$$

Answer. It takes Achilles $11\frac{1}{9}$ seconds to catch up with the tortoise.

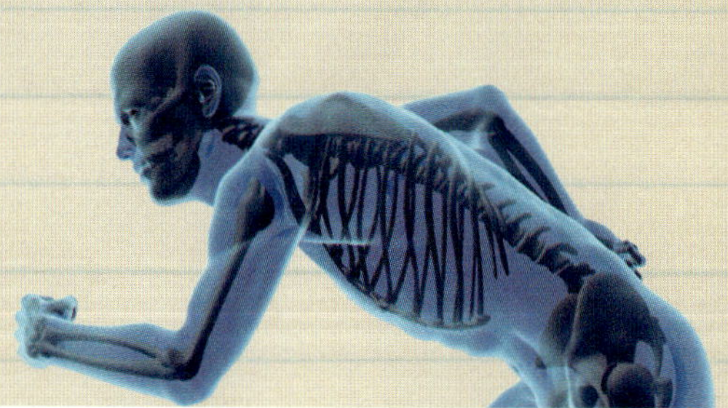

STEP 4 **Look Back.** Does this answer make sense? How long does it take a person to run 100 meters? The problem says Achilles runs at 10 m/sec, so at that rate it would take 10 seconds. The answer seems about right.

Figure 3.7 Achilles and tortoise problem

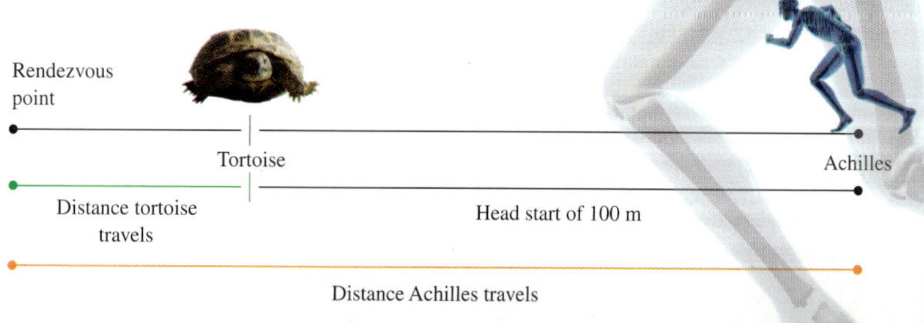

Evolve

The side is one-half the length of pipe, so it is 0.5 mile. Also, since the expansion is 1 inch, one-half the arc would have length 0.5 mile + 0.5 inch.

$$\text{(SIDE)}^2 + \text{(HEIGHT)}^2 = \text{(HYPOTENUSE)}^2$$
$$\downarrow \qquad\qquad\qquad \downarrow$$
$$(0.5 \text{ mile})^2 + \text{(HEIGHT)}^2 = (0.5 \text{ mile} + 0.5 \text{ in.})^2$$

There is a single unknown, so let h = HEIGHT. Also, notice that there is a mixture of units. Let us convert all measurements to inches. We know that

$$1 \text{ mile} = 5{,}280 \text{ ft} = 5{,}280(12 \text{ in.}) = 63{,}360 \text{ in.}$$
$$\tfrac{1}{2} \text{ mile} = 31{,}680 \text{ in.}$$
$$(0.5 \text{ mile})^2 + \text{(HEIGHT)}^2 = (0.5 \text{ mile} + 0.5 \text{ in.})^2$$
$$\downarrow \qquad\qquad\qquad \downarrow$$
$$(31{,}680)^2 + h^2 = (31{,}680 + 0.5)^2$$

Solve

$$h^2 = (31{,}680.5)^2 - (31{,}680)^2$$
$$h = \sqrt{(31{,}680.5)^2 - (31{,}680)^2}$$
$$\approx 177.99$$

Answer

The pipe rises about 180 in. in the middle.

STEP 4 ***Look Back.*** The solution, 177.99 in., is approximately 14.8 ft (roughly 5 yards). This is an extraordinary result if you consider that the pipe expanded only 1 *inch*. The pipe would bow approximately 14.8 ft at the middle. This answer may not seem correct, but in re-examining the steps, we see that it is! This answer is paradoxical or, at least, counterintuitive.

3.7 Ratios and Proportions

RATIOS AND PROPORTIONS ARE POWERFUL PROBLEM-SOLVING TOOLS IN ALGEBRA.

Ratios are a way of comparing two numbers or quantities, whereas a proportion is a statement of equality between two ratios.

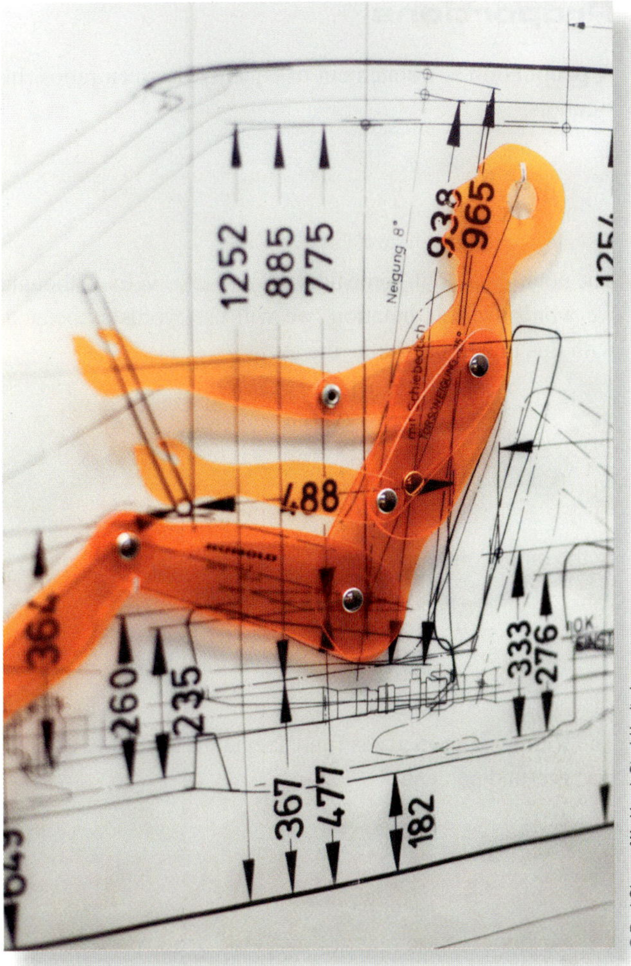

© Paul Giamou/Workbook Stock/Jupiterimages

Ratios

A **ratio** expresses a size relationship between two sets and is defined as the quotient of two numbers. Some examples include the compression ratio of a car, the gear ratio of a transmission, the pitch of a roof, the steepness of a road, or a player's batting average. It is written using the word *to,* a colon, or a fraction; that is, if the ratio of men to women is 5 to 4, this could also be written as 5:4 or $\frac{5}{4}$.

> The expression $\frac{a}{b}$ is called the **ratio** of a to b. The two parts a and b are called its terms.

We will emphasize the idea that a ratio can be written as a fraction (or as a quotient of two numbers). Since a fraction can be reduced, a ratio can also be reduced.

Proportions

A **proportion** is a statement of equality between ratios. In symbols,

$$\frac{a}{b} = \frac{c}{d}$$

"a is to b" "as" "c is to d"

The notation used in some books is $a : b :: c : d$. Even though we won't use this notation, we will use words associated with this notation to name the terms:

Extremes: a and d; Means: b and c

$$a : b :: c : d$$

In the more common fractional notation, we have

Extremes: a and d; Means: b and c

$$\frac{a}{b} = \frac{c}{d}$$

The following property is fundamental to our study of proportions and percents.

PROPERTY OF PROPORTIONS

If the product of the means equals the product of the extremes, then the ratios form a proportion.

Also, if the ratios form a proportion, then the product of the means equals the product of the extremes.

In symbols,

$$\frac{a}{b} = \frac{c}{d}$$

$$b \times c = a \times d$$

Product of means = Product of extremes

You can use the cross-product method not only to see whether two fractions form a proportion, but also to compare the sizes of two fractions. For example, if a and c are whole numbers, and b and d are counting numbers, then the following property can be used to compare the sizes of two fractions:

If $ad = bc$, then $\frac{a}{b} = \frac{c}{d}$.

If $ad < bc$, then $\frac{a}{b} < \frac{c}{d}$.

If $ad > bc$, then $\frac{a}{b} > \frac{c}{d}$.

Comparing the size of fractions when they are written as decimal numbers can sometimes be confusing; for example, which is larger,

0.6 or 0.58921?

The larger number is 0.6. To see this, simply write each decimal with the same number of places by affixing trailing zeros, and then compare. That is, write

0.60000
0.58921

Now, it is easy to see that $0.60000 > 0.58921$ because 60,000 hundred thousandths is larger than 58,921 hundred thousandths.

Solving Proportions

The usual setting for a proportion problem is that three of the terms of the proportion are known and one of the terms is unknown. It is always possible to find the missing term by solving an equation. However, when given a proportion, we first use the property of proportions (which is equivalent to multiplying both sides of the equation by the same number).

Find the missing term of each proportion. Since there are four positions in a proportion, there are four places in which an unknown can appear:

Top left: $\frac{t}{15} = \frac{3}{5}$ **Top right:** $\frac{3}{4} = \frac{w}{20}$

Bottom right: $\frac{3}{4} = \frac{27}{y}$ **Bottom left:** $\frac{2}{x} = \frac{8}{9}$

Solve: $\frac{t}{15} = \frac{3}{5}$

PRODUCT OF MEANS = PRODUCT OF EXTREMES

$$3(15) = 5t$$

$$\frac{3(15)}{5} = t$$ Divide both sides by 5. Notice that 5 is the number opposite the unknown.

$$9 = t$$

Solve: $\frac{3}{4} = \frac{w}{20}$

PRODUCT OF MEANS = PRODUCT OF EXTREMES

$$4w = 3(20)$$

$$w = \frac{3(20)}{4}$$ Solve by dividing both sides by 4. Notice that 4 is the number opposite the unknown.

$$w = 15$$

PROCEDURE: Solving Proportions

Given a proportion:

STEP 1 Find the product of the means or the product of the extremes, whichever does not contain the unknown term.

STEP 2 Divide this product by the number that is opposite the unknown term.

Solve: $\frac{3}{4} = \frac{27}{y}$

$$\text{PRODUCT OF MEANS} = \text{PRODUCT OF EXTREMES}$$

$$4(27) = 3y$$

$$\frac{4(27)}{3} = y$$

Divide both sides by 3. Notice that 3 is the number opposite the unknown.

$$36 = y$$

Solve: $\frac{2}{x} = \frac{8}{9}$

$$\text{PRODUCT OF MEANS} = \text{PRODUCT OF EXTREMES}$$

$$8x = 2(9)$$

$$x = \frac{2(9)}{8}$$

Divide both sides by 8. Notice that 8 is the number opposite the unknown.

$$x = \frac{9}{4}$$

Notice that the unknown term can be in any one of four positions, as illustrated above. But even though you can find the missing term of a proportion (called **solving the proportion**) by the technique used above, it is easier to think in terms of **the cross-product divided by the number opposite the unknown**. This method is easier than actually solving the equation because it can be done quickly using a calculator, as shown in the following examples.

Many applied problems can be solved using a proportion. Whenever you are working an applied problem, you should estimate an answer so that you will know whether the result you obtain is reasonable.

When setting up a proportion with units, be sure that like units occupy corresponding positions. The proportion is obtained by applying the sentence "a is to b as c is to d" to the quantities in the problem.

If 4 cans of cola sell for $1.89, how much will 6 cans cost?

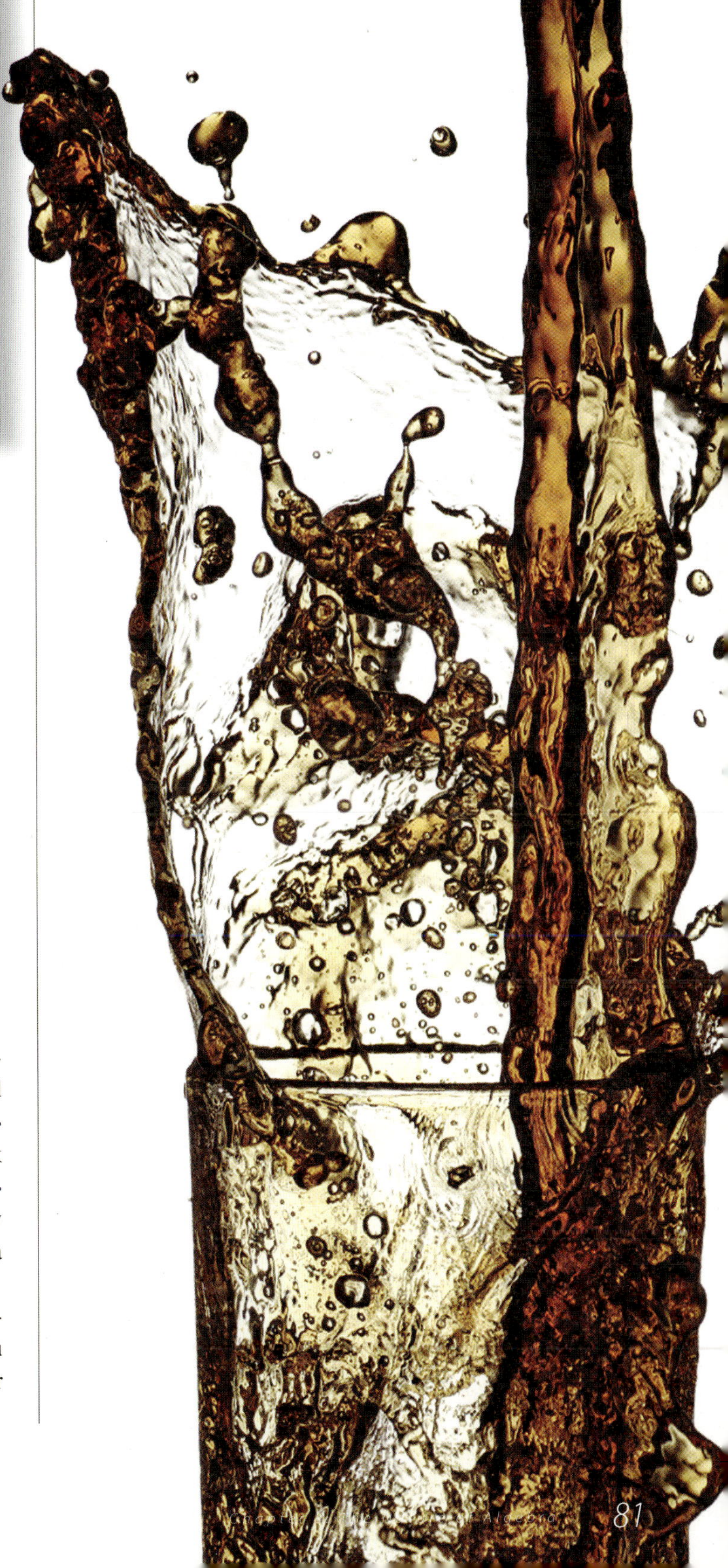

STEP 1 ***Understand the Problem.*** We see that 4 cans sell for \$1.89 and 8 cans sell for 2(\$1.89) = \$3.78. We need to find the cost for 6 cans, which must be somewhere between \$1.89 and \$3.78.

STEP 2 ***Devise a Plan.*** There are many possible plans for solving this problem. We will form a proportion.

STEP 3 ***Carry Out the Plan.*** Solve "4 cans is to \$1.89 as 6 cans is to what?"

$$\frac{4 \text{ cans}}{1.89 \text{ dollars}} = \frac{6 \text{ cans}}{x \text{ dollars}}$$

$$x = \frac{1.89 \times 6}{4}$$

$$= 2.835$$

STEP 4 ***Look Back.*** We see that 6 cans will cost \$2.84.

Sometimes we use proportions to formulate a mixture problem. In a can of mixed nuts, the ratio of cashews to peanuts is 1 to 6. If a machine releases 46 cashews into a can, how many peanuts should it release? First, understand the problem. This problem is comparing two quantities, cashews and peanuts, so consider writing a proportion.

TRANSLATE This is the given ratio. ↓

$$\frac{\text{NUMBER OF CASHEWS}}{\text{NUMBER OF PEANUTS}} = \frac{1}{6}$$

EVOLVE The number of cashews = 46, so by substitution

$$\frac{46}{\text{NUMBER OF PEANUTS}} = \frac{1}{6}$$

Let p = number of peanuts; then the equation is

$$\frac{46}{p} = \frac{1}{6}$$

SOLVE $6(46) = p$

$276 = p$

ANSWER Thus, 276 peanuts should be released.

3.8 Percents

WE FREQUENTLY USE PERCENTS, AND YOU HAVE, NO DOUBT, WORKED WITH PERCENTS IN YOUR PREVIOUS MATHEMATICS CLASSES.

However, we include this section to review percents and the equivalence of the decimal, fraction, and percent forms.

> **Percent** is the ratio of a given number to 100. This means that a percent is the numerator of a fraction whose denominator is 100.

Percent

The symbol % is used to indicate percent. Since a percent is a ratio, percents can easily be written in fractional form.

Fractions/Decimals/Percents

Percents can also be written as decimals. Since a percent is a ratio of a number to 100, we can divide by 100 by moving the decimal point.

STOP *Spend some time with Table 3.1. In fact, you may want to place a marker on page 83 for future reference.*

PROCEDURE: Percents to Decimals

To express a percent as a decimal, shift the decimal point two places to the *left* and delete the % symbol. If the percent involves a fraction, write the fraction as a decimal; *then* shift the decimal point.

Every number can be written as a fraction or a decimal, but every number can also be written as a percent. That means that every number can be written in three forms. Even though we discussed changing from fraction to decimal form earlier in the text, we'll review the three forms in this section. The procedure for changing from one form to another is given in Table 3.1.

Estimation

Percent problems are very common. We conclude this section with a discussion of estimation and some percent calculations.

The first estimation method is the *unit fraction-conversion method,* which can be used to estimate the common percents of 10%, 25%, $33\frac{1}{3}\%$, and 50%. To estimate the size of a part of a whole quantity, which is sometimes called a **percentage**, rewrite the percent as a fraction and mentally multiply, as shown by the following example.

Unit Fraction Comparison

Percent	Fraction
10%	$\frac{1}{10}$
25%	$\frac{1}{4}$
$33\frac{1}{3}\%$	$\frac{1}{3}$
50%	$\frac{1}{2}$

50% of 800: $\frac{1}{2} \times 800 = 400$ THINK: $800 \div 2 = 400$

25% of 1,200: $\frac{1}{4} \times 1{,}200 = 300$ THINK: $1{,}200 \div 4 = 300$

$33\frac{1}{3}\%$ of 600: $\frac{1}{3} \times 600 = 200$ THINK: $600 \div 3 = 200$

10% of 824: $\frac{1}{10} \times 824 = 82.4$ THINK: $824 \div 10 = 82.4$

If the numbers for which you are finding a percentage are not as "nice" as those given here, you can estimate by rounding the number.

A second estimation procedure uses a multiple of a unit fraction. For example,

Think of 75% as $\frac{3}{4}$, which is $3 \times \frac{1}{4}$.

Think of $66\frac{2}{3}\%$ as $\frac{2}{3}$, which is $2 \times \frac{1}{3}$.

Think of 60% as $\frac{6}{10}$, which is $6 \times \frac{1}{10}$.

The Percent Problem

Many percentage problems are more difficult than those above. The following quotation was found in a recent publication: "An elected official is one who gets 51 percent of the vote cast by 40 percent of the 60 percent of voters who registered." Certainly, most of us will have trouble understanding the percent given in this quotation, but you can't pick up a newspaper without seeing dozens of examples of ideas that require some understanding of percents. A difficult job for most of us is knowing whether to multiply or divide by the given numbers. In this section, I will provide you with a sure-fire method for knowing what to do. The first step is to understand what is meant by **the percent problem**.

Table 3.1 Fraction/Decimal/Percent Conversion Chart

From: \ To:	Fraction	Decimal	Percent
Fraction		Divide the numerator (top) by the denominator (bottom). Write as a terminating or as a repeating decimal (bar notation).	First change the fraction to a decimal by carrying out the division to two decimal places and writing the remainder as a fraction. *Then* move the decimal point two places to the right, and affix a percent symbol.
Terminating Decimal	Write the decimal without the decimal point, and multiply by the decimal name of the last digit (rightmost digit).		Shift the decimal point two places to the *right*, and affix a percent symbol.
Percent	Write as a ratio to 100 and reduce the fraction. If the percent involves a decimal, first write the decimal in fractional form, and then multiply by $\frac{1}{100}$. If the percent involves a fraction, delete the percent symbol and multiply by $\frac{1}{100}$.	Shift the decimal point two places to the *left*, and delete the percent symbol. If the percent involves a fraction, first write the fraction as a decimal, and then shift the decimal point.	

The Percent Problem

A is **P%** of **W**

- **A**: This is the given amount.
- **P%**: The percent is written $\frac{P}{100}$.
- **W**: This is the whole quantity. It always follows the word "of."

Study this percent problem. If you learn this, you get a written guarantee for correctly working percent problems.

The percent problem won't always be stated in this form, but notice that three quantities are associated with it:

1. The *amount*—sometimes called the **percentage**
2. The *percent*—sometimes called the **rate**
3. The *whole quantity*—sometimes called the **base**

Now, regardless of the form in which you are given the percent problem, follow the steps at right to write a proportion. Look over this procedure before going through the example below.

read these three steps—SLOWLY!

PROCEDURE: Solving Percent Problems

STEP 1 Identify the *percent* first; it will be followed by the symbol % or the word *percent*. Write it as a fraction:

$$\frac{P}{100}$$

STEP 2 Identify the *whole quantity* next; it is preceded by the word "of." It is the denominator of the second fraction in the proportion:

$$\frac{P}{100} = \frac{}{W}$$ ← This is the quantity following the word "of."

STEP 3 The remaining number is the partial amount; it is the numerator of the second fraction in the proportion:

$$\frac{P}{100} = \frac{A}{W}$$ ← This is the last quantity to be inserted into the proportion.

Since there are only three letters in the proportion

$$\frac{P}{100} = \frac{A}{W}$$

there are three types of percent problems. These possible types are illustrated in the Example box shown here. To answer a question involving a percent, write a proportion and then solve the proportion. The answers are: $B = 36$; $C = 36$; $D = 1{,}250$; $E = 15$; $F = 400$; $G = 200$.

→ Example	Percent P(%)	Whole W ("of")	Amount A (part)	Proportion $\frac{P}{100} = \frac{A}{W}$
What number is 18% of 200?	18	200	unknown	$\frac{18}{100} = \frac{B}{200}$
18% of 200 is what number?	18	200	unknown	$\frac{18}{100} = \frac{C}{200}$
150 is 12% of what number?	12	unknown	150	$\frac{12}{100} = \frac{150}{D}$
63 is what percent of 420?	unknown	420	63	$\frac{F}{100} = \frac{63}{420}$
18% of what number is 72?	18	unknown	72	$\frac{18}{100} = \frac{72}{F}$
120 is what percent of 60?	unknown	60	120	$\frac{G}{100} = \frac{120}{60}$

↑ Regardless of the arrangement of the question, identify *P* first.
↑ Second, identify the number following the word "of."
↑ This number is identified last.

Consider another example from the news:

EXTRA
FINAL SPORTS EXTRA
DAILY PRESS

Teen drug use soars 105%

WASHINGTON —Teen drug use rose 105% between 1995 and 1997.

A national survey showed that between 1995 and 1996 youth drug use rose 30%, but between 1996 and 1997 usage soared 75%.

Over the two-year period, the rise of 105% was attributed to...

Atom tests 'affected IQ'

WIFE-STEALING HORSE

Pioneer heads for the unknown

What is wrong with the headline? We are not given all the relevant numbers, but consider the following possibility: Suppose there are 100 drug users, so a rise of

100 to 130 is a 30% increase

130 to 227 is a 75% increase

100 to 227 is a 127% increase, NOT 105%

Remember, adding percents can give faulty results.

For example, suppose you have $100 and spend 50%. How much have you spent, and how much do you have left?

Amount Spent	*Remainder*
$50	$50

Now, suppose you spend 50% of the remainder. How much have you spent, and how much is left?

New Spending	*Old Spending*	*Remainder*
$25	$50	$25

This means you have spent $75 or 75% of your original bankroll. A common ERROR is to say "50% spending + 50% spending = 100% spending."

***remember**

If you add percents, you often obtain incorrect results.

3.9 Modeling Uncategorized Problems

ONE MAJOR CRITICISM OF STUDYING THE COMMON TYPES OF WORD PROBLEMS PRESENTED IN MOST TEXTBOOKS IS THAT STUDENTS CAN FALL INTO THE HABIT OF SOLVING PROBLEMS BY USING A TEMPLATE OR PATTERN AND BE SUCCESSFUL IN CLASS WITHOUT EVER DEVELOPING INDEPENDENT PROBLEM-SOLVING ABILITIES.

Be careful not to fall into the habit of just using a template or pattern in problem solving. Make sure you actually think about what you're doing.

IF YOU WORK HARD MASTERING THIS SECTION, YOU WILL HAVE GAINED AN IMPORTANT LIFE SKILL.

Even though problem solving may require algebraic skills, it also requires many other skills; a goal of this book is to help you develop a general problem-solving ability so that when presented with a problem that does not fit a template, you can apply techniques that will lead to a solution.

Most problems that do not come from textbooks are presented with several variables, along with one or more relationships among those variables. In some instances, insufficient information is given; in others there may be superfluous information or inconsistent information. A common mistake when working with these problems is to assume that you know which variable to choose as the unknown in the equation *at the beginning of the problem.* This leads to trying to take too much into your memory at the start, and as a result it is easy to get confused.

Now you are in a better position to practice Pólya's problem-solving techniques because you have had some experience in carrying out the second step of the process, which we repeat here for convenience.

Guidelines for Problem Solving

STEP 1 ***Understand the problem.*** **Ask questions, experiment, or otherwise rephrase the question in your own words.**

STEP 2 ***Devise a plan.*** **Find the connection between the data and the unknown. Look for patterns, relate to a previously solved problem or a known formula, or simplify the given information to give you an easier problem.**

STEP 3 ***Carry out the plan.*** **Check the steps as you go.**

STEP 4 ***Look back.*** **Examine the solution obtained.**

Remember that the key to becoming a problem solver is to develop the skill to solve problems *that are not like the examples shown in the text.* For this reason, the problems used as examples in this section will require that you go beyond copying the techniques developed in the first part of this chapter.

In California, state funding of education is based on the average daily attendance (ADA). Develop a formula for determining the ADA at your school.

Most attempts at mathematical modeling come from a real problem that needs to be solved. There is no "answer book" to tell you when you are correct. There is often the need to do additional research to find necessary information, and the need *not* to use certain information that you have to arrive at a solution.

STEP 1 ***Understand the Problem.*** What is meant by ADA? The first step might be a call to your school registrar to find out how ADA is calculated. For example, in California it is based on weekly student contact hours (WSCH), and 1 ADA = 525 WSCH. Thus, you might begin by writing the formula

$$\frac{\text{WSCH}}{525} = \text{TOTAL ADA}$$

This means that 525 WSCH is 525/525 = 1 ADA or 1050 WSCH is $\frac{1050}{525}$ = 2 ADA. In other words, we divide the WSCH by 525 to find the ADA.

STEP 2 ***Devise a Plan.*** Mathematical modeling requires that we check this formula to see whether it properly models the TOTAL ADA at your school. How is the WSCH determined? In California, the roll sheets are examined at two census dates, and WSCH is calculated as the average of the census numbers. In mathematical modeling, you often need formulas that are not specified as part of the problem. In this case, we need a formula for calculating an average. We use the *mean*:

$$\text{WSCH} = \frac{\text{Census 1} + \text{Census 2}}{2}$$

We now have a second attempt at a formula for TOTAL ADA:

$$\frac{\text{Census 1} + \text{Census 2}}{2} \div 525 = \text{TOTAL ADA}$$

STEP 3 ***Carry Out the Plan.*** Does this properly model the TOTAL ADA? Perhaps, but suppose a taxpayer or congressperson brings up the argument that funding should take into account absent people, because not all classes have 100% attendance each day. You might include an *absence factor* as part of the formula. In California, the agreed absence factor for funding purposes is 0.911. How would we incorporate this into the TOTAL ADA calculation?

$$\frac{\text{Census 1} + \text{Census 2}}{2} \cdot \frac{\text{Absence factor}}{525} = \text{TOTAL ADA}$$

This formula could be simplified to

$$\text{TOTAL ADA} = 0.0008676190476(c_1 + c_2)$$

where c_1 and c_2 are the numbers of students on the roll sheets on the first and second census dates, respectively.

STEP 4 ***Look Back.*** In fact, a Senate bill in California states this formula as

$$\frac{\text{Census 1 WSCH} + \text{Census 2 WSCH}}{2} \times \frac{0.911 \text{ Absence factor}}{525} = \text{TOTAL ADA}$$

This is equivalent to the formula we derived.

We have refrained from working so-called age problems because they seem to be a rather useless type of word problem—one that occurs only in algebra books. They do, however, give us a chance to practice our problem-solving skill, so they are worth considering. The age problem given in the next example was found in the first three frames of a *Peanuts* cartoon published September 14, 1972.

A man has a daughter and a son. The son is three years older than the daughter. In one year the man will be six times as old as the daughter is now, and in ten years he will be fourteen years older than the combined ages of his children. What is the man's present age?

STEP 1 ***Understand the Problem.*** There are three people: a man, his daughter, and his son. We are concerned with their ages now, in one year, and in ten years.

STEP 2 ***Devise a Plan.*** Does this look like any of the problems we have solved? We need to distinguish among the persons' ages now and some time in the future. Let us begin by translating the known information:

Ages Now	Ages in One Year	Ages in Ten Years
MAN'S AGE NOW	MAN'S AGE NOW + 1	MAN'S AGE NOW + 10
DAUGHTER'S AGE NOW	DAUGHTER'S AGE NOW + 1	DAUGHTER'S AGE NOW + 10
SON'S AGE NOW	SON'S AGE NOW + 1	SON'S AGE NOW + 10

We are given that

First equation:

$$\text{SON'S AGE NOW} = \text{DAUGHTER'S AGE NOW} + 3$$

and

$$\text{MAN'S AGE NOW} + 1 = 6(\text{DAUGHTER'S AGE NOW})$$

This is the same as

Second equation:

$$\text{MAN'S AGE NOW} = 6(\text{DAUGHTER'S AGE NOW}) - 1$$

Finally, we are given that

$$\text{MAN'S AGE NOW} + 10 = (\text{SON'S AGE NOW} + 10) + (\text{DAUGHTER'S AGE NOW} + 10) + 14$$

↑ 14 years older

If we simplify this equation we obtain:

Third equation:

$$\text{MAN'S AGE NOW} = \text{SON'S AGE NOW} + \text{DAUGHTER'S AGE NOW} + 24$$

The plan is to begin with the third equation and evolve it into an equation we can solve.

STEP 3 ***Carry Out the Plan.***

MAN'S AGE NOW = SON'S AGE NOW + DAUGHTER'S AGE NOW + 24

↑ (SON'S AGE NOW) SON'S AGE NOW = DAUGHTER'S AGE NOW + 3

↑ (MAN'S AGE NOW) MAN'S AGE NOW = 6(DAUGHTER'S AGE NOW) − 1

$$6(\text{DAUGHTER'S AGE NOW}) - 1 = \text{DAUGHTER'S AGE NOW} + 3 + \text{DAUGTER'S AGE NOW} + 24$$

$$6d - 1 = d + 3 + d + 24 \qquad \text{Let } d = \text{DAUGHTER'S AGE NOW}$$

$$6d - 1 = 2d + 27$$

$$4d = 28$$

$$d = 7$$

$$\text{DAUGHTER'S AGE NOW} = 7$$

$$\text{MAN'S AGE NOW} = 6\,(\text{DAUGHTER'S AGE NOW}) - 1$$

$$\text{MAN'S AGE NOW} = 6(7) - 1 = 41$$

The man's present age is 41.

STEP 4 ***Look Back.*** From the first equation, SON'S AGE NOW = 7 + 3 = 10. In one year the man will be 42, and this is 6 times the daughter's present age. In ten years the man will be 51 and the children will be 20 and 17; the man will be 14 years older than 20 + 17 = 37.

LEARN YOUR WAY

With ***MATH,*** you have a multitude of study aids at your fingertips. After reviewing and practicing the examples, be sure to check your work!

The **Students Solutions Manual** contains the worked out solutions to every odd-numbered exercise, further reinforcing students understanding of mathematical concepts in ***MATH.***

In addition to the Student Solutions Manual, **4ltrpress.cengage.com/math** offers exercises and questions that correspond to every section and chapter in the text for students to practice the concepts they learned under the **Practice It, Solve It,** and **Quiz It** links. They can also click on **Watch It** to view video tutorials that show some of the key problems being worked out to better understand the mathematical concepts.

The Nature of Geometry

4.1 Geometry

WHEN WE REFER TO EUCLIDEAN GEOMETRY, WE ARE TALKING ABOUT THE GEOMETRY KNOWN TO THE GREEKS AS SUMMARIZED IN A WORK KNOWN AS EUCLID'S *ELEMENTS*.

topics

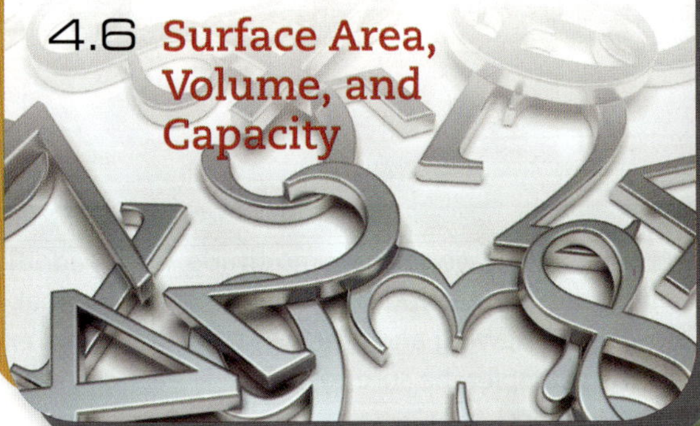

"I wish I could see the expression on the faces of my students who said there was no value in studying geometry."

This 13-volume set of books collected all the material known about geometry and organized it into a logical deductive system. It is the most widely used and studied book in history, with the exception of the Bible. An overview of the history of mathematics, and of geometry in particular, is presented in the prologue of this book, and it includes the geometry of both the Egyptians and the Greeks. We do not know very much about the life of Euclid except that he was the first professor of mathematics at the University of Alexandria (which opened in 300 BC).

Greek (Euclidean) Geometry

Geometry involves **points** and sets of points called **lines**, **planes**, and **surfaces**. Certain concepts in geometry are called **undefined terms**. For example, what is a line? You might say, "I know what a line is!" But try to define a line. Is it a set of points? Any set of points? What is a point?

1. A point is something that has no length, width, or thickness.
2. A point is a location in space.

Certainly these are not satisfactory definitions because they involve other terms that are not defined. We will therefore take the terms *point*, *line*, and *plane* as undefined.

Early civilization observed from nature certain simple shapes such as triangles, rectangles, and circles. The study of geometry began with the need to measure and understand the properties of these simple shapes.

Figure 4.1 An old woman or a young woman?

We often draw physical models or pictures to represent these concepts; however, we must be careful not to try to prove assertions by looking at pictures, since a picture may contain hidden assumptions or ambiguities. For example, consider Figure 4.1 above.

Do you see an old woman or a young woman? Is the fly in Figure 4.2 on the cube or in the cube? The point we are making is that although we may use a figure in geometry to help us understand a problem, we cannot use what we see in a figure as a basis for our reasoning.

Geometry can be separated into two categories:

1. Traditional (which is the geometry of Euclid)
2. Transformational (which is more algebraic than the traditional approach)

Figure 4.2 Is the fly on the cube or in it? On which face?

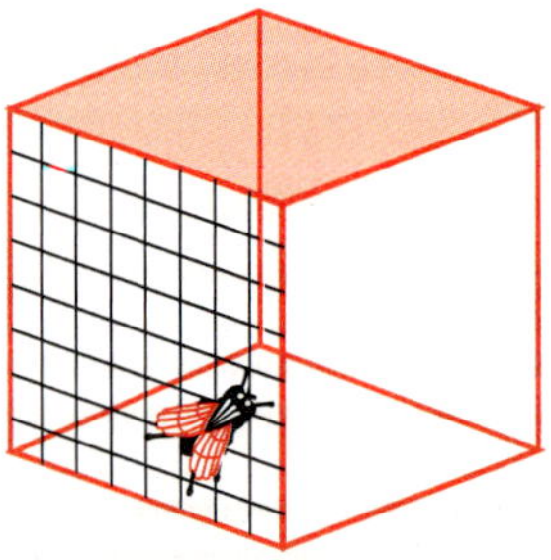

When Euclid was formalizing traditional geometry, he based it on five postulates, which have come to be known as **Euclid's postulates**. A **postulate** or **axiom** is a statement accepted without proof. In mathematics, a result that is proved on the basis of some agreed-upon postulates is called a **theorem**.

The first four of these postulates were obvious and noncontroversial, but the fifth one was different. This fifth postulate looked more like a theorem than a postulate. It was much more difficult to understand than the other four postulates, and for more than 20 centuries mathematicians tried to derive it from the other postulates or to replace it by a more acceptable equivalent. Two straight lines in the same plane are said to be **parallel** if they do not intersect.

Today we can either accept it as a postulate (without proof) or deny it. If it is denied, it turns out that no contradiction results; in fact, if it is not accepted, other geometries called **non-Euclidean geometries** result. If it is accepted, then the geometry that results is consistent with our everyday experiences and is called **Euclidean geometry**.

Let's look at each of Euclid's postulates. The first one says that a straight line can be drawn from any point to any other point. To connect two points, you need a device called a **straightedge** (a device that we assume has no markings on it; you will use a ruler, but not to measure, when you are treating it as a straightedge). The portion

Euclid's Postulates

1. A straight line can be drawn from any point to any other point.
2. A straight line extends infinitely far in either direction.
3. A circle can be described with any point as center and with a radius equal to any finite straight line drawn from the center.
4. All right angles are equal to each other.
5. Given a straight line and any point not on this line, there is one and only one line through that point that is parallel to the given line.*

* The fifth postulate stated here is the one usually found in high school geometry books. It is sometimes called Playfair's axiom and is equivalent to Euclid's original statement as translated from the original Greek by T. L. Heath: "If a straight line falling on two straight lines makes the interior angle on the same side less than two right angles, the two straight lines, if produced infinitely, meet on that side on which the angles are less than the two right angles."

Figure 4.4 A compass

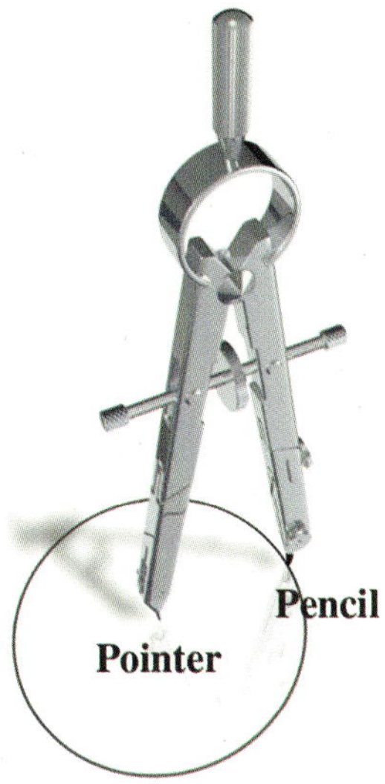

of the line that connects points A and B in Figure 4.3 is called a **line segment**. We write $\overline{AB}$ (or $\overline{BA}$). We contrast this notation with $\overleftrightarrow{AB}$, which is used to name the line passing through the points A and B. We use the symbol $|\overline{AB}|$ for the length of segment $\overline{AB}$.

The second postulate says that we can draw a straight line. This seems straightforward and obvious, but we should point out that we will indicate a line by putting arrows on each end. If we consider a point on a line, that point separates the line into parts: two **half-lines** and the point itself. If the arrow points in only one direction, the figure is called a **ray**. We write $\overrightarrow{AB}$ (or $\overleftarrow{BA}$) for the ray with endpoint A passing through B. These definitions are illustrated in Figure 4.3.

To construct a line segment of length equal to the length of a given line segment, we need a device called a **compass**. Figure 4.4 shows a compass, which is used to mark off and duplicate lengths, but not to measure them.

If objects have exactly the same size and shape, they are called **congruent**. We can use a straightedge and compass to **construct** a figure so that it meets certain requirements. To *construct a line segment congruent to a given line segment*, copy a segment $\overline{AB}$ on any line ℓ. First fix the compass so that the pointer is on point A and the pencil is on B, as shown in Figure 4.5a. Then, on line ℓ, choose a point C. Next, without changing the compass setting, place the pointer on C and strike an arc at D, as shown in Figure 4.5b.

Euclid's third postulate leads us to a second construction. The task is to construct a circle, given its center and radius. These steps are summarized in Figure 4.6.

Figure 4.3 Portions of lines

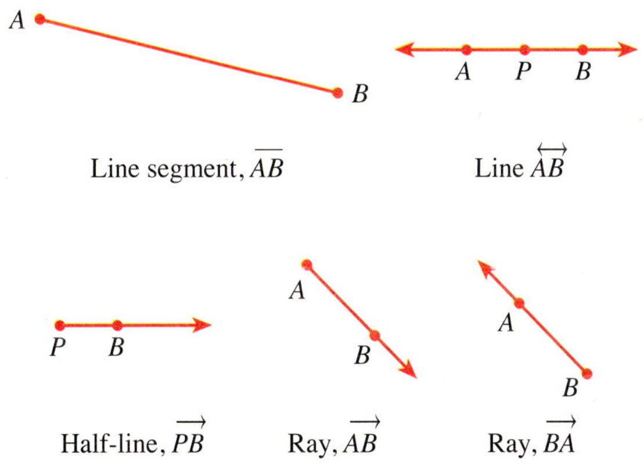

Figure 4.5 Constructing a line segment

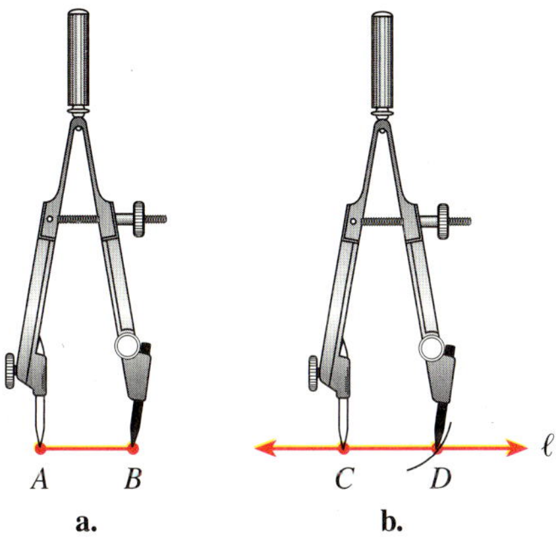

Figure 4.6 Construction of a circle

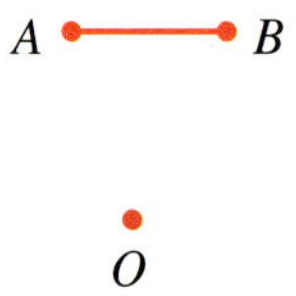

a. Given, a point and a radius of length $|\overline{AB}|$.

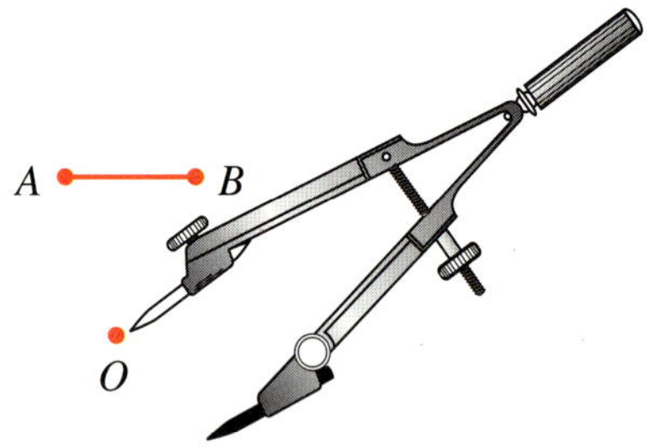

b. Set the legs of the compass on the ends of radius $\overline{AB}$; move the pointer to point O without changing the setting.

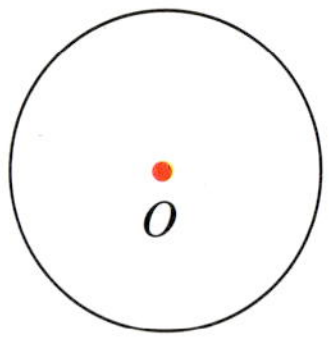

c. Hold the pointer at point O and move the pencil end to draw the circle.

Figure 4.7 Construction of a line parallel to a given line through a given point

a. Given line

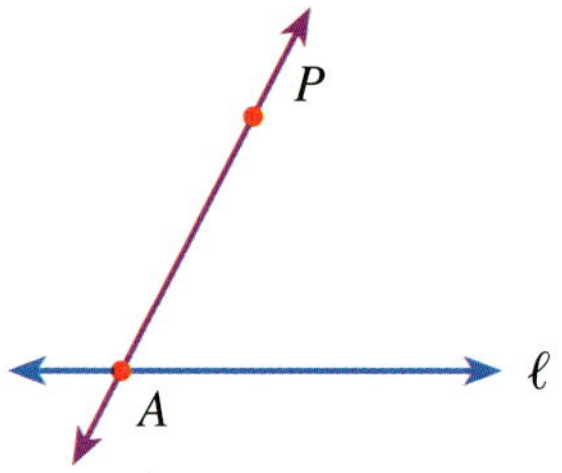

b. Draw line

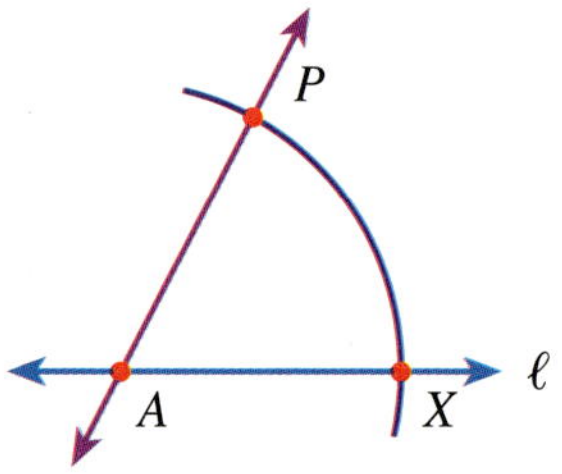

c. Strike arc

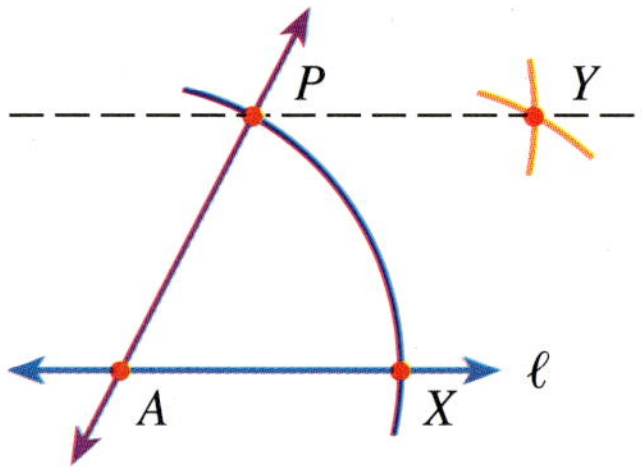

d. Determine point Y

We will demonstrate the fourth postulate in the next section when we consider angles.

The final construction of this section will demonstrate the fifth postulate. The task is to construct a line through a point P parallel to a given line ℓ, as shown in Figure 4.7a. First, draw any line through P that intersects ℓ at a point A, as shown in Figure 4.7b.

Now draw an arc with the pointer at A and radius $\overline{AP}$, and label the point of intersection of the arc and the line X, as shown in Figure 4.7c. With the same opening of the compass, draw an arc first with the pointer at P and then with the pointer at X. Their point of intersection will determine a point Y (Figure 4.7d). Draw the line through both P and Y. This line is parallel to ℓ.

Transformational Geometry

We now turn our attention to the second category of geometry. **Transformational geometry** is quite different from traditional geometry in that it deals with the study of *transformations*.

A **transformation** is the passage from one geometric figure to another by means of reflections, translations, rotations, contractions, or dilations. For example, given a line L

and a point P, as shown in Figure 4.8, we call the point P' the **reflection** of P about the line L if $\overline{PP'}$ is perpendicular to L and is also bisected by L.

Figure 4.8 A reflection

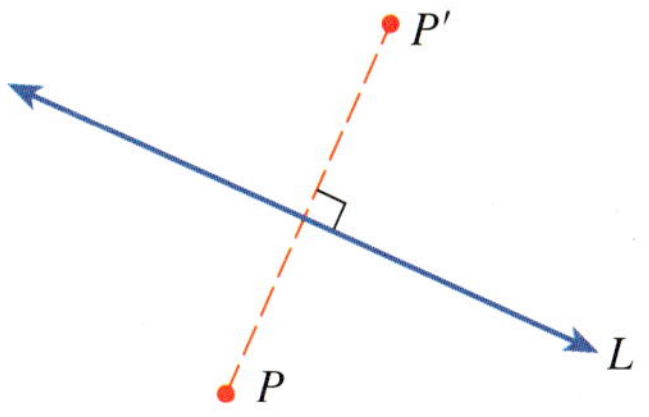

Each point in the plane has exactly one reflection point corresponding to a given line L. A reflection is called a *reflection transformation*, and the line of reflection is called the **line of symmetry**. The easiest way to describe a line of symmetry is to say that if you fold a paper along its line of symmetry, then the figure will fold onto itself to form a perfect match, as shown in Figure 4.9.

Figure 4.9 Line symmetry on the Maple Leaf of Canada

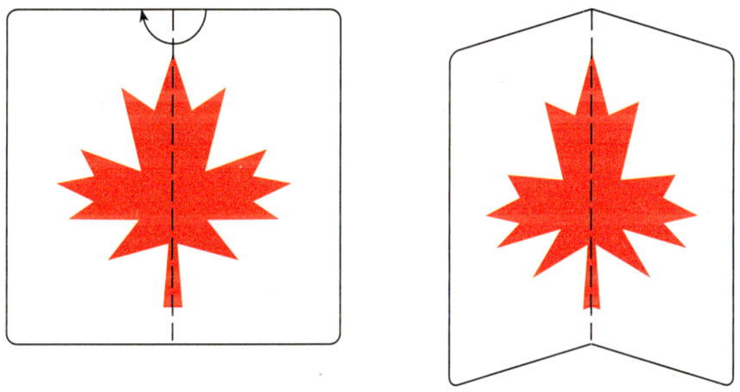

Many everyday objects exhibit a line of symmetry. From snowflakes in nature, to the Taj Mahal in architectural design, to many flags and logos, we see examples of lines of symmetry (see Figure 4.10).

Other transformations include *translations*, *rotations*, *dilations*, and *contractions*, which are illustrated in Figure 4.11 on the next page.

A REFLECTION IS CALLED A *REFLECTION TRANSFORMATION*, AND THE LINE OF REFLECTION IS CALLED THE LINE OF SYMMETRY.

Figure 4.10 Examples of line symmetry

Figure 4.11 Transformations of a fixed geometric figure

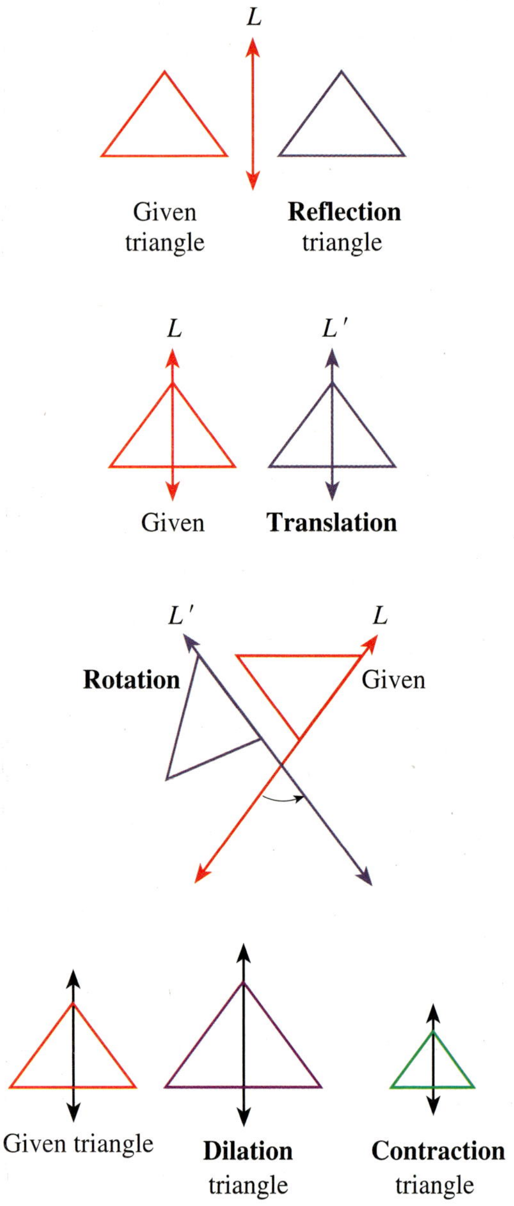

Similarity

Geometry is also concerned with the study of the relationships between geometric figures. A primary relationship is that of *congruence*. A second relationship is called **similarity**. Two figures are said to be **similar** if they have the same shape, although not necessarily the same size. These ideas are considered in Section 4.3.

If we were to develop this text formally, we would need to be very careful about the statement of our postulates. The notion of mathematical proof requires a very precise formulation of all postulates and theorems. However, since we are not formally developing geometry, we simply accept the general drift of the statement. Remember, though, that you cannot base a mathematical proof on general drift. On the other hand, there are some facts that we *know to be true* that tell us that certain properties are impossible. For example, if someone claims to be able to trisect an angle with a straightedge and compass, we know *without looking at the construction* that the construction is wrong. This can be frustrating to someone who believes that he or she has accomplished the impossible. In fact, it was so frustrating to Daniel Wade Arthur that he was motivated to take out a paid advertisement in the *Los Angeles Times*.

© Mikael Damkier/iStockphoto.com

You can learn a lot about geometry just through simple observation and using your instincts. Look over this city scape, for instance. Can you break the images here down into their basic geometric components?

4.2 Polygons and Angles

WHEN THE EUCLIDEAN GEOMETRY INTRODUCED IN THE PRECEDING SECTION IS STUDIED IN HIGH SCHOOL AS AN ENTIRE COURSE, IT IS USUALLY PRESENTED IN A *FORMAL* MANNER USING DEFINITIONS, AXIOMS, AND THEOREMS.

The development of this chapter is *informal*, which means that we base our results on observations and intuition. We begin by assuming that you are familiar with the ideas of *point*, *line*, and *plane*.

Polygons

A **polygon** is a geometric figure that has three or more straight sides, all of which lie on a flat surface or plane so that the starting point and the ending point are the same. Polygons can be classified according to their number of sides, as shown in Figure 4.12. We say any polygon is **regular** if its sides are the same length.

Figure 4.12 Polygons classified according to number of sides

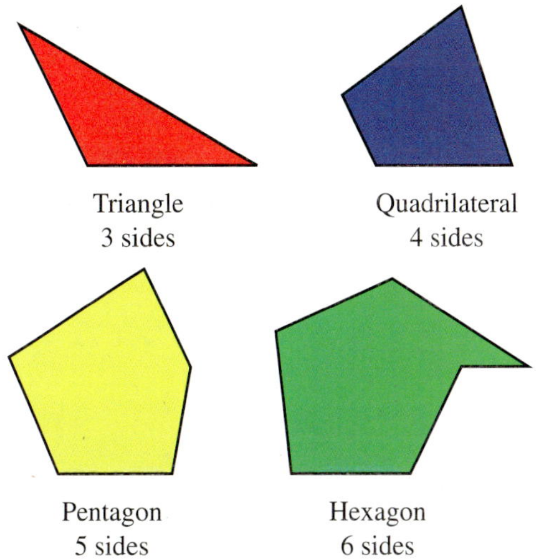

Polygons (not pictured)
Heptagon: 7 sides
Octagon: 8 sides
Nonagon: 9 sides
Decagon: 10 sides
Dodecagon: 12 sides
n-gon: n sides

A polygon with four sides is a **quadrilateral.** Quadrilaterals are classified as follows:

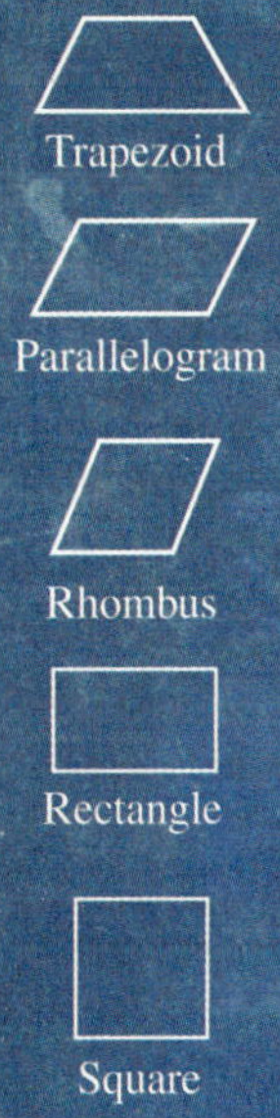

A **trapezoid** is a quadrilateral with exactly one pair of parallel sides.

A **parallelogram** is a quadrilateral with opposite sides parallel.

A **rhombus** is a parallelogram with adjacent sides equal.

A **rectangle** is a parallelogram that contains a right angle.

A **square** is a rectangle with two adjacent sides of equal length.

Angles

A connecting point of two sides is called a **vertex** (plural **vertices**) and is usually designated by a capital letter. An **angle** is composed of two rays or segments with a common endpoint. The angles between the sides of a polygon are sometimes also denoted by a capital letter, but other ways of denoting angles are shown in Figure 4.13.

Figure 4.13 Ways of denoting angles

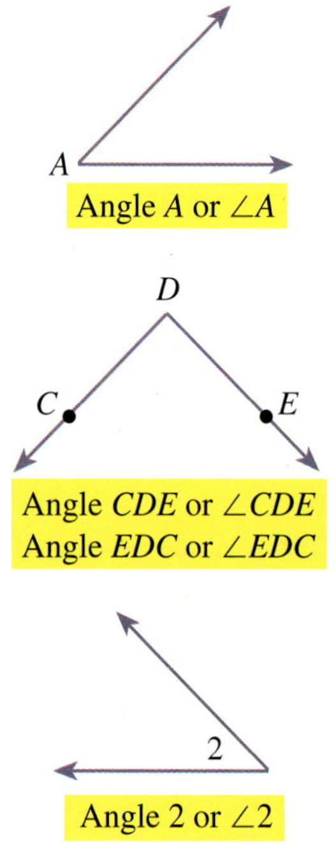

We return to the constructions first introduced in the last section. To construct an angle with the same size as a given angle B, first draw a ray from B', as shown in Figure 4.14a. Next, mark off an arc with the pointer at the vertex of the given angle and label the points A and C. Without changing the compass, mark off a similar arc with the pointer at B', as shown in Figure 4.14b. Label the point C' where this arc crosses the ray from B'. Place the pointer at C and set the compass to the distance from C to A. Without changing the compass, put the pointer at C' and strike an arc to make a point of intersection A' with the arc from C', as shown in Figure 4.14c. Finally, draw a ray from B' through A'.

Two angles are said to be **equal** if they describe the same angle. If we write m in front of an angle symbol, we mean the measure of the angle rather than the angle itself.

Angles are usually measured using a unit called a **degree**, which is defined to be $\frac{1}{360}$ of a full revolution. The symbol ° is used to designate degrees. To measure an angle, you can use a **protractor**, but in this book the angle whose measures we need will be labeled as in Figure 4.15.

Angles are sometimes classified according to their measures, as shown in Table 4.1.

Experience leads us to see the plausibility of Euclid's fourth postulate that all right angles are congruent to one another.

Figure 4.14 Construction of an angle congruent to a given angle

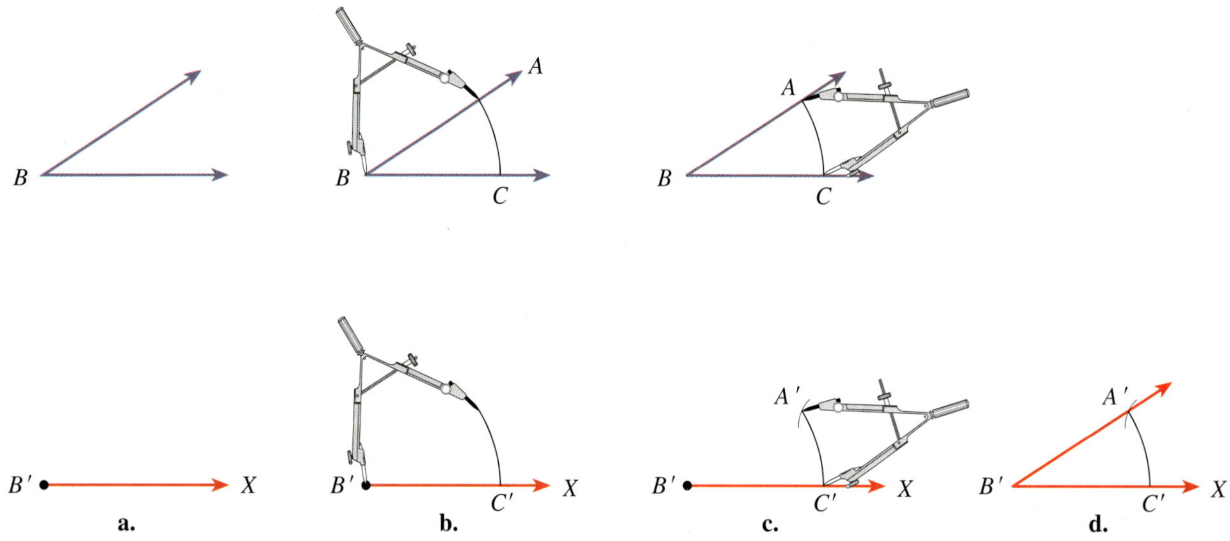

Figure 4.15 Labeling angles

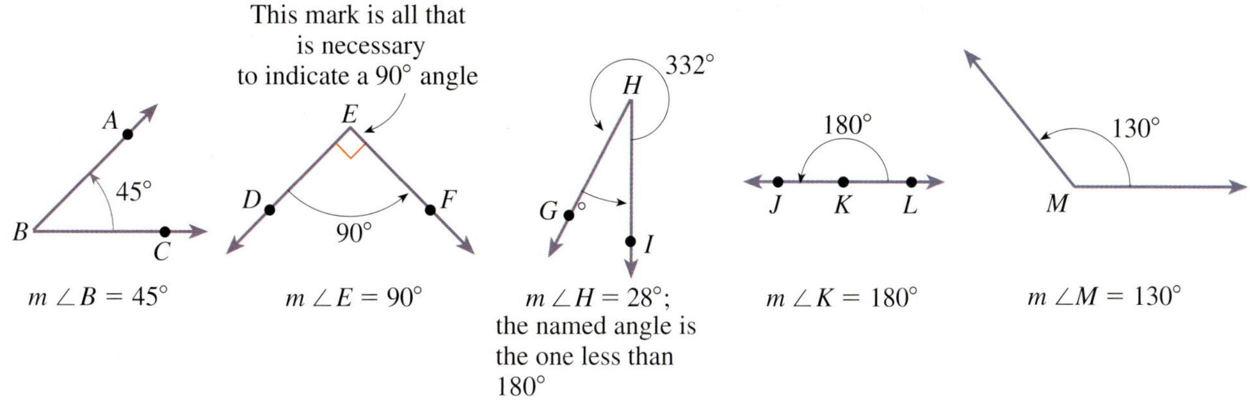

Table 4.1 Types of Angles

Angle Measure	Classification
Less than 90°	**Acute**
Equal to 90°	**Right**
Between 90° and 180°	**Obtuse**
Equal to 180°	**Straight**

*Remember these names for types of angles.

Figure 4.16 Angles formed by intersecting lines

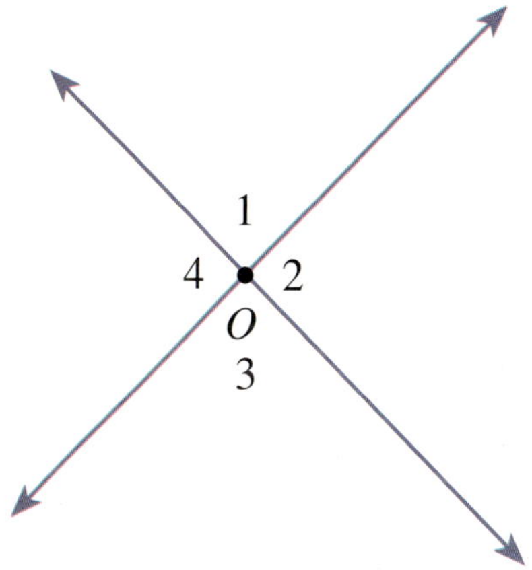

Two angles with the same measure are said to be **congruent**. If the sum of the measures of two angles is 90°, they are called **complementary angles**, and if the sum is 180°, they are called **supplementary angles**.

Consider any two distinct (different) intersecting lines in a plane, and let O be the point of intersection as shown in Figure 4.16.

These lines must form four angles. Angles with a common ray, common vertex, and on opposite sides of their common sides are called **adjacent angles**. We say that $\angle 1$ and $\angle 2$, $\angle 2$ and $\angle 3$, $\angle 3$ and $\angle 4$, as well as $\angle 4$ and $\angle 1$ are pairs of adjacent angles. We also say that $\angle 1$ and $\angle 3$ as well as $\angle 2$ and $\angle 4$ are pairs of **vertical angles**—that is, two angles for which each side of one angle is a prolongation through the vertex of a side of the other.

5 RELATIONSHIPS BETWEEN ANGLES

1 Complementary
2 Supplementary
3 Alternate interior
4 Alternate exterior
5 Corresponding

Angles with Parallel Lines

Consider three lines. Suppose that two of the lines, say, ℓ_1 and ℓ_2, are *parallel* (that is, they lie in the same plane and never intersect), and also that a third line ℓ_3 intersects the parallel lines at points P and Q, as shown in Figure 4.17. The line ℓ_3 is called a **transversal**. The notation we use for parallel lines is $\ell_1 \parallel \ell_2$.

Figure 4.17 Parallel lines cut by a transversal

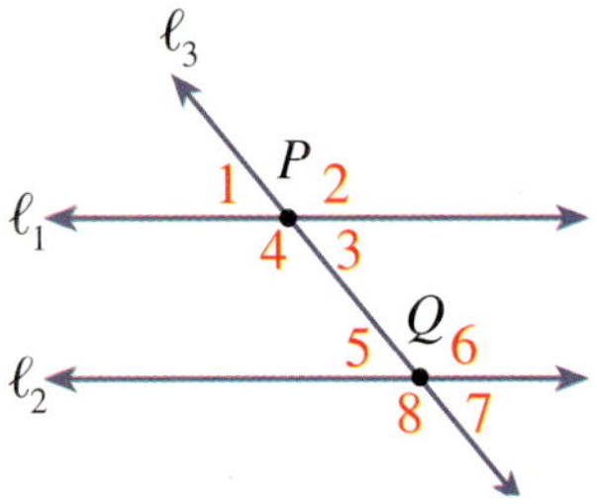

We make some observations about angles:

Vertical angles are congruent.

Alternate interior angles are pairs of angles whose interiors lie between the parallel lines, but on opposite sides of the transversal, each having one of the lines for one of its sides. Alternate interior angles are congruent.

Alternate exterior angles are pairs of angles that lie outside the parallel lines, but on opposite sides of the transversal, each with one side adjacent to each parallel. Alternate exterior angles are congruent.

Corresponding angles are two nonadjacent angles whose interiors lie on the same side of the transversal such that one angle lies between the parallel lines and the other does not. Corresponding angles are congruent.

Perpendicular Lines

If two lines intersect so that the adjacent angles are equal, then the lines are **perpendicular**. Simply, lines that intersect to form angles of 90° (right angles) are called perpendicular lines. In Figure 4.18, lines ℓ_3 and ℓ_4 intersect to form a right angle, and therefore they are perpendicular lines.

In a diagram on a printed page, any line that is parallel to the top and bottom edge of the page is considered **horizontal**. Lines that are perpendicular to a horizontal line are considered to be **vertical**. In Figure 4.18, line ℓ_5 is a horizontal line and line ℓ_6 is a vertical line.

Figure 4.18 Horizontal, vertical, and perpendicular lines

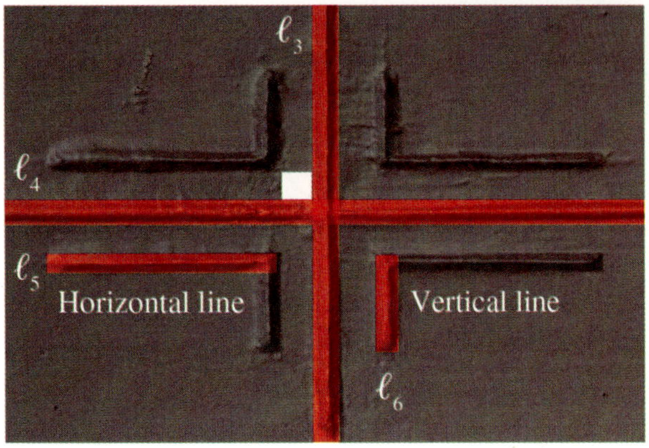

4.3 Triangles

ONE OF THE MOST FREQUENTLY ENCOUNTERED POLYGONS IS THE **TRIANGLE**.

In this section we take a closer look at them.

Terminology

Every triangle has six parts: three sides and three angles. We name the sides by naming the endpoints of the line segments, and we name the angles by identifying the vertex (see Figure 4.19).

Figure 4.19 A standard triangle showing the six parts

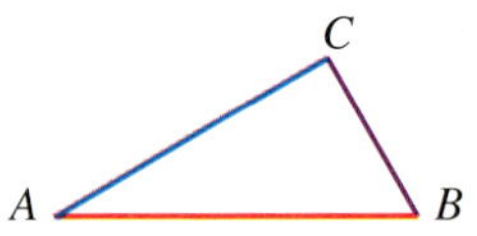

Sides	Angles
$\overline{AC}$	$\angle A$
$\overline{CB}$	$\angle B$
$\overline{AB}$	$\angle C$

STOP *A triangle and the parts of a triangle are essential ideas.*

We say that two triangles are **congruent** if they have the same size and shape. Suppose that we wish to construct a triangle with vertices D, E, and F, congruent to $\triangle ABC$

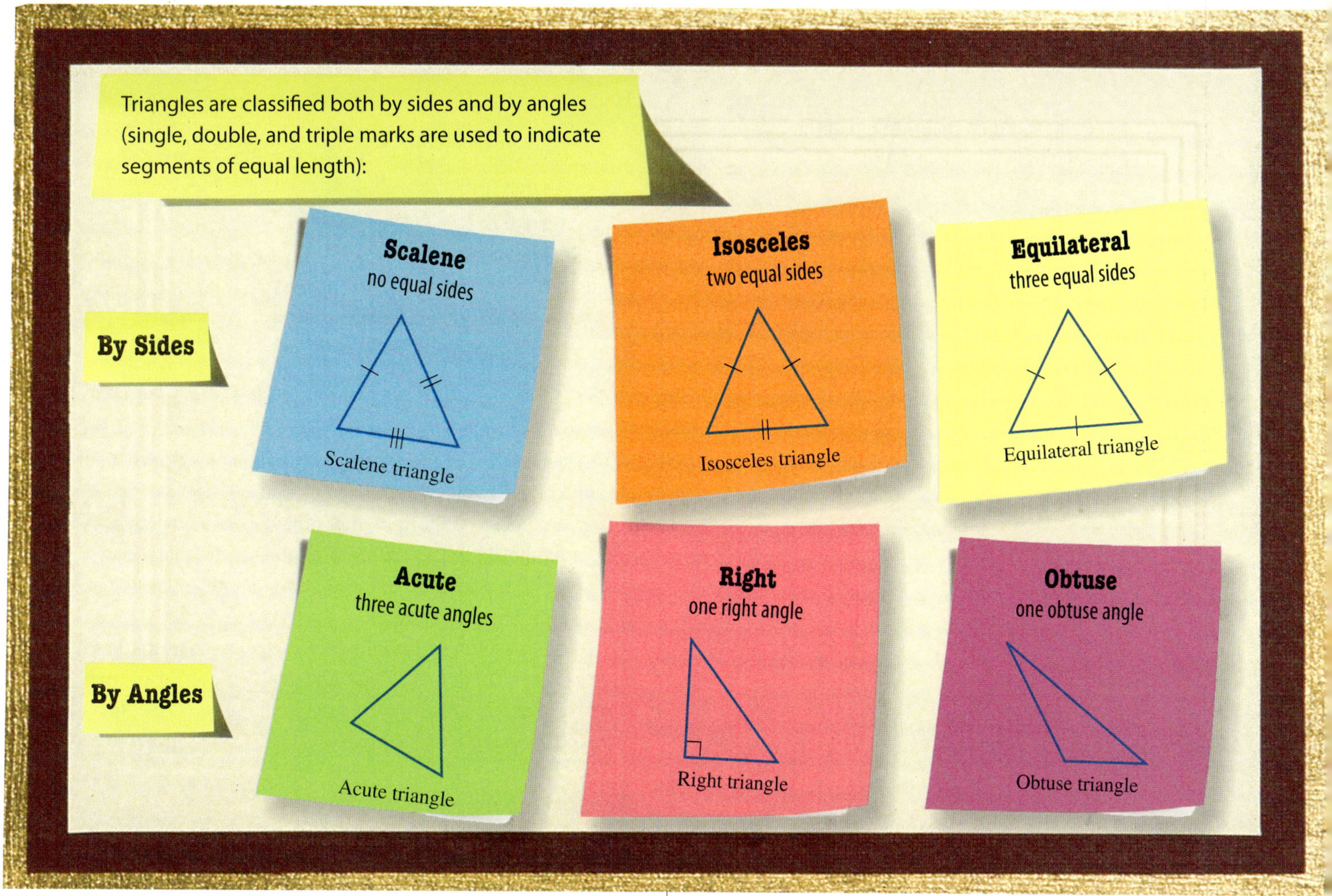

as shown in Figure 4.19. We would proceed as follows (as shown in Figure 4.20):

1. Mark off segment $\overline{DE}$ so that it is congruent to $\overline{AB}$. We write this as $\overline{DE} \simeq \overline{AB}$.
2. Construct angle E so that it is congruent to angle B. We write this as $\angle E \simeq \angle B$.
3. Mark off segment $\overline{EF} \simeq \overline{BC}$.

You can now see that if you connect points D and F with a straightedge, the resulting $\triangle DEF$ has the same size and shape as $\triangle ABC$. The procedure we used here is called Side-Angle-Side (SAS), meaning we constructed two sides and an *included angle* (an angle between two sides) congruent to two sides and an included angle of another triangle. We call these **corresponding parts**. There are other procedures for constructing congruent triangles. For this example, we say $\triangle ABC \simeq \triangle DEF$. From this we conclude that all six corresponding parts are congruent.

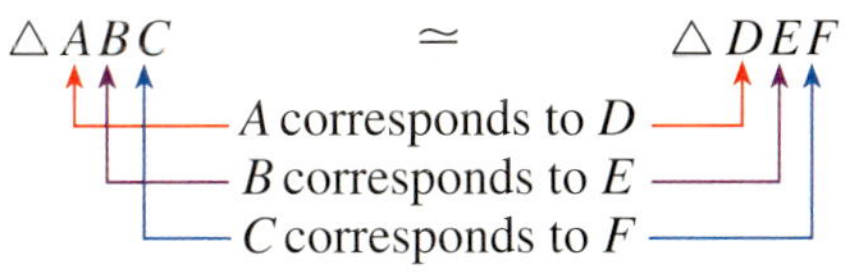

Figure 4.20 Constructing congruent triangles

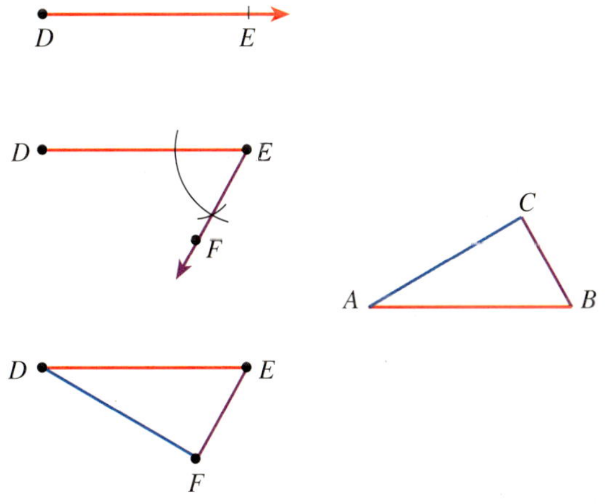

Angles of a Triangle

One of the most basic properties of a triangle involves the sum of the measures of its angles. To discover this property for yourself, place a pencil with an eraser along one side of any triangle as shown in Figure 4.21a on the next page.

Figure 4.21 Demonstration that the sum of the measures of the angles in a triangle is 180°

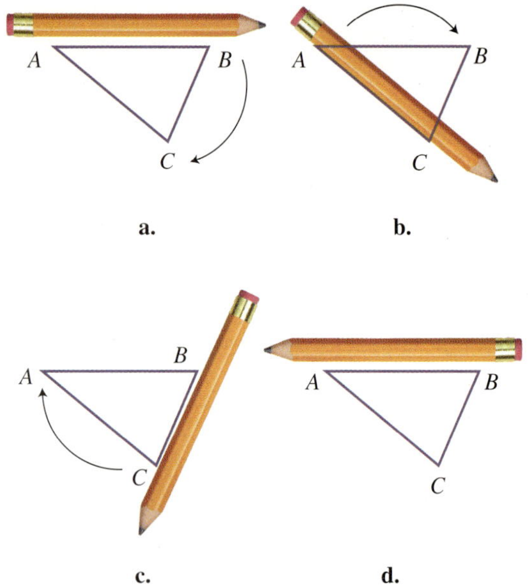

Now rotate the pencil to correspond to the size of $\angle A$ as shown in Figure 4.21b. You see your pencil is along $\overline{AC}$. Next, rotate the pencil through $\angle C$, as shown in Figure 4.21c. Finally, rotate the pencil through $\angle B$. Notice that the pencil has been rotated the same amount as the sum of the angles of the triangle. Also notice that the orientation of the pencil is exactly reversed from the starting position. This leads us to the following important theorem regarding the angles in a triangle. The sum of the measures of the angles in any triangle is 180°.

An **exterior angle** of a triangle is the angle on the other side of an extension of one side of the triangle. An example is the angle whose measure is marked as x in Figure 4.22.

Figure 4.22 Exterior angle *x*

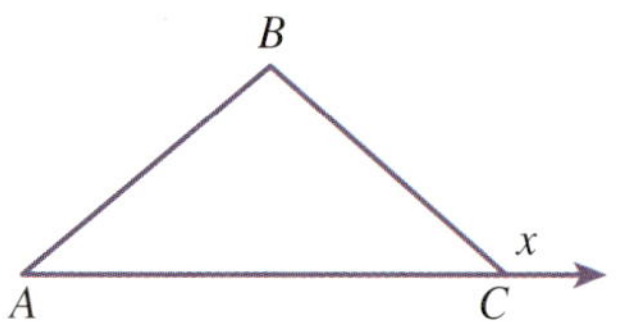

Notice that the following relationships are true for any $\triangle ABC$ with exterior angle x:

$$m\angle A + m\angle B + m\angle C = 180°$$

and

$$m\angle C + x = 180°$$

Thus,

$$m\angle A + m\angle B + m\angle C = m\angle C + x$$

$$m\angle A + m\angle B = x \quad \text{Subtract } m\angle C \text{ from both sides.}$$

That is, the measure of the exterior angle of a triangle equals the sum of the measures of the two interior angles.

Isosceles Triangle Property

In an isosceles triangle, there are two sides of equal length and the third side is called its **base**. The angle included by its legs is called the **vertex angle**, and the angles that include the base are called **base angles**.

There is an important theorem in geometry that is known as the **isosceles triangle property**. It states that if two sides of a triangle have the same length, then angles opposite them are congruent.

In other words, if a triangle is isosceles, then the base angles have equal measures. The converse is also true; namely, if two angles of a triangle are congruent, the sides opposite them have equal length.

Similar Triangles

Congruent figures have exactly the same size and shape. However, it is possible for figures to have exactly the same shape without necessarily having the same size. Such figures are called *similar figures*. In this section we will focus on **similar triangles**. If $\triangle ABC$ is similar to $\triangle DEF$, we write

$$\triangle ABC \sim \triangle DEF$$

Similar triangles are shown in Figure 4.23.

Since these figures have the same shape, we talk about **corresponding angles** and **corresponding sides**. The corresponding angles of similar triangles are those angles that have equal measure. The corresponding sides are those sides that are opposite equal angles.

Even though corresponding angles are equal, corresponding sides do not need to have the same length. If they do have the same length, the triangles are congruent. However, when they are not the same length, we can say they are proportional. From Figure 4.23 we see that the lengths of the sides are labeled a, b, c and d, e, f. When we say the sides are proportional, we mean

Primary ratios:

$$\frac{a}{b} = \frac{d}{e} \qquad \frac{a}{c} = \frac{d}{f} \qquad \frac{b}{c} = \frac{e}{f}$$

Reciprocals:

$$\frac{b}{a} = \frac{e}{d} \qquad \frac{c}{a} = \frac{f}{d} \qquad \frac{c}{b} = \frac{f}{e}$$

Figure 4.23 Similar triangles

$m\angle A = m\angle D$, so these are corresponding angles.
$m\angle B = m\angle E$, so these are corresponding angles.
$m\angle C = m\angle F$, so these are corresponding angles.
Side $\overline{BC}$ is opposite $\angle A$ and side $\overline{EF}$ is opposite $\angle D$, so we say that $\overline{BC}$ corresponds to $\overline{EF}$.
$\overline{AC}$ corresponds to $\overline{DF}$.
$\overline{AB}$ corresponds to $\overline{DE}$.

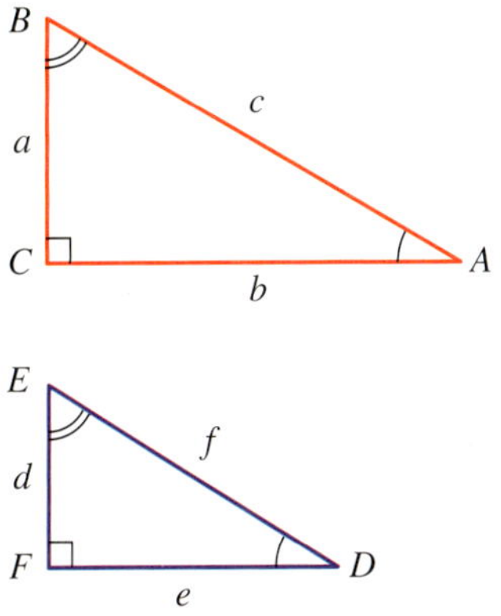

to recap

ANGLES IN A TRIANGLE

The sum of the measures of the angles in any triangle is 180°.

* You will frequently need to use this property.

EXTERIOR TRIANGLE PROPERTY

The measure of the exterior angle of a triangle equals the sum of the measures of the two interior angles.

ISOSCELES TRIANGLE PROPERTY

If two sides of a triangle have the same length, then angles opposite them are congruent.

SIMILAR TRIANGLE THEOREM

Two triangles are similar if two angles of one triangle are congruent to two angles of the other triangle. If the triangles are similar, then their corresponding sides are proportional.

We summarize with an important property of similar triangles called the **similar triangle theorem**: Two triangles are similar if two angles of one triangle are congruent to two angles of the other triangle. If the triangles are similar, then their corresponding sides are proportional.

WATCH YOUR STEP *This result is used in many applications.*

Identifying similar triangles is simplified even further if we know that the triangles are right triangles, because then the triangles are similar if one of the acute angles of one triangle has the same measure as an acute angle of the other. Let's see how this works by finding the height of a tree that is difficult to measure directly.

Understand the Problem. We need to find the height of some tree without measuring it directly.

Devise a Plan. We assume that it is a sunny day, and we will measure the height of the tree by measuring its shadow on the ground. For reference, we also measure the length of shadow of an object of known height (say our own height, a meterstick, or a yardstick). We will then use similar triangles and proportions to find the height of the tree.

Carry Out the Plan. Suppose that a tree and a yardstick are casting shadows as shown in Figure 4.24. If the shadow of the yardstick is 3 yards long and the shadow of the tree is 12 yards long, we use similar triangles to estimate h, the height of the tree, if we know that

$$m\angle S = m\angle S'$$

Figure 4.24 Finding the height of a tall object by using similar triangles

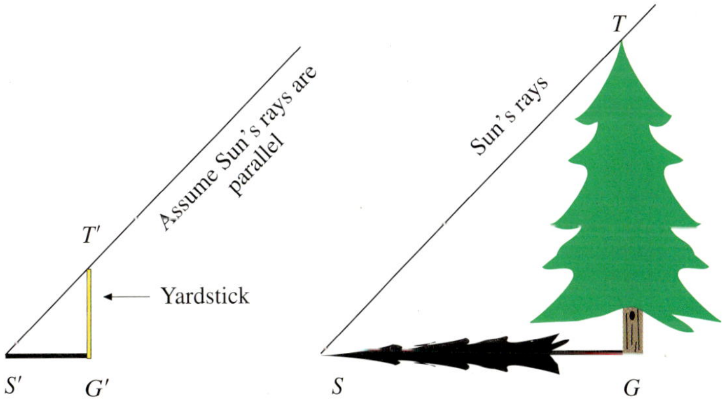

Since $\angle G$ and $\angle G'$ are right angles, and since $m\angle S = m\angle S'$, $\triangle SGT \sim \triangle S'G'T'$. Therefore corresponding sides are proportional.

$$\frac{1}{3} = \frac{h}{12}$$

$$h = \frac{1(12)}{3}$$

$$h = 4$$

You solved proportions like this in the previous chapter.

Look Back. The tree is 4 yards, or 12 ft, tall.

There is a relationship between the sizes of the angles of a right triangle and the ratios of the lengths of the sides. In a right triangle, the side opposite the right angle is called the **hypotenuse**. Each of the acute angles of a right triangle has one side that is the hypotenuse; the other side of that angle is called the **adjacent side** (see Figure 4.25).

Figure 4.25 A right triangle

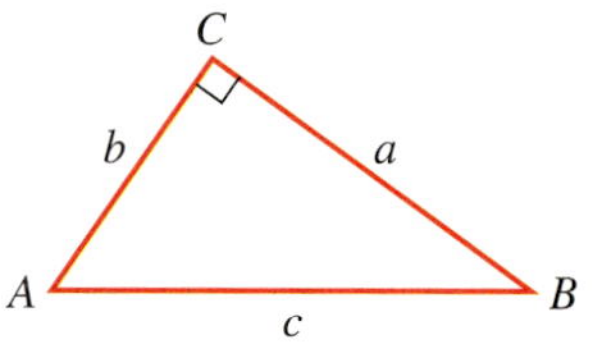

In $\triangle ABC$ with right angle at C:
the hypotenuse is c;
the side adjacent to $\angle A$ is b;
the side adjacent to $\angle B$ is a.

We also talk about an **opposite side**. The side opposite $\angle A$ is a, and the side opposite $\angle B$ is b.

4.4 Mathematics, Art, and Non-Euclidean Geometries

THE TOPIC OF THIS SECTION IS CERTAINLY AMBITIOUS, AND IF TREATED THOROUGHLY WOULD TAKE VOLUMES.

In this section, we will simply introduce some of the connections between art and mathematics.

Golden Rectangles

Certain rectangles hold some special interest because of the relationship between their height and width. Consider a rectangle with height h and width w, as shown in Figure 4.26.

Figure 4.26 Golden rectangle

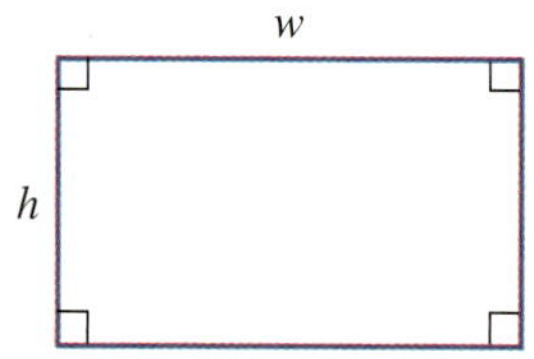

Consider the proportion

$$\frac{h}{w} = \frac{w}{h+w}$$

This relationship is called the **divine proportion**. If $h = 1$, we can solve the resulting equation for w:

$$\frac{1}{w} = \frac{w}{1+w}$$

$$1 + w = w^2$$

$$w^2 - w - 1 = 0$$

$$w = \frac{1 \pm \sqrt{(-1)^2 - 4(1)(-1)}}{2(1)} \quad \text{Quadratic formula}$$

$$= \frac{1 \pm \sqrt{5}}{2}$$

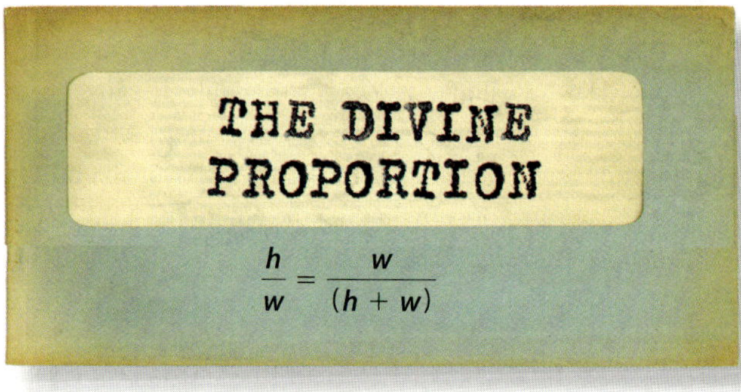

Since w is a length, we disregard the negative value to find

$$w = \frac{1 + \sqrt{5}}{2} \approx 1.618033989$$

This number is called the **golden ratio**, and is denoted by ϕ (pronounced *phi*) or τ (pronounced *tau*). We will use τ in this book.

A rectangle that satisfies this proportion for finding the golden ratio is called a **golden rectangle** and can easily be constructed using a straightedge and a compass. Consider the proportion

$$\frac{h}{w} = \frac{w}{h + w}$$

which means the ratio of the height (h) to the width (w) is the same as the ratio of the width (w) to the sum of its height and width. To draw such a rectangle, we can begin with *any* square $CDHG$, as shown in Figure 4.27.

Figure 4.27 Constructing a golden rectangle $EFGH$

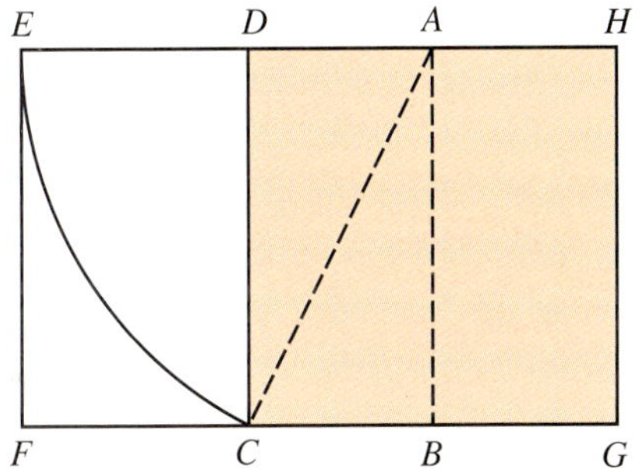

This square is shown with its interior shaded. Now divide the square into two equal parts, as shown by the dashed segment $\overline{AB}$. Set your compass so that it measures the length of $\overline{AC}$. Draw an arc, with center at A and radius equal to the length of $\overline{AC}$, so that it intersects the extension of side $\overline{HD}$; label this point E. Now draw side $\overline{EF}$. The resulting rectangle $EFGH$, is a golden rectangle; $CDEF$ is also a golden rectangle.

There are many interesting properties associated with the golden ratio τ. Consider the pattern of numbers

1, 1, 2, 3, 5, 8, 13, 21, 34, 55, 89, 144, . . .

which is formed by adding the first two terms for the third term, and then continues by adding successive pairs of numbers. Suppose we consider the ratios of the successive terms in this list:

> A RECTANGLE THAT SATISFIES THIS PROPORTION FOR FINDING THE GOLDEN RATIO IS CALLED A GOLDEN RECTANGLE

$\frac{1}{1} = 1.0000;$ $\qquad \frac{2}{1} = 2.0000;$

$\frac{3}{2} = 1.5000;$ $\qquad \frac{5}{3} \approx 1.667;$

$\frac{8}{5} = 1.6000;$ $\qquad \frac{13}{8} = 1.625;$

$\frac{21}{13} \approx 1.615;$ $\qquad \frac{34}{21} \approx 1.619;$

$\frac{55}{34} \approx 1.618;$ $\qquad \frac{89}{55} \approx 1.618.$

If you continue to find these ratios, you will notice that the sequence oscillates about a number approximately equal to 1.618, which is τ.

Suppose we repeat this same procedure, except we start with *any* two nonzero numbers, say 4 and 7:

4, 7, 11, 18, 29, 47, 76, 123, 199, 322, . . .

Next, form the ratios of the successive terms:

$\frac{7}{4} = 1.750;$ $\qquad \frac{11}{7} \approx 1.571;$ $\qquad \frac{18}{11} \approx 1.636;$

$\frac{29}{18} \approx 1.611;$ $\qquad \frac{47}{29} \approx 1.621; \ldots$

These ratios are oscillating about the same number, τ.

It has been said that many everyday rectangular objects have a length-to-width ratio of about 1.6:1. Many cereal boxes have dimensions of 30 cm by 19 cm, for a ratio of 1.6. You might also find a 1-lb box of sugar that is 17 cm by 10 cm, for a ratio of 1.7. A standard business card is 2 in. by 2.5 in. for a ratio of 1.75. Some animal carriers have dimensions yielding these ratios as well. What other objects can you find with dimensions in these ratios?

Mathematics and Art

Psychologists have tested individuals to determine the rectangles they find most pleasing; the results are those rectangles whose length-to-width ratios are near the golden ratio. George Markowsky, on the other hand, in the article "Misconceptions About the Golden Ratio," suggests that among rectangles with greatly different length-to-width ratios, the golden rectangle is the most pleasing; but when confronted

Figure 4.28 *La Parade* by the French impressionist Georges Seurat

with rectangles with ratios "close" to the golden ratio, subjects are unable to select the "best" rectangle.

We can see evidence of golden rectangles in many works of art. Whether the artist had such rectangles in mind is open to speculation, but we can see golden rectangles in the work of Albrecht Dürer, Leonardo da Vinci, George Bellows, Pieter Mondrian, and Georges Seurat (see Figure 4.28).

The Parthenon in Athens has been used as an example of a building with a height-to-width ratio that is almost equal to the golden ratio.

Figure 4.29 Proportions of the human body

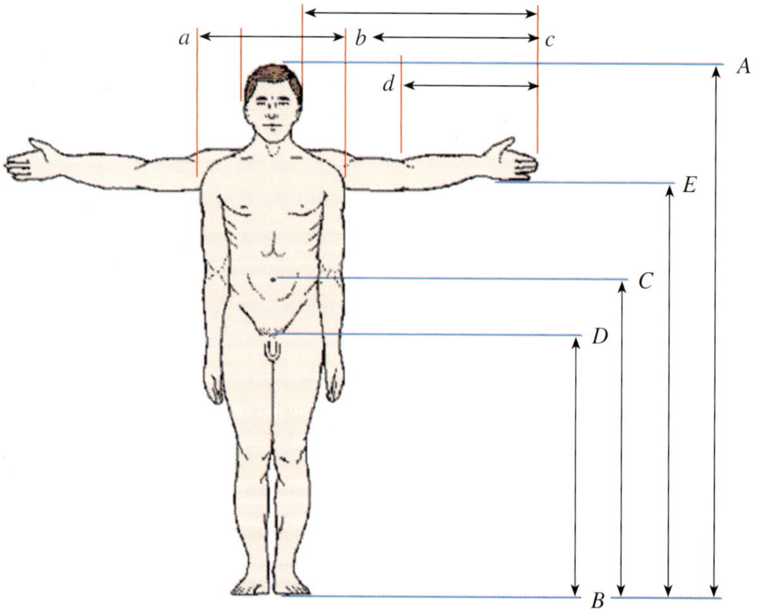

Many studies of the human body itself involve the golden ratio (remember $\tau \approx 1.62$). Figure 4.29 shows a drawing of an idealized athlete.

Let

$$|AC| = \text{distance from the top of the head to the navel;}$$
$$|CB| = \text{distance from the navel to the floor; and}$$
$$|AB| = \text{height.}$$

Then

$$\frac{|CB|}{|AC|} \approx \tau \quad \text{and} \quad \frac{|AB|}{|CB|} \approx \tau.$$

Also, let

$$|ab| = \text{shoulder width and } |bc| = \text{arm length.}$$

Then

$$\frac{|bc|}{|ab|} \approx \tau$$

***David* (1501–1504) by Michelangelo illustrates many golden ratios.**

Figure 4.30 Golden rectangles used in art

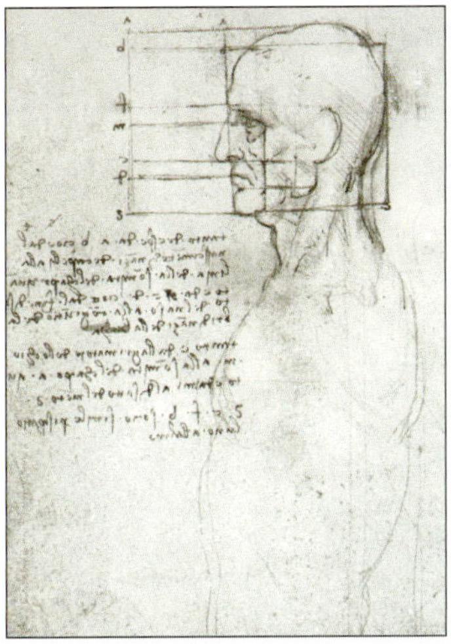

Dynamic symmetry of a human face by Leonardo da Vinci

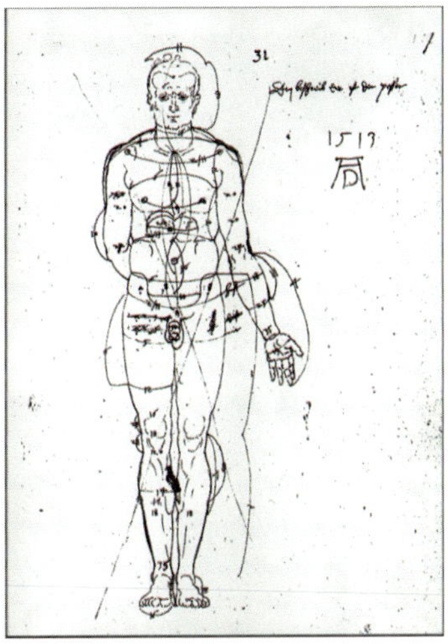

Proportions of the human body by Albrecht Dürer

In The Chambered Nautilus, Oliver Wendell Holmes wrote:

"Year after year beheld the silent toil
That spread his lustrous coil;
Still, as the spiral grew,
He left the past year's dwelling
for the new."

See if you can find other ratios on the human body that approximate τ. Figure 4.30 shows studies of the human body by da Vinci and Dürer, in which the rectangles approximate golden rectangles.

The last application of the golden rectangle we will consider in this section is related to the manner in which a chambered nautilus grows. The spiral of the chambered nautilus can be seen in the photograph above, and can be constructed by following the steps in Figure 4.31.

Projective Geometry

As Europe passed out of the Middle Ages and into the Renaissance, artists were at the forefront of the intellectual revolution. No longer satisfied with flat-looking scenes, they wanted to portray people and objects as they looked

Figure 4.31 A spiral is constructed using a golden rectangle.

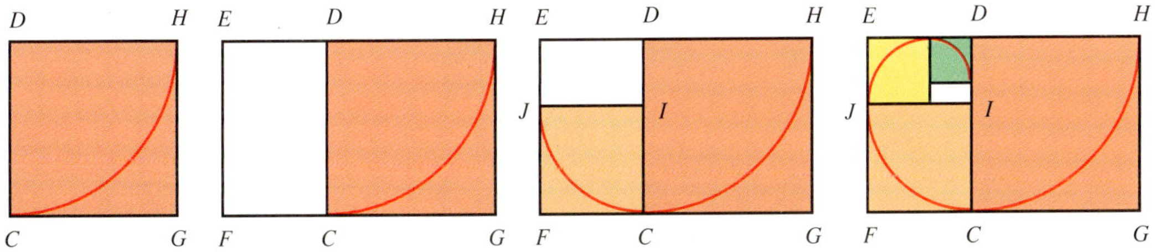

Begin with any square and draw a quarter circle as shown.

Form a golden rectangle.

Draw a square within the new rectangle *CDEF*; draw a quarter circle as shown.

Repeat the process. The resulting curve is called a logarithmic spiral.

Figure 4.32 Duccio's *Last Supper* illustrates perspective that is incorrect.

Figure 4.33 Hogarth's *Perspective Absurdities*

in real life. The artists' problem was one of dimension, and dimension is related to mathematics, so many of the Renaissance artists had to solve some original mathematics problems. How could a flat surface be made to look three-dimensional?

One of the first (but rather unsuccessful) attempts at portraying depth in a painting is shown in Figure 4.32, Duccio's *Last Supper.*

Notice that the figures are in a boxed-in room. This technique is characteristic of the period, and was an attempt to make perspective easier to define.

Most errors in perspective were attributed to carelessness of the artists. In 1754, the artist William Hogarth forced artists to confront their inadequacies with his engraving *Perspective Absurdities* (Figure 4.33), in which he challenged the viewer to find all the perspective mistakes.

The first great painter of the Italian Renaissance was Masaccio (1401–1428), whose painting *The Holy Trinity* (Figure 4.34) shows mathematical perspective. The pane at the right shows the structure of

Figure 4.34 Masaccio's *The Holy Trinity* is a study in perspective.

perspective. The ideas of shapes, rectangles, triangles, and circles, and how these figures relate to each other were of importance not only to mathematicians, but also to artists and architects.

The *B.C.* cartoon shown above even pokes fun at the idea of perspective.

Artists finally solved the problem of perspective by considering the surface of the picture to be a window through which the object was painted. This technique was pioneered by Paolo Uccello (1397–1475), Piero della Francesca (1415–1492), Leonardo da Vinci (1452–1519), and Albrecht Dürer (1471–1528). As the lines of vision from the object converge at the eye, the picture captures a cross section of them, as shown in Figure 4.35.

The mathematical study of vanishing points and perspective is part of a branch of mathematics called **projective geometry**, the study of those properties of geometric configurations that do not change (are invariant) under projections.

Non-Euclidean Geometry

Euclid's so-called fifth postulate (see Section 4.1) caused problems from the time it was stated. It somehow doesn't seem like the other postulates but, rather, like a theorem that should be proved. In fact, this postulate even bothered Euclid himself, since he didn't use it until he had proved his 29th theorem. Many mathematicians tried to find a proof for this postulate.

One of the first serious attempts to prove Euclid's fifth postulate was made by Girolamo Saccheri (1667–1733), an Italian Jesuit. Saccheri's plan was simple. He constructed a quadrilateral, later known as a **Saccheri quadrilateral**,

Dürer's woodcut shows how the problem of perspective can be overcome. The point in front of the artist's eye fixes the point of viewing the painting. The grid on the window corresponds to the grid on the artist's canvas.

Figure 4.35 Albrecht Dürer's *Draughtsman Drawing a Recumbent Woman*

with base angles A and B right angles, and with sides $\overline{AC}$ and $\overline{BD}$ the same length, as shown in Figure 4.36.

Figure 4.36 A Saccheri quadrilateral

As you may know from high school geometry, the summit angles C and D are also right angles. However, this result uses Euclid's fifth postulate. Now it is also true that *if* the summit angles are right angles, *then* Euclid's fifth postulate holds. The problem, then, was to establish the fact that angles C and D are right angles. Here is the plan:

1. Assume that the angles are obtuse and deduce a contradiction.
2. Assume that the angles are acute and deduce a contradiction.
3. Therefore, by the first two steps, the angles must be right angles.
4. From step 3, Euclid's fifth postulate can be deduced.

It turned out not to be as easy as he thought, because he was not able to establish a contradiction. He gave up the search because, he said, it "led to results that were repugnant to the nature of a straight line."

Saccheri never realized the significance of what he had started, and his work was forgotten until 1889. However, in the meantime, Johann Lambert (1728–1777) and Adrien-Marie Legendre (1752–1833) similarly investigated the possibility of eliminating Euclid's fifth postulate by proving it from the other postulates.

By the early years of the 19th century, three accomplished mathematicians began to suspect that the parallel postulate was independent and could not be eliminated by deducing it from the others. The great mathematician Karl Gauss was the first to reach this conclusion, but since he didn't publish this finding of his, the credit goes to two others. In 1811, an 18-year-old Russian named Nikolai Lobachevsky pondered the possibility of a "non-Euclidean" geometry—that is, a geometry that did not assume Euclid's fifth postulate. In 1840, he published his ideas in an article entitled "Geometrical Researches on the Theory of Parallels." The postulate he used was subsequently named after him.

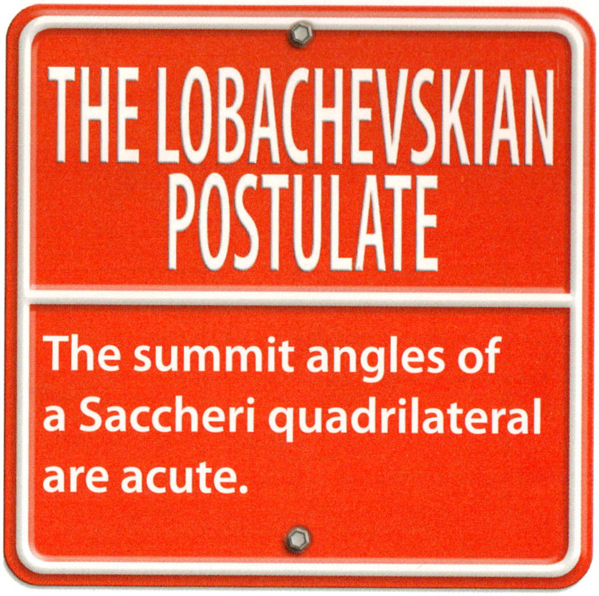

This axiom, in place of Euclid's fifth postulate, leads to a geometry that we call **hyperbolic geometry**. If we use the plane as a model for Euclidean geometry, what model could serve for hyperbolic geometry? A rough model for this geometry can be seen by placing two trumpet bells together as shown in Figure 4.37a. It is called a **pseudosphere** and is generated by a curve called a *tractrix* (as shown in Figure 4.37b). The tractrix is rotated about the line $\overleftrightarrow{AB}$. The

Figure 4.37 A tractrix can be used to generate a pseudosphere.

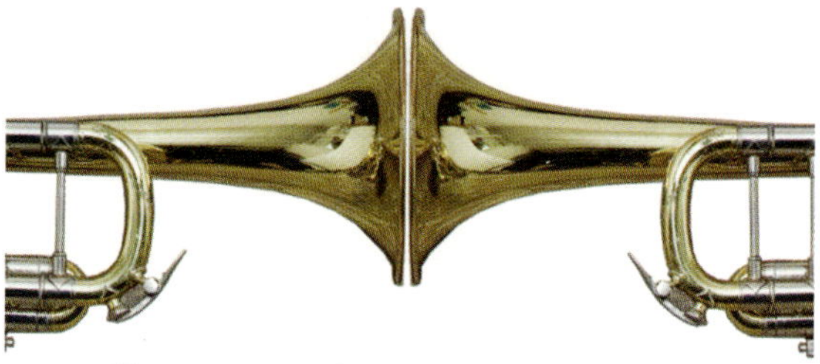

Two trumpets placed end to end serve as a physical model of a pseudosphere.

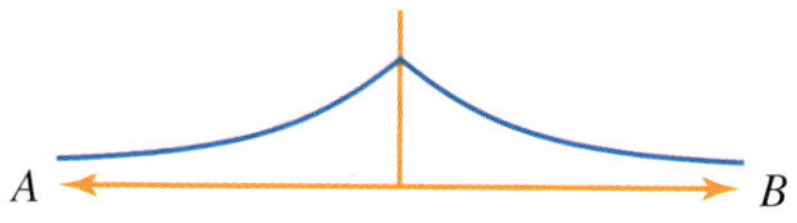

a. A tractrix

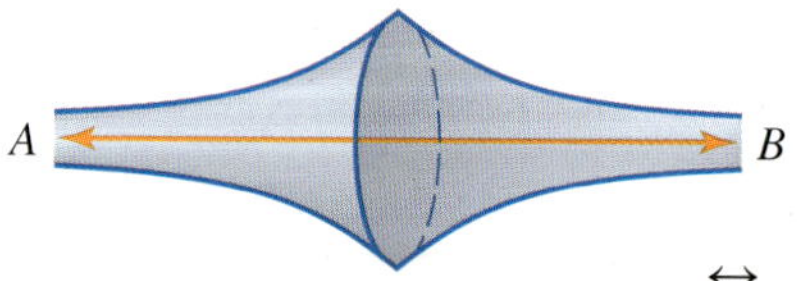

b. A tractrix rotated about the line $\overleftrightarrow{AB}$

pseudosphere has the property that, through a point not on a line, there are many lines parallel to a given line.

Georg Riemann (1826–1866), who also worked in this area, pointed out that, although a straight line may be extended indefinitely, it need not have infinite length. It could instead be similar to the arc of a circle, which eventually begins to retrace itself. Such a line is called *re-entrant*. An example of a re-entrant line is found by considering a great circle on a sphere. A **great circle** is a circle on a sphere with a diameter equal to the diameter of the sphere. With this model, a Saccheri quadrilateral is constructed on a sphere with the summit angles obtuse. The resulting geometry is called **elliptic geometry**. The shortest path between any two points on a sphere is an arc of the great circle through those points; these arcs correspond to line segments in Euclidean geometry. In 1854, Riemann showed that, with some other slight adjustments in the remaining postulates, another consistent non-Euclidean geometry can be developed. Notice that the fifth, or parallel, postulate fails to hold because any two great circles on a sphere must intersect at two points (see Figure 4.38).

Figure 4.38 A sphere showing the intersection of two great circles

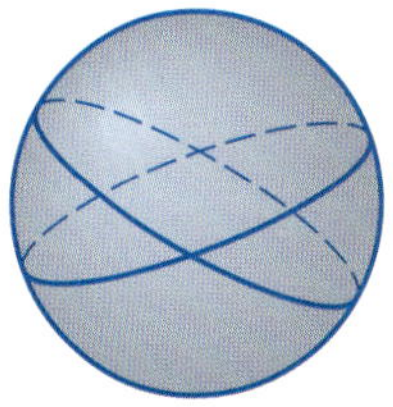

We have not, by any means, discussed all possible geometries. We have merely shown that the Euclidean geometry that is taught in high school is not the only possible model. A comparison of some of the properties of these geometries is shown in Table 4.2.

Table 4.2 Comparison of Major Two-Dimensional Geometries

Euclidean Geometry	Hyperbolic Geometry	Elliptic Geometry
Euclid (about 300 BC)	Gauss, Bolyai, Lobachevsky (ca. 1830)	Riemann (ca. 1850)
Given a point not on a line, there is one and only one line through the point parallel to the given line.	Given a point not on a line, there are an infinite number of lines through the point that do not intersect the given line.	There are no parallels.
A representative line in each geometry is shown in color for each model, and the shaded portion showing a Saccheri quadrilateral is shown directly below the representative models.		
Geometry is on a plane: 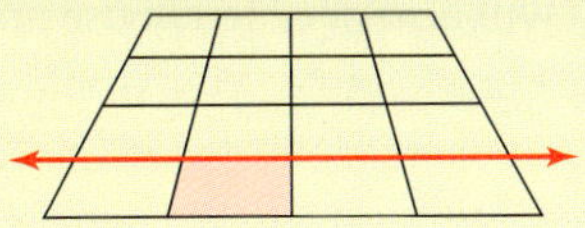 Lines are infinitely long. 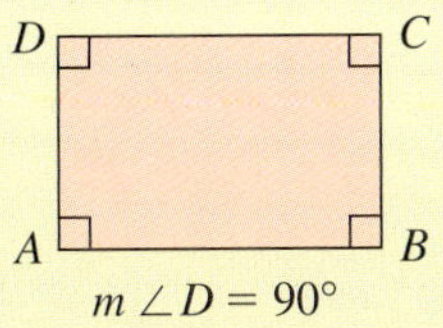	**Geometry is on a pseudosphere:** 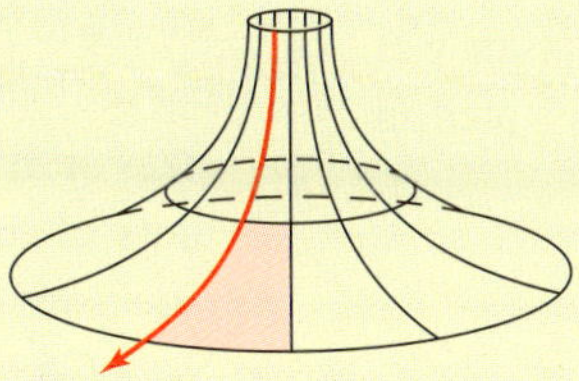 Lines are infinitely long. 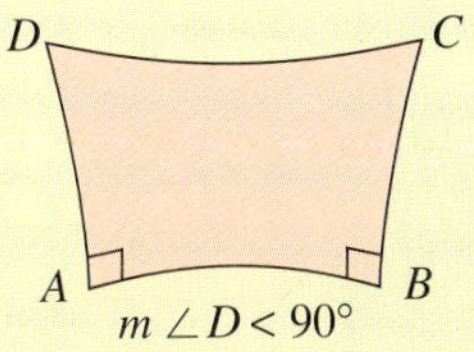	**Geometry is on a sphere:** 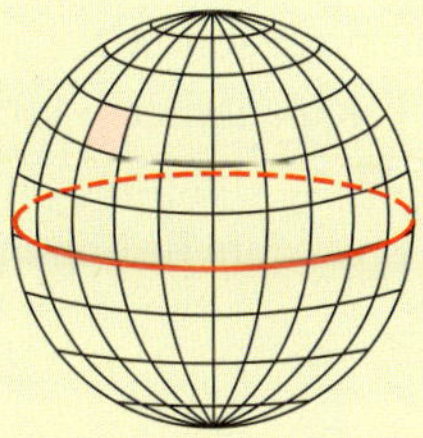 Lines are finite in length. 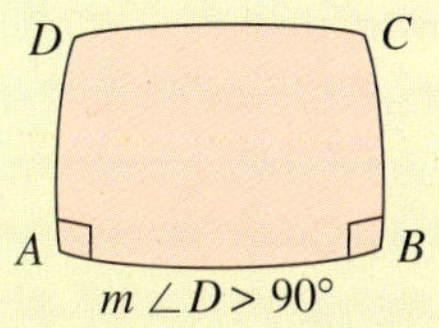
The sum of the angles of a triangle is 180°.	The sum of the angles of a triangle is less than 180°.	The sum of the angles of a triangle is more than 180°.

4.5 Perimeter and Area

IN THIS TOPIC WE ARE CONCERNED WITH THE NOTION OF MEASUREMENT.

To **measure** an object is to assign a number to its size. Measurement is never exact, and you therefore need to decide how **precise** the measure should be. For example, the measurement might be to the nearest inch, nearest foot, or even nearest mile. The precision of a measurement depends not only on the instrument used but also on the purpose of your measurement. For example, if you are measuring the size of a room to lay carpet, the precision of your measurement might be different than if you are measuring the size of an airport hangar.

The **accuracy** refers to your answer. Suppose that you measure with an instrument that measures to the nearest tenth of a unit. You find one measurement to be 4.6 and another measurement to be 2.1. If, in the process of your work, you need to multiply these numbers, the result you obtain is

$$4.6 \times 2.1 = 9.66$$

This product is calculated to two decimal places, but it does not seem quite right that you obtain an answer that is more accurate (two decimal places) than the instrument you are using to make your measurements (one decimal place). In this book, we will require that the accuracy of your answers not exceed the precision of the measurement. This means that after the calculations are completed, the final answer should be rounded. The principle we will use is stated in the Accuracy Procedure box on the right.

WATCH YOUR STEP

Spend a few moments thinking about the ideas of precision and accuracy.

ACCURACY PROCEDURE USED IN THIS BOOK

All measurements are as precise as given in the text. If you are asked to make a measurement, the precision will be specified.

STEP 1 Carry out all calculations without rounding.

STEP 2 After you obtain a final answer, round this answer to be as accurate as *the least precise* measurement.

STEP 3 If you are working with money, round your final answer to the nearest cent.

STOP *The answers we give will conform to this procedure.*

This accuracy procedure specifies that, to avoid round-off error, you should round only once (at the end). This is particularly important if you are using a calculator, which will display 8, 10, 12, or even more decimal places.

You will also be asked to *estimate* the size of many objects in this chapter. As we introduce different units of measurement, you should remember some reference points so that you can make intelligent estimates. Many comparisons will be mentioned in the text, but you need to remember only those that are meaningful for you to estimate other sizes or distances. You will also need to choose appropriate units of measurement. For example, you would not measure your height in yards or miles, or the distance to New York City in inches.

Measuring Length

What is your height? To answer that question, you must take a measurement.

The number representing the linear dimension of an object, as measured from end to end, is its **length**.

The most common system of measurement used in the world is what we call the **metric system**. There have been numerous attempts to make the metric system mandatory in the United States. Today, big business is supporting the drive toward metric conversion, and it appears inevitable that the metric system will eventually come into use in the United States. In the meantime, it is important that we understand how to use both the United States and metric systems.

The most difficult problem in changing from the **United States system** (the customary system of measurement in the United States) to the metric system is not mathematical, but psychological. Many people fear that changing to the metric system will require complex multiplying and dividing and the use of confusing decimal points. For example, James Collier made the comments below in a recent popular article.

The author of this article has missed the whole point. Why are kilometers hard to calculate? How does he know that it's 400 miles to Cleveland? He knows because the odometer on his car or a road sign told him. Won't it be just as easy to read an odometer calibrated to kilometers or a metric road sign telling him how far it is to Cleveland?

The real advantage of using the metric system is the ease of conversion from one unit of measurement to another. How many of you remember the difficulty you had in learning to change tablespoons to cups? Or pints to gallons?

In this book we will work with both the U.S. and the metric measurement systems. You should be familiar with both and be able to make estimates in both systems. The following box gives the standard units of length.

Standard Length Units

U.S. System	Metric System
inch (in.)	**meter (m)**
foot (ft, 12 in)	centimeter (cm, $\frac{1}{100}$ m)
yard (yd, 36 in.)	kilometer (km; 1,000 m)
mile (mi, 63,360 in.)	

To understand the size of any measurement, you need to see it, have experience with it, and take measurements using it as a standard unit.

The basic unit of measurement for the U.S. system is the inch; it is shown in Figure 4.39 on the next page. You can remember that an inch is about the distance from the joint of your thumb to the tip of your thumb.

The basic unit of measurement for the metric system is the meter; it is also shown in Figure 4.39. You can remember that a meter is about the distance from your left ear to the tip of the fingers on the end of your outstretched right arm.

For instance, if someone tells me it's 250 miles up to Lake George, or 400 out to Cleveland, I can pretty well figure out how long it's going to take and plan accordingly. Translating all of this into kilometers is going to be an awful headache. A kilometer is about 0.62 miles, so to convert miles into kilometers you divide by six and multiply by ten, and even that isn't accurate. Who can do that kind of thing when somebody is asking me are we almost there, the dog is beginning to drool and somebody else is telling you you're driving too fast?

Of course, that won't matter, because you won't know how fast you're going anyway. I remember once driving in a rented car on a superhighway in France, and every time I looked down at the speedometer we were going 120. That kind of thing can give you the creeps. What's it going to be like when your wife keeps shouting, "Slow down, you're going almost 130"? But if you think kilometers will be hard to calculate...

Figure 4.39 Standard units of measurement for length

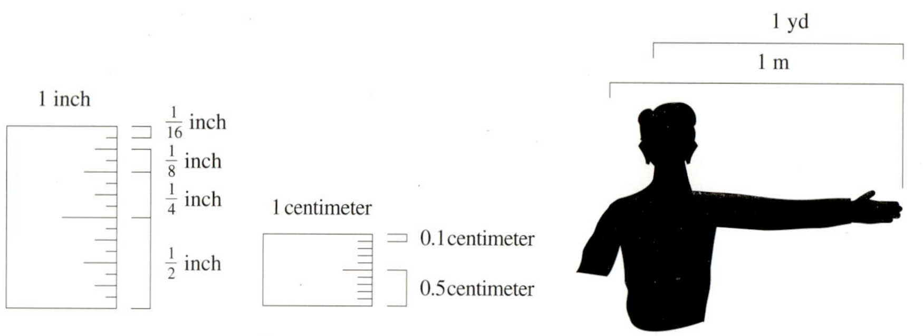

a. Basic unit of length in the U.S. system is the inch.

b. In the metric system, a distance comparable to the inch is the centimeter.

c. Basic unit of length in the metric system is the meter. In the U.S. system, a comparable unit is the yard.

For the larger distances of a mile and a kilometer, you will need to look at maps or the odometer of your car. However, you should have some idea of these distances.*

It might help to have a visual image of certain prefixes as you progress through this chapter. Greek prefixes **kilo-**, **hecto-**, and **deka-** are used for measurements larger than the basic metric unit, and Latin prefixes **deci-**, **centi-**, and **milli-** are used for smaller quantities (see Figure 4.40). As you can see from Figure 4.40, a centimeter is $\frac{1}{100}$ of a meter; this means that 1 meter is equal to 100 centimeters.

Now we will measure given line segments with different levels of precision. We will consider two different rulers, one marked to the nearest centimeter and another marked to the nearest $\frac{1}{10}$ centimeter.

* We could tell you that a mile is 5,280 ft or that a kilometer is 1,000 m, but to do so does not give you any feeling for what these distances really are. You need to get into a car and watch the odometer to see how far you travel in going 1 mile. Most cars in the United States do not have odometers set to kilometers, and until they do it is difficult to measure in kilometers. You might, however, be familiar with a 10-kilometer race. It takes a good runner about 30 minutes to run 10 kilometers and an average runner about 45 minutes. You can walk a kilometer in about 6 minutes.

Figure 4.40 Metric prefixes

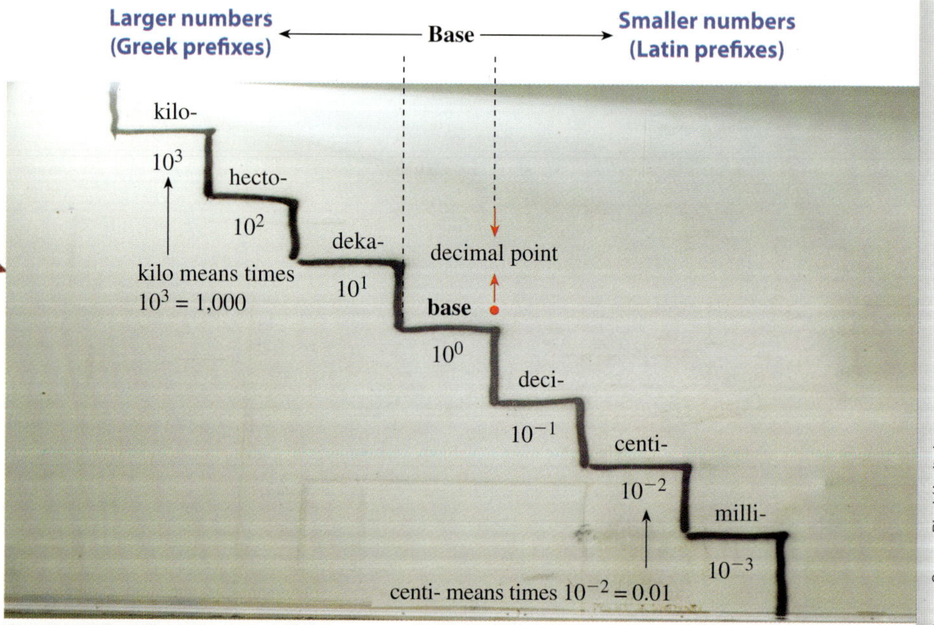

Greek prefixes for larger quantities | Latin prefixes for smaller quantities

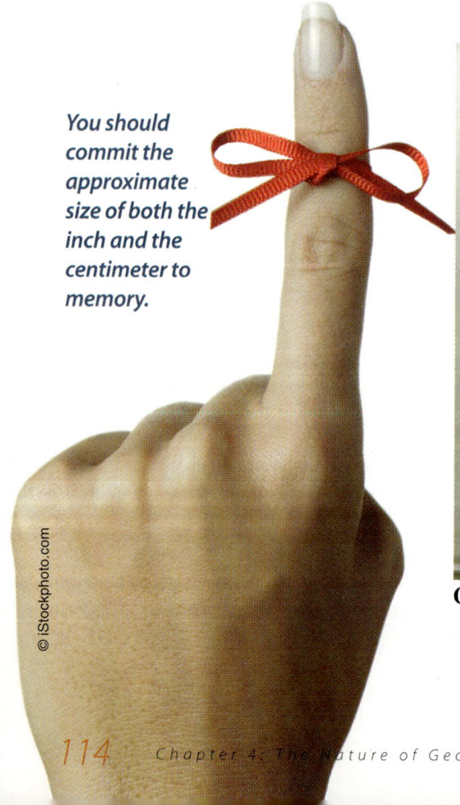

You should commit the approximate size of both the inch and the centimeter to memory.

Perimeter

One application of both measurement and geometry involves finding the distance around a polygon. This distance is called the **perimeter** of the polygon.

> The **perimeter** of a polygon is the sum of the lengths of the sides of that polygon.
>
> *Remember this term.

Following are some formulas for finding the perimeters of the most common polygons. An **equilateral triangle** is a triangle with all sides equal in length.

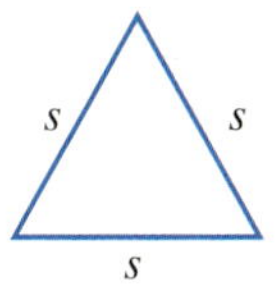

$$\text{PERIMETER} = 3(\text{SIDE})$$
$$P = 3s$$

Equilateral triangle

A **rectangle** is a quadrilateral with opposite sides parallel and equal in length.

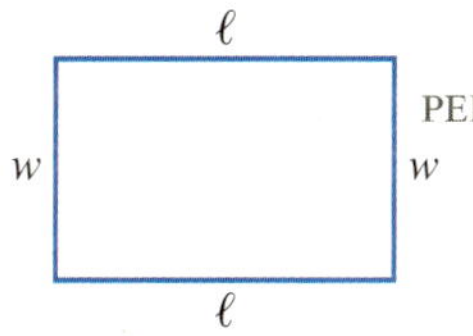

$$\text{PERIMETER} = 2(\text{LENGTH}) + 2(\text{WIDTH})$$
$$P = 2\ell + 2w$$

Rectangle

A **square** is a quadrilateral with all sides equal in length.

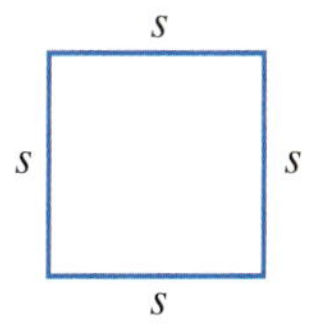

$$\text{PERIMETER} = 4(\text{SIDE})$$
$$P = 4s$$

Square

Circumference

A **circle** is the set of all points in a plane a given distance, called the **radius**, from a given point, called the **center**. Although a circle is not a polygon, sometimes we need to find the distance around a circle. This distance is called the **circumference**. For *any circle*, if you divide the circumference by the diameter, you will get the *same number* (see Figure 4.41). This number is given the name π (**pi**). The number π is an irrational number and is sometimes approximated by 3.14 or $\frac{22}{7}$. We need this number π to state a formula for the circumference C:

$$C = d\pi \quad \text{where} \quad d = \text{DIAMETER}$$

or

$$C = 2\pi r \quad \text{where} \quad r = \text{RADIUS}$$

For a circle, the **diameter** is twice the radius. This means that, if you know the radius and want to find the diameter, you simply multiply by 2. If you know the diameter and want to find the radius, divide by 2.

Figure 4.41 Circle

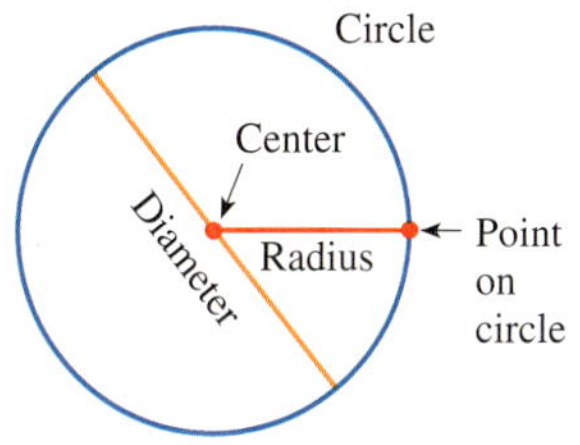

Many calculators have a single key marked π. If you press it, the display shows an approximation correct to several decimal places (the number of places depends on your calculator):

Press: $\boxed{\pi}$ *Display:* `3.141592654`

If your calculator doesn't have a key marked π, you may want to use this approximation to obtain the accuracy you want. In this book, the answers are found by using the π key on a calculator and then rounding the answer.

The measurement of length, discussed in the previous section, is sometimes considered to be a *one-dimensional measurement* (back and forth, i.e., end to end). In this section, we consider a *two-dimensional measurement* (end to end and top to bottom, i.e., back/forth and up/down).

Area

Suppose that you want to carpet your living room. The price of carpet is quoted as a price per square yard. A square yard is a measure of **area**. To measure the area of a plane figure, you fill it with **square units** (see Figure 4.42).

Figure 4.42 Common units of measurement for area

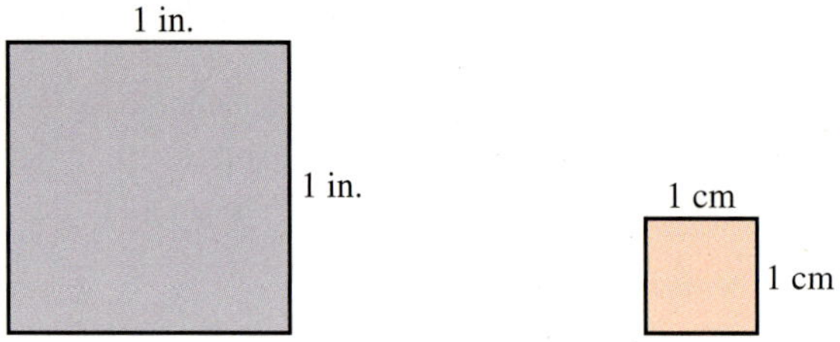

a. 1 **square inch** (actual size); abbreviated 1 sq in. or 1 in.^{2}

b. 1 **square centimeter** (actual size); abbreviated 1 sq cm or 1 cm^2

Rectangles

The area of a rectangular or square region is the product of the distance across (length) and the distance down (width).

Figure 4.43 Parallelograms

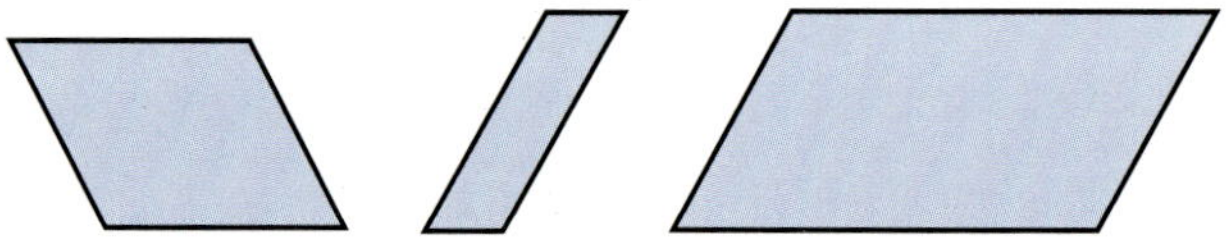

Parallelograms

A **parallelogram** is a quadrilateral with two pairs of parallel sides, as shown in Figure 4.43.

To find the area of a parallelogram, we can estimate the area by counting the number of square units inside the parallelogram (which may require estimation of partial square units), or we can show that the formula for the area of a parallelogram is the same as the formula for the area of a rectangle.

The justification of the parallelogram formula is given in geometric form below.

Triangles

You can find the area of a triangle by filling in and approximating the number of square units, by rearranging the parts, or by noticing that *every* triangle has an area that is exactly half that of a corresponding parallelogram.

The justification of the triangle formula is given in geometric form below.

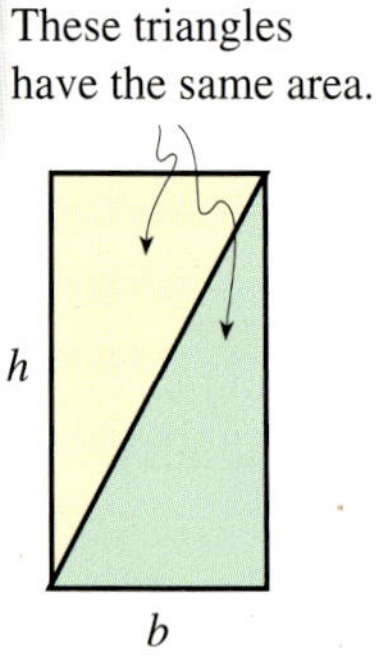

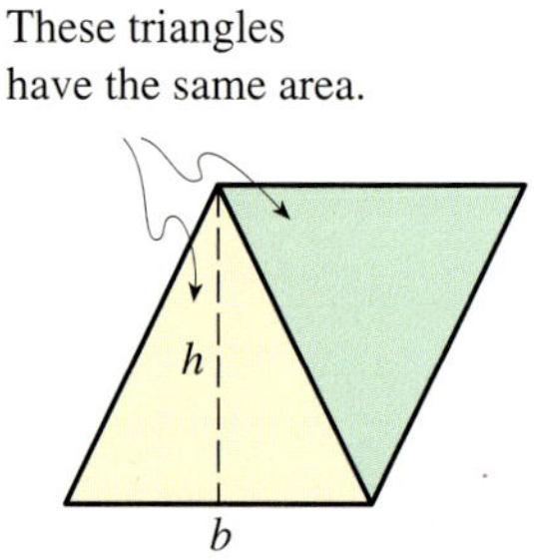

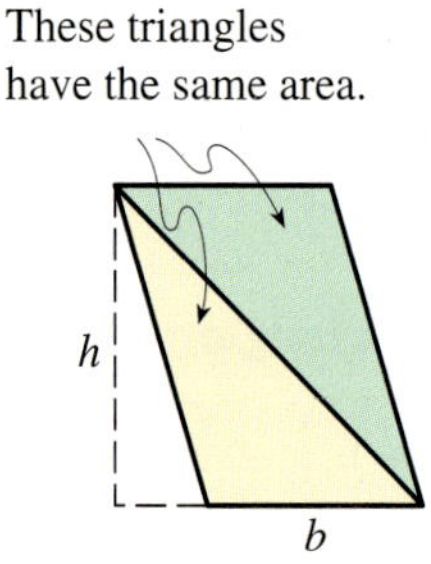

Trapezoids

A **trapezoid** is a quadrilateral with two sides parallel. These sides are called the *bases*, and the perpendicular distance between the bases is the *height*. We can find the area of a trapezoid by finding the sum of the areas of two triangles,

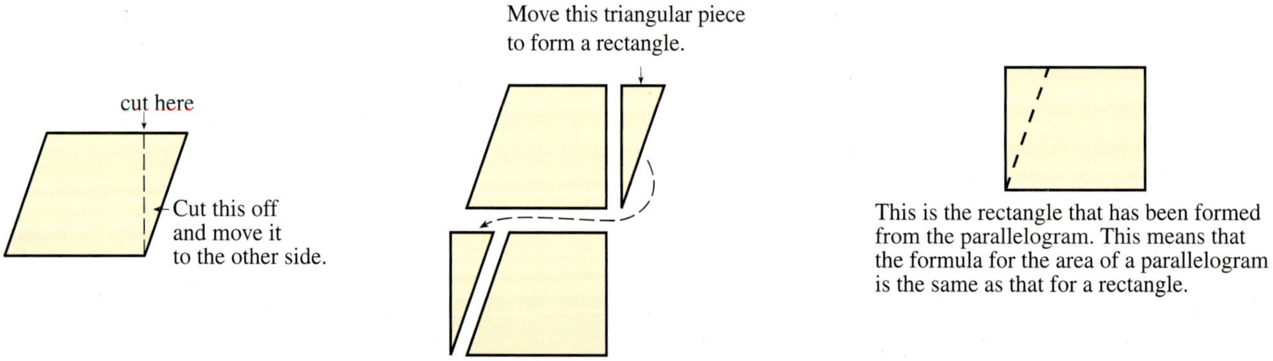

AREA OF A . . .

Rectangle and Square

The formulas for the area, A, of a rectangle of length ℓ and width w and the area, A, of a square of side with length s are:

$$A = \ell w$$

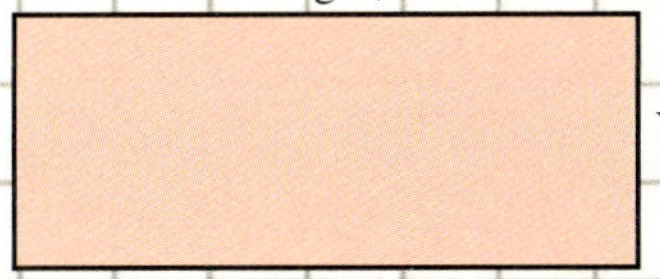

$$A = s^2$$

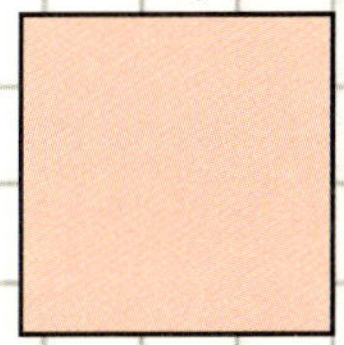

Parallelogram

The area, A, of a parallelogram with base b and height h is

$$A = bh$$

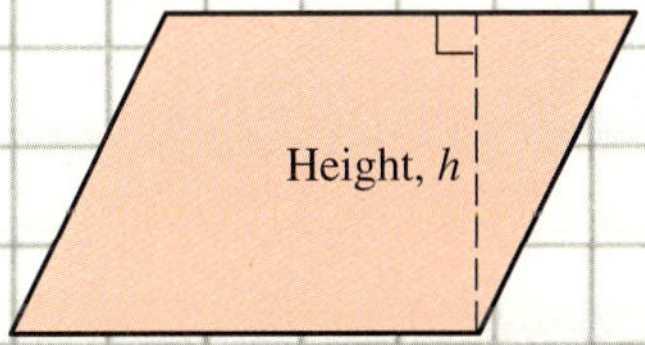

Triangle

The area, A, of a triangle with base b and height h is*

$$A = \frac{1}{2}bh$$

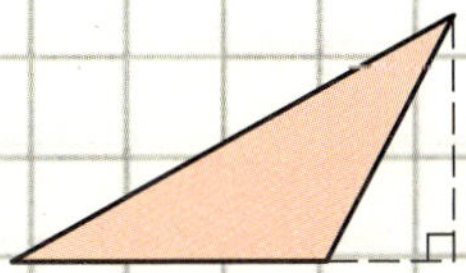

*The height of a triangle is the perpendicular distance from the vertex to the base.

Trapezoid

The area, A, of a trapezoid with bases b and B and height h is

$$A = \frac{1}{2}h(b + B)$$

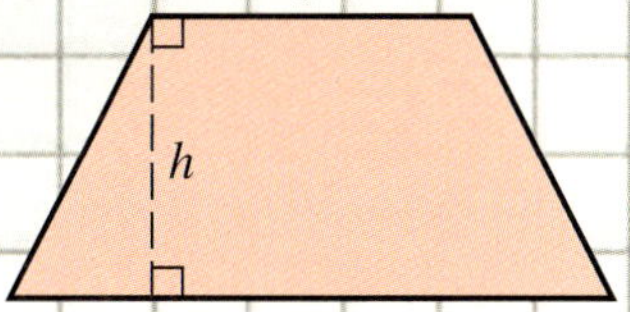

Circle

The area, A, of a circle with radius r is

$$A = \pi r^2$$

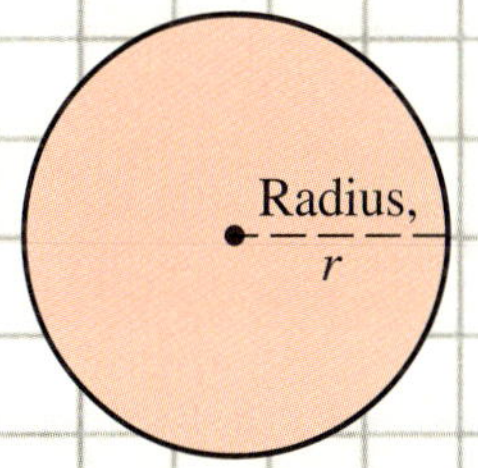

STOP *You will need these formulas not only for this text, but also for real-world problems.*

as shown in Figure 4.44. If we use the distributive property, we obtain the area formula for a trapezoid.

Figure 4.44 Trapezoid

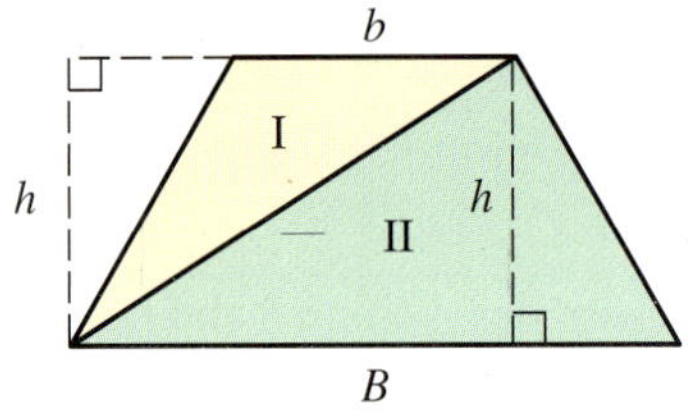

Area of triangle I: $\frac{1}{2}bh$

Area of triangle II: $\frac{1}{2}Bh$

Total area: $\frac{1}{2}bh + \frac{1}{2}Bh$

Circles

The last of our area formulas is for the area of a circle. Historically, we know from the Rhind papyrus that the Egyptians knew of the formula for the area of a circle. We state this formula using modern notation.

Even though it is beyond the scope of this course to derive a formula for the area of a circle, we can give a geometric justification that may appeal to your intuition.

Consider a circle with radius r:

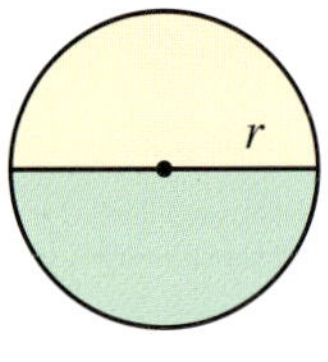

$C = 2\pi r$

Fit these two pieces together:

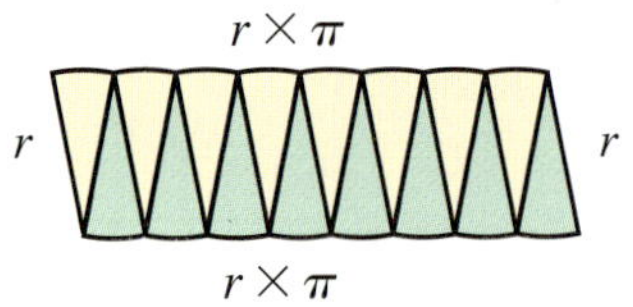

Therefore, it looks as if the area of a circle of radius r is about the same as the area of a rectangle of length πr and width r—that is, πr^2.

Cut the circle in half:

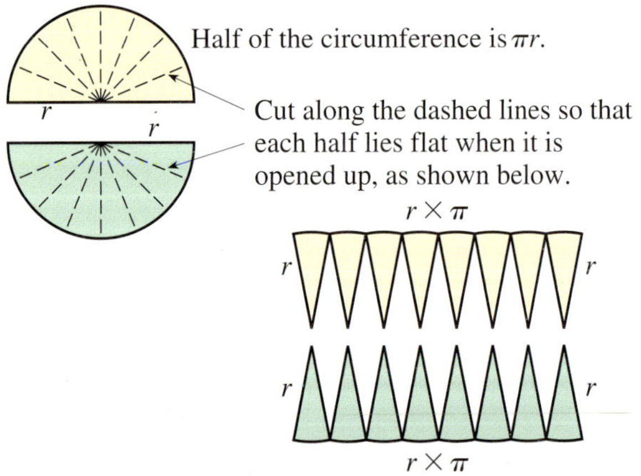

Acres

If the area is large, as with property, a larger unit is needed. This unit is called an acre. An **acre** is 43,560 ft^2. This definition leads us to a procedure for changing square feet to acres. To convert square feet to acres, divide by 43,560.

For simplicity, real estate brokers estimate an acre as 200 ft by 200 ft or 40,000 ft^2.

4.6 Surface Area, Volume, and Capacity

IN THIS SECTION WE COMPLETE OUR TRILOGY OF DIMENSIONS BY LOOKING AT A *THREE-DIMENSIONAL MEASUREMENT*.

We have considered length (a *one-dimensional measurement*, say back and forth), area (a *two-dimensional measurement*, say back/forth and up/down). Now, the measurement of volume has a third direction of measurement: back/forth; up/down; in/out. Before we consider volume, we begin by measuring the surface area of three dimensional objects, and after considering volume, we measure the contents of a three-dimensional object.

Surface Area

Suppose you wish to paint a box whose edges are each 3 ft, and you need to know how much paint to buy. To determine this you need to find the sum of the areas of all the faces—this is called the **surface area**. Find the amount of paint needed for a box with edges 3 ft.

A box (cube) has 6 faces of equal area.

Number of faces of cube

$6 \times 9 \text{ ft}^2 = 54 \text{ ft}^2$

Area of each face

You need enough paint to cover 54 ft^2.

Some boxes have tops and others are open at the top. Note that the above box has a top. The soup can pictured below has a lid, but how would we find the surface area if we popped the top and removed it?

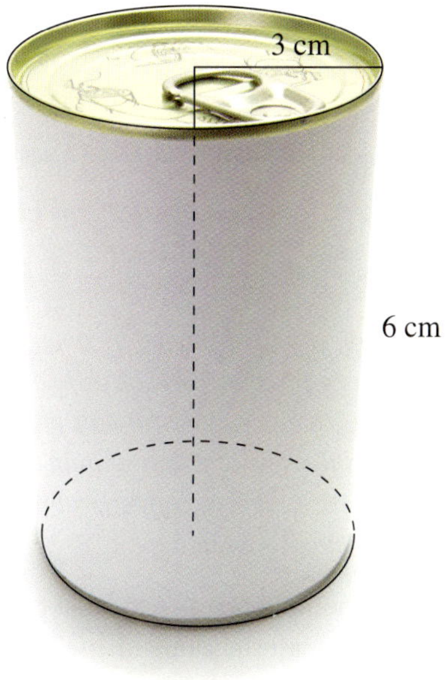

To find the surface area, find the area of a circle (the bottom) and think of the sides of the can as being "rolled out." The length of the resulting rectangle is the circumference of the can and the width of the rectangle is the height of the can.

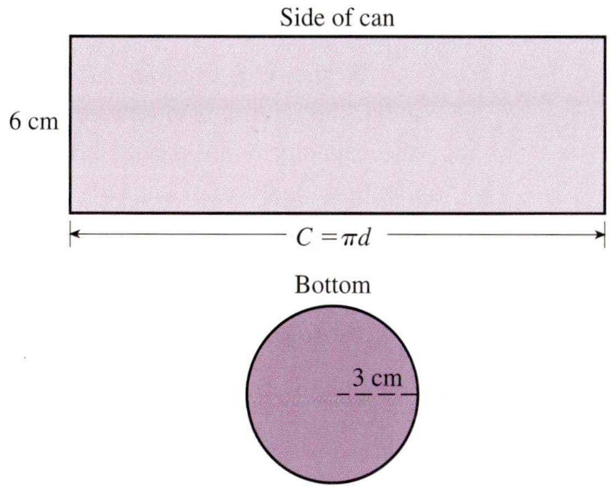

Side: $A = \ell w = (\pi d)w - \pi(6)(6) = 36\pi$

Bottom: $A = \pi r^2 = \pi(3)^2 = 9\pi$

Surface area: $36\pi + 9\pi = 45\pi \approx 141.37167$

The surface area is about 141 cm^2.

Volume

To measure area, we covered a region with square units and then found the area by using a mathematical formula. A similar procedure is used to find the amount of space inside a solid object, which is called its **volume**. We can imagine filling the space with **cubes**. A **cubic inch** and a **cubic centimeter** are shown in Figure 4.45.

Figure 4.45 Cubic units used for measuring volume

a. 1 cubic inch (1 cu in. or 1 in.^{3})

b. 1 cubic centimeter (1 cu cm, cc, or 1 cm^3)

Volume of a Cube

The volume, V, of a cube with edge s is

$$V = s^3.$$

If the solid is not a cube but is a box with edges of different lengths (called a **rectangular parallelepiped**), the volume can be found similarly.

VOLUME OF A BOX

The volume V of a box (parallelepiped) with edges ℓ, w, and h is

$$V = \ell wh$$

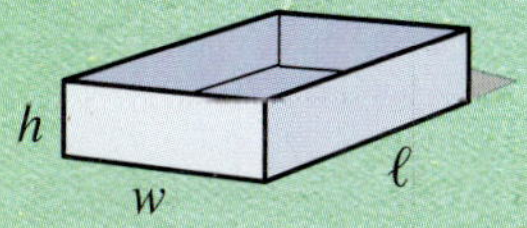

Capacity

One of the most common applications of volume involves measuring the amount of liquid a container holds, which we refer to as its **capacity**. For example, if a container is 2 ft by 2 ft by 12 ft, it is fairly easy to calculate the volume:

$$2 \times 2 \times 12 = 48 \text{ ft}^3$$

But this still doesn't tell us how much water the container holds. The capacities of a can of cola, a bottle of milk, an aquarium tank, the gas tank in your car, and a swimming pool can all be measured by the amount of fluid they can hold.

Standard Capacity Units

U.S. System	Metric System
gallon (gal)	**liter (L)**
ounce (oz, $\frac{1}{128}$ gal.)	kiloliter (kl, 1,000 L)
cup (c, 8 oz)	milliliter (ml, $\frac{1}{1,000}$ L)
quart (qt, $\frac{1}{4}$ gal, 32 oz)	

Most containers of liquid that you buy have capacities stated in both milliliters and ounces, or quarts and liters (see Figure 4.46).

Figure 4.46 Standard capacities

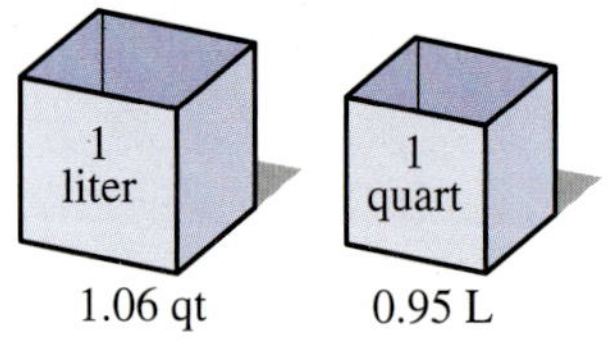

Some capacity statements from purchased products are listed in Table 4.3. The U.S. Bureau of Alcohol, Tobacco, and Firearms has made metric bottle sizes for liquor mandatory, so the half-pint, fifth, and quart have been replaced by 200-ml, 750-ml, and 1-L sizes. A typical dose of cough medicine is 5 ml, and 1 kl is 1,000 L, or about the amount of water one person would use for all purposes in two or three days.

Table 4.3 Capacities of Common Grocery Items, as Shown on Labels

Item	U.S. Capacity	Metric Capacity
Milk	**$\frac{1}{2}$ gal**	1.89 L
Milk	1.06 qt	**1 L**
Budweiser	**12 oz**	355 ml
Coke	67.6 oz	**2 L**
Hawaiian Punch	**1 qt**	0.95 L
Del Monte pickles	1 pt 6 oz	**651 ml**

WATCH YOUR STEP *You should remember some of these references for purposes of estimation. For example, remember that a can of Coke is 355 ml, and the size of a liter of milk is about the same as a quart of milk. A cup of coffee is about 300 ml and a spoonful of medicine is about 5 ml.*

Since it is common practice to label capacities in both U.S. and metric measuring units, it will generally not be necessary for you to make conversions from one system to another. But if you do, it is easy to remember that a liter is just a little larger than a quart, just as a meter is a little larger than a yard. To measure capacity, you use a measuring cup.

Some common relationships among volume and capacity measurements in the U.S. system are shown in Figure 4.47 to the left.

Figure 4.47 U.S. measurement relationship between volume and capacity

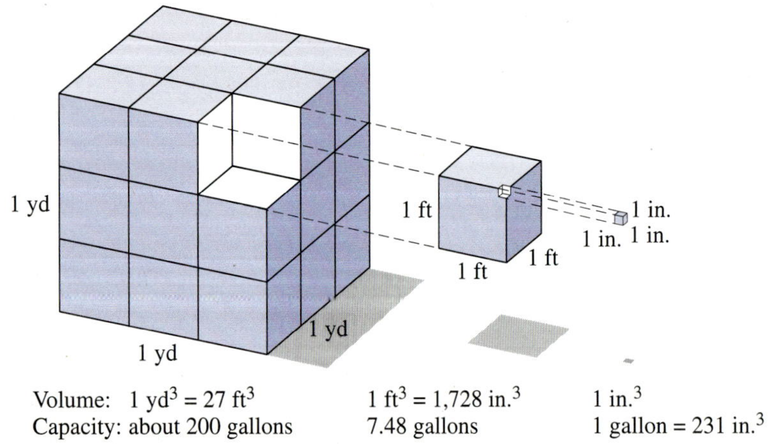

In the U.S. system of measurement, the relationship between volume and capacity is not particularly convenient. One gallon of capacity occupies 231 in^3.

To find the capacity of the 2-ft by 2-ft by 12-ft box mentioned earlier, we must change 48 ft^3 to cubic inches:

Estimate: Since $1 \text{ ft}^3 \approx 7.5$ gal,
$48 \text{ ft}^3 \approx 50 \text{ ft}^3$
$\approx (50 \times 7.5)$ gal
≈ 375 gal

$$\begin{aligned} 48 \text{ ft}^3 &= 48 \times (1 \text{ ft}) \times (1 \text{ ft}) \times (1 \text{ ft}) \\ &= 48 \times 12 \text{ in.} \times 12 \text{ in.} \times 12 \text{ in.} \\ &= 82{,}944 \text{ in.}^3 \end{aligned}$$

A calculator would help here.

Since 1 gallon is 231 in^3, the final step is to divide 82,944 by 231 to obtain approximately 359 gallons.

The relationship between volume and capacity in the metric system is easier to remember. One cubic centimeter is one-thousandth of a liter. Notice that this is the same as a milliliter. For this reason, you will sometimes see cc used to mean cm^3 or ml. These relationships are shown in Figure 4.48.

Figure 4.48 Metric measurement relationship between volume and capacity

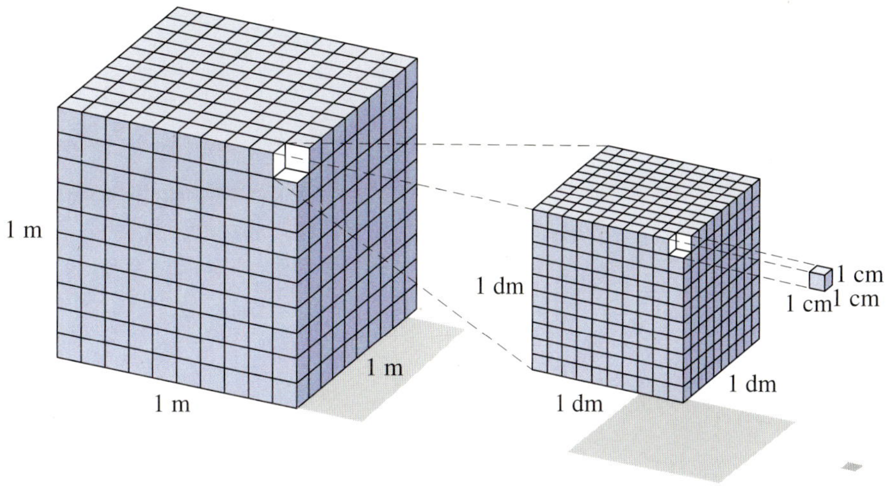

Volume: $1\text{ m}^3 = 1{,}000\text{ dm}^3$ | $1\text{ dm}^3 = 1{,}000\text{ cm}^3$ | $1\text{ cm}^3 = 1\text{ cc}$

Capacity: 1,000 L = 1 kl | 1 L = 1,000 ml | 1 ml = 1 cc

Relationship between Volume and Capacity

Chapter 5

The Nature of Networks

5.1 Euler Circuits and Hamiltonian Cycles

WE NOW TURN TO ONE OF THE NEWER BRANCHES OF GEOMETRY KNOWN AS *GRAPH THEORY*, WHICH INCLUDES *CIRCUITS*, *CYCLES*, AND *TREES*.

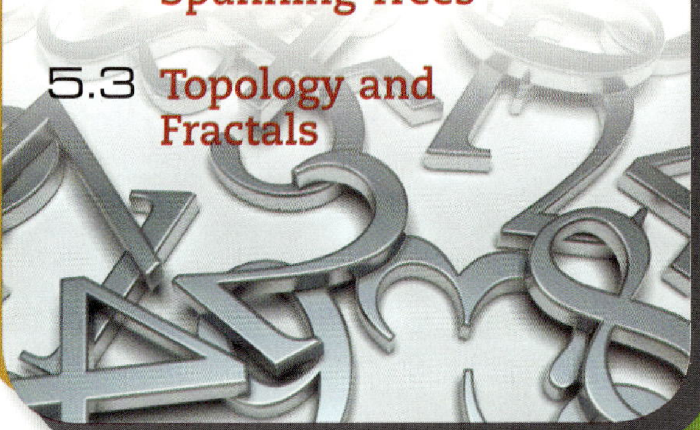

topics

Euler Circuits

In the 18th century, in the German town of Königsberg (now a Russian city), a popular pastime was to walk along the bank of the Pregel River and cross over some of the seven bridges that connected two islands, as shown in Figure 5.1.

One day a native asked a neighbor this question: "How can you take a walk so that you cross each of our seven bridges once and only once and

end up where you started?" The problem intrigued the neighbor, and soon caught the interest of many other people of Königsberg as well. Whenever people tried it, they ended up either not crossing a bridge at all or else crossing one bridge twice. This problem was brought to the attention of the Swiss mathematician Leonhard Euler, who was serving at the court of the Russian empress Catherine the Great in St. Petersburg. The method of solution we discuss here was first developed by Euler, and it led to the development of two major topics in geometry. The first is *networks*, which we discuss in this

Figure 5.1 Königsberg bridges

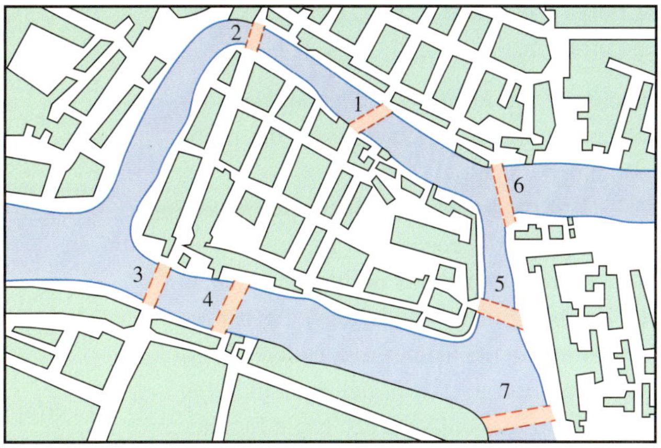

section, and the second is *topology*, which we discuss in Section 5.3.

We will use Pólya's problem-solving method for the Königsberg bridge problem.

STEP 1 ***Understand the Problem.*** To understand the problem, Euler began by drawing a diagram for the problem, as shown in Figure 5.2a below.

Next, Euler used one of the great problem-solving procedures—namely, to change the conceptual mode. That is, he **let the land area be represented as points (sometimes called *vertices* or *nodes*), and let the bridges be represented by arcs or line segments (sometimes called *edges*) connecting the given points.** As part of understanding the problem, we can do what Euler did—we can begin by tracing a diagram like the one shown in Figure 5.2b.

STEP 2 ***Devise a Plan.*** To solve the bridge problem, we need to draw the figure without lifting the pencil from the paper. Figures similar to the one in Figure 5.2b are called **networks** or **graphs**. In a network, the points where the line segments meet (or cross) are called **vertices**, and the lines representing bridges are called **edges** or **arcs**. Each separated part of the plane formed by a network is called a **region**. We say that a graph is **connected** if there is at least one path between each pair of vertices.

A network is said to be **traversable** if it can be traced in one sweep without lifting the pencil from the paper and without tracing the same edge more than once. Vertices may be passed through more than once. The **degree** of a vertex is the number of edges that meet at that vertex.

First, note that *the sum of the degrees of the vertices equals twice the number of edges*. Do you see why this must always be true? Consider any graph. Each edge must be connected at both ends, so the sum of all of those ends must be twice the number of vertices.

Now, consider a second observation regarding traversability. You might begin by actually tracing out some simple networks. However, a more complicated network, such as the Königsberg bridge problem, will require some analysis. The goal is to begin at some vertex, travel on each edge exactly once, and then return to the starting vertex. Such a path is called an **Euler circuit**. We can now rephrase the Königsberg bridge problem: "Does the network in Figure 5.2 have an Euler circuit?"

To answer this question, we will follow Euler's lead and classify vertices. Vertex A in Figure 5.2 is degree 3, so the vertex A is called an **odd vertex**. In the same way, D is an odd vertex, because it is degree 5. A vertex with even degree is called an **even vertex**. Euler discovered that only a certain number of odd vertices can exist in any network if you are to travel it in one journey without retracing any edge. You may start at any vertex and end at any other vertex, as long as you travel the entire network. Also, the network must connect each point (this is called a **connected network**).

Let's examine networks more carefully and look for a pattern, as shown in Table 5.1.

We see that, if the vertex is odd, then it must be a starting point or an ending point. What is the largest number of starting and ending points in any network? [*Answer*: Two—one starting point and one ending point.] This discussion allows us to now formulate the step we have called **devise a plan**, which we now state without proof. How did we get to that conclusion so quickly? By counting the number of odd vertices. You can see how this works in the box on the next page.

© Andrew Johnson/iStockphoto.com / © Interfoto/Alamy

DEPARTURE

ARRIVAL

Figure 5.2 Königsberg bridge problem

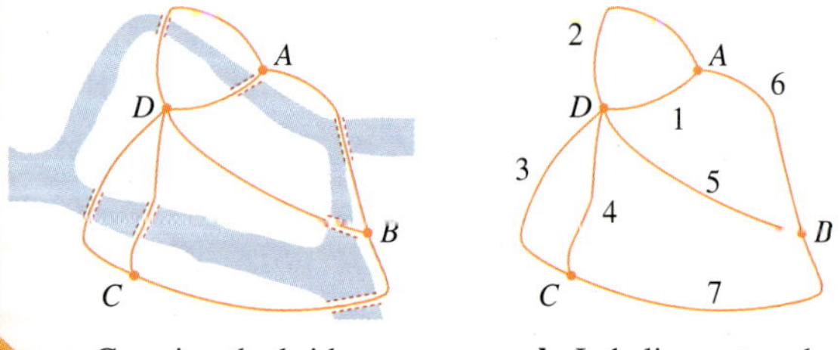

a. Crossing the bridges **b.** Labeling network

Table 5.1 Arrivals and Departures for Networks

Number of Arcs	Description	Possibilities
1	1 departure (starting point) 1 arrival (ending point)	
2	1 arrival (arrive then depart) and I departure (depart then arrive)	
3	1 arrival, 2 departures 2 arrivals, 1 departure	
4	2 arrivals, 2 departures	
5	2 arrivals, 3 departures (starting point) 3 arrivals, 2 departures (ending point)	

STEP 3 ***Carry Out the Plan.*** Classify the vertices; there are four odd vertices, so the network is not traversable.

Counting the number of odd vertices:

0 If there are no odd vertices, the network is traversable and any point may be a starting point. The point selected will also be the ending point.

1 If there is one odd vertex, the network is not traversable. A network cannot have only one starting or ending point without the other.

2 If there are two odd vertices, the network is traversable; one odd vertex must be a starting point and the other odd vertex must be the ending point.

2+ If there are more than two odd vertices, the network is not traversable. A network cannot have more than one starting point and one ending point.

Euler's Circuit Theorem

Every vertex on a graph with an Euler circuit has an even degree, and, conversely, if in a connected graph every vertex has an even degree, then the graph has an Euler circuit.

STEP 4 ***Look Back.*** We have solved the Königsberg bridge problem, but you should note that saying it cannot be done is not the same thing as saying "I can't do the problem." We can do the problem, and the solution is certain.

We summarize this investigation.

Applications of Euler Circuits

Euler circuits have a wide variety of applications. We will mention a few.

- *Supermarket problem* Set up the shelves in a market or convenience store so that it is possible to enter the store at the door and travel in each aisle exactly once (once and only once) and leave by the same door.
- *Police patrol problem* Suppose a police car needs to patrol a gated subdivision and would like to enter the gate, cruise all the streets exactly once, and then leave by the same gate.
- *Floor-plan problem* Suppose you have a floor plan of a building with a security guard who needs to go through the building and lock each door at the end of the day.
- *Water-pipe problem* Suppose you have a network of water pipes, and you wish to inspect the pipeline. Can you pass your hand over each pipe exactly once without lifting your hand from a pipe, and without going over some pipe a second time?

We will examine one of these applications and leave the others for the problem set. Let's look at the *floor-plan problem*. This problem, which is related to the Königsberg bridge problem, involves taking a trip through all the rooms and passing through each door only once. There is, however, one important difference between these two problems. The Königsberg bridge problem requires an Euler circuit, but the floor-plan problem does not. In other words, with the bridges we must end up where we started, but the floor plan problem seeks only traversability. Let's draw a floor-plan problem as shown in Figure 5.3a below.

Label the rooms as *A*, *B*, *C*, *D*, *E*, and *F*. In Figure 5.3a, rooms *A*, *C*, *E*, and *F* have two doors, and rooms *B* and *D* have three doors; in Figure 5.3b, it looks as if there are five rooms, but since there are doors that lead to the "outside," we must count the outside as a room. So this figure also has six rooms labeled *A*, *B*, *C*, *D*, *E*, and *F*. Rooms *A*, *B*, and *C* each have 5 doors, rooms *D* and *E* each have 4 doors, and room *F* has 9 doors.

Make a conjecture about the solution to the floor-plan problem. If there are no rooms with an odd number of doors, then it will be traversable. If there are two rooms

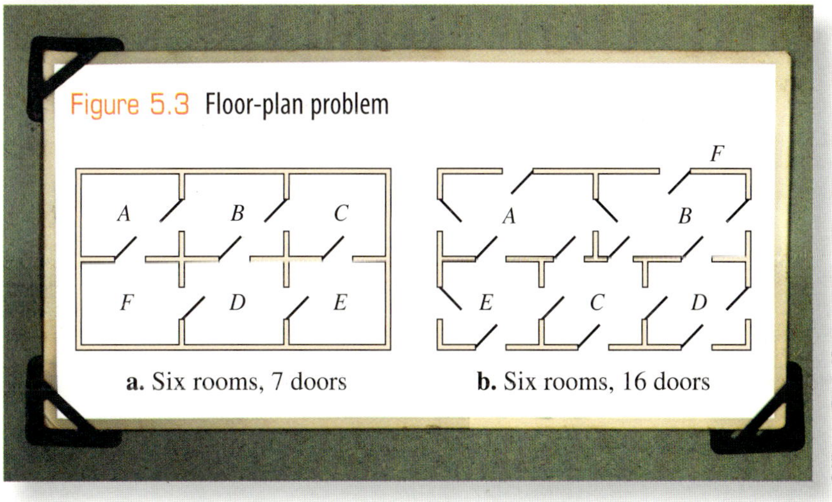

Figure 5.3 Floor-plan problem

a. Six rooms, 7 doors **b.** Six rooms, 16 doors

with an odd number of doors, then it will be traversable: Start in one of those rooms, and end up in the other.

Hamiltonian Cycles

One application that cannot be solved using Euler circuits is the so-called **traveling salesperson problem**: A salesperson starts at home and wants to visit several cities without going through any city more than once, and then return to the starting city. This problem is so famous with so many people working on its solution that it is often referred to in the literature as **TSP**. The salesperson would like to do this in the most efficient way (that is, least distance, least time, smallest cost, . . .). To answer this question, we reverse the roles of the vertices and edges of an Euler circuit. Now, we ask whether we can visit each vertex exactly once and end at the original vertex. Such a path is called a **Hamiltonian cycle**.

Find a Hamiltonian cycle for the network in Figure 5.4.

Figure 5.4 Network

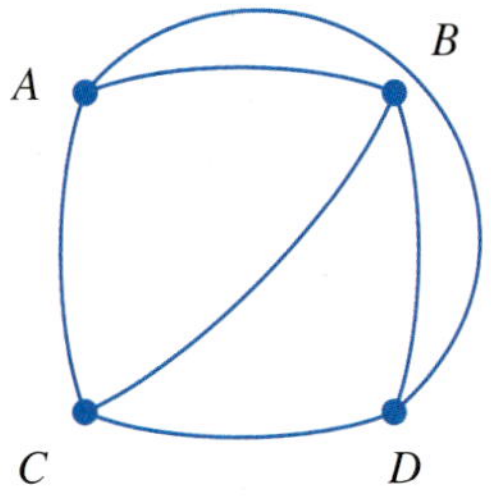

We found that there was *not* an Euler circuit for this network. On the other hand, it is easy to find a Hamiltonian cycle:

$$A \rightarrow C \rightarrow B \rightarrow D \rightarrow A$$

Use Figure 5.5 to decide if the given cycle is Hamiltonian. If it is not, tell why.

It seems as if the problem of deciding whether a network has a Hamiltonian cycle should have a solution similar to that of the Euler circuit problem, but such is not the case. In fact, no solution is known at this time, and it is one of the great unsolved problems of mathematics. In this book, the best we will be able to do is a trial-and-error solution. If you are interested in seeing some of the different attempts at finding a solution to this problem, visit www.mathnature.com.

We conclude this section with an example. A salesman wants to visit four California cities: San Francisco, Sacramento, San Jose, and Fresno. Driving distances are shown in Figure 5.6. What is the shortest trip starting and ending in San Francisco that visits each of these cities?

Since the best we can do is to offer some possible methods of attack, we will use this example to help build

Figure 5.5 Network with 6 vertices

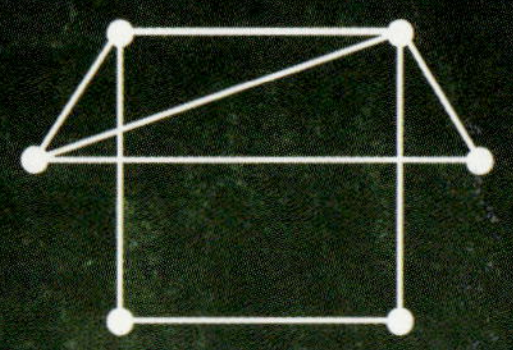

a. $A \rightarrow B \rightarrow C \rightarrow D \rightarrow A$; This is not a Hamiltonian cycle because it does not visit each vertex.
b. $C \rightarrow D \rightarrow A \rightarrow B \rightarrow F \rightarrow E \rightarrow A$; This is not a Hamiltonian cycle because it does not return to the starting point.
c. $D \rightarrow C \rightarrow B \rightarrow A \rightarrow E \rightarrow F$; This is not a Hamiltonian cycle because it does not return to the starting point.
d. $F \rightarrow E \rightarrow B \rightarrow F \rightarrow E \rightarrow B \rightarrow F$; This is not a Hamiltonian cycle because it does not visit each vertex, but repeats the same vertices, which is sometimes called a **loop**.
e. $B \rightarrow C \rightarrow D \rightarrow A \rightarrow E \rightarrow F \rightarrow B$; This is a Hamiltonian cycle.

Figure 5.6 TSP for four cities

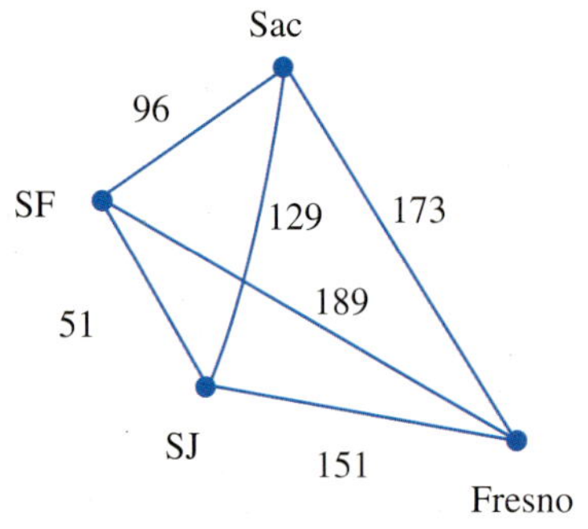

your problem-solving skills. We use Pólya's problem-solving guidelines for this example.

STEP 1 ***Understand the Problem.*** Part of understanding the problem is to decide what we mean by the "best" solution. For this problem, let us assume it is the least miles traveled. We also note that, in terms of miles traveled, each route and its reverse are equivalent. That is,

SF → San Jose → Fresno → Sacramento → SF

is the same as

SF → Sacramento → Fresno → San Jose → SF

STEP 2 ***Devise a Plan.*** There are several possible methods of attack for this problem: *brute force* (listing all possible routes); *nearest neighbor* (at each city, go to the nearest neighbor which has not been previously visited); sometimes the nearest-neighbor plan will form a loop without going to some city, so we repair this problem using a method called the *sorted-edge method.* In the sorted-edge method, we sort the choices by selecting the nearest neighbor that does not form a loop.

STEP 3 ***Carry Out the Plan.***

Brute force:

$\text{SF} \xrightarrow{96} \text{S} \xrightarrow{173} \text{F} \xrightarrow{151} \text{SJ} \xrightarrow{51} \text{SF}$ Total: 471 miles

$\text{SF} \xrightarrow{96} \text{S} \xrightarrow{129} \text{SJ} \xrightarrow{151} \text{F} \xrightarrow{189} \text{SF}$ Total: 565 miles

$\text{SF} \xrightarrow{51} \text{SJ} \xrightarrow{129} \text{S} \xrightarrow{173} \text{F} \xrightarrow{189} \text{SF}$ Total: 542 miles

Here are the reverse trips (so we don't need to calculate these).

$\text{SF} \to \text{SJ} \to \text{F} \to \text{S} \to \text{SF}$

$\text{SF} \to \text{F} \to \text{SJ} \to \text{S} \to \text{SF}$

$\text{SF} \to \text{F} \to \text{S} \to \text{SJ} \to \text{SF}$

We see that 471 is the minimum number of miles.

Nearest neighbor:

$\text{SF} \xrightarrow{51} \text{SJ} \xrightarrow{129} \text{S} \xrightarrow{96} \text{SF}$ A loop is formed; Fresno is not included because it is never the nearest neighbor if we start in San Francisco.

Sorted edge:

For this method, we sort the distances (edges of the graph) from smallest to largest: 51, 96, 129, 151, 173, and 189. This gives the following trip (skipping 96 and 151 because these choices would form a loop):

$\text{SF} \xrightarrow{51} \text{SJ} \xrightarrow{129} \text{S} \xrightarrow{173} \text{F} \xrightarrow{189} \text{SF}$ Total: 542 miles

STEP 4 ***Look Back.*** With this simple problem, it is easy to see that the best overall solution is a trip with 471 miles, but as you can imagine, for a larger number of cities the solution may not be obvious at all.

We summarize the **sorted-edge method** for finding an approximate solution to a traveling salesperson problem.

The sorted-edge method may not produce the optimal solution, so you should also check other methods.

PROCEDURE: Sorted-Edge Method

Draw a graph showing the cities and the distances; identify the starting vertex.

STEP 1 Choose the edge attached to the starting vertex that has the shortest distance or the lowest cost. Travel along this edge to the next vertex.

STEP 2 At the second vertex, travel along the edge with the shortest distance or lowest cost. Do not choose a vertex that would lead to a vertex already visited.

STEP 3 Continue until all vertices are visited until arriving back at the original vertex.

5.2 Trees and Minimum Spanning Trees

IN THE LAST SECTION, WE CONSIDERED GRAPHS WITH CIRCUITS.

An Euler circuit (which is a round-trip path traveling all the edges) and a Hamiltonian cycle (a path that visits each vertex exactly once).

Recall that circuits are paths or routes that begin and end at the same vertex. In this section, we'll examine another type of graph, without circuits, called a tree.

Trees

Let us begin with an example. Suppose you wish to draw a family tree showing yourself, your parents, and your maternal and paternal grandparents.

One possibility for showing this family tree is shown in Figure 5.7.

Figure 5.7 Personal family tree

The family tree shown in the example has two obvious properties. It is a **connected graph** because there is at least one path between each pair of vertices, and there are no circuits in this family tree. A simplified *tree* diagram for this example is shown below.

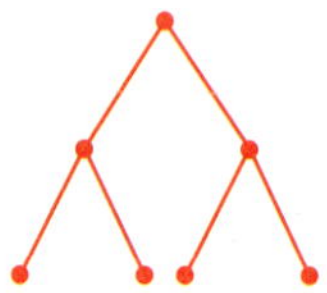

Simplified family tree

A **tree** is a graph that is connected and has no circuits.

In a tree, there is always exactly one path from each vertex in the graph to any other vertex in the graph. We illustrate this property of trees with the following example.

Ben wishes to install a sprinkler system to water the areas shown in Figure 5.8. Show how this might be done.

Figure 5.8 Locations of a faucet and sprinkler heads

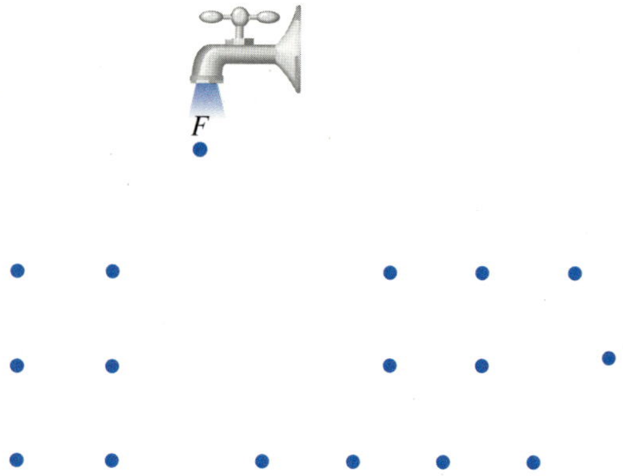

We know there is at least one way to build a tree from each vertex (in this case, the faucet, labeled *F*). We show one such way in Figure 5.9.

Figure 5.9 Sprinkler system

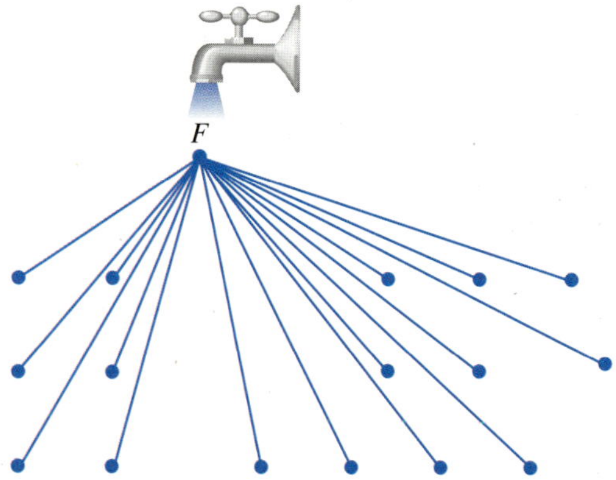

The solution shown for this example may or may not be an efficient solution to the sprinkler system problem. Suppose we connect the vertices in Figure 5.8 without regard to whether the graph is a tree, as shown in Figure 5.10a. Next, we remove edges until the resulting graph is a tree. A tree that is created from another graph by removing edges but keeping a path to each vertex is called a **spanning tree**. Can you form a spanning tree for the graph in Figure 5.10a? If you think about it for a moment, you will see that any connected graph will have a spanning tree, and that if the original graph has at least one circuit, then it will have several different spanning trees. Figure 5.10b shows a spanning tree for the sprinkler problem.

Figure 5.10 Comparison of a graph and spanning tree for the sprinkler problem

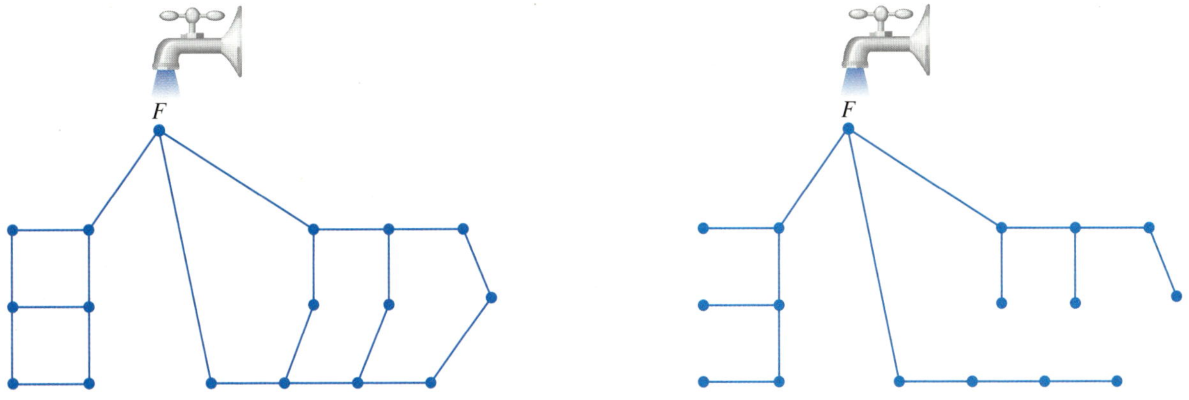

a. A graph **b.** A spanning tree

Minimum Spanning Trees

Sometimes the length of each edge in a spanning tree is associated with a cost or a length, called the edge's **weight**. In such cases we are often interested in minimizing the cost or the distance. If the edges of a graph have weight, then we refer to the graph as a **weighted graph**. When the number associated with the edges is a minimum, the tree is called a **minimum spanning tree**.

> A **minimum spanning tree** is a spanning tree for which the sum of the numbers associated with the edges is a minimum.

Figure 5.11 Portion of campus

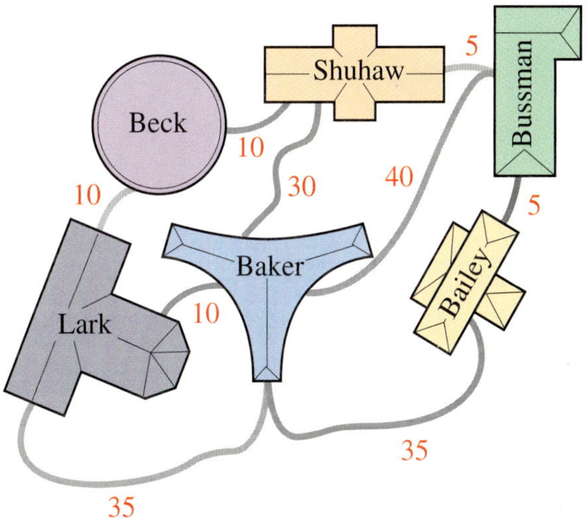

A portion of the Santa Rosa Junior College campus, along with some walkways (lengths shown in feet) connecting the buildings, is shown in Figure 5.11.

Suppose the decision is made to connect each building with a brick walkway, and the only requirement is that there be one brick walkway connecting each of the buildings. We assume that the cost of installing a brick walkway is \$100/ft. What is the minimum cost for this project?

We use Pólya's problem-solving guidelines for this example.

STEP 1 ***Understand the Problem.*** To make sure we understand the problem, we consider a simpler problem. Consider this sample graph with costs shown in color.

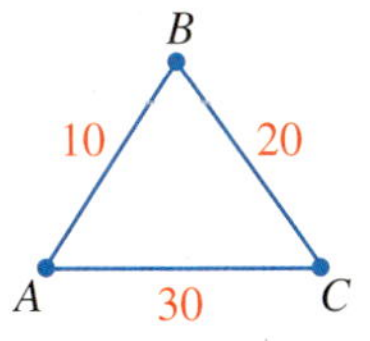

We consider the vertices to be buildings since the only requirement is that there be one brick walkway connecting each of the buildings. To find the best way to construct the walkways, we consider minimum spanning trees. Since this is a circuit, we can break this circuit in one of three ways: eliminate one of the sides, *AB*, *BC*, or *AC*.

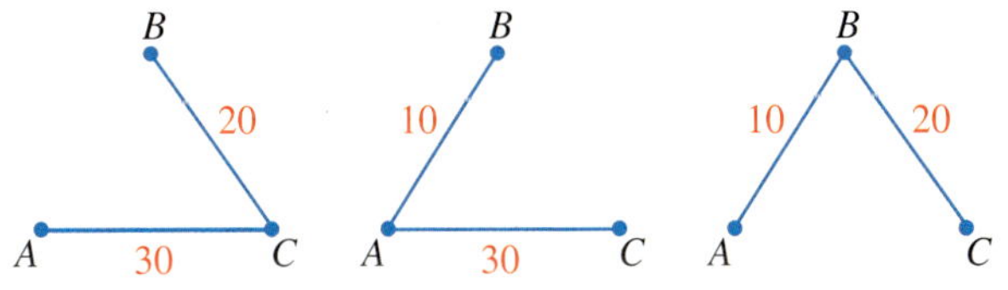

We see that the cost associated with each of these trees is:

$$20 + 30 = 50 \quad 10 + 30 = 40 \quad 10 + 20 = 30$$

The minimal cost for this simplified problem is 30.

STEP 2 ***Devise a Plan.*** We will carry out the steps for the Santa Rosa campus as follows: Look at Figure 5.11 and find the side with the smallest weight (because we wish to keep the smaller weights). We see there are two sides labeled 5; select either of these. Next, select a side with the smallest remaining weight (it is also 5). Continue by each time selecting the smallest remaining weight until every vertex is connected, but *do not select any edge that creates a circuit.*

STEP 3 ***Carry Out the Plan.*** Following this procedure, we select both of the edges labeled 5, as well as the three labeled 10. The resulting pathways are shown in Figure 5.12.

Figure 5.12 Minimum spanning tree

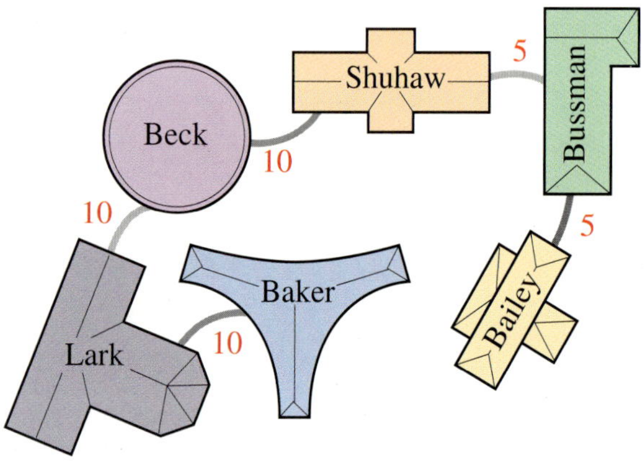

We see that the graph in Figure 5.12 is a minimum spanning tree, so the total distance is

$$5 + 5 + 10 + 10 + 10 = 40$$

with a total cost of

$$40 \times \$100 = \$4{,}000$$

STEP 4 ***Look Back.*** We can try other possible routes connecting all of the buildings, but in each case, the cost is more than $4,000.

The process used in this example illustrates a procedure called **Kruskal's algorithm** found in the box to the right.

The next example is adapted from a standardized test given in the United Kingdom in 1995.

A company is considering building a gas pipeline network to connect seven wells (*A, B, C, D, E, F, G*) to a processing plant *H*. The possible pipelines that it can construct and their costs (in thousands of dollars) are listed in the following table.

PROCEDURE:

Kruskal's Algorithm

To construct a minimum spanning tree from a weighted graph, use the following procedure:

STEP 1 Select any edge with minimum weight.

STEP 2 Select the next edge with minimum weight among those not yet selected.

STEP 3 Continue to choose edges of minimum weight from those not yet selected, but make sure not to select any edge that forms a circuit.

STEP 4 Repeat the process until the tree connects all the vertices of the original graph.

STOP *Pay attention to this procedure (algorithm).*

Pipeline	AB	AD	AE	BC	BE	BF	CG	DE	DF	EH	FG	FH
Cost	23	19	17	15	30	27	10	14	20	28	11	35

What pipelines do you suggest be built, and what is the total cost of your suggested pipeline network? Begin by drawing a graph to represent the data. This graph is shown in Figure 5.13.

Figure 5.13 Building a gas pipeline

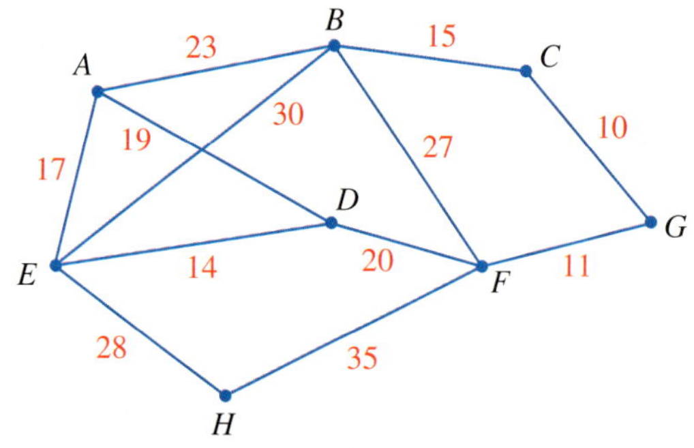

We now apply Kruskal's algorithm (in table form).

	Link	Cost	Decision
STEP 1	*CG*	10	Smallest value: add to tree
STEP 2	*FG*	11	Next smallest value; add to tree
STEP 3	*DE*	14	Add to tree; note that the graph does not need to be connected at this step.
	BC	15	Add to tree
	AE	17	Add to tree
	AD	19	Reject; it forms a circuit *ADE*
	DF	20	Add to tree
	AB	23	Reject; it forms a circuit *ABCGFDE*
	BF	27	Reject; it forms a circuit *BFGC*
STEP 4	*EH*	28	Add to tree; stop because all vertices are now included.

The completed minimal spanning tree is shown in Figure 5.14.

Figure 5.14 Minimal spanning tree for pipeline problem

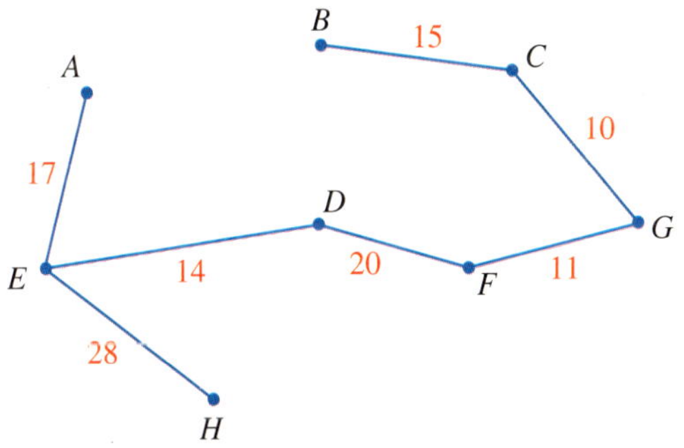

The minimal cost is

$$10 + 11 + 14 + 15 + 17 + 20 + 28 = 115$$

so the cost of the pipeline is $115,000.

Note in this example that there were eight given vertices, and that there were seven links added to form the minimal spanning tree. This is a general result.

Number-of-Vertices-and-Edges-in-a-Tree Theorem

If a graph is a tree with *n* vertices, then the number of edges is *n* − 1.

There is another related property that says the converse of this property holds for connected graphs. If the number of edges is one less than the number of vertices in a connected graph, then the graph is a tree.

5.3 Topology and Fractals

A BRIEF LOOK AT THE HISTORY OF GEOMETRY ILLUSTRATES, IN A VERY GRAPHICAL WAY, THE HISTORICAL EVOLUTION OF MANY MATHEMATICAL IDEAS AND THE NATURE OF CHANGES IN MATHEMATICAL THOUGHT.

The geometry of the Greeks included very concrete notions of space and geometry. They considered space to be a locus in which objects could move freely about, and their geometry, known as Euclidean geometry, was a geometry of congruence. In this section we investigate two very different branches of geometry that question, or alter, the way we think of space and dimension.

THE GOLDEN AGE OF MATHEMATICS—THAT WAS NOT THE AGE OF EUCLID, IT IS OURS.

Topology

In the 17th century, space came to be conceptualized as a set of points, and, with the non-Euclidean geometries of the 19th century, mathematicians gave up the notion that geometry had to describe the physical universe. The existence of multiple geometries was accepted, but space was still thought of as a geometry of congruence. The emphasis shifted to sets, and geometry was studied as a mathematical system. Space could be conceived as a set of points together with an abstract set of relations in which these points are involved. The time was right for geometry to be considered as the theory of such a space, and in 1895 Jules Henri Poincaré published a book using this notion of space and geometry in a systematic development. This book was called *Vorstudien zur Topologie* (*Introductory Studies in Topology*). However, topology was not the invention of any one person, and the names of Cantor, Euler, Fréchet, Hausdorff, Möbius, and Riemann are associated with the origins of **topology**. Today it is a broad and fundamental branch of mathematics.

To obtain an idea about the nature of topology, consider a device called a *geoboard*, which you may have used in elementary school. Suppose we stretch one rubber band over the pegs to form a square and another to form a triangle, as shown in Figure 5.15.

In high school geometry, the square and the triangle in Figure 5.15 would be seen as different. However, in topology, these figures are viewed as the same object. Topology is concerned with discovering and analyzing the essential similarities and differences between sets and figures. One important idea is called *elastic motion*, which includes bending, stretching, shrinking, or distorting the figure in any way that allows the points to remain distinct. It does not include cutting a figure unless we "sew up" the cut *exactly* as it was before.

Figure 5.15 Creating geometric figures with a geoboard

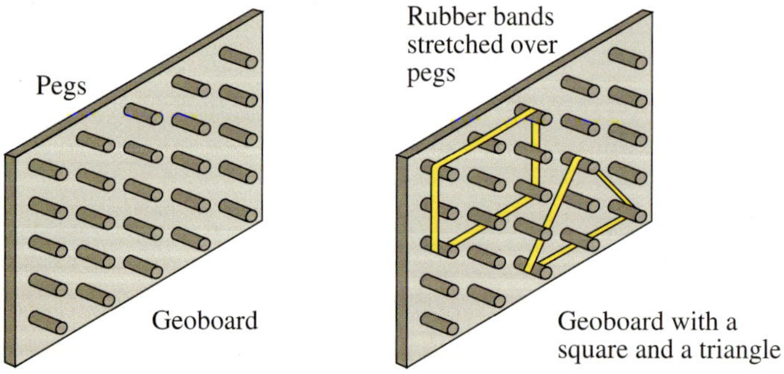

Two geometric figures are said to be **topologically equivalent** if one figure can be elastically twisted, stretched, bent, shrunk, or straightened into the same shape as the other. One can cut the figure, provided at some point the cut edges are "glued" back together again to be exactly the same as before.

For example, rubber bands can be stretched into a wide variety of shapes. All forms in Figure 5.16 are topologically equivalent. We say that a curve is **planar** if it lies flat in a plane.

All of the curves in Figure 5.16 are *planar simple closed curves*. A curve is **closed** if it divides the plane into three disjoint subsets: the set of points on the curve itself, the set of points *interior* to the curve, and the set of points *exterior* to the curve. It is said to be **simple** if it has only one interior. Sometimes a simple closed curve is called a **Jordan curve**. Notice that, to pass from a point in the interior to a point in the exterior, it is necessary to cross over the given curve an odd number of times. This property remains the same for any distortion, and is therefore called an *invariant* property.

Figure 5.16 Topologically equivalent curves

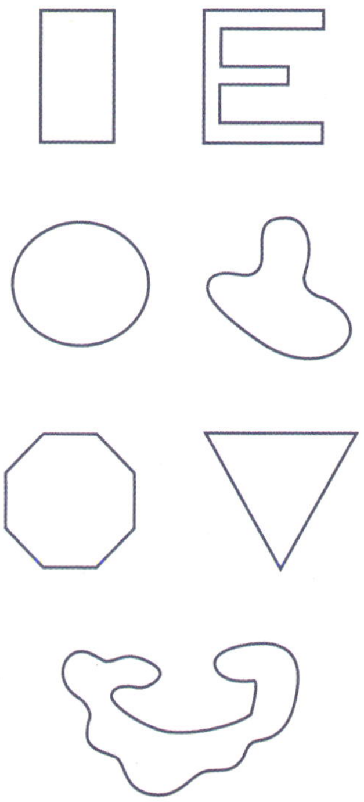

Figure 5.17 Genus of the surfaces of some everyday objects. Look at the number of holes in the objects.

Two-dimensional surfaces in a three-dimensional space are classified according to the number of cuts possible without slicing the object into two pieces. The number of cuts that can be made without cutting the figure into two pieces is called its **genus**. The genus of an object is the number of holes in the object (see Figure 5.17).

For example, no cut can be made through a sphere without cutting it into two pieces, so its genus is 0. In three dimensions, you can generally classify the genus of an object by looking at the number of holes the object has. A doughnut, for example, has genus 1 since it has 1 hole. In mathematical terms, we say it has genus 1 since only one closed cut can be made without dividing it into two pieces. All figures with the same genus are topologically equivalent. Figure 5.18 shows that a doughnut and a coffee cup are topologically equivalent, and Figure 5.19 shows objects of genus 0, genus 1, and genus 2.

Figure 5.18 A doughnut is topologically equivalent to a coffee cup.

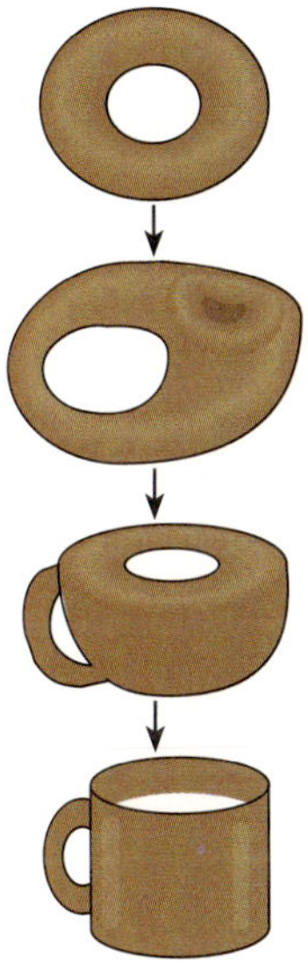

Courtesy of Karl J. Smith

The children and their distorted images are topologically equivalent.

Figure 5.19 Genus of a sphere, a doughnut, and a two-holed doughnut

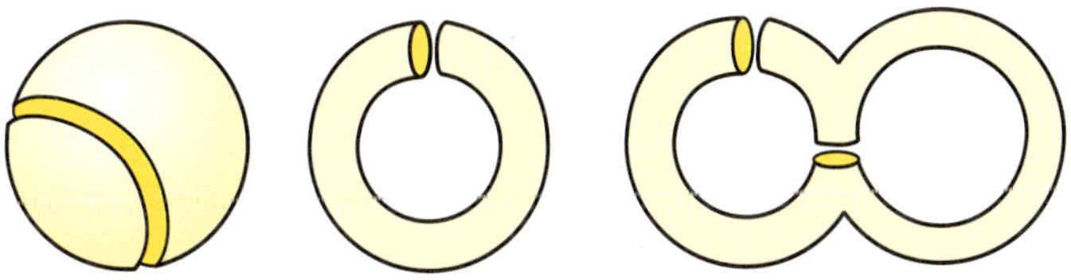

A sphere has genus 0.

A doughnut has genus 1.

Two holes allow two cuts, so this form has genus 2.

Figure 5.20 Every map can be colored with four colors.

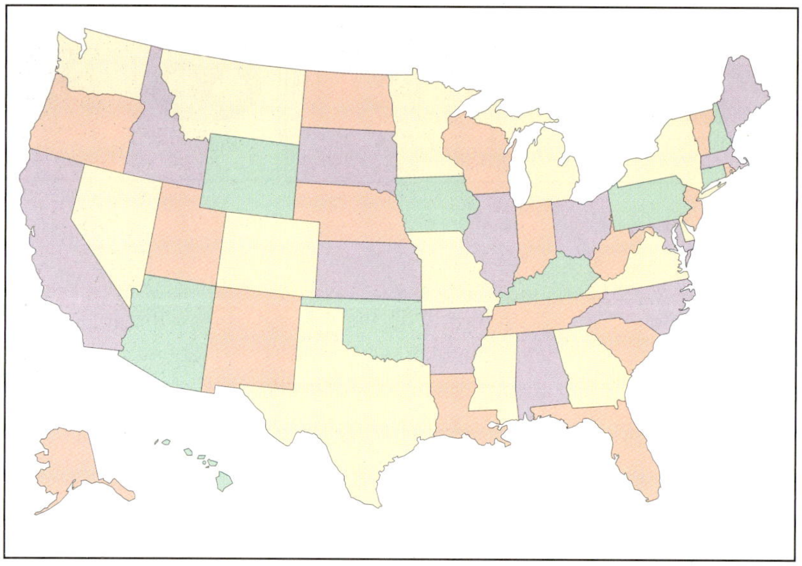

Four-Color Problem

One of the earliest and most famous problems in topology is the **four-color problem**. It was first stated in 1850 by the English mathematician Francis Guthrie. It states that any map on a plane or a sphere can be colored with at most four colors so that any two countries that share a common boundary are colored differently. (See Figure 5.20, for example.)

All attempts to prove this conjecture had failed until Kenneth Appel and Wolfgang Haken of the University of Illinois announced their proof in 1976. The university honored their discovery using the illustrated postmark.

Since the theorem was first stated, many unsuccessful attempts have been made to prove it. The first published "incorrect proof" is due to Kempe, who enumerated four cases and disposed of each. However, in 1990, an error was found in one of those cases, which it turned out could actually be divided into 1,930 subcases. Appel and Haken reduced the map to a graph as Euler did with the Königsberg bridge problem. They reduced each country to a point and used computers to check every possible arrangement of four colors for each case, requiring more than 1,200 hours of computer time to verify the proof.

Fractal Geometry

One of the newest and most exciting branches of mathematics is called **fractal geometry**. Fractals have been used recently to produce realistic computer images in the movies, and the new super crisp high-definition television (HDTV) uses fractals to squeeze the HDTV signal into existing broadcast channels. In February 1989, Iterated System, Inc., began marketing a $32,500 software package for creating models of biological systems from fractals. Today you can find hundreds of fractal generators online, most of them free.

Fractals were invented by Benoit B. Mandelbrot over 30 years ago, but have become important only in the last few years because of computers. Mandelbrot's first book on fractals appeared in 1975; in it he used computer graphics to illustrate the fractals. The book inspired Richard Voss, a physicist at IBM, to create stunning landscapes, earthly and otherworldly (see Figure 5.21). "Without computer graphics, this work could have been completely disregarded," Mandelbrot acknowledges.

What exactly is a fractal? We are used to describing the dimension of an object without having a precise definition: A point has 0 dimensions; a line, 1 dimension; a plane, 2 dimensions; and the world around us, 3 dimensions. We can even stretch our imagination to believe that Einstein used a four-dimensional model. However, what about a dimension of 1.5? Fractals allow us to define objects with non-integer dimension. For example, a jagged line is given a fractional dimension between 1 and 2, and the exact value is determined by the line's "jaggedness."

We will illustrate this concept by constructing the most famous fractal curve, the so-called "snowflake curve." Start with a line segment $\overline{AB}$:

Here we say the number of segments is $N = 1$; $r = 1$ is the length of this segment.

Divide this segment into thirds, by marking locations C and D:

$N = 3$; $r = \frac{1}{3}$ is the length of each segment.

Figure 5.21 Fractal images of a mountainscape (generated by Richard Voss) and a fern

Now construct an equilateral triangle $\triangle CED$ on the middle segment and then remove the middle segment $\overline{CD}$.

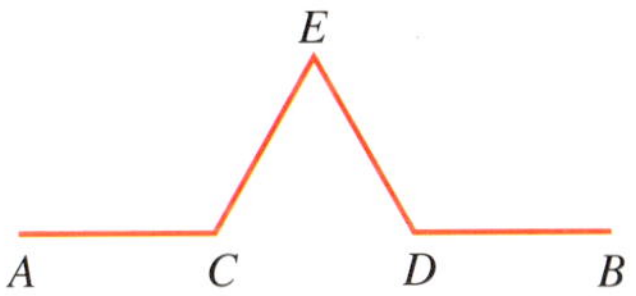

$N = 4; r = \frac{1}{3}$ is the length of each segment.

Now, repeat the above steps for each segment:

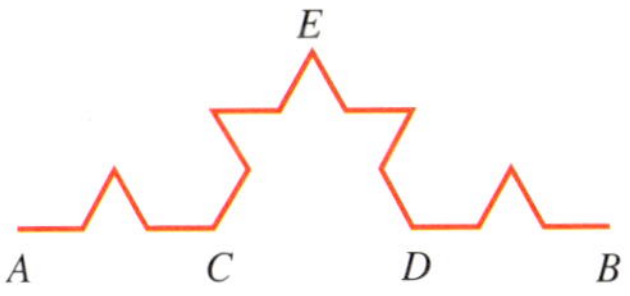

$N = 16$ segments, $r = \frac{1}{9}$

Again, repeat the process:

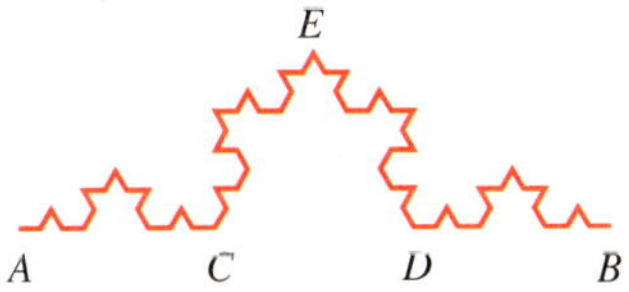

$N = 64, r = \frac{1}{27}$

If you repeat this process (until you reach any desired level of complexity), you have a fractal curve with dimension between 1 and 2.

The actual description of the dimension is more difficult to understand. Mandelbrot defined the dimension as follows:

$$D = \frac{\log N}{\log \frac{1}{r}}$$

where N is any integer and r is the length of each segment.*

For the illustrations to the left, we can calculate the dimension:

$N = 3,\ r = \frac{1}{3};\ D = 1$

$N = 4,\ r = \frac{1}{3};\ D \approx 1.26$

$N = 16,\ r = \frac{1}{9};\ D \approx 1.26$

$N = 64,\ r = \frac{1}{27};\ D \approx 1.26$

* Mandelbrot defined r as the ratio L/N, where L is the sum of the lengths of the N line segments. Logarithms are defined in most algebra courses, but at this point, it is not necessary that you understand this formula.

Tessellations

The construction of the snowflake curve reminds us of another interesting mathematical construction, called a **tessellation**. By skillfully altering a basic polygon (such as a triangle, rectangle, or hexagon), the artist Escher was able to produce artistic tessellations such as that shown in Figure 5.22.

We can describe a procedure for reproducing a simple tessellation based on the Escher print in Figure 5.22.

STEP 1 Start with an equilateral triangle $\triangle ABC$. Mark off the same curve on sides $\overline{AB}$ and $\overline{AC}$, as shown in Figure 5.23. Mark off another curve on side $\overline{BC}$ that is symmetric about the midpoint P. If you choose the curves carefully, as Escher did, an interesting figure suitable for tessellating will be formed.

Figure 5.23 Tessellation pattern

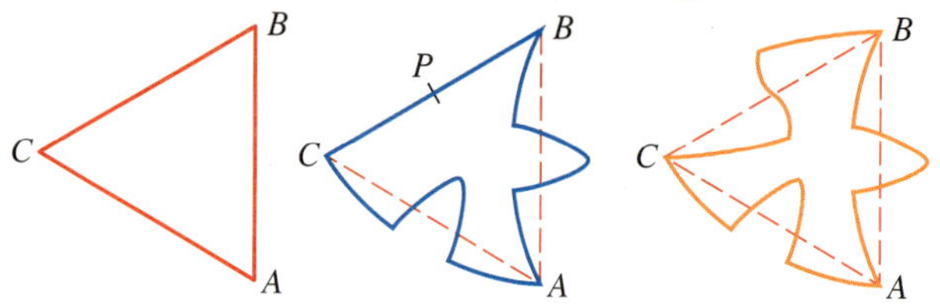

STEP 2 Six of these figures accurately fit together around a point, forming a hexagonal array (see Figure 5.24). If you trace and cut one of these basic figures, you can continue the tessellation over as large an area as you wish.

Figure 5.22 Escher print: *Circle Limit III*

Figure 5.24 Tessellation pattern

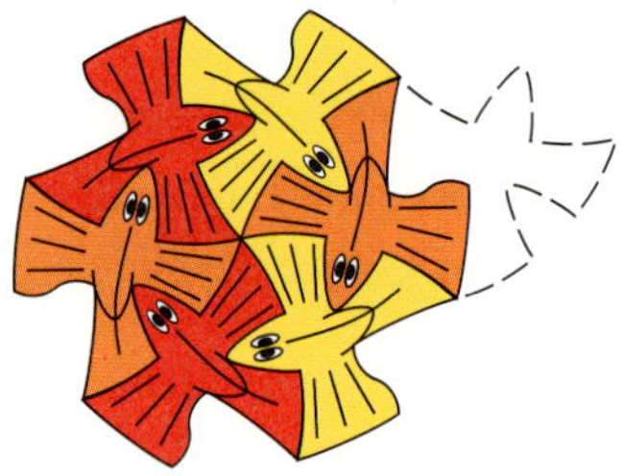

***remember**

Practice problems and homework for the concepts in this chapter are available online at 4ltrpress.cengage.com/math.

The Nature of Growth

topics

6.1 Exponential Equations

THE MEASUREMENT OF GROWTH AND DECAY OFTEN INVOLVES THE STUDY OF RELATIVELY LARGE OR RELATIVELY SMALL QUANTITIES.

The difficulties with scaling measurements are often of primary concern when describing and measuring figures and data. In this section, we investigate solving equations known as *exponential equations*. An equation of the form $b^x = N$ in which an unknown value is included as part of the exponent is called an **exponential equation**.

> An equation of the form $b^x = N$ in which an unknown value is included as part of the exponent is called an **exponential equation**.

An **exponential** is an expression of the form b^x; we begin by using a calculator to evaluate some exponentials. We have defined b^x for integer values of x, but in more advanced courses, b^x is defined for all real numbers. We will use a calculator to approximate these values. We will also frequently approximate two irrational numbers

$$\pi \approx 3.1416 \quad \text{and} \quad e \approx 2.7183$$

Using a calculator is essential when evaluating exponentials. We show the calculator steps on the next page.

Exponential

For any nonzero number b and any counting number n,

$$b^n = \underbrace{b \cdot b \cdot b \cdot \ldots \cdot b}_{n \text{ factors}}, \qquad b^0 = 1, \qquad b^{-n} = \frac{1}{b^n}$$

The number b is called the **base**, the number n in b^n is called the **exponent**, and the number b^n is called a **power** or **exponential.**

don't skip this example!

Test each of these on your calculator because these evaluations set the groundwork for the rest of this chapter. In other words, actually press keys on your own calculator to verify that you obtain what is shown here.

	Given	*Keys Pressed*	*Evaluation*	*Approximation*
a.	2^8	2 ^ 8 =	256 (exact)	256.00
b.	$3^{2.5}$	3 ^ 2.5 =	15.58845727	15.59
c.	$4^{\sqrt{2}}$	4 ^ √ 2 =	7.102993301	7.10
d.	π^3	π ^ 3 =	31.00627668	31.01
e.	e^2	e ^ 2 =	7.389056099	7.39
		Note: If you want to evaluate e, find e^1:		
		e ^ 1 =	2.718281828	2.72
f.	e^{π}	e ^ π =	23.14069263	23.14
g.	π^e	π ^ e =	22.45915772	22.46

Let's solve the exponential equation $2^x = 14$. To solve an equation means to find the replacement(s) for the variable that make the equation true. You might try certain values:

$x = 1$: $2^x = 2^1 = 2$ *Too small*
$x = 2$: $2^x = 2^2 = 4$ *Too small*
$x = 3$: $2^x = 2^3 = 8$ *Still too small*
$x = 4$: $2^x = 2^4 = 16$ *Too big*

It seems as if the number you are looking for is between 3 and 4. Our task in this section is to find both an approximate as well as an exact value for x. To answer this problem, we need some preliminary information.

Definition of Logarithm

The solution of the equation $2^x = 14$ seeks an x value. What is this x-value? We express the idea in words:

x is the exponent on a base 2 that gives the answer 14

This can be abbreviated as

x = exp on base 2 to give 14

We further shorten this notation to

$$x = \exp_2 14$$

This statement is read, "x is the exponent on a base 2 that gives the answer 14." It appears that the equation is now solved for x, but this is simply a notational change. The expression "exponent of 14 to the base 2" is called, for historical reasons, "the log of 14 to the base 2." That is,

$$x = \exp_2 14 \quad \text{and} \quad x = \log_2 14$$

mean exactly the same thing. This leads us to the following definition of **logarithm**.

> For positive b and A, $b \neq 1$
>
> $x = \log_b A$ means $b^x = A$
>
> x is called the **logarithm** and A is called the **argument**.
>
> *Spend some time with this definition.

If you're having trouble understanding the principle of logarithms, go back through the development of the definition, but this time, do it more slowly to let each transition sink in. The statement $x = \log_b A$ should be read as "x is the log (exponent) on a base b that gives the value A." *Do not forget that a logarithm is an exponent.*

In $5^2 = 25$, 5 is the base and 2 is the exponent, so we write

$$2 = \log_5 25$$

Remember, the logarithmic expression "solves" for the exponent. With $\frac{1}{8} = 2^{-3}$, the base is 2 and the exponent is -3:

$$-3 = \log_2 \frac{1}{8}$$

With $\sqrt{64} = 8$, the base is 64 and the exponent is $\frac{1}{2}$ (since $\sqrt{64} = 64^{1/2}$):

$$\frac{1}{2} = \log_{64} 8$$

It is important to know what logarithmic expressions mean. For example, $\log_{10} 100$ is the exponent on a base 10 that gives 100. We see that the exponent is 2, so we write $\log_{10} 100 = 2$; the base is 10 and the exponent is 2, so $10^2 = 100$. Also, $\log_{10} \frac{1}{1{,}000}$ is the exponent on a base 10 that gives $\frac{1}{1{,}000}$; this exponent is -3. The base is 10 and the exponent is -3, so we write

$$10^{-3} = \frac{1}{1{,}000}$$

Finally, $\log_3 1$ is the exponent on a base 3 that gives 1; this exponent is 0. The base is 3 and the exponent is 0, so we write

$$3^0 = 1$$

In elementary work, the most commonly used base is 10, so we call a logarithm to the base 10 a **common logarithm**, and we agree to write it without using a subscript 10. That is, $\log x$ is a *common logarithm*. A logarithm to the base e is called a **natural logarithm** and is denoted by $\ln x$. The expression $\ln x$ is often pronounced "ell en x" or "lon x."

Logarithmic Notations

Common logarithm: $\log x$ means $\log_{10} x$

Natural logarithm: $\ln x$ means $\log_e x$

The solution for the equation $10^x = 2$ is $x = \log 2$, and the solution for the equation $e^x = 0.56$ is $x = \ln 0.56$.

Evaluating Logarithms

To **evaluate** a logarithm means to find a numerical value for the given logarithm. Calculators have, to a large extent, eliminated the need for logarithm tables. You should find two logarithm keys on your calculator. One is labeled LOG for common logarithms, and the other is labeled LN for natural logarithms. Use your own calculator to verify these answers because the number of digits shown may vary.

$$\log 5.03 \approx 0.7015679851^*$$
$$\ln 3.49 \approx 1.249901736$$
$$\log 0.00728 \approx -2.137868621$$

These examples are fairly straightforward evaluations, since they involve common or natural logarithms and because your calculator has both LOG and LN keys. However, suppose we wish to evaluate a logarithm to some base *other than* base 10 or base e. The first method uses the definition of logarithm, and the second method uses what is called the **change of base theorem**. Before we state this theorem, we consider its plausibility with the following example. Evaluate the given expressions.

a. $\log_2 8, \dfrac{\log 8}{\log 2}$, and $\dfrac{\ln 8}{\ln 2}$ **b.** $\log_3 9, \dfrac{\log 9}{\log 3}$, and $\dfrac{\ln 9}{\ln 3}$

* Calculator answers are more accurate than were the old table answers, but it is important to realize that any answer (whether from a table or a calculator) is only as accurate as the input numbers. However, in this book we will not be concerned with significant digits, but instead will use all the accuracy our calculator gives us, rounding only once (if requested) at the end of the problem.

a. From the definition of logarithm, $\log_2 8 = x$ means $2^x = 8$ or $x = 3$. Thus, $\log_2 8 = 3$. By calculator,

$$\frac{\log 8}{\log 2} \approx \frac{0.903089987}{0.3010299957} \approx 3$$

Also,

$$\frac{\ln 8}{\ln 2} \approx \frac{2.079441542}{0.6931471806} \approx 3$$

b. $\log_3 9 = x$ means $3^x = 3^2$, so that $x = \log_3 9 = 2$. By calculator,

$$\frac{\log 9}{\log 3} \approx \frac{0.9542425094}{0.4771212547} \approx 2$$

and

$$\frac{\ln 9}{\ln 3} \approx \frac{2.197224577}{1.098612289} \approx 2$$

Change of Base

$$\log_a x = \frac{\log_b x}{\log_b a}$$

Evaluate (round to the nearest hundredth):

a. $\log_7 3$ **b.** $\log_3 3.84$

a. $\log_7 3 = \dfrac{\log 3}{\log 7}$

$$\approx \underbrace{\frac{0.4771212547}{0.84509804} \approx 0.5645750341}_{} \approx 0.56$$

This is all done by calculator and not on your paper.

b. $\log_3 3.84 = \dfrac{\log 3.84}{\log 3}$

$$\approx \underbrace{\frac{0.5843312244}{0.4771212547} \approx 1.224701726}_{} \approx 1.22$$

Calculator work

We now return to the problem of solving

$2^x = 14$ Given equation

$x = \log_2 14$ Solution

We call $\log_2 14$ the **exact solution** for the equation, and we can use a calculator to find an approximate solution. We use the definition of logarithm and the change of base theorem to write

$$x = \log_2 14 = \underbrace{\frac{\log 14}{\log 2} \approx 3.807354922}_{} \approx 3.81$$

Calculator work

Remember the change of base formula so you can evaluate logarithms to bases other than 10 or e.

© Sport/Jupiterimages

Exponential Equations

We now turn to solving *exponential equations*. Exponential equations will fall into one of three types:

Common log	Natural log	Arbitrary
base 10	base e	base b
Example: $10^x = 5$	Example: $e^{-0.06x} = 3.456$	Example: $8^x = 156.8$

The following example illustrates the procedure for solving each type of exponential equation. Solve the following exponential equations:

a. $10^x = 5$ **b.** $e^{-0.06x} = 3.456$ **c.** $8^x = 156.8$

Regardless of the base, we use the definition of logarithm to solve an exponential equation.

a.

$10^x = 5$	Given equation
$x = \log 5$	Definition of logarithm; this is the exact answer.
≈ 0.6989700043	Approximate calculator answer

b.

$e^{-0.06x} = 3.456$	Given equation
$-0.06x = \ln 3.456$	Definition of logarithm
$x = \dfrac{\ln 3.456}{-0.06}$	Exact answer; this can be simplified to $x = -\frac{50}{3}\ln 3.456$.
≈ -20.66853085	Approximate calculator answer

c.

$8^x = 156.8$	Given equation
$x = \log_8 156.8$	Definition of logarithm; this is the exact answer.
≈ 2.43092725	Approximate calculator answer. Use the change of base theorem: $\log_8 156.8 = \dfrac{\log 156.8}{\log 8}$.

Note: Many people will solve $8^x = 156.8$ by "taking the log of both sides":

$8^x = 156.8$	Given equation
$\log 8^x = \log 156.8$	Take the "log of both sides."
$x \log 8 = \log 156.8$	This property of logarithms will be developed in the next section.
$x = \dfrac{\log 156.8}{\log 8}$	Divide both sides by log 8.
≈ 2.43092725	This answer agrees with the first solution.

Did you notice that this result is the same? It simply involves several extra steps and some additional properties of logarithms. It is rather like solving quadratic equations by completing the square each time instead of using the quadratic formula. You can see that, before calculators, there were good reasons to avoid representations such as $\log_8 156.8$. Whenever you *see* an expression such as $\log_8 156.8$, you *know* how to calculate it: log 156.8/log 8.

We now consider some more general exponential equations. Some algebraic steps will be required to put the equations into the correct form. That is, before we use the definition of logarithm, we first solve for the exponential form.

Solve:

a. $\dfrac{10^{5x+3}}{5} = 39$

b. $1 = 2e^{-0.000425x}$

c. $8 \cdot 6^{3x+2} = 1{,}600$

Note that, in each case, we use the definition of logarithm.

a.

$\dfrac{10^{5x+3}}{5} = 39$	Given equation
$10^{5x+3} = 195$	Multiply both sides by 5. (Solve for exponential.)
$5x + 3 = \log 195$	Definition of logarithm
$x = \dfrac{\log 195 - 3}{5}$	Solve linear equation for x. This is the exact answer.
≈ -0.1419930777	Approximate calculator answer

b.

$1 = 2e^{-0.000425x}$	Given equation
$\dfrac{1}{2} = e^{-0.000425x}$	Divide both sides by 2. (Solve for exponential.)
$-0.000425x = \ln \dfrac{1}{2}$	Definition of logarithm
$x = \dfrac{\ln 0.5}{-0.000425}$	Solve linear equation for x. This is the exact answer.
$\approx 1{,}630.934542$	Approximate calculator answer

c.
$$
\begin{aligned}
8 \cdot 6^{3x+2} &= 1{,}600 && \text{Given equation}\\
6^{3x+2} &= 200 && \text{Divide both sides by 8. (Solve for exponential.)}\\
3x + 2 &= \log_6 200 && \text{Definition of logarithm}\\
x &= \frac{\log_6 200 - 2}{3} && \text{Solve linear equation for } x\text{. This is the exact answer.}\\
&\approx 0.3190157417 && \text{Approximate calculator answer. You will need the change of base theorem.}
\end{aligned}
$$

Growth and decay problems are common examples of exponential equations. We will consider growth and decay applications in Topic 6.3.

6.2 Logarithmic Equations

IN 2005, AN EARTHQUAKE MEASURING 7.6 ON THE RICHTER SCALE STRUCK PAKISTAN, INDIA, AND THE KASHMIR REGION.

The intensity of this quake was similar to the one that devastated San Francisco in 1906, but the death toll for this earthquake was measured in the tens of thousands, and the number of homeless was measured in the millions. What is the amount of energy released (in ergs) by this earthquake? How would you answer this question? Where would you begin?

Fundamental Properties

With a little earthquake research, you could find information on the *Richter scale*, which was developed by Gutenberg and Richter. The formula relating the energy E (in ergs) to the magnitude of the earthquake, M, is given by

$$M = \frac{\log E - 11.8}{1.5}$$

This equation is called a *logarithmic equation*, and the topic of this section is to solve such equations. To answer the question, we first solve for log E, and then we use the definition of logarithm to write this as an exponential equation.

$$
\begin{aligned}
M &= \frac{\log E - 11.8}{1.5} && \text{Given equation}\\
1.5M &= \log E - 11.8 && \text{Multiply both sides by 1.5.}\\
1.5M + 11.8 &= \log E && \text{Add 11.8 to both sides.}\\
10^{1.5M+11.8} &= E && \text{Definition of logarithm}
\end{aligned}
$$

We can now answer the question. Since $M = 7.6$,

$$E = 10^{1.5(7.6)+11.8} \approx 1.58 \times 10^{23}$$

However, to solve certain logarithmic equations, we must first develop some properties of logarithms.

We begin with two *fundamental properties of logarithms*. If you understand the definition of logarithm, you can see that these two properties are self-evident, so we call these the **Grant's tomb properties** of logarithms.

FUNDAMENTAL PROPERTIES OF LOGARITHMS

1. $\log_b b^x = x$
   In words, x is the exponent on a base b that gives b^x. That is, $b^x = b^x$.
2. $b^{\log_b x} = x \quad x > 0$
   In words, $\log_b x$ is the exponent on a base b that gives x, which is the definition of logarithm.

*Spend some time making sure you understand these properties. Do you see why we call them the Grant's tomb properties?

© rackerman/iStockphoto.com / © Mark Evans/iStockphoto.com

© Paula Bronstein/Getty Images

Logarithmic Equations

A **logarithmic equation** is an equation for which there is a logarithm on one or both sides. The key to solving logarithmic equations is the following theorem, which we will call the **log of both sides theorem**.

Log of Both Sides Theorem

If A, B, and b are positive real numbers with $b \neq 1$, then

$\log_b A = \log_b B$ is equivalent to $A = B$

STOP The proof of this theorem is not difficult, and it depends on the two fundamental properties of logarithms given in the previous subsection.

Basically, all logarithmic equations in this book fall into one of four types:

		Example:
TYPE I:	The unknown is the logarithm.	$\log_2 \sqrt{3} = x$
TYPE II:	The unknown is the base.	$\log_x 6 = 2$
TYPE III:	The logarithm of an unknown is equal to a number.	$\ln x = 5$
TYPE IV:	The logarithm of an unknown is equal to the log of a number.	$\log_5 x = \log_5 72$

The following example illustrates the procedure for solving each type of logarithmic equation.

TYPE I: $\log_2 \sqrt{3} = x$. If the logarithmic expression does not contain a variable, you can use your calculator to evaluate. Remember, this type was evaluated in Topic 6.1. If it is a common logarithm (base 10), use the LOG key; if it is a natural logarithm (base e), use the LN key; if it has another base, use the change of base theorem:

$$\log_a N = \frac{\log N}{\log a} \quad \text{or} \quad \log_a N = \frac{\ln N}{\ln a}$$

For this example, we see

$$x = \log_2 \sqrt{3} = \frac{\log \sqrt{3}}{\log 2} \approx 0.7924812504$$

TYPE II: $\log_x 6 = 2$. If the unknown is the base, then use the definition of logarithm to write an equation that is not a logarithmic equation.

$$\log_x 6 = 2 \quad \text{Given}$$
$$x^2 = 6 \quad \text{Definition of logarithm}$$
$$x = \pm\sqrt{6} \quad \text{Solve quadratic equation.}$$

When solving logarithmic equations, make sure your answers are in the domain of the variable. Remember that, by definition, the base must be positive. For this example, $x = -\sqrt{6}$ is not in the domain, so the solution is $x = \sqrt{6}$.

TYPE III: The third and fourth types of logarithmic equations are the most common, and both involve the logarithm of an unknown quantity on one side of an equation. For the third type, use the definition of logarithm (and a calculator for an approximate solution, if necessary).

$$\ln x = 5 \quad \text{Given}$$
$$e^5 = x \quad \text{5 is the exponent on } e \text{ that gives } x.$$

This is the exact solution. An approximate solution is $x \approx 148.4131591$.

TYPE IV: When a logarithm occurs on both sides, use the log of both sides theorem. *Make sure the log on both sides has the same base:*

$$\log_5 x = \log_5 72$$
$$x = 72$$

This example illustrates the procedures for solving logarithmic equations, but most logarithmic equations are not as easy. Usually, you must do some algebraic simplification to put the problem into the form of one of the four types of logarithmic equations. You might also have realized that Type IV is a special case of Type III. For example, to solve

$$\log_5 x = \log_3 72$$

which looks like Type IV, we see that we cannot use the log of both sides theorem because the bases are not the same. We can, however, treat this as a Type III equation by using the definition of logarithm to write

$$x = 5^{\log_3 72}$$

This can be evaluated using a calculator. However, you may find it easier to visualize if we write

$$\log_5 x = \log_3 72 \approx 3.892789261$$

so that 3.892789261 is the exponent on a base 5 that gives x. In other words,

$$x \approx 5^{3.892789261} \approx 525.9481435$$

Laws of Logarithms

To simplify logarithmic expressions, we remember that a logarithm is an exponent and the laws of exponents correspond to the **laws of logarithms**. Take a moment to review these on the next page.

The proofs of these laws of logarithms are easy. The additive law of logarithms comes from the additive law of exponents:

$$b^x b^y = b^{x+y}$$

Let $A = b^x$ and $B = b^y$, so that $AB = b^{x+y}$. Then from the definition of logarithm, these three equations are equivalent to

$$x = \log_b A,\ y = \log_b B, \text{ and } x + y = \log_b(AB)$$

Therefore, by putting these pieces together, we have

$$\log_b (AB) = x + y = \log_b A + \log_b B$$

LAWS OF LOGARITHMS

If A, B, and b are positive numbers, p is any real number, and $b \neq 1$:

First Law (Additive)

$$\log_b (AB) = \log_b A + \log_b B$$

The log of the product of two numbers is the sum of the logs of those numbers.

Second Law (Subtractive)

$$\log_b \left(\frac{A}{B}\right) = \log_b A - \log_b B$$

The log of the quotient of two numbers is the log of the numerator minus the log of the denominator.

Third Law (Multiplicative)

$$\log_b A^p = p \log_b A$$

The log of the pth power of a number is p times the log of that number.

Similarly, for the subtractive law of logarithms,

$$\frac{A}{B} = \frac{b^x}{b^y}$$

$$= b^{x-y} \quad \text{Subtractive law of exponents}$$

$$x - y = \log_b \left(\frac{A}{B}\right) \quad \text{Definition of logarithm}$$

$$\log_b A - \log_b B = \log_b \left(\frac{A}{B}\right) \quad \text{Since } x = \log_b A \text{ and } y = \log_b B$$

The proof of the multiplicative law of logarithms follows from the multiplicative law of exponents and you are asked to do this in the problem set. We can also prove this multiplicative law by using the additive law of logarithms for p a positive integer:

$$\log_b A^p = \log_b \underbrace{(A \cdot A \cdot A \cdot \ldots \cdot A)}_{p \text{ factors}} \quad \text{Definition of } A^p$$

Additive law of logarithms

$$= \underbrace{\log_b A + \log_b A + \log_b A + \ldots + \log_b A}_{p \text{ terms}}$$

When logarithms were used for calculations, the laws of logarithms were used to expand an expression such as $\log\left(\frac{6 \cdot 45.62^2}{84.2}\right)$. Calculators have made such problems obsolete. Today, logarithms are important in solving equations, and the procedure for solving logarithmic equations requires that we take an algebraic expression involving logarithms and write it as a single logarithm. We might call this *contracting* a logarithmic expression.

Contract: $\log_2 3x - 2\log_2 x + \log_2(x + 3)$

$$\log_2 3x - 2\log_2 x + \log_2(x + 3)$$

$$= \log_2 3x - \log_2 x^2 + \log_2(x + 3)$$

$$= \log_2 \frac{3x(x + 3)}{x^2}$$

$$= \log_2 \frac{3(x + 3)}{x}$$

Solve: $\log_8 3 + \frac{1}{2}\log_8 25 = \log_8 x$

The goal here is to make this look like a Type IV logarithmic equation so that there is a single log expression on both sides.

$$\log_8 3 + \frac{1}{2}\log_8 25 = \log_8 x \quad \text{Given equation}$$

$$\log_8 3 + \log_8 25^{1/2} = \log_8 x \quad \text{Third law of logarithms}$$

$$\log_8 3 + \log_8 5 = \log_8 x \quad 25^{1/2} = (5^2)^{1/2} = 5$$

$$\log_8 (3 \cdot 5) = \log_8 x \quad \text{First law of logarithms}$$

$$15 = x \quad \text{Log of both sides theorem}$$

The solution is 15. (Check to be sure 15 is in the domain of the variable.)

When solving logarithmic equations, you must look for extraneous solutions because the logarithm requires that the arguments be positive, but when solving an equation, we may not know the signs of the arguments. For example, if you solve an equation involving $\log x$ and obtain two answers, for example $x = 3$ and $x = -4$, then the value $x = -4$ must be extraneous because $\log(-4)$ is not defined.

We conclude this section by proving the change of base theorem.

Prove: $\log_a x = \dfrac{\log_b x}{\log_b a}$

Let $y = \log_a x$.

$$a^y = x \quad \text{Definition of logarithm}$$

$$\log_b a^y = \log_b x \quad \text{Log of both sides theorem}$$

$$y \log_b a = \log_b x \quad \text{Third law of logarithms}$$

$$y = \frac{\log_b x}{\log_b a} \quad \text{Divide both sides by } \log_b a \; (\log_b a \neq 0).$$

Thus, by substitution, $\log_a x = \dfrac{\log_b x}{\log_b a}$.

6.3 Applications of Growth and Decay

IN POPULATIONS, BANK ACCOUNTS, AND RADIOACTIVE DECAY, WHERE THE *RATE OF CHANGE* IS HELD CONSTANT, THE AVERAGE GROWTH RATE IS A CONSTANT PERCENT OF THE CURRENT VALUE.

In calculus, a **growth formula** is derived, and this formula is presented below.

Growth/Decay Formula

Exponential **growth** or **decay** can be described by the equation

$$A = A_0 e^{rt}$$

where r is the annual growth/decay rate, t is the time (in years), A_0 is the amount present initially (present value), and A is the target (future) value. If r is positive, this formula models growth, and if r is negative, the formula models decay.

STOP *This is one of the most useful formulas from mathematics.*

Note: You can use this formula as long as the units of time are the same. That is, if the time is measured in years, then the growth/decay rate is in years, but if the time is measured in days, then the growth/decay rate is a daily growth/decay rate.

Population Growth

According to the U.S. Census Bureau in mid-2009 the world population was about 6.77 billion and would reach 7 billion in early 2012. If we assume a growth rate of 1.5%, when will the population reach 8 billion?

We are given the growth rate $r = 0.015$, the initial population $A_0 = 7$ (in billions), and the target population $A = 8$ (in billions).

$A = A_0 e^{rt}$	Growth formula
$8 = 7e^{0.015t}$	Substitute known values.
$\frac{8}{7} = e^{0.015t}$	Solve for the exponential.
$0.015t = \ln\frac{8}{7}$	Definition of logarithm
$t = \frac{\ln 8/7}{0.015}$	Divide both sides by 0.015.
≈ 8.9020928	Approximate answer by calculator

This means that we should pass the 8 billion mark in $2012 + 9 = 2021$.

Suppose we do not know the growth rate but have some population data. Consider the following example, assuming an exponential growth model.

According to the Centers for Disease Control in Atlanta, Georgia, at the end of January 1992, the total number of AIDS-related U.S. deaths for all ages was 209,693. At that time, it was predicted that by January 1996 there would be from 400,000 to 450,000 cumulative deaths from the disease. Assuming these numbers are correct, estimate the cumulative number of AIDS-related deaths at the end of January 2002.

We assume that the growth rate will remain constant over the years of our study and also that the growth takes place continuously. From the end of January 1992 to January 1996 is 4 years, so $t = 4$. Furthermore, we will work with the more conservative estimate of cumulative deaths; that is, we let $A_0 = 209{,}693$ and $A = 400{,}000$.

$A = A_0e^{rt}$	Growth formula
$400{,}000 = 209{,}693e^{r(4)}$	Substitute known values.
$\dfrac{400{,}000}{209{,}693} = e^{r}$	Solve for the exponential.
$4r = \ln\left(\dfrac{400{,}000}{209{,}693}\right)$	Definition of logarithm
$r = \dfrac{1}{4}\ln\left(\dfrac{400{,}000}{209{,}693}\right)$	Solve for the unknown, r.
≈ 0.1614549977	Calculator approximation

Thus, at the end of January 2002, we have (for $t = 10$), $A = 209{,}693e^{10r} \approx 1{,}053{,}839$. A graph is shown in Figure 6.1.

Figure 6.1 Cumulative deaths from AIDS, 1992–2002

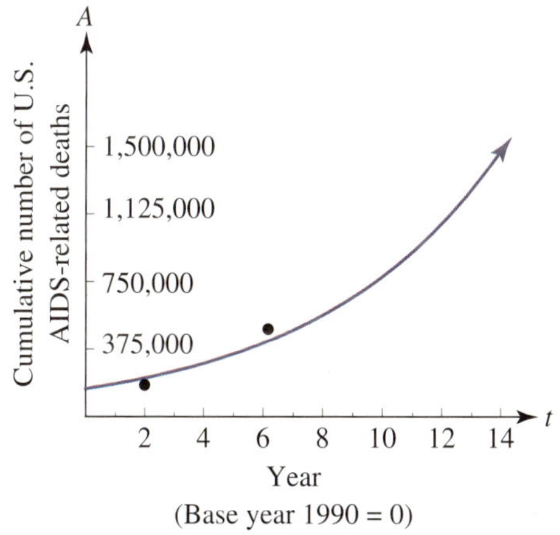

Radioactive Decay

We now consider another application involving decay. Radioactive materials decay over time (see Figure 6.2).

Each substance has a different decay rate. In the following example, when we say the decay rate of neptunium-239 is 31%, we imply that the rate is negative—that is, growth implies positive rate and decay implies negative rate; or, saying it another way, positive rate is growth and negative rate is decay.

We often specify radioactive decay in terms of what is called the **half-life**. This is the time that it takes for a particular radioactive substance to decay to half of its original amount.

Figure 6.2 Radioactive decay

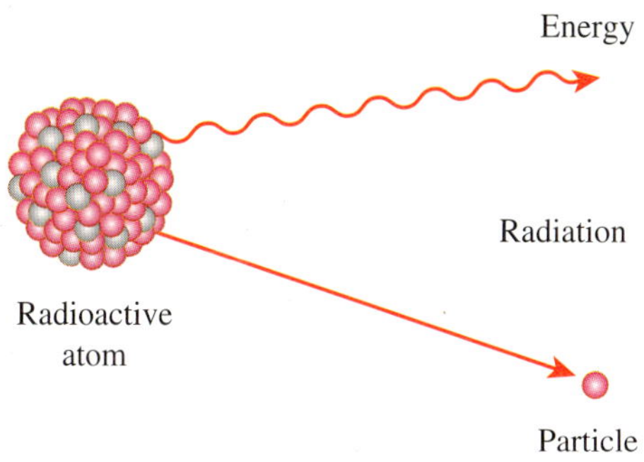

Carbon-14, used for archaeological dating, has a half-life of 5,730 years. Find the decay rate for carbon-14. (We will use the decay rate we find in this example in other examples and in the problem set.)

If 100 mg of carbon-14 ($A_0 = 100$) is present, we are given that in 5,730 years ($t = 5{,}730$) there will be 50 mg present ($A = 50$). We use the growth/decay formula:

$A = A_0e^{rt}$	Growth/decay formula
$50 = 100e^{r(5{,}730)}$	Substitute known values.
$0.5 = e^{5{,}730r}$	Solve for the exponential.
$5{,}730r = \ln 0.5$	Definition of logarithm
$r = \dfrac{\ln 0.5}{5{,}730}$	Solve for the unknown.
$\approx -1.209680943\text{E} - 4$	Approximate answer by calculator

Use this value of r for carbon-14 calculations.

We can use the decay rate for carbon-14 to date an artifact, as illustrated by the following example.

An archaeologist has found a fossil in which the ratio of ^{14}C to ^{12}C is 20% of the ratio found in the atmosphere. Approximately how old is the fossil?

As the radioactive isotope carbon-14 (denoted by ^{14}C) decays, it changes to a stable form of carbon, called carbon-12. Once again, we use the

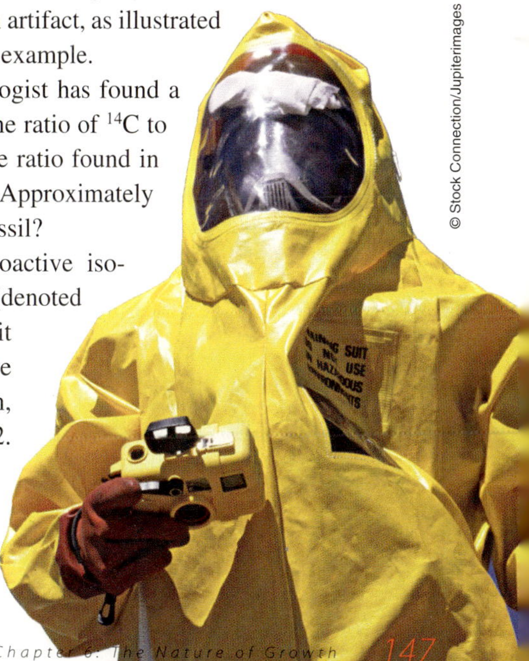

growth/decay formula with the ratio of ^{14}C to ^{12}C to be 20% as follows:

$$
\begin{aligned}
A &= A_0e^{rt} && \text{Growth/decay formula}\\
\frac{A}{A_0} &= e^{rt} && \text{Divide both sides by } A_0.\\
0.20 &= e^{rt} && \text{The given ratio is 20\%.}\\
rt &= \ln 0.20 && \text{Definition of logarithm}\\
t &= \frac{\ln 0.20}{r} && \text{Solve for the unknown; use the value of } r \text{ from the previous example.}\\
&\approx 13{,}304.64798 && \text{Approximate answer by calculator}
\end{aligned}
$$

The fossil is approximately 13,000 years old.

Logarithmic Scales

Growth and decay examples are exponential models, but as we have seen, a logarithm is an exponent and is therefore directly related to growth and decay. A **logarithmic scale** is a scale in which logarithms are used to make data more manageable by expanding small variations and compressing large ones.

For example, prior to 1935, *seismographs* were used to record the amount of earth movement generated by an earthquake's seismic wave; this movement was recorded on a *seismogram*. The *amplitude* of a seismogram is the vertical distance between the peak or valley of the recording of the seismic wave and a horizontal line formed if there is no earth movement. This amplitude is measured using a very small unit, *micrometer* (denoted by μm), which is one-millionth of a meter. This small movement on a seismograph is used to measure a very large amount of energy released by an earthquake, and it must be done in such a way that the location of the seismograph relative to the earthquake's location (called the *epicenter*) is not relevant. You have, no doubt, heard of the well-known *Richter scale* used today as a means of measuring the magnitude, M, of an earthquake.

In 1935, Charles F. Richter, a seismologist at the California Institute of Technology, declared that the magnitude M of an earthquake with amplitude A on a seismograph was

$$M = \log \frac{A}{A_0}$$

where A_0 is the amplitude of a "standard earthquake." This number M is called the **Richter number** or **Richter scale** to denote the size of an earthquake. Richter measured a large number of extremely small southern California earthquakes, and *defined* $\log A_0$ to be -1.7 for a seismograph located 20 km from the epicenter. Using the properties of logarithms, we know

$$
\begin{aligned}
M &= \log A - \log A_0\\
&= \log A - (-1.7)\\
&= \log A + 1.7
\end{aligned}
$$

If the seismograph is located 300 km from the epicenter, then $\log A_0$ is *defined* to be -4.0, so

$$
\begin{aligned}
M &= \log A - \log A_0\\
&= \log A + 4.0
\end{aligned}
$$

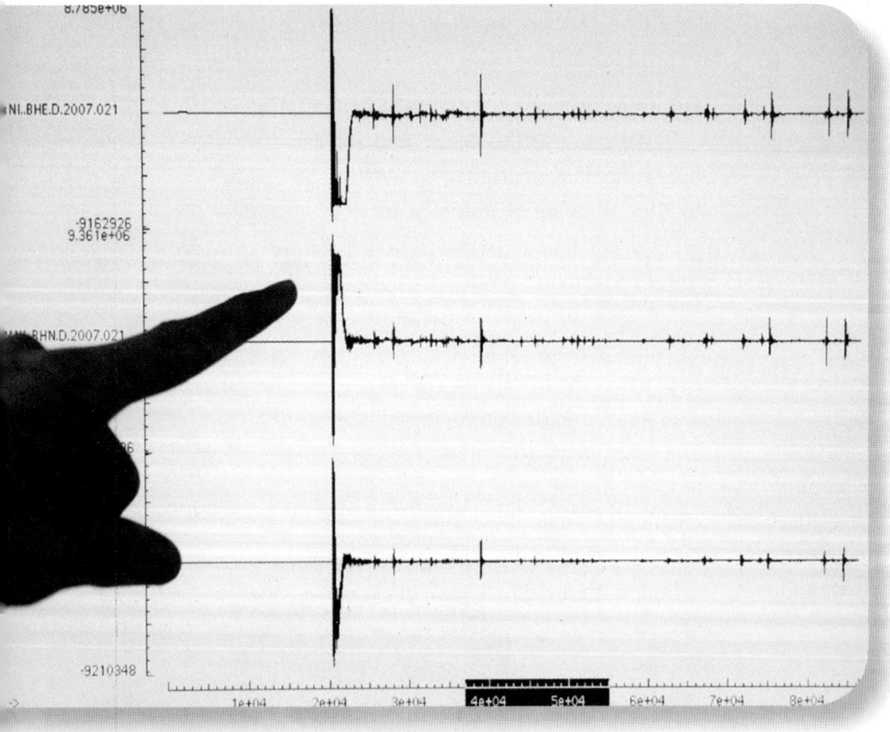

© Dimas Ardian/Getty Images

Since the calculation of the magnitude depends on the distance of the seismograph from the epicenter, and since for a particular earthquake the distance of the seismograph from the epicenter is not known, an actual earthquake is usually measured at three different locations in order to determine the epicenter. The Richter scale ratings for some well-known quakes are shown in Table 6.1, but it should be noted that if you search the web you will find that earthquakes are common. In 1998 there were more than 10 quakes recorded with a magnitude of over 7.0.

Why is the Richter scale called logarithmic? The reason is that if you increase the magnitude by 1, then the quake is 10 times stronger; if you increase the magnitude by 2, then the quake is $10^2 = 100$ times stronger; if you increase the magnitude by 3, then the quake is 10^3 times stronger. We illustrate an increase of magnitude by 4 with the following example.

Table 6.1 Magnitudes of Major World Earthquakes

Date	Location	Magnitude
1906	San Francisco	7.8
1906	Valparaiso, Chile	8.2
1915	Avezzano, Italy	7.0
1933	Japan	8.4
1946	Honshu, Japan	8.1
1952	Kamchatka	9.0
1960	Chile	9.5
1985	Mexico	8.0
1989	Loma Prieta	7.1
1995	Kobe, Japan	6.9
1998	Balleny Islands	8.1
1999	Turkey	7.2
2003	Colima, Mexico	7.6
2004	Sumatra	9.1
2005	Indonesia	8.6
2007	Indonesia	8.5
2008	Sichuan, China	7.9
2008	Italy	6.3

Note: It is customary to give Richter scale readings rounded to the nearest tenth.
Source: U.S. Geological Survey, "Historic Worldwide Earthquakes," U.S. Department of the Interior. http://earthquake.usgs.gov/regional/world/historical.php (accessed 6/10/2009).

Compare the strengths of earthquakes with magnitudes 4 and 8. Let M_1 and M_2 be the two given magnitudes. Then

$$\begin{aligned} M_1 - M_2 &= (\log A_1 - \log A_0) - (\log A_2 - \log A_0) \\ &= \log A_1 - \log A_2 \\ &= \log \frac{A_1}{A_2} \end{aligned}$$

For this problem, in particular, we have

$$\begin{aligned} 8 - 4 &= \log \frac{A_1}{A_2} \\ 4 &= \log \frac{A_1}{A_2} \\ 10^4 &= \frac{A_1}{A_2} \\ A_1 &= 10{,}000 A_2 \end{aligned}$$

A doubling of the magnitude from 4 to 8 means that the stronger earthquake's amplitude is $10^4 = 10{,}000$ times greater.

The amount of earth movement from an earthquake is measured by the amount of energy released by the earthquake. Consider the following example. Compare the amount of earth movement (the energy released) by earthquakes of magnitudes of 4 and 8.

Use the formula

$$M = \frac{\log E - 11.8}{1.5}$$

from Topic 6.2. We solve for E:

$1.5M = \log E - 11.8$	Multiply both sides by 1.5.
$1.5M + 11.8 = \log E$	Add 11.8 to both sides.
$E = 10^{1.5M+11.8}$	Definition of logarithm

Let $M_1 = 4$ and $M_2 = 8$ with corresponding energies E_1 and E_2, respectively. We now compare these energies:

$\frac{E_1}{E_2} = \frac{10^{1.5(4)+11.8}}{10^{1.5(8)+11.8}}$	Same bases, subtract exponents.
$E_1 = 10^{-6} E_2$	Multiply both sides by E_2.
$10^6 E_1 = E_2$	Multiply both sides by 10^6.

The earthquake with magnitude 8 releases a million times more energy than an earthquake with magnitude 4.

A second example of a logarithmic scale is the decibel rating used for measuring the intensity of sounds. To measure the intensity of sound, we need to understand that a sound is a vibration received by the ear and processed by the brain. We can place a listening device in the path of the sound and measure the amount of energy on that device per unit of area per second. This listening device acts like an eardrum, but the problem is that experiments have shown that humans perceive loudness on the basis of the ratio of intensities of two different sounds. For this reason, the unit of measurement for measuring sounds, called the **decibel**, in honor of Alexander Graham Bell, the inventor of the telephone, is defined as a ratio of the intensity of one sound, I, and another sound, $I_0 \approx 10^{-16}$ watt/cm^2, the intensity of a barely audible sound for a person with normal hearing.

The issue is further complicated by the fact that a human ear can hear an incredible range of sounds. A painful sound is 10^{14} (100 trillion) times more intense than a barely audible sound. This leads us to define the number of decibels, D, by

$$D = 10 \log \frac{I}{I_0}$$

for a sound of intensity I. This is called the **decibel formula**. The decibel rating, abbreviated dB, for various sounds is shown in Table 6.2.

A link for a sound test of decibel changes can be found at the following site: www.phys.unsw.edu.au/jw/hearing.html

Table 6.2 Decibel Ratings

Sound	dB Rating
threshold of hearing	0
recording studio	20
whisper	25
quiet room	30
conversation	60
traffic	70
train	100
orchestra	110
rock music	115
pain threshold	120
rocket	125

A scale for loudness of sounds begins at 0 dB (threshold of hearing) and extends to the threshold of pain, 120 dB. Each increase of 10 decibels is perceived as a doubling of loudness. A sound of 70 dB is twice as loud as a 60-dB sound. The noise in a classroom varies from 50 dB to 62 dB. Find the corresponding variation in intensities.

We are given $D_1 = 50$ and $D_2 = 62$, and we wish to compare I_1 and I_2:

$$\begin{aligned}
D_2 - D_1 &= 10 \log \frac{I_2}{I_0} - 10 \log \frac{I_1}{I_0} \\
&= 10 \log I_2 - 10 \log I_0 - 10 \log I_1 + 10 \log I_0 \\
&= 10(\log I_2 - \log I_1) \\
&= 10 \log \frac{I_2}{I_1} \\
62 - 50 &= 10 \log \frac{I_2}{I_1} && \text{Substitute given values.} \\
1.2 &= \log \frac{I_2}{I_1} \\
10^{1.2} &= \frac{I_2}{I_1} && \text{Definition of logarithm} \\
15.85 &\approx \frac{I_2}{I_1} && \text{Calculator approximation of } 10^{1.2} \\
I_2 &\approx 16 I_1
\end{aligned}$$

The louder room is about 16 times noisier than the quiet room.

The Nature of Money

7.1 It's Simple

IT SEEMS THAT EVERYONE HAS MONEY PROBLEMS. EITHER WE HAVE TOO MUCH (YOU'VE READ STORIES OF PEOPLE WHO DON'T KNOW WHAT TO DO WITH ALL THEIR MONEY) OR WE HAVE TOO LITTLE.

topics

Very few people believe that they have "just the right amount of money."

Certain arithmetic skills enable us to make intelligent decisions about how we spend the money we earn.

© Bruce Shippee/Shutterstock

Amount of Simple Interest

One of the most fundamental mathematical concepts that consumers, as well as business people, must understand is *interest*. Simply stated, **interest** is money paid for the use of money. We receive interest when we let others use our money (when we deposit money in a savings account, for example), and we pay interest when we use the money of others (for example, when we borrow from a bank).

The amount of the deposit or loan is called the **principal** or **present value**, and the interest is stated as a percent of the

3 CRITICAL FORMULAS

1 Simple Interest
2 Future Value
3 Annual Percentage Rate (APR)

© Nic Taylor/iStockphoto.com / © Brand X Pictures/Jupiterimages

principal, called the **interest rate**. The **time** is the length of time for which the money is borrowed or lent. The interest rate is usually an *annual interest rate*, and is stated in years unless otherwise indicated.

The following **simple interest formula** provides a basis for many financial formulas.

Simple Interest Formula

INTEREST = PRESENT VALUE × RATE × TIME

$I = Prt$ where I = AMOUNT OF INTEREST

P = PRESENT VALUE (or PRINCIPAL)

r = ANNUAL INTEREST RATE

t = TIME (in years)

* This is a crucial formula to remember.

Sometimes you know the amount of interest but need to find the principal, the rate, or the time. These can be easily found by solving the formula $I = Prt$ for the unknown.

What You Want	What You Know	Formula
I, amount of interest	P, r, and t	$I = Prt$
P, present value (principal)	I, r, and t	$P = \frac{I}{rt}$
r, rate	I, P, and t	$r = \frac{I}{Pt}$
t, time	I, P, and r	$t = \frac{I}{Pr}$

* These are all variations of the simple interest formula. Using algebra, you can derive them all by solving for the desired variable.

Future Value

There is a difference between asking for the amount of interest and asking for the **future value**. The future amount is the amount you will have after the interest is added to the principal, or present value. Let A = FUTURE VALUE.

$$A = P + I \quad \text{or} \quad P = A - I \quad \text{or} \quad I = A - P$$

Once again, all these are algebraic variations of the same formula.

Interest for Part of a Year

The length of time for an investment is not always a whole number of years. There are two ways to convert a number of days to a portion of a year:

Exact interest: 365 days per year
Ordinary interest: 360 days per year

Most applications and businesses use ordinary interest. So in this book, unless it is otherwise stated, assume ordinary interest; that is, use 360 for the number of days in a year.

$$t = \frac{\text{ACTUAL NUMBER OF DAYS}}{360}$$

It is worthwhile to derive a formula for future value because sometimes we will not calculate the interest separately.

$$\text{FUTURE VALUE} = \text{PRESENT VALUE} + \text{INTEREST}$$
$$A = P + I$$
$$= P + Prt \quad \text{Substitute } I = Prt.$$
$$= P(1 + rt) \quad \text{Distributive property}$$

This is a formula that will be used frequently when working with finances.

You might notice that this is the same procedure we used to find the sales tax and total price in the previous section. We call this the **future value formula**.

Future Value Formula (Simple Interest)

$$A = P(1 + rt)$$

7.2 Closed-End Credit—Installment Loans

TWO TYPES OF CONSUMER CREDIT ALLOW YOU TO MAKE INSTALLMENT PURCHASES.

The first, called **closed-end**, is the traditional installment loan (We will discuss the second, called open-end, in Topic 7.3.). An **installment loan** is an agreement to pay off a loan or a purchase by making equal payments at regular intervals for some specific period of time. In this book, it is assumed that all installment payments are made monthly.

A loan is said to be **amortized** if it is completely paid off by these payments; and the payments are called **installments**. If the loan is not amortized, there is a larger final payment, called a **balloon payment**. With an **interest-only loan**, there is a monthly payment equal to the interest, with a final payment equal to the amount received when the loan was obtained.

Add-On Interest

The most common method for calculating interest on installment loans is by a method known as **add-on interest**. It is nothing more than an application of the simple interest formula. It is called *add-on interest* because the interest is *added* to the amount borrowed so that both interest and the amount borrowed are paid for over the length of the loan. You should be familiar with the following variables, so spend some time reviewing them and the installment loan formulas.

P = AMOUNT TO BE FINANCED (present value)
r = ADD-ON INTEREST RATE
t = TIME (in years) TO REPAY THE LOAN
I = AMOUNT OF INTEREST
A = AMOUNT TO BE REPAID (future value)
m = AMOUNT OF THE MONTHLY PAYMENT
N = NUMBER OF PAYMENTS

We use these variables in the following summary of **installment loan formulas**.

AMOUNT OF INTEREST: $I = Prt$

AMOUNT TO BE REPAID: $A = P + I$ or $A = P(1 + rt)$

NUMBER OF PAYMENTS: $N = 12t$

AMOUNT OF EACH PAYMENT: $m = \frac{A}{N}$

When figuring monthly payments in everyday life, most businesses and banks round up for any fraction of a cent. However, for consistency in this book, we will continue to use the rounding procedures developed in Chapter 1. This means we will round money answers to the nearest cent.

Among the most common applications of installment loans are the purchase of a car and the purchase of a home. Interest for purchasing a car is add-on interest, but interest for purchasing a home is not. We will, therefore, delay our discussion of home loans until after we have discussed compound interest.

Suppose that you have decided to purchase a 2007 Honda Civic Hybrid and want to determine the monthly payment if you pay for the car in 4 years. Assume that this car will get 70 miles per gallon of gasoline, and that you will drive it for 100,000 miles. How much will it cost to drive this car for 100,000 miles if you assume that the average price of gasoline is \$3.10/gal?

Not enough information is given, so you need to ask some questions of the car dealer:

Sticker price of the car (as posted on the window):	\$20,650
Dealer's preparation charges (as posted on the window):	\$650
Tax rate (determined by the state):	7%
Add-on interest rate:	8%

You must make an offer. If you are serious about getting the best price, find out the **dealer's cost**—the price the dealer paid for the car you want to buy. In this book, we will tell you the dealer's cost, but in the real world you will need to do some research to find it (consult a reporting service, an automobile association, a credit union, or the April issue of *Consumer Reports*). Assume that the dealer's cost for this car is \$18,867. You decide to offer the dealer 5% *over* this cost. We will call this a **5% offer**:

$$\$18,867(1 + 0.05) = \$19,810.35$$

You will notice that we ignored the sticker price and the dealer's preparation charges. Our offer is based only on the *dealer's cost*. Most car dealers will accept an offer that is between 3% and 10% over what they actually paid for the car. For this example, we will assume that the dealer accepted a price of \$19,800. We also assume that we have a trade-in with a value of \$7,500. Here is a list of calculations shown on the sales contract:

Sales price of Honda:	\$19,800.00
Destination charges:	200.00
Subtotal:	20,000.00
Tax (7%) rate:	1,400.00
Less trade-in:	7,500.00
Amount to be financed:	13,900.00

© Image Source Pink/Jupiterimages

We now calculate several key amounts:

Interest: $I = Prt = 13{,}900(0.08)(4) = 4{,}448.00$

Amount to be repaid: $A = P + I$

$$= 13{,}900.00 + 4{,}448.00$$
$$= 18{,}348.00$$

Monthly payment: $m = \dfrac{18{,}348.00}{48} = 382.25$

The monthly payment for the car is \$382.25.

The cost to drive this car for 100,000 miles is found by dividing the number of miles by the miles per gallon to give the number of gallons:

$$\frac{100{,}000}{70} = 1{,}428.57$$

The cost per gallon is \$3.10, so the total cost of gasoline is:

$$1{,}428.57 \times \$3.10 = \$4{,}428.57$$

Annual Percentage Rate (APR)

An important aspect of add-on interest is that you are paying a rate that exceeds the quoted add-on interest rate. The reason for this is that you are not keeping the entire amount borrowed for the entire time. For the car payments calculated above, the amount to be repaid was \$13,900.00, but you do not *owe* this entire amount for 4 years. After the first payment, you owe *less* than this amount. In fact, after you make 47 payments, you will owe only \$382.25; but the calculation shown assumes that the principal remains constant for 4 years.

To see this a little more clearly, consider a simpler example. Suppose you borrow \$2,000 for 2 years with 10% add-on interest. The amount of interest is

$$\$2{,}000 \times 0.10 \times 2 = \$400$$

Now, if you pay back \$2,000 + \$400 at the end of two years, the annual interest rate is 10%. However, if you make a partial payment of \$1,200 at the end of the first year and \$1,200 at the end of the second year, your total paid back is still the same (\$2,400), but you have now paid a higher annual interest rate. Why? Take a look at Figure 7.1.

On the left we see that the interest on \$2,000 is \$400. But if you make a partial payment (figure on the right), we see that \$200 for the first year is the correct interest, but the remaining \$200 interest piled on the remaining balance of \$1,000 is 20% interest (not the stated 10%). Note that since you did not owe \$2,000 for 2 years, the interest rate, r, necessary to give \$400 interest can be calculated using $I = Prt$:

Figure 7.1 Interest on a \$2,000 two-year loan

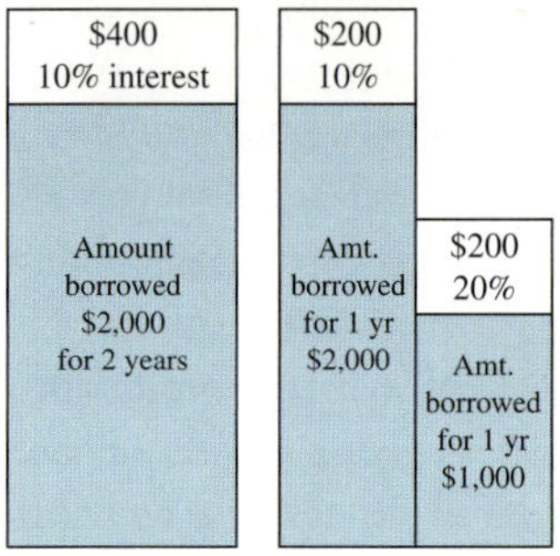

$$(2{,}000)r(1) + (1{,}000)r(1) = 400$$
$$3{,}000r = 400$$
$$r = \frac{400}{3{,}000} = 0.1\overline{3} \text{ or } 13.3\%$$

This number, 13.3%, is called the *annual percentage rate*. This number is too difficult to calculate, as we have just done here, if the number of months is very large. We will, instead, use the annual percentage rate, which can be found for an add-on interest rate, r, with N payments made at equal time intervals by using the following formula:

Annual Percentage Rate

$$APR = \frac{2Nr}{N + 1}$$

In 1968, the Truth-in-Lending Act was passed by Congress; it requires all lenders to state the true annual interest rate, which is called the *annual percentage rate* (APR) and is based on the actual amount owed. Regardless of the rate quoted, when you ask a salesperson what the APR is, the law requires that you be told this rate. This regulation enables you to compare interest rates *before* you sign a contract, which must state the APR even if you haven't asked for it.

Consider a 2007 Blazer with a price of \$28,505 that is advertised at a monthly payment of \$631.00 for 60 months. What is the APR (to the nearest tenth of a percent)?

WATCH YOUR STEP

Use the APR formula to compare interest rates.

We are given $P = 28{,}505$, $m = 631.00$, $t = 5$ (60 months is 5 years), and $N = 60$. The APR formula requires that we know the rate r. Think about the problem before using a calculator. We will use the formula $I = Prt$ to find r by first substituting the values for I, P, and t. We know P and t, but need to calculate I. The future value is the total amount to be repaid ($A = P + I$) and we know $A = 631.00(60) = 37{,}860$, so $I = A - P = 37{,}860 - 28{,}505 = 9{,}355$. Now we are ready to use the formula $I = Prt$:

$$\begin{aligned} I &= Prt \\ 9{,}355 &= 28{,}505(r)(5) && \text{Substitute known values.} \\ 1{,}871 &= 28{,}505r && \text{Divide both sides by 5.} \\ 0.0656376 &\approx r && \text{Divide both sides by 28,505.} \end{aligned}$$

Finally, for the APR formula,

$$APR = \frac{2Nr}{N+1} = \frac{2(60)(0.065637607437)}{61}$$

Don't round until the last step.

This is a calculation for your calculator:

Find A.

631 × 60 − 28505

Find I.

= ÷ 5 ÷ 28505

Find r.

= × 2 × 60 ÷ 61

Find APR.

= Display: .129123162172

The APR is 12.9%.

7.3 Open-End Credit—Credit Cards

THE SECOND TYPE OF CONSUMER CREDIT IS CALLED **OPEN-END**, **REVOLVING CREDIT**, OR MORE COMMONLY, A **CREDIT CARD** LOAN.

MasterCard, VISA, and Discover cards, as well as those from department stores and oil companies, are examples of open-ended loans. This type of loan allows for purchases or cash advances up to a specified maximum **line of credit** and has a flexible repayment schedule. Because you don't have to apply for credit each time you want to charge an item, this type of credit is very convenient.

Calculating Credit Card Interest

When comparing the interest rates on loans, you should use the APR. In the previous section, we introduced a formula for add-on interest; but for credit cards, the stated interest rate *is* the APR. However, the APR on credit cards is often stated as a daily or a monthly rate. For credit cards, we use a 365-day year, rather than a 360-day year.

Note: The agreement in this book for the number of days in a year to use when working with credit card interest is 365.

Many credit cards charge an annual fee; some charge $1 every billing period the card is used; others are free. These charges affect the APR differently, depending on how much the credit card is used during the year and on the monthly balance. If you always pay your credit card bill in full as soon as you receive it, the card with no yearly fee would obviously be the best for you. On the other hand, if you use your credit card to stretch out your payments, the APR is more important than the flat fee. For our purposes, we won't use the yearly fee in our calculations of APR on credit cards.

Like annual fees, the interest rates or APRs for credit cards vary greatly. Because VISA and MasterCard credit cards are issued by many different banks, the terms even in one locality can vary greatly. Some common examples are shown below.

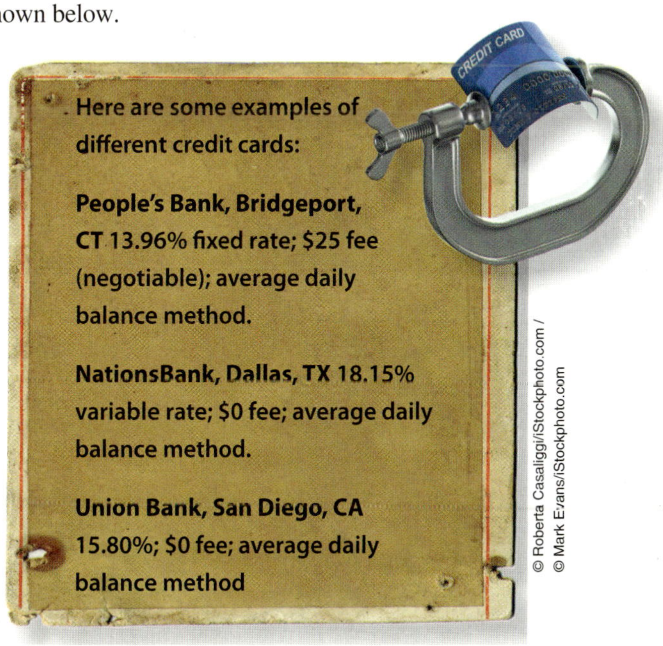

© Roberta Casaliggi/iStockphoto.com / © Mark Evans/iStockphoto.com

3 METHODS FOR CALCULATING FINANCE CHARGES

1 Previous balance
2 Adjusted balance
3 Average daily balance

If you use credit cards, you should be familiar with these methods for calculating interest. They are all based on the simple interest formula.

The finance charges can vary greatly even on credit cards that show the *same* APR, depending on the way the interest is calculated. There are three generally accepted methods for calculating these charges: *previous balance*, *adjusted balance*, and *average daily balance*.

Credit Card Interest

For credit card interest, use the simple interest formula, $I = Prt$.

PREVIOUS BALANCE METHOD: Interest is calculated on the previous month's balance. With this method, P = previous balance, r = annual rate, and $t = \frac{1}{12}$.

ADJUSTED BALANCE METHOD: Interest is calculated on the previous month's balance *less* credits and payments. With this method, P = adjusted balance, r = annual rate, and $t = \frac{1}{12}$.

AVERAGE DAILY BALANCE METHOD: Add the outstanding balance each day in the billing period, and then divide by the number of days in the billing period to find what is called the *average daily balance*. With this method, P = average daily balance, r = annual rate, and t = number of days in the billing period divided by 365.

Let us compare the finance charges on a \$1,000 credit card purchase, using these three different methods. Assume that a bill for \$1,000 is received on April 1 and a \$50 payment is made. Assume that it takes 10 days for the payment to be received and credited to the account. Then another bill is received on May 1, and this bill shows some finance charges. The stated APR is 18% and what we are calculating is the finance charge shown on the May 1 bill.

Previous Balance Method

The first method for calculating credit card finance charges is the previous balance method. Cards that use this method calculate interest based on the previous month's balance. That means the payment doesn't affect the finance charge for this month unless the bill is paid in full. We have $P = \$1{,}000$, $r = 0.18$, and $t = \frac{1}{12}$. Thus,

$$\begin{aligned} I &= Prt \\ &= \$1{,}000(0.18)\left(\frac{1}{12}\right) \\ &= \$15 \end{aligned}$$

The interest is \$15 for this month.

Adjusted Balance Method

First, find the adjusted balance:

Previous balance:	\$1,000
Less credits and payments:	50
Adjusted balance:	\$ 950 ← This is P.

We have $P = \$950$, $r = 0.18$, and $t = \frac{1}{12}$. Thus,

$$\begin{aligned} I &= Prt \\ &= \$950(0.18)\left(\frac{1}{12}\right) \\ &= \$14.25 \end{aligned}$$

The interest is \$14.25 for this month.

Average Daily Balance Method

For the first 10 days the balance is \$1,000, but then the balance drops to \$950. Add the balance for *each day*:

10 days @ \$1,000:	\$10,000
20 days @ \$950:	\$19,000
Total:	\$29,000

Divide by the number of days in the month (30 in April):

$\$29{,}000 \div 30 = \$966.67$ ← This is the average daily balance.

For this problem we have $P = \$966.67$, $r = 0.18$, and $t = \frac{30}{365}$. Thus,

$$\begin{aligned} I &= Prt \\ &= \$966.67(0.18)\left(\frac{30}{365}\right) \\ &= \$14.30 \end{aligned}$$

You can do this calculation with one calculator session, starting at the top. When using your calculator, think of what you are doing, rather than thinking in terms of individual buttons pressed:

Number of days at first balance

[10] [×] [1000] [+]

Number of days at second balance — Divide by number of days for average.

[20] [×] [950] [=] [÷] [30] [=]

This gives *P* in the simple interest formula.

[×] [.18] [×] [30] [÷] [365]

This is *r*, the rate. — This is time; number of days divided by 365.

[=] *Display:* 14.30136986

The interest is \$14.30 for this month.

You can sometimes make good use of credit cards by taking advantage of the period during which no finance charges are levied. Many credit cards charge no interest if you pay in full within a certain period of time (usually 20 or 30 days). This is called the **grace period**. On the other hand, if you borrow cash on your credit card, you should know that many credit cards have an additional charge for cash advances—and these can be as high as 4%. This 4% is *in addition to* the normal finance charges.

7.4 Compound Interest

A CRITICAL TOOL IN MAKING SOUND FINANCIAL DECISIONS IS UNDERSTANDING HOW COMPOUND INTEREST WORKS.

Imagine you receive a large inheritance. You should probably use the money to pay off \$206,000 of your home loan, but you'd also like to put the money in the bank. Would you believe that it's possible to set up an account that would pay off that \$206,000 and generate over \$250,000 in cash? Let's see how that can be done by examining a detailed example on compound interest. (Who ever said math is not worthwhile!)

How Compounding Works

Most banks do not pay interest according to the simple interest formula; instead, after some period of time, they add the interest to the principal and then pay interest on this new, larger amount. When this is done, it is called **compound interest**.

Let's compare simple and compound interest for a \$1,000 deposit at 8% interest for 3 years.

First, calculate the future value of the simple interest:

$$\begin{aligned} A &= P(1 + rt) \\ &= 1{,}000(1 + 0.08 \times 3) \\ &= 1{,}000(1.24) \quad \text{Order of operations, multiplication first.} \\ &= 1{,}240 \end{aligned}$$

Using simple interest, the future value in three years is \$1,240.

Next, assume that the interest is **compounded annually**. This means that the interest is added to the principal after 1 year has passed. This new amount then becomes the principal for the following year. Since the time period for each calculation is 1 year, we let $t = 1$ for each calculation.

First year ($t = 1$): $A = P(1 + r)$
$= 1{,}000(1 + 0.08)$
$= 1{,}080$
↓
Second year ($t = 1$): $A = P(1 + r)$ One year's principal is previous year's balance.
$= 1{,}080(1 + 0.08)$
$= 1{,}166.40$
↓
Third year ($t = 1$): $A = P(1 + r)$
$= 1{,}166.40(1 + 0.08)$
$= 1{,}259.71$

Using interest compounded annually, the future value in 3 years is $1,259.71. The earnings from compounding are $19.71 more than from simple interest.

The problem with compound interest relates to the difficulty of calculating it. What if we wanted to compound annually for 20 years instead of for 3 years?

Simple interest (20 years):

$$\begin{aligned} A &= P(1 + rt) \\ &= 1{,}000(1 + 0.08 \times 20) \\ &= 1{,}000(1 + 1.6) \\ &= 1{,}000(2.6) \\ &= 2{,}600 \end{aligned}$$

Annual compounding (20 years):

$A = P(1 + r)$ — First year
↓
$= P(1 + r)(1 + r)$ — Second year
$= P(1 + r)^2$ — Second year simplified
↓
$= P(1 + r)^2(1 + r)$ — Third year
$= P(1 + r)^3$ — Third year simplified
⋮
$= P(1 + r)^{20}$ — Twentieth year simplified

For a period of 20 years, starting with $1,000 at 8% compounded annually, we have

$$A = 1{,}000(1.08)^{20}$$

The difficulty lies in calculating this number. You will need to have a calculator with an exponent key. These are labeled in different ways, depending on the brand. It might be [y^x] or [x^y] or [^]. In this book we will show exponents by using [^], but you should press the appropriate key for your own brand of calculator.

[1000] [×] [1.08] [^] [20] [=] *Display:* 4660.957144

Round money answers to the nearest cent: $4,660.96 is the future value of $1,000 compounded annually at 8% for 20 years. This compares with $2,600 from simple interest. The effect of compounding yields $2,060.96 *more* than simple interest.

Compounding Periods

Most banks compound interest more frequently than once a year. For instance, a bank may pay interest as follows:

Semiannually: twice a year or every 180 days
Quarterly: 4 times a year or every 90 days
Monthly: 12 times a year or every 30 days
Daily: 360 times a year

WATCH YOUR STEP *Remember these compounding period names.*

To write a formula for various compounding periods, we must introduce three new variables. First, let

n = NUMBER OF TIMES INTEREST IS CALCULATED EACH YEAR

That is,

$n = 1$ for *annual* compounding
$n = 2$ for *semiannual* compounding
$n = 4$ for *quarterly* compounding
$n = 12$ for *monthly* compounding
$n = 360$ for *daily* compounding

Second, let

N = NUMBER OF COMPOUNDING PERIODS

That is,

$$N = nt$$

Third, let

i = RATE PER PERIOD

That is,

$$i = \frac{r}{n}$$

We can now summarize the variables we use for interest.

Interest Variables

A = FUTURE VALUE	This is the principal plus interest.
P = PRESENT VALUE	This is the same as the principal.
r = INTEREST RATE	This is the *annual* interest rate.
t = TIME	This is the time *in years*.

Calculated variables:

$N = nt$	This is the number of periods.
$i = \frac{r}{n}$	This is the rate per period.

STOP It is tempting to skip past this box, but you must take some time to study what these variables represent.

We are now ready to state the **future value formula** for compound interest, which is sometimes called the **compound interest formula**.

Future Value (Compound Interest)

$$A = P(1 + i)^N$$

where A is future value, P is present value, $i = \frac{r}{n}$, and $N = nt$.

WATCH YOUR STEP *To use this formula, follow the procedure described in the following box.*

PROCEDURE: Future Value Formula

Follow this procedure for finding the future value for compound interest.

STEP 1 Identify the present value, P.

STEP 2 Identify the rate, r.

STEP 3 Identify the time, t.

STEP 4 Identify the number of times interest is compounded each year, n.

STEP 5 Calculate $N = nt$.

STEP 6 Calculate $i = \frac{r}{n}$.

STEP 7 Use the future value formula using the calculated values of i and N.

Future value calculations aren't just for textbooks. You can use these calculations in the real world. Imagine you have \$206,000 left to pay on a home mortgage. Your monthly payment of \$1,950 takes a significant chunk out of your monthly budget, and there are 10 more years on your mortgage. If you had the money (the entire \$206,000), would it be better to pay off the whole mortgage or invest the money? Let's find out.

The first question is, "How much principal would you need to generate interest income of \$1,950 per month (to make your mortgage payments) if you are able to invest it at 12% interest?" "Wait! Where can you find 12% interest? My bank pays only 5% interest!" There are investments you could make (not a deposit into a savings account) that could yield a 12% return on your money. Problem solving often requires that you make certain assumptions to have sufficient information to answer a question that you might have. This first question is an application of simple interest, because the interest is withdrawn each month and is not left to accumulate:

I is the amount withdrawn each month.

$$I = Prt \leftarrow t = \frac{1}{12} \text{ because it is monthly income.}$$

$$1{,}950 = P(0.12)\left(\frac{1}{12}\right)$$

$$23{,}400 = 0.12P \quad \text{Multiply both sides by 12.}$$

$$195{,}000 = P \quad \text{Divide both sides by 0.12.}$$

This means that a deposit of $195,000 will be sufficient to generate enough income to cover the monthly payments for 10 remaining years of the term. Because the payments are covered by the interest, the principal will remain untouched, so when your home is eventually paid for, you will still have the $195,000!

Remember, you have $206,000 to invest, so you can also allow the remaining $11,000 to grow at 12% interest. This is an example of compound interest because the interest is not withdrawn, but instead accumulates. Since there are 10 years left on the home loan, we have $P = 11{,}000$; $r = 0.12$, $t = 10$, and $n = 12$ (assume monthly compounding). Calculate:

$$N = nt = (12)(10) = 120, \quad i = \frac{r}{n} = \frac{0.12}{12} = 0.01$$

Thus,

$$A = 11{,}000(1 + 0.01)^{120} \approx 36{,}304.26$$

WATCH YOUR STEP *If you ever said, "When will I ever use this?" here is a real-life example that could save you a great deal of money.*

This means that you have two options:

1. Use your $206,000 to pay off the home loan. You will have the home paid for and will not need to make any further payments.
2. Dispose of your $206,000 as follows: Deposit $195,000 into an account to make your house payments. You won't need to make any further payments. At the end of 10 years you'll still have the $195,000. Deposit the excess $11,000 into an account and let it grow for 10 years. The accumulated value will be $36,304.26.

   Under Option 2 you'll have

   $$\$36{,}304.26 + \$195{,}000 = \$231{,}304.26$$

   in 10 years in addition to all the benefits gained under Option 1.

Inflation

Any discussion of compound interest is incomplete without a discussion of inflation. When there is an increase in the amount of money in circulation, there is a fall in its value which, in turn, causes a rise in prices. This is called **inflation**. The same procedure we used to calculate compound interest can be used to calculate the effects of inflation. The government releases reports of monthly and annual inflation rates. In 1981, the inflation rate was nearly 9%, but in 2004 it was less than 2%. Keep in mind that inflation rates can vary tremendously and that the best we can do in this section is to assume different constant inflation rates. For our purposes in this book, we will assume $n = 1$ (annual compounding) when working inflation problems.

Consider a day worker who is earning $30,000 per year and would like to know what salary he could expect in 20 years if inflation continues at an average of 9%.

$P = 30{,}000$, $r = 0.09$, and $t = 20$.

In this book, assume $n = 1$ for inflation problems. This means that $N = 20$ and $i = 0.09$. Find

$$A = P(1 + i)^N$$

$$= 30{,}000(1 + 0.09)^{20}$$

$$\approx 168{,}132.32 \quad \text{Use a calculator.}$$

The answer means that, if inflation continues at a constant 9% rate, an annual salary of $168,000 will have about the same purchasing power in 20 years as a salary of $30,000 today.

Present Value

Sometimes we know the future value of an investment and wish to know its present value. Such a problem is called a **present value** problem. The **present value formula** follows directly from the future value formula (by division).

Present Value Formula

$$P = \frac{A}{(1 + i)^N}; \text{ on a calculator this is } A \div (1 + i)^N$$

where P is present value, A is future value, $i = r/n$, and $N = nt$.

STOP *This is the same as the future value formula, algebraically solved for* P.

Consider an insurance agent who wishes to sell you a policy that will pay you \$100,000 in 30 years. What is the value of this policy in today's dollars, if we assume a 9% inflation rate? This is a present value problem for which $A = 100{,}000$, $r = 0.09$, and $t = 30$. We calculate

$$N = nt = 1(30) = 30 \qquad i = \frac{r}{n} = \frac{0.09}{1} = 0.09$$

To find the present value, calculate

$$P = \frac{100{,}000}{(1 + 0.09)^{30}} \approx \$7{,}537.11$$

This means that the agent is offering you an amount comparable to \$7,537.11 in terms of today's dollars.

7.5 Buying a Home

IT IS LIKELY THAT YOU WILL PURCHASE A HOME AT LEAST ONCE IN YOUR LIFE, AND THE PURPOSE OF THIS SECTION IS TO HELP YOU THROUGH THAT PROCESS.

A portion of a mortgage application is shown in Figure 7.2.

Home Loans

To purchase a home, you will probably need a lender to agree to provide the money you need. You, in turn, promise to repay the money based on terms set forth in an agreement, or loan contract, called a **mortgage**. As the borrower, you pledge your home as security. It remains pledged until the loan is paid off. If you fail to meet the terms of the contract, the lender has the right to **foreclose**, which means that the lender may take possession of the property.

There are three types of mortgage loans: (1) conventional loans made between you and a private lender; (2) VA loans made to eligible veterans (these are guaranteed by the Veterans Administration, so they cost less than the other types of loans); and (3) FHA loans made by private lenders and insured by the Federal Housing Administration. Regardless of the type of loan you obtain, you will pay certain lender costs. By *lender costs*, we mean all the charges required by the lender: closing costs plus interest.

When you shop around for a loan, certain rates will be quoted:

1. **Interest rate**. This is the annual interest rate for the loan; it fluctuates on a daily basis. The APR, as stated on the loan agreement, is generally just a little higher

Figure 7.2 Portion of a mortgage application

I. TYPE OF MORTGAGE AND TERMS OF LOAN

Mortgage Applied for: ☐ V.A. ☐ Conventional ☐ Other: ☐ FHA ☐ FmHA	Agency Case Number	Lender Case Number

Amount $	Interest Rate %	No. of Months	Amortization Type:	☐ Fixed Rate ☐ Other (explain): ☐ GPM ☐ ARM (type):

II. PROPERTY INFORMATION AND PURPOSE OF LOAN

Subject Property Address (street, city, state, ZIP)	No. of Units
Legal Description of Subject Property (attach description if necessary)	Year Built

Purpose of Loan ☐ Purchase ☐ Construction ☐ Other (explain): ☐ Refinance ☐ Construction-Permanent	Property will be: ☐ Primary Residence ☐ Secondary Residence ☐ Investment

Complete this line if construction or construction-permanent loan.

Year Lot Acquired	Original Cost	Amount Existing Liens	(a) Present Value of Lot	(b) Cost of Improvements	Total (a + b)
	$	$	$	$	$

Complete this line if this is a refinance loan.

Year Acquired	Original Cost	Amount Existing Liens	Purpose of Refinance	Describe Improvements ☐ made ☐ to be made
	$	$		Cost: $

Title will be held in what Name(s)	Manner in which Title will be held	Estate will be held in: ☐ Fee Simple ☐ Leasehold (show expiration date)
Source of Down Payment, Settlement Charges and/or Subordinate Financing (explain)		

than the quoted interest rate. This is because the quoted interest rate is usually based on ordinary interest (360-day year), whereas the APR is based on exact interest (365-day year).

2. **Down payment**. This is the amount that is paid when the loan is obtained. The purchase price minus the down payment is equal to the amount financed.

3. **Origination fee**. This is a one-time charge to cover the lender's administrative costs in processing the loan. It may be a flat $100 to $300 fee, or it may be expressed as a percentage of the loan.

4. **Points**. This refers to discount points, a one-time charge used to adjust the yield on the loan to what the market conditions demand. It offsets constraints placed on the yield by state and federal regulations. Each point is equal to 1% of the amount of the loan.

Suppose that Lender A quotes 8.5% + 2.5 points + $250, and Lender B quotes 8.8% + 1 point + $100. Which lender should you choose? It is desirable to incorporate these three charges—interest rate, origination fee, and points—into one formula so that you can decide which lending institution is offering you the best terms on your loan. This could save you thousands of dollars over the life of your loan. The **comparison rate** formula shown in the following box can be used to calculate the combined effects of these fees. Even though it is not perfectly accurate, it is usually close enough to permit meaningful comparison among lenders.* The lower the rate, the better the offer.

Comparison Rate

$$\text{COMPARISON RATE} = \text{APR} + 0.125\left(\text{POINTS} + \frac{\text{ORIGINATION FEE}}{\text{AMOUNT OF LOAN}}\right)$$

Suppose that you wish to obtain a home loan for $120,000, and you obtain the following quotations from lenders:

Lender A: 8.5% + 2.5 points + $250

Lender B: 8.8% + 1 point + $100

Which lender is making you the better offer? Calculate the comparison rate for both lenders (a calculator is helpful for this calculation).

* The 0.125 is a weighting factor. Since the points and origination fee are one-time factors, they should not be weighted as heavily as the interest rate. Since the decimal 0.125 is equivalent to $\frac{1}{8}$, we see that the one-time fees are weighted to be one-eighth as important as the interest rate.

Lender A:

$$\text{COMPARISON RATE} = \text{APR} + 0.125\left(\text{POINTS} + \frac{\text{FEE}}{\text{AMT OF LOAN}}\right)$$

$$= \underbrace{0.085}_{\text{APR}} + 0.125\left(\underset{\uparrow}{0.025} + \frac{250}{120{,}000}\right) \quad \text{Write points as a decimal.}$$

$$= 0.0884 \text{ or } 8.84\% \quad \text{Use a calculator.}$$

Lender B:

$$\text{COMPARISON RATE} = \text{APR} + 0.125\left(\text{POINTS} + \frac{\text{FEE}}{\text{AMT OF LOAN}}\right)$$

$$= 0.088 + 0.125\left(0.01 + \frac{100}{120{,}000}\right)$$

$$= 0.0894 \text{ or } 8.94\%$$

Lender A is making the better offer, because its comparison rate of 8.84% is less than the comparison rate of Lender B (8.94%).

Monthly Payments

Now imagine that you have selected a lender; next, you need to calculate the monthly payments. Several factors influence the amount of the *monthly payment*:

1. *Length of the loan.*
   Most lenders assume a 30-year period. The shorter the period, the greater the monthly payment; however, the greater the monthly payment, the less the finance charges.

In November 2008, during the housing crisis, Nevada registered the highest foreclosure rate in the nation with 1 in every 74 houses, like this one in North Las Vegas, receiving foreclosure filings.

© Ethan Miller/Getty Images

2. Amount of the *down payment*.
The greater the down payment, the less the amount to finance; and the less the amount to finance, the smaller the monthly payment.

3. The *APR*.
The smaller the interest rate (APR), the smaller the finance charge and consequently the smaller the monthly payment.

The effect of some of these factors is shown in Table 7.1. Some financial counselors suggest making as large a down payment as you can afford, whereas others suggest making as small a down payment as is allowed. You will have to assess many factors, such as your tax bracket and your investment potential, to determine how large a down payment you should make.

If you are obtaining a \$120,000 30-year 8% loan, what would you save in monthly payments and in total payments by increasing your down payment from \$12,000 to \$24,000? From Table 7.1 we see that the monthly payments for a 30-year 8% loan with a 10% (\$12,000) down payment are \$792.47, and with a 20% (\$24,000) down payment the monthly payments are \$704.41. This is a *monthly* savings of \$88.06. The total savings are also found by subtracting the amounts shown in Table 7.1:

$$\$285{,}289 - \$253{,}588 = \$31{,}701$$

The amount of the down payment and the monthly payments are calculated in Table 7.1. However, it is unlikely that you will buy a home with a loan of exactly \$120,000 and an interest rate of exactly 8%. Let's now consider these calculations.

Since the down payment is simply a percent of the purchase price, we encountered the necessary procedures in the first part of this text. The home you select costs \$145,500 and you pay 20% down. What is your down payment? How much will be financed?

$$\text{DOWN PAYMENT} = \$145{,}500 \times 0.20 = \$29{,}100$$

$$\begin{aligned}\text{AMOUNT TO BE FINANCED} &= \text{TOTAL AMOUNT} - \text{DOWN PAYMENT}\\ &= \$145{,}500 - \$29{,}100\\ &= \$116{,}400\end{aligned}$$

You can also find the amount to be financed by using the complement of the down payment. The complement of a 20% down payment is 0.80.

$$\begin{aligned}\text{AMOUNT TO BE FINANCED} &= \text{TOTAL AMOUNT} \times \text{COMPLEMENT}\\ &= \$145{,}500(0.80)\\ &= \$116{,}400\end{aligned}$$

We can use Table 7.2 to calculate the amount of the monthly payment for a loan. You will need to know the amount to be financed, the interest rate, and the length of time the loan is to be financed. The formula for finding the monthly payment uses Table 7.2 as follows:

Monthly Payment

$$\text{MONTHLY PAYMENT} = \frac{\text{AMOUNT OF LOAN}}{1{,}000} \times \text{TABLE 7.2 ENTRY}$$

Table 7.1 Effect of Down Payment on the Cost of a \$120,000 Home with Interest at 8%

Down Payment	Percent	Monthly Payment			Total Payment (nearest dollar)		
		20 Years	25 Years	30 Years	20 Years	25 Years	30 Years
\$0	0%	\$1,003.73	\$926.18	\$880.52	\$240,895	\$277,854	\$316,987
\$6,000	5%	\$953.54	\$879.87	\$836.49	\$228,850	\$263,961	\$301,136
\$12,000	10%	\$903.36	\$833.56	\$792.47	\$216,806	\$250,068	\$285,289
\$24,000	20%	\$802.98	\$740.94	\$704.41	\$192,715	\$222,282	\$253,588
\$30,000	25%	\$752.80	\$694.63	\$660.39	\$180,672	\$208,389	\$237,740
\$36,000	30%	\$702.61	\$648.33	\$616.36	\$168,626	\$194,499	\$221,890

The Nature of Sets and Logic

8.1 Introduction to Sets

IN MATHEMATICS, WE DO NOT DEFINE THE WORD **SET**.

It is what, in mathematics, is called an **undefined term**. It is impossible to define all terms, because every definition requires other terms, so some *undefined terms* are necessary to get us started. To illustrate this idea, let's try to define the word *set* by using dictionary definitions:

"*Set:* a *collection* of objects." What is a collection?

"*Collection:* an *accumulation*." What is an accumulation?

"*Accumulation:* a *collection,* a *pile,* or a *heap*." We see that the word *collection* gives us a **circular definition**. What is a *pile*?

"*Pile:* a *heap*." What is a heap?

"*Heap:* a *pile*."

Do you see that a dictionary leads us in circles? In mathematics, we do not allow circular definitions, and this forces us to accept some words without definition. The term *set* is undefined. Remember, the fact that we do not define *set* does not prevent us from having an intuitive grasp of how to use the word.

Denoting Sets

Sets are usually specified in one of two ways. The first is by *description*, and the other is by the *roster* method. In the **description method**, we specify the set by describing it in such a way that we know exactly which elements belong to it. An example is the set of 50 states in the United States of America. We say that this set is **well defined**, since there is no doubt that the state of California belongs to it and that the state of Germany does not; neither does the state of confusion. Lack of confusion, in fact, is necessary in using sets (see Figure 8.1). The distinctive property that determines the inclusion or exclusion of a particular element is called the *defining property* of the set.

Consider the example of *the set of good students in this class.* This set is not well defined, since it is a matter of opinion whether a student is a "good" student. If we agree, however, on the meaning of the words

Figure 8.1 A well defined set?

© Jim Jurica/iStockphoto.com

Are interior and exterior areas of this building well defined?

Objects in a set are said to be contained in a set of which they are members.

good students, then the set is said to be *well defined*. A better (and more precise) formulation is usually required—for example, *the set of all students in this class who received a C or better on the first examination*. This is well defined, since it can be clearly determined exactly which students received a C or better on the first test.

In the **roster method**, the set is defined by listing the members. The objects in a set are called **members** or **elements** of the set and are said to **belong to** or **be contained in** the set. For example, instead of defining a set as *the set of all students in this class who received a C or better on the first examination*, we might simply define the set by listing its members: {Howie, Mary, Larry}.

Sets are usually denoted by capital letters, and the notation used for sets is braces. Thus, the expression

$$A = \{4, 5, 6\}$$

means that A is the name for the set whose members are the numbers 4, 5, and 6.

Sometimes we use braces with a defining property, as in the following examples:

{states in the United States of America}
{all students in this class who received an A on the first test}

If we try to list the set of rational numbers by roster, we will find that this is a difficult task. A new notation called **set-builder notation** was invented to allow us to combine both the roster and the description methods. Consider:

The set of all x

$$\{x \quad | \quad x \text{ is an even counting number}\}$$

↑ such that

We now use this notation for the set of rational numbers:

$$\left\{ \frac{a}{b} \,\middle|\, a \text{ is an integer and } b \text{ is a nonzero integer} \right\}$$

Read this as: "The set of all $\frac{a}{b}$ such that a is an integer and b is a nonzero integer." We can further shorten this notation. Here are the names for some common sets of numbers:

$\mathbb{N} = \{1, 2, 3, 4, \ldots\}$	Set of **natural**, or **counting, numbers**
$\mathbb{W} = \{0, 1, 2, 3, 4, \ldots\}$	Set of **whole numbers**
$\mathbb{I} = \{\ldots, -2, -1, 0, 1, 2, \ldots\}$	Set of **integers**
$\mathbb{Q} = \left\{ \frac{a}{b} \,\middle|\, a \in \mathbb{I}, b \in \mathbb{I}, b \neq 0 \right\}$	Set of **rational numbers**

Notice that we used a new symbol in the set-builder notation for the set $\mathbb{Q}$. If S is a set, we write $a \in S$ if a is a member of the set S, and we write $b \notin S$ if b is not a member of the set S. Thus, "$a \in \mathbb{I}$" means that the variable a is an integer, and the statement "$b \in \mathbb{I}, b \neq 0$" means that the variable b is a nonzero integer.

Equal and Equivalent Sets

We say that two sets are **equal** if they contain exactly the same elements. Thus, if $E = \{2, 4, 6, 8, \ldots\}$, then

$$\{x | x \text{ is an even counting number}\} = \{x | x \in E\}$$

The order in which you represent elements in a set has no effect on set membership. Thus,

$$\{1, 2, 3\} = \{3, 1, 2\} = \{2, 1, 3\} = \ldots$$

Also, if an element appears in a set more than once, it is not generally listed more than a single time. For example,

$$\{1, 2, 3, 3\} = \{1, 2, 3\}$$

Another possible relationship between sets is that of *equivalence*. Two sets are **equivalent** if they have the same *number* of elements. Don't confuse this concept with equality. Equivalent sets do not need to be equal sets, but equal sets are always equivalent.

The number of elements in a set is often called its **cardinality**. The cardinality of the sets {5, 8, 11} and {1, 2, 3} is 3; that is, the common property of the sets is the **cardinal number** of the set. The cardinality of a set S is denoted by $|S|$. Equivalent sets with four elements each have in common the property of "fourness," and thus we would say that their cardinality is 4.

Certain sets such as $\mathbb{N}$, $\mathbb{I}$, $\mathbb{W}$, or $A = \{1000, 2000, 3000, \ldots\}$ have a common property. We call these *infinite*

sets. If the cardinality of a set is 0 or a counting number, we say the set is **finite**. Otherwise, we say it is **infinite**. We can also say that a set is finite if it has a cardinality less than some counting number, even though we may not know its precise cardinality. For example, we can safely assert that the set of students attending the University of Hawaii is finite even though we may not know its cardinality, because the cardinality is certainly less than a million.

You use the ideas of cardinality and of equivalent sets every time you count something, even though you don't use the term *cardinality*. For example, a set of sheep is counted by finding a set of counting numbers that has the same cardinality as the set of sheep. These equivalent sets are found by using an idea called a *one-to-one correspondence*. If the set of sheep is placed into a one-to-one correspondence with a set of pebbles, the set of pebbles can then be used to represent the set of sheep.

Since infinity is not a number, we cannot correctly say that the cardinality of the counting numbers is infinity. In the late 18th century, Georg Cantor assigned a cardinal number $\aleph_0$ (pronounced "aleph-null") to the set of counting numbers. That is, $\aleph_0$ is the cardinality of the set of counting numbers

$$\mathbb{N} = \{1, 2, 3, 4, \ldots\}$$

The set

$$\mathbb{E} = \{2, 4, 6, 8, \ldots\}$$

also has cardinality $\aleph_0$, since it can be put into a one-to-one correspondence with set $\mathbb{N}$:

$$\begin{array}{l} \mathbb{N} = \{1, 2, 3, 4, \ldots, n \ldots\} \\ \quad\;\; \updownarrow\;\updownarrow\;\updownarrow\;\updownarrow \qquad\;\; \updownarrow \\ \mathbb{E} = \{2, 4, 6, 8, \ldots, 2n \ldots\} \end{array}$$

Universal and Empty Sets

We conclude this section by considering two special sets. The first is the set that contains every element under consideration, and the second is the set that contains no elements. A **universal set**, denoted by U, contains all the elements under consideration in a given discussion; and the **empty set** contains no elements, and thus has cardinality 0. The empty set is denoted by { } or $\varnothing$. Do not confuse the notations $\varnothing$, 0, and $\{\varnothing\}$. The symbol $\varnothing$ denotes a *set* with no elements; the symbol 0 denotes a *number*; and the symbol $\{\varnothing\}$ is a set with one element (namely, the set containing $\varnothing$).

For example, if $U = \{1, 2, 3, 4, 5, 6, 7, 8, 9\}$, then all sets we would be considering would have elements only among the elements of U. No set could contain the number 10, since 10 is not in that agreed-upon universe.

For every problem, a universal set must be specified or implied, and it must remain fixed for that problem. However, when a new problem is begun, a new universal set can be specified.

Notice that we defined *a* universal set and *the* empty set; that is, a universal set may vary from problem to problem, but there is only one empty set. After all, it doesn't matter whether the empty set contains no numbers or no people—it is still empty. The following are examples of descriptions of the empty set:

{living saber-toothed tigers}
{counting numbers less than 1}

8.2 Set Relationships

NOW THAT WE HAVE INTRODUCED SETS, LET'S INVESTIGATE WHAT WE CAN DO WITH THEM.

Subsets

To deal effectively with sets, you must understand certain relationships among sets. A set A is a **subset** of a set B, denoted by $A \subseteq B$, if every element of A is an element of B. Consider the following sets:

$$U = \{1, 2, 3, 4, 5, 6, 7, 8, 9\}$$
$$A = \{2, 4, 6, 8\}, B = \{1, 3, 5, 7\}, C = \{5, 7\}$$

Now, A, B, and C are subsets of the universal set U (*all* sets we consider are subsets of the universe, by definition of a universal set). We also note that $C \subseteq B$ since every element of C is also an element of B. However, C is not a subset of A, written $C \nsubseteq A$. In this case, we merely note that $5 \in C$ and $5 \notin A$.

Do not confuse the notions of "element" and "subset." In the present example, 5 is an *element* of C, since it is listed in C. By the same token, {5} is a *subset* of C, but it is not an element, since we do not find {5} contained in C; if we did, C might look like this: {5,{5},7}. We must therefore be careful to distinguish between a subset and an element. Remember, 5 and {5} mean different things.

The subsets of C can be classified into two categories: *proper* and *improper*. Since every set is a subset of itself, we immediately know one subset for *any* given set: the set itself. A *proper subset* is a subset that is not equal to the original set; that is, A is a **proper subset** of a set B, written $A \subset B$, if A is a subset of B and $A \neq B$. An **improper subset** of a set A is the set A.

We see there are three proper subsets of $C = \{5, 7\}$: $\varnothing$, {5}, and {7}. There is one improper subset of C: {5, 7}.

A set of 2 elements has four subsets, a set of 3 elements has eight subsets, and a set with cardinality 4 has 16 subsets.

The **number of subsets** of a set of size n is 2^n.

Venn Diagrams

A useful way to depict relationships among sets is to let the universal set be represented by a rectangle, with the proper sets in the universe represented by circular or oval regions, as shown in Figure 8.2. These figures are called **Venn diagrams**, after John Venn (1834–1923).

We can also illustrate other relationships between two sets: A and B may have no elements in common, in which case they are **disjoint** (as depicted by Figure 8.3a), or they may be **overlapping sets** that have some elements in common (as depicted in Figure 8.3b).

Sometimes we are given two sets X and Y, and we know nothing about how they are related. In this situation, we draw a general figure, shown in Figure 8.4. In it, there are four regions, labeled I, II, III, and IV.

Figure 8.2 Venn diagrams for subset

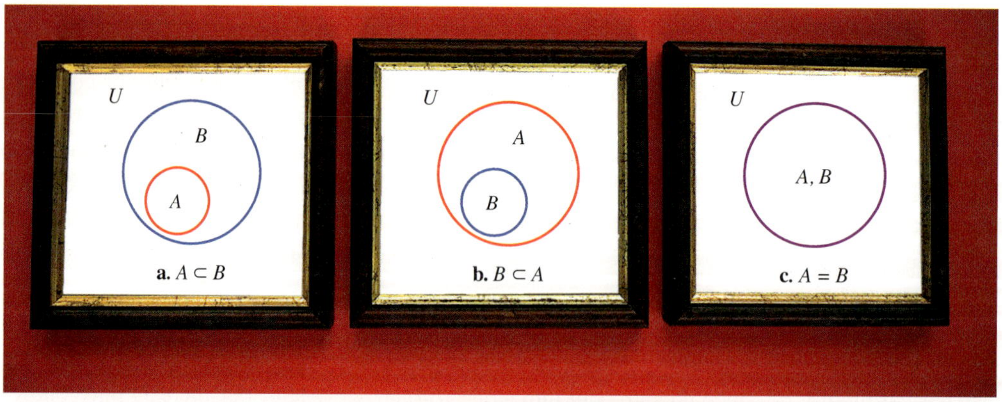

Figure 8.3 Set relationships

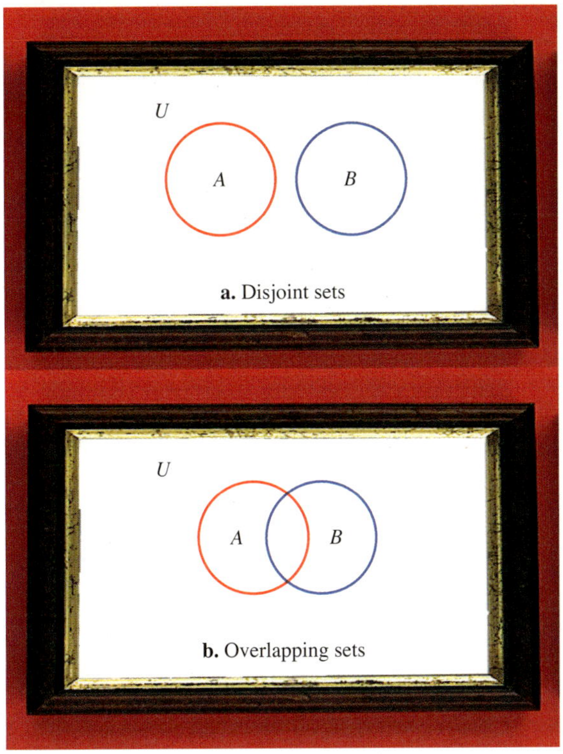

Figure 8.4 Two general sets

If $X \subseteq Y$, then region II is empty.
If $Y \subseteq X$, then region IV is empty.
If $X = Y$, then regions II and IV are empty.
If X and Y are disjoint, then region III is empty.

8.3 Operations with Sets

THERE ARE THREE COMMON OPERATIONS WITH SETS: *UNION*, *INTERSECTION*, AND *COMPLEMENTATION*.

Union

Union is an operation for sets A and B in which a set is formed that consists of all the elements that are in A or B or both. The symbol for the operation of union is $\cup$, and we write $A \cup B$. The operation of union is sometimes translated by the English word "**or**."

> The **union** of sets A and B, denoted by $A \cup B$, is the set consisting of all elements of A or B or both.
>
> *Make sure you understand the set operation of union.

If $A = \{2, 4, 6, 8\}$, $B = \{1, 3, 5, 7\}$, then

$$\begin{aligned}(A \cup B) \cup \{9\} &= \{1, 2, 3, 4, 5, 6, 7, 8\} \cup \{9\} \\ &= \{1, 2, 3, 4, 5, 6, 7, 8, 9\} \\ &= U\end{aligned}$$

We can use Venn diagrams to illustrate union. In Figure 8.5, we first shade A (horizontal lines) and then shade B (vertical lines). *The union is all parts that have been shaded* (either horizontal or vertical) *at least once*; this region is shown as a color screen.

> THE OPERATION OF UNION IS SOMETIMES TRANSLATED BY THE ENGLISH WORD "OR."

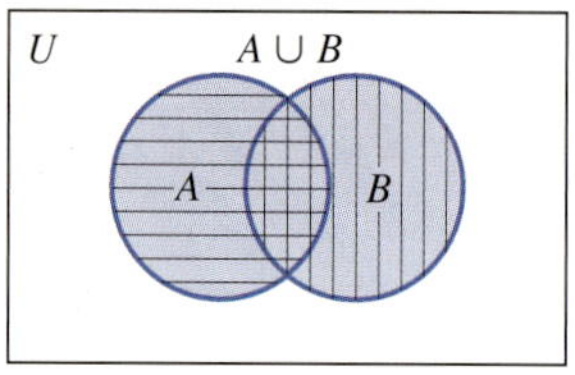

Figure 8.5 Venn diagram for union

Intersection

A second operation is called **intersection**.

The **intersection** of sets *A* and *B*, denoted by $A \cap B$, is the set consisting of all elements common to both *A* and *B*.

*Make sure you understand the set operation of intersection.

The operation of intersection can be translated by the English word "**and**." If $A = \{a, c, e\}$, $B = \{c, d, e\}$, $C = \{e\}$, then

$$\begin{aligned}(A \cap B) \cap C &= \{c, e\} \cap \{e\} && \text{Parentheses first} \\ &= \{e\} && \text{Intersection} \\ &= C\end{aligned}$$

The intersection of sets can also be easily shown using a Venn diagram as in Figure 8.6. The intersection is all parts shaded twice (both horizontal and vertical) as shown with a color screen.

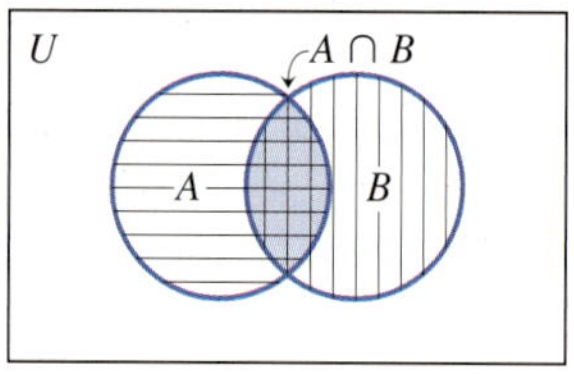

Figure 8.6 Venn diagram for intersection

Complementation

Complementation is an operation on a set that must be performed in reference to a universal set. It can be translated into English by the word "**not**."

Complementation, too, can be shown using a Venn diagram. In a Venn diagram, *the complement is everything*

The **complement** of a set *A*, denoted by $\overline{A}$, is the set of all elements in *U* that are not in the set *A*.

*Make sure you understand the set operation of complementation.

in U that is not in the set under consideration (in this case, everything not in *A*). To find the complement of the set *A*, shade *A* (diagonal lines in Figure 8.7); the complement of *A* is everything in the universe not shaded by the lines as shown with a color screen.

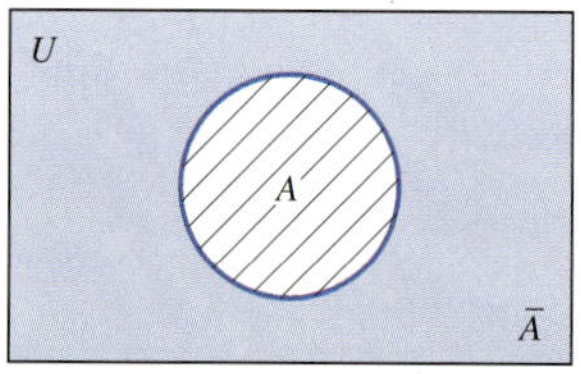

Figure 8.7 Venn diagram for complementation

A survey of 140 students asked the following questions: 1) Are you enrolled in at least one math class, and 2) Are you enrolled in at least one English class? We can draw a Venn diagram to represent students' responses. There are two sets, M = {students enrolled in at least one math class} and E = {students enrolled in at least one English class}. Assume that 50 students are enrolled in math, 60 are enrolled in English, and 20 are enrolled in both. These results are shown in Figure 8.8.

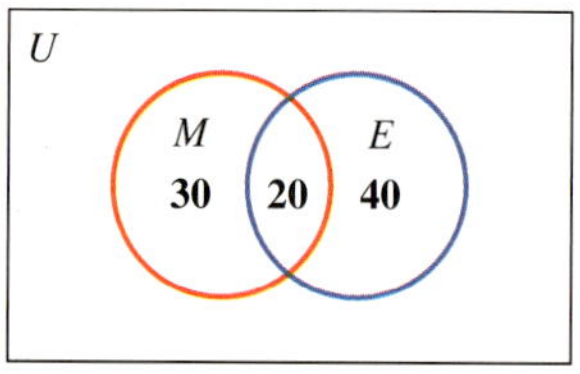

Figure 8.8 Results of survey question

THE COMPLEMENT IS EVERYTHING IN *U* THAT IS NOT IN THE SET UNDER CONSIDERATION.

8.4 Venn Diagrams

IN THE PREVIOUS SECTION, WE DEFINED UNION, INTERSECTION, AND COMPLEMENTATION OF SETS.

However, the real payoff for studying these relationships comes when dealing with combined operations or with several sets at the same time.

Combined Operations with Sets

Draw a Venn diagram for $\overline{A \cup B}$ and contrast it with the Venn diagram for $\overline{A} \cup \overline{B}$. Verify your diagrams for the following particular example: Let $U = \{1, 2, 3, 4, 5, 6, 7, 8, 9, 10\}$ and let $A = \{1, 2\}$, $B = \{4, 5, 6, 7, 8\}$. These are combined operations; in $\overline{A \cup B}$ we first find the union and then find the complement; and for $\overline{A} \cup \overline{B}$, we first find the complements and then find the union.

The answer in the example below is shown as the shaded portion; the lines show the intermediate steps. In your own work, you will generally find it easier to show the *final answer* only in a second color (pen or a highlighter) as shown above. For the particular example at hand, we find

$$\overline{A \cup B} = \overline{\{1, 2\} \cup \{4, 5, 6, 7, 8\}}$$
$$= \overline{\{1, 2, 4, 5, 6, 7, 8\}}$$
$$= \{3, 9, 10\}$$

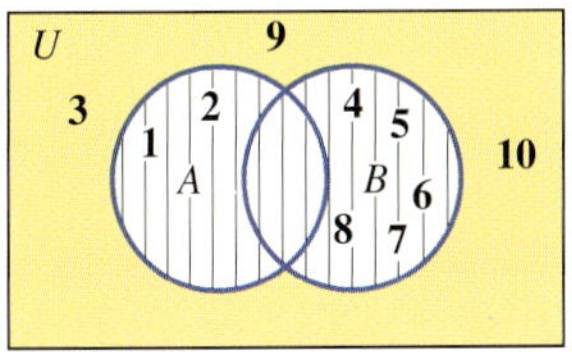

For $\overline{A} \cup \overline{B}$, first find $\overline{A}$ and $\overline{B}$:

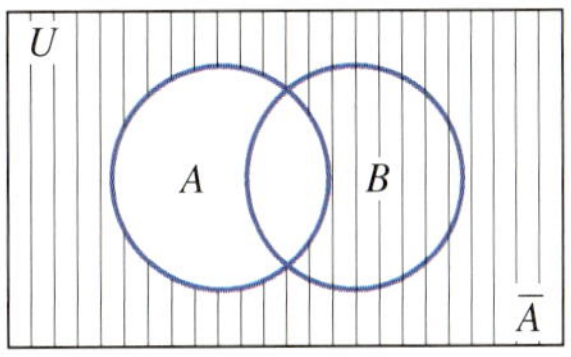

$\overline{A}$ (vertical lines)

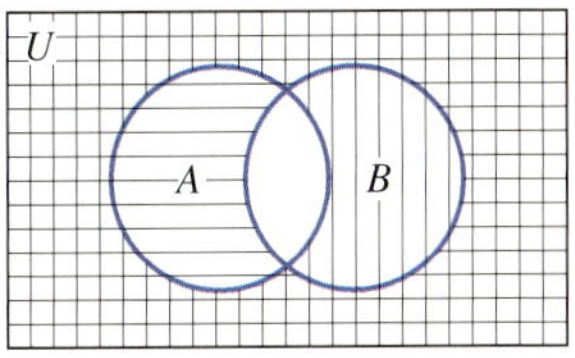

$\overline{A}$ with $\overline{B}$ (horizontal lines)

What you should show is the final step only (using a highlighter) for the union of $\overline{A}$ and $\overline{B}$, which is all parts that have horizontal or vertical lines (or both). This illustration is shown below.

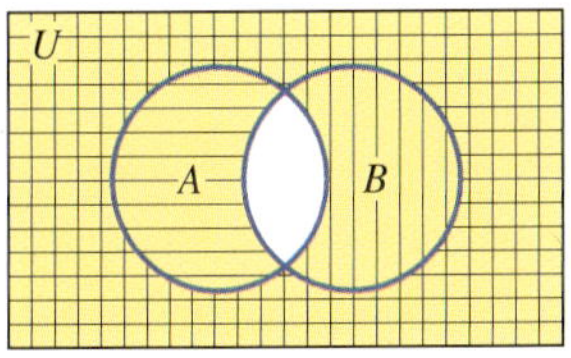

$\overline{A} \cup \overline{B}$

For this particular example, we find

$$\begin{aligned}\overline{A} \cup \overline{B} &= \overline{\{1, 2\}} \cup \overline{\{4, 5, 6, 7, 8\}}\\ &= \{3, 4, 5, 6, 7, 8, 9, 10\} \cup \{1, 2, 3, 9, 10\}\\ &= \{1, 2, 3, 4, 5, 6, 7, 8, 9, 10\}\end{aligned}$$

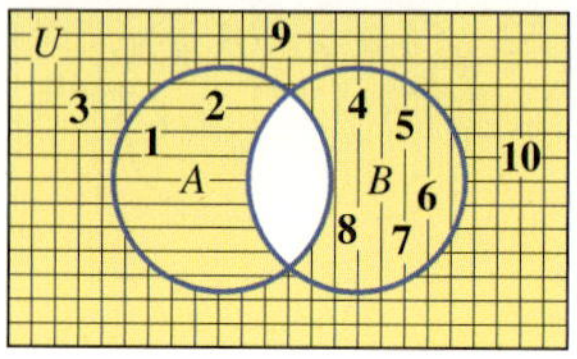

Notice from the Venn diagram that the shaded portion is not the entire universe. *For this example, $\overline{A} \cup \overline{B} = U$, but this is not true in general, since (as the Venn diagram shows) the entire region is not shaded.*

Cardinality of a Union

Venn diagrams can be useful in making general statements about sets. We see for the Venn diagrams above that $\overline{A \cup B} \neq \overline{A} \cup \overline{B}$. If they were equal, the final *shaded* portions of the Venn diagrams would be the same. Suppose that a survey indicates that 45 students are taking mathematics and that 41 are taking English. How many students are taking math or English?

At first, it might seem that all we need to do is add 41 and 45, but such is not the case, as you can see by looking at Figure 8.9.

Figure 8.9 Using a Venn diagram to find the numbers in regions

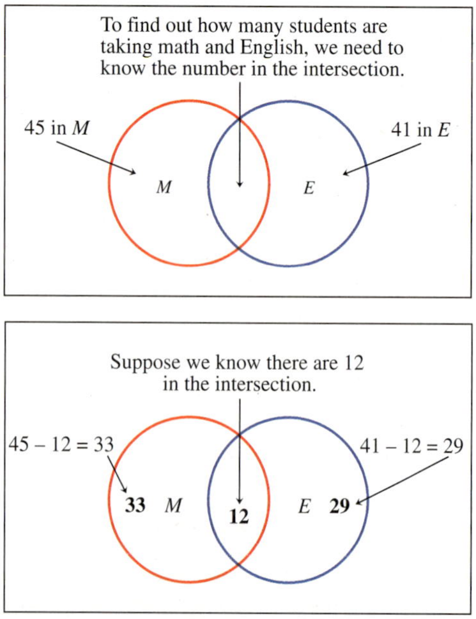

We see that there are 33 + 29 + 12 = 74 students enrolled in mathematics or in English or in both (see Figure 8.9). We see that the proper procedure is to fill in the number in the intersection and then to find the numbers in the other regions by subtraction. This result is summarized with the following property.

Cardinality of a Union

For any two sets X and Y,

$$|X \cup Y| = |X| + |Y| - |X \cap Y|$$

The property of cardinality will be essential to working with survey problems, which we consider in the next section. It will also be used in the chapter on probability.

Show that $\overline{A \cup B} = \overline{A} \cap \overline{B}$. The procedure is to draw a Venn diagram for the left side and a separate diagram for the right side, and then to look to see whether they are the same.

Venn diagrams:

Left side of equal sign | Right side of equal sign

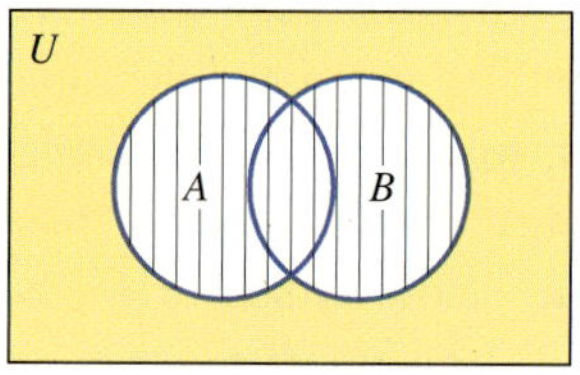

$\overline{A \cup B}$

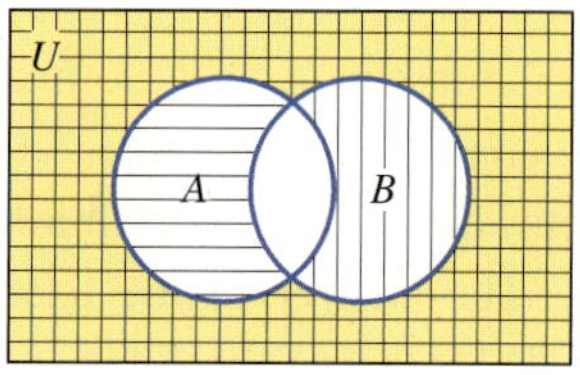

$\overline{A} \cap \overline{B}$

Detail:

$A \cup B$ (vertical lines)
Use a highlighter to show the complement.

$\overline{A}$ (vertical lines)
$\overline{B}$ (horizontal lines)
$\overline{A} \cap \overline{B}$ is the intersection of the horizontal and vertical lines; use a highlighter to show this intersection.

Compare the highlighted portions of the two Venn diagrams. They are the same, so $\overline{A \cup B} = \overline{A} \cap \overline{B}$.

This result is one part of a result known as **De Morgan's laws**, which are important in set theory, logic, and even in the design of circuits.

De Morgan's Laws

$$\overline{X \cup Y} = \overline{X} \cap \overline{Y} \quad \text{and} \quad \overline{X \cap Y} = \overline{X} \cup \overline{Y}$$

The *order* of operations for sets is from left to right, unless there are parentheses. Operations within parentheses are performed first.

Venn Diagrams with Three Sets

Sometimes you will be asked to consider the relationships among three sets. The general Venn diagram is shown in Figure 8.10. Notice that the three sets divide the universe into eight regions. Can you number each part?

Figure 8.10 Three general sets

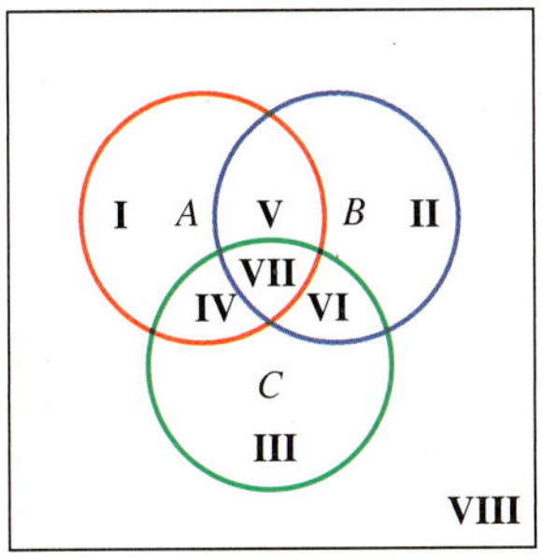

Perform the following combination of operations among three sets:

$\overline{A \cup B} \cap C$

Overbars "act like" parentheses, so do $\overline{A \cup B}$ first (vertical); then fill in C (horizontal). The intersection is all parts that show *both* vertical and horizontal lines; the answer is the part that is highlighted.

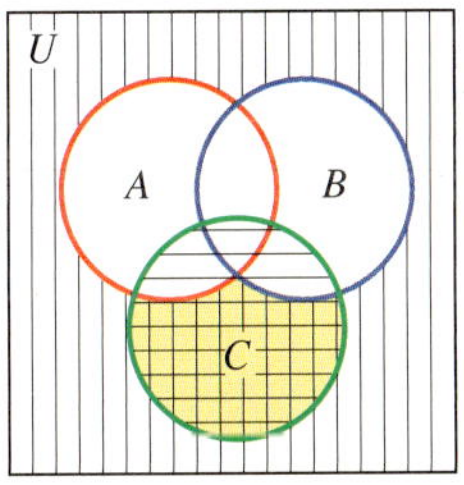

8.5 Survey Problems Using Sets

VENN DIAGRAMS CAN SOMETIMES BE USED TO SOLVE SURVEY PROBLEMS.

We will consider survey problems with two or three sets.

Cardinality with Two Sets

If there are two sets in the survey, then we draw two overlapping sets, as shown in Figure 8.11.

Figure 8.11 Survey problem with two sets, A and B

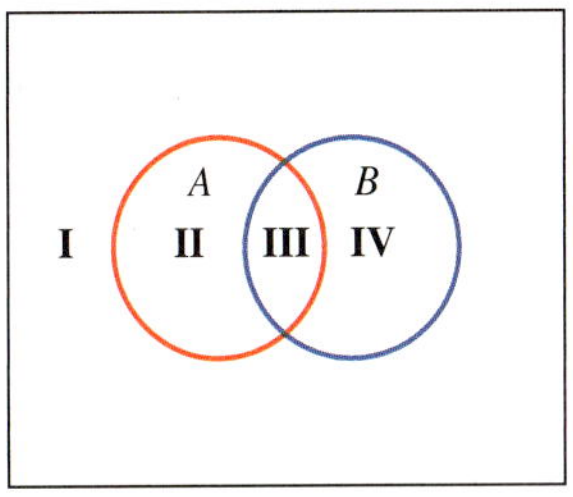

WATCH YOUR STEP *This diagram can be used whenever you are dealing with two sets.*

In the previous section we considered finding the number of elements in the union of two sets. We repeat that property here for convenience: For any two sets X and Y,

$$|X \cup Y| = |X| + |Y| - |X \cap Y|$$

However, when doing survey problems, it is generally easier to use Venn diagrams. For example, give the numbers of elements in the regions marked I, II, III, and IV in Figure 8.11 when $|U| = 100$, $|A| = 30$, $|B| = 40$, and $|A \cap B| = 12$. We draw a Venn diagram with two overlapping sets, as shown in Figure 8.11. Begin with the intersection, and fill in the number of elements in Region III:

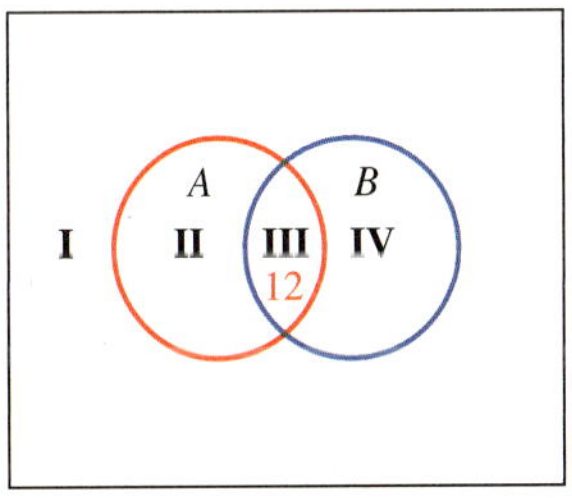

Next, find the numbers of elements in Regions II and IV. For Region II,

$30 - 12 = 18$ Fill in this number in the Venn diagram in Region II.

For Region IV,

$40 - 12 = 28$ Fill in this number in the Venn diagram in Region IV.

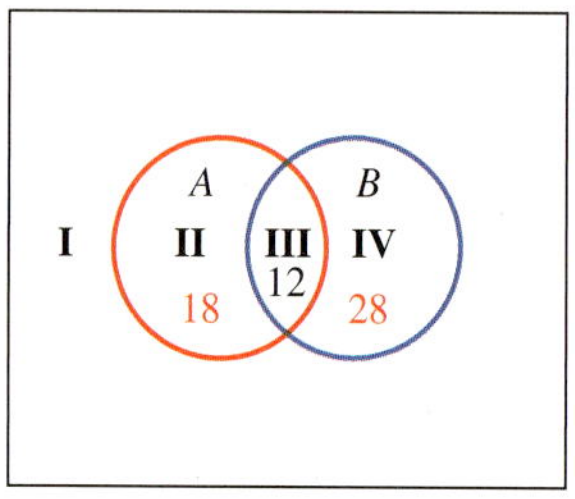

Finally, for Region I,

$$100 - (30 + 40 - 12) = 100 - 58 = 42$$

Cardinality with Three Sets

For three sets, the situation is a little more involved. As we did with two sets, begin with a Venn diagram showing three overlapping sets, as shown in Figure 8.12.

Figure 8.12 Survey problem with three sets *A*, *B*, and *C*

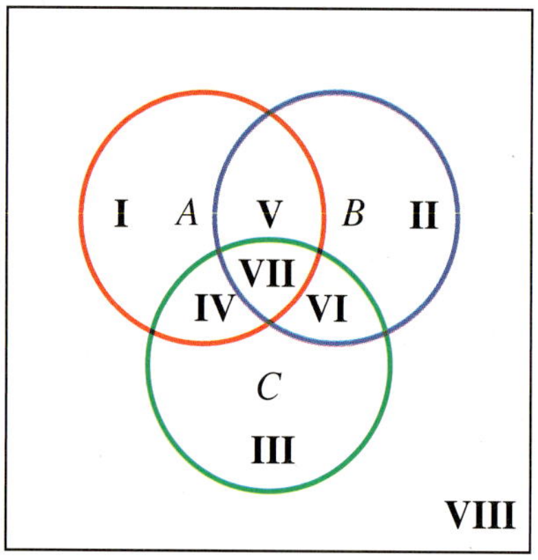

This diagram can be used whenever you are dealing with three sets.

The overall procedure is to fill in the number in the innermost set first and work your way out through the rest of the Venn diagram by using subtraction. We summarize this procedure in the box on the right.

PROCEDURE: Venn Diagram Problems

The procedure for finding the number of elements in each of the eight regions formed by three sets (numbered as shown in Figure 8.12) is given:

STEP 1 Draw a Venn diagram with three overlapping sets.

STEP 2 Fill in the number of elements in the innermost region (Region VII).

STEP 3 Fill in the numbers of elements in those regions with two overlapping parts (Regions IV, V, and VI).

STEP 4 Fill in the numbers of elements in those regions with one part (Regions I, II, and III).

STEP 5 Finally, subtract all the numbers in the Venn diagram from $|U|$ to find the number of elements in none of the sets (Region VIII).

Give the numbers of elements in the regions marked I, II, . . . , VII, and VIII in Figure 8.12 when $|U| = 100$, $|A| = 30$, $|B| = 40$, $|C| = 35$, $|A \cap B| = 12$, $|A \cap C| = 14$, $|B \cap C| = 15$, and $|A \cap B \cap C| = 3$.

STEP 1 Draw a Venn diagram with three overlapping sets, as shown in Figure 8.12.

STEP 2 Fill in the number of elements in Region VII, as shown in Figure 8.12.

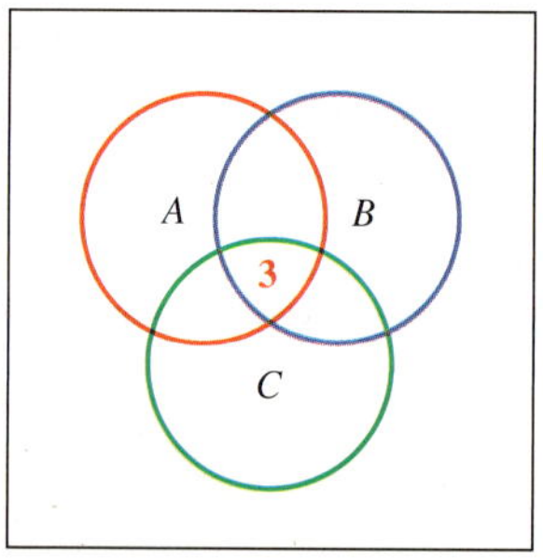

STEP 3 Fill in the numbers in Regions IV, V, and VI.

For Region IV,
$|A \cap C| - |A \cap B \cap C| = 14 - 3 = 11.$
For Region V,
$|A \cap B| - |A \cap B \cap C| = 12 - 3 = 9.$
For Region VI,
$|B \cap C| - |A \cap B \cap C| = 15 - 3 = 12.$

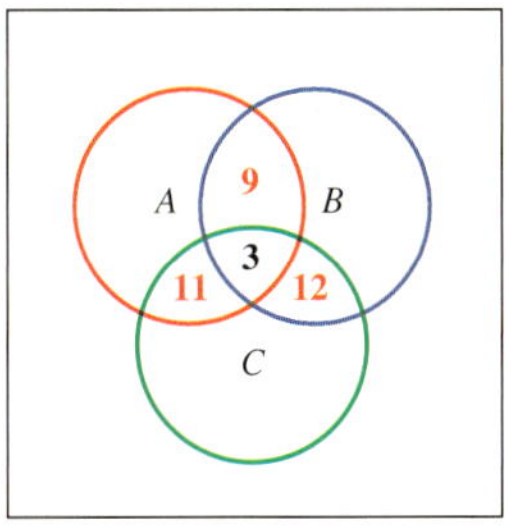

STEP 4 Fill in the numbers in Regions I, II, and III.

For Region I,
$|A| - (9 + 3 + 11) = 30 - (23) = 7.$
For Region II,
$|B| - (9 + 3 + 12) = 40 - (24) = 16.$
For Region III,
$|C| - (11 + 3 + 12) = 35 - (26) = 9.$

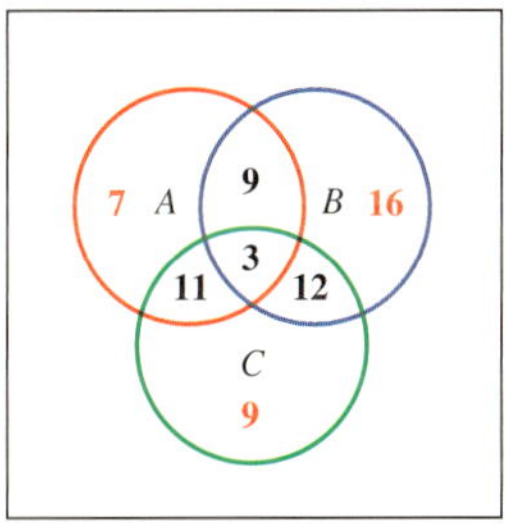

STEP 5 Finally, for Region VIII, subtract all of the numbers in the Venn diagram from $|U|$:

$$100 - (7 + 9 + 3 + 11 + 16 + 12 + 9)$$
$$= 100 - 67 = 33$$

We now apply this procedure to an applied problem which we call a survey problem.

A survey of 100 randomly selected students gave the following information:

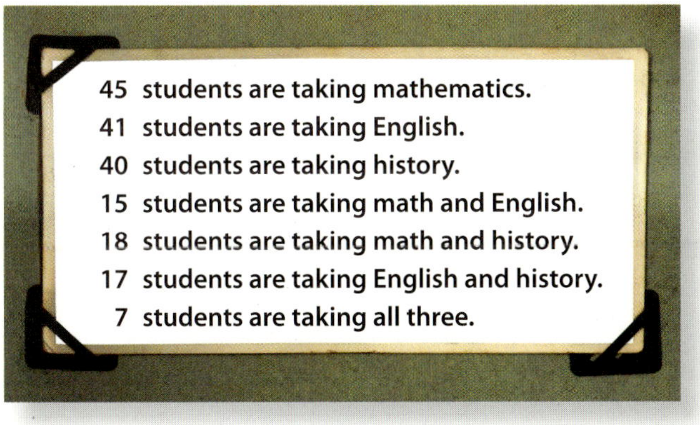

Use Figure 8.12 (with Regions I to VIII) to answer the following questions, which are designed to follow the steps in the procedure for Venn diagram problems.

a. Name the three sets (A, B, and C) in this survey problem.

b. How many students are taking all three subjects (Region VII)?

c. How many are taking mathematics and history, but not English (Region IV)?

d. How many are taking mathematics and English, but not history (Region V)?

e. How many are taking English and history, but not mathematics (Region VI)?

f. How many are taking only mathematics (Region I)?

g. How many are taking only English (Region II)?

h. How many are taking only history (Region III)?

i. How many are taking none of the three subjects (Region VIII)?

Draw a Venn diagram and fill in the various regions.

STEP 1 **a.** Let the three sets be:

$M = \{\text{students taking mathematics}\}$
$E = \{\text{students taking English}\}$
$H = \{\text{students taking history}\}$

Notice that even though the sets in Figure 8.12 are labeled A, B, and C, we relabel those sets M, E, and H, for easy reference in this survey problem.

STEP 2 **b.** Start by filling in the innermost section first; there are 7 in the region $M \cap E \cap H$. Notice that we have filled in a 7 in this region. There are 7 people taking all three subjects.

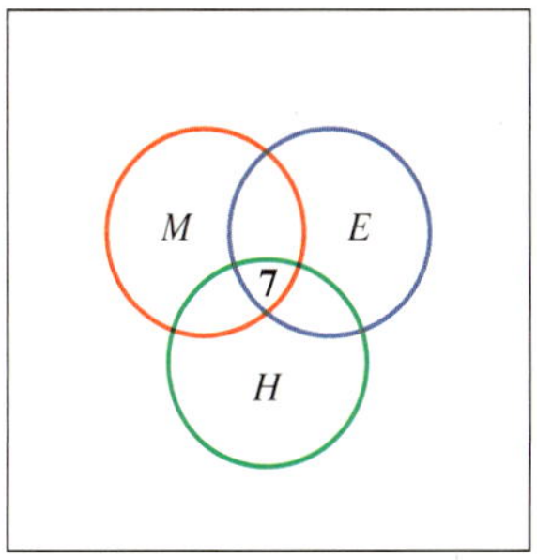

STEP 3 Now fill in the portions of intersection of each pair of two sets, using subtraction:

c. $|M \cap H| = 18$; but 7 have previously been accounted for, so only the *remaining* 11 are added to the Venn diagram ($18 - 7 = 11$). There are 11 students taking mathematics and history, but not English. Fill in 11 into Region IV.

d. $|M \cap E| = 15$; so fill in 8 students ($15 - 7 = 8$). There are 8 students taking mathematics and English, but not history. Fill in 8 into Region V.

e. $|E \cap H| = 17$, so fill in an additional 10 students ($17 - 7 = 10$). There are 10 students taking English and history, but not mathematics. Fill in 10 into Region VI.

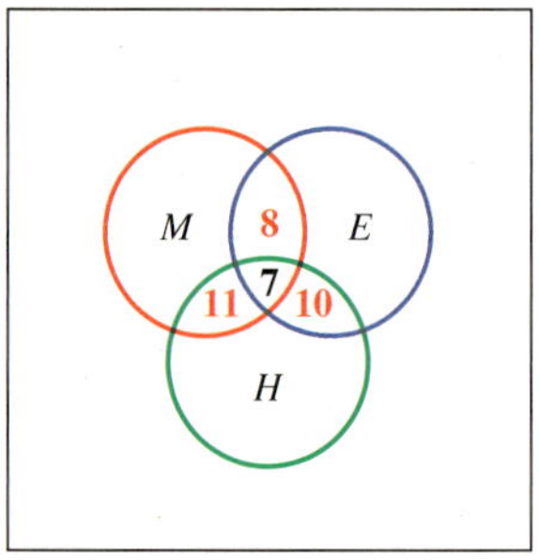

STEP 4 The next step is to fill in the regions of the Venn diagram representing single sets:

f. $|M| = 45$; but 26 (namely, $8 + 7 + 11$) have previously been accounted for, so in this case we subtract 26 from 45, leaving us with 19. Fill this number into Region I. There are 19 students taking only mathematics.

g. $|E| = 41$; but here we subtract 25 ($7 + 10 + 8$) and fill in 16 into Region II.

h. $|H| = 40$; and we subtract 28 ($7 + 10 + 11$) and fill in 12 into Region III.

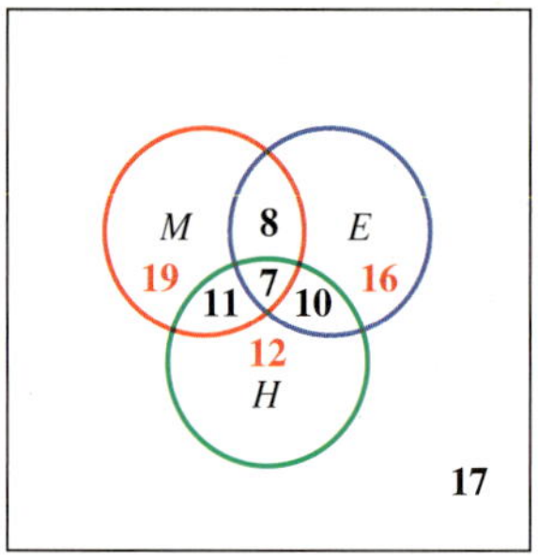

STEP 5 Finally, for Region VIII, subtract all of the numbers in the Venn diagram from $|U|$.

i. Add all the numbers in the diagram and confirm that 83 persons have been accounted for: $19 + 8 + 16 + 11 + 7 + 10 + 12 = 83$. Since 100 students were surveyed, we see that $100 - 83 = 17$ are not taking any of the three courses. We fill in 17 as the number outside the three interlocking circles.

8.6 Inductive and Deductive Reasoning

IN SECTION 8.4 WE USED VENN DIAGRAMS TO PROVE DE MORGAN'S LAWS.

Here we will introduce other methods of proof using what is called **logic**. Logic is a method of reasoning that accepts only those conclusions that are inescapable. We will look at two types of logical reasoning and then we conclude by using Venn diagrams to reach certain conclusions.

Inductive Reasoning

One type of logical reasoning, called **inductive reasoning**, reaches conclusions by observing patterns and then predicting other results based on those observations. It is the type of reasoning used in much of scientific investigation, and it involves reasoning from particular facts or individual cases to a general *conjecture*. A **conjecture** is a guess or generalization predicted from incomplete or uncertain evidence.

> **Inductive reasoning** is reasoning from the particular to the general.

The more individual occurrences you observe, the better able you are to make a correct generalization. As you

2 ESSENTIAL FORMS OF LOGICAL REASONING

1 Inductive reasoning
2 Deductive reasoning

reason from the particular to the general, you must keep in mind that an inductive (tentative) conclusion may have to be revised in light of new evidence. For example, consider this pattern:

$$\left.\begin{aligned} 1 \times 9 &= 9 \\ 2 \times 9 &= 18 \\ 3 \times 9 &= 27 \\ 4 \times 9 &= 36 \\ 5 \times 9 &= 45 \\ 6 \times 9 &= 54 \\ 7 \times 9 &= 63 \\ 8 \times 9 &= 72 \\ 9 \times 9 &= 81 \\ 10 \times 9 &= 90 \end{aligned}\right\}$$

Conjecture: The sum of the digits of the answer of any product involving 9 is always 9.

Evidence: The first ten examples shown here substantiate this speculation.

The conjecture based on this pattern is suspect because it is based on so few cases. In fact, it is shattered by the very next case, where we get $11 \times 9 = 99$. An example that contradicts a conjecture is called a **counterexample**.

Sometimes you must formulate a conjecture based on inductive reasoning. For example, what is the 100th consecutive positive odd number? Use this information to find the sum of the first 100 consecutive positive odd numbers.

Positive odd numbers are 1, 3, 5, ... What is the 100th consecutive odd number?

1 is the 1st odd number;
3 is the 2nd odd number;
5 is the 3rd odd number;
7 is the 4th odd number;
9 is the 5th odd number;
↑
This seems to be one less than twice the term number.

$2(6) - 1 = 11$ is the 6th odd number;
$2(7) - 1 = 13$ is the 7th odd number;
$2(100) - 1 = 199$ is the 100th odd number.

We now look for a pattern to find $1 + 3 + 5 + \cdots + 199$; certainly it is too large an equation to do by brute force (even with a calculator).

$1 = 1$	One term
$1 + 3 = 4$	Two terms
$1 + 3 + 5 = 9$	Three terms
$1 + 3 + 5 + 7 = 16$	Four terms
$1 + 3 + 5 + 7 + 9 = 25$	Five terms

It appears that the sum of 2 terms is $4 = 2^2$; of 3 terms is $9 = 3^2$; of 4 terms is $16 = 4^2$; and of 5 terms is $25 = 5^2$. Thus, the sum of the first 100 consecutive odd numbers seems to be 100^2.

Conjecture: $1 + 3 + 5 + \cdots + 199 = 100^2 = 10{,}000$

Deductive Reasoning

Although mathematicians often proceed by inductive reasoning to formulate new ideas, they are not content to stop at the "probable" stage. Often they formulate their predictions into conjectures and then try to prove these *deductively*. *Deductive reasoning* is a formal structure based on a set of *unproved* statements and a set of *undefined* terms, as well as being a logical process of deriving new results. The unproved statements are called **premises** or **axioms**. For example, consider the following argument:

1. If you read the *Times*, then you are well informed.
2. You read the *Times*.
3. Therefore, you are well informed.

Statements 1 and 2 are the *premises* of the argument; statement 3 is called the **conclusion**. If you accept statements 1 and 2 as true, then you *must* accept statement 3 as true. Such reasoning is called **deductive reasoning**; and if the conclusion follows from the premises, the reasoning is said to be **valid**.

Deductive reasoning consists of reaching a conclusion by using a formal structure based on a set of *undefined terms* and on a set of accepted unproved *axioms* or *premises*. The conclusions are said to be *proved* and are called **theorems**.

WATCH YOUR STEP

Reasoning that is not valid is called **invalid** reasoning. Logic accepts no conclusions except those that are inescapable. This is possible because of the strict way in which concepts are defined. Difficulty in simplifying arguments may arise because of their length, the vagueness of the words used, the literary style, or the possible emotional impact of the words used.

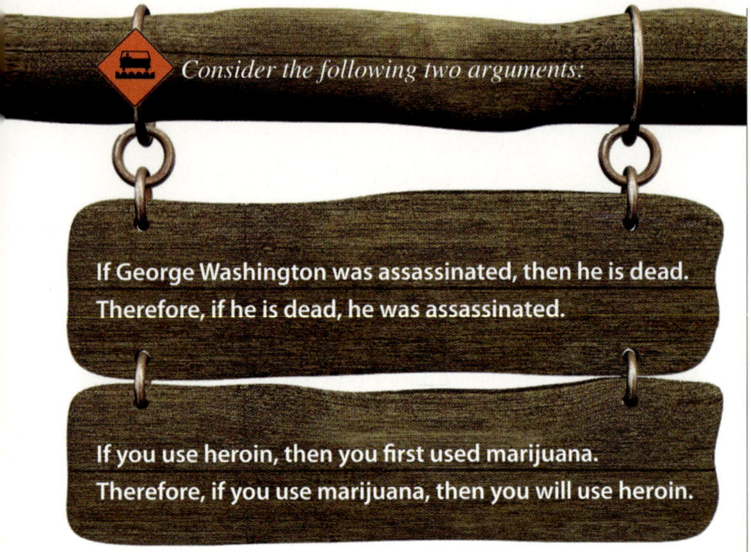

Logically, these two arguments are exactly the same, and both are *invalid* forms of reasoning. Nearly everyone would agree that the first is invalid, but many people see the second as valid. The reason lies in the emotional appeal of the words used.

To avoid these difficulties, we look at the *form* of the arguments and not at the independent truth or falsity of the statements. One type of logic problem is called a **syllogism**. A syllogism has three parts: two *premises*, or hypotheses, and a *conclusion*. The premises give us information from which we form a conclusion. With the syllogism, we are interested in knowing whether the conclusion *necessarily follows* from the premises. If it does, it is called a *valid syllogism*; if not, it is called *invalid*. Consider the following examples:

Valid Forms of Reasoning		Invalid Forms of Reasoning
All Chevrolets are automobiles.	Premise	Some people are nice.
All automobiles have four wheels.	Premise	Some people are broke.
Therefore, all Chevrolets have four wheels.	Conclusion	Therefore, there are some nice broke people.
All teachers are crazy.	Premise	All dodos are extinct.
Karl Smith is a teacher.	Premise	No dinosaurs are dodos.
Therefore, Karl Smith is crazy.	Conclusion	Therefore, all dinosaurs are extinct.

To analyze such arguments, we need to have a systematic method of approach. We will use Venn diagrams.* For two sets p and q, the interpretations are summarized in Figure 8.13.

* In logic, Venn diagrams are often called *Euler circles*, after the famous mathematician Leonhard Euler, who used circles and ovals to analyze this type of argument. However, Venn used these circles in a more general way.

Figure 8.13 Venn diagrams for syllogisms

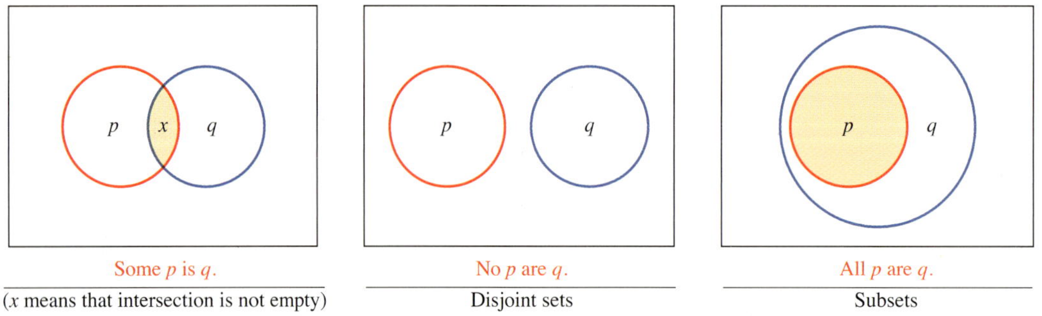

Chapter 9

The Nature of Counting

© Jan Tyler/iStockphoto.com

9.1 Permutations

WE NOW TURN TO AN INVESTIGATION OF THE NATURE OF COUNTING.

It may seem like a simple topic for a college math book, since everyone knows how to count in the usual "one, two, three, . . ." method. However, there are many times we need to know "How many?" but can't find out by direct counting.

Election Problem

Consider a club with five members:

$A = \{\text{Alfie, Bogie, Calvin, Doug, Ernie}\}$

© Travel File/Alamy

Figure 9.1 Tree diagram for five choices

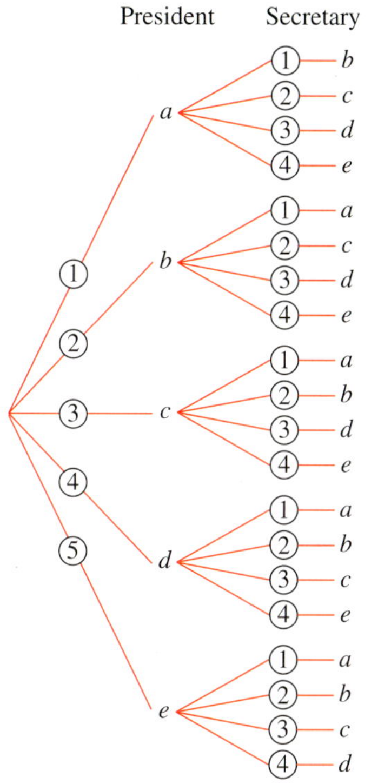

In how many ways could they elect a president and secretary? We call this the *election problem*. There are several ways to solve this problem. The first, and perhaps the easiest, is to make a picture, or a **tree diagram**, listing all possibilities (see Figure 9.1).

We see there are 20 possibilities for choosing a president and a secretary from five club members. This method is effective for "small" tree diagrams, but the technique quickly gets out of hand. For example, if we wished to see how many ways the club could elect a president, secretary, and treasurer, this technique would be very lengthy.

A second method of solution is to use boxes or "pigeonholes" representing each choice separately. Here we determine the number of ways of choosing a president, and then the number of ways of choosing a secretary.

Ways of choosing a president	Ways of choosing a secretary
5	4

↑ Since we have chosen a president, only 4 remain.

We multiply the numbers in the pigeonholes,

$$5 \cdot 4 = 20$$

and we see that the result is the same as from the tree diagram.

A third method is to use the fundamental counting principle, which we'll discuss further in Chapter 10. For now, let's look at a basic definition.

FUNDAMENTAL COUNTING PRINCIPLE

The fundamental counting principle gives the number of ways of performing two or more tasks. If task A can be performed in *m* ways, and if after task A is performed, a second task B can be performed in *n* ways, then task A followed by task B can be performed in $m \times n$ ways.

****You can guess that something with this title is important.***

When set symbols { } are used, the order in which the elements are listed is not important. Suppose now that you wish to select elements from $A = \{a, b, c, d, e\}$ by picking them in a certain order. The selected elements are enclosed in parentheses to signify order and are called an **arrangement** of elements of A. For example, if the elements a and b are selected from A, then there are two pairs, or arrangements:

(a, b) and (b, a)

These arrangements are called **ordered pairs**. Remember, when parentheses are used, the order in which the elements are listed *is* important. This example shows ordered pairs, but you could also select an **ordered triple** such as (d, c, a). These arrangements are said to be selected *without repetition*, since a symbol cannot be used twice in the same arrangement.

If we are given some set of elements and we are to choose *without repetition* a certain number of elements from the set, we can choose them so that the order in which the choices are made is important, or so that it is not. If the *order is important*, we call our result a **permutation**, and if the order is not important it is called a **combination**. We now consider permutations, and we will consider combinations in the next section.

Suppose we consider the election problem for a larger set than A; we wish to elect a president, secretary, and treasurer from among

{Frank, George, Hans, Iris, Jane, Karl}

We could use one of the previously mentioned three methods, but we wish to generalize, so we ask, "Is it possible to count the number of arrangements without actually counting them?"

In answering this question, we note that we are selecting 3 persons from a group of 6 people. If an arbitrary finite set S has n elements and r elements are selected without repetition from S (where $r \leq n$), then an arrangement of the r selected elements is called a *permutation*.

Permutation

A permutation of *r* elements selected from a set *S* with *n* elements is an ordered arrangement of those *r* elements selected without repetition.

How many permutations of two elements can be selected from a set of six elements?

Let $B = \{a, b, c, d, e, f\}$ and select two elements:

$(a, b), (a, c), (a, d), (a, e), (a, f), (b, a), (b, c), (b, d), (b, e), (b, f), (c, a), (c, b), (c, d), (c, e), (c, f), (d, a), (d, b), (d, c), (d, e), (d, f), (e, a), (e, b), (e, c), (e, d), (e, f), (f, a), (f, b), (f, c), (f, d), (f, e)$

STOP *Remember that since we are considering permutations, the order is important; that is,* (a, b) *is NOT the same as* (b, a)*.*

There are 30 permutations of two elements selected from a set of six elements.

This example brings up two difficulties. The first is the lack of notation for the phrase, "the number of permutations of two elements selected from a set of six elements," and the second is the inadequacy of relying on direct counting, especially if the sets are very large.

Notation for Permutations

The symbol $_nP_r$ is used to denote the number of permutations of r elements selected from a set of n elements.

The preceding example can now be shortened by writing

$_6P_2 = 30$ — Actual number of permutations is 30.

↑ Total number in set; ↑ Number we are selecting from the set

From the fundamental counting principle, we can also write

$$_6P_2 = \underbrace{6 \cdot 5}_{\text{Two factors}} = 30.$$

Evaluate:

a. $_{52}P_2 = \underbrace{52 \cdot 51}_{\text{Two factors}} = 2{,}652$

b. $_7P_3 = \underbrace{7 \cdot 6 \cdot 5}_{\text{Three factors}} = 210$

c. $_{10}P_4 = \underbrace{10 \cdot 9 \cdot 8 \cdot 7}_{\text{Four factors}} = 5{,}040$

d. $_{10}P_1 = \underbrace{10}_{\text{One factor}}$

e. $_nP_r = \underbrace{n(n-1)(n-2)\cdot\cdots\cdot(n-r+1)}_{r \text{ factors}}$

Factorial

In our work with permutations, we will frequently encounter products such as

$6 \cdot 5 \cdot 4 \cdot 3 \cdot 2 \cdot 1$ or
$10 \cdot 9 \cdot 8 \cdot 7 \cdot 6 \cdot 5 \cdot 4 \cdot 3 \cdot 2 \cdot 1$ or
$52 \cdot 51 \cdot 50 \cdot 49 \cdot\cdots\cdot 4 \cdot 3 \cdot 2 \cdot 1$

Since these are rather lengthy, we use *factorial notation.*

Factorial

For any counting number n, the factorial of n is defined by

$$n! = n(n-1)(n-2)\cdot\cdots\cdot 3 \cdot 2 \cdot 1$$

Also, $0! = 1$.

If you actually carry out some factorial calculations, you will discover a useful property of factorials: $3! = 3 \cdot 2!$, $4! = 4 \cdot 3!$, $5! = 5 \cdot 4!$; that is, to calculate $11!$ you would not need to "start over" but simply multiply 11 by the answer found for $10!$. This property is called the **multiplication property of factorials** or the **count-down property**.

COUNT-DOWN PROPERTY

$$n! = n \cdot (n-1)!$$

Using factorials, we can find a formula for $_nP_r$.

$$\begin{aligned} _nP_r &= n(n-1)(n-2)\cdot\cdots\cdot(n-r+1) \\ &= n(n-1)(n-2)\cdot\cdots\cdot(n-r+1)\cdot\frac{(n-r)!}{(n-r)!} \\ &= \frac{n(n-1)(n-2)\cdot\cdots\cdot(n-r+1)(n-r)!}{(n-r)!} \\ &= \frac{n!}{(n-r)!} \end{aligned}$$

This is the general formula for $_nP_r$.

Permutation Formula

$$_nP_r = \frac{n!}{(n-r)!}$$

Evaluate:

a. $_{10}P_2 = \dfrac{10!}{(10-2)!} = \dfrac{10!}{8!} = \dfrac{10 \cdot 9 \cdot 8!}{8!} = 90$

b. $_nP_0 = \dfrac{n!}{(n-0)!} = \dfrac{n!}{n!} = 1$

c. $_8P_8 = \dfrac{8!}{(8-8)!} = \dfrac{8!}{0!} = 8! = 40{,}320$

We return to the situation at the beginning of this section. In how many ways can we select a president, secretary, and treasurer from a club of six members?

The election is a permutation problem:

$$_6P_3 = \frac{6!}{(6-3)!} = 120$$

Distinguishable Permutations

We now consider a generalization of permutations in which one or more of the selected items are *indistinguishable* from the others.

Find the number of arrangements of letters in the given word:

a. MATH; this is a permutation of four objects taken four at a time:

$$_4P_4 = 4! = 24$$

b. HATH; this is different from part **a** because not all the letters in the word HATH are distinguishable; that is, the first and last letters are both H so they are *indistinguishable*. If we make the letters distinguishable by labeling them as HATH, we see that now the list is the same as in part **a.** Let us list the possibilities.

Possibilities if Hs are indistinguishable
(First and second columns are the same.)

HATH	HATH
HAHT	HAHT
HTAH	HTAH
HTHA	HTHA
HHTA	HHTA
HHAT	HHAT
AHHT	AHHT
AHTH	AHTH
ATHH	ATHH
THHA	THHA
THAH	THAH
TAHH	TAHH

We see that there are 24 possibilities, but notice how we have arranged this listing. If we consider H = H (that is, the Hs are indistinguishable), we see that the first and the second columns are the same. Since there are *two* indistinguishable letters, we divide the total by 2:

$$\frac{4!}{2} = \frac{24}{2} = 12$$

This example suggests a general result.

Formula for Distinguishable Permutations

The number of **distinguishable permutations** of n objects in which n_1 are of one kind, n_2 are of another kind, . . . , and n_k are of a further kind, so that $n = n_1 + n_2 + \cdots + n_k$ is denoted by

$\binom{n}{n_1, n_2, \ldots, n_k}$ and is defined by the formula

$$\binom{n}{n_1, n_2, \ldots, n_k} = \frac{n!}{n_1!n_2! \cdot \cdots \cdot n_k!}$$

What is the number of distinguishable permutations of the letters in the words NATURE OF MATHEMATICS?

There are 19 letters: A and T (3 times each), E and M (2 times each), and 9 letters each appearing once. We use the formula for distinguishable permutations.

$$\frac{19!}{3!3!2!2!1!1!1!1!1!1!1!1!1!} = 8.447576417 \times 10^{14}$$

By calculator; note the sum of the numbers on the bottom is 19.

If we also consider the spaces and where they occur (which would be necessary if you were programming this on a computer), then the number of possibilities is found by

$$\frac{21!}{3!3!2!2!2!1!1!1!1!1!1!1!1!1!1!} = 1.773991048 \times 10^{17}$$

9.2 Combinations

IN THE LAST SECTION, WE INTRODUCED THE SITUATION IN WHICH WE ARE GIVEN SOME SET OF ELEMENTS AND WE ARE TO CHOOSE *WITHOUT REPETITION* A CERTAIN NUMBER OF ELEMENTS FROM THE SET.

We can choose them so that the order in which the choices are made is important, or so that it is not. If the *order is important*, the selection was called a permutation, and if the order is not important it was called a combination. We consider combinations in this section.

© iStockphoto.com

Committee Problem

Reconsider the club example given at the beginning of the previous section:

$$A = \{\text{Alfie, Bogie, Calvin, Doug, Ernie}\}$$

In how many ways could they elect a committee of two persons? We call this the *committee problem*.

One method of solution is easy (but tedious) and involves the enumeration of all possibilities:

$\{a, b\}$	$\{b, c\}$	$\{c, d\}$	$\{d, e\}$
$\{a, c\}$	$\{b, d\}$	$\{c, e\}$	
$\{a, d\}$	$\{b, e\}$		
$\{a, e\}$			

We see there are ten possible two-member committees. Do you see why we cannot use the fundamental counting principle for this committee problem in the same way we did for the election problem?

We have presented two different types of counting problems, the *election problem* and the *committee problem*. For the election problem, we found an easy numerical method of counting, using the fundamental counting principle. For the committee problem, we did not; further investigation is necessary.

Let us compare the committee and election problems. We saw in the preceding section, while considering the election problem, that the following arrangements are *different*:

President	Secretary	Treasurer
Alfie	Bogie	Calvin
Bogie	Alfie	Calvin

That is, the order was important. However, in the committee problem, the three-member committees listed above are the *same*.

In this case, the order *is not important*. When the order in which the objects are listed is not important, we call the list a **combination** and represent it as a *subset* of A.

As shown in the table below, we've selected two elements from the set $A = \{a, b, c, d, e\}$, and listed all possible arrangements as well as all possible subsets.

Permutations—arrangements Order important	Combinations—subsets Order not important
(a, b), (a, c), (a, d), (a, e),	$\{a, b\}$, $\{a, c\}$, $\{a, d\}$, $\{a, e\}$,
(b, a), (b, c), (b, d), (b, e),	$\{b, c\}$, $\{b, d\}$, $\{b, e\}$,
(c, a), (c, b), (c, d), (c, e),	↑ $\{c, d\}$, $\{c, e\}$,
(d, a), (d, b), (d, c), (d, e),	**Do not list** $\{b, a\}$ since $\{a, b\} = \{b, a\}$. $\{d, e\}$
(e, a), (e, b), (e, c), (e, d)	
Note that ordered pair notation is used. There are 20 permutations.	Note that set notation is used. There are 10 combinations.

We now state a definition of a combination.

A **combination** of r elements of a finite set S of n elements is a subset of S that contains r distinct elements. The notations $\binom{n}{r}$ and ${}_nC_r$ are both used to denote the number of combinations of r elements selected from a set of n elements ($r \leq n$).

The notation ${}_nC_r$ is similar to the notation used for permutations, but since $\binom{n}{r}$ is more common in your later work in mathematics, we will usually use this notation for combinations. The notation $\binom{n}{r}$ is read as "n choose r." The formula for the number of permutations leads directly to a formula for the number of combinations since each subset of r elements has $r!$ permutations of its members. Thus, by the fundamental counting principle,

$$\binom{n}{r} \cdot r! = {}_nP_r \quad \text{so} \quad \binom{n}{r} = \frac{{}_nP_r}{r!} = \frac{n!}{r!(n-r)!}$$

Combination Formula

$$\binom{n}{r} = \frac{n!}{r!(n-r)!}$$

In how many ways can a club of five members select a three-person committee? In an election, the order of selection is important, but in choosing a committee, the order of selection is not important, so this is a combination. Three members are selected from five, so we have "5 choose 3":

$$\binom{5}{3} = \frac{5!}{3!2!} = \frac{5 \cdot 4}{2!} = 10$$

Many applications deal with an ordinary **deck of cards**, as shown in Figure 9.2 on the next page.

Find the number of five-card hands that can be drawn from an ordinary deck of cards.

$$\binom{52}{5} = \frac{52!}{5!47!} = \frac{52 \cdot 51 \cdot 50 \cdot 49 \cdot 48 \cdot 47!}{5 \cdot 4 \cdot 3 \cdot 2 \cdot 1 \cdot 47!} = 2{,}598{,}960$$

In how many ways can a heart flush be drawn in poker? (A heart flush is any hand of five hearts.) We need to determine the number of combinations of 13 objects (hearts) taken 5 at a time. Thus,

$$\binom{13}{5} = \frac{13!}{5!8!} = \frac{13 \cdot 12 \cdot 11 \cdot 10 \cdot 9 \cdot 8!}{5 \cdot 4 \cdot 3 \cdot 2 \cdot 1 \cdot 8!} = 1{,}287$$

In how many ways can a flush be drawn in poker? (A flush is five cards of one suit.) There are four possible suits, so we use the fundamental counting principle, along with the above result.

Number of suits

$$4 \cdot 1{,}287 = 5{,}148$$

Number of ways for a particular suit

Figure 9.2 A deck of cards

Pascal's Triangle

For many applications, if n and r are relatively small (which will be the case for most of the problems for this course) you should notice the following relationship:

$$\binom{0}{0} = 1$$

$$\binom{1}{0} = 1 \quad \binom{1}{1} = 1$$

$$\binom{2}{0} = 1 \quad \binom{2}{1} = 2 \quad \binom{2}{2} = 1$$

$$\binom{3}{0} = 1 \quad \binom{3}{1} = 3 \quad \binom{3}{2} = 3 \quad \binom{3}{3} = 1$$

$$\binom{4}{0} = 1 \quad \binom{4}{1} = 4 \quad \binom{4}{2} = 6 \quad \binom{4}{3} = 4 \quad \binom{4}{4} = 1$$

$$\vdots$$

That is, $\binom{n}{r}$ is the number in the nth row, rth diagonal of Pascal's triangle (see Figure 9.3).

Figure 9.3 Pascal's triangle

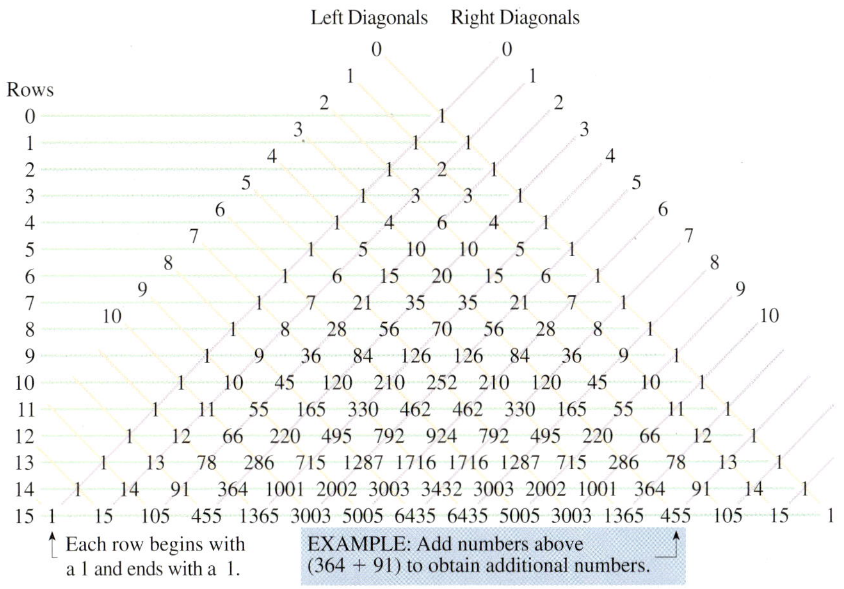

"Five trillion, four hundred eighty billion, five hundred twenty-three million, two hundred ninety-seven thousand, one-hundred and sixty-two . . ."

In practice, we are usually required to decide whether a given counting problem is a **permutation** or a **combination** before we can find a solution. For the sake of review, recall the difference between the election and committee problems of the previous sections. The election problem is a permutation problem, and the committee problem is a combination problem. We summarize and compare the concepts of permutation and combination.

9.3 Counting Without Counting

ONE OF THE IMPORTANT TOPICS OF THIS CHAPTER IS TO UNDERSTAND THAT THERE ARE MORE EFFICIENT WAYS OF COUNTING THAN THE OLD "ONE, TWO, THREE, . . . " TECHNIQUE.

There are many ways of counting. We saw that some counting problems can be solved by using the fundamental counting principle, some by using permutations, and some by using combinations. Other problems required that we combine some of these ideas. However, it is important to keep in mind that not all counting problems fall into one of these neat categories.

Keep in mind, therefore, as we go through this section, that, although some problems may be permutation problems and some may be combination problems, there are many counting problems that are neither.

Permutations and Combinations

A **permutation** of a set of objects is an arrangement of a certain number of these objects in a *specific order*. A **combination** of a set of objects is an arrangement of a certain number of these objects *without regard to their order.*

STOP *remember

Permutation—Order is important. Combination—Order is not important.

License Plate Problem

States issue vehicle license plates, and as the number of registered vehicles increases, new plates are designed with more numerals and letters. For example, the state of California has some plates consisting of three letters followed by three digits. When they ran out of these possibilities, they began making license plates with three digits followed by three letters. Most recently they have issued plates with

Figure 9.4 Preamble to the U. S. Constitution using license plates

one digit followed by three letters in turn followed by three more digits.

Many states issue personalized plates. Figure 9.4 shows a work by Mike Wilkins, who not only assembled the plates to spell out the preamble of the U.S. Constitution, but also did it by using all 50 states in *alphabetical order!*

How many license plates can be formed if repetition of letters or digits is not allowed, and the state uses the scheme of three numerals followed by three letters?

To make sure you understand the question, which of the following plates would be considered a success (no repetition)?

123ABC	Success
122ABC	Failure; repeated digit
456AAB	Failure; repeated letter
111AAA	Failure; repeated letter and repeated numeral
890XYZ	Success

We can use the fundamental counting principle to count the number of license plates that *do not* have a repetition:

Number of digits ↓ (10); Letters in the alphabet ↓ (26)

$$10 \times 9 \times 8 \times 26 \times 25 \times 24 = 11{,}232{,}000$$

Digits left ↑ (9); Letters left after the first one (no repetitions) ↑ (25)

Which Method?

We have now looked at several counting schemes: tree diagrams, pigeonholes, the fundamental counting principle, permutations, distinguishable permutations, and combinations. In practice, you will generally not be told what type of counting problem you are dealing with—you will need to decide. Table 9.1 should help with that decision. Remember, tree diagrams and pigeonholes are applications of the fundamental counting principle, so they are not listed separately in the table.

Using a different approach, what is the number of license plates possible if each license plate consists of three letters followed by three digits, and we add the condition that repetition of letters or digits is not permitted? This is a permutation problem since the *order* in which the elements are arranged is important, and the choice is without

Table 9.1 Counting Methods

Fundamental Counting Principle	Permutations	Combinations	Distinguishable Permutations
Counts the total number of separate tasks.	Number of ways of selecting r items out of n items		n elements divided into k categories
Repetitions are allowed.	Repetitions are not allowed.		Repetitions are not allowed.
If tasks $1, 2, 3, \ldots, k$ can be performed in $n_1, n_2, n_3, \ldots, n_k$ ways, respectively, then the total number of ways the tasks can be done is $n_1 \cdot n_2 \cdot n_3 \cdot \cdots \cdot n_k$	Order important; called *arrangements* Formula: $_nP_r = \dfrac{n!}{(n-r)!}$	Order not important; called *subsets* Formula: $\dbinom{n}{r} = \dfrac{n!}{r!(n-r)!}$	Order of categories is important. $\dbinom{n}{n_1, n_2, \ldots, n_k} = \dfrac{n!}{n_1!n_2! \cdots n_k!}$ where $n = n_1 + n_2 + \cdots + n_k$

© Bob Daemmrich/PhotoEdit

repetition. The number is found by using permutations along with the fundamental counting principle:

$${}_{26}P_3 \cdot {}_{10}P_3 = 26 \cdot 25 \cdot 24 \cdot 10 \cdot 9 \cdot 8 = 11{,}232{,}000$$

Notice that this method and the one used to solve this problem in the previous example produce the same result.

Consider another example. Suppose a quartet is to be selected from a choir. There is to be one soprano selected from a group of six sopranos, two tenors selected from a group of five tenors, and a bass selected from three basses.

a. In how many ways can the quartet be formed? Begin with the fundamental counting principle:

$$\underbrace{\binom{6}{1}}_{\text{Soprano}} \cdot \underbrace{\binom{5}{2}}_{\text{Two tenors}} \cdot \underbrace{\binom{3}{1}}_{\text{Bass}} = 6 \cdot 10 \cdot 3 = 180$$

b. In how many ways can the quartet be formed if one of the tenors is designated lead tenor? Since the order of selecting the tenors is important, the middle factor from part a is replaced by

$${}_5P_2 = \frac{5!}{3!} = 20$$

The number of ways of selecting the quartet is $6 \cdot 20 \cdot 3 = 360$.

The principle of counting without counting is particularly useful when the results become more complicated, as illustrated by the following example.

Find the number of ways of obtaining at least one diamond when drawing five cards from an ordinary deck of cards. This is very difficult if we proceed directly, but we can compute the number of ways of not drawing a diamond:

$${}_{39}C_5 = \frac{39 \cdot 38 \cdot 37 \cdot 36 \cdot 35}{5 \cdot 4 \cdot 3 \cdot 2 \cdot 1} = 575{,}757$$

In the last section, we found there is a total of 2,598,960 possibilities, so the number of ways of drawing at least one diamond is

$$2{,}598{,}960 - 575{,}757 = 2{,}023{,}203$$

9.4 Rubik's Cube and Instant Insanity

THIS SECTION DISCUSSES TWO FAMOUS PUZZLES, THE INSTANT INSANITY AND RUBIK'S CUBE PUZZLES.*

If you are not familiar with these fascinating puzzles, check them out on the web. You can reach them via **www.mathnature.com**.

Rubik's cube:

http://www.schubart.net/rc/

Instant Insanity:

http://mysite.verizon.net/msmammek/markspuz.html

Rubik's Cube

In the summer of 1974, a Hungarian architect invented a three-dimensional object that could rotate about *all three axes* (sounds impossible, doesn't it?). He wrote up the details of the cube and obtained a patent in 1975. The cube is now known worldwide as **Rubik's cube**. In case you have not seen one of these cubes, it is shown in Figure 9.5.

When you purchase the cube, it is arranged so that each face is showing a different color, but after a few turns it seems next to impossible to return to the start. In fact, the manufacturer claims there are 8.86×10^{22} possible arrangements, of which there is only one correct solution. This claim is incorrect; there are 2,048 possible solutions among the 8.86×10^{22} claimed arrangements (actually,

* The term "Rubik's Cube" is a trademark of Ideal Toy Corporation, Hollis, New York. The term "Rubik's cube" as used in this book means the cube puzzle sold under any trademark. "Instant Insanity" is a trademark of Parker Brothers, Inc.

Figure 9.5 Rubik's cube

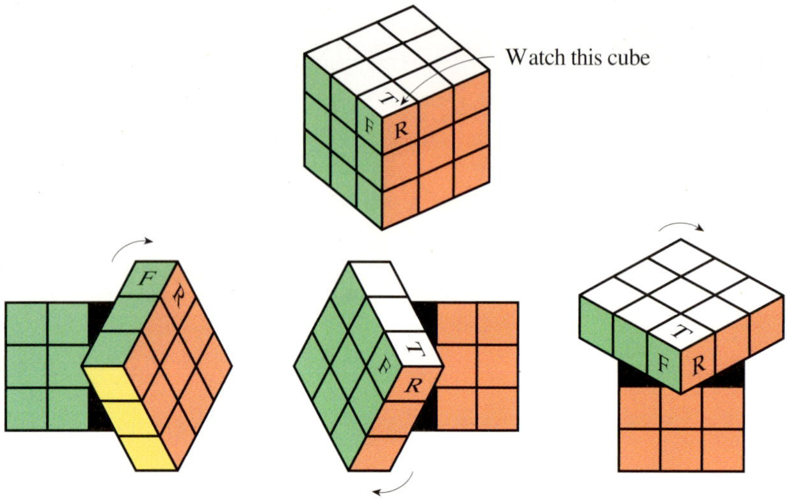

a. Rotate the top right corner with the right face.

b. Rotate the top right corner with the front face.

c. Rotate the top right corner with the top face.

$8.85801027 \times 10^{22}$). This means there is one solution for each 4.3×10^{19} (actually 43,252,003,274,489,856,000) arrangements.

Let's consider what we call the *standard-position cube*, as shown in Figure 9.6. Label the faces Front (F), Right (R), Left (L), Back (B), Top (T), and Under (U), as shown. Hold the cube in your left hand with T up and F toward you so that L is against your left palm. Now describe the results of the moves in the following example.

Figure 9.6 Standard-position Rubik's cube

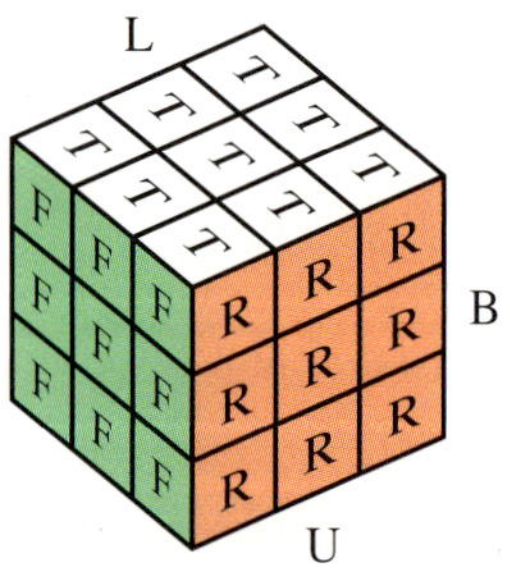

a. Rotate the right face 90° clockwise; denote this move by R. Return the cube to standard position; we denote this move by R^{-1}.

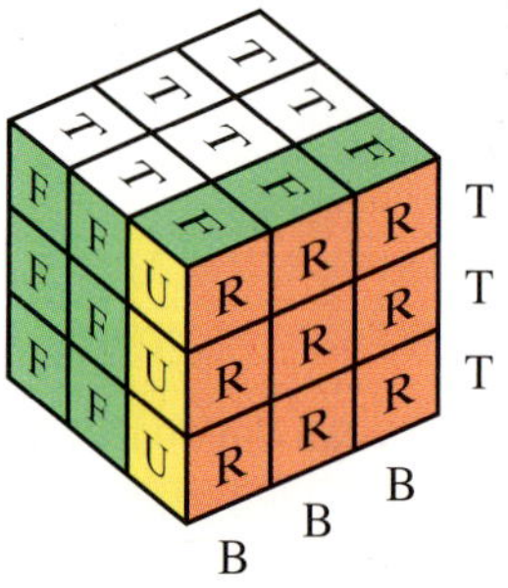

b. Rotate the right face 180° clockwise; denote this by R^2. Return the cube to standard position by doing another R^2. Notice that $R^2R^2 = R^4$, which returns the cube to standard position.

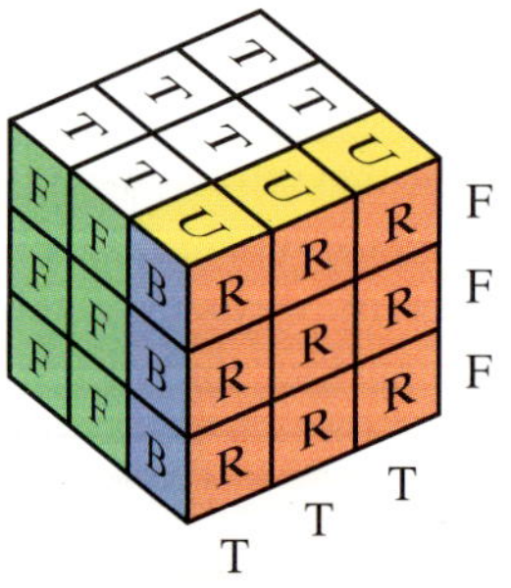

c. Rotate the top 90° clockwise; call this T. Return the cube by doing T^{-1}.

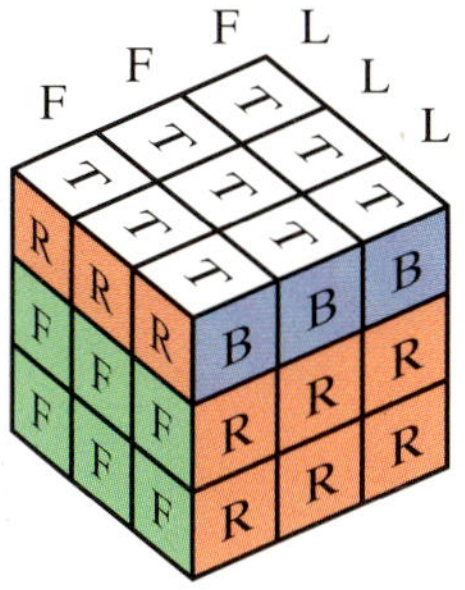

d. *TR* means rotate the top face 90° clockwise, *then* rotate the right face 90° clockwise. Describe the steps necessary to return the cube to standard position.

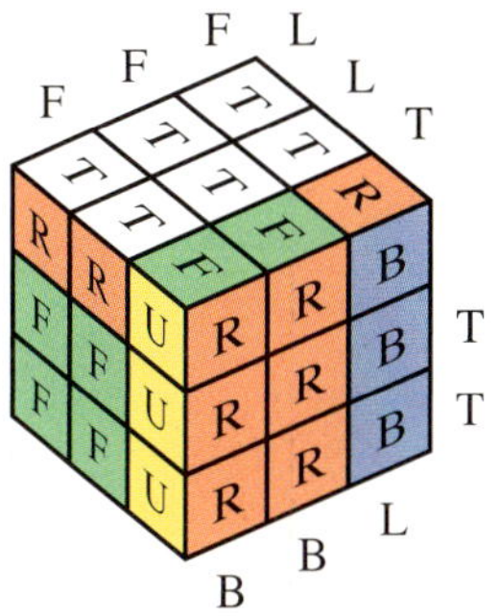

To return this cube to standard position you need $R^{-1}T^{-1}$.

A rearrangement of the 54 colored faces of a small cube is a *permutation*.

Instant Insanity

An older puzzle, simpler than Rubik's cube, is called **Instant Insanity**. It provides four cubes colored red, yellow, blue, and green, as indicated in Figure 9.7. The puzzle is to assemble them into a 1 × 1 × 4 block so that all four colors appear on each side of the block.

Figure 9.7 Instant Insanity

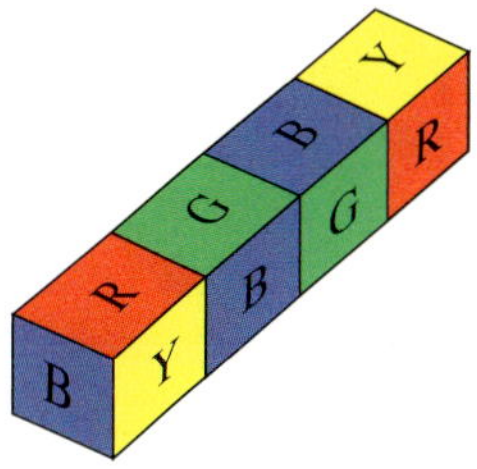

In how many ways can this Instant Insanity puzzle be arranged? A common mistake is to assume that a cube can have 6 different arrangements (because of our experience with dice). In the case of Instant Insanity, we are interested not only in the top, but also in the other sides. There are 6 possible faces for the top and *then* 4 possible faces for the front. Thus, by the fundamental counting principle, there are

$6 \cdot 4 = 24$ arrangements for one cube

Now, for four cubes, again use the fundamental counting principle to find

$24 \cdot 24 \cdot 24 \cdot 24 = 331{,}776$

This is *not* the number of *different* possibilities.

The Nature of Chance

topics

10.1 It's Not Certain

AN **EXPERIMENT** IS AN OBSERVATION OF ANY PHYSICAL OCCURRENCE. THE **SAMPLE SPACE** OF AN EXPERIMENT IS THE SET OF ALL ITS POSSIBLE OUTCOMES. AN **EVENT** IS A SUBSET OF THE SAMPLE SPACE.

If an event is the empty set, it is called the **impossible event**; and if it has only one element, it is called a **simple event**. Consider the experiment of tossing a coin and rolling a die.

A coin is considered **fair** if the outcomes of head and tail are **equally likely**. We also note that a fair die is one for which the outcomes from rolling it are *equally likely*. A sample space for a die is shown in Figure 10.1.

Figure 10.1 Sample space for a single die

A die for which one outcome is more likely than the others is called a **loaded die**. In this book, we will assume fair dice and fair coins unless otherwise noted. Now consider the experiment of tossing a coin and rolling a die. In cases like this where the sample space becomes larger, it can be helpful to build sample spaces by using what is called a **tree diagram**.

For our tree diagram, we see that S (the sample space) is

$S = \{H1, H2, H3, H4, H5, H6, T1, T2, T3, T4, T5, T6\}$

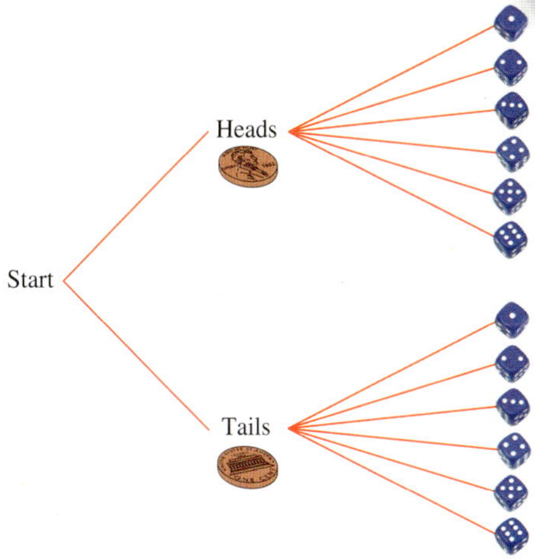

An event must be a *subset* of the sample space. Consider the three subsets E, H, and X.

E = {rolling an even number on the die}
H = {tossing a head}
X = {rolling a six and tossing a tail}

Notice that E, H, and X are all subsets of S. Therefore,

E = {H2, H4, H6, T2, T4, T6}
H = {H1, H2, H3, H4, H5, H6}
X = {T6}

X is a simple event, because it has only one element. Two events E and F are said to be **mutually exclusive** (that is, the sets E and F are disjoint) if $E \cap F = \varnothing$.

Probability

If the sample space can be divided into *mutually exclusive* and *equally likely* outcomes, we can define the probability of an event. Let's consider the experiment of tossing a single coin. A suitable sample space is

S = {heads, tails}

Suppose we wish to consider the event of obtaining heads; we'll call this event A. Then,

A = {heads}

and this is a simple event.

We wish to define the probability of event A, which we denote by $P(A)$. Notice that the outcomes in the sample space are mutually exclusive; that is, if one occurs, the other cannot occur. If we flip a coin, there are two possible outcomes, and *one and only one* outcome can occur on a toss. If each outcome in the sample space is equally likely, we define the probability of A as

$$P(A) = \frac{\text{NUMBER OF SUCCESSFUL RESULTS}}{\text{NUMBER OF POSSIBLE RESULTS}}$$

A "successful" result is a result that corresponds to the event whose probability we are seeking—in this case, {heads}.

Since we can obtain a head (success) in only one way, and the total number of possible outcomes is two, the probability of heads is given by this definition as

$$P(\text{heads}) = P(A) = \frac{1}{2}$$

This must correspond to the empirical results you would obtain if you repeated the experiment a large number of times.

If an experiment can occur in any of n mutually exclusive and equally likely ways, and if s of these ways are considered favorable, then the **probability** of an event E, denoted by $P(E)$, is

Probability

$$P(E) = \frac{s}{n} = \frac{\text{NUMBER OF OUTCOMES FAVORABLE TO } E}{\text{NUMBER OF ALL POSSIBLE OUTCOMES}}$$

Reduced fractions are used to state probabilities when the fractions are fairly simple. If, however, the fractions are not simple, and you have a calculator, it is acceptable to state the probabilities as decimals.

Consider two spinners as shown in Figure 10.2. You and an opponent are to spin your spinners simultaneously, and the one with the higher number wins. Which spinner should you choose, and why?

Figure 10.2 Spinner game

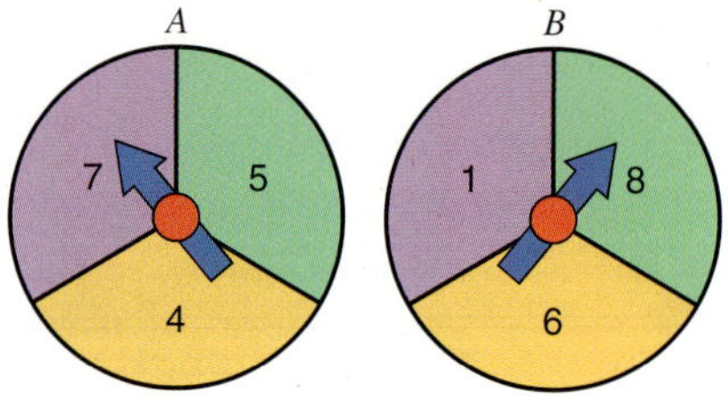

Begin by listing the sample space:

A \ B	1	6	8
4	(4,1)	(4,6)	(4,8)
5	(5,1)	(5,6)	(5,8)
7	(7,1)	(7,6)	(7,8)

The times that A wins are highlighted. $P(A \text{ wins}) = \frac{4}{9}$; $P(B \text{ wins}) = \frac{5}{9}$. We would choose spinner B because it has a greater probability of winning.

Suppose you are just beginning a game of Monopoly® (see Figure 10.3). You roll a pair of dice. What is the probability that you land on a railroad on the first roll of the dice?

Figure 10.3 Monopoly playing board

There are four railroads on a Monopoly playing board, and these are positioned so that only one can be reached on one roll of a pair of dice. The required number to roll is a 5. We begin by listing the sample space. You might try

$$\{2, 3, 4, 5, 6, 7, 8, 9, 10, 11, 12\},$$

but these possible outcomes are not equally likely, which you can see by considering a tree diagram. The roll of the first die has 6 possibilities, and then *each* of these in turn can combine with any of 6 possibilities for a total of 36 possibilities. The **sample space for a pair of dice** is summarized in Figure 10.4. We will refer to the sample space in Figure 10.4 for many of the examples that follow.

Thus, $n = 36$ for the definition of probability. We need to look at Figure 10.4 to see how many possibilities there are for obtaining a 5. We find (1, 4), (2, 3), (3, 2), and (4, 1), so $s = 4$. Then

$$P(\text{five}) = \frac{4}{36} \quad \begin{array}{l}\leftarrow \text{4 ways to obtain a 5}\\ \leftarrow \text{36 ways to roll a pair of dice}\end{array}$$
$$= \frac{1}{9}$$

Figure 10.4 Sample space for a pair of dice

You should use Figure 10.4 when working probability problems that deal with rolling a pair of dice.

You might recall in Chapter 9 when we first introduced a deck of cards. A sample space for a deck of cards is shown in Figure 9.2 on page 190. Here are some examples:

- $P(\text{ace}) = \frac{4}{52} = \frac{1}{13}$ ← An ace is a card with one spot
- $P(\text{heart}) = \frac{13}{52} = \frac{1}{4}$
- $P(\text{face card}) = \frac{12}{52} = \frac{3}{13}$ ← 12: A face card is a jack, queen, or king. ← 52: Number of cards in the sample space

Probabilities of Unions and Intersections

The word *or* is translated as ∪ (union), and the word *and* is translated as ∩ (intersection). We will find the probabilities of combinations of events involving the words *or* and *and* by finding unions and intersections of events.

Suppose that a single card is selected from an ordinary deck of cards.

$P(\text{two or a king}) = P(\text{two} \cup \text{king})$

two = {two of hearts, two of spades, two of diamonds, two of clubs}

king = {king of hearts, king of spades, king of diamonds, king of clubs}

two ∪ king = {two of hearts, two of spades, two of diamonds, two of clubs, king of hearts, king of spades, king of diamonds, king of clubs}

There are 8 possibilities for success. It is usually not necessary to list all of these to know that there are 8 possibilities—simply recall the sample space for a deck of cards.

$$P(\text{two} \cup \text{king}) = \frac{8}{52} = \frac{2}{13}$$

$P(\text{two and a heart}) = P(\text{two} \cap \text{heart})$

two = {**two of hearts**, two of spades, two of diamonds, two of clubs}

heart = {ace of hearts, **two of hearts**, three of hearts, . . . , king of hearts}

two ∩ heart = {**two of hearts**}

There is one element in common (as shown in boldface), so

$$P(\text{two} \cap \text{heart}) = \frac{1}{52}$$

$P(\text{two or a heart}) = P(\text{two} \cup \text{heart})$; this is very similar to first two situations, but there is one important difference. Look at the sample space and notice that although there are 4 twos and 13 hearts, the total number of successes is *not* $4 + 13 = 17$, *but rather* 16.

two = {**two of hearts**, two of spades, two of diamonds, two of clubs}

heart = {ace of hearts, **two of hearts**, three of hearts, . . . , king of hearts}

two ∪ heart = {**two of hearts**, two of spades, two of diamonds, two of clubs, ace of hearts, three of hearts, four of hearts, five of hearts, six of hearts, seven of hearts, eight of hearts, nine of hearts, ten of hearts, jack of hearts, queen of hearts, king of hearts}

It is not necessary to list these possibilities. The purpose of doing so in this case was to reinforce the fact that there are *actually* 16 (not 17) possibilities. The reason for this is that there is one common element:

$$P(\text{two} \cup \text{heart}) = \frac{16}{52} = \frac{4}{13}$$

The probability of an empty set is 0, which means that the event *cannot* occur. The probability of an event that *must* occur is 1. These are the two extremes. All other probabilities fall somewhere in between. The closer a probability is to 1, the more likely the event is to occur; the closer a probability is to 0, the less likely the event is to occur.

Now let's summarize the procedure for finding the probability of an event E when all simple events in the sample space are equally likely:

STEP 1 Describe and identify the sample space, S. The number of elements in S is n.

STEP 2 Count the number of occurrences that interest us; call this the number of successes and denote it by s.

STEP 3 Compute the probability of the event using the formula

$$P(E) = \frac{s}{n}$$

The procedure just outlined will work only when the simple events in S are equally likely. If the equally likely model does not apply to your experiments, you need a more complicated model, or else you must proceed experimentally. This model will, however, be sufficient for the problems you will find in this book.

10.2 Probability Models

IN THE LAST SECTION, WE LOOKED AT THE PROBABILITY OF AN EVENT *E*. NOW WE WISH TO EXPAND OUR DISCUSSION.

Complementary Probabilities

Let

s = NUMBER OF GOOD OUTCOMES (successes)
f = NUMBER OF BAD OUTCOMES (failures)
n = TOTAL NUMBER OF POSSIBLE OUTCOMES $(s + f = n)$

Then the probability that event E occurs is

$$P(E) = \frac{s}{n}$$

The probability that event E does not occur is

$$P(\overline{E}) = \frac{f}{n}$$

That is, some event either happens or does not.

An important property of probability is found by adding these probabilities:

$$P(E) + P(\overline{E}) = \frac{s}{n} + \frac{f}{n} = \frac{s+f}{n} = \frac{n}{n} = 1$$

Probabilities whose sum is 1 are called **complementary probabilities**, and the following box shows what is known as the **property of complements**.

PROPERTY OF COMPLEMENTS

The property of complements can be stated in two ways:

$$P(E) = 1 - P(\overline{E}) \quad \text{or} \quad P(\overline{E}) = 1 - P(E)$$

What is the probability of obtaining at least one head when a coin is flipped three times? Let F = {receive at least one head when a coin is flipped three times}.

Method I. Work directly; use the tree diagram below to find the possibilities.

$$P(F) = \frac{7}{8}$$

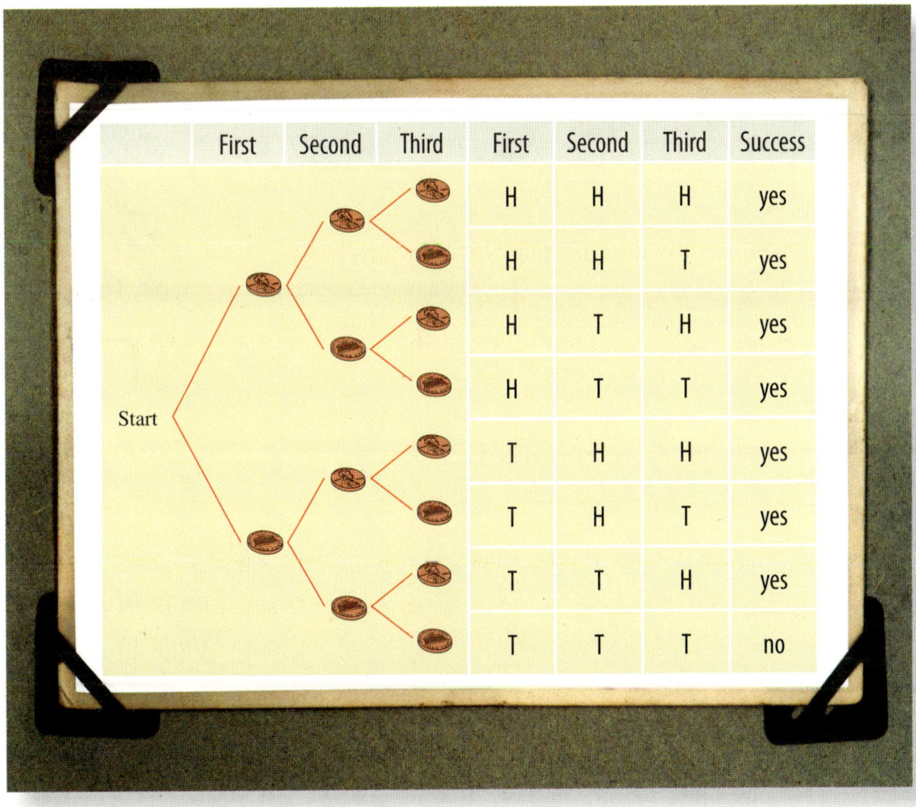

			First	Second	Third	Success
First	Second	Third				
			H	H	H	yes
			H	H	T	yes
			H	T	H	yes
			H	T	T	yes
			T	H	H	yes
			T	H	T	yes
			T	T	H	yes
			T	T	T	no

Method II. For one coin there are 2 outcomes (head and tail); for two coins there are 4 outcomes (HH, HT, TH, TT); and for three coins there are 8 outcomes. We answer the question by finding the complement; $\overline{F}$ is the event of receiving no heads (that is, of obtaining all tails). *Without* drawing the tree diagram, we note that there is only one way of obtaining all tails (TTT). Thus

$$P(F) = 1 - P(\overline{F}) = 1 - \frac{1}{8} = \frac{7}{8}$$

Fundamental Counting Principle

For one coin there are 2 possible outcomes, and for 2 coins there are 4 possible outcomes. We have considered flipping a coin three times, and by drawing a tree diagram we found 8 possibilities. These are applications of a counting technique called the **fundamental counting principle**, which can be understood by looking at tree diagrams.

FUNDAMENTAL COUNTING PRINCIPLE

If task *A* can be performed in *m* ways, and if, after task *A* is performed, a second task *B* can be performed in *n* ways, then task *A* followed by task *B* can be performed in

$$m \times n$$

ways.

What is the probability that, in a family with two children, the children are of opposite sexes? The fundamental counting principle tells us that, since there are 2 ways of having a child (B or G), for 2 children there are

$2 \cdot 2 = 4$ ways

We verify this by looking at a tree diagram:

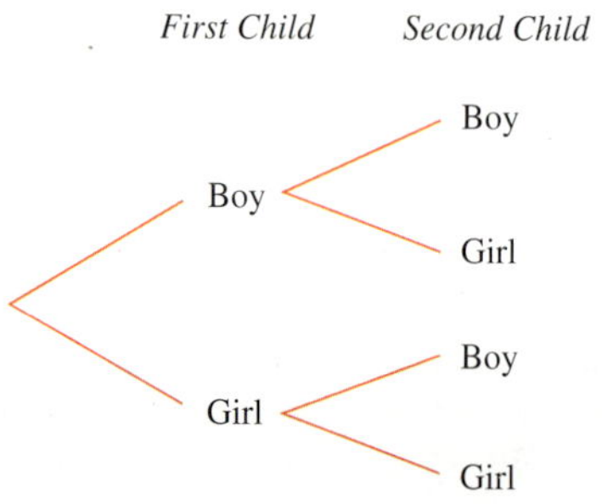

There are 4 equally likely outcomes: BB, BG, GB, and GG. Thus, the probability of having a boy and a girl in a family of two children is

$$\frac{\text{NUMBER OF SUCCESSFUL OUTCOMES}}{\text{TOTAL NUMBER OF POSSIBLE OUTCOMES}} = \frac{2}{4} = \frac{1}{2}$$

In Section 9.3, we considered the license plate problem. We will now use that problem to find the probability (rounded to the nearest percent) of getting a license plate that has a repeated letter. On page 192, we found the number of license plates that *do not* have a repetition; it is 11,232,000. Now, to find the probability, we need to find n (the total number of possibilities):

Number of digits ↓ Letters in the alphabet ↓

$$\underbrace{10 \times 10 \times 10}_{\text{Three digits}} \times \underbrace{26 \times 26 \times 26}_{\text{Three letters}} = 17{,}576{,}000$$

Let R be the event that a repetition is received.

$$P(R) = 1 - P(\overline{R}) = 1 - \frac{11{,}232{,}000}{17{,}576{,}000} \approx 0.36$$

This means that about 36% of all license plates in the state have at least one repeated letter or digit.

10.3 Odds and Conditional Probability

IN MANY PLACES YOU WILL SEE THE WORD *ODDS*, AND MANY PEOPLE INCORRECTLY ASSUME THAT ODDS ARE THE SAME AS PROBABILITY.

Odds

Related to probability is the notion of odds. Instead of forming ratios

$$P(E) = \frac{s}{n} \quad \text{and} \quad P(\overline{E}) = \frac{f}{n}$$

we form the following ratios:

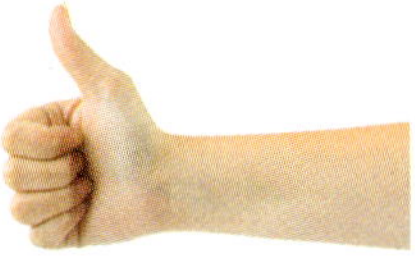

Odds in favor of an event *E*:

$\frac{s}{f}$ (ratio of successes to failures);

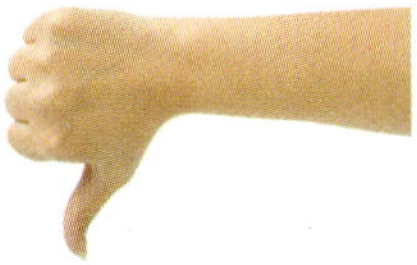

Odds against an event *E*:

$\frac{f}{s}$ (ratio of failures to successes);

where

s = NUMBER OF SUCCESSES
f = NUMBER OF FAILURES
n = NUMBER OF POSSIBILITIES

Sometimes you know the probability and want to find the odds, or you may know the odds and want to find the probability. These relationships are easy if you remember:

$$s + f = n$$

First, we show

$$\frac{P(E)}{P(\overline{E})} = \frac{\frac{s}{n}}{\frac{f}{n}} = \frac{s}{n} \cdot \frac{n}{f} = \frac{s}{f} = \text{odds in favor}$$

Similarly, it can be shown that $\frac{P(\overline{E})}{P(E)}$ = odds against. This leads us to the procedure for finding odds when we know the probability. This procedure, along with the procedure for finding the probability when we know the odds, is shown in the box to the right.

PROCEDURE:

Probability to Odds

Suppose you know the probability of an event, *P*(*E*), and wish to find the odds.

STEP 1 Use $P(\overline{E}) = 1 - P(E)$ to find the probability of the complementary event.

STEP 2 To find the odds in favor, divide the probability by its complementary probability: $\frac{P(E)}{P(\overline{E})}$

STEP 3 To find the odds against, divide the complementary probability by the probability: $\frac{P(\overline{E})}{P(E)}$

On the other hand, if we know the odds and wish to find the probability, use the following procedure:

Odds to Probabilty

Suppose you know the odds in favor (*s* to *f*) of event *E*, or the odds against (*f* to *s*), and wish to find $P(E)$ and $P(\overline{E})$.

STEP 1 Calculate $s + f$

STEP 2 $P(E) = \frac{s}{s + f}$

STEP 3 $P(\overline{E}) = \frac{f}{s + f}$

Conditional Probability

Frequently, we wish to compute the probability of an event but we have additional information that will alter the sample space. For example, suppose that a family has two children. What is the probability that the family has two boys?

$$P(2 \text{ boys}) = \frac{1}{4}$$ Sample space: BB, BG, GB, GG; 1 success out of 4 possibilities

Now, let's complicate the problem a little. Suppose that we know that the older child is a boy. We have *altered* the sample space as follows:

Original sample space: BB, BG, GB, GG; but we need to cross out the last two possibilities because we *know* that the older child is a boy.

Success ↓ — These are crossed out.

Altered sample space: BB, BG, ~~GB, GG~~

Altered sample space has two elements.

Therefore,

$$P(2 \text{ boys given the older is a boy}) = \frac{1}{2}$$

This is a problem involving a **conditional probability**—namely, the *probability of an event E, **given** that another event F has occurred.* We denote this by

$P(E|F)$ Read this as "probability of *E* given *F*."

Suppose that you toss two coins (or a single coin twice). What is the probability that two heads are obtained if you know that at least one head is obtained? Consider an altered sample space:

HH, HT, TH, ~~TT~~

The probability is $\frac{1}{3}$.

Suppose that you draw two cards from a deck of cards. The first card selected is not returned to the deck before the second card is drawn. Let $H = \{$the second card drawn is a heart$\}$. Find $P(H|$a heart is drawn on the first draw). Since the first card is a heart, the number of remaining cards is $n = 51$, and $s = 12$ (because a heart was drawn on the first draw):

$$P(H|\text{a heart is drawn on the first draw}) = \frac{12}{51} \approx 0.235$$

Find $P(H|$a heart is not drawn on the first draw). We still have $n = 51$, but this time $s = 13$:

$$P(H|\text{a heart is not drawn on the first draw}) = \frac{13}{51} \approx 0.255$$

Finally, find $P(H)$. This time we do not know the first card drawn, so it is as if it is still in the deck of cards, so $n = 52$ this time, and $s = 13$, so

$$P(H) = \frac{13}{52} = \frac{1}{4} = 0.250$$

Remember, it does not matter what happened on the first draw because we do not know what happened on that draw. The second card "does not remember" what is drawn on the first draw.

10.4 Mathematical Expectation

IN THIS SECTION, YOU'LL LEARN HOW TO ANALYZE A VARIETY OF GAMBLING SITUATIONS.

Whether you enjoy gambling and games of chance or are opposed to them and would never play a gambling game, you should find some valuable information in this section. Gambling situations range from dice, cards, and slot machines, to buying insurance and selling a home. By analyzing these games, you can show that without proper analysis, a person could be destined for financial ruin, given enough time and limited resources. You can also find situations that should not be considered gambling—situations in which you can't lose.

Expectation

Smiles toothpaste is giving away \$10,000. All you must do to have a chance to win is send a postcard with your name on it (the fine print says you do not need to buy a tube of toothpaste). Is it worthwhile to enter?

Suppose the contest receives 1 million postcards (a conservative estimate). We wish to compute the **expected value** (or your **expectation**) of entering this contest. The expected value of this contest is obtained by multiplying the amount to win by the probability of winning:

$$\begin{aligned} E &= (\text{AMOUNT TO WIN}) \times (\text{PROBABILITY OF WINNING}) \\ &= \$10{,}000 \times \frac{1}{1{,}000{,}000} \\ &= \$0.01 \end{aligned}$$

What does this expected value mean? It means if you were to play this "game" a large number of times, you would expect your *average winnings per game* to be \$0.01. A game is said to be **fair** if the expected value equals the cost of playing the game. If the expected value is positive, then the game is in your favor; if the expected value is negative, then the game is not in your favor. Is this game fair? If the toothpaste company charges you 1¢ to play the game, then it is fair. But how much does the postcard cost? We see that this is not a fair game.

Sometimes there is more than one possible payoff, and we define the expected value (or expectation) as the sum of the expected values from each separate payoff.

A recent contest offered one grand prize worth \$10,000, two second prizes worth \$5,000 each, and ten third prizes worth \$1,000 each. What is the expected value if you assume that there are 1 million entries and that the winners' names are replaced after being drawn?

$$P(\text{1st prize}) = \frac{1}{1{,}000{,}000};\ P(\text{2nd prize}) = \frac{2}{1{,}000{,}000};$$
$$P(\text{3rd prize}) = \frac{10}{1{,}000{,}000}$$

$$E = \underbrace{\$10{,}000}_{\text{Amount of 1st prize}} \times \underbrace{\frac{1}{1{,}000{,}000}}_{P(\text{1st prize})} + \underbrace{\$5{,}000 \times \frac{2}{1{,}000{,}000}}_{\text{2nd prize}} + \underbrace{\$1{,}000 \times \frac{10}{1{,}000{,}000}}_{\text{3rd prize}}$$

$$= \$0.01 + \$0.01 + \$0.01$$

$$= \$0.03$$

Sometimes we use expected value to help us make a decision. Consider two games:

> Game A: Two dice are rolled. You will be paid \$3.60 if you roll two ones, and you will not receive anything for any other outcome.
>
> Game B: Two dice are rolled. You will be paid \$36.00 if you roll any pair, but you must pay \$3.60 for any other outcome.

Which game should you play?

You might say, "I'll play the first game because, if I play that game, I cannot lose anything." This strategy involves *minimizing your losses*. On the other hand, you can use a strategy that *maximizes your winnings*. In this book, we will base our decisions on maximizing the winnings—that is, we wish to select the game that provides the larger expectation.

Game A: $E = \$3.60 \times \frac{1}{36} = \$0.10$

Game B: When calculating the expected value with a charge (a loss), write that charge as a negative number (a negative payoff is a loss).

$$E = \$36.00 \times \frac{6}{36} + (-\$3.60) \times \frac{30}{36}$$

$$= \$6.00 + (-\$3.00)$$

$$= \$3.00$$

This means that, if you were to play each game 100 times, you would expect your winnings for Game A to be about 100(\$0.10) or \$10 and those from playing Game B to be about 100(\$3.00) or \$300. *You should choose to play Game B.*

Now we give a formal definition of expectation.

STOP *Use this definition to help you decide whether to place a bet, play a game, or enter a business venture.*

Mathematical Expectation

If an event E has several possible outcomes with probabilities $p_1, p_2, p_3, \ldots$, and if for each of these outcomes the amount that can be won is $a_1, a_2, a_3, \ldots$, respectively, then the mathematical expectation (or expected value) of E is

$$E = a_1p_1 + a_2p_2 + a_3p_3 + \cdots$$

Expectation with a Cost of Playing

Many games charge you a fee to play. If you must pay to play, this cost of playing should be taken into consideration when you calculate the expected value. Remember, if the expected value is 0, it is a fair game; if the expected value is positive, you should play; but if it is negative, you should not.

PROCEDURE:

Finding Expectation

In order to find the mathematical expectation with a cost of playing, use the following procedure.

STEP 1 Decide whether there is a cost, c, for playing the game. If not, then let $c = 0$.

STEP 2 Determine the amount to win, a, and the probability of winning, p.

STEP 3 Use the expectation formula:

$$\text{EXPECTATION} = ap - c$$

Walt, who is a realtor, knows that if he takes a listing to sell a house, it will cost him \$1,000. However, if he sells the house, he will receive 6% of the selling price. If another realtor sells the house, Walt will receive 3% of the selling price. If the house remains unsold after 3 months, he will lose the listing and receive nothing. Suppose that the probabilities for selling a particular \$200,000 house are as follows: the probability that Walt will sell the house is 0.4;

the probability that another agent will sell the house is 0.2; and the probability that the house will remain unsold is 0.4. What is Walt's expectation if he takes this listing?

First, we must decide whether there is a "cost for playing" for this problem. Is Walt required to pay the \$1,000 before the "game" of selling the house is played? The answer is yes, so the \$1,000 must be subtracted from the payoffs. Now let's calculate those payoffs:

$$6\% \text{ of } \$200{,}000 = 0.06(\$200{,}000) = \$12{,}000$$
$$3\% \text{ of } \$200{,}000 = 0.03(\$200{,}000) = \$6{,}000$$

Now we can use the procedure for calculating the expectation with a cost of playing, $c = \$1{,}000$.

$$E = \overbrace{(\$12{,}000)(0.4)}^{\text{Walt sells the house.}} + \overbrace{(\$6{,}000)(0.2)}^{\text{Another agent sells.}} - \overbrace{(\$1{,}000)}^{\text{House doesn't sell.}}$$
$$= \$5{,}000$$

Walt's expectation is \$5,000.

You must understand the nature of the game to know whether the cost of playing, c, is 0 or whether it is not. If you surrender your money to play, then c is nonzero, but if you "leave it on the table," then $c = 0$. Consider the following example of a U.S. roulette game. In this game, your bet is placed on the table but is not collected until after the play of the game and it is determined that you lost. A U.S. roulette wheel has 38 numbered slots (1–36, 0, and 00), as shown in Figure 10.5.

Some of the more common bets and payoffs are shown. If the payoff is listed as 6 to 1, you would receive \$6 for each \$1 bet. In addition, you would keep the \$1 you originally wagered. One play consists of having the dealer spin the wheel and a little ball in opposite directions. As the ball slows to a stop, it lands in one of the 38 numbered slots, which are colored black, red, or green. A single-number bet has a payoff of 35 to 1. The \$1 you bet is collected only if you lose.

What is the expectation for playing roulette if you bet \$1 on number 5? Calculate the expected value:

$$E = \overbrace{35\left(\frac{1}{38}\right)}^{\text{win}} + \overbrace{(-1)\left(\frac{37}{38}\right)}^{\text{lose}} - \underset{\text{cost of playing}}{0}$$
$$\approx -\$0.05$$

The expected loss is about 5¢ per play.

10.5 Frequency Distributions and Graphs

WE ARE SOMETIMES CONFRONTED WITH LARGE AMOUNTS OF DATA, WHICH CAN BE DIFFICULT TO UNDERSTAND.

Figure 10.5 U.S. roulette wheel and board

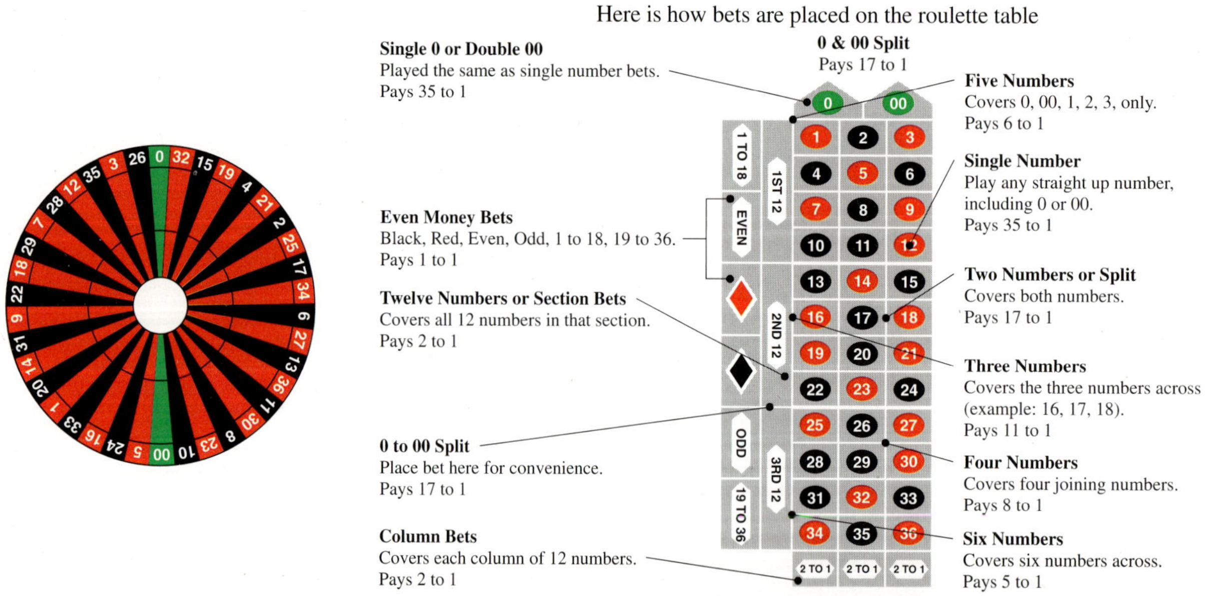

Computers, spreadsheets, and simulation programs have done a lot to help us deal with hundreds or thousands of pieces of information at the same time.

Frequency Distribution

We can deal with large batches of data by organizing them into groups, or **classes**. The difference between the lower limit of one class and the lower limit of the next class is called the **interval** of the class. After determining the number of values within a class, termed the **frequency**, you can use this information to summarize the data. The end result of this classification and tabulation is called a **frequency distribution**. For example, suppose that you roll a pair of dice 50 times and obtain these outcomes:

3, 2, 6, 5, 3, 8, 8, 7, 10, 9, 7, 5, 12, 9, 6, 11, 8,
11, 11, 8, 7, 7, 7, 10, 11, 6, 4, 8, 8, 7, 6, 4, 10,
7, 9, 7, 9, 6, 6, 9, 4, 4, 6, 3, 4, 10, 6, 9, 6, 11

We can organize these data in a convenient way by using a frequency distribution, as shown in Table 10.1.

A graphical method that is useful for organizing large sets of data is a **stem-and-leaf plot**. Consider the data shown in Table 10.2.* For these data we form stems representing decades of the ages of the actors. For example, Jamie Foxx, who won the 2004 best actor award in 2005 for his role in *Ray*, was 38 years of age when he won the award. We would say that the stem for this age is 3 (for 30), and the leaf is 8.

The plot below is useful because it is easy to see that most best actor winners received the award in their forties.

* The idea for this example came from "Ages of Oscar-Winning Best Actors and Actresses" by Richard Brown and Gretchen Davis, *The Mathematics Teacher*, 1990, pp. 96–102.

Table 10.1 Frequency Distribution for 50 Rolls of a Pair of Dice

Outcome	Tally	Frequency
2	/	1
3	///	3
4	卌	5
5	//	2
6	卌 ////	9
7	卌 ///	8
8	卌 /	6
9	卌 /	6
10	////	4
11	卌	5
12	/	1

The data sets {32, 56, 47, 30, 41} and {3.2, 5.6, 4.7, 3.0, 4.1} have the same stem-and-leaf plots with the first set having a leaf unit of 1 and the second set having a leaf unit of 0.1.

To help us understand the relationship between and among variables, we use a diagram called a **graph**. In this section, we consider *bar graphs*, *line graphs*, *circle graphs*, and *pictographs*.

Stem-and-Leaf Plot of Ages of Best Actor, 1928–2007

2	9
3	0 1 1 1 2 2 3 3 4 4 5 5 5 5 6 7 7 7 8 8 8 8 8 8 8 8 8 9 9
4	0 0 0 0 1 1 1 1 1 2 2 2 3 3 3 3 3 4 4 5 5 6 6 6 6 7 7 7 8 8 8 8 8 9 9 9
5	0 1 1 2 2 3 5 5 6 6 6 9
6	0 1 2
7	6

Table 10.2 Best Actors, 1928–2008

Year	Actor	Age	Movie
1928	Emil Jannings	44	*The Way of All Flesh*
1929	Warner Baxter	38	*In Old Arizona*
1930	George Arliss	46	*Disraeli*
1931	Lionel Barrymore	53	*A Free Soul*
1932	Fredric March Wallace Beery	35 47	*Dr. Jekyll and Mr. Hyde* *The Champ* tie
1933	Charles Laughton	34	*The Private Life of Henry VIII*
1934	Clark Gable	33	*It Happened One Night*
1935	Victor McLaglen	49	*The Informer*
1936	Paul Muni	41	*The Story of Louis Pasteur*
1937	Spencer Tracy	37	*Captains Courageous*
1938	Spencer Tracy	38	*Boys' Town*
1939	Robert Donat	34	*Goodbye Mr. Chips*
1940	James Stewart	32	*The Philadelphia Story*
1941	Gary Cooper	40	*Sergeant York*
1942	James Cagney	48	*Yankee Doodle Dandy*
1943	Paul Lukas	48	*Watch on the Rhine*
1944	Bing Crosby	43	*Going My Way*
1945	Ray Milland	40	*The Lost Weekend*
1946	Fredric March	49	*The Best Years of Our Lives*
1947	Ronald Colman	56	*A Double Life*
1948	Laurence Olivier	41	*Hamlet*
1949	Broderick Crawford	38	*All the King's Men*
1950	Jose Ferrer	38	*Cyrano de Bergerac*
1951	Humphrey Bogart	52	*The African Queen*
1952	Gary Cooper	51	*High Noon*
1953	William Holden	35	*Stalag 17*
1954	Marlon Brando	30	*On the Waterfront*
1955	Ernest Borgnine	38	*Marty*
1956	Yul Brynner	41	*The King and I*
1957	Alec Guinness	43	*The Bridge on the River Kwai*
1958	David Niven	49	*Separate Tables*
1959	Charlton Heston	35	*Ben Hur*
1960	Burt Lancaster	47	*Elmer Gantry*
1961	Maximilian Schell	31	*Judgment at Nuremburg*
1962	Gregory Peck	46	*To Kill a Mockingbird*
1963	Sidney Poitier	39	*Lilies of the Field*
1964	Rex Harrison	56	*My Fair Lady*
1965	Lee Marvin	41	*Cat Ballou*
1966	Paul Scofield	44	*A Man for All Seasons*
1967	Rod Steiger	42	*In the Heat of the Night*
1968	Cliff Robertson	43	*Charly*
1969	John Wayne	62	*True Grit*
1970	George C. Scott	43	*Patton*
1971	Gene Hackman	40	*The French Connection*
1972	Marlon Brando	48	*The Godfather*
1973	Jack Lemmon	48	*Save the Tiger*
1974	Art Carney	56	*Harry and Tonto*
1975	Jack Nicholson	38	*One Flew over the Cuckoo's Nest*
1976	Peter Finch	60	*Network*
1977	Richard Dreyfuss	32	*The Goodbye Girl*
1978	Jon Voight	40	*Coming Home*
1979	Dustin Hoffman	42	*Kramer vs Kramer*
1980	Robert De Niro	37	*Raging Bull*
1981	Henry Fonda	76	*On Golden Pond*
1982	Ben Kingsley	39	*Gandhi*
1983	Robert Duvall	55	*Tender Mercies*
1984	F. Murray Abraham	45	*Amadeus*
1985	William Hurt	35	*Kiss of the Spider Woman*
1986	Paul Newman	61	*The Color of Money*
1987	Michael Douglas	33	*Wall Street*
1988	Dustin Hoffman	51	*Rain Man*
1989	Daniel Day-Lewis	31	*My Left Foot*
1990	Jeremy Irons	42	*Reversal of Fortune*
1991	Anthony Hopkins	55	*Silence of the Lambs*
1992	Al Pacino	52	*Scent of a Woman*
1993	Tom Hanks	37	*Philadelphia*
1994	Tom Hanks	38	*Forrest Gump*
1995	Nicholas Cage	31	*Leaving Las Vegas*
1996	Geoffrey Rush	45	*Shine*
1997	Jack Nicholson	59	*As Good As It Gets*
1998	Roberto Benigni	46	*Life Is Beautiful*
1999	Kevin Spacey	41	*American Beauty*
2000	Russell Crowe	36	*Gladiator*
2001	Denzel Washington	47	*Training Day*
2002	Adrien Brody	29	*The Pianist*
2003	Sean Penn	43	*Mystic River*
2004	Jamie Foxx	38	*Ray*
2005	Philip Seymour Hoffman	38	*Capote*
2006	Forest Whitaker	46	*The Last King of Scotland*
2007	Daniel Day-Lewis	50	*There Will Be Blood*
2008	Sean Penn	48	*Milk*

Bar Graphs

A **bar graph** compares several related pieces of data using horizontal or vertical bars of uniform width. There must be some sort of scale or measurement on both the horizontal and vertical axes. An example of a bar graph is shown in Figure 10.6, which shows the data from Table 10.1.

Figure 10.6 Outcomes of experiment of rolling a pair of dice

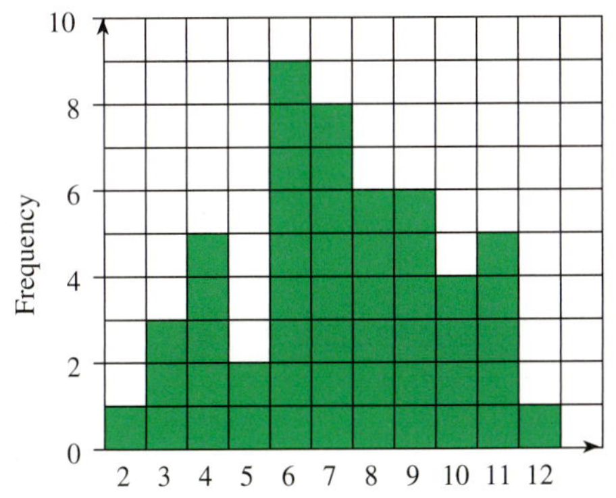

You will frequently need to look at and interpret bar graphs in which bars of different lengths are used for comparison purposes.

Line Graph

A graph that uses a broken line to illustrate how one quantity changes with respect to another is called a **line graph**. A line graph is one of the most widely used kinds of graph.

Just as with bar graphs, you need to be able to read and interpret line graphs. Refer to Figure 10.7 to answer the following questions.

In which year was the voter turnout in a presidential election the greatest? Voter turnout was the greatest (63.1%) in 1960. During the period 1932–2004, were there more periods of economic growth or economic decline? Growth is shown as a white region and decline as a shaded region; there are 13 periods of each, but the growth periods are of greater duration.

Circle Graphs

Another type of commonly used graph is the **circle graph**, also known as a **pie chart**. This graph is particularly useful in illustrating how a whole quantity is divided into parts — for example, income or expenses in a budget.

To create a circle graph, first express the number in each category as a percentage of the total. Then convert this percentage to an angle in a circle. Remember that a circle is divided into 360°, so we multiply the percent by 360 to find the number of degrees for each category. You can use a protractor to construct a circle graph.

Figure 10.7 Voter turnout in presidential elections, 1932–2004

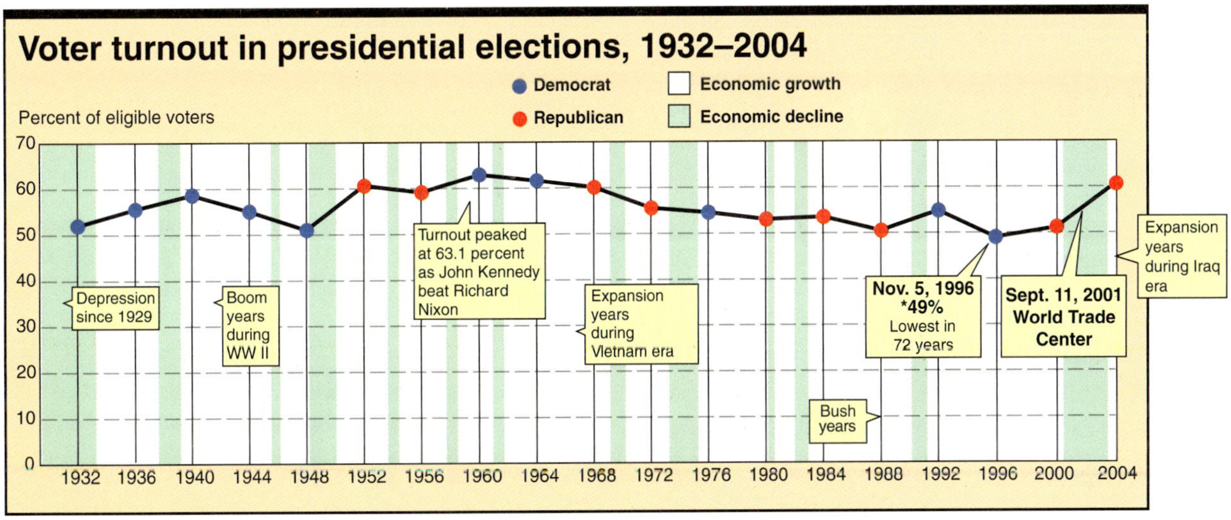

Pictographs

A **pictograph** is a representation of data that uses pictures to show quantity. Consider the raw data shown in Table 10.3.

Table 10.3 Marital Status*
(for persons age 65 and older)

	Married	Widowed	Divorced	Never Married
Women	5.4	7.2	0.4	0.8
Men	7.5	1.4	0.3	0.6

*In millions, rounded to the nearest 100,000.

A pictograph uses a picture to illustrate data; it is normally used only in popular publications, rather than for scientific applications. For these data, suppose that we draw pictures of a woman and a man so that each picture represents 1 million persons, as shown in Figure 10.8.

Figure 10.9 Examples of misuses in pictographs

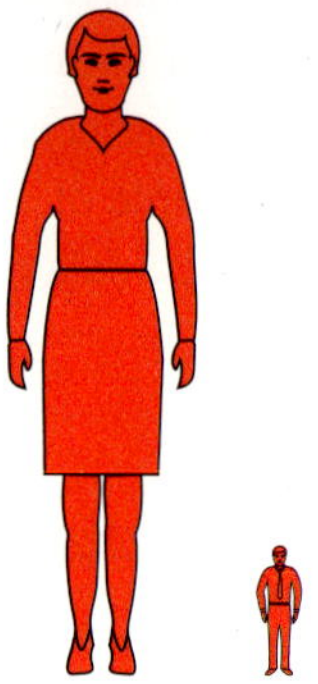

a. Pictograph representing values as heights

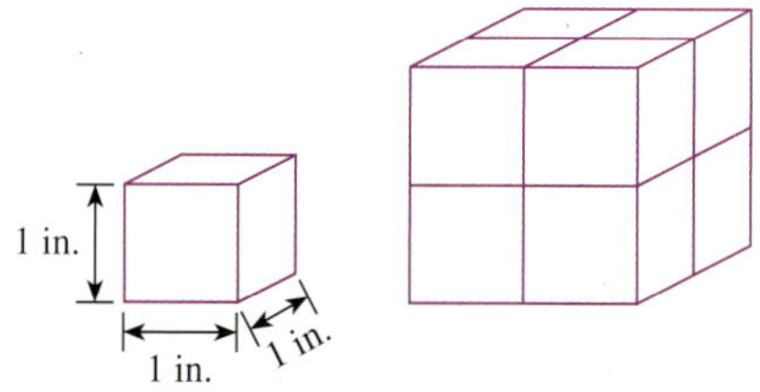

b. Doubling height and width increases volume 8-fold

Misuses of Graphs

The most misused type of graph is the pictograph. Consider the data from Table 10.3. Such data can be used to determine the height of a three-dimensional object, as in part **a** of Figure 10.9. When an object (such as a person) is viewed as three-dimensional, differences seem much larger than they actually are. Look at part **b** of Figure 10.9 and notice that, as the height and width are doubled, the volume is actually increased eightfold.

This pictograph fallacy carries over to graphs of all kinds, especially since software programs easily change two-dimensional scales to three-dimensional scales. For example, percentages are represented as heights on the scale shown in Figure 10.10a, but the software has incorrectly drawn the graph as three-dimensional bars. Another fallacy is to choose the scales to exaggerate or diminish real differences. Even worse, graphs are sometimes presented with no scale whatsoever as illustrated in a graphical "comparison" between Anacin and "regular strength aspirin" shown in Figure 10.10b.

Figure 10.8 Pictograph showing the marital status of persons age 65 and older

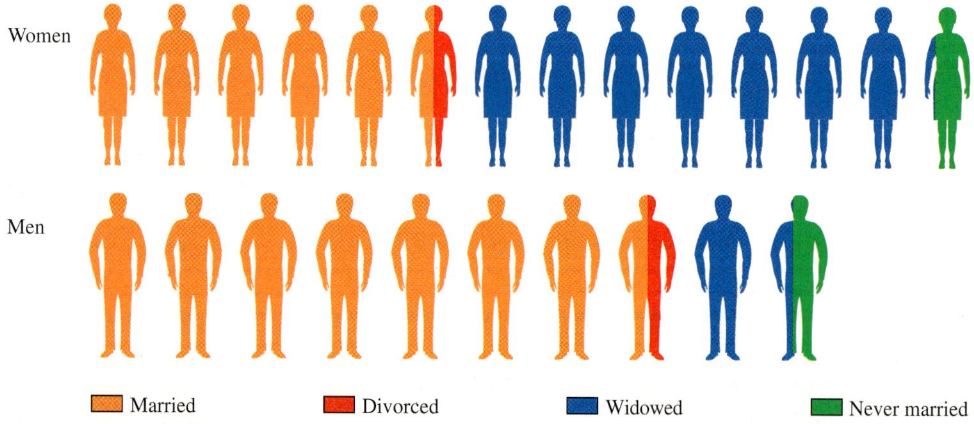

Figure 10.10 Misuses of graphs

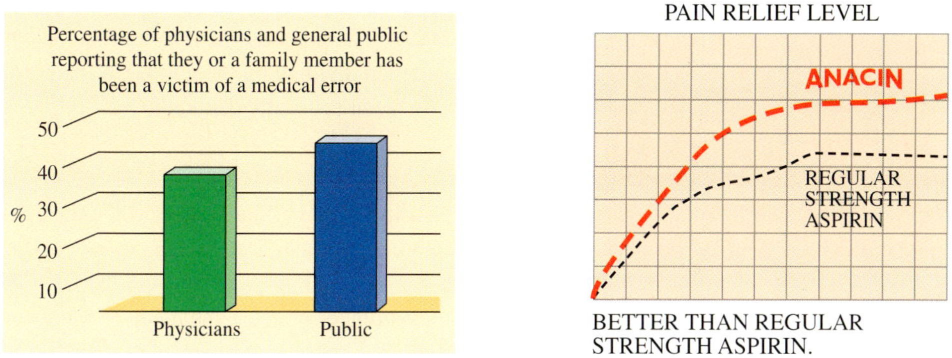

a. Heights are used to graph three-dimensional objects.

b. No scale is shown in this Anacin advertisment.

10.6 Descriptive Statistics

DESCRIPTIVE STATISTICS IS CONCERNED WITH THE ACCUMULATION OF DATA, MEASURES OF CENTRAL TENDENCY, AND DISPERSION.

6 IMPORTANT IDEAS

1 Mean
2 Median
3 Mode
4 Range
5 Variance
6 Standard Deviation

Measures of Central Tendency

In the preceding section, we organized data into a frequency distribution and then discussed their presentation in graphical form. However, some properties of data can help us interpret masses of information. We will use the *Peanuts* cartoon below to introduce the notion of *average*.

Do you suppose that Violet's dad bowled better on Monday nights (185 avg) than on Thursday nights (170 avg)? Don't be too hasty to say "yes" before you look at the scores that make up these averages:

	Monday Night	Thursday Night
Game 1	175	180
Game 2	150	130
Game 3	160	161
Game 4	180	185
Game 5	160	163
Game 6	183	185
Game 7	287	186
Totals	1,295	1,190

To find the averages used by Violet in the cartoon, we divide these totals by the number of games:

Monday Night	*Thursday Night*
$\frac{1{,}295}{7} = 185$	$\frac{1{,}190}{7} = 170$

If we consider the averages, Violet's dad did better on Mondays; but if we consider the games separately, we see that Violet's dad typically did better on Thursday (five out of seven games). Would any other properties of the bowling scores tell us this fact?

Since we must often add up a list of numbers in statistics, as we did above, we use the symbol $\sum x$ to mean *the sum of all the values that* x *can assume*. Similarly, $\sum x^2$ means to square each value that x can assume, and then add the results; $(\sum x)^2$ means to first add the values and then square the result. The symbol $\sum$ is the Greek capital letter sigma (which is chosen because S reminds us of "sum").

The average used by Violet is only one kind of statistical measure that can be used. It is the measure that most of us think of when we hear someone use the word *average*. It is called the *mean*. There are three statistical measures called **averages** or **measures of central tendency**: the mean, the median, and the mode.

The **mean** is the most sensitive average. It reflects the entire distribution and is the most common average.

The **median** gives the middle value. It is useful when there are a few extraordinary values to distort the mean.

The **mode** is the average that measures "popularity." It is possible to have no mode or more than one mode.

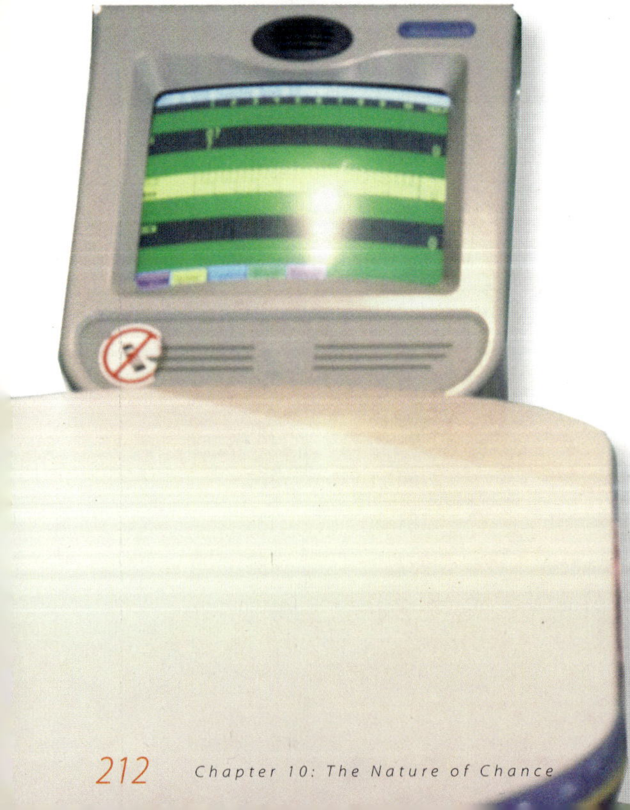

Measures of Central Tendency

1. **Mean** The number found by adding the data and then dividing by the number of data values. The mean is usually denoted by $\bar{x}$:
$$\bar{x} = \frac{\sum x}{n}$$
2. **Median** The middle number when the numbers in the data values are arranged in order of size. If there are two middle numbers (in the case of an even number of data), the median is the mean of these two middle numbers.
3. **Mode** The value that occurs most frequently. If no number occurs more than once, there is no mode. It is possible to have more than one mode.

Violet used the *mean* and called it the average. Let us consider the other measures of central tendency for Violet's dad's bowling scores.

MEDIAN Rearrange the data values from smallest to largest when finding the median:

Monday Night		*Thursday Night*
150		130
160		161
160		163
175	← Middle number is the median. →	**180**
180		185
183		185
287		186

© Rainer Holz/zefa/Corbis

MODE Look for the number that occurs most frequently:

Monday Night		*Thursday Night*
150		130
160	← Most frequent is the mode.	161
160		163
175		180
180	Most frequent is the mode. →	**185**
183		**185**
287		186

If we compare the three measures of central tendency for the bowling scores, we find the following:

	Monday Night	Thursday Night
Mean	185	170
Median	175	180
Mode	160	185

We are no longer convinced that Violet's dad did better on Monday nights than on Thursday nights. (See highlighted parts for the winning night, according to each measure of central tendency—Thursday wins two out of three.)

A rather nice physical model illustrates the idea of the mean. Consider a seesaw that consists of a plank and a movable support (called a *fulcrum*). We assume that the plank has no weight and is marked off into units as shown in Figure 10.11.

Figure 10.11 Fulcrum and plank model for mean

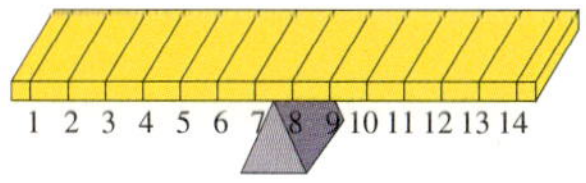

Now let's place some 1-lb weights in the position of the numbers in some given distribution. The balance point for the plank is the mean. If weights are placed on 3, 5, 5, 8, and 9 on the plank, the balance point is 6, as shown in Figure 10.12.

Figure 10.12 Balance point for the data set 3, 5, 5, 8, 9 is 6.

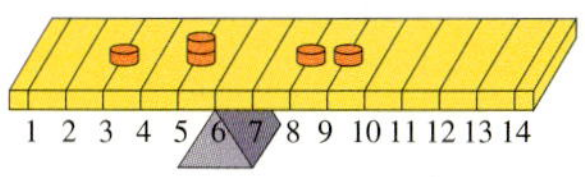

The graph shown in Figure 10.13 represents the distribution of grades in Clark's math class.

Figure 10.13 Grade distribution for Clark's math class

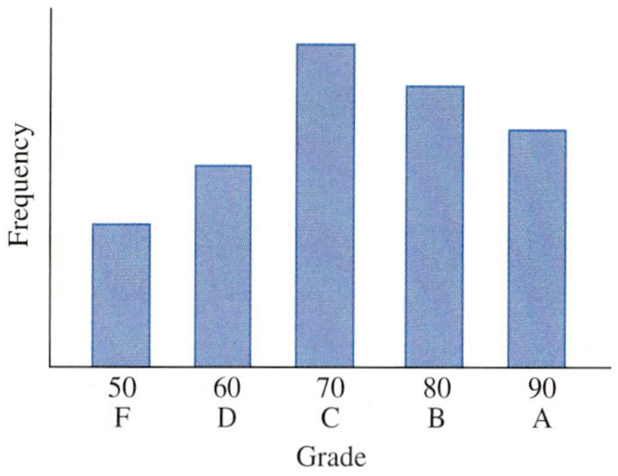

Which of the statements is true?

a. The mean and the mode are the same.
b. The mean is greater than the mode.
c. The median is less than the mode.
d. The mean is less than the mode.

WATCH YOUR STEP *Notice that you are given data values, but are not given the corresponding frequencies or relative frequencies. Therefore, we are not able to compute the values of the mean and median.*

The only measure of central tendency we can determine exactly is the mode: *The mode is the value under the tallest bar.* We see the mode is 70. We now estimate the mean. In finding the mean, the number 70 would be added most frequently. If the value of 60 occurred the same number of times as 80, the data would have a mean of 70, but we see there are more 80s than there are 60s, so the mean must be greater than 70. Similarly, we see that adding the 50s and 90s would give us a mean of more than 70. Thus, the mean is greater than 70, and the correct answer is B.

When finding the mean from a frequency distribution, you are finding what is called a weighted mean.

Weighted Mean

If a list of scores $x_1, x_2, x_3, \ldots, x_n$ occurs $w_1, w_2, \ldots, w_n$ times, respectively, then the **weighted mean** is

$$\bar{x} = \frac{\sum(w \cdot x)}{\sum w}$$

A sociology class is studying family structures and the professor asks each student to state the number of

Table 10.4 Family Data

Number of Children	Number of Students
1	11
2	7
3	3
4	2
5	1
6	1

children in his or her family. The results are summarized in Table 10.4.

What is the average number of children in the families of students in this sociology class? We need to find the weighted mean where x represents the number of students and w the population (number of families).

$$\begin{aligned}\bar{x} &= \frac{\Sigma(w \cdot x)}{\Sigma w}\\ &= \frac{1 \cdot 11 + 2 \cdot 7 + 3 \cdot 3 + 4 \cdot 2 + 5 \cdot 1 + 6 \cdot 1}{11 + 7 + 3 + 2 + 1 + 1}\\ &= \frac{53}{25}\\ &= 2.12\end{aligned}$$

There is an average of two children per family.

Measures of Position

The median divides the data into two equal parts, with half the values above the median and half below the median, so the median is called a **measure of position**. Sometimes we use benchmark positions that divide the data into more than two parts. **Quartiles**, denoted by $Q1$ (first quartile), $Q2$ (second quartile), and $Q3$ (third quartile), divide the data into four equal parts. **Deciles** are nine values that divide the data into ten equal parts, and **percentiles** are 99 values that divide the data into 100 equal parts. For example, when you take the Scholastic Assessment Test (SAT), your score is recorded as a percentile score. If you scored in the 92nd percentile, it means that you scored better than approximately 92% of those who took the test.

Measures of Dispersion

The measures we've been discussing can help us interpret information, but they do not give the entire story. For example, consider these sets of data:

Set A: {8, 9, 9, 9, 10}

Mean: $\dfrac{8 + 9 + 9 + 9 + 10}{5} = 9$

Median: 9

Mode: 9

Set B: {2, 9, 9, 12, 13}

Mean: $\dfrac{2 + 9 + 9 + 12 + 13}{5} = 9$

Median: 9

Mode: 9

Notice that, for sets A and B, the measures of central tendency do not distinguish the data. However, if you look at the data placed on planks, as shown in Figure 10.14, you will see that the data in set B are relatively widely dispersed along the plank, whereas the data in set A are clumped around the mean.

We'll consider three **measures of dispersion**: the *range*, the *standard deviation*, and the *variance*.

The **range** of a set of data is the difference between the largest and the smallest numbers in the set.

Figure 10.14 Visualization of dispersion of sets of data

a. $A = \{8, 9, 9, 9, 10\}$ **b.** $B = \{2, 9, 9, 12, 13\}$

The **range** is used, along with quartiles, to construct a statistical tool called a *box plot*. For a given set of data, a **box plot** consists of a rectangular box positioned above a numerical scale, drawn from $Q1$ (the first quartile) to $Q3$ (the third quartile). The median ($Q2$, or second quartile) is shown as a dashed line, and a segment is extended to the left to show the distance to the minimum value; another segment is extended to the right for the maximum value.

A box plot for the ages of the actors who received the Best Actor award at the Academy Awards, as reported in Table 10.2, is shown in Figure 10.15.

Figure 10.15 Box plot

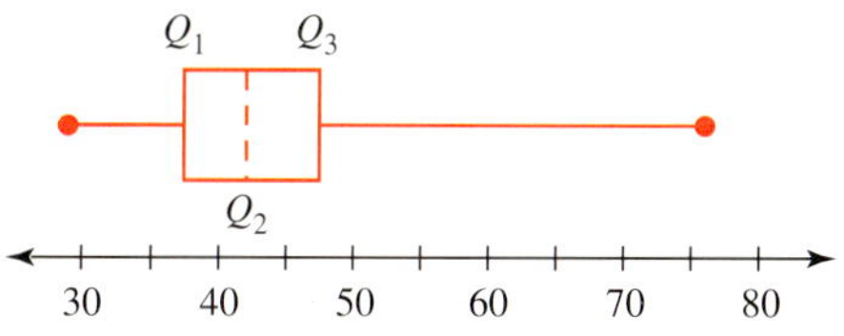

Sometimes a box plot is called a *box-and-whisker plot*. Its usefulness should be clear when you look at Figure 10.15. It shows:

1. the median (a measure of central tendency);
2. the location of the middle half of the data (represented by the extent of the box);
3. the range (a measure of dispersion);
4. the skewness (the nonsymmetry of both the box and the whiskers).

The *variance* and *standard deviation* are measures that use all the numbers in the data set to give information about the dispersion. When finding the variance, we must make a distinction between the **variance of the entire population** and the **variance of a random sample** from the population. When the variance is based on a set of sample scores, it is denoted by s^2; and when it is based on all scores in a population, it is denoted by σ^2 (σ is the lowercase Greek letter sigma). The variance for a random sample is found by

$$s^2 = \frac{\Sigma(x - \bar{x})^2}{n - 1}$$

To understand this formula for the sample variance, we will consider an example before summarizing a procedure. Let's consider two data sets.

Set $A = \{8, 9, 9, 9, 10\}$	Set $B = \{2, 9, 9, 12, 13\}$
Mean is 9.	Mean is 9.

Find the deviations by subtracting the mean from each term:

$8 - 9 = -1$	$2 - 9 = -7$
$9 - 9 = 0$	$9 - 9 = 0$
$9 - 9 = 0$	$9 - 9 = 0$
$9 - 9 = 0$	$12 - 9 = 3$
$10 - 9 = 1$	$13 - 9 = 4$
↑ Mean	↑ Mean

If we sum these deviations (to obtain a measure of the total deviation), in each case we obtain 0, because the positive and negative differences "cancel each other out." Next we calculate the *square of each of these deviations*:

Set $A = \{8, 9, 9, 9, 10\}$	Set $B = \{2, 9, 9, 12, 13\}$
$(8 - 9)^2 = (-1)^2 = 1$	$(2 - 9)^2 = (-7)^2 = 49$
$(9 - 9)^2 = 0^2 = 0$	$(9 - 9)^2 = 0^2 = 0$
$(9 - 9)^2 = 0^2 = 0$	$(9 - 9)^2 = 0^2 = 0$
$(9 - 9)^2 = 0^2 = 0$	$(12 - 9)^2 = 3^2 = 9$
$(10 - 9)^2 = 1^2 = 1$	$(13 - 9)^2 = 4^2 = 16$

PROCEDURE:

Standard Deviation

The standard deviation of a sample, denoted by s, is the square root of the variance. To find it, carry out these steps:

STEP 1 Determine the mean of the set of numbers.

STEP 2 Subtract the mean from each number in the set.

STEP 3 Square each of these differences.

STEP 4 Find the sum of the squares of the differences.

STEP 5 Divide this sum by one less than the number of pieces of data. This gives the *variance* of the sample.

STEP 6 Take the square root of the variance. This is the *standard deviation* of the sample.

*Spend some time with this box; make sure you understand not only the procedure, but also the concept.

Finally, we find the sum of these squares and divide by one less than the number of items to obtain the variance:

$$\text{Set } A: \quad s^2 = \frac{1 + 0 + 0 + 0 + 1}{5 - 1} = \frac{2}{4} = 0.5$$

$$\text{Set } B: \quad s^2 = \frac{49 + 0 + 0 + 9 + 16}{5 - 1} = \frac{74}{4} = 18.5$$

The larger the variance, the more dispersion there is in the original data. However, we will continue to develop a true picture of the dispersion. Since we squared each difference (to eliminate the canceling effect of positive and negative differences), it seems reasonable that we should find the square root of the variance as a more meaningful measure of dispersion. This number, called the **standard deviation**, is denoted by the lowercase Greek letter sigma (σ) when it is based on a population and by s when it is based on a sample. You will need a calculator to find square roots.

$$\text{Set } A: \quad s = \sqrt{0.5} \approx 0.707 \qquad \text{Set } B: \quad s = \sqrt{18.5} \approx 4.301$$

We summarize these steps in the procedure box on the next page.

How can we use the standard deviation? We will begin the discussion in Section 10.7 with this question. For now, however, we will give one example. Suppose that Hannah obtained 65 on an examination for which the mean was 50 and the standard deviation was 15, whereas Søren in another class scored 74 on an examination for which the mean was 80 and the standard deviation was 3. Did Hannah or Søren do better in her respective class? We see that Hannah scored one standard deviation *above* the mean ($50 + 15 = 65$), whereas Søren scored two standard deviations *below* the mean ($80 - 2 \times 3 = 74$); therefore Hannah did better compared to her classmates than did Søren.

10.7 It's Normal

SOMETIMES WE REPRESENT FREQUENCIES IN A CUMULATIVE WAY, ESPECIALLY WHEN WE WANT TO FIND THE POSITION OF ONE CASE RELATIVE TO THE PERFORMANCE OF THE GROUP.

Cumulative Distributions

A **cumulative frequency** is the sum of all preceding frequencies in which some order has been established. A judge ordered a survey to determine how many of the offenders appearing in her court during the past year had three or more previous appearances. The accumulated data is shown in Table 10.5.

Table 10.5 Number of Previous Appearances

Number	Percent	Cumulative Percent
0	21%	21%
1	25%	46%
2	24%	70%
3	13%	83%
4	8%	91%
5	5%	96%
6 or more	4%	100%

Note the last column showing the *cumulative relative frequency*.

Bell-Shaped Curves

The cartoon below suggests that most people do not like to think of themselves or their children as having "normal intelligence." But what do we mean by *normal* or *normal intelligence*?

Suppose we survey the results of 20 children's scores on an IQ test. The scores (rounded to the nearest 5 points) are 115, 90, 100, 95, 105, 95, 105, 105, 95, 125, 120, 110, 100, 100, 90, 110, 100, 115, 105, and 80. We can find $\bar{x} = 103$ and $s \approx 10.93$. A frequency graph of these data is shown in part **a** of Figure 10.16. If we consider 10,000 scores instead of only 20, we might obtain the frequency distribution shown in part **b** of Figure 10.16.

Figure 10.16 Frequency distributions for IQ scores

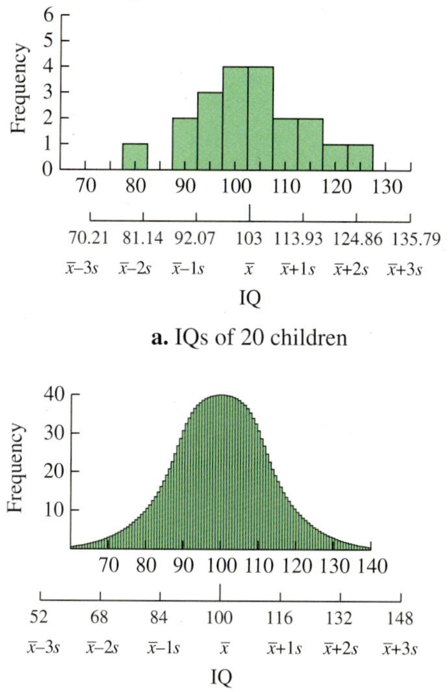

a. IQs of 20 children

b. IQs of 10,000 children

The data illustrated in Figure 10.16 approximate a commonly used curve called a *normal frequency curve*, or simply a **normal curve**. (see Figure 10.17).

WATCH YOUR STEP *This curve is important in many different applications and when observing many natural phenomena.*

Figure 10.17 A normal curve

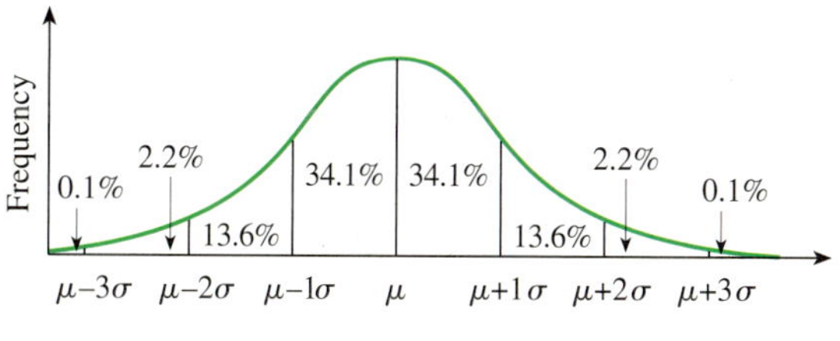

If we obtain the frequency distribution of a large number of measurements (as with IQ), the corresponding graph tends to look normal, or **bell-shaped**. The normal curve has some interesting properties. In it, the mean, the median, and the mode all have the same value, and all occur exactly at the center of the distribution; we denote this value by the Greek letter mu (μ). The standard deviation for this distribution is σ (sigma). Roughly 68% of all values lie within the region from 1 standard deviation below to 1 standard deviation above the mean. About 95% lie within 2 standard deviations on either side of the mean, and virtually all (99.8%) values lie within 3 standard deviations on either side. These percentages are the same regardless of the particular mean or standard deviation.

The normal distribution is a **continuous** (rather than a discrete) **distribution**, and it extends indefinitely in both directions, never touching the x-axis. It is symmetric about a vertical line drawn through the mean, μ. Graphs of this curve for several choices of σ are shown in Figure 10.18.

Figure 10.18 Variations of normal curves

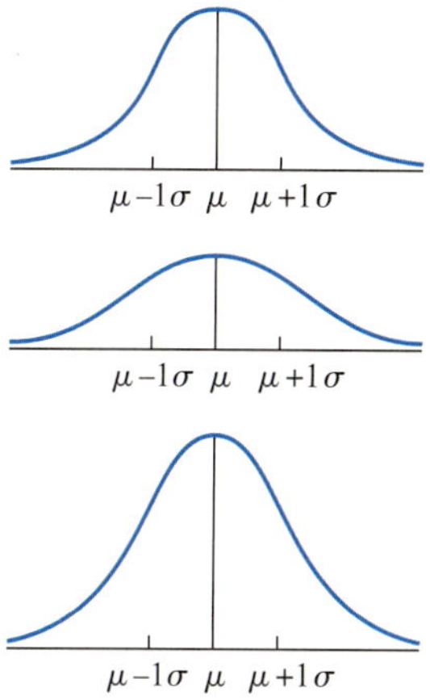

z-Scores

Sometimes we want to know the percent of occurrence for scores that do not happen to be 1, 2, or 3 standard deviations from the mean. For example, 34.1% of the scores are between the mean and 1 standard deviation above the mean. Suppose we wish to find the percent of scores that are between the mean and 1.2 standard deviations above the mean. To find this percent, we use Table 10.6.

First, we introduce some terminology. We use *z-scores* (sometimes called *standard scores*) to determine how far, in terms of standard deviations, a given score is from the mean of the distribution.

We use the z-score to translate any normal curve into a *standard normal* curve (the particular normal curve with a mean of 0 and a standard deviation of 1) by using the definition.

z-Score

If x is a value from a normal distribution with mean μ and standard deviation σ, then its **z-score** is

$$z = \frac{x - \mu}{\sigma}$$

Table 10.6 Standard Normal Distribution

***z*-scores**

For a particular value, this table gives the percent of scores between the mean and the *z*-value of a normally distributed random variable.

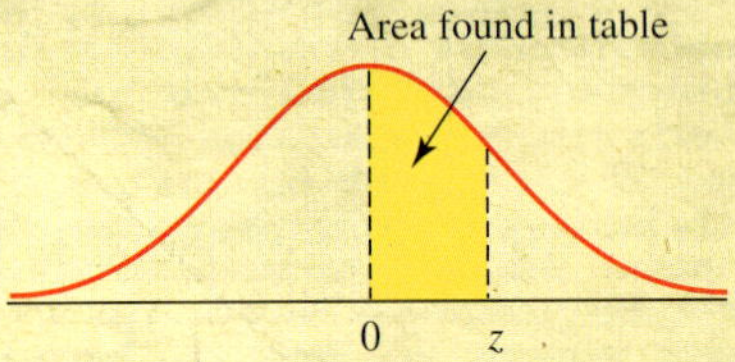

z	0.00	0.01	0.02	0.03	0.04	0.05	0.06	0.07	0.08	0.09
0.0	0.0000	0.0040	0.0080	0.0120	0.0160	0.0199	0.0239	0.0279	0.0319	0.0359
0.1	0.0398	0.0438	0.0478	0.0517	0.0557	0.0596	0.0636	0.0675	0.0714	0.0753
0.2	0.0793	0.0832	0.0871	0.0910	0.0948	0.0987	0.1026	0.1064	0.1103	0.1141
0.3	0.1179	0.1217	0.1255	0.1293	0.1331	0.1368	0.1406	0.1443	0.1480	0.1517
0.4	0.1554	0.1591	0.1628	0.1664	0.1700	0.1736	0.1772	0.1808	0.1844	0.1879
0.5	0.1915	0.1950	0.1985	0.2019	0.2054	0.2088	0.2123	0.2157	0.2190	0.2224
0.6	0.2257	0.2291	0.2324	0.2357	0.2389	0.2422	0.2454	0.2486	0.2517	0.2549
0.7	0.2580	0.2611	0.2642	0.2673	0.2704	0.2734	0.2764	0.2794	0.2823	0.2852
0.8	0.2881	0.2910	0.2939	0.2967	0.2995	0.3023	0.3051	0.3078	0.3106	0.3133
0.9	0.3159	0.3186	0.3212	0.3238	0.3264	0.3289	0.3315	0.3340	0.3365	0.3389
1.0	0.3413	0.3438	0.3461	0.3485	0.3508	0.3531	0.3554	0.3577	0.3599	0.3621
1.1	0.3643	0.3665	0.3686	0.3708	0.3729	0.3749	0.3770	0.3790	0.3810	0.3830
1.2	0.3849	0.3869	0.3888	0.3907	0.3925	0.3944	0.3962	0.3980	0.3997	0.4015
1.3	0.4032	0.4049	0.4066	0.4082	0.4099	0.4115	0.4131	0.4147	0.4162	0.4177
1.4	0.4192	0.4207	0.4222	0.4236	0.4251	0.4265	0.4279	0.4292	0.4306	0.4319
1.5	0.4332	0.4345	0.4357	0.4370	0.4382	0.4394	0.4406	0.4418	0.4429	0.4441
1.6	0.4452	0.4463	0.4474	0.4484	0.4495	0.4505	0.4515	0.4525	0.4535	0.4545
1.7	0.4554	0.4564	0.4573	0.4582	0.4591	0.4599	0.4608	0.4616	0.4625	0.4633
1.8	0.4641	0.4649	0.4656	0.4664	0.4671	0.4678	0.4686	0.4693	0.4699	0.4706
1.9	0.4713	0.4719	0.4726	0.4732	0.4738	0.4744	0.4750	0.4756	0.4761	0.4767
2.0	0.4772	0.4778	0.4783	0.4788	0.4793	0.4798	0.4803	0.4808	0.4812	0.4817
2.1	0.4821	0.4826	0.4830	0.4834	0.4838	0.4842	0.4846	0.4850	0.4854	0.4857
2.2	0.4861	0.4864	0.4868	0.4871	0.4875	0.4878	0.4881	0.4884	0.4887	0.4890
2.3	0.4893	0.4896	0.4898	0.4901	0.4904	0.4906	0.4909	0.4911	0.4913	0.4916
2.4	0.4918	0.4920	0.4922	0.4925	0.4927	0.4929	0.4931	0.4932	0.4934	0.4936
2.5	0.4938	0.4940	0.4941	0.4943	0.4945	0.4946	0.4948	0.4949	0.4951	0.4952
2.6	0.4953	0.4955	0.4956	0.4957	0.4959	0.4960	0.4961	0.4962	0.4963	0.4964
2.7	0.4965	0.4966	0.4967	0.4968	0.4969	0.4970	0.4971	0.4972	0.4973	0.4974
2.8	0.4974	0.4975	0.4976	0.4977	0.4977	0.4978	0.4979	0.4979	0.4980	0.4981
2.9	0.4981	0.4982	0.4982	0.4983	0.4984	0.4984	0.4985	0.4985	0.4986	0.4986
3.0	0.4987	0.4987	0.4987	0.4988	0.4988	0.4989	0.4989	0.4989	0.4990	0.4990

Note: For values of *z* above 3.09, use 0.4999.

The z-score is used with Table 10.6 to find the percent of occurrence between the mean and the number of standard deviations above the mean specified by the z-score, as illustrated in Figure 10.19.

Figure 10.19 Percent of occurrence using a z-score

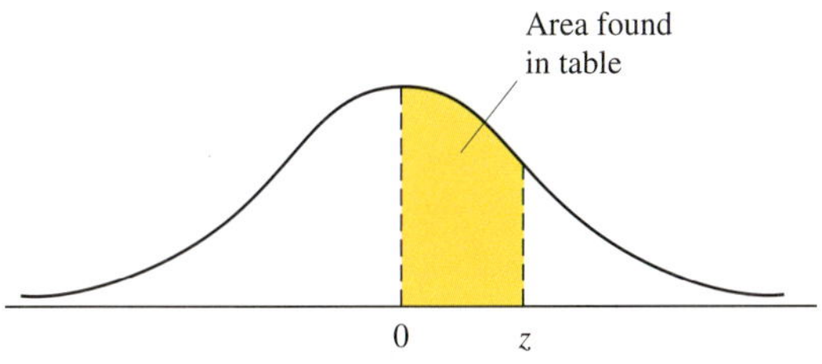

There are three equivalent ideas associated with the normal curve. These are summarized in the box to the right.

Sometimes data do not fall into a normal distribution, but are **skewed**, which means their distribution has more tail on one side or the other. For example, Figure 10.20a shows that the 1941 scores on the SAT exam (when the test was first used) were normally distributed. However, by 1990, the scale had become skewed to the left, as shown in Figure 10.20b.

Normal Curve Interpretations

In a standard normal curve, the following three quantities are equivalent:

> ***Probability*** **of a randomly chosen item lying in an interval;**
>
> ***Percentage*** **of total items that lie in an interval;**
>
> ***Area*** **under a normal curve along an interval.**

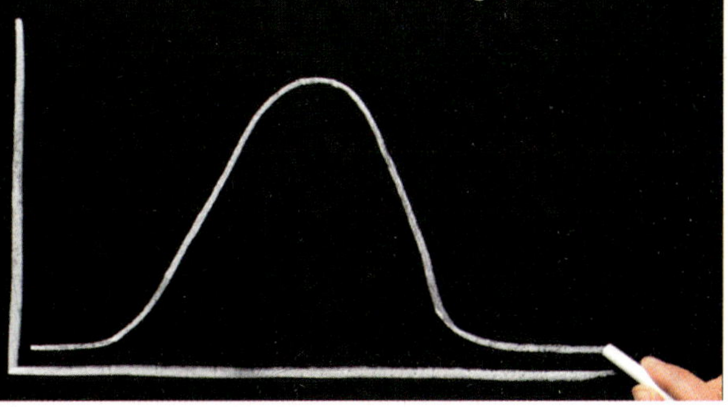

© Stephen Rees/iStockphoto.com

In a normal distribution, the mean, median, and mode all have the same value, but if the distribution is skewed, the relative positions of the mean, median, and mode would be as shown in Figure 10.21.

Figure 10.20 Distribution of SAT scores

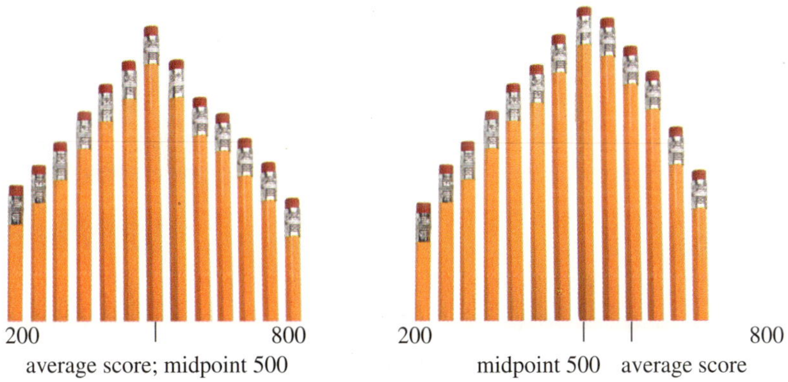

a. 1941 SAT scale **b.** 1990 SAT scale

© Brand X Pictures/Jupiterimage

Figure 10.21 Comparison of three distributions

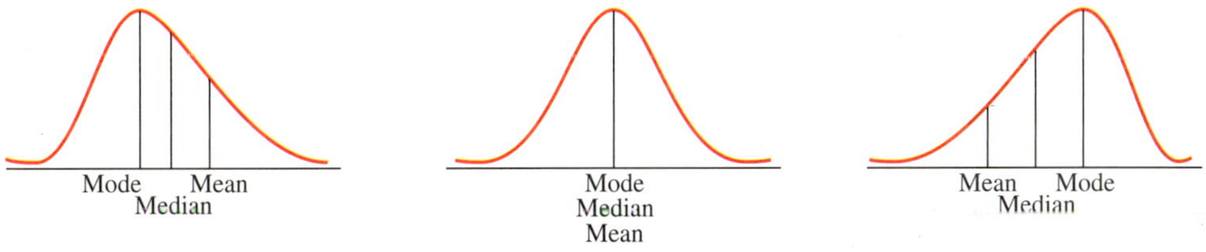

a. Skewed to the right **b.** Normal distribution **c.** Skewed to the left

The Nature of Graphs—The Marriage of Algebra and Geometry

11.1 Cartesian Coordinate System

HAVE YOU EVER DRAWN A PICTURE BY CONNECTING THE DOTS OR FOUND A CITY OR STREET ON A MAP?

topics

If you have, then you've used the ideas we'll be discussing in this section.

Ordered Pairs

How can you find Fisherman's Wharf by looking at the map shown in Figure 11.1?

Figure 11.1 Map of San Francisco

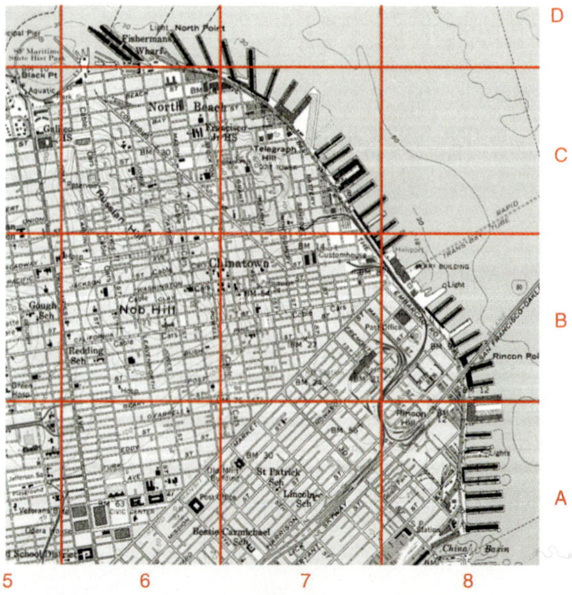

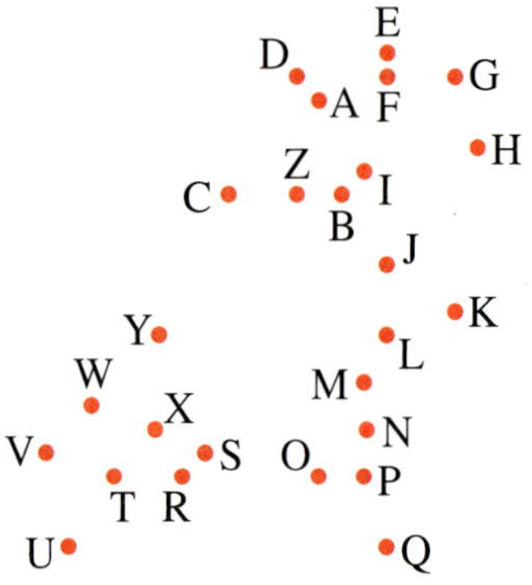

Can you connect the dots?

If you looked at an index for the map, you would find Fisherman's Wharf listed as (6, D). Can you locate section (6, D) in Figure 11.1? Did you find it? Next, see if you can find Main Street—located at (7, B). Hard to find, right? How could we improve the map to make our task easier? We could create a map with a smaller grid. However, a smaller grid means that a lot of letters are needed for the vertical scale, and we might need more letters than there are in the alphabet. So let's use a notation that will allow us to represent points on the map with pairs of numbers. A pair of numbers written as (2, 3) is called an **ordered pair** to remind you that the order in which the numbers 2 and 3 are listed is important. That is, (2, 3) specifies a different location than does (3, 2). For the ordered pair (2, 3), 2 is the **first component** and 3 is the **second component**. The ordered pair is referred to as the **coordinates** for location on a map or a graph.

Figure 11.2 Map of San Francisco with mathematical coordinates

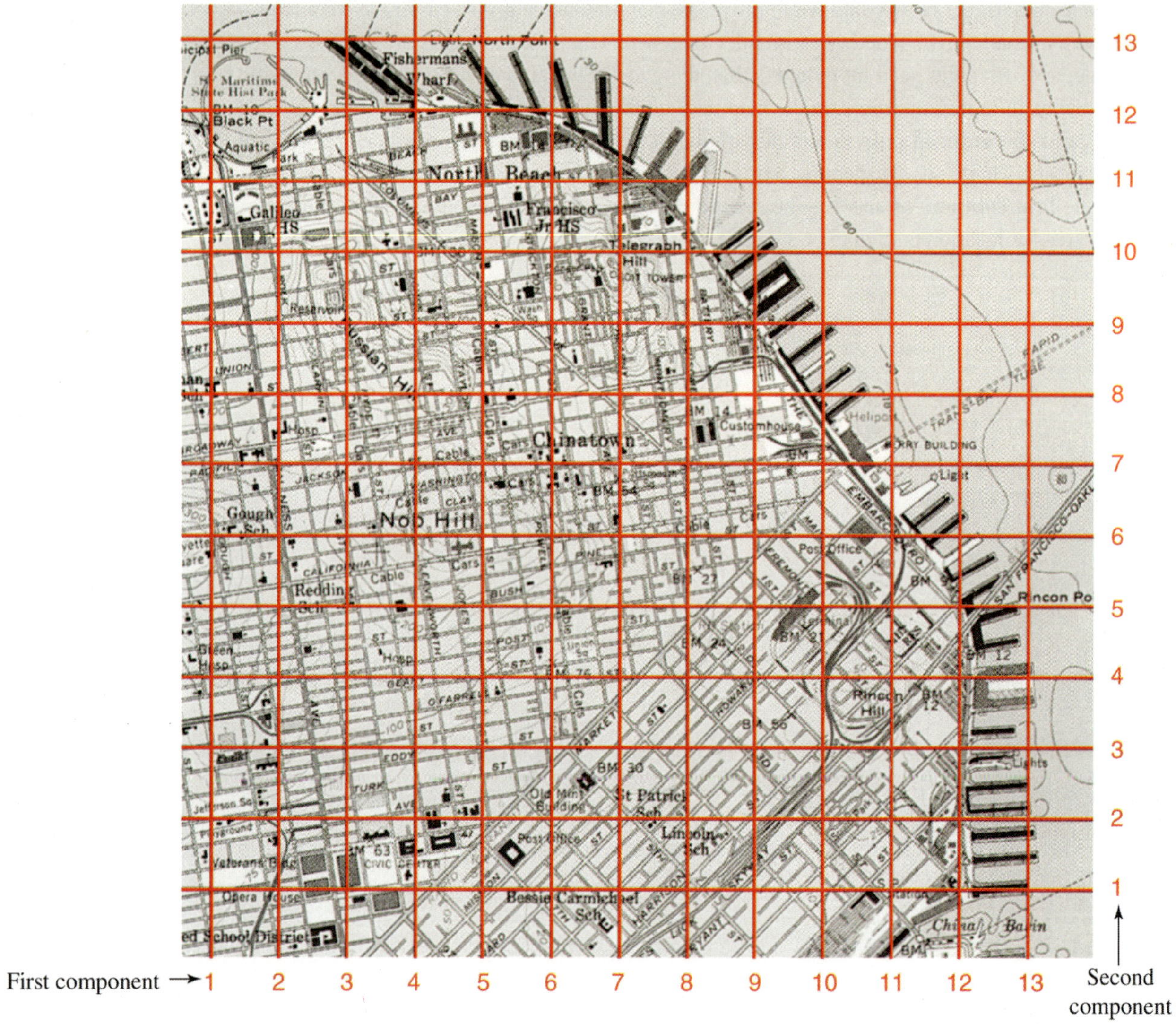

STOP *Don't forget the meaning of this notation.*

first component
↓
(x, y)
↑
second component

For our map, suppose that we relabel the vertical scale with numbers and change both scales so that we label the *lines instead of the spaces*, as shown in Figure 11.2. (By the way, most technical maps number lines instead of spaces.)

Now we can fix the location of any street on the map quite precisely. Notice that if we use an ordered pair of numbers (instead of a number and a letter), it is important to know which component of the ordered pair represents the horizontal distance and which component represents the vertical distance. If we use Figure 11.2, we see that the coordinates of Main Street are about (9.5, 6.3); we can even say that Main Street runs from about (9.5, 6.3) to (11.2, 4.5). Notice that, by using ordered pairs and numbering the lines instead of the spaces, we have refined our grid. We've refined it even more with decimal components.

When using ordered pairs of numbers, remember that the first component is on the horizontal axis and the second component is on the vertical axis.

There are many ways to use ordered pairs to find particular locations. For example, a teacher may make a seating chart like the one shown in Figure 11.3.

In the grade book, the teacher records

Anderson (3, 4)	Remember, first component is horizontal direction;
Atz (1, 3)	second component is vertical direction.

Anderson's seat is in column 3, row 4. Can you think of some other ways in which ordered pairs could be used to locate a position?

Figure 11.3 Classroom seating chart

5	Hannah Becker	Susan Reiland		Jeff Clark	Søren Sovndal
4	Sharon Boschen	Linda Smith	Bob Anderson	Josephine Lee	Milt Hoehn
3	Jeff Atz	Laurie Pederson	Tim Selbo	Todd Humann	Brian Claasen
2	Terry Shell	Arnie Norman	Clint Stevenson	Steve Switzer	
1	Theron Sovndal	Beverly Schaap	Niels Pedersen	Cole Becker	Eva Mikalson
	1	2	3	4	5

Coordinates

The idea of using an ordered pair to locate a certain position requires particular terminology. **Axes** are two perpendicular real number lines, such as those shown in Figure 11.4. The point of intersection of the axes is called the **origin**. In Chapter 2, we associated direction to the right or up with positive numbers. The upward and rightward arrows in Figure 11.4 are pointing in the positive directions. These perpendicular lines are usually drawn so that one is horizontal and the other is vertical. The horizontal axis is called the ***x*-axis**, and the vertical axis is called the ***y*-axis**.

Figure 11.4 Cartesian coordinate system

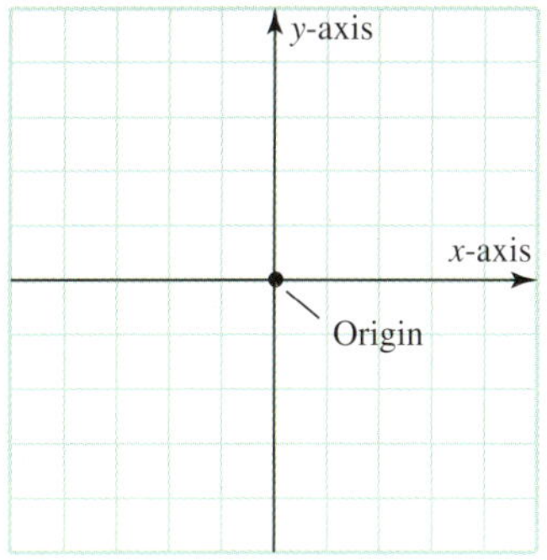

Notice that the axes of a Cartesian coordinate system divide the plane into four parts. These parts are called **quadrants** and are labeled as shown in Figure 11.5.

Figure 11.5 Quadrants

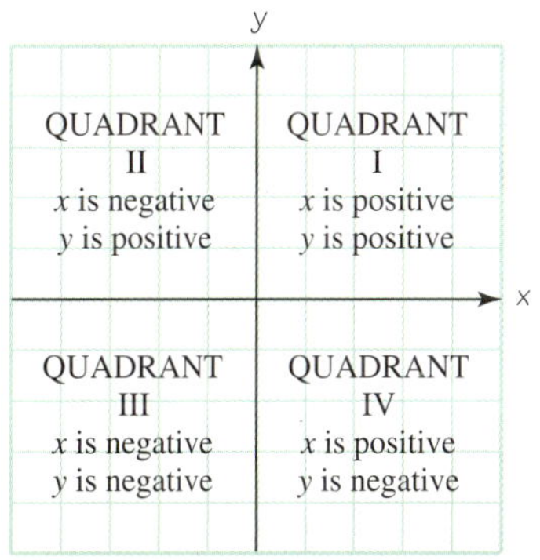

We can now label points in the plane by using ordered pairs. The first component of the pair gives the horizontal distance, and the second component gives the vertical distance, as shown in Figure 11.6.

Figure 11.6 (x, y) are coordinates of a point

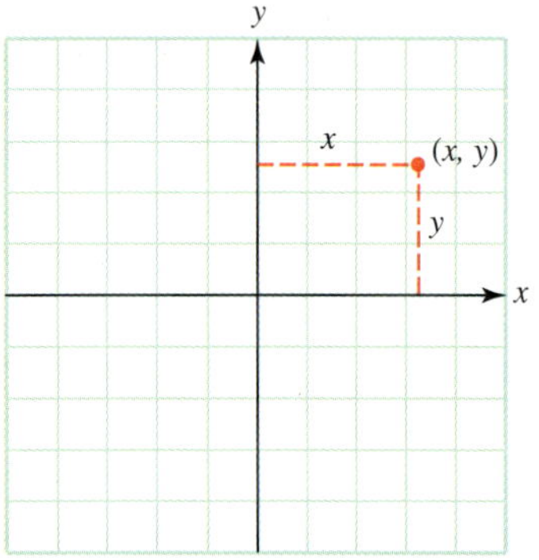

If x and y are components of a point, representation of the point (x, y) is called the **rectangular** or **Cartesian coordinates** of the point. To **plot** (or **graph**) a point means to show the coordinates of the ordered pair by drawing a dot at the specified location.

11.2 Functions

THE IDEA OF LOOKING AT TWO SETS OF VARIABLES AT THE SAME TIME WAS INTRODUCED IN THE PREVIOUS SECTION.

Sets of ordered pairs provide a very compact and useful way to represent relationships between various sets of numbers. To consider this idea, let's look at the cartoon below.

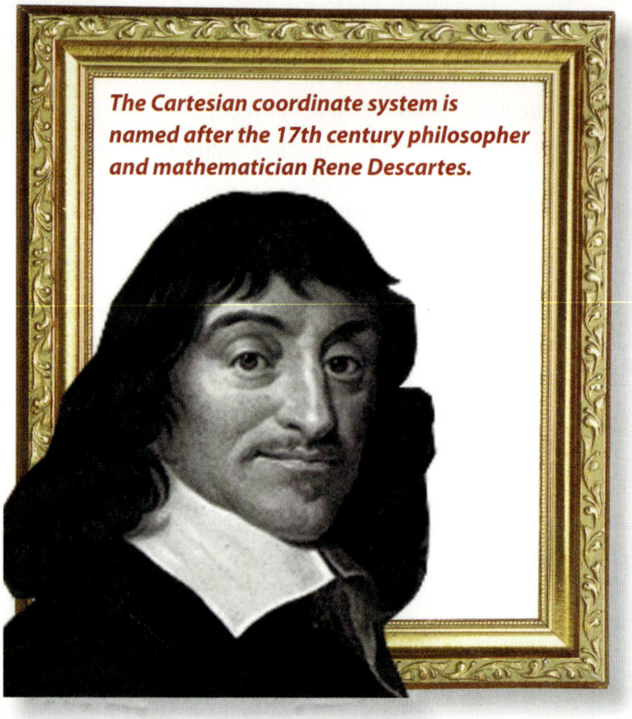

The distance an object will fall depends on (among other things) the length of time it falls. If we let the variable d be the distance the object has fallen and the variable t be the time it has fallen (in seconds), and if we disregard air resistance, the formula is

$$d = 16t^2$$

Therefore, in the *B.C.* cartoon, if the well is 16 seconds deep (and we neglect the time it takes for the sound to come back up), we know that the depth of the well (in feet) is

$$\begin{aligned} d &= 16(16)^2 \\ &= 16(256) \\ &= 4{,}096 \end{aligned}$$

The formula $d = 16t^2$ gives rise to a set of data:

Time (in seconds)	0	1	2	3	4	···	15	16
Distance (in ft)	0	16	64	144	256	···	3,600	4,096

B.C. cartoon reprinted by permission of Johnny Hart and Creators Syndicate.

For every nonnegative value of t, there is a corresponding value for d.

first component (values for t)
↓
(x, y)
↑
second component (values for d)

We can represent the data in the table as a set of ordered pairs in which the first component represents a value for t and the second component represents a corresponding value for d. For this example, we have (0, 0), (1, 16), (2, 64), (3, 144), (4, 256), . . . , (15, 3,600), (16, 4,096).

Whenever we have a situation comparable to the one illustrated by this example—namely, whenever the first component of an ordered pair is associated with exactly one second component—we call the set of ordered pairs a **function**.

> A **function** is a set of ordered pairs in which the first component is associated with exactly one second component.

This definition is one of the unifying ideas in all of mathematics.

Consider the following example.

$\{(0, 0), (1, 2), (2, 4), (3, 9), (4, 16)\}$

For this set, we see that

$0 \rightarrow 0$
$1 \rightarrow 2$
$2 \rightarrow 4$
$3 \rightarrow 9$
$4 \rightarrow 16$

Sometimes it is helpful to think of the first component as the "picker" and the second component as the "pickee." Given an ordered pair (x, y), we find that each replacement for x "picks" a partner, or a second value. We can symbolize this by $x \rightarrow y$.

Since each first component is associated with exactly one second component, the set is a function. Not all sets of ordered pairs are functions. Consider another example.

$\{(0, 0), (1, 1), (1, -1), (4, 2), (3, -2)\}$

For this set,

$0 \rightarrow 0$
$1 \rightarrow 1$ and $1 \rightarrow -1$
$4 \rightarrow 2$
$3 \rightarrow -2$

Since 1 picks two values as a partner or second component, we call the number 1 a "fickle picker."

A function is a set of ordered pairs for which there are no fickle pickers.

Since the first component can be associated with more than one second component, the set is not a function.

$\{(1, 3), (2, 3), (3, 3), (4, 3)\}$

For this set,

$1 \rightarrow 3$
$2 \rightarrow 3$
$3 \rightarrow 3$
$4 \rightarrow 3$

There are no fickle pickers, so it is a function.

This is an example of a function.

$\{(3, 1), (3, 2), (3, 3), (3, 4)\}$

Finally,

$3 \rightarrow 1$
$3 \rightarrow 2$
$3 \rightarrow 3$
$3 \rightarrow 4$

The number 3 is a fickle picker, so this set is not a function.

Since the first component is associated with several second components, the set is not a function.

Another way to consider functions is with the idea of a function machine. Think of a function machine as shown in Figure 11.7.

Figure 11.7 Function machine

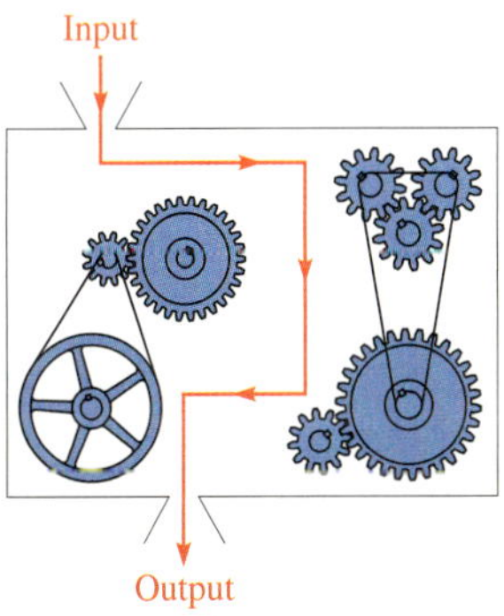

Think of this machine as having an input where items are entered and an output where results are obtained, much like a vending machine. If the number 2 is dropped into the input, a function machine will output a single value. If the name of the function machine is f, then the output value is called "f of 2" and is written as $f(2)$. This is called **functional notation**. If a function machine f squares the input value, we write $f(x) = x^2$, where x represents the input value. We usually define functions by simply saying "Let $f(x) = x^2$."

Identify the value of f for the given value.

$f(2) = 2^2 = 4;$
$f(8) = 8^2 = 64;$
$f(-3) = (-3)^2 = 9;$
$f(t) = t^2.$

11.3 Lines

LET'S CONSIDER AN EQUATION WITH TWO VARIABLES, SAY *X* AND *Y*.

Solving Equations with Two Variables

If there are two values X and Y that make an equation true, then we say that the ordered pair (X, Y) **satisfies** the equation and that it is a **solution** of the equation.

Graphing a Line

The process of graphing a line requires that you find ordered pairs that make an equation true. To do this, *you*, the student, must choose convenient values for x and then solve the resulting equation to find a corresponding value for y. Find three ordered pairs that satisfy the equation $y = -2x + 3$. *You* choose any x value—say, $x = 1$. Substitute this value into the given equation to find a corresponding value of y:

$$\begin{aligned} y &= -2x + 3 && \text{Given equation} \\ &= -2(1) + 3 && \text{Substitute chosen value.} \\ &= -2 + 3 \\ &= 1 \end{aligned}$$

You choose this value.
↓
The first ordered pair is (1, 1).
↑
You find this value by substitution into the equation.

Choose a second value—say, $x = 2$. Then

$$\begin{aligned} y &= -2x + 3 && \text{Start with given equation.} \\ &= -2(2) + 3 && \text{Substitute} \\ &= -4 + 3 \\ &= -1 \end{aligned}$$

The second ordered pair is $(2, -1)$. Choose a third value—say, $x = -1$. Then

$$\begin{aligned} y &= -2x + 3 \\ &= -2(-1) + 3 \\ &= 2 + 3 \\ &= 5 \end{aligned}$$

The third ordered pair is $(-1, 5)$. We plot these points (shown in blue) in Figure 11.8.

Figure 11.8 Some points that satisfy $y = -2x + 3$

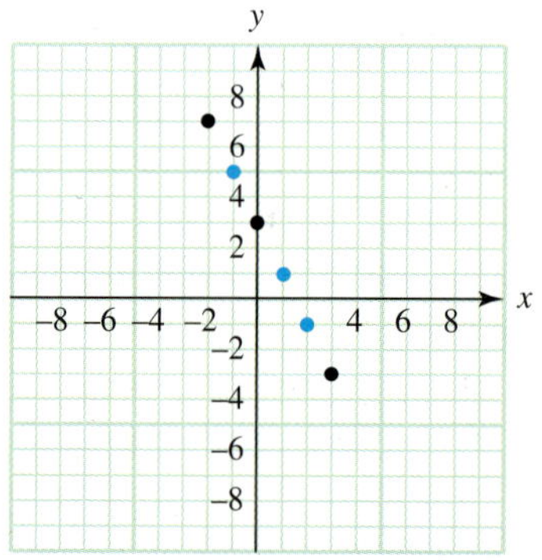

Have we found *all* the ordered pairs that satisfy the equation $y = -2x + 3$? Can you find others? Three more are shown in black in Figure 11.8. Do you notice anything about the arrangement of these points in the plane? Suppose that we draw a line passing through these points in Figure 11.8, as shown in Figure 11.9. This line represents the set of *all* ordered pairs that satisfy the equation.

Figure 11.9 Representation of all points satisfying $y = -2x + 3$

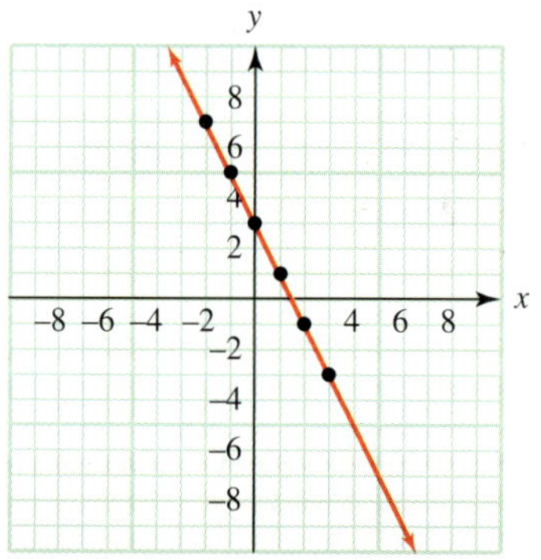

The Process of Graphing a Line

If we carry out the process of finding three ordered pairs that satisfy an equation with two first-degree variables, and then we draw a line through those points to find the representation of all ordered pairs satisfying the equation, we say that we are *graphing the line*, and the final set of points we have drawn represents the **graph** of the line.

PROCEDURE:

Graphing a Line

In order to graph a line by plotting points, follow these steps.

STEP 1 First find two ordered pairs that lie on the line.

STEP 2 Two points determine a line. As a check, find a third ordered pair.

STEP 3 Draw the line (using a straightedge) passing through these three points.

*If three points don't lie on a line, then you have made an error.

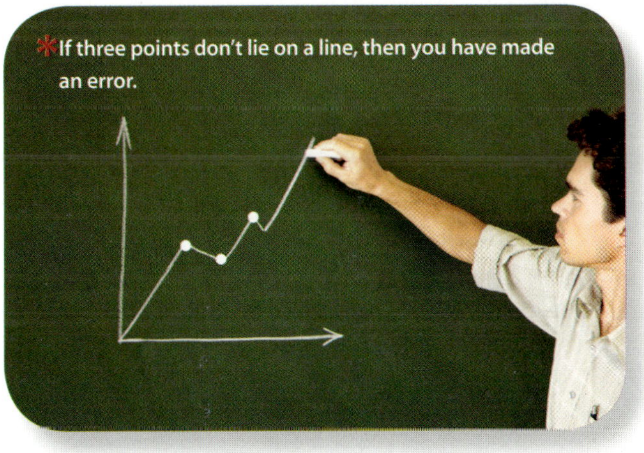

Graph $y = 2x + 2$. It is generally easier to pick x and find y.

If $x = 0$: $y = 2x + 2$ Given equation.
$= 2(0) + 2$ Substitute.
$= 2$ Plot the point (0, 2).

If $x = 1$: $y = 2x + 2$
$= 2(1) + 2$
$= 4$ Plot the point (1, 4).

If $x = 2$: $y = 2x + 2$
$= 2(2) + 2$
$= 6$ Plot the point (2, 6).

Draw the line through the plotted points, as shown in Figure 11.10.

Figure 11.10 Graph of $y = 2x + 2$

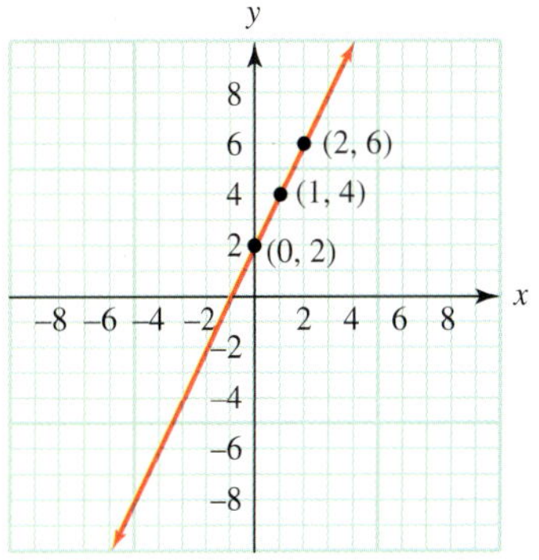

Horizontal and Vertical Lines

Graph $y = 4$. Since the only requirement is that y (the second component) equal 4, we see that there is no restriction on the choice for x. Thus, (0, 4), (1, 4), and $(-2, 4)$ all satisfy the equation $y = 4$.

If you plot and connect these points, you will see that the line formed is shown in Figure 11.11. This line, described as parallel to the x-axis, is called a **horizontal line**.

Figure 11.11 Graph of $y = 4$

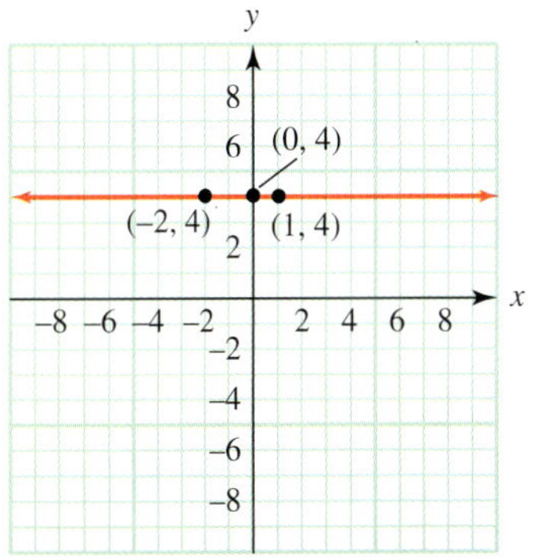

Graph $x = 3$. Since the only requirement is that x (the first component) equal 3, we see that there is no restriction

on the choice for y. Thus, (3, 2), (3, −1), and (3, 0) all satisfy the equation $x = 3$.

If you plot and connect these points, you will see that the line formed is shown in Figure 11.12. This line, described as parallel to the y-axis, is called a **vertical line**.

Figure 11.12 Graph of $x = 3$

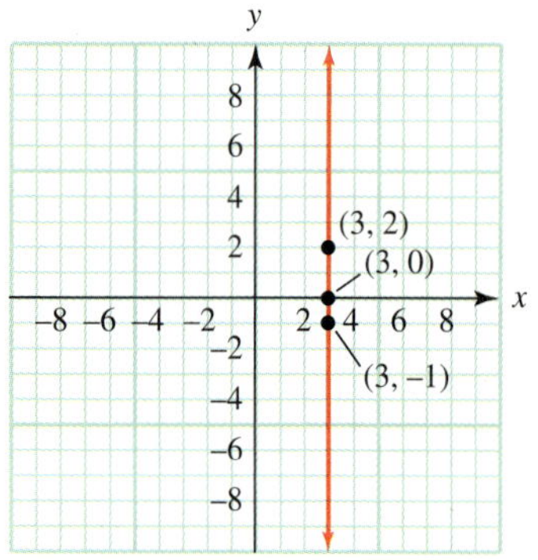

11.4 Systems and Inequalities

MANY SITUATIONS INVOLVE TWO VARIABLES OR UNKNOWNS THAT ARE RELATED IN SOME SPECIFIC FASHION.

Linda is on a business trip and needs to rent a car for the day. The car rental agency has the following options on the car she wants to rent:

Option A: $40/day plus 50¢ per mile

Option B: Flat rate of $60/day with unlimited mileage

Which car should she rent?

Solving Systems of Equations by Graphing

The cost c of a car rental is related to the number of miles driven, in the following way:

Option A: COST = BASIC CHARGE + MILEAGE CHARGE

50¢ per mile ↓

COST = 40 + 0.5(NUMBER OF MILES)

Let COST = c NUMBER OF MILES = m

$$c = 40 + 0.5m$$

Option B: COST = FLAT FEE

$$c = 60$$

Suppose that we represent these relationships in a graph, as described by a Cartesian coordinate system. We

Option A

Option B

will find ordered pairs (m, c) that make these equations true.

Option A: $c = 40 + 0.5m$

Let $m = \mathbf{20}$: $c = 40 + 0.5(\mathbf{20})$
$= 40 + 10 = 50$ This means that if Linda drives 20 miles, the cost of the rental is \$50; plot (20, 50).

Let $m = \mathbf{50}$: $c = 40 + 0.5(\mathbf{50})$
$= 40 + 25 = 65$ Plot (50, 65).

Let $m = \mathbf{100}$: $c = 40 + 0.5(\mathbf{100})$
$= 40 + 50 = 90$ Plot (100, 90).

We now have three ordered pairs, so we plot those three points as shown in Figure 11.13.

Figure 11.13 Graphs for the rental car problem

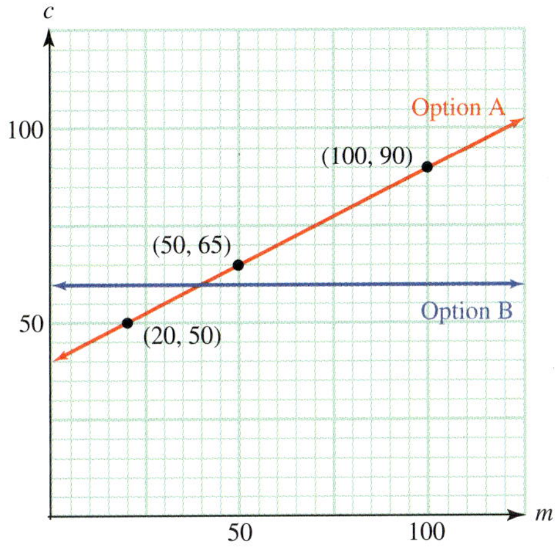

Next, notice that these points all lie on the same line. Draw a line through these points. This line is shown in red in Figure 11.13.

Next, we consider Option B:

Option B: $c = 60$

The second component of the ordered pair (m, c) is always 60 regardless of the number of miles, m. This is shown as a blue horizontal line in Figure 11.13. Estimate the mileage for which both rates are the same. The solution is the point of intersection of the graphs shown in Figure 11.13. We estimate the coordinates to be (40, 60), as shown in Figure 11.14.

This point of intersection means that, if Linda drives 40 miles, the rates are the same. It also means that, if Linda expects to drive more than 40 miles, she should take the fixed rate (Option B). She should choose Option A if she expects to drive less than 40 miles.

When two or more equations are considered together, we call them a **system of equations**. The intersection point

Figure 11.14 Comparing car rental rates

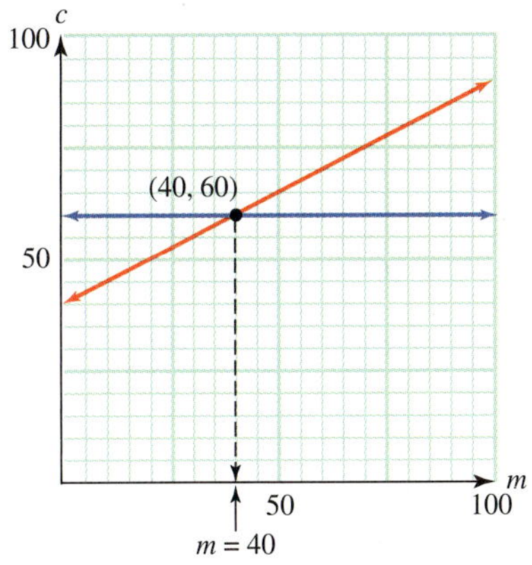

on the graph is called the **simultaneous solution** of a system of equations.

Solve the following system of equations by graphing:

$$\begin{cases} x + 2y = 5 \\ 3x - y = 8 \end{cases}$$

The brace is used to signify that we want to find the simultaneous solution of the system of equations. The method of graphing involves looking for the point of intersection for the two lines. Graph both lines on the same coordinate axes.

Line $x + 2y = 5$		Line $3x - y = 8$	
x	y	x	y
1	2	0	−8
3	1	1	−5
5	0	2	−2

Remember, to find these points, you choose the x-value and then calculate the corresponding y-value.

Plot these points and draw each line passing through them, as shown in Figure 11.15.

Figure 11.15 Graphs of $x + 2y = 5$ and $3x - y = 8$

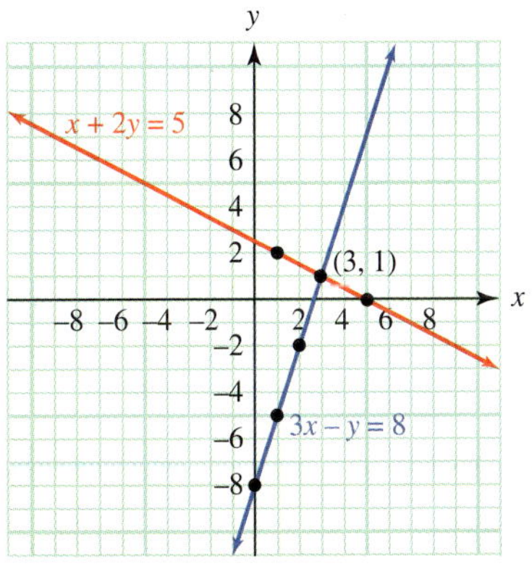

The solution to the system of equations is the point of intersection; it looks like the point (3, 1). We can check this point to see whether it satisfies *both* equations:

$$\begin{aligned} x + 2y &= 5 \\ (3) + 2(1) &= 5 \\ 5 &= 5 \text{ is true} \end{aligned} \qquad \begin{aligned} 3x - y &= 8 \\ 3(3) - (1) &= 8 \\ 8 &= 8 \text{ is true} \end{aligned}$$

The point (3, 1) satisfies both of the given equations, so we say that (3, 1) checks.

An interesting application of graphing systems of equations has to do with **supply and demand**. If supply greatly exceeds demand, money will be lost because of unsold items. On the other hand, if demand greatly exceeds supply, money will be lost because of insufficient inventory. The most desirable situation is when supply and demand are equal. If we assume that supply and demand are linear, then the solution of the system is called the **equilibrium point** and represents the point at which supply and demand are equal. In more advanced courses, it is shown that the price that maximizes the profit occurs at this equilibrium point.

Graphing Linear Inequalities*

A second application of graphing lines involves extending the concept to graphing linear inequalities. We begin by noting that every line divides a plane into three parts, as shown in Figure 11.16.

* Before reading this section, you might review Topic 3.5.

Figure 11.16 Half-planes

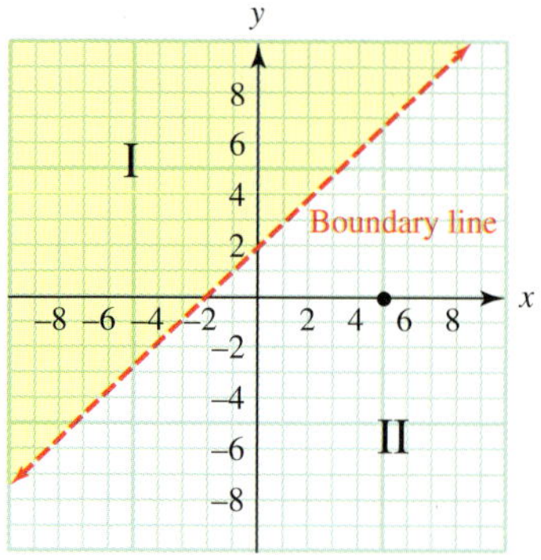

Two parts are labeled I and II; these are called **half-planes**. The third part is called the **boundary** and is the line separating the half-planes. The solution of a first-degree inequality in two unknowns is the set of all ordered pairs that satisfy the given inequality. A half-plane is **closed** if it includes its boundary line and is **open** if it does not. This solution set is a half-plane.

The following table offers some examples of first-degree inequalities with two unknowns, along with associated terminology.

Example	Inequality Symbol	Boundary Included	Term
$3x - y > 5$	$>$	no	**open half-plane**
$3x - y < 5$	$<$	no	open half-plane
$3x - y \geq 5$	$\geq$	yes	**closed half-plane**
$3x - y \leq 5$	$\leq$	yes	closed half-plane

We can now summarize the procedure for graphing a first-degree inequality in two unknowns.

SCALE 1/8" = 1 FT. DRAWN BY: TRACED BY: CHECKED BY: SKETCH SHEET DATE

PROCEDURE:

Graphing Inequalities

The procedure for graphing an equality can be summarized in two steps.

STEP 1 Graph the boundary. Replace the inequality symbol with an equality symbol and draw the resulting line. This is the boundary line. Use a solid line when the boundary is included ($\leq$ or $\geq$). Use a dashed line when the boundary is not included ($<$ or $>$).

STEP 2 Test a point. Choose any point in the plane that is not on the boundary line; the point (0, 0) is usually the simplest choice. If this point, called a test point, makes the *inequality* true, shade in that half-plane for the solution.*

If the test point makes the *inequality* false, shade in the other half-plane for the solution.

*A highlighter pen does a nice job of shading your work.

REVISION 1 2 3 BY DATE

This process sounds complicated, but if you know how to draw lines from equations, you will not find it difficult. Graph $3x - y \geq 5$. Note that the inequality symbol is $\geq$, so the boundary is included.

STEP 1 Graph the boundary; draw the (solid) line corresponding to

$3x - y = 5$ Replace the inequality symbol with an equality symbol.

Let $x = 0$; then $3(0) - y = 5$ or $y = -5$.
Plot the point $(0, -5)$.

Let $x = 1$; then $3(1) - y = 5$ or $y = R - 2$.
Plot the point $(1, -2)$.

Let $x = 2$; then $3(2) - y = 5$ or $y = 1$.
Plot the point $(2, 1)$.

The boundary line is shown in Figure 11.17.

Figure 11.17 Graph of $3x - y \geq 5$

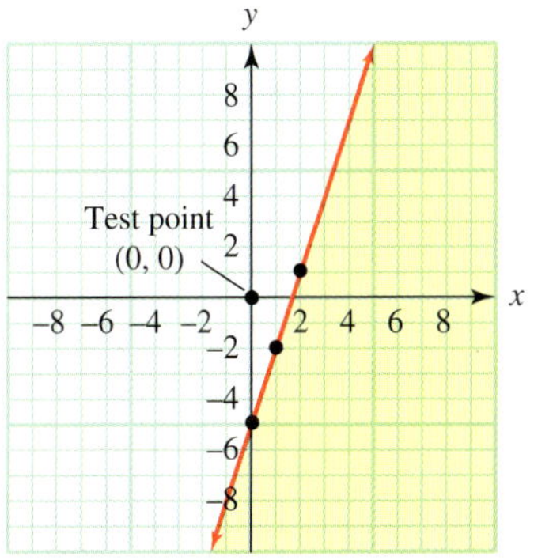

STEP 2 Choose a test point; we choose (0, 0). Plot (0, 0) in Figure 11.17 and note that it lies in one of the half-planes determined by the boundary line. We now check this test point with the given *inequality*.

$3(0) - (0) \geq 5$ You can usually test this in your head.
$0 \geq 5$ This is false.

Therefore, shade the half-plane that does *not* contain (0, 0), as shown in Figure 11.17.

11.5 Graphing Curves

WHEN CANNONS WERE INTRODUCED IN THE 13TH CENTURY, THEIR PRIMARY USE WAS TO DEMORALIZE THE ENEMY.

It was much later that they were used for strategic purposes. In fact, cannons existed nearly three centuries before enough was known about the behavior of projectiles to use them with any accuracy. The cannonball does not travel in a

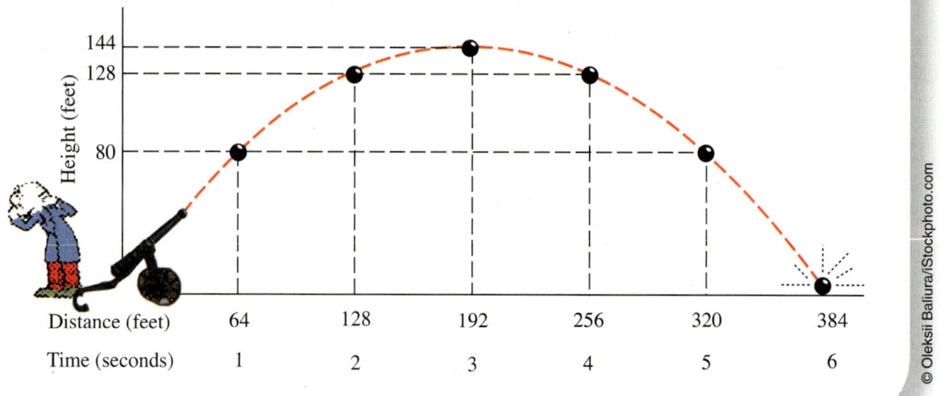

Figure 11.18 Path of a cannonball

straight line, it was discovered, because of an unseen force that today we know as *gravity*. Consider Figure 11.18. It is a scale drawing (graph) of the path of a cannonball fired in a particular way.

Graphing Curves by Plotting Points

The path described by a projectile is called a **parabola**. Any projectile—a ball, an arrow, a bullet, a rock from a slingshot, even water from the nozzle of a hose or sprinkler—will travel a parabolic path. Note that this parabolic curve has a maximum height and is symmetric about a vertical line through that height. In other words, the ascent and descent paths are symmetric.

For example, graph $y = x^2$. We will choose x-values and find corresponding y-values.

Let $x = 0$
$y = 0^2 = 0$; plot $(0, 0)$

Let $x = 1$
$y = 1^2 = 1$; plot $(1, 1)$

Let $x = -1$
$y = (-1)^2 = 1$; plot $(-1, 1)$

Notice in Figure 11.19 that these points do not fall in a straight line. If we find two more points, we can see the shape of the graph.

Let $x = 2$: $y = 2^2 = 4$; plot $(2, 4)$

Let $x = -2$: $y = (-2)^2 = 4$; plot $(-2, 4)$

These two additional points are also shown in Figure 11.19. We can now connect the points to form a smooth curve, as shown in Figure 11.20.

Figure 11.19 Points that satisfy the equation $y = x^2$

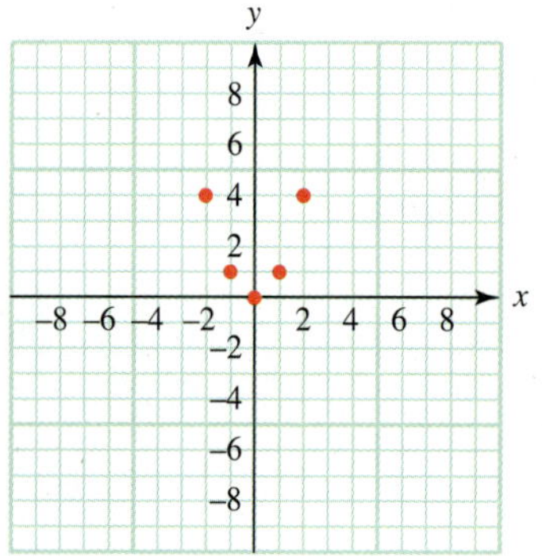

Figure 11.20 Graph of $y = x^2$

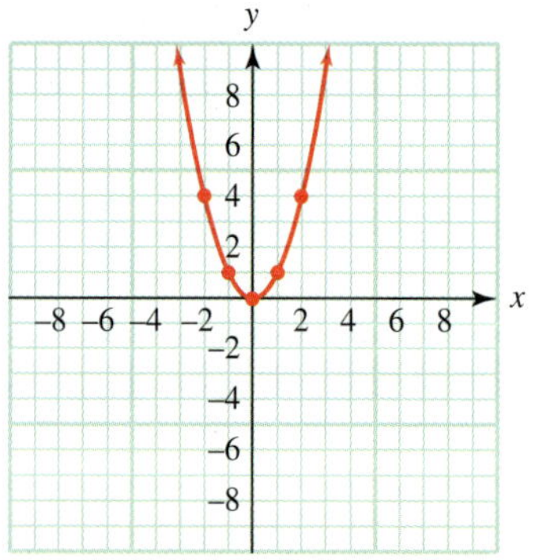

The curve shown in Figure 11.20 is a parabola that is said to *open upward*. The lowest point, (0, 0) in Figure 11.20, is called the **vertex**. The following example is a parabola that *opens downward*.

Sketch $y = -\frac{1}{2}x^2$

Let $x = 0$; then $y = -\frac{1}{2}(0)^2 = 0$ or $y = 0$; plot the point $(0, 0)$.

Let $x = 1$; then $y = -\frac{1}{2}(1)^2 = -\frac{1}{2}$; plot the point $\left(1, -\frac{1}{2}\right)$.

Let $x = -1$; then $y = -\frac{1}{2}(-1)^2 = -\frac{1}{2}$; plot the point $\left(-1, -\frac{1}{2}\right)$.

Let $x = 2$; then $y = -\frac{1}{2}(2)^2 = -2$; plot the point $(2, -2)$.

Let $x = -2$; then $y = -\frac{1}{2}(-2)^2 = -2$; plot the point $(-2, -2)$.

Let $x = 4$; then $y = -\frac{1}{2}(4)^2 = -8$; plot the point $(4, -8)$.

First, plot the points. Next, connect these points to form a smooth curve, as shown in Figure 11.21.

Figure 11.21 Graph of $y = -\frac{1}{2}x^2$

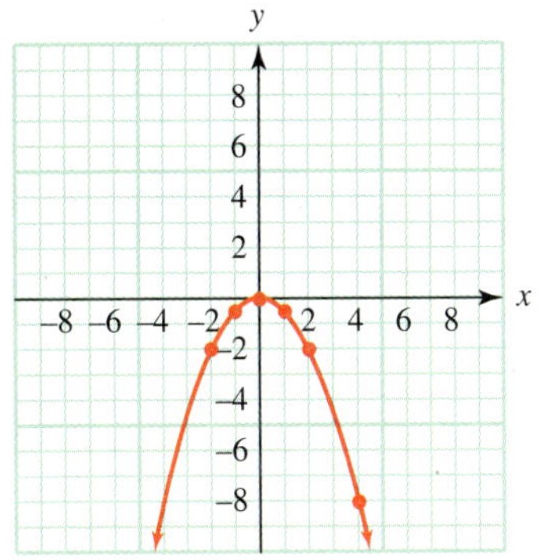

You can sketch many different curves by plotting points. The procedure is to decide whether you should pick x-values and find the corresponding y-values, or pick y-values and find the corresponding x-values. Find enough ordered pairs so that you can connect the points with a smooth graph. Many graphs in mathematics are not smooth, but we will not consider those in this course.

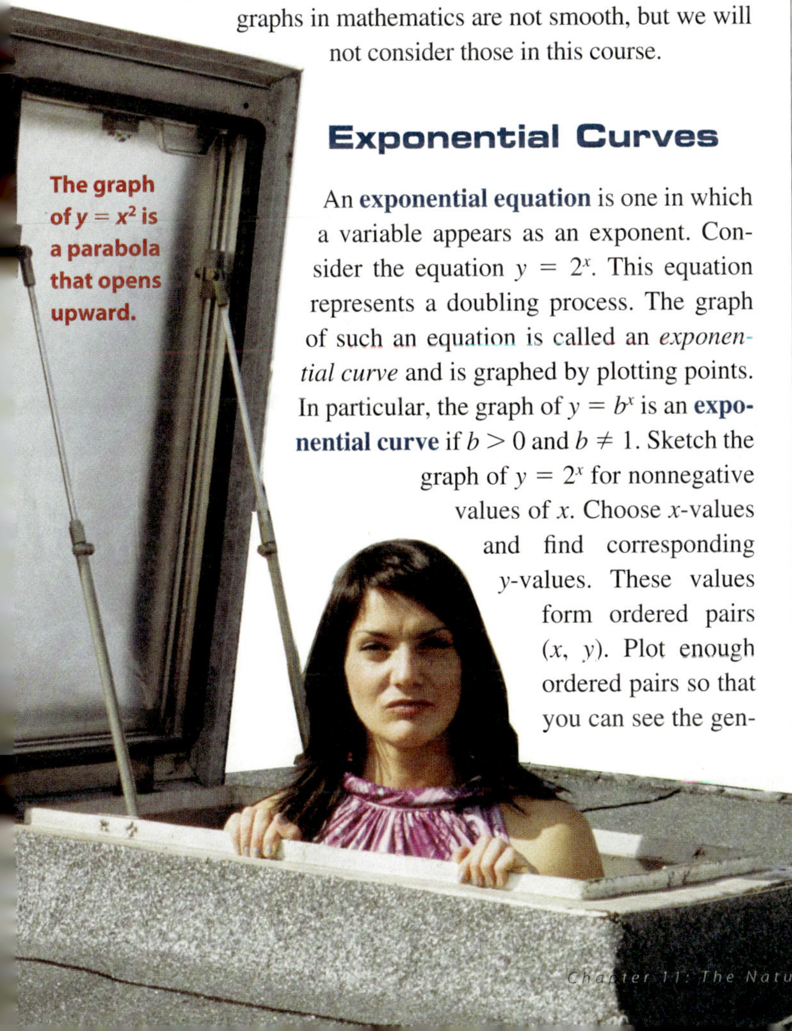

The graph of $y = x^2$ is a parabola that opens upward.

Exponential Curves

An **exponential equation** is one in which a variable appears as an exponent. Consider the equation $y = 2^x$. This equation represents a doubling process. The graph of such an equation is called an *exponential curve* and is graphed by plotting points. In particular, the graph of $y = b^x$ is an **exponential curve** if $b > 0$ and $b \neq 1$. Sketch the graph of $y = 2^x$ for nonnegative values of x. Choose x-values and find corresponding y-values. These values form ordered pairs (x, y). Plot enough ordered pairs so that you can see the general shape of the curve, and then connect the points with a smooth curve, as shown in Figure 11.22.

Let $x = 0$; then $y = 2^0 = 1$; plot the point $(0, 1)$.

Let $x = 1$; then $y = 2^1 = 2$; plot the point $(1, 2)$.

Let $x = 2$; then $y = 2^2 = 4$; plot the point $(2, 4)$.

Let $x = 3$; then $y = 2^3 = 8$; plot the point $(3, 8)$.

Let $x = 4$; then $y = 2^4 = 16$; plot the point $(4, 16)$.

Figure 11.22 Graph of $y = 2^x$

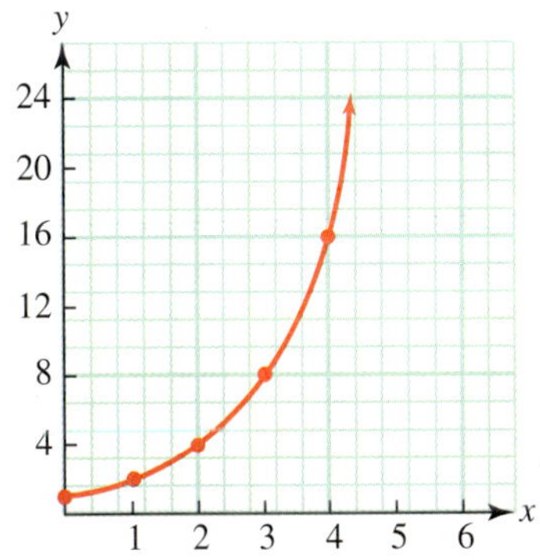

Population growth is described by an exponential equation. The population P at some future date can be predicted if you know the present population, P_0, and the growth rate, r. In more advanced courses, it is shown that the predicted population in t time periods is approximated by the equation $P = P_0(2.72)^{rt}$.

Tony calls his local Chamber of Commerce and finds that the population growth rate of his town is now 5%.

Also, according to the 1990 census, the population is 2,500. Find the growth equation, and draw a graph showing the population between the years 1990 and 2010.

$P_0 = 2{,}500$ and $r = 5\% = 0.05$ — Remember, to change a percent to a decimal, move the decimal point two places to the left.

The equation of the graph is $\mathbf{P = 2{,}500(2.72)^{0.05t}}$.

If $t = 0$: $P = 2{,}500(2.72)^0 = 2{,}500$; plot the point $(0, 2{,}500)$. This is the 1990 population; 1990 is called the base year. It is called the "present time" (even though it is not now 1990). Thus, if $t = 5$, then the population corresponds to the year 1995. If $t = 10$, the population is for the year 2000.

If $t = 10$: $P = 2{,}500(2.72)^{0.05(10)} \approx 4{,}123$

Display: `4123.105626`

This means that the predicted population in the year 2000 is 4,123. Plot the point (10, 4,123).

If $t = 20$: $P = 2{,}500(2.72)^{0.05(20)} = 6{,}800$

Display: `6800` Plot the point (20, 6,800).

We have plotted these points in Figure 11.23.

Figure 11.23 Graph showing population P from 1990 to 2010 (base year, $t = 0$, is 1990)

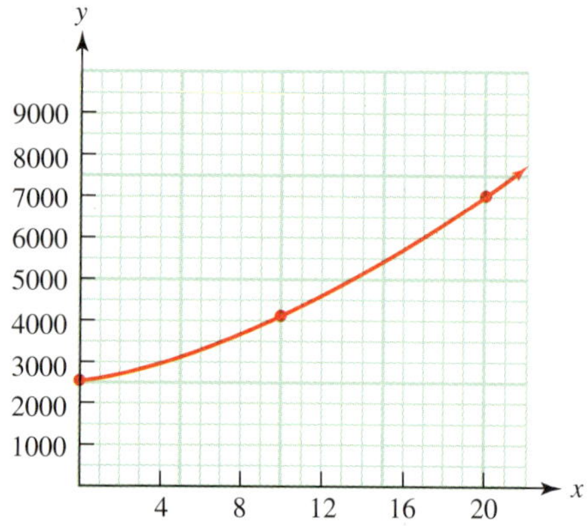

MORE AND MORE PROBLEM SETS

MATH puts a multitude of study aids at your fingertips. After reading the chapters, check out these resources for further help.

- Downloadable problem sets per chapter and chapter section that allow you to apply the math concepts you learned in the text.
- Online printable flashcards give you two additional ways to check your comprehension of key mathematics concepts.

Other great ways to help you study include **Watch It** video tutorials, **Practice It** worked-out examples, **Solve It** downloadable homework problem sets, an online glossary, and **Quiz It** interactive quizzing.

You can find all of the above at **4ltrpress.cengage.com/math.**

Chapter 12

The Nature of Voting and Apportionment

topics

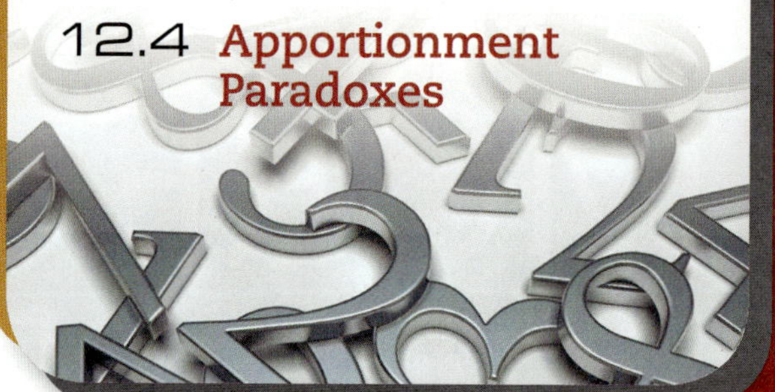

12.1 Voting

THE PROCESS OF SELECTION CAN BE ACCOMPLISHED IN MANY DIFFERENT WAYS.

If one person alone makes the decision, we call it a **dictatorship**. If the decision is made by a group, it is called a **vote**. The different methods of selection using a vote, such as voting on a proposal, resolution, law, or a choice between candidates is an area of study called *social choice theory*. In this section we will discuss several ways of counting the votes to declare a winner.

Majority Rule

One common method of voting is by *majority rule*. By **majority rule**, we mean voting to find an alternative that receives more than 50% of the vote. Be careful how you interpret this. If there are 11 voters with two alternatives A and B, then 6 votes for A is a majority. If there are 12 voters and A receives 6 votes, then A does not have a majority. Finally, if there are more than two alternatives, say, A, B, and C, with 12 voters and A receives 5 votes, B receives 3 votes, and C receives 4 votes, then no alternative has a majority. We summarize with the box to the right.

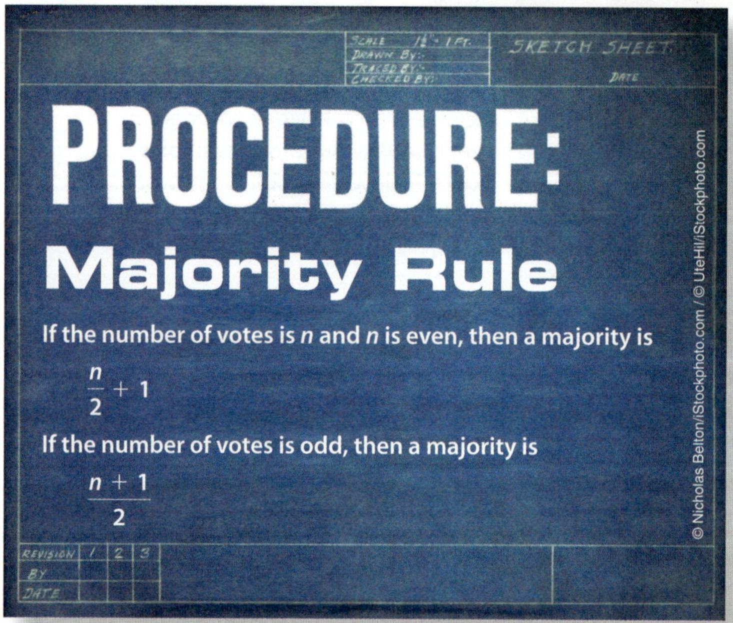

Consider an election with three alternatives. These might be Republican, Democrat, and Green party candidates. To keep our notation simple, we will designate the candidates as A, B, and C. There are 6 possible rankings, regardless of the number of voters. We list these using the following notation:

Choices: (ABC) (ACB) (BAC) (BCA) (CAB) (CBA)

The symbol "(ACB)" means that the ranking of a voter is candidate A for first place, C for second place, and B for third place. The six sets of three letters here indicate all possible ways for a voter to rank three candidates. Now, suppose there are 12 voters and we list the rankings of these voters using the following notation:

Choices:	(ABC)	(ACB)	(BAC)	(BCA)	(CAB)	(CBA)
No. of votes:	5	0	2	1	0	4

This means that 5 of the 12 voters ranked the candidates ABC, while none of the voters ranked the candidates in the order ACB. Notice that we have accounted for all 6 possibilities even though in some cases some possibilities have no voters. The sum of the number of votes for all possibilities equals the number of voters—12 for this example. Use the majority rule to find a winner.

For majority rule, we look only at first choices (even though the voters ranked all the candidates). We see A received 5 votes ($5 + 0 = 5$), B received 3 votes ($2 + 1 = 3$), and C received 4 votes ($0 + 4 = 4$). If we use the majority rule, $\frac{12}{2} + 1 = 7$ votes, and we see that there is no winner.

Notice that with three candidates, we listed 6 possibilities. In social choice theory, the principle that asserts that any set of individual rankings is possible is called the *principle of unrestricted domain.* If there are n candidates, then there are n first choices, $n - 1$ second choices, and so on. So, by the fundamental counting principle, the total number of choices is

$$n(n-1)(n-2)\cdot\cdots\cdot 3\cdot 2\cdot 1$$

We denote this product by writing $n!$. That is, $5! = 5\cdot 4\cdot 3\cdot 2\cdot 1$.

The majority rule satisfies a principle called **symmetry**. This principle ensures that if one voter prefers choice A to choice B and another prefers choice B to A, then their votes should cancel each other out.

Pluralty Method

In the case of no winner by majority rule, we often want to have an alternative way to select a winner. With the **plurality method**, the winner is the candidate with the highest number of votes.

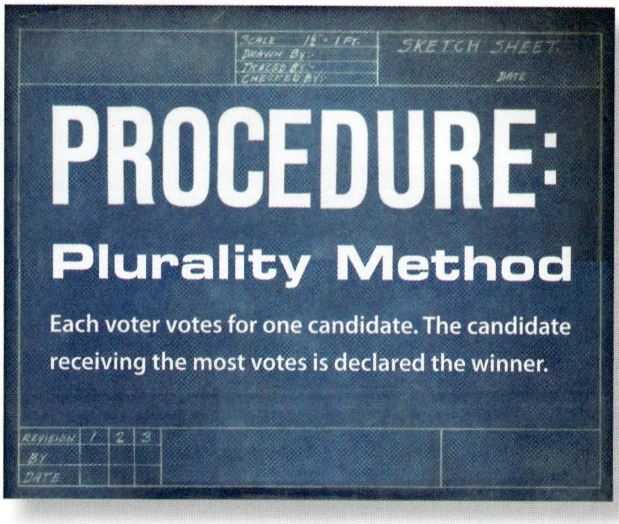

If we use the plurality method for the above election, we find:

A: $5 + 0 = 5$ votes; B: $2 + 1 = 3$ votes;
C: $0 + 4 = 4$ votes

The winner is the candidate with the most votes, namely, candidate A.

The chairperson is allowed to vote to make or break a tie.

Sometimes the result of an election produces a tie vote. The very nature of voting seems to imply that we want a winner, so we need some set of tie-breaking rules. In situations governed by *Robert's Rules of Order*, the chairperson is allowed to vote to make or break a tie. Social choice theory calls this the *principle of decisiveness*.

Borda Count

A common way of determining a winner when there is no majority is to assign a point value to each voter's ranking. The last-place candidate is given 1 point, each next-to-the-last candidate is given 2 points, and so on. This counting scheme, called a **Borda count**, is defined in the following box.

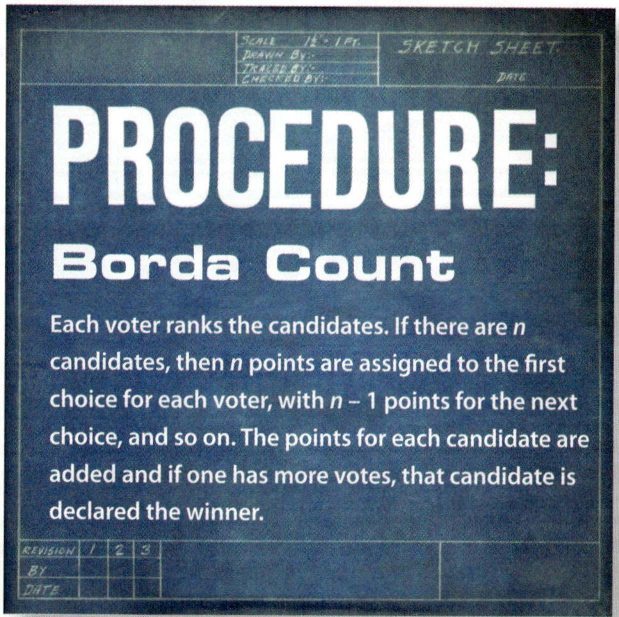

An example of voting using the Borda method with which you may be familiar is the annual voting for the Heisman Trophy in collegiate football. In 2005, the winner Reggie Bush of USC was selected after 870 ballots were mailed to media personnel across the country and 51 still-living Heisman winners for a total of 921 electors. Each elector votes for three choices and a point total is reached by a system of three points for a first place vote, two for a second, and one for a third. It was reported that Bush received 2,541 points, with the runner-up Vince Young of the University of Texas garnering 1,608 points.

The principle of decisiveness forces us to consider a structure for selecting a winner when the method we use does not produce a winner. One such method is to hold a *runoff election*. A **runoff election** is an attempt to obtain a majority vote by eliminating one or more alternatives and voting again on the remaining choices.

Hare Method

The first runoff method we will consider was proposed in 1861 by Thomas Hare (1806–1891). In this method, votes are transferred from eliminated candidates to remaining candidates. We summarize this method in the following box.

PROCEDURE:

Hare Method

Each voter votes for one candidate. If a candidate receives a majority of the votes, that candidate is declared to be a *first-round winner*. If no candidate receives a majority of the votes, then with the **Hare method**, also known as the *plurality with an elimination runoff method*, the candidate(s) with the fewest number of first-place votes is (are) eliminated.

Each voter votes for one candidate in the second round. If a candidate receives a majority, that candidate is declared to be a *second-round winner*. If no candidate receives a majority of the second-round votes, then eliminate the candidate(s) with the fewest number of first-place votes. Repeat this process until a candidate receives a majority.

Consider the following voting situation:

Choices:	(ABC)	(ACB)	(BAC)	(BCA)	(CAB)	(CBA)
No. of votes:	3	2	2	0	1	4

There is neither a majority winner nor a plurality winner. We find a solution using the Hare method. We see that A received 5 (3 + 2 = 5) first-round votes; B received 2 votes; and C received 5 votes. We hold a runoff election by eliminating the alternative with the fewest votes; this is choice B. For convenience, in this book we assume that a voter's order of preference will remain the same for subsequent rounds of voting. Thus, we now have the following possibilities, where we have crossed out candidate B:

Choices:	(A~~B~~C)	(AC~~B~~)	(~~B~~AC)	(~~B~~CA)	(CA~~B~~)	(C~~B~~A)
No. of votes:	3 ↓	2 ↓	2 ↓	0 ↓	1 ↓	4 ↓
Choices:		(AC)			(CA)	
No. of votes:		3 + 2 + 2 = 7			0 + 1 + 4 = 5	

We now declare a second-round winner, A, using the *majority rule*.

The assumption that we made in the above example about consistent voting has a name in social choice theory. It is called the *principle of independence of irrelevant alternatives*. In other words, we assume consistent voting, which means that if a voter prefers A to B with C a possible choice, then the voter still prefers A to B when C is not a possible choice.

In countries with many political parties, such as France, the Hare method is used for electing their president.

Pairwise Comparison Method

Runoff elections are not always appropriate. It seems reasonable that if everyone in a group of voters prefers candidate X over candidate Y, then under its voting method, the group should prefer X to Y. Social choice theory calls this the *Pareto principle*. Thus, it is desirable that the pairwise methods we consider satisfy this principle. The characteristic property of these pairwise methods is that they pair up the competitors, two at a time. Such methods are called **binary voting**. We begin with the most important of these methods.

PROCEDURE:

Pairwise Comparison Method

In the **pairwise comparison method** of voting, the voters rank the candidates by making a series of comparisons in which each candidate is compared to each of the other candidates. If choice A is preferred to choice B, then A receives 1 point. If B is preferred to A, then B receives 1 point. If the candidates tie, each receives $\frac{1}{2}$ point. The candidate with the most points is declared the winner.

Tournament Method

Another form of binary voting is a *king-of-the-hill* situation in which the competitors are paired, the winner of one pairing taking on the next competitor. This type of runoff election is sometimes called **sequential voting**.

One of the most common examples of sequential voting is called the **tournament method**, or **tournament elimination method**. With this method, candidates are teamed head-to-head, with the winner of one pairing facing a new opponent for the next election. Tennis matches and other sporting events are often decided in this fashion.

Consider the following election:

Choices:	(ABC)	(ACB)	(BAC)	(BCA)	(CAB)	(CBA)
No. of votes:	5	0	3	0	0	4

We find the winner using the tournament method.

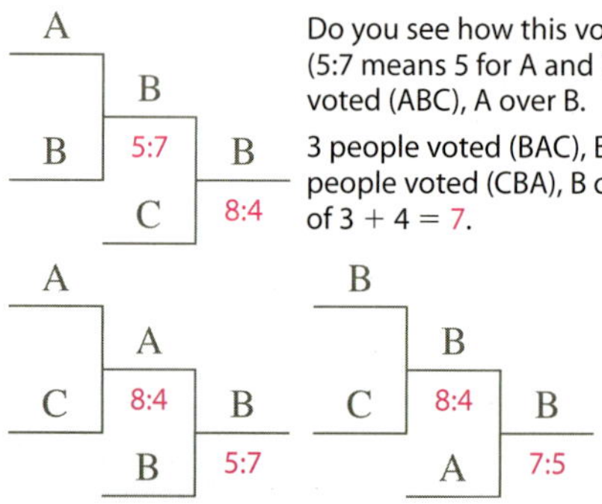

Do you see how this vote of 5:7 is found? (5:7 means 5 for A and 7 for B.) 5 people voted (ABC), A over B.

3 people voted (BAC), B over A, and 4 people voted (CBA), B over A; this is a total of 3 + 4 = 7.

Since all three possible tournaments result in B as the winner, we see the tournament method finds B to be the winner. We will see later that different pairings *may* result in different winners.

In this example, there were three candidates, and the number of comparison charts was three (A with B, A with C, and B with C). In general, the number of necessary comparisons for n candidates is

$$\frac{n(n-1)}{2}$$

In this book we will not have examples with more than 5 candidates, so Table 12.1 shows the number of choices for n between 3 and 6 (inclusive).

Table 12.1 Number of Pairwise Comparisons

n	Number
3	3
4	6
5	10
6	15

Even though we can use some tie-breaking voting procedures, ties may still exist. Decisiveness requires that we specify some method for breaking ties. Sometimes *breaking a tie* can be accomplished by using another voting method, by choosing the candidate with the most first-place votes, by voting by the presiding officer, or even by flipping a coin. If the voting process is to be fair, the tie-breaking procedure should be specified before the vote.

Approval Voting

Historically, the most recent voting method replaces the "one person, one vote" method with which we are familiar in the United States with a system that allows a voter to cast one vote for each of the candidates. There is no limit on the number of candidates for whom an individual can vote.

This is the method used to select the secretary general of the United Nations and is popular in those countries in which there are many candidates. It was designed, in part, to prevent the election of minority candidates in multicandidate contests.

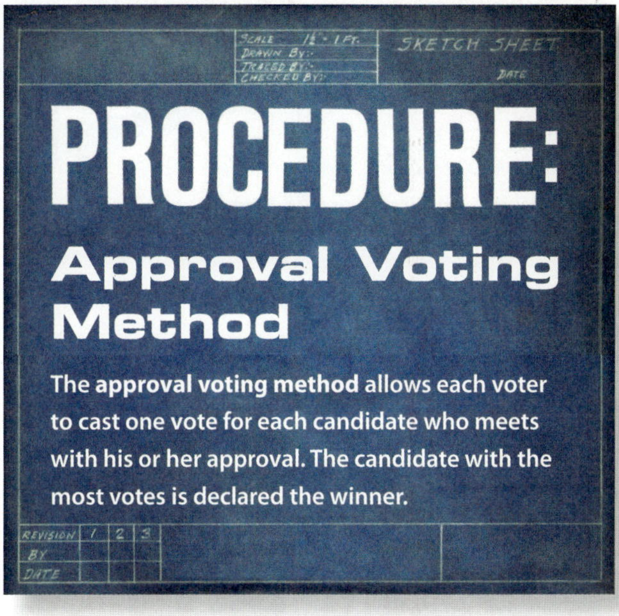

We conclude on the next page with an example comparing some of the voting methods introduced in this section. These methods are summarized in Table 12.2.

Table 12.2 Summary of Voting Methods

Method	Description
Majority Method	Each voter votes for one candidate. If the number of voters is n and n is even, then the candidate with $\frac{n}{2} + 1$ or more votes wins. If the number n is odd, then the candidate with $\frac{n+1}{2}$ or more votes wins.
Plurality Method	Each voter votes for one candidate. The candidate receiving the most votes wins.
Borda Count Method	Each voter ranks the candidates. Each last-place candidate is given 1 point, each next-to-last candidate is given 2 points, and so on. The candidate with the highest number of points wins.
Hare Method	Each voter votes for one candidate. If a candidate receives a majority of the votes, that candidate is the winner. If no candidate receives a majority, eliminate the candidate with the fewest first-place votes and repeat the process until there is a majority candidate, who wins.
Pairwise Comparison Method	Each voter ranks the candidates. Each candidate is compared to each of the other candidates. If choice A is preferred to choice B, then A receives 1 point. If B is preferred to A, then B receives 1 point. If the candidates tie, then each receives $\frac{1}{2}$ point. The candidate with the most points wins.
Tournament Method	This method compares the entire slate of candidates two at a time, in a predetermined order. The first and second candidates are compared, the candidate with the fewer votes is eliminated, and the winner is then compared with the third candidate. These pairwise comparisons continue until the final pairing, which selects the winner.
Approval Method	Each voter casts one vote for all the candidates who meet with his or her approval. The candidate with the most votes is declared the winner.

Voting Methods in Action

The town of Ferndale has four candidates running for mayor: the town barber, Darrell; the fire chief, Clough; the grocer, Abel; and a housewife, Belle. A poll of 1,000 of the voters shows the following results:

Choices:	(DABC)	(CABD)	(CADB)	(BADC)
No. of votes:	225	190	210	375

- ✔ How many different votes are possible (4 are shown)? What is the vote for the possibilities not shown? There are $4! = 24$ possibilities; there are no votes for the 20 possibilities not shown.
- ✔ Is there a majority winner? A: 0 votes; B: 375 votes; C: $190 + 210 = 400$ votes; D: 225 votes. A majority is $\frac{1000}{2} + 1 = 501$ or more votes; there is no majority winner.
- ✔ Is there a winner using the plurality method? The plurality winner is C (because it has the most votes).
- ✔ What is the Borda count, and is there a winner using this method? We show the Borda count in the following table:

					Total			
	A	B	C	D	A	B	C	D
225:	3	2	1	4	675	450	225	900
190:	3	2	4	1	570	380	760	190
210:	3	1	4	2	630	210	840	420
375:	3	4	1	2	1,125	1,500	375	750
TOTAL:					3,000	2,540	2,200	2,260

The Borda count declares A the winner.

12.2 Voting Dilemmas

PRINCIPLES IN SOCIAL CHOICE THEORY DO NOT BEHAVE IN THE SAME FASHION AS PRINCIPLES OF MATHEMATICS.

In mathematics, a correctly stated principle has no exceptions. On the other hand, we frequently find exceptions to voting principles. In the last section, we considered four reasonable and often-used voting methods. In this section, we will consider four voting principles that most would agree are desirable, and then we will show that all of the voting methods will fail one or more of the principles. We will call these **fair voting principles**: *majority criterion, Condorcet criterion, monotonicity criterion*, and *irrelevant alternatives criterion*. Let us consider these voting principles, one at a time.

Majority Criterion

The first and most obvious criterion is called the **majority criterion**.

> According to the **majority criterion**, if a candidate receives a majority of the first-place votes, then that candidate should be declared the winner.

Only a Borda count method can violate this criterion. Consider the following example. The South Davis Faculty Association is using the Borda count method to vote for their collective bargaining representative. Their choices are the All Faculty Association (A), American Federation of Teachers (B), and California Teachers Association (C). Here are the results of the voting:

Choices:	(ABC)	(ACB)	(BAC)	(BCA)	(CAB)	(CBA)
No. of votes:	16	0	0	8	0	7

Which organization is selected for collective bargaining and does this selection violate the majority criterion? Here is the tally of the Borda count:

				Total		
	A	B	C	A	B	C
(ABC) 16:	3	2	1	48	32	16
(BCA) 8:	1	3	2	8	24	16
(CBA) 7:	1	2	3	7	14	21
TOTAL:				63	70	53

The highest Borda count number goes to choice B, the American Federation of Teachers. However, choice A received 16 votes, which is a majority of the 31 votes that were cast, so the Borda count violates the majority criterion.

Even though the Borda count violates this criterion, all the other methods must satisfy it. Suppose that a candidate X is the first choice for more than half the voters. It follows that X will have more first-place votes than any other single candidate and must win by the plurality method. If the Hare method is used, then X would always have at least the votes that it started with, and since that is more than half the votes, X could never be eliminated and would wind up the winner. And finally, since X has the majority of the votes in each of its pairwise matchups, X would win in each of those matchups. So no other candidate can win as many pairs as X does, so X wins the election.

Thus we conclude that the Borda count method presents a dilemma. Although it takes into account voters' preferences by having all candidates ranked, a candidate with a majority of first-place votes can lose an election!

Condorcet Criterion

About a decade after Borda proposed his counting procedure, the mathematician Marquis de Condorcet became interested in some of the apparent dilemmas raised by the Borda count methods. He proposed a head-to-head election to rank the candidates. The candidate who wins all the one-to-one matchups is the **Condorcet candidate**. The *Condorcet criterion* asserts that the Condorcet candidate should win the election. Some elections do not yield a Condorcet candidate because none of the candidates can win over *all* the others.

According to the **Condorcet criterion**, if a candidate is favored when compared one-on-one with every other candidate, then that candidate should be declared the winner.

Before most major elections in the United States, we hear the results of polls for each of the political parties pairing candidates and telling preferences in a one-on-one election. Is this a valid way of considering the candidates? Consider the following example.

The seniors at Weseltown High School are voting on where to go for their senior trip. They are deciding on Angel Falls (A), Bend Canyon (B), Cedar Lake (C), or Danger Gap (D). The results of the preferences are:

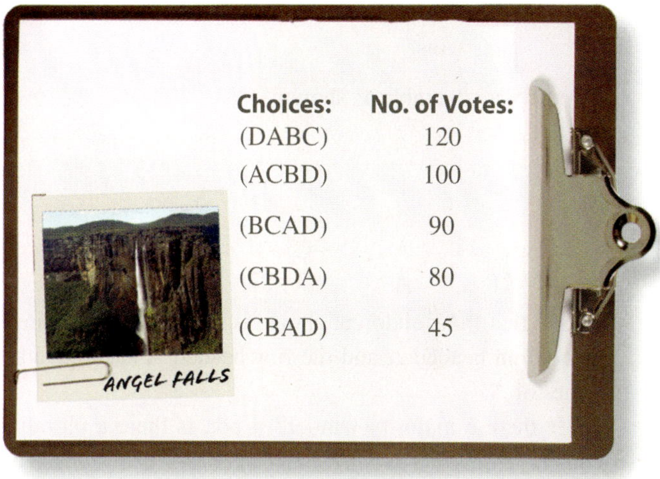

First, we seek the Condorcet candidate. The best way to examine the one-on-one matchups is to construct a table with all possibilities listed as the row and column headings. Start by comparing A with B, one-on-one:

	A	B	C	D
A	—	*		
B	*	—		
C			—	
D				—

(DABC)(ACBD) — A wins (BCAD)(CBDA)(CBAD) — B wins

Look at the line right under the preferences.

$120 + 100 = 220 \quad 90 + 80 + 45 = 215$

A wins, since $220 > 215$, so we fill in these entries in the table.

	A	B	C	D
A	—	A		
B	A	—		
C			—	
D				—

We similarly fill in the rest of the table by comparing the items, one-on-one:

A with C: A: 120 + 100 = 220; C: 90 + 80 + 45 = 215; A wins.
A with D: A: 100 + 90 + 45 = 235; D: 120 + 80 = 200; A wins.
B with C: B: 120 + 90 = 210; C: 100 + 80 + 45 = 225; C wins.
B with D: B: 100 + 90 + 80 + 45 = 315; D: 120; B wins.
C with D: C: 100 + 90 + 80 + 45 = 315; D: 120; C wins.

We complete the table as shown:

	A	B	C	D
A	—	A	A	A
B	A	—	C	B
C	A	C	—	C
D	A	B	C	—

We see that the Condorcet choice is A (Angel Falls) since the column headed A and the row headed A each have all entries of A.

Is there a majority winner? If not, is there a plurality winner? *Does this violate the Condorcet criterion?* The first place votes are:

A: 100
B: 90
C: 80 + 45 = 125
D: 120

Since there were 435 votes cast, a majority would be

$$\frac{435 + 1}{2} = 218 \text{ votes}$$

There is no majority. The winner of the plurality vote is C, Cedar Lake. This example shows that the plurality method can violate the Condorcet criterion.

Who wins the Borda count? *Does this violate the Condorcet criterion?* The Borda count is shown in the following table.

					Total			
	A	B	C	D	A	B	C	D
120:	3	2	1	4	360	240	120	480
100:	4	2	3	1	400	200	300	100
90:	2	4	3	1	180	360	270	90
80:	1	3	4	2	80	240	320	160
45:	2	3	4	1	90	135	180	45
TOTAL:					1,110	1,175	1,190	875

Location C, Cedar Lake, wins the Borda count. This example shows that the Borda count can violate the Condorcet criterion.

Who wins using the Hare method? *Does this violate the Condorcet criterion?* Using the Hare method, there is no majority, so we eliminate the candidate with the fewest first-place votes; this is choice B. The remaining tally is

A: 100   C: 90 + 80 + 45 = 215   D: 120

Since a majority vote is 218, there is still no majority, so we now eliminate A. The result now is:

C: 100 + 90 + 80 + 45 = 315   D: 120

The declared winner is C, Cedar Lake. This example demonstrates that the Hare method can violate the Condorcet criterion.

Who wins using the pairwise comparison method? *Does this violate the Condorcet criterion?* For the pairwise comparison method, we can use the table of pairings we had when we found the Condorcet candidate:

A is favored over B, C, and D, giving A 3 points.
B is favored over D, giving B 1 point.
C is favored over B and D, giving C 2 points.
D is not favored.

The choice is A, Angel Falls. Note that if a certain choice is favored over all other candidates, then this candidate will have the largest point value. Thus, the pairwise comparison method can never violate the Condorcet criterion.

Monotonicity Criterion

Another property of voting has to do with elections that are held more than once. Historically, there have been many pairings of the same two candidates, and at a personal level, we are often part of a process in which a nonbinding vote is taken before all the discussion takes place. Such a vote is known as a **straw vote**. It would seem obvious that if a winning candidate in the first election gained strength before the second election, then that candidate should win the second election. A statement of this property is called the **monotonicity criterion**.

> According to the **monotonicity criterion**, a candidate who wins a first election and then gains additional support, without losing any of the original support, should also win a second election.

As obvious as this criterion may seem, the following example introduces another voting dilemma by showing it is possible for the winner of the first election to gain additional support before a second election, and then lose that second election.

In 1995 the 105th International Olympic Committee (IOC) met in Budapest to select the 2002 Winter Olympics site. The cities in the running were Québec (Q), Salt Lake City (L), Ostersund (T), and Sion (S). Consider the following fictional account of how the voting might have been conducted. The voting takes place over a two-day period using the Hare method. The first day, the 87 members of the IOC take a nonbinding vote, and then on the second day they take a binding vote. On the first day, the rankings of the IOC members were

(TLSQ)	(LQTS)	(QSTL)	(TQSL)	(TSLQ)
21	24	30	6	6

Suppose we use the Hare method for the first (nonbinding) day of voting.

A majority is $\dfrac{87 + 1}{2} = 44$ votes.

On the first day,

Round 1: T: 21 + 6 + 6 = 33   L: 24   Q: 30   S: 0

No city has a majority (44) of votes, so Sion is eliminated from the voting.

Round 2: T: 21 + 6 + 6 = 33   L: 24   Q: 30

No city has a majority, so now Salt Lake City is eliminated from the voting.

Round 3: T: 21 + 6 + 6 = 33   Q: 24 + 30 = 54

© Jonathan Selkowitz/NewSport/Corbis

Québec has a majority of the votes and is the winner from the first (nonbinding) day of voting using the Hare method.

On the evening of the first day of voting, representatives from Salt Lake City offered bribes to the 12 members with the bottom votes. They were able to convince these IOC members to move Québec to the top of their list, because, after all, Québec won the day's straw votes anyway. Now for the second day, the rankings of the IOC committee were:

(TLSQ)	(LQTS)	(QSTL)	(QTSL)	(QTSL)
21	24	30	6	6

What are the results of the election using the Hare method for the second (binding) day of voting? On the second day,

Round 1: T: 21   L: 24   Q: 30 + 6 + 6 = 42   S: 0

No city has a majority (44) of votes, so Sion is eliminated from the voting.

Round 2: T: 21   L: 24   Q: 30 + 6 + 6 = 42

No city has a majority, so now Ostersund (T) is eliminated from the voting.

Round 3: L: 21 + 24 = 45 votes
Q: 30 + 6 + 6 = 42

Salt Lake City has a majority of the votes and is the winner from the second (binding) day of voting using the Hare method.

As you can see from this remarkable example, it is possible for the winning candidate on a first vote (Québec) to receive more votes and end up losing the election! We see that the Hare method can violate the monotonicity criterion. It is also possible to find examples showing that the pairwise comparison method can also violate the monotonicity criterion. The plurality and Borda count methods cannot violate the monotonicity criterion.

Irrelevant Alternatives Criterion

In the controversial 2000 presidential election, there was much talk about the final vote of the election. Although there is no such thing as an official final figure, the numbers in Table 12.3 are an aggregate of state numbers that appear to be final.

Suppose the president were selected by popular vote (rather than the Electoral College). As close as the election was, if we use the numbers in Table 12.3, we see that the winner would have been Al Gore. Now, suppose that another election were held, and this time Ralph Nader dropped out before the vote. Since Nader really had no chance of winning, we might conclude this action should not have any effect on the outcome. But as you can see from these numbers, such is not the case. The Nader voters could have swung the election either way. We might consider this a voting dilemma because it would violate the following criterion, called the **irrelevant alternatives criterion**.

Table 12.3 Summary of Popular and Electoral Vote in the 2000 U.S. Presidential Election

Candidate	Party	Vote	Percentage	Electoral College Vote
Harry Browne	Libertarian	386,024	0.37	0
Pat Buchanan	Reform	448,750	0.42	0
George W. Bush	Republican	50,456,167	47.88	271
Al Gore	Democrat	50,996,277	48.39	267
Ralph Nader	Green	2,864,810	2.72	0
14 others		238,300	0.23	0
TOTAL		105,390,328		538

According to the **irrelevant alternatives criterion**, if a candidate is declared the winner of an election, and in a second election one or more of the other candidates is removed, then the previous winner should still be declared the winner.

An outstanding factual example illustrating this dilemma occurred in the 1991 Louisiana gubernatorial race. The candidates were the incumbent Governor "Buddy" Roemer and his challengers, former governor Edwin Edwards and David Duke. Now, David Duke was a former leader of the Ku Klux Klan, and the former governor was indicted for corruption, so it is reasonable to assume that Roemer would have beaten either of his opponents in a one-on-one race, but instead he came in last.

Arrow's Impossibility Theorem

We have now considered four criteria that would seem to be desirable properties of any voting system. We refer to these four criteria as the **fairness criteria**.

FAIRNESS CRITERIA

Majority criterion

If a candidate receives a majority of the first-place votes, then that candidate should be declared the winner.

Condorcet criterion

If a candidate is favored when compared one-on-one with every other candidate, then that candidate should be declared the winner.

Monotonicity criterion

A candidate who wins a first election and then gains additional support, without losing any of the original support, should also win a second election.

Irrelevant alternatives criterion

If a candidate is declared the winner of an election, and in a second election one or more of the other candidates is removed, then the previous winner should still be declared the winner.

SPEND A FEW MINUTES WITH THESE CRITERIA. READ, THEN REREAD; CREATE SOME SMALL EXAMPLES AND TEST THEM.

Table 12.4 Comparison of Voting Methods and Fairness Criteria

Voting Method	Plurality	Hare	Borda Count	Pairwise Comparison
Majority criterion	Satisfied	Satisfied	Not satisfied	Satisfied
Condorcet criterion	Not satisfied	Not satisfied	Not satisfied	Satisfied
Monotonicity criterion	Satisfied	Not satisfied	Satisfied	Not satisfied
Irrelevant alternatives criterion	Not satisfied	Not satisfied	Not satisfied	Not satisfied

We compare these criteria with the voting methods we have considered in Table 12.4.

In 1951, the economist Kenneth Arrow (1921–) proved that there is exactly one method for voting that satisfies all four of these principles, and this method is a *dictatorship*. Stated in another way, it is known as *Arrow's paradox*: Perfect democratic voting is, not just in practice but in principle, impossible.

Essentially this says that there is no perfect voting method.

The following example illustrates a situation in which any of the candidates A, B, or C could be declared the winner using the tournament method!

Consider the following election:

Choices:	(ABC)	(ACB)	(BAC)	(BCA)	(CAB)	(CBA)
No. of votes:	1	0	0	1	1	0

Determine the winner using the tournament method.

The pairing AB gives A one point; the pairing AC gives C one point; and the pairing BC gives B one point. All three are tied in points.

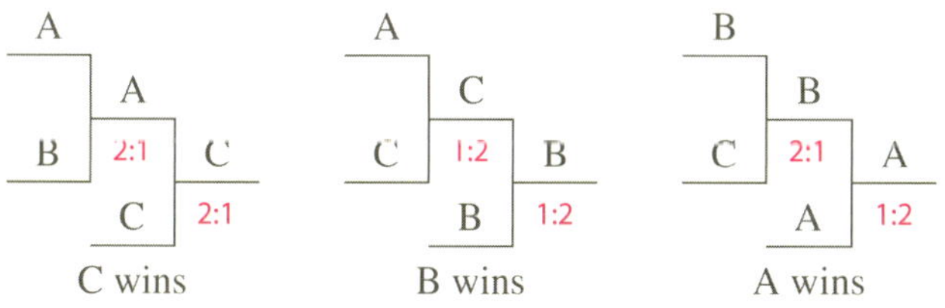

However, if we play this as a tournament, we see that any of A, B, or C could win, depending on the initial pairing. This shows that there is tremendous power in the hands of the tournament director or committee chair who has the opportunity to set the agenda, if the group choice is to be made using a tournament (pairwise) voting method.

Different agendas may produce different winners. This is called the agenda effect.

A variation of the agenda effect is **insincere voting**, or the offering of amendments with the purpose of changing an election. Consider the following example.

Assume that Tom, Ann, and Linda each have the choice of voting on whether to lower the drinking age to 18. The current law sets the drinking age at 21. Voting against the new law (age 18) means that the old law (age 21) will prevail. Let's assume that Tom and Ann are in favor of the new law, but Linda is against it. Here is a table of their preferences:

	First Choice	Second Choice
Tom:	New law (age 18)	Old law (age 21)
Ann:	New law (age 18)	Old law (age 21)
Linda:	Old law (age 21)	New law (age 18)

Let's also assume that this law will pass or fail, depending on the outcome of the votes of these three people. If the vote is taken now, all three persons know the vote will be 2 for the new law and 1 against the new law. However, Linda decides to defeat the new law by insincere voting, and she introduces an amendment that she knows Tom would like most of all, but Ann likes least of all. Suppose that Linda knows Tom would like to have no law regarding drinking, but that Ann would find that offensive. Linda offers an amendment *pretending* to prefer the old law (age 21) over the amendment (no age) and the amendment (no age) over the new law (age 18). Here are the choices:

	First Choice	Second Choice	Third Choice
Tom:	Amendment (no age)	New law (age 18)	Old law (age 21)
Ann:	New law (age 18)	Old law (age 21)	Amendment (no age)
Linda:	Old law (age 21)	Amendment (no age)	New law (age 18)

The vote is taken first for the amendment, and it passes with a vote of 2 to 1 because Tom votes for it and Linda votes insincerely by voting for the amendment. Now, the vote on the floor is for no age limitation or for the old law. Tom votes for no limitation and Linda and Ann vote for the old law, which carries by a vote of 2 to 1.

What does this say? If you are sitting through a meeting conducted by *Robert's Rules of Order*, it may be better to enter the more preferred outcomes at a later stage of the discussion. The chances of success are better when there are fewer remaining votes.

There is a curious possibility that seems to violate the transitive law in mathematics. The **transitive law** states:

If A beats B, and B beats C, then A should beat C.

The tournament method example on the previous page violates this law and leads to a paradox. Notice that A beats B by a vote of 2 to 1; B beats C by a vote of 2 to 1. The transitive law says that A should beat C, but that is NOT the case! C beats A by a vote of 2 to 1. This paradox was first described by Marquis de Condorcet. He wrote a treatise, *Essay on the Application of Analysis to the Probability of Majority Decisions*, in 1785, and he described this paradox, which today is known as **Condorcet's paradox** or *the paradox of voting*.

In the right-hand column, we state the result known as **Arrow's impossibility theorem**, which Kenneth Arrow proved in 1951.

arrow's impossibility theorem

No social choice rule satisfies all of the following conditions.

1. **unrestricted domain** Any set of rankings is possible; if there are n candidates, then there are $n!$ possible rankings.
2. **decisiveness** Given any set of individual rankings, the method produces a winner.
3. **symmetry and transitivity** The voting system should be symmetric and transitive over the set of all outcomes.
4. **independence of irrelevant alternatives** If a voter prefers A to B with C as a possible choice, then the voter still prefers A to B when C is not a possible choice.
5. **Pareto principle** If each voter prefers A over B, then the group chooses A over B.
6. There should be **no dictator**.

12.3 Apportionment

THE FRAMING OF THE UNITED STATES CONSTITUTION DURING THE CONSTITUTIONAL CONVENTION IN 1787 HAS BEEN THE SUBJECT OF BOOKS, MOVIES, AND PLAYS.

Many issues of grave importance were introduced and debated, but one of the most heated and important debates concerned how the states would be represented in the new legislature. The large states wanted proportional representation based on population, and the smaller states wanted representation by state. From this debate came the Great Compromise, which led to the formation of two sides of the legislative branch of government. The compromise allowed the Senate to have two representatives per state (advantageous for the smaller states) and the House of Representatives to determine the number of representatives for a particular state by the size of the population (advantageous for the larger states). The accompanying box on the right gives the exact wording from the United States Constitution, and if you read it you will notice that it does not specify *how* to determine the number of representatives for each state. The process of making this decision is called **apportionment**. To *apportion* means to divide or share out according to a plan. It usually refers to dividing representatives in Congress or taxes to the states, but it can refer to judicial decisions or to the assignment of goods or people to different jurisdictions. In this section, we will consider five apportionment plans: *Adams's plan, Jefferson's plan, Hamilton's plan, Webster's plan*, and *Huntington-Hill's plan (HH plan)*. You recognize, no doubt, some of these names from American history.

ARTICLE 1, SECTION 2
United States Constitution

Representation and direct taxes shall be apportioned among the several states which may be included in the Union, according to the respective numbers . . . . The number of Representatives shall not exceed one for every thirty thousand, but each state shall have at least one representative.

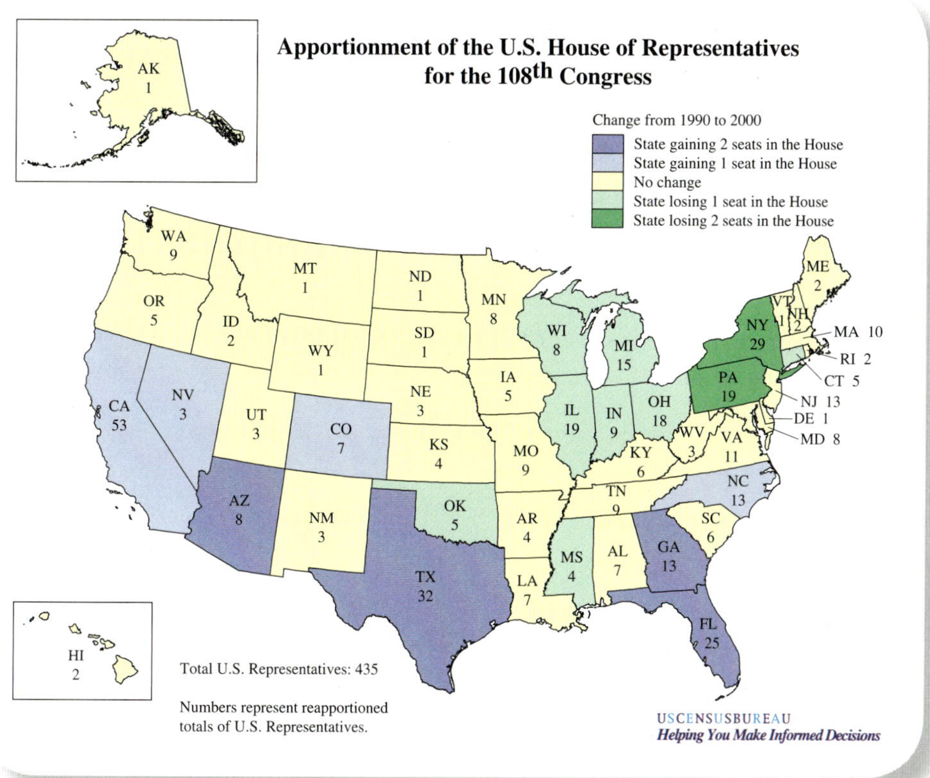

If the assignment of council seats is proportional to the borough's population, use Table 12.5 to allocate the council seats. To find the appropriate representation, we need to divide the population of each borough by the standard divisor; the resulting number is known as the *standard quota*. Round your results to the nearest hundredth. We show rounding the standard quota to the nearest whole number, and we also show the result of rounding up and of rounding down. The result of rounding up is called the **upper quota** and the result of rounding down is called the **lower quota**.

The Apportionment Process

We begin with a simple example to introduce us to some of the terminology used with apportionment. Table 12.5 shows the population (in thousands) over the years for five New York Boroughs.

One of the recurring problems with apportionment is working with approximate data and the problems caused by rounding. For example, if you look at the total population for the five New York Boroughs in the year 2000, you will find the total to be 8,008,000. If you add the numbers in Table 12.5, you will find the total to be 8,007,000. The discrepancy is caused by rounding, and we should not just sweep it under the rug and ignore such discrepancies. How we handle rounding is a large part of distinguishing apportionment problems. Consider the following example based on Table 12.5.

In 1790 the population in New York City was 49,000. Suppose the city council at that time consisted of 8 members. How many people did each city council member represent? Since the population was 49,000, each council member should represent

$$\frac{49{,}000}{8} = 6{,}125$$

This number is called the *standard divisor*.

	Standard Quota	*Nearest*	*Upper Quota*	*Lower Quota*
Manhattan:	$\frac{32{,}000}{6{,}125} \approx 5.22$	5	6	5
Bronx:	$\frac{2{,}000}{6{,}125} \approx 0.33$	0	1	0
Brooklyn:	$\frac{5{,}000}{6{,}125} \approx 0.82$	1	1	0
Queens:	$\frac{6{,}000}{6{,}125} \approx 0.98$	1	1	0
Staten Island:	$\frac{4{,}000}{6{,}125} \approx 0.65$	1	1	0
TOTAL:		8	10	5

Table 12.5 Populations of New York Boroughs (in thousands)

Year	Total	Manhattan	Bronx	Brooklyn	Queens	Staten Island
1790	49	32	2	5	6	4
1800	81	61	2	6	7	5
1840	697	516	8	139	19	15
1900	3,438	1,850	201	1,167	153	67
1940	7,454	1,890	1,395	2,698	1,297	174
1990	7,324	1,488	1,204	2,301	1,952	379
2000	8,007	1,537	1,333	2,465	2,229	443

Now, seats on a city council must be whole numbers, so we should use the numbers from one of the columns of rounded numbers. But which column? Since we need to fill 8 seats, we see for this example that if we round to the nearest unit, we will fill the 8 seats.

This example raises some questions. First, how would you like it if you lived in the Bronx? You would have no representation. On the other hand, if you rounded each of the numbers up, the number of seats would increase to 10, and certainly rounding down for this example would not satisfy anyone (except perhaps those from Manhattan). There are other difficulties caused by the rounding in this example, but before we take a closer look, we need the following definitions.

Standard Divisor/Standard Quota

The standard divisor is defined to be the quotient

$$\text{STANDARD DIVISOR} = \frac{\text{TOTAL POPULATION}}{\text{NUMBER OF SHARES}}$$

The standard quota is defined to be the quotient

$$\text{STANDARD QUOTA} = \frac{\text{TOTAL POPULATION}}{\text{STANDARD DIVISOR}}$$

The apportionment we seek must be either the upper quota or the lower quota. This is known as the **quota rule**.

Quota Rule

The number assigned to each represented unit must be either the standard quota rounded down to the nearest integer or the standard quota rounded up to the nearest integer.

Before we decide on a rounding scheme, we will consider one more historical example from the United States Congress. The first congressional apportionment was to occur after the 1790 census. (It actually occurred in 1794.) The results of the census of 1790 are shown in Table 12.6.

Table 12.6 U.S. Population in the 1790 Census*

State	Population
Connecticut	237,655
Delaware	59,096
Georgia	82,548
Kentucky	73,677
Maryland	319,728
Massachusetts	475,199
New Hampshire	141,899
New Jersey	184,139
New York	340,241
North Carolina	395,005
Pennsylvania	433,611
Rhode Island	69,112
South Carolina	249,073
Vermont	85,341
Virginia	747,550
TOTAL	3,893,874

*We are using demographic information from the Consortium for Political and Social Research, Study 00003. The population numbers actually used for the 1794 apportionment were slightly different from these, so the historical record does not exactly match these academic examples. Among the reasons for this discrepancy is that prior to 1870, the population base included the total free population of the states and three-fifths of the number of slaves, and it excluded American Indians not taxed.

Use the results of Table 12.6, and the fact that the number of seats in the House of Representatives was to be raised from 65 to 105. Find the standard divisor and the standard quota for each state. Round each of the standard quotas to the nearest number, as well as to give the lower and upper quotas.

The quota rule tells us that the actual representation for each state must be the lower quota or the upper quota.

The First Congress of the United States needed to decide how to round the standard quotas, q. There were three plans proposed initially, and we will consider them one at a time. One of them rounded up, one rounded down, and a third rounded down with some additional conditions.

Standard divisor: $d = \frac{3{,}893{,}874}{105} \approx 37{,}084.51$

	Standard Quota	*Nearest*	*Lower Quota*	*Upper Quota*
Connecticut:	$\frac{237{,}655}{d} \approx 6.41$	6	6	7
Delaware:	$\frac{59{,}096}{d} \approx 1.59$	2	1	2
Georgia:	$\frac{82{,}548}{d} \approx 2.23$	2	2	3
Kentucky:	$\frac{73{,}677}{d} \approx 1.99$	2	1	2
Maryland:	$\frac{319{,}728}{d} \approx 8.62$	9	8	9
Massachusetts:	$\frac{475{,}199}{d} \approx 12.81$	13	12	13
New Hampshire:	$\frac{141{,}899}{d} \approx 3.83$	4	3	4
New Jersey:	$\frac{184{,}139}{d} \approx 4.97$	5	4	5
New York:	$\frac{340{,}241}{d} \approx 9.17$	9	9	10
North Carolina:	$\frac{395{,}005}{d} \approx 10.65$	11	10	11
Pennsylvania:	$\frac{433{,}611}{d} \approx 11.69$	12	11	12
Rhode Island:	$\frac{69{,}112}{d} \approx 1.86$	2	1	2
South Carolina:	$\frac{249{,}073}{d} \approx 6.72$	7	6	7
Vermont:	$\frac{85{,}341}{d} \approx 2.30$	2	2	3
Virginia:	$\frac{747{,}550}{d} \approx 20.16$	20	20	21
TOTAL:		106	96	111

Adams's Plan

The first plan we will consider was proposed by the sixth President of the United States, John Quincy Adams, so it is known as **Adams's plan**.

Back in 1790 the process of finding the modified quota was quite a task, but with the help of spreadsheets today it is not very difficult. Look at the previous example and note that the upper quotas total 111 and we are looking for a total of 105 seats. Look at the spreadsheet in Figure 12.1 on page 253. Note that $d = 37{,}084.51$ and if we raise this to $D = 38{,}000$ the total number of seats is 108, so we raised d too little. Next, we raise d to $D = 40{,}000$ and the total number of seats is now 103, so we raised d too much. (Remember, the goal is 105.) Finally, you will see that if we choose $D = 39{,}600$ we obtain the target number of seats, which is 105. The number

PROCEDURE: Adams's Plan

Any standard quota with a decimal portion must be *rounded up* to the next whole number. To find the appropriate number of seats, use the following procedure.

STEP 1 Compute the standard divisor, *d*.

STEP 2 Compute the standard quota, *q*, for each state.

STEP 3 Round the standard quotas up and add these quotas to find the total number of seats. It will be correct, or it will be too large. Raise the standard divisor in small increments until the rounded quotas provide the appropriate total; this divisor is called a **modified divisor**, *D*. The number *Q* for each state is called the **modified quota.**

PROCEDURE: Jefferson's Plan

Any standard quota with a decimal portion must be *rounded down* to the next whole number. To find the appropriate number of seats, use the following procedure.

STEP 1 Compute the standard divisor, *d*.

STEP 2 Compute the standard quota, *q*, for each state.

STEP 3 Round the standard quotas down and add these quotas to find the total number of seats. It will be correct, or it will be too small. Lower the standard divisor in small increments to find a modified divisor that will give modified quotas that provide the appropriate total.

of seats for each of the original states according to Adams's apportionment plan is shown in Figure 12.1.

Jefferson's Plan

Since the second plan was proposed by the third president of the United States, Thomas Jefferson, it is known as **Jefferson's plan**. It is the same as Adams's plan, except you round down instead of rounding up.

We again turn to the historical 1790 census for the U.S. House of Representatives and note that the lower quotas total 96 and we are looking for a total of 105 seats. Look at the spreadsheet in Figure 12.2 on page 253. This time we look at the lower quotas. Note that $d = 37{,}084.51$ (from Table 12.6) and if we lower this to $D = 36{,}000$ the total number of seats is 104, so we lowered d too little. (Remember, the goal is 105.) Next, we lower d to $D = 33{,}000$ and the total number of seats is now 111, so we lowered d too much. Finally, if we choose $D = 35{,}000$, we obtain the target number of seats, which is 105. The number of seats for each of the original states according to Jefferson's apportionment plan is shown in Figure 12.2.

Figure 12.1 Apportionment calculations for Adams's apportionment plan

	A	B	C	D	E	F	G	H	I	J	K
1		CN	DE	GA	KY	MD	MS	NH	NJ	NY	
2	Population	237,655	59,096	82,548	73,677	319,728	475,199	141,899	184,139	340,241	
3	*q*	6.41	1.59	2.23	1.99	8.62	12.81	3.83	4.97	9.17	
4	Nearest	6	2	2	2	9	13	4	5	9	
5	Round up	7	2	3	2	9	13	4	5	10	
6	Round dn	6	1	2	1	8	12	3	4	9	
7	Trial 1	7	2	3	2	9	13	4	5	9	
8	Q	6.25	1.56	2.17	1.94	8.41	12.51	3.73	4.85	8.95	
9	Trial 2	6	2	3	2	8	12	4	5	9	
10	Q	5.94	1.48	2.06	1.84	7.99	11.88	3.55	4.60	8.51	
11	Adams	6	2	3	2	9	13	4	5	9	
12	Q	6.00	1.49	2.06	1.86	8.07	12.00	3.58	4.65	8.59	
13											
14											
15		NC	PA	RI	SC	VT	VA	TOTAL	No. of Seats	*d*	
16	Population	395,005	433,611	69,112	249,073	85,341	747,550	3,893,874	105	37,084.51	
17	*q*	10.65	11.69	1.86	6.72	2.30	20.16	105			
18	Nearest	11	12	2	7	2	20	106			
19	Round up	11	12	2	7	3	21	111			
20	Round dn	10	11	1	6	2	20	96		*D*	
21	Trial 1	11	11	2	7	3	20	106	Raise *d* to:	38,000	too little
22	Q	10.39	11.41	1.82	6.55	2.25	19.67				
23	Trial 2	10	11	2	7	3	19	103	Raise *d* to:	40,000	too much
24	Q	9.88	10.84	1.73	6.23	2.13	18.69				
25	Adams	10	11	2	7	3	19	105	Raise *d* to:	39,600	just right
26	Q	9.97	10.95	1.75	6.29	2.16	18.88				

Figure 12.2 Apportionment calculations for Jefferson's apportionment plan

	A	B	C	D	E	F	G	H	I	J	
1		CN	DE	GA	KY	MD	MS	NH	NJ	NY	
2	Population	237,655	59,096	82,548	73,677	319,728	475,199	141,899	184,139	340,241	
3	*q*	6.41	1.59	2.23	1.99	8.62	12.81	3.83	4.97	9.17	
4	Nearest	6	2	2	2	9	13	4	5	9	
5	Round up	7	2	3	2	9	13	4	5	10	
6	Round dn	6	1	2	1	8	12	3	4	9	
7	Trial 1	6	1	2	2	8	13	3	5	9	
8	Q	6.80	1.64	2.29	2.05	8.88	13.20	3.94	5.11	9.45	
9	Trial 2	7	1	2	2	9	14	4	5	10	
10	Q	7.20	1.79	2.50	2.23	9.69	14.40	4.30	5.58	10.31	
11	Jefferson	6	1	2	2	9	13	4	5	9	
12	Q	6.79	1.69	2.36	2.11	9.14	13.58	4.05	5.26	9.72	
13											
14											
15		NC	PA	RI	SC	VT	VA	TOTAL	No. of Seats	*d*	
16	Population	395,005	433,611	69,112	249,073	85,341	747,550	3,893,874	105	37,084.51	
17	*q*	10.65	11.69	1.86	6.72	2.30	20.16	105			
18	Nearest	11	12	2	7	2	20	106			
19	Round up	11	12	2	7	3	21	111			
20	Round dn	10	11	1	6	2	20	96		*D*	
21	Trial 1	10	12	1	6	2	20	100	Lower *d* to:	36,000	too little
22	Q	10.97	12.04	1.92	6.92	2.37	20.77				
23	Trial 2	11	13	2	7	2	22	111	Lower *d* to:	33,000	too much
24	Q	11.97	13.14	2.09	7.55	2.59	22.65				
25	Jefferson	11	12	1	7	2	21	105	Lower *d* to:	35,000	just right
26	Q	11.29	12.39	1.97	7.12	2.44	21.36				

Hamilton's Plan

As you might have guessed by now, both Adams's and Jefferson's plans are a bit complicated. Historically, many complained that using this "modified divisor" to "tweak" the numbers is a bit "like magic." Alexander Hamilton, secretary of the treasury under George Washington, proposed the next plan we will consider, which is called, of course, **Hamilton's plan**. It is easier and more straightforward than the previous two plans we have considered.

© Pan America/Jupiterimages

> **PROCEDURE:**
> **Hamilton's Plan**
>
> To find the appropriate number of seats, use the following procedure.
>
> **STEP 1** Compute the standard divisor, *d*.
>
> **STEP 2** Compute the standard quota, *q*, for each state.
>
> **STEP 3** Round the standard quotas down to the nearest integer, but each *must be at least one*.
>
> **STEP 4** Give any additional seats, one at a time (until no seats are left) to the states with the largest fractional parts of their standard quotas.

© Nicholas Belton/iStockphoto.com / © UteHil/iStockphoto.com

Note that Hamilton took into account the problem we discovered in the 1790 apportionment of the New York City Borroughs. It just does not seem right that a district should have no representation, so if Hamilton's plan is used, all voters will have *some* representation.

Once again, look at the table on page 251 and note that the lower quotas total 96 and we are looking for a total of 105 seats. In the spreadsheet in Figure 12.3, we show you all three methods for easy comparison.

To carry out Hamilton's plan, start by looking at the value of q in the second row. Look across and locate the one with the greatest decimal portion; it is Kentucky (1.99, but look just at the decimal portion; 0.99); add one seat to Kentucky (see #1). Next, pick New Jersey (0.97); add one seat to New Jersey (see #2). Next, pick Rhode Island because it has the next largest decimal portion (0.86); add one seat to Rhode Island (see #3). Continue to add seats in order (see #4 to #9). Note that now the total is 105 seats, so the process is complete.

The following example projects these mathematical methods of apportionment into the political process. Take a good look at Figure 12.3 to answer the following questions.

If you were from a small state, which plan would you probably favor? There are seven states (out of 15) for which the representation changes depending on the adopted plan. Adams's plan favors Delaware and Georgia, but hurts North Carolina and Pennsylvania. Jefferson's plan hurts Rhode Island. It seems as if *Adams's plan favors the smaller states.*

If you were from a large state, which plan would you probably favor? By the analysis for small states, it seems that the larger states would favor Jefferson's plan. It is not a coincidence that *Jefferson's plan favors the larger states* and that Jefferson was from Virginia.

Figure 12.3 Apportionment calculations for Adams's, Jefferson's, and Hamilton's apportionment plans

	A	B	C	D	E	F	G	H	I	J
1		CN	DE	GA	KY	MD	MS	NH	NJ	NY
2	Population	237,655	59,096	82,548	73,677	319,728	475,199	141,899	184,139	340,241
3	*q*	6.41	1.59	2.23	1.99	8.62	12.81	3.83	4.97	9.17
4	Nearest	6	2	2	2	9	13	4	5	9
5	Round up	7	2	3	2	9	13	4	5	10
6	Round dn	6	1	2	1	8	12	3	4	9
7	Adams	6	2	3	2	9	13	4	5	9
8	Jefferson	6	1	2	2	9	13	4	5	9
9	Hamilton	6	1	2	2	9	13	4	5	9
10					#1	#9	#5	#4	#2	
11										
12		NC	PA	RI	SC	VT	VA	TOTAL	No. of Seats	*d*
13	Population	395,005	433,611	69,112	249,073	85,341	747,550	3,893,874	105	37,084.51
14	*q*	10.65	11.69	1.86	6.72	2.30	20.16	105		
15	Nearest	11	12	2	7	2	20	106		
16	Round up	11	12	2	7	3	21	111		
17	Round dn	10	11	1	6	2	20	96		
18	Adams	10	11	2	7	3	19	105		
19	Jefferson	11	12	1	7	2	21	105		
20	Hamilton	11	12	2	7	2	20	105		
21		#8	#7	#3	#6					

Which plan do you think was the first plan to be adopted by the First Congress? (*Hint*: remember, the First Congress was the congress of compromise.) It would seem that the plan to compromise the positions should be Hamilton's plan.

By considering this last example, we can understand why the first apportionment plan to pass was Hamilton's plan. When the bill that would have adopted Hamilton's plan reached President Washington's desk, it became the first presidential veto in the history of our country. Washington objected to the fourth step in Hamilton's plan. Congress was not able to override the veto, so with a second bill Congress adopted Jefferson's plan, which was used until 1840 when it was replaced because flaws in Jefferson's plan showed up after the 1820 and 1830 censuses. We will discuss these flaws in the next section.

Webster's Plan

Daniel Webster, a senator from Massachusetts, ran for president under the Whig party, and was appointed secretary of state by President William H. Harrison. When the reapportionment based on the 1830 census was done, New

© Hulton Archive/Getty Images

PROCEDURE: Webster's Plan

Any standard quota with a decimal portion must be *rounded to the nearest whole number*. To find the appropriate number of seats, use the following procedure.

STEP 1 Compute the standard divisor, *d*.

STEP 2 Compute the standard quota, *q*, for each state.

STEP 3 Round the standard quotas down if the fractional part is less than 0.5 and up if the fractional part is greater than or equal to 0.5. The total will be correct, or it will not.

STEP 4 If it is not, lower or raise the standard divisor in small increments to find a modified divisor that will give modified quotas that provide the appropriate total.

York had a standard quota of 38.59 but was awarded 40 seats using Jefferson's plan. Webster argued that this was unconstitutional (violated the *quota rule*) and suggested a compromise, which became known as **Webster's plan**. His plan is similar to both Adams's and Jefferson's plans. Instead of rounding up or down from the modified quota, Webster proposed that any quota with a decimal portion must be rounded to the *nearest* whole number. This method, described above, is based on the *arithmetic mean*; round down if the standard quota is less than the *arithmetic mean* and round up otherwise.

At the time that Webster's plan was adopted, no one suspected that it had the same flaw as Jefferson's plan. It was used after the 1840 census and from 1900 to 1941, when it was replaced by Huntington-Hill's plan. Oddly enough, from 1850 to 1900 Hamilton's plan was used, so the only method never actually used in Congress was Adams's plan.

Huntington-Hill's Plan

Edward Huntington, a professor of mechanics and mathematics at Harvard University, and Joseph Hill, chief statistician for the Bureau of the Census, devised a rounding method currently used by the U.S. legislature. From 1850 to 1911, the size of the House of Representatives (number of seats) changed as states were added. In 1911, the House size was fixed at 433, with a provision for the addition of one seat each for Arizona and New Mexico. The House size has remained at 435 since, except for a temporary increase to 437 at the time of admission of Alaska and Hawaii. The seats went back to 435 after the subsequent census. In 1910, a plan called *Huntington-Hill's plan*, which we will abbreviate as the *HH plan*, was adopted. It is the same as Webster's plan except it rounds using the *geometric mean*, rather than the arithmetic mean used by Webster's plan.

PROCEDURE: Huntington-Hill's Plan

To find the appropriate number of seats, use the following procedure.

STEP 1 Compute the standard divisor, *d*.

STEP 2 Compute the standard quota, *q*, for each state. Let a = lower quota and b = upper quota for each state.

STEP 3 Round the standard quotas down if the fractional part is less than $\sqrt{ab}$ and up if the fractional part is greater than or equal to $\sqrt{ab}$. Add these rounded numbers; the total will be correct, or it will not.

STEP 4 If it is not, lower or raise the standard divisor in small increments to find a modified divisor that will give modified quotas that provide the appropriate total.

Let's look at an example now reviewing the concept of geometric mean.

If a and b are two numbers, then

arithmetic mean (A.M.) $= \frac{a+b}{2}$

geometric mean (G.M.) $= \sqrt{ab}$

Find the upper and lower quotas, and the arithmetic and geometric means of the upper and lower quotas. Then round the modified quota by comparing it to the arithmetic mean and then to the geometric mean.

a. 9.49 **b.** 1.42 **c.** 4.53 **d.** 6.42

	Q	Down	Up	A.M.	A.M. round	G.M.	G.M. round
a.	9.49	9	10	$\frac{9+10}{2} = 9.5$	9	$\sqrt{9 \times 10} \approx 9.486$	10
b.	1.42	1	2	$\frac{1+2}{2} = 1.5$	1	$\sqrt{1 \times 2} \approx 1.414$	2
c.	4.53	4	5	$\frac{4+5}{2} = 4.5$	5	$\sqrt{4 \times 5} \approx 4.472$	5
d.	6.42	6	7	$\frac{6+7}{2} = 6.5$	6	$\sqrt{6 \times 7} \approx 6.48$	6

We conclude this topic with Table 12.7, which allows us to compare and contrast the apportionment methods introduced in this section.

12.4 Apportionment Paradoxes

AS WE SAW IN THE LAST SECTION, THE U.S. CONSTITUTION MANDATED THAT REPRESENTATION IN THE HOUSE OF REPRESENTATIVES BE BASED ON PROPORTIONAL REPRESENTATION BY STATE.

The first three apportionment plans, Adams's, Jefferson's, and Hamilton's plans, were debated in Congress in regard to implementing this mandate using the population numbers from the 1790 census. The easiest to apply was Hamilton's plan, which, as we saw, was vetoed by Washington. This left two plans that relied on modified divisors. Remember, the quota rule states that the actual number of seats assigned to each state must be the lower or the upper quota.

Consider the following historical example. In the 1830 election, New York's population was 1,918,578 and the U.S. population was 11,931,000. At that time, there were 240 seats in the House of Representatives. Determine the

Table 12.7 Summary of Apportionment Methods

Method	Divisor	Apportionment
Adams's Plan	Round **up**; **raise** the standard divisor to find the modified divisor.	Round the standard quotas up. Apportion to each group its modified upper quota. It favors the smaller states.
Jefferson's Plan	Round **down**; **lower** the standard divisor to find the modified divisor.	Round the standard quotas down. Apportion to each group its modified lower quota. It favors the larger states.
Hamilton's Plan	Use the standard divisor. Round **down**.	Round the standard quotas down. Distribute additional seats one at a time until all items are distributed.
Webster's Plan	Use modified divisors. May round up or down.	Round by comparing with the **arithmetic mean** of the upper and lower quotas.
HH's Plan	Use modified divisors. May round up or down.	Round by comparing with the **geometric mean** of the upper and lower quotas.

standard, upper, and lower quotas for New York in the 1830 election.

$$d = \frac{11{,}931{,}000}{240} = 49{,}712.5$$

The standard quota was

$$\frac{1{,}918{,}578}{d} \approx 38.59.$$

The lower quota is 38 and the upper quota is 39.

Remember, in 1830 Jefferson's plan was in place and the modified divisor used for that election produced a number with a standard quota that rounded down to 40; this violated the quota rule. Daniel Webster was outraged, and he argued that the result was unconstitutional. Unfortunately, he proposed a method that had the same flaw (namely, it violated the quota rule). Any plan that uses a modified divisor can violate the quota rule.

The same kind of inconsistencies can happen with any of the methods that use modified divisors and modified quotas to form the sum. Only Hamilton's plan is immune to this behavior, and all the other plans may violate the quota rule. You might ask, Why, then, don't we use Hamilton's plan? We have another paradox to consider.

Alabama Paradox

A serious inconsistency in Hamilton's plan was discovered in the 1880 census. Before the number of seats in the House of Representatives was fixed at 435, there was a debate on whether to have 299 or 300 seats in the House. Using Hamilton's method with 299 members, Alabama was to receive eight seats. But if the total number of representatives were *increased* to 300, Alabama would receive only seven seats! This became known as the **Alabama paradox**.

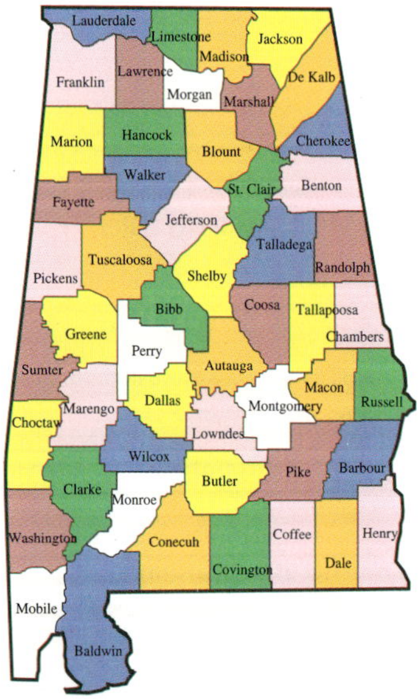

A reapportionment in which an increase in the total number of seats results in a loss in the seats for some state is known as the **Alabama paradox**.

It is easy to see how this paradox can occur. Raising the number can cause a decimal part of one number to increase faster than the decimal part of another, changing their "rank" in their decimal parts.

Population Paradox

Shortly after the discovery of the Alabama paradox, another paradox (the **population paradox**) was discovered around 1900 while Congress was still using Hamilton's plan. It is possible for the population of one state to be growing at a faster rate than another state, but still lose seats to the slower-growing state.

When there is a fixed number of seats, a reapportionment that causes a state to lose a seat to another state even though the percent increase in the population of the state that loses the seat is larger than the percent increase of the state that wins the seat is called the **population paradox**.

Consider the following example of the population paradox. Suppose there are 100 new teachers to be apportioned to the three boroughs according to their 1990 population using Hamilton's plan. The population of each borough is shown in the table below.

	1990	2000
Anderson Valley	3,755	3,800
Bennett Valley	10,250	10,350
Central Valley	36,100	36,150
TOTAL	50,105	50,300

Show that this example illustrates the population paradox.

In 1990, $d = \frac{50{,}105}{100} = 501.05$. The standard quotas are (in thousands).

Borough	Population	q	Lower Quota	Hamilton's Plan
A	3,755	7.49	7	8 (#1)
B	10,250	20.46	20	20
C	36,100	72.05	72	72
TOTAL	50,105		99	100

In 2000, $d = \dfrac{50{,}300}{100} = 503.$

Borough	Population	q	Lower Quota	Hamilton's Plan
A	3,800	7.55	7	7
B	10,350	20.58	20	21 (#2)
C	36,150	71.87	71	72 (#1)
TOTAL	50,300		98	100

Now, here are the percent increases:

Borough	1990	2000	Increase	Percent Increase
A	3,755	3,800	45	$\frac{45}{3{,}755} \approx 1.20\%$
B	10,250	10,350	100	$\frac{100}{10{,}250} \approx 0.98\%$
C	36,100	36,150	50	$\frac{50}{36{,}100} \approx 0.14\%$

Anderson Valley had the largest percent increase, but lost one teacher to Bennett Valley. This is an example of the population paradox.

New States Paradox

The last paradox we will discuss was discovered in 1907 when Oklahoma joined the Union. If a new state is added to the existing states and the number of seats being apportioned is increased to prevent decreasing the existing apportionment, addition may cause a shift in some of the original allocations. This is the **new states paradox**.

A reapportionment in which an increase in the total number of seats causes a shift in the apportionment of the existing states is known as the **new states paradox**.

Balinski and Young's Impossibility Theorem

In 1980 two mathematicians proved that if any apportionment plan satisfies the quota rule, then it must permit the possibility of some other paradox. Here is a statement of **Balinski and Young's impossibility theorem**.

Balinski and Young's Impossibility Theorem

Any apportionment plan that does not violate the quota rule must produce paradoxes. And any apportionment plan that does not produce paradoxes must violate the quota rule.

There is a footnote, however, to this theorem. It must be qualified that the second part of this theorem is true only when the number of seats to be apportioned is fixed up front, as it is fixed with the U.S. House of Representatives to be 435.

We conclude with a summary of the paradoxes of this section, along with the quota rule, in Table 12.8.

Table 12.8 Comparison of Apportionment Paradoxes

Paradox	Comment	Adams's	Jefferson's	Hamilton's	Webster's	HH
Quota Rule	Apportionment must be either the lower or upper quota.	Yes	Yes	No	Yes	Yes
Alabama Paradox	An increase in the total may result in a loss for a state.	No	No	Yes	No	No
Population Paradox	One state may lose seats to another even though its percent increase is larger.	No	No	Yes	No	No
New States Paradox	The addition of a new state may change the apportionment of another group.	No	No	Yes	No	No

Note: "Yes" means that the apportionment method may violate the stated paradox. "No" means that the apportionment method may not violate the stated paradox.

PROBLEM HANDBOOK

FOR

MATH

FOR LIBERAL ARTS

Karl J. Smith
Brooks/Cole Cengage Learning
20 Davis Drive
Belmount, CA 94002-3098

1.1 Math Anxiety

In this section, there are some hints for success. **IN YOUR OWN WORDS,** *discuss the statements which refer to these hints.*

1. You must make a commitment to attend each class. Do you think this means each and every class?
1. If it is impossible to attend class (doctor's visit, for example), it is acceptable to skip over the day's activities and pick up with the material when you return.
2. If it is impossible to turn in one or two assignments (because of illness, for example), it is acceptable to skip those assignments and pick up with the material when you return.
3. You must read the text carefully. Do you think this means read every word?

1.2 What is the Problem?

Simplify the numerical expressions given in Problems 1-1, and classify each as a sum, difference, product, or quotient.

1. Simplify

a. $2 \times 18 + 9 \div 3 - 5 \times 2$ 29; difference

b. $2 \times (18 + 9) \div 3 - 5 \times 2$ 8; difference

2. Simplify$(18 + 2)(82 - 2)$ 1,600; product

3. Write in scientific notation.

a. 15,824 1.5824×10^4

b. 0.00081 7 8.17×10^{-4}

c. 6.34 E9 6.34×10^9

d. 8.291029292 12 $8.291029292 \times 10^{12}$

4. Write each of the numbers without using exponents.

a. 7.2×10^{10} 72,000,000,000

b. 4.6×10^{-7} 0.00000 046

c. 3.2×10^0 3.2

d. 0.0000329 07 329

1.3 Early Numeration Systems

1. Tell which of the named properties apply to the Egyptian, Roman, and Babylonian numeration systems.

a. grouping system Egyptian, Roman

b. positional system Roman, Babylonian

c. repetitive system Egyptian, Roman, Babylonian

d. additive system Egyptian, Roman, Babylonian

e. subtractive system Roman, Babylonian

f. multiplicative system Roman

2. Kathy had a dream in which she was selling roses in an international market. She started out with 143 roses. Then her first customer, an Egyptian, bought ∩||||| of them. Soon afterward, a Babylonian asked to buy ◁◁◁▼ ▼▼▼▼▼ roses; later XIV roses were bought by (you guessed it) a Roman. How many roses did she have left to sell at the end of her dream? 78

3. In a strange mix-up, several people (no two of whom spoke the same language) needed to pool their resources to survive the scorching desert heat. Eric had 45 bottles of water; Dimetrius had ∩ ∩ ∩|||| bottles; Sparticus had ◁◁◁◁◁▼▼▼▼ bottles. How many bottles of water did they have all together? 133

4. **Historical Quest** The Yale tablet from the Babylonian collection, written between 1900 BC and 1600 BC, contains the following problem::

> The length of a rectangle exceeds the width by 10 and the area is 600. What are the dimensions of the rectangle?

Give your answer using Babylonian notation. ◁◁ by ◁◁◁

1.4 Hindu-Arabic Numeration System

1. Write the numbers in decimal notation.

a. 10^{-4} 0.0001 **b.** 10^{-3} 0.001

c. 6×10^{-2} 0.06

d. $2 \times 10^4 + 6 \times 10^2 + 4 \times 10^{-1} + 7 \times 10^{-3} + 6 \times 10^{-4} + 9 \times 10^{-5}$

20,600.40769

2. Write each of the numbers in expanded notation.

a. 0.096421

$9 \times 10^{-2} + 6 \times 10^{-3} + 4 \times 10^{-4} + 2 \times 10^{-5} + 1 \times 10^{-6}$

b. 27.572

$2 \times 10^1 + 7 \times 10^0 + 5 \times 10^{-1} + 7 \times 10^{-2} + 2 \times 10^{-3}$

c. 893.0001

$8 \times 10^2 + 9 \times 10^1 + 3 \times 10^0 + 1 \times 10^{-4}$

3. **Historical Quest** One of the oldest devices used for calculation is the abacus, as shown below. Each rod names one of the positions we use in counting. Each bead on the bottom represents one unit in that column and each bead on the top represents 5 units in that column. The number illustrated is 1,734.

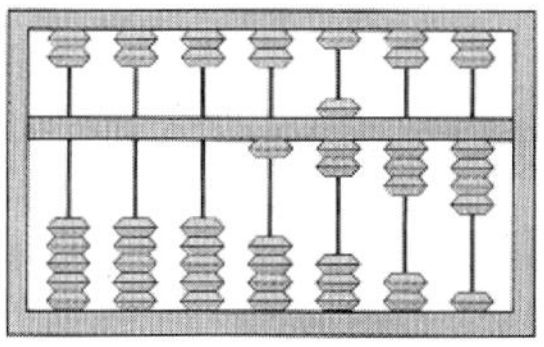

What number is illustrated by

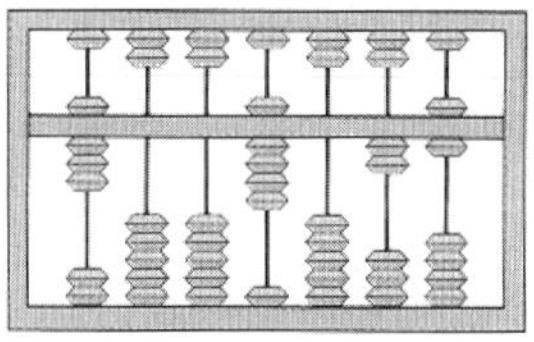

8,009,026

4. Sketch an abacus to show 8,007,009

1.5 Different Numeration Systems

1. Count the number of people in the indicated base.

a. base ten 13

b. base five 23_{five}

c. base thirteen $10_{thirteen}$

d. base eight 15_{eight}

e. base two 1101_{two}

f. base twelve 11_{twelve}

2. Write 110111.1001_{two} in expanded notation.

$1 \times 2^5 + 1 \times 2^4 + 1 \times 2^2 + 1 \times 2^1 + 1 \times 2^0 + 1 \times 2^{-1} + 1 \times 2^{-4}$

3. a. Change 412 to base five. 3122_{five}

b. Change 615 to base eight. 1147_{eight}

4. If you keep one investment for 1 year, 7 months, 11 days, and then roll it over into another investment for 1 year, 6 months, 26 days, how long was the total investment (if you assume that all months are 30 days long)? 3 years, 2 months, 7 days

1.6 Binary Numeration System

1. What decimal number is represented by the light bulbs?

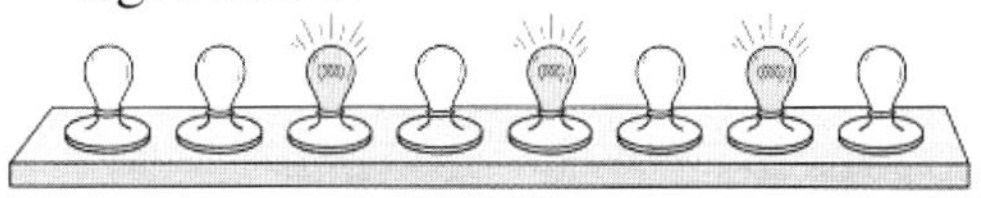

42

2. Write each number as a decimal numeral.

a. 1101_{two} 13

b. 1100011_{two} 99

3. Write each number as a binary numeral.

a. 51 110011_{two}

b. 95 1100011011_{two}

4.
$$\begin{array}{r} 111_{two} \\ \times\ 101_{two} \\ \hline \end{array}$$

100011_{two}

1.7 History of Calculating Devices

1. Arrange the development of the following computers in chronological order of their first appearance.

Altair, Cray, ENIAC, Apple, and UNIVAC

ENIAC (1942), UNIVAC (1951), Cray (1958), Altair (1975), Apple (1976)

2. **IN YOUR OWN WORDS** Have you ever been told that something cannot be

changed because "that is the way the computer does it"? Discuss this issue.

3. **IN YOUR OWN WORDS** Definitions for "thinking" are given. *According to each of the given definitions*, answer the question, "Can computers think?"
   a. To remember [yes]
   b. To subject to the process of logical thought [yes]
   c. To form a mental picture of [perhaps]
   d. To perceive or recognize [perhaps]
   e. To have feeling or consideration for [no]
   f. To create or devise [perhaps]
   g. To have the ability to learn [yes]
4. **IN YOUR OWN WORDS** What do you mean by "thinking" and "reasoning"? Try to formulate these ideas as clearly as possible, and then discuss the following question: "Can computers think or reason?"

2.1 It's Natural

1. In the English language, the meanings of certain phrases can be very different depending on the association of the words. For example,

   (MAN EATING) TIGER

   is not the same as

   MAN (EATING TIGER)

   Decide whether each of the following groups of words is associative.
   [None are associative.]
   a. HIGH SCHOOL STUDENT
   b. SLOW CURVE SIGN
   c. BARE FACTS PERSON
   d. RED FIRE ENGINE
   e. TRAVELING SALESMAN JOKE
   f. BROWN SMOKING JACKET
2. Consider the set $A = \{1, 4, 7, 9\}$ with an operation $\otimes$ defined by the table.

$\otimes$	1	4	7	9
1	9	7	1	4
4	7	9	4	1
7	1	4	7	9
9	4	1	9	7

   $a \otimes b$ means find the entry in row a and column b; for example,

   $$7 \otimes 9 = 9$$

   (the entry in row 7 and column 9). Find each of the following.
   a. $7 \otimes 4$ [4]
   b. $9 \otimes 1$ [4]
   c. $1 \otimes 7$ [1]
   d. $9 \otimes 9$ [7]
   e. $4 \otimes 7$ [4]
   f. $1 \otimes 9$ [4]
   g. $7 \otimes 1$ [1]
   h. $7 \otimes 7$ [7]
3. Consider the set A and the operation $\otimes$ from Problem 2. Is the set A closed for the operation of $\otimes$? Give reasons for your answer. [yes]
4. Consider the set A and the operation $\otimes$ from Problem 2. Does the set A satisfy the given property for the operation of $\otimes$? Give reasons for your answer.
   a. Associative [no]
   b. Commutative [yes]

2.2 Prime Numbers

1. Find all prime numbers less than or equal to 300. [See *IM*.]
2. Find the canonical representation for each of the numbers.
   a. 105 [$3 \cdot 5 \cdot 7$]
   b. 67 [prime]
3. Find the g.c.f. and l.c.m. of $\{60, 72\}$. [12; 360]
4. Bill and Sue both work at night. Bill has every sixth night off and Sue has every eighth night off. If they are both off tonight, how many nights will it be before they are both off again at the same time? [3 weeks, 3 days]

2.3 Numbers — Up and Down

Simplify the expressions in Problems 1-4.

1. a. $6 + (-8) - 5$ [-7]

b. $-2(-3)+(-1)(6)$ $\boxed{0}$

c. $6-(-2)$ $\boxed{8}$

2. **a.** . $-5-(-3)$ $\boxed{-2}$

b. $\frac{-32}{-8}-5-(-7)$ $\boxed{6}$

c. . $\frac{-15}{-5}-4-(-8)$ $\boxed{7}$

3. **a.** $|-3|-[-(-2)]$ $\boxed{1}$

b. $15-(-7)$ $\boxed{22}$

c. $[48\div(-6)]\div(-2)$ $\boxed{4}$

4. **a.** $48\div[(-6)\div(-2)]$ $\boxed{16}$

b. . $-5(2)+(-3)(-4)-6(-7)$ $\boxed{44}$

c. $-8(3)-6(-4)-2(-8)$ $\boxed{16}$

2.4 It's a Long Way From Zero to One

Perform the indicated operations in Problems 1-4. *(Recall that negative exponents are sometimes used to denote fractions. For example,* $\frac{1}{7}=7^{-1}$.*)*

1. **a.** $\frac{-12}{35}-\frac{8}{15}$ $\boxed{\frac{-92}{105}}$

b. $2^{-1}+3^{-1}$ $\boxed{\frac{5}{6}}$

2. **a.** $\frac{2}{3}\times\frac{5}{7}$ $\boxed{\frac{10}{21}}$

b. $\left(\frac{3}{7}\cdot\frac{3}{5}\right)\div\frac{1}{2}$ $\boxed{\frac{18}{35}}$

3. **a.** $\frac{2^{-1}+3^{-2}}{2^{-1}+3^{-1}}$ $\boxed{\frac{11}{15}}$ **b.** $\frac{6+2^{-1}}{\frac{1}{2}+\frac{1}{3}}$ $\boxed{\frac{39}{5}}$

4. **a.** $\frac{-3}{4}\cdot\frac{119}{200}+\frac{-3}{4}\cdot\frac{81}{200}$ $\boxed{\frac{-3}{4}\text{; use dist. prop.}}$

b. $\frac{-3}{4}\left(\frac{119}{200}+\frac{81}{200}\right)$ $\boxed{\frac{-3}{4}}$

2.5 It's Irrational

1. A computer approximation for $\sqrt{2}$ is 1.41421356237309504880168872420969807856967187537694
Give a brief argument showing why that can't be $\sqrt{2}$.

2. Write the following limerick in symbols, and then tell whether it is true or false:*

A dozen, a gross, and a score
Plus three times the square root of four
Divided by seven
Plus five times eleven
Is nine squared and not a bit more.

$\boxed{\frac{12+144+20+3\sqrt{4}}{7}+5\cdot 11=9^2+0}$

$\boxed{\text{is a true statement.}}$

3. If a carpenter wants to be sure that the corner of a building is square and measures out 6 ft and 8 ft along the sides, how long should she make the diagonal? $\boxed{10\text{ ft}}$

4. Find an irrational number between 1 and 3. $\boxed{1.2323323332\cdots}$

2.6 Be Real

1. Tell whether each number is an element of $\mathbb{N}$ (a natural number), $\mathbb{Z}$ (an integer), $\mathbb{Q}$ (a rational number), $\mathbb{Q}'$ (an irrational number), or $\mathbb{R}$ (a real number). Since these sets are not all disjoint, you may need to list more than one set for each answer.

a. 19 $\boxed{\mathbb{N},\mathbb{Z},\mathbb{Q},\mathbb{R}}$

b. 6.48 $\boxed{\mathbb{Q},\mathbb{R}}$

c. $1.868686868\cdots$ $\boxed{\mathbb{Q},\mathbb{R}}$

d. $\sqrt{8}$ $\boxed{\mathbb{Q}',\mathbb{R}}$

e. π $\boxed{\mathbb{Q}',\mathbb{R}}$

f. $0.00\overline{12}$ $\boxed{\mathbb{Q},\mathbb{R}}$

g. $\sqrt{16}$ $\boxed{\mathbb{N},\mathbb{Z},\mathbb{Q},\mathbb{R}}$

h. $\sqrt{1{,}000}$ $\boxed{\mathbb{Q}',\mathbb{R}}$

i. $\frac{1}{7}$ $\boxed{\mathbb{Q},\mathbb{R}}$

2. Identify each of the properties illustrated.

a. $5\cdot 1=1\cdot 5$ $\boxed{\text{commutative}}$

b. $3(4+8)=3(4)+3(8)$ $\boxed{\text{distributive}}$

c. $a+(10+b)=(a+10)+b$ $\boxed{\text{associative}}$

d. $a+(10+b)=(10+b)+a$ $\boxed{\text{commutative}}$

e. $\frac{x^2+x-1}{x^2-1}=\frac{x^2+x-1}{x^2-1}\cdot\frac{\frac{1}{x^2}}{\frac{1}{x^2}}$

$\boxed{\text{identity}}$

3. Check whether each of the sets form

---

*From *Omni*, March 1995, "Games" department, p. 104.

a group.

a. $\mathbb{N}$ for $-$ $\boxed{\text{no}}$

b. $\mathbb{W}$ for $\times$ $\boxed{\text{no}}$

c. $\mathbb{Q}$ for $\times$ $\boxed{\text{no}}$

4. a. Given the set $\{1, 2, 3, 4\}$ and the operation $\times$, construct a multiplication table showing all possible answers for the numbers in the set.

b. Given the set $\{1, 2, 3, 4\}$ and the operation $*$ defined by $a*b = 2a$, construct a table for $*$ showing all possible answers for numbers in the set.

c. Verify as many of the field properties as possible for the operations of $\times$ and $*$.

operation $\times$: not closed, assoc., identity is 1, no inverse, commutative; operation $*$: not closed, not assoc., no identity, no inverse, not commutative

2.7 Mathematical Modeling

1. IN YOUR OWN WORDS Prepare a personal budget for a college student.

A good example of mathematics modeling in the natural sciences, but with implications to history and the social sciences (not to mention golf!), is modeling the path of a cannonball. The real-world problem is to hit a target.

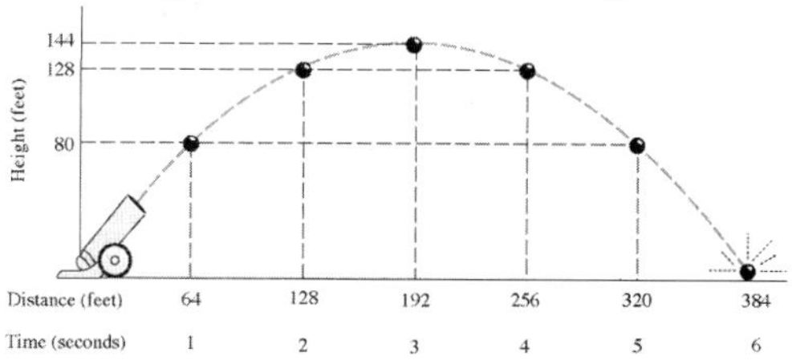

Fire a cannonball at 50 m/s at a 60° angle. We might begin by using trial and error. One possible trial is shown.

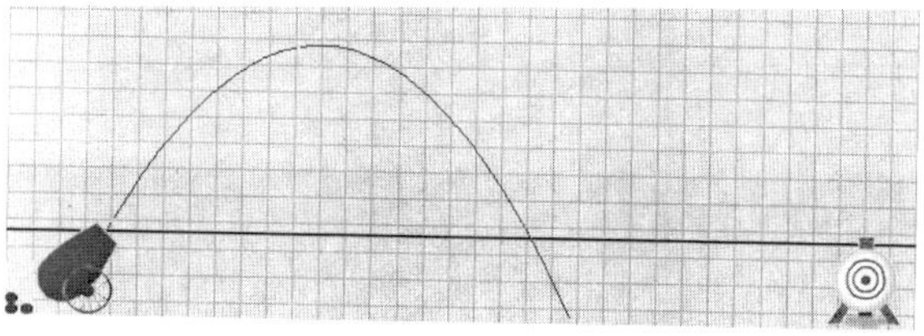

Trying to hit a target by trial and error

2. Use the above trial as a basis of comparison for projecting the trajectories.

a. Decrease the angle to 45°.

b. Increase the velocity to 60 m/s.

c. Increase the angle to 75°.

d. Decrease the velocity to 30 m/s.

3. Now, we will try to hit the target; use 45° with 60 m/s.

4. Draw a path to the bullseye of the target. Estimate the angle and the velocity.

3.1 Polynomials

1. Multiply mentally.

a. $(x + 3)(x + 2)$ $\boxed{x^2 + 5x + 6}$

b. $(y + 1)(y + 5)$ $\boxed{y^2 + 6y + 5}$

c. $(x + 4)^2$ $\boxed{x^2 + 8x + 16}$

d. $(y - 3)^2$ $\boxed{y^2 - 6y + 9}$

2. Simplify

a. $(5x + 1)(3x^2 - 5x + 2)$ $\boxed{15x^3 - 22x^2 + 5x + 2}$

b. $(5x + 1)(x^3 - 2x^2 + 3x)$ $\boxed{5x^4 - 9x^3 + 13x^2 + 3x}$

3. Expand $(x + y)^5$.

4. If a boat is traveling at a rate of $6b + 15$ miles per hour for a time of $10 - 2b$ hours, what is the distance traveled by the boat? $\boxed{150 + 30b - 12b^2}$

3.2 Factoring

If possible, completely factor the expressions in Problems 1-3.

1. a. $x^2 - 4x + 3$ $\boxed{(x - 3)(x - 1)}$

b. $x^2 - 5x + 6$ $\boxed{(x - 3)(x - 2)}$

c. $3x^2 - 5x - 2$ $\boxed{(3x + 1)(x - 2)}$

d. $2x^2 + 9x + 4$ $\boxed{(2x+1)(x+4)}$

2. **a.** $5x^3 + 7x^2 - 6x$ $\boxed{x(5x-3)(x+2)}$

b. $7x^4 - 11x^3 - 6x^2$ $\boxed{x^2(7x+3)(x-2)}$

c. $x^2 - 64$ $\boxed{(x-8)(x+8)}$

d. $25x^2 + 50$ $\boxed{25(x^2+2)}$

3. **a.** $(x+2)(x+4) + (5x+6)(x-1)$ $\boxed{(3x+2)(2x+1)}$

b. $x^6 - 13x^4 + 36x^2$ $\boxed{x^2(x-3)(x+3)(x-2)(x+2)}$

4. The area of a rectangle is $x^2 - 2x - 143$ square feet. What are the dimensions of the figure? $\boxed{(x-13) \text{ feet by } (x+11) \text{ feet}}$

3.3 Evaluation

1. Write each expression in spreadsheet notation. Let x be in cell A1, y in A2, and z in A3.

a. $\frac{2}{3}x^2$ $\boxed{\text{+(2/3)*A1^2}}$

b. $5x^2 - 6y^2$ $\boxed{\text{+5*A1^2 – 6*A2^2}}$

c. $(5-x)(x+3)^2$ $\boxed{\text{+(5 – A1)*(A1+3)^2}}$

d. $\frac{2}{3}x^2 + \frac{1}{3}x - 17$ $\boxed{\text{+(2/3)*A1^2+(1/3)*A1 – 17}}$

2. Write each spreadsheet expression in ordinary algebraic notation. Let cell A1 represent the variable x, A2 the variable y, A3 is the variable z, B1 is a, B2 is b, and B3 is c.

a. +4*A1+3 $\boxed{4x+3}$

b. +5*A1^2 – 3*A1+4 $\boxed{5x^2 - 3x + 4}$

c. +(5/4)*A1+14^2 $\boxed{\frac{5}{4}x + 14^2}$

d. +(5/4*A1+14)^2 $\boxed{(\frac{5}{4}x + 14)^2}$

3. Let $w = 2, x = 1, y = 2$, and $z = 4$. Find the values of the given capital letters.

a. $A = x + z + 8$ $\boxed{13}$

b. $E = 25 - y^2$ $\boxed{21}$

c. $I = 5y - 2z$ $\boxed{2}$

d. $U = \dfrac{3wyz}{x}$ $\boxed{48}$

4. Suppose that a spreadsheet contains the following values:

Spreadsheet Application

	A	B	C	D	E
1	6	-4	2	3	
2					
3					
4					
5					

Determine the value of cell E1 if it contains the given formula.

a. +A1 – B1/C1 $\boxed{8}$

b. +(A1 – B1)/C1 $\boxed{5}$

c. +A1/C1*D1 $\boxed{9}$

d. +(A1+...+D1)/2 or @sum(A1..D1)/2 $\boxed{3.5}$

3.4 Equations

Solve the equations in Problems 1-3.

1. **a.** $16F - 5 = 11$ $\boxed{1}$

b. $6 = 5G - 24$ $\boxed{6}$

c. $7 = \frac{2N}{3} + 11$ $\boxed{-6}$

d. $-5 = \frac{2P+1}{3}$ $\boxed{-8}$

2. **a.** $5(6S - 81) = -3(15 + 5S)$ $\boxed{8}$

b. $3(U-3) - 2(U-12) = 18$ $\boxed{3}$

c. $5(W+3) - 6(W+5) = 0$ $\boxed{-15}$

d. $5(Z-2) - 3(Z+3) = 9$ $\boxed{14}$

3. **a.** $x^2 = 10x$ $\boxed{0, 10}$

b. $x^3 = 4x$ $\boxed{0, 2, -2}$

c. $x^2 - 6x + 7 = 0$ $\boxed{3 \pm \sqrt{2}}$

d. $3x^2 = 11x + 4$ $\boxed{4, -\frac{1}{3}}$

4. **Historical Quest** Al-Khwârizmî solved the equation

$$x^2 + 10x = 39$$

a. Solve this equation. $\boxed{x = -13, 3}$

b. Here is a translation of his solution:

... a square and 10 *roots are equal to* 39 *units. The question therefore in this type of equation is about as follows: What is the square which combined with ten of its roots will give a sum total of* 39*? The manner of solving this type of equation is to take one-half of the roots just mentioned. Now the roots in the problem before us are* 10*. Therefore take* 5*, which multiplied by itself gives* 25*, an amount which you add to* 39 *giving* 64*. Having*

taken then the square root of this which is 8, subtract from it half the roots, 5, leaving 3. The number three therefore represents one root of this square, which itself, of course is 9. Nine therefore gives the square.

Follow these directions to find a solution. Show each step using modern algebraic notation.

3.5 Inequalities

1. Graph the solution sets.
   a. $x < 5$ **b.** $x \geq -3$ **c.** $\frac{x}{2} > 3$
2. Solve the inequalities.
   a. $x - 2 \leq 5$ $\boxed{x \leq 7}$
   b. $3y - 6 \geq 9$ $\boxed{y \geq 5}$
   c. $2 - x \geq 3x + 10$ $\boxed{x \leq -2}$
3. Solve the inequalities.
   a. $B > 3(1 + B)$ $\boxed{B < -\frac{3}{2}}$
   b. $2(D + 7) > 2 - D$ $\boxed{D > -4}$
   c. $7(J - 2) + 5 \leq 3(2 + J)$ $\boxed{J \leq \frac{15}{4}}$
4. If the opposite of a number must be greater than twice the number, what are the possible numbers?
   $\boxed{\text{The number is any number less than 0.}}$

3.6 Algebra in Problem Solving

Solve Problems 1–4. Because you are practicing a ***procedure****, you must show all of your work. Start with a verbal description and end with a sentence answering the question.*

EXAMPLE 1 Find consecutive numbers

Find three consecutive integers whose sum is 42.

Solution Read the problem. Write down a verbal description of the problem, using operation signs and an equal sign:

INTEGER + NEXT INTEGER + THIRD INTEGER = 42

This problem has three variables, but they are related. If

x = INTEGER, then

$x + 1$ = NEXT INTEGER

$x + 2$ = THIRD INTEGER

Substitute the variables into the verbal equation:

INTEGER + NEXT INTEGER + THIRD INTEGER = 42

$$x + (x + 1) + (x + 2) = 42$$

Solve the equation.

$$x + x + 1 + x + 2 = 42$$
$$3x + 3 = 42$$
$$3x = 39$$
$$x = 13$$

Check: 13 + 14 + 15 = 42; the integers are 13, 14, and 15. □

1. The sum of four consecutive integers is 74. What are the integers? $\boxed{17, 18, 19, 20}$
2. Two persons are to run a race, but one can run 10 meters per second, whereas the other can run 6 meters per second. If the slower runner has a 50-meter head start, how long will it be before the faster runner catches the slower runner, if they begin at the same time? $\boxed{12.5 \text{ sec}}$
3. A diagonal brace is to be placed in the wall of a room. The height of the wall is 8 ft, and the wall is 14 ft long. What is the exact length of the brace, and what is the length of the brace to the nearest foot? $\boxed{2\sqrt{65}; 16 \text{ ft}}$
4. ***Historical Quest*** (from Bhaskara, ca. AD 1120) "In a lake the bud of a water lily was observed, one cubit above the water, and when moved by the gentle breeze, it sank in the water at two cubits' distance." Find the depth of the water. $\boxed{1\frac{1}{2} \text{ cubits}}$

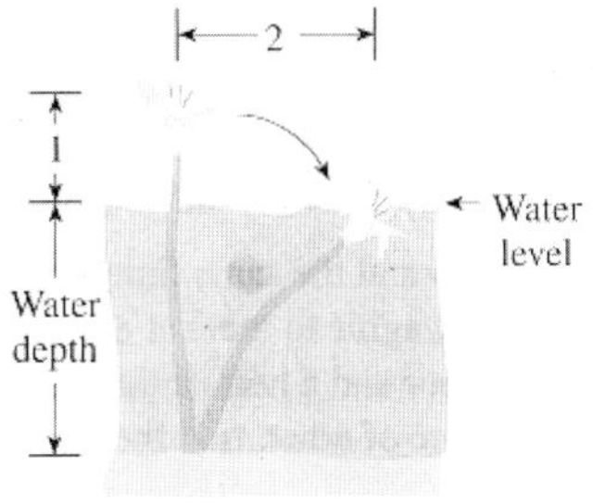

3.7 Ratios and Proportions

1. Solve each proportion for the item represented by a letter.

   a. $\frac{5}{1} = \frac{A}{6}$ 30 b. $\frac{C}{2} = \frac{5}{1}$ 10

   c. $\frac{5}{R} = \frac{7}{12\frac{3}{5}}$ 9 d. $\frac{33}{2\frac{1}{5}} = \frac{3\frac{3}{4}}{T}$ 0.25

2. The *pitch* of a roof is the ratio of the rise to the half-span. If a roof has a rise of 8 feet and a span of 24 feet, what is the pitch? 2 ft to 3 ft or 2/3

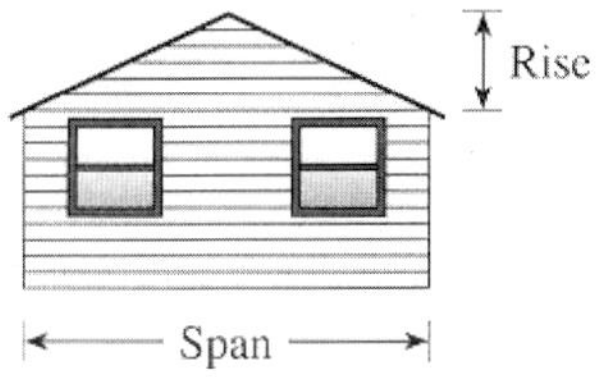

3. You've probably seen advertisements for posters that can be made from any photograph. If the finished poster will be 2 ft by 3 ft, it's likely that part of your original snapshot will be cut off. Suppose you send in a photo that measures 3 in. by 5 in. If the shorter side of the enlargement will be 2 ft, what size should the longer side of the enlargement be so that the entire snapshot is shown in the poster? $3\frac{1}{3}$ ft or 3 ft, 4 in.

3.8 Percents

1. Change the given form into the two missing forms.

	Fraction	*Decimal*	*Percent*
a.	$\frac{3}{4}$	0.75	75%
b.	$\frac{2}{5}$	0.4	40%
c.	$\frac{1}{3}$	$0.\overline{3}$	$33\frac{1}{3}\%$
d.	$\frac{6}{5}$	1.2	120%

2. If the sales tax is 6% and the purchase price is \$181, what is the amount of tax? \$10.86
3. If Brad's monthly salary is \$8,200, and 32% is withheld for taxes and Social Security, how much money is withheld each month? \$2,624
4. If Carlos answered 18 out of 20 questions on a test correctly, what was his percentage right? 90%

3.9 Modeling Uncategorized Problems

1. The product of two consecutive positive even numbers is 440. What are the numbers? 20 and 22
2. The combined area of New York and California is 204,192 square miles. The area of California is 108,530 square miles more than that of New York. Find the land area of each state. CA, 156,361 mi^2; NY, 47,831 mi^2
3. A survey of 100 persons at Better Widgets finds that 40 jog, 25 swim, 16 cycle, 15 both swim and jog, 10 swim and cycle, 8 jog and cycle, and 3 persons do all three. How many people at Better Widgets do not take part in any of these three exercise programs? 49
4. An inlet pipe on a swimming pool can be used to fill the pool in 24 hours. The drain pipe can be used to empty the pool in 30 hours. If the pool is two-thirds filled and then the drain pipe is accidentally opened, how long will it take to fill the pool? 56 hours

4.1 Geometry

1. Is the woman in the figure a young woman or an old woman? both

Edwund Boring, You See My Wife, and Mother-In-Law, 1941

2. Find at least one line of symmetry for each of the illustrations. If there is no line of symmetry, so state.

a.

symmetric

b.

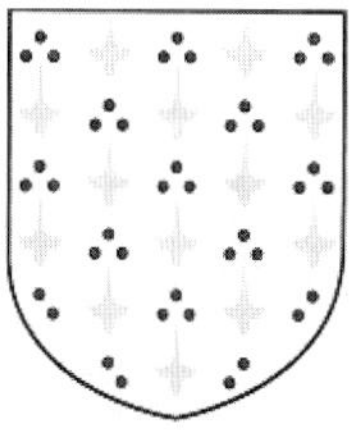

symmetric

c.

symmetric

d.

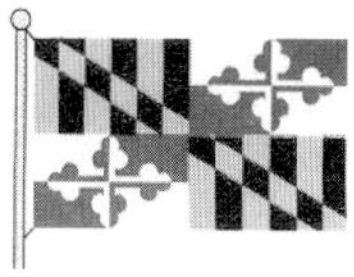

not symmetric

3. Which of the pictures illustrate a line symmetry?

a. Chambered nautilus

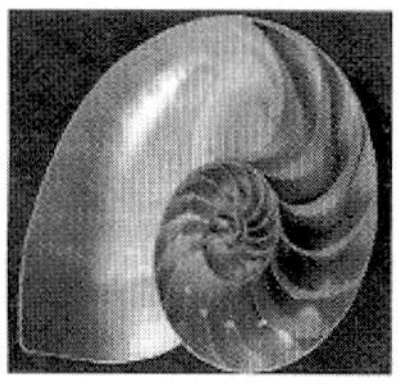

© Susan Van Etten/Stock Boston

not symmetric

b. Butterfly

© Tim Zurowski/CORBIS

not symmetric

c. Human brain

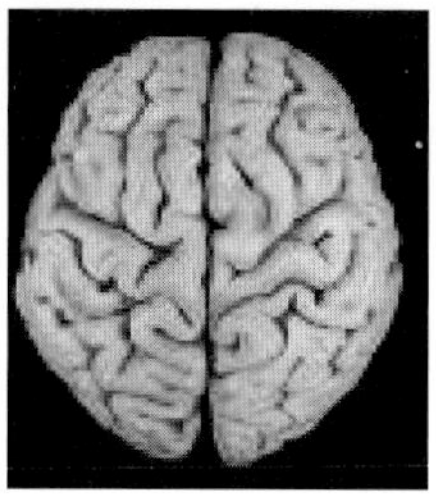

www.morphonix.com

not symmetric

d. Human face

www.photoshoptalent.com

symmetric

4. Start with the given cube and then rotate this cube 90° in the directions indicated by the arrows, as shown. Select the cube marked A, B, C, or D to indicate which most closely matches the result.

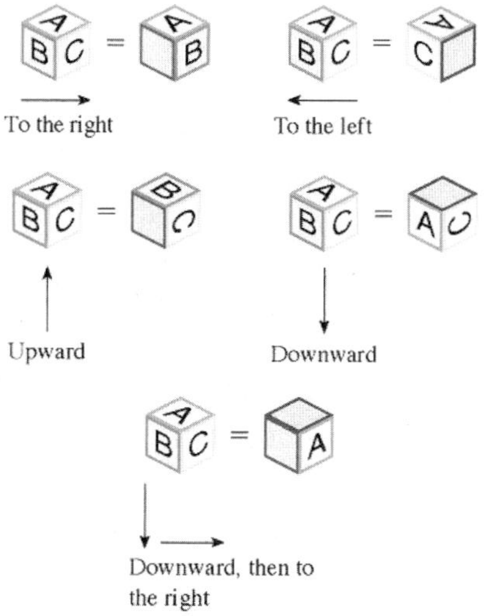

Rotating a cube

a.

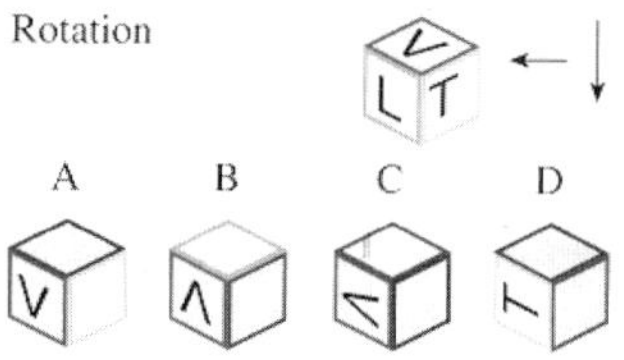

C

b. [D]

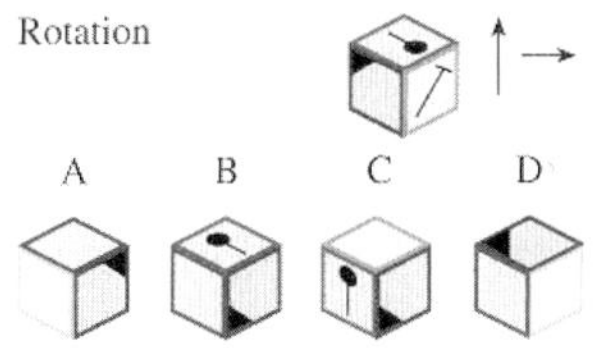

4.2 Polygons and Angles

1. Use the following figure to classify the requested angles shown, where ℓ_1 and ℓ_2 are parallel.

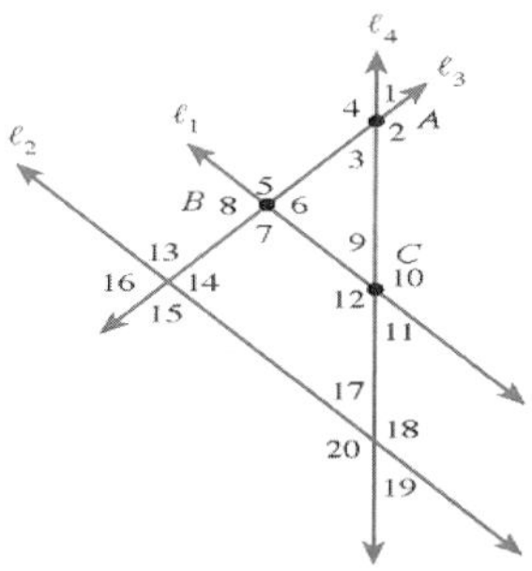

Parallel lines cut by transversals

a. $\angle BAC$ if $m\angle 1$ is 30° [acute]
b. $\angle ABC$ if $m\angle 5$ is 90° [right]
c. $\angle 18$ if $m\angle 17$ is 105° [acute]
d. $\angle 19$ if $m\angle 11$ is 70° [acute]
e. $\angle 10$ if $m\angle 11$ is 90° [right]
f. $\angle 16$ if $m\angle 15$ is 30° [obtuse]
g. $\angle 1$ if $m\angle 2$ is 130° [acute]
h. $\angle 5$ if $m\angle 15$ is 88° [acute]

2. Find the measures of all the angles.

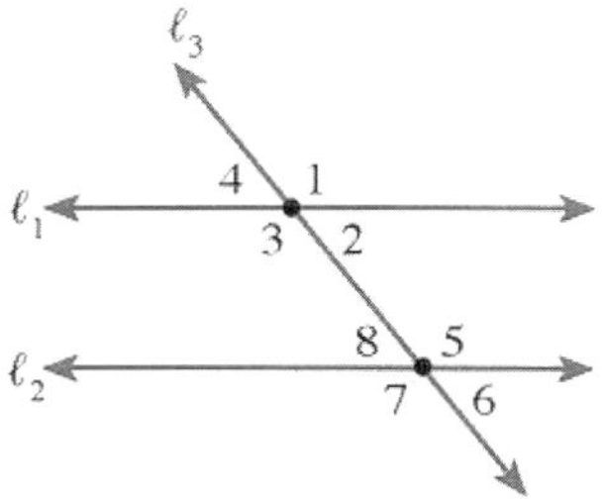

ℓ_1 is parallel to ℓ_2

[$m\angle 1 = m\angle 3 = m\angle 5 = m\angle 7$]

[$m\angle 2 = m\angle 4 = m\angle 6 = m\angle 8$]

a. Given $m\angle 2 = 65°$ [$m\angle 7 = 115°$]
b. Given $m\angle 1 = 153°$ [$m\angle 8 = 27°$]
c. Given $m\angle 5 = 120°$ [$m\angle 8 = 60°$]
d. Given $m\angle 3 = 163°$ [$m\angle 8 = 17°$]

3. Consider the angles in the accompanying figure. Classify the named angles as acute, right, straight, or obtuse.

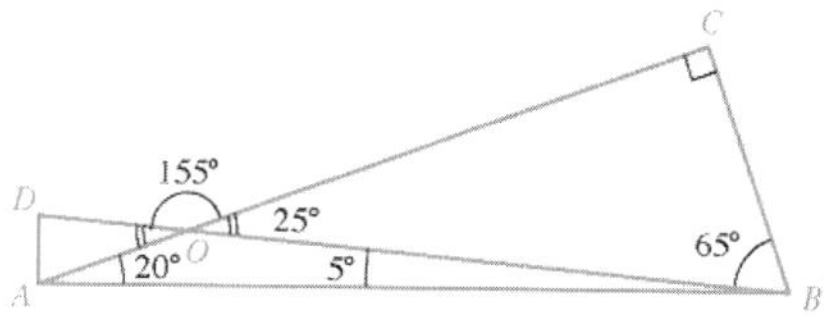

a. $\angle DOC$ [obtuse]
b. $\angle AOB$ [obtuse]
c. $\angle DBC$ [acute]
d. $\angle CAB$ [acute]
e. $\angle DOB$ [straight]
f. $\angle C$ [right]
g. $\angle COB$ [acute]
h. $\angle AOC$ [straight]
i. $\angle DOA$ [acute]
j. Name an angle congruent to $\angle DOB$.
[$\angle AOC$]

4. This problem anticipates a major result derived in the next section. Show that *the sum of the measures of the interior angles of any triangle is* 180°.

a. Draw three triangles, one with all acute angles, one with a right angle, and a third with an obtuse angle. A triangle with all acute angles is shown here:

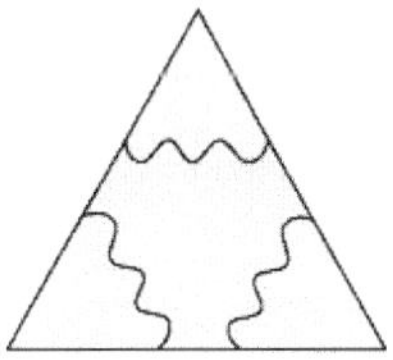

b. Tear apart the angles of each triangle you've drawn, and place them together to form a straight angle at the bottom, as shown here:

4.3 Triangles

1. Use algebra to find the value of x in each of the triangles. Notice that the measurement of the angle is not necessarily the same as the value of x.

a. $x = 20°$

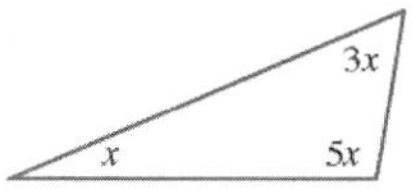

b. $x = 21°$

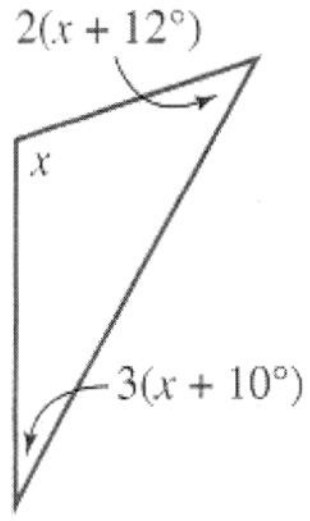

c. $x = 12.5°$

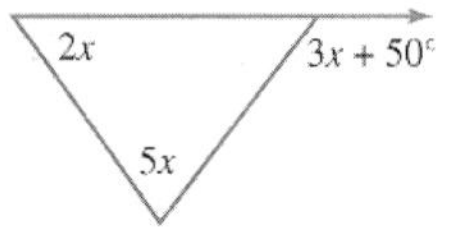

d. $x = 6°$

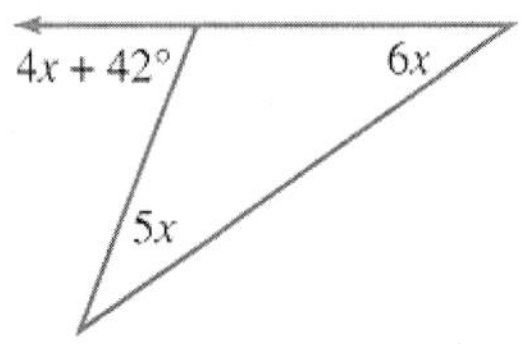

2. Find the numerical measures of the angles of the triangle whose angle measures are given.

a. x, x, x 60°, 60°, 60°

b. $x, x + 10°, x + 20°$ 50°, 60°, 70°

c. $x, 14° + 3x, 3(x + 25°)$ 13°, 53°, 114°

d. $x, 3x - 10°, 3(55° - x)$ 25°, 65°, 90°

3. Assume that the given angles have been measured, and calculate the angles (marked as x) that could not be found by direct measurement.

a. 50°

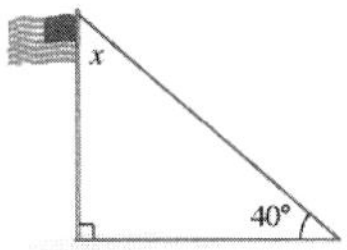

b. 120°

4. The legs of a picnic table form a triangle where $\overline{AC}$ and $\overline{BC}$ have the same length, as shown.

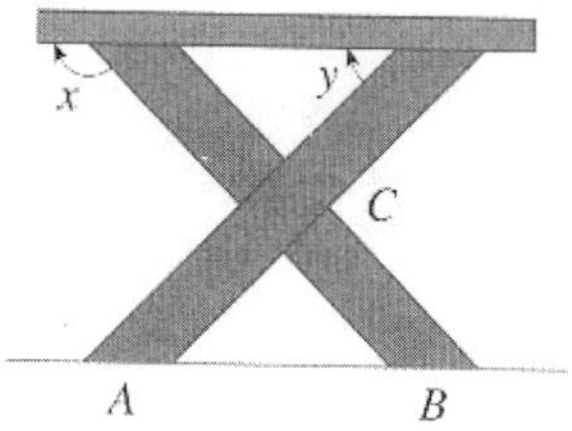

Picnic table

Find the measures of the angles x and y so that the top of the table will be parallel to the ground, given the following measurements.

a. $m\angle ACB = 90°$ $x = 135°; y = 45°$

b. $m\angle ACB = 85°$ $x = 132.5°; y = 47.5°$

c. $m\angle ACB = 92°$ $x = 136°; y = 44°$

4.4 Mathematics, Art, and Non-Euclidean Geometries

1. **Historical Quest** If the Parthenon in Greece is 60 ft tall (at the apex) and 97 ft wide, find the ratio of width to height and compare it with τ. $1.61\overline{6}$; close to τ

2. How closely does the ratio of the dimensions of a basketball court (36 ft by 78 ft) approximate τ?
2.17; not too close

3. Which of the figures (if any) are Saccheri quadrilaterals?

a. yes

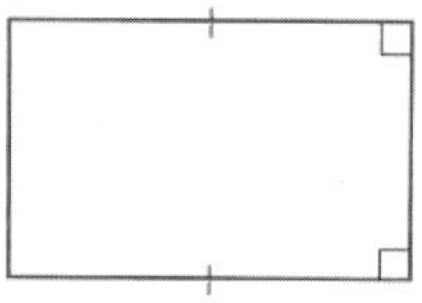

b. no

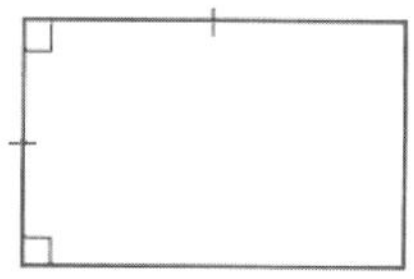

4. A plant grows for two months and then adds a new branch. Each new branch grows for two months, and then adds another branch. After the second month, each branch adds a new branch every month. Assume that the growth begins in January.

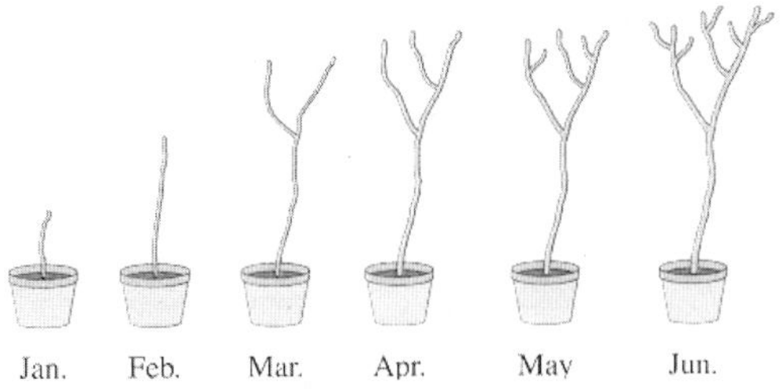

a. How many branches will there be in March? [2]

b. How many branches will there be in June? [8]

c. How many branches will there be after 12 months? [144]

d. Form a sequence of ratios of successive terms by considering the number of branches for the first 12 months. How do these numbers compare with τ?

[1, 2, 1.50, 1.67, 1.60, 1.63, 1.62, $\cdots$; close to τ]

4.5 Perimeter and Area

1. Find the perimeter, circumference, or distance around the figures by using the appropriate formula. Round approximate answers to the least accurate of the given measurements.

a. [18 in.]

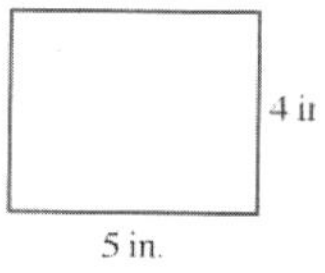

b. [9 dm]

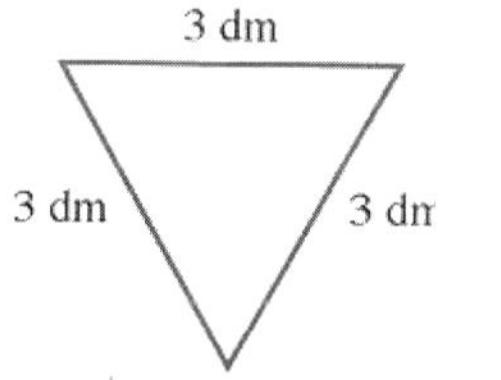

c. [15.08 m]

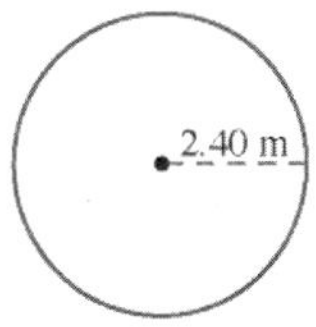

d. [397.0 ft]

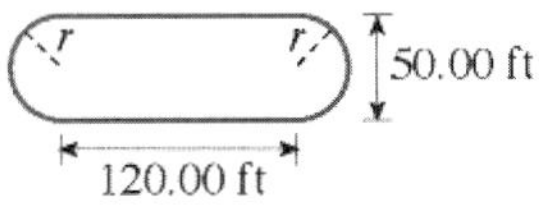

2. Find the area of each shaded region. (Assume that given measurements are exact, and round approximate answers to the nearest tenth of a square unit.)

a. [15 in.^{2}]

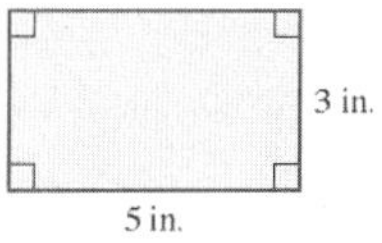

b. [7,560 ft^2]

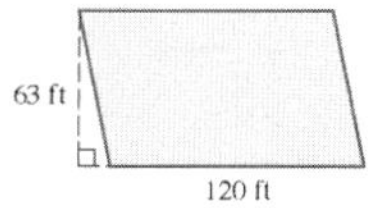

c. [5,550 cm^2]

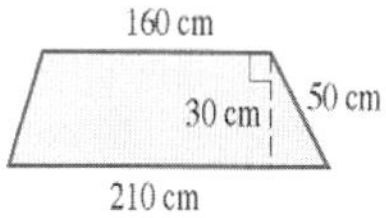

d. [7.6 cm^2]

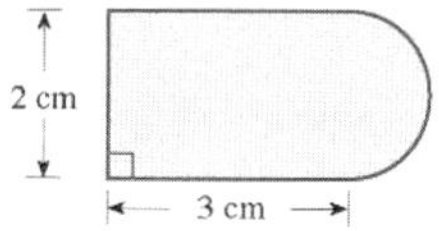

3. **Historical Quest** One of the first recorded units of measurement is the **cubit,** shown.

Musée du Louvre, by M. Chuzeville, Paris.

An ancient cubit, from the Louvre, Paris. The original measures 52.5 cm.

If we define a *cubit* as the distance from your elbow to your fingertips, then we may find that the cubit defined for your body is a little different from the Egyptian cubit on display at the Louvre. How does your cubit compare with this Egyptian cubit?

[Answers vary; probably smaller.]

4. What is the cost of seeding a rectangular lawn 100 ft by 30 ft if 1 pound of seed costs \$5.85 and covers 150 square feet? Use estimation to decide whether your answer is reasonable. [20 pounds; \$117]

4.6 Surface Area, Volume, and Capacity

1. Find the outside surface area. Note that some boxes have tops and others do not.

EXAMPLE 1 Find the outside surface area

Find the outside surface area.

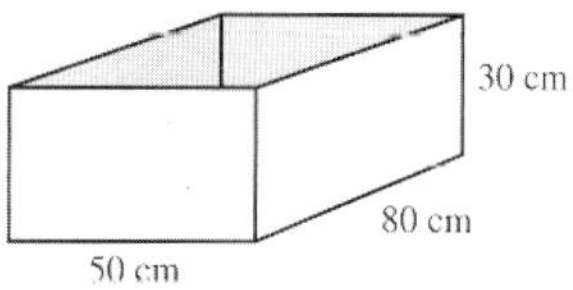

Solution

We find the sum of the areas of all the faces:

Front: $30 \times 50 = 1{,}500$
Back: 1,500 *Same as front*
Side: $80 \times 30 = 2{,}400$
Side: 2,400 *Sides are the same size.*
Bottom: $80 \times 50 = 4{,}000$
Total: $11{,}800 \text{ cm}^2$

a. $\boxed{3{,}125 \text{ cm}^2}$ **b.** $\boxed{780 \text{ cm}^2}$

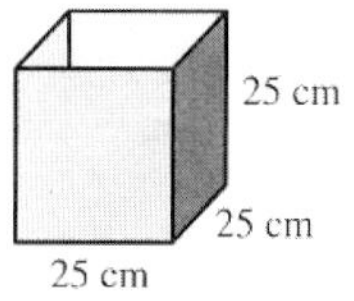

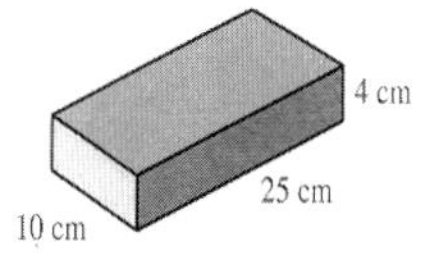

c. $\boxed{36\pi \text{ cm}^2}$

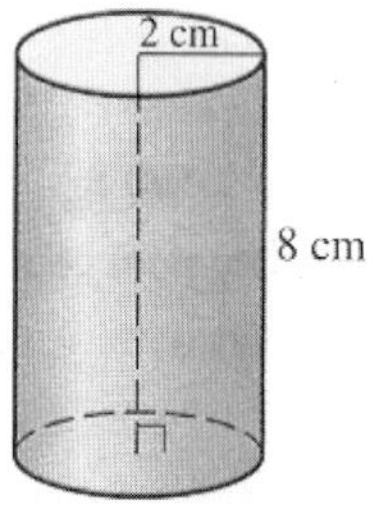

2. Find the volume of each solid.

a. $\boxed{125 \text{ ft}^3}$ **b.** $\boxed{8{,}000 \text{ cm}^3}$

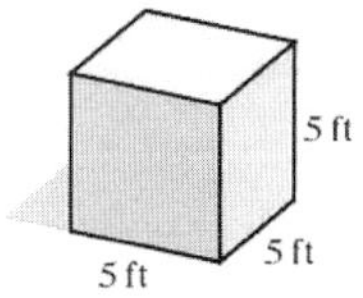

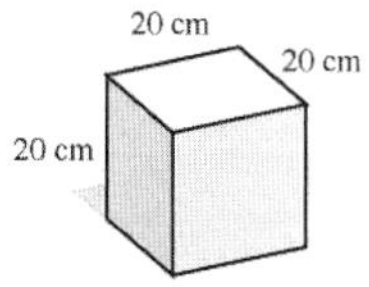

c. $\boxed{24 \text{ ft}^3}$ **d.** $\boxed{96{,}000 \text{ cm}^3}$

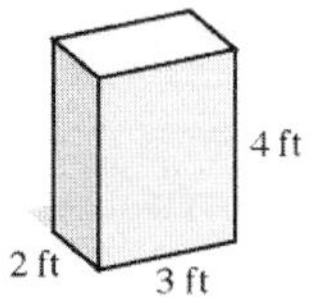

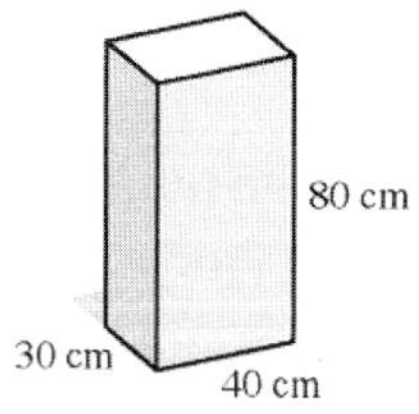

3. Measure each amount.

EXAMPLE 2 Measure the quantity of a liquid

Measure the amount of liquid in the measuring cup in Figure 4.1, both in the U.S. system and in the metric system.

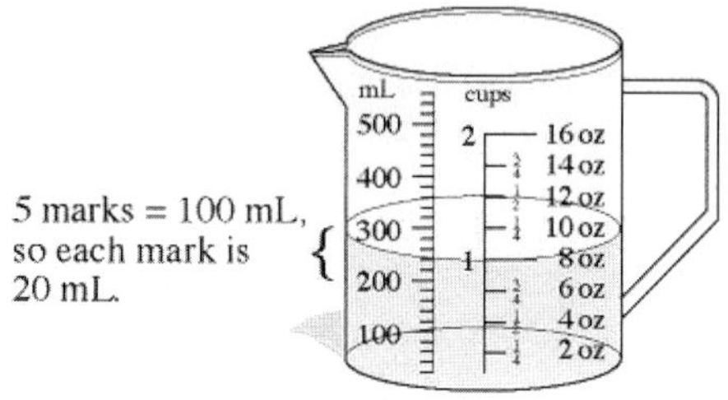

Figure 4.1 Standard measuring cup with both metric and U.S. measurements

Solution Metric: 240 mL U.S.: About 1 c or 8 oz □

a. Container A in cups $\boxed{2 \text{ c}}$
b. Container A in ounces $\boxed{16 \text{ oz}}$
c. Container B in ounces $\boxed{11 \text{ oz}}$
d. Container B in milliliters $\boxed{320 \text{ ml}}$

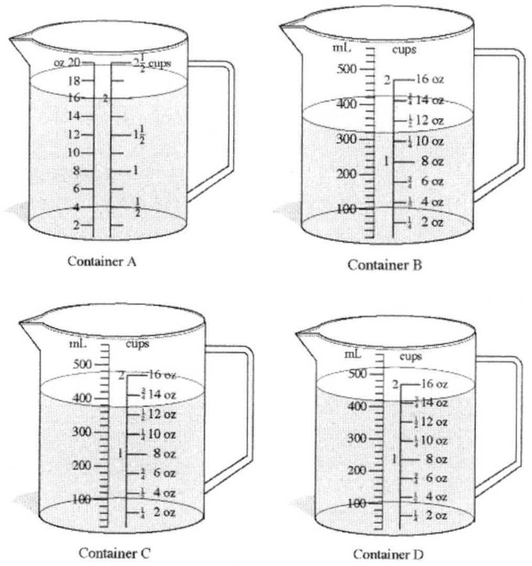

e. Container C in ounces $\boxed{13 \text{ oz}}$
f. Container C in milliliters $\boxed{380 \text{ ml}}$
g. Container D in cups $\boxed{1\frac{3}{4} \text{ c}}$
h. Container D in ounces $\boxed{14 \text{ oz}}$
i. Container D in milliliters $\boxed{420 \text{ ml}}$

4. The exterior dimensions of a refrigerator/freezer are shown.

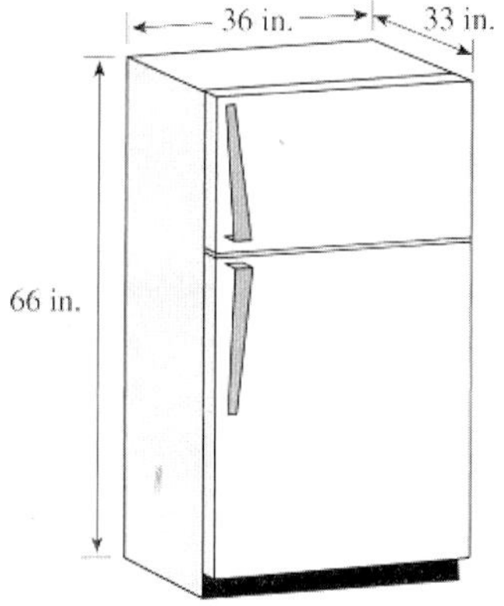

Refrigerator/freezer

a. How many cubic feet are contained within the refrigerator/freezer?
45.375 ft^3

b. If it is advertised as a 19-cu-ft refrigerator, how much space is taken up by the motor, insulation, and so on?
26.375 ft^3

5.1 Euler Circuits and Hamiltonian Cycles

1. Which of the networks are Euler circuits? If a network can be traversed, show how.

a.

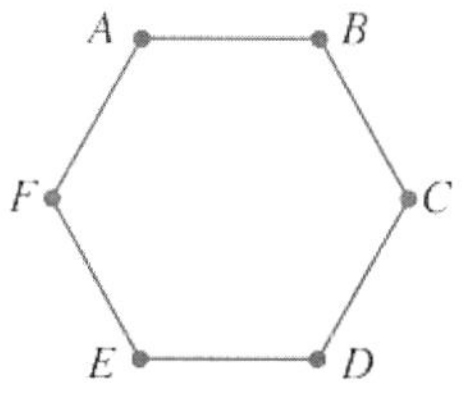

Euler circuit;
$A \to B \to C \to D$
$\to E \to F \to A$

b.

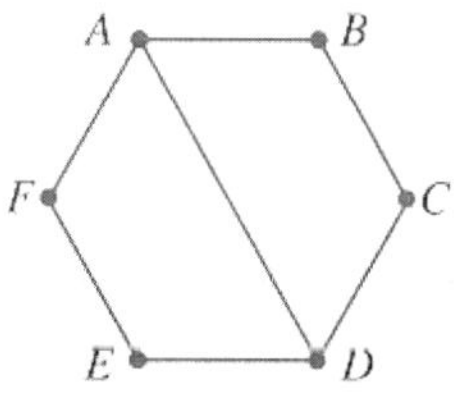

not an Euler circuit;
$A \to B \to C \to D$
$\to A \to F \to E \to D$

2. Which of the networks have Hamiltonian cycles? If a network has one, describe it.
All are Hamiltonian cycles.
Routes may vary; start and end at *A*.

a.

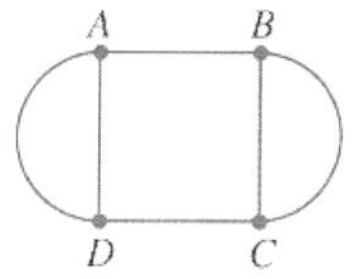

$A \to B \to C$
$\to D \to A$

b.

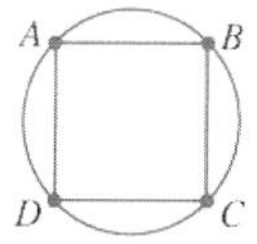

$A \to B \to C \to D \to A$

3. After Euler solved the Königsberg bridge problem, an eighth bridge was built as shown. Is this network traversable? If so, show how. yes; paths vary

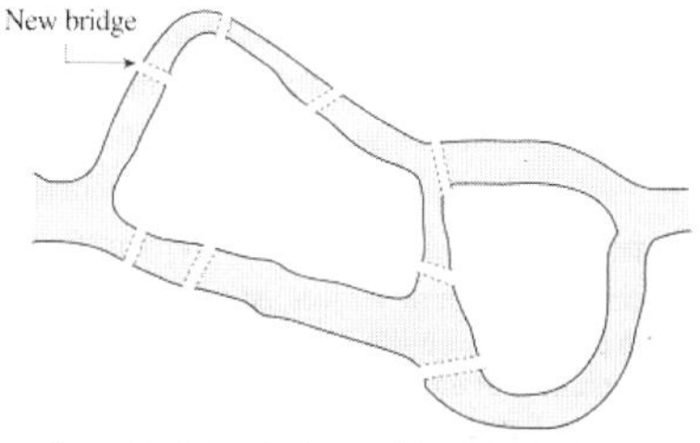

Königsberg with eight bridges

4. A saleswoman wants to visit eastern cities, New York City, Boston, Cleveland, and Washington, D.C. Driving distances are as shown. What is the shortest trip starting in New York that visits each of these cities?
1,493 mi

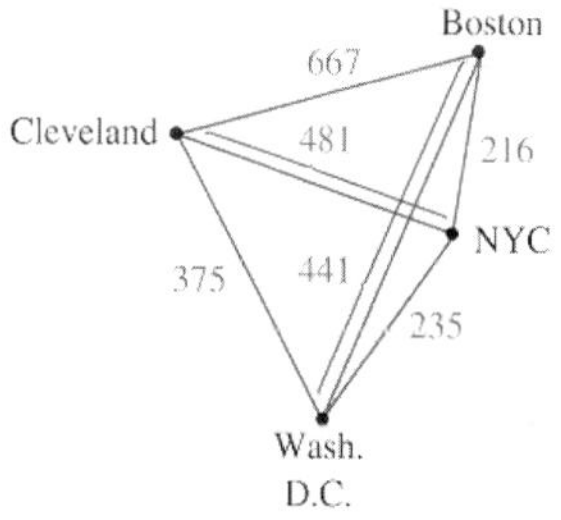

TSP for four cities

a. Find a solution using the brute-force method.

b. Find a solution, if possible, using the nearest-neighbor method.
NYC → Boston → D.C. → NYC; 892 mi

c. Find a solution, if possible, using the sorted-edge method.
NYC → Boston → D.C. →
Cleveland → NYC; 1,513 mi

5.2 Trees and Minimum Spanning Trees

1. Determine whether each of the graphs is a tree. If it is not, explain why.

a. not a tree

b. not a tree

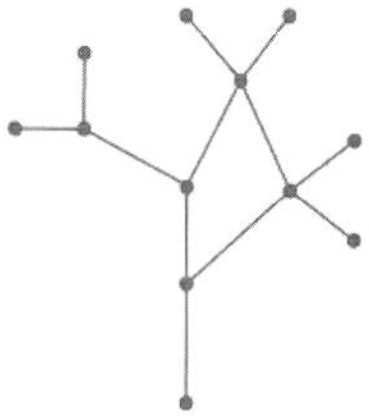

c. not a tree

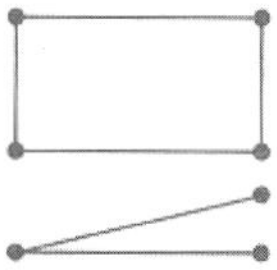

d. tree

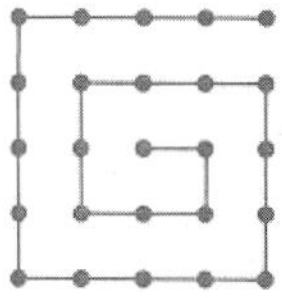

2. Find two different spanning trees for each graph.

a.

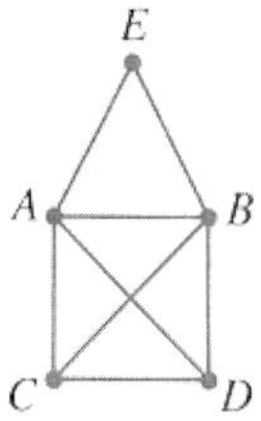

b.

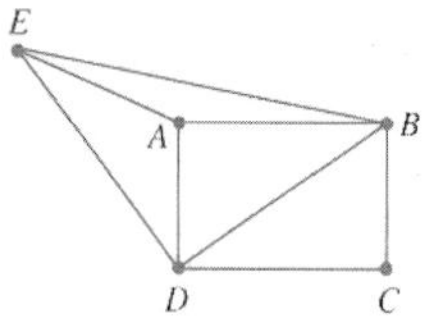

c.

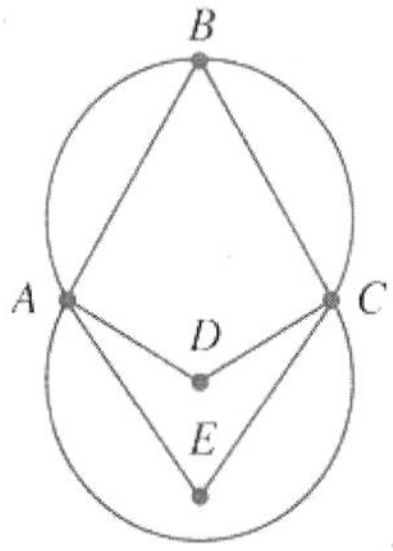

3. Find the minimum spanning tree for each of the graphs.

a. 60

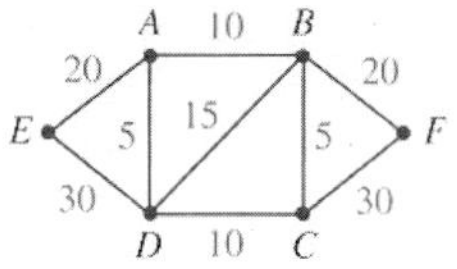

b. 65

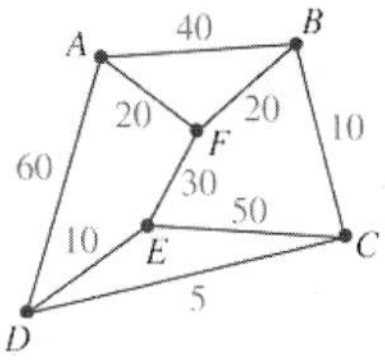

4. Suppose *XYZ* drilling has four oil wells that must be connected via pipelines to a storage tank. The cost of each pipeline (in millions of dollars) is shown in the following table:

From\To	#1	#2	#3	#4	Tank
#1	—	1	4	2	3
#2	1	—	3	1	2
#3	4	3	—	1	4
#4	2	1	1	—	1
Tank	3	2	4	1	—

a. Represent this information with a weighted graph.

b. Use Kruskal's algorithm to find a minimum spanning tree.

c. What is the minimum cost that links together all of the wells and the tank?
$4,000,000

5.3 Topology and Fractals

1. Group the figures into classes so that all the elements within each class are topologically equivalent, and no elements from different classes are topologically equivalent. Which are simple closed curves?
A and F; B and G; C and D
A and F are simple closed curves.

A.

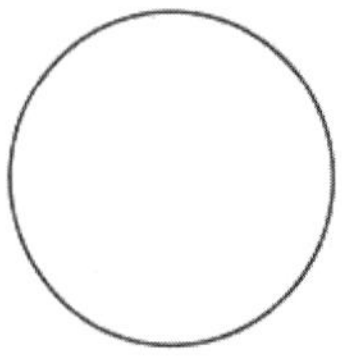

B.

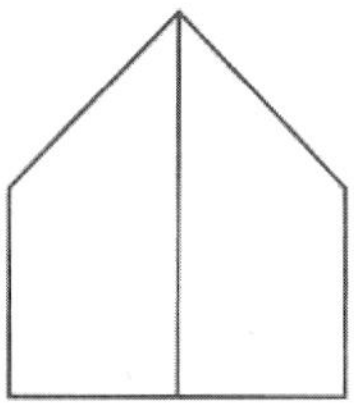

C.

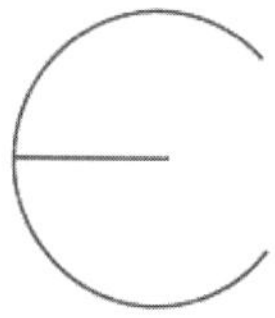

D.

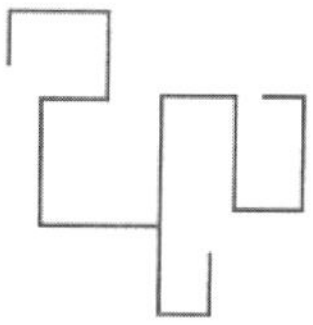

E.

F.

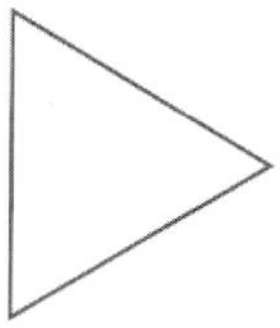

G.

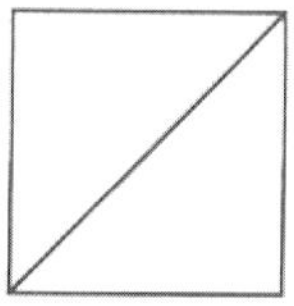

H.

2. One of the simplest map-coloring rules of topology involves a map of "countries" with straight lines as boundaries. How many colors would be necessary for the 4-corner area on a U.S. map? Note that a common point is not considered a common boundary. $\boxed{\text{two colors}}$

How many colors are needed for the 4-corners area?

3. Construct a fractal curve by forming squares (rather than triangles as shown in the text). The first step is shown here.

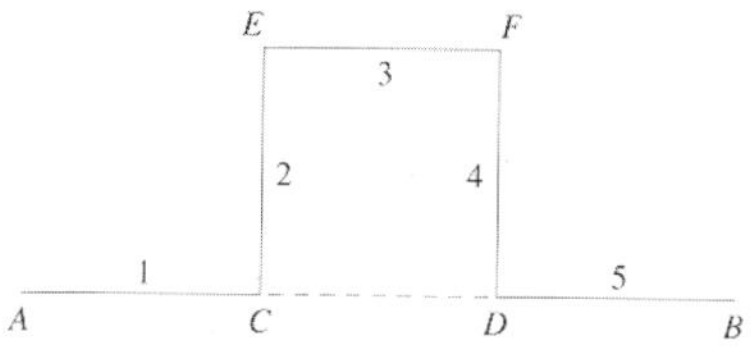

4. **IN YOUR OWN WORDS** Construct a tessellation using triangles.

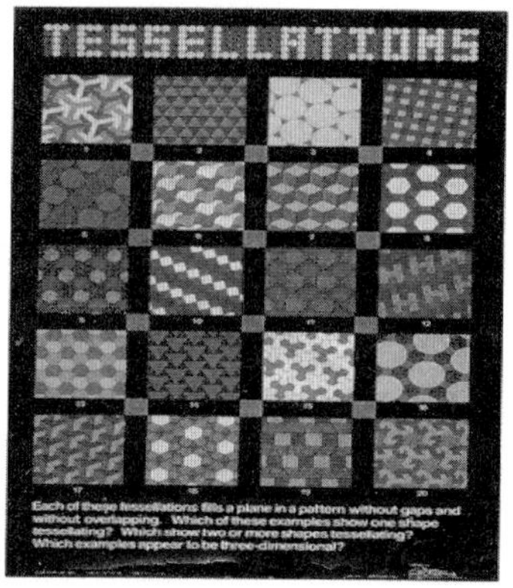

Dale Seymour Publications

6.1 Exponential Equations

1. Solve each exponential equation. Give the exact value for x.
   a. $4^x = \frac{1}{16}$ $\boxed{-2}$ **b.** $5^x = 8$ $\boxed{\log_5 8}$
   c. $216^x = 36$ $\boxed{\frac{2}{3}}$ **d.** $10^x = 2.5$ $\boxed{\log 2.5}$
2. Evaluate the given expressions (to two decimal places).
   a. $\log 4.27$ $\boxed{0.63}$ **b.** $\log_b b^2$ $\boxed{2.00}$
   c. $\ln 10$ $\boxed{2.30}$ **d.** $\log 0.321$ $\boxed{-1.14}$
3. **a.** Write $\log_3 45$ in terms of common logarithms, and then give a calculator approximation (correct to four decimal places). $\boxed{\frac{\log 45}{\log 3} \approx 3.4650}$
   b. Write $\log_2 0.0056$ in terms of natural logarithms, and then give a calculator approximation (correct to four decimal places). $\boxed{\frac{\ln 0.0056}{\ln 2} \approx -7.4804}$
   b. $\log_{8.3} 105$ $\boxed{\frac{\ln 105}{\ln 8.3} \approx 2.1991}$
4. Solve the exponential equations. Show the approximation you obtain with your calculator without rounding.
   a. $8^x = 3$ $\boxed{0.528320834}$
   b. $10^x = 0.0234$ $\boxed{-1.630784143}$

c. $e^{-x} = 8$ $\boxed{-2.07944154168}$
d. $10^{5-3x} = 0.041$ $\boxed{2.129072048}$

6.2 Logarithmic Equations

1. Find a simplified value for x by inspection. Do not use a calculator.
   a. $e^{\ln 23}$ $\boxed{23}$ **b.** $10^{\log 3.4}$ $\boxed{3.4}$
   c. $\log 10^{4.2}$ $\boxed{4.2}$ **d.** $\ln e^3$ $\boxed{3}$
   e. $\log_5 25 = x$ $\boxed{2}$ **f.** $\ln x = 3$ $\boxed{e^3}$
2. Solve the equations by finding the exact solution.
   a. $\frac{1}{2}\log x - \log 100 = 2$ $\boxed{10^8}$
   b. $\frac{1}{2}\log_b x = 3\log_b 5 - \log_b x$ $\boxed{25}$
   c. $\ln e = \ln\frac{\sqrt{2}}{x} - \ln e$ $\boxed{\sqrt{2}/e^2}$
   d. $\log 2 = \frac{1}{4}\log 16 - x$ $\boxed{0}$
3. The "forgetting curve" for memorizing nonsense syllables is given by

$$R = 80 - 27\ln t \quad (t \geq 1)$$

   where R is the percentage who remember the syllables after t seconds.
   a. In how many seconds would only 10% ($R = 10$) of the students remember? $\boxed{13 \text{ sec}}$
   b. Solve for t. $\boxed{t = e^{(80-R)/27}}$
4. Prove the multiplicative law of logarithms using the multiplicative law of exponents. That is, prove

$$\log_b A^p = p\log_b A$$

6.3 Applications of Growth and Decay

1. Figure 6.1 uses a growth rate of AIDS-related deaths and uses this information to predict the cumulative number of AIDS-related deaths at the end of January 2002. Repeat this example for the number of deaths at the turn of the century, January 2001.
   $\boxed{896{,}716}$
2. Tests of an artifact discovered at the Debert site in Nova Scotia show that 28% of the original ^{14}C is still present. What is the probable age of the artifact? $\boxed{10{,}500 \text{ yr}}$
3. A satellite has an initial radioisotope power supply of 50 watts (W). The power output in watts is given by

$$P = 50e^{-t/250}$$

   where t is the time in days. Solve for t to find the time when the power supply is 30 W. $\boxed{128 \text{ days}}$
4. In 1986, it was determined that the *Challenger* disaster was caused by failure of the primary O-rings. Linda Tappin gives a formula in "Analyzing Data Relating to the *Challenger* Disaster" (*The Mathematics Teacher*, Vol. 87, No. 6, Sept. 1994, pp. 423-426) that relates the temperature x (in degrees Fahrenheit) around the O-rings and the expected number y of eroded or leaky primary O-rings:

$$y = \frac{6e^{5.085-0.1156x}}{1 + e^{5.085-0.1156x}}$$

   a. What is the predicted number of eroded or leaky O-rings at a temperature of 75°F? $\boxed{\text{no failures}}$
   b. What is the predicted number of eroded or leaky O-rings at a temperature of 32°F? $\boxed{5 \text{ failures}}$

7.1 It's Simple

1 Suppose you see a car advertised with a price of $32,450 and payments of $627.35 per month for 5 years. What is the amount of interest paid? $\boxed{\$5{,}191}$
2. Theron wants to save $3,900. If he has $3,000 and invests it at 5% simple interest, how long will it take him to obtain $3,900? $\boxed{6 \text{ years}}$

3. What is the future value of $890 invested at 6% simple interest for 83 days? $902.31
4. If Cole wants to retire with $1,000 per month, how much principal is necessary to generate this amount of monthly interest income if the interest rate is 6%? $200,000

7.2 Buying on Credit

In Problems 1-2, round your answer to the nearest tenth of a percent.

1. A newspaper advertisement offers a $9,000 car for nothing down and 36 easy monthly payments of $317.50. What is the APR?
17.5% (0.1751351351)
2. A car dealer will sell you the $16,450 car of your dreams for $3,290 down and payments of $339.97 per month for 48 months. What is the APR?
11.8% (0.1175569754)
3. A car dealer carries out the following calculations:

List price	$5,368.00
Options	$1,625.00
Destination charges	$ 200.00
Subtotal	$7,193.00
Tax	$ 431.58
Less trade-in	$2,932.00
Amount to be financed	$4,692.58
8% interest; 48 months	$1,501.63
MONTHLY PAYMENT	$ 129.05

What is the annual percentage rate? Round to the nearest tenth percent.
8% add-on rate; APR is about 15.7%

7.3 Credit Card Interest

1. Calculate the monthly finance charge for each credit card transaction. Assume that it takes 10 days for a payment to be received and recorded and that the month is 30 days long.

	Balance	*Rate*	*Payment*	*Method*
a.	$300	18%	$50	Previous balance
	$4.50			
b.	$300	18%	$50	Average daily balance
	$3.95			
c.	$300	18%	$250	Adjusted balance
	$0.75			
d.	$500	20%	$50	Previous balance
	$8.33			

2 Most credit cards provide for a minimum finance charge of 50¢ per month. Suppose that you buy a $30 item, make five monthly payments of $5, and then pay the remaining balance. What are the payments and the total interest for this purchase if the interest rate is 12% but you pay the minimum finance charge?
5 payments of $5 plus a last payment of $7.50;
total payments of $32.50 with interest of $2.50

3. Suppose you have a $1,000 charge on a credit card charging 1.5% monthly interest using the adjusted balance method. The minimum payment due in May is $30. How much will you save in interest charges in June by paying $60 instead?
You will save $0.45.

7.4 Compound Interest

1. Find the future value, using the future value formula and a calculator
   - **a.** $35 at 17.65% compounded annually for 20 years $903.46
   - **b.** $835 at 3.5% compounded semiannually for 6 years $1,028.25
   - **c.** $575 at 5.5% compounded quarterly for 5 years $755.59
   - **d.** $89,500 at 6.2% compounded monthly for 30 years $572,177.99
   - **e.** $355,000 at 9.5% compounded daily for 30 years $6,134,855.57

2. How much would you have in 5 years if you purchased a \$1,000 5-year savings certificate that paid 4% compounded quarterly? $\boxed{\$1{,}220.19}$
3. Find the cost of the monthly rent for a two-bedroom apartment in 30 years, assuming an annual inflation rate of 4%, if the current rent is \$650. $\boxed{\$2{,}108.21}$
4. Suppose that an insurance agent offers you a policy that will provide you with a yearly income of \$50,000 in 30 years. What is the comparable annual salary today, assuming an inflation rate of 6%? $\boxed{\$8{,}705.51}$

7.5 Buying a Home

1. Determine the down payment and the amount to be financed for each home described.

EXAMPLE 1 Down payment

What is the down payment for a home costing \$148,500 requiring 5% down?

Solution
DOWN PAYMENT:
\$148,500 × 0.05 = \$7,425 □

   a. \$169,900; 20% down $\boxed{\$33{,}980}$
   b. \$250,250; 10% down $\boxed{\$25{,}025}$
   c. \$950,000; 20% down $\boxed{\$190{,}000}$

2. What are the bank charges for the points?

EXAMPLE 2 Points

\$53,200; 3 points
Solution \$53,200 × 0.03 = \$1,596 □

   a. \$85,000; $\frac{1}{2}$ point $\boxed{\$425}$
   b. \$64,350; 5 points $\boxed{\$3{,}217.50}$
   c. \$112,000; $\frac{3}{4}$ point $\boxed{\$840}$

3. Determine the comparable interest rate (to two decimal places) for a \$50,000 loan when the quoted information is given.
   a. 11.5% + 2 pts + \$450 $\boxed{11.86\%}$
   b. 9.3% + $\frac{3}{4}$ pt + \$150 $\boxed{9.43\%}$
4. Use Table 7.1 to estimate the monthly payment for each loan.
   a. \$48,500; 30 years; 6% $\boxed{\$291.00}$
   b. \$112,000; 30 years; 7% $\boxed{\$744.80}$
5. Suppose that you want to purchase a home for \$375,000, with a 30-year mortgage at 7% interest. Suppose that you can put 20% down.
   a. What is the amount of the down payment? $\boxed{\$75{,}000}$
   b. What is the amount to be financed? $\boxed{\$300{,}000}$
   c. What are the monthly payments? $\boxed{\$1{,}995.00}$
   d. What is the total amount of interest paid on the 30-year loan? $\boxed{\$418{,}200}$
   e. What is the necessary monthly income for you to be able to afford this home? $\boxed{\$5{,}541.67}$

8.1 Introduction to Sets

1. Consider the sets
   $A = \{\text{distinct letters in the word } pipe\}$
   $B = \{4\}$
   $C = \{p, i, e\}$
   $D = \{2 + 1\}$
   $E = \{\text{three}\}$
   $F = \{3\}$
   a. What is the cardinality of each set?
   $\boxed{|A| = 3;\ |B| = 1;\ |C| = 3;\ |D| = 1;\ |E| = 1;\ |F| = 1}$
   b. Which of the sets can be placed into a one-to-one correspondence?
   $\boxed{A \leftrightarrow C;\ B \leftrightarrow D \leftrightarrow E \leftrightarrow F}$
   c. Which of the given sets are equal?
   $\boxed{A = C;\ D = E = F}$
2. List the set of rational numbers between 0 and 1 by roster. List the elements systematically, and do not list elements that have been previously listed.
   $\boxed{\left\{\frac{1}{2}, \frac{1}{3}, \frac{2}{3}, \frac{1}{4}, \frac{3}{4}, \frac{1}{5}, \frac{2}{5}, \frac{3}{5}, \frac{4}{5}, \frac{1}{6}, \frac{5}{6}, \frac{1}{7}, \cdots\right\}}$

3. **IN YOUR OWN WORDS** Show that the following sets have the same cardinality, by placing the elements into a one-to-one correspondence. $\{1, 2, 3, 4, \cdots, 999, 1000\}$ and $\{7964, 7965, 7966, 7967, \cdots, 8962, 8963\}$.
4. Classify the sets as finite or infinite.
   - **a.** The set of shoes in my closet finite
   - **b.** The number of married people in the world finite
   - **c.** The set of stars in the Milky Way finite
   - **d.** The set of drops of water in all the oceans on earth finite

8.2 Set Relationships

1. List all subsets of $\{m, y\}$. $\emptyset$, $\{m\}$, $\{y\}$, $\{m, y\}$
2. Draw a Venn diagram showing male and female where the universe is the set of all people.
3. Draw a Venn diagram showing people wearing blue and those wearing black.
4. Draw a Venn diagram showing that all ducks are birds.
5. Draw a Venn diagram showing people who are over 30, people who are 30 or under, and people who drive a car.

8.3 Operations with Sets

1. **a.** Draw a Venn diagram for union. See Figure 8.5.
   b. Draw a Venn diagram for intersection. See Figure 8.6.
   c. Draw a Venn diagram for complement. See Figure 8.7.
2. Let $U = \{1, 2, 3, 4, 5, 6, 7\}$; $A = \{1, 2, 3, 4\}$; $B = \{1, 2, 5, 6\}$; and $C = \{3, 5, 7\}$. List all members of each of the sets.
   - **a.** $A \cup B$ $\{1, 2, 3, 4, 5, 6\}$
   - **b.** $B \cup C$ $\{1, 2, 3, 5, 6, 7\}$
   - **c.** $A \cap C$ $\{3\}$
   - **d.** $\overline{A}$ $\{5, 6, 7\}$

3. One question in a survey of 450 members of a club asked the following:

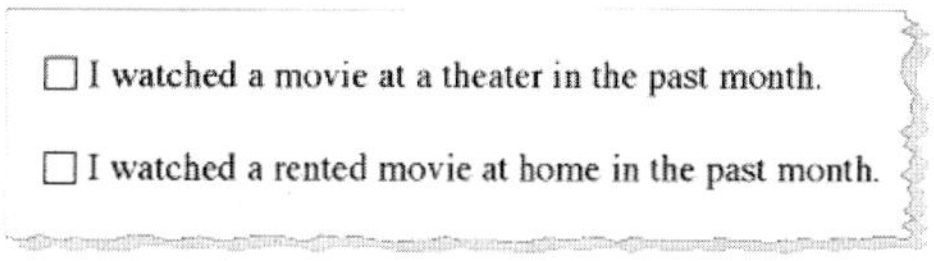
☐ I watched a movie at a theater in the past month.

☐ I watched a rented movie at home in the past month.

   - **a.** If 135 respondents checked the first box, what percent of the respondents watched a movie at a theater in the past month? 30%
   - **b.** If 72 checked both boxes, what percent of the respondents watched movies both in a theater and at home? 16%
4. A glazed doughnut contains 235 calories and a slice of apple pie contains 405 calories. Use the given table to list all possible sets of exercises (with no exercise combinations) that will burn off the calories

Exercise	Calories/hr
Sitting	75
Walking	150
Golfing	300
Biking	420
Jogging	500

   - **a.** Two doughnuts and one hour of exercise jogging
   - **b.** One hour of exercise and a slice of apple pie (405 calories). biking; jogging

8.4 Venn Diagrams

1. Use set notation to identify the shaded portion of the following Venn diagrams.
   a. $A \cap B$

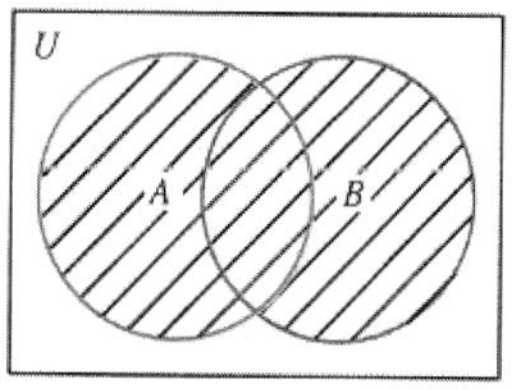

b. $\boxed{\overline{A}}$

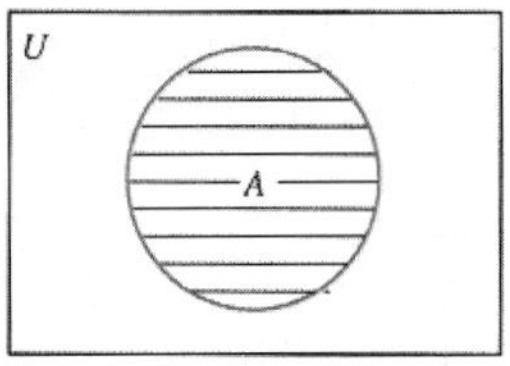

c. $\boxed{A \cup B}$

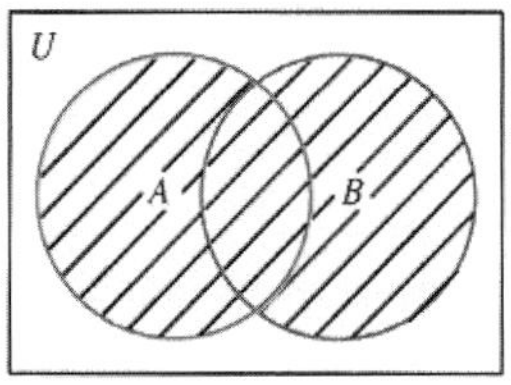

2. **a.** Write in symbols: the complement of the union of sets A and B. Draw a Venn diagram. $\boxed{\overline{A \cup B}}$
   b. Write in symbols: the union of the complements of sets A and B. Draw a Venn diagram. $\boxed{\overline{A} \cup \overline{B}}$
3. Let
   $U = \{1, 2, 3, 4, 5, 6, 7, 8, 9, 10\}$
   $A = \{2, 4, 6, 8\}$
   $B = \{5, 9\}$
   $C = \{2, 5, 8, 9, 10\}$
   List all the members of each set.
   a. $(A \cup B) \cup C$ $\boxed{\{2, 4, 5, 6, 8, 9, 10\}}$
   b. $\overline{A} \cap (B \cup C)$ $\boxed{\{5, 9, 10\}}$
   c. $\overline{A \cap B} \cup C$
   $\boxed{U \text{ or } \{1, 2, 3, 4, 5, 6, 7, 8, 9, 10\}}$
   d. $\overline{A \cup (B \cap C)}$ $\boxed{\{1, 3, 7, 10\}}$
4. Use Venn diagrams to prove De Morgan's law: $\overline{X \cap Y} = \overline{X} \cup \overline{Y}$ $\boxed{\text{T}}$

8.5 Survey Problems Using Sets

1. Give the numbers of elements in the regions marked I, II, III, and IV in Figure 8.11.
   $|U| = 25, |A| = 6, |B| = 14, |A \cap B| = 2$
   $\boxed{\text{I: 7; II: 4; III: 2; IV: 12}}$
2. Give the numbers of elements in the regions marked I, II, III, IV, V, VI, VII, and VIII in Figure 8.12.

EXAMPLE 1 Number of elements

$|U| = 25, |A| = 10, |B| = 8, |C| = 12,$
$|A \cap B| = 4, |A \cap C| = 3, |B \cap C| = 2,$
$|A \cap B \cap C| = 1$

Solution

Start by filling in 24 in Region III; that is, start with the intersection.
Next, fill in Region II by noting $|A| = 42$, and 24 of these are accounted for in Region III, so fill $42 - 24 = 18$ in Region II.
Similarly, since $|B| = 46$; fill in $46 - 24 = 22$ in Region IV.
Add together the number in Regions II, III, and IV: $18 + 24 + 22 = 64$, so region I has $74 - 64 = 10$.
The answer is: I: 10; II: 18; III: 24; IV: 22. □

$|U| = 100, |A| = 45, |B| = 20, |C| = 36,$
$|A \cap B| = 2, |A \cap C| = 2, |B \cap C| = 8,$
$|A \cap B \cap C| = 2$
$\boxed{\text{I: 43; II: 12; III: 28; IV: 0; V: 0; VI: 6; VII: 2; VIII: 9}}$

3. Human blood is typed Rh^+ (positive blood) or Rh^- (negative blood). This Rh factor is called an *antigen*. There are two other antigens known as A and B types. Blood lacking both A and B types is called type O. Sketch a Venn diagram showing the three types of antigens, A, B, and Rh, and label each of the eight regions. For example, O^+ is inside the Rh set (anything in Rh is positive), but outside both A and B. On the other hand, O^- is that region outside all three circles.
4. In a recent survey of 100 women, the following information was gathered:
   59 use shampoo A.
   51 use shampoo B.
   35 use shampoo C.

24 use shampoos A and B.
19 use shampoos A and C.
13 use shampoos B and C.
11 use all three.

Use Figure 8.12 (with Regions I to VIII) to answer the questions.

a. Name the three sets (A, B, and C) in this survey problem.
$A = \{$women who use shampoo A$\}$;
$B = \{$women who use shampoo B$\}$;
$C = \{$women who use shampoo C$\}$

b. How many are using shampoos A and C, but not B (Region IV)? 8

c. How many are using shampoos B and C, but not A (Region VI)? 2

d. How many are using shampoo B only (Region II)? 25

e. How many are not using any of the three listed shampoos (Region VIII)? 0

8.6 Inductive and Deductive Reasoning

Use Venn diagrams to check the validity of the arguments in Problems 1-3.

1.. All mathematicians are eccentrics.
All eccentrics are rich.
Therefore, all mathematicians are rich. valid

2. Some women are tall.
No men are strong.
Therefore, some tall people are not strong.
Set of men is the complement of the set of women; not valid

3. All red hair is pretty.
No pretty things are valuable.
Therefore, no red hair is valuable. valid

4. Does the news story illustrate inductive or deductive reasoning?
Explain your answer.
Deductive reasoning; explanations vary.

> The young man in charge of the checkroom in a fancy restaurant was known for his memory. He never used the usual markers to identify the hats and coats. One day a guest decided to put him to a test, and said to the clerk, "How do you know this is my hat?" "I don't," was the response. "But why did you return it to me?" asked the guest. "Because," said the clerk, "it's the one you gave to me."

9.1 Permutations

1. Evaluate each expression.
a. ${}_9P_1$ 9 **b.** ${}_{52}P_3$ 132,600
c. ${}_{92}P_0$ 1 **d.** ${}_gP_h$ $\dfrac{g!}{(g-h)!}$

2. How many permutations are there of the word MISSISSIPPI? 34,650

3. In how many ways can a president, a vice president, and a secretary be elected from a group of 10 people? 720

4. A DNA molecule is shown here.

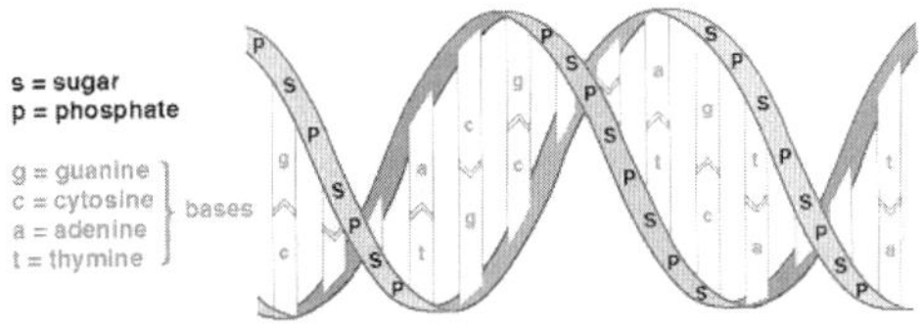

anthro.palomar.edu/biobasis/bio_5.htm

A nucleotide is represented by one of the letters $\{a, t, c, g\}$. A *codon* is defined to be a triplet of nucleotides. The order of the nucleotides in a codon is significant, and the nucleotides can be repeated. These codons are important in determining how DNA is transformed into protein. How many different codons are possible? 64

9.2 Combinations

1. Evaluate each expression.
a. $\binom{9}{1}$ 9 **b.** $\binom{52}{3}$ 22,100
c. $\binom{4}{4}$ 1 **d.** $\binom{g}{h}$ $\frac{g!}{h!(g-h)!}$
e. $\binom{10}{4, 3, 3}$ 4,200

2. A bag contains 12 pieces of candy. In how many ways can five pieces be selected? $\boxed{792}$
3. If a family has five children, in how many ways could the parents have two boys and three girls? $\boxed{10}$
4. Prove: $\binom{n}{r} = \binom{n}{n-r}$

9.3 Counting Without Counting

1. How many skirt-blouse outfits can a woman wear if she has three skirts and five blouses? $\boxed{15}$

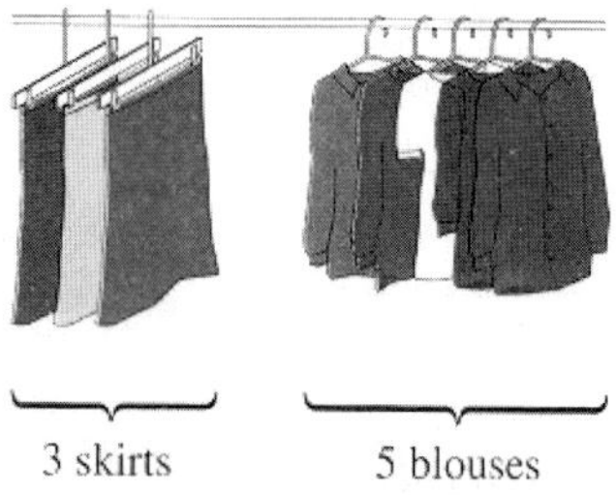

2. Many states offer personalized license plates. The state of California, for example, allows personalized plates with seven spaces for numerals or letters, or one of the following four symbols:

What is the total number of license plates possible using this counting scheme? (Assume that each available space is occupied by a numeral, letter, symbol, or space.) $\boxed{1.95 \times 10^{11}}$

3. The News Clip below presents an argument proving that at least two New Yorkers must have *exactly* the same number of hairs on their heads! For this problem, just *suppose* you knew the number of hairs on your head, as well as the *exact* number of hairs on anyone else's head. Now multiply the number of hairs on your head by the number of hairs on your neighbor's head. Take this result and multiply by the number of hairs on the heads of each person in your town or city. Continue this process until you have done this for everyone in the entire world! Make a guess (you can use scientific notation, if you like) about the size of this answer. (*Hint*: The author has worked this out and claims to know the exact answer.) $\boxed{0}$

> An example about reaching a conclusion about the number of objects in a set is given by M. Cohen and E. Nagel in *An Introduction to Logic*. They conclude that there are at least two people in New York City who have the same number of hairs on their heads. This conclusion was reached not through counting the hairs on the heads of 8 million inhabitants of the city, but through studies revealing that: (1) the maximum number of hairs on the human scalp could never be as many as 5,000 per square centimeter, and (2) the maximum area of the human scalp could never reach 1,000 square centimeters. We can now conclude that no human head could contain even
> $$5{,}000 \times 1{,}000 = 5{,}000{,}000$$
> hairs. Since this number is less than the population of New York City, it follows that at least two New Yorkers must have the same number of hairs on their heads!

9.4 Rubik's Cube and Instant Insanity

1. Determine whether each of the figures will be a solution to an Instant Insanity puzzle.

a. $\boxed{\text{yes}}$

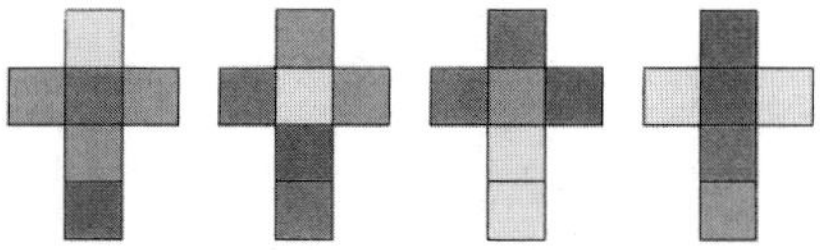

b. $\boxed{\text{no}}$

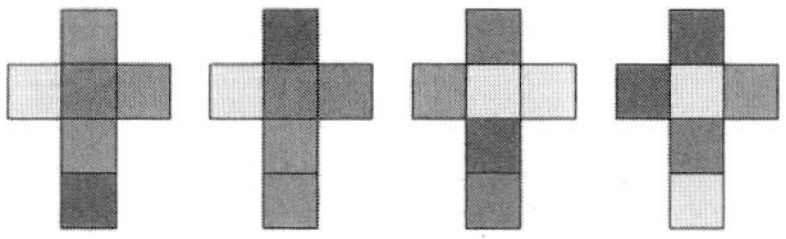

c. $\boxed{\text{no}}$

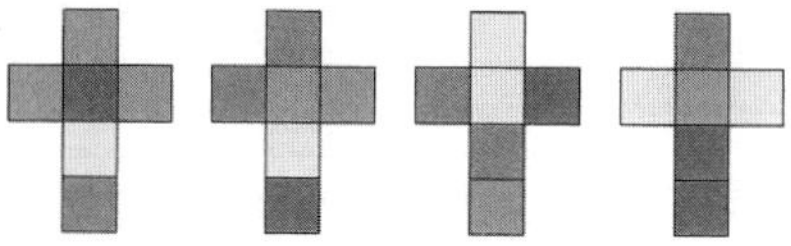

2. Name the move or moves that will return the Rubik's cube to standard position after making the move shown.

a. U $\boxed{U^{-1}}$ **b.** B^3 $\boxed{B \text{ or } (B^{-1})^3}$

c. BU $\boxed{U^{-1}B^{-1}}$ **d.** $F^{-1}B^{-1}$ $\boxed{BF}$

3. Are three consecutive moves M_1, M_2, and M_3 on Rubik's cube associative; that is
$$M_1(M_2M_3) = (M_2M_1)M_3? \quad \boxed{\text{no}}$$
4. Find the number of *different* arrangements for the Instant Insanity blocks. $\boxed{41{,}472}$

10.1 It's Not Certain

1. Find the probability using the given spinners. Assume that the pointer can never lie on a border line.

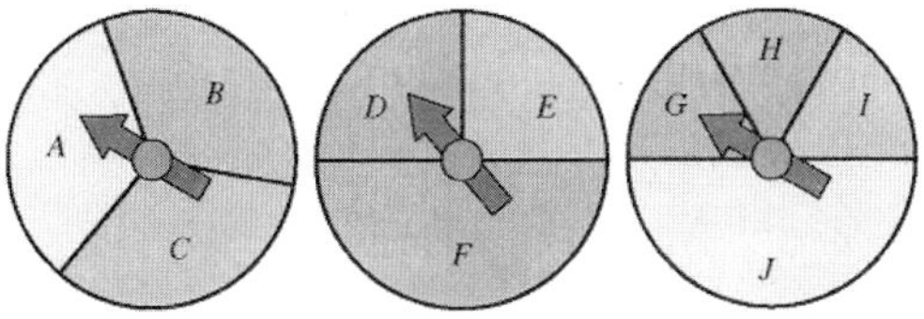

a. P(A) $\boxed{\frac{1}{3}}$ **b.** $P(B)$ $\boxed{\frac{1}{3}}$ **c.** $P(C)$ $\boxed{\frac{1}{3}}$
d. $P(D)$ $\boxed{\frac{1}{4}}$ **e.** $P(E)$ $\boxed{\frac{1}{4}}$ **f.** $P(F)$ $\boxed{\frac{1}{2}}$
g. $P(G)$ $\boxed{\frac{1}{6}}$ **h.** $P(H)$ $\boxed{\frac{1}{6}}$ **i.** $P(J)$ $\boxed{\frac{1}{2}}$

2. Consider the jar containing marbles as shown.

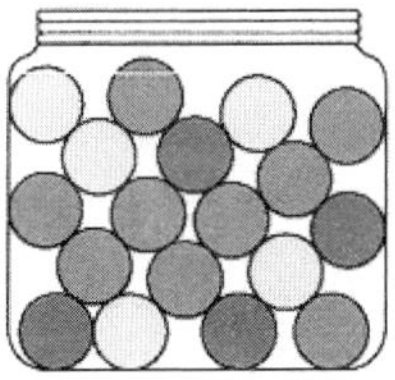

Find the probabilities of picking each color; assume that each marble has an equal chance of being picked from the jar.
a. P(yellow) $\boxed{\frac{5}{18}}$ **b.** P(blue) $\boxed{\frac{2}{9}}$
c. P(green) $\boxed{\frac{1}{2}}$ **d.** P(black) $\boxed{0}$

3. *Dice* is a popular game in gambling casinos. Two dice are tossed, and various amounts are paid according to the outcome.
   a. If a seven or eleven occurs on the first roll, the player wins. What is the probability of winning on the first roll? $\boxed{\frac{2}{9}}$
   b. The player loses if the outcome of the first roll is a two, three, or twelve. What is the probability of losing on the first roll? $\boxed{\frac{1}{9}}$

4. We see examples of probability every day. Weather forecasts, stock market analyses, contests, children's games, television game shows, and gambling all involve ideas of probability. If you are beginning to play a game of Monopoly™, what space are you most likely to land on with your first roll of the dice?
$\boxed{\text{Chance, since the most likely number to roll is 7}}$

10.2 Probability Models

1 Find $P(\overline{A})$ if $P(A) = 0.6$ $\boxed{0.4}$
2. Three fair coins are tossed. What is the probability that at least one is a head? $\boxed{\frac{7}{8}}$
3. What is the probability of obtaining a sum that is at least 7 when rolling a pair of dice? $\boxed{\frac{21}{36} = \frac{7}{12}}$
4.[*] One roulette system is to bet $1 on black. If black comes up on the first spin of the wheel, you win $1 and the game is over. If black does not come up, double your bet ($2). If you win, the game is over and your net winnings for two spins is still $1 (show this). If black does not come up, double your bet again ($4). If you win, the game is over and your net winnings for three spins is still $1 (show this). Continue this doubling procedure until you eventually win; in every case your net winnings amount to $1 (show this). What is the fallacy with this betting system?
$\boxed{\text{The betting limit imposed on the game}}$
5. [†]Suppose you like to bet on a silly card game. If you and a friend each select a card, the card with the higher value wins. If you bet 25¢ and win, you stop playing. On the other hand, if you lose, you raise

---

[*]You do not need to know anything about roulette to answer this question.
[†]You do not need to know anything about cards to answer this question.

your bet to 50¢. If you win, you stop playing with winnings of 25¢, ($-\$0.25 + \$0.50 = \$0.25$). If you lose, you raise your bet to \$1.00. If you continue with this process, eventually you will stop with a net gain of 25¢. What is the fallacy with the betting system?
At some point, your friend will decide to stop and at that point you will have a net loss.

10.3 Odds and Conditional Probability

1. Find the odds in favor of the events whose probabilities are given.
   a. $P(E) = \frac{1}{2}$ 1 to 1 **b.** $P(E) = \frac{3}{4}$ 3 to 1
   c. $P(E) = 0.3$ 3 to 7 **d.** $P(E) = 0.04$ 1 to 24
2. Find the probabilities whose odds are given.
   a. Odds against are 100 to 1 $\frac{1}{101}$
   b. Odds against are 10,000 to 1 $\frac{1}{10{,}001}$
   c. Odds in favor are 3 to 2 $\frac{3}{5}$
   d. Odds in favor are 10,000 to 1 $\frac{10{,}000}{10{,}001}$
3. What are the odds against flipping a coin three times and obtaining heads all three times? 7 to 1
4. Consider the following table showing the results of a survey of TV network executives asking their opinion of current programming.

	Satisfied, S	Not satisfied, $\overline{S}$	Total
NBC, N	18	7	25
CBS, C	21	9	30
ABC, A	15	10	25
Total	54	26	80

Suppose one network executive is selected at random. Find the indicated probabilities (rounded to the nearest hundredth).
   a. What is the probability that it is an NBC executive?
   $P(N) = \frac{25}{80} \approx 0.31$
   b. What is the probability that the selected person is satisfied?
   $P(S) = \frac{54}{80} \approx 0.68$
   c. What is the probability the selected person is from CBS if we know the person is satisfied with current programming?
   $P(C \mid S) = \frac{21}{54} \approx 0.39$
   d. What is the probability the selected person is satisfied, if we know the person is from CBS?
   $P(S \mid C) = \frac{21}{30} = 0.70$

10.4 Mathematical Expectation

1. What is the expectation for the \$1 bets on a U.S. roulette wheel?

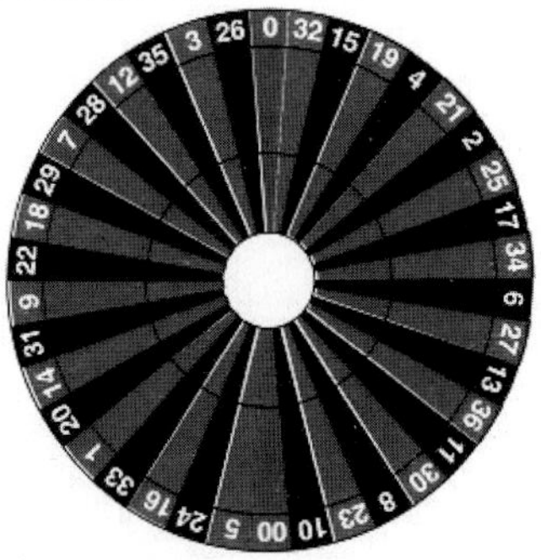

   See Figure 10.5 on page 206.
   a. Black $-\$0.05$
   b. Single-number bet $-\$0.05$
   c. Three-number bet $-\$0.05$
   d. Five-number bet $-\$0.08$
2. Suppose that you roll two dice. You will be paid \$5 if you roll a double. You will not receive anything for any other outcome. How much should you be willing to pay for the privilege of rolling the dice? \$0.83
3. A game involves drawing a single card from an ordinary deck. If an ace is drawn, you receive 50¢; if a heart is drawn, you receive 25¢; if the queen of spades is drawn, you receive \$1. If the cost of playing is 10¢, should you play?
   $E \approx \$0.02$; yes, you should play the game.
4. A company held a contest, and the following information was included in the fine print:

$ WIN$ WIN$		
PRIZE	NUMBER OF PRIZES	PROBABILITY OF WINNING INDICATED PRIZE
$10,000	13	0.000005
$1,000	52	0.00002
$100	520	0.0002
$10	28,900	0.010886
TOTAL	29,485	0.011111

$E \approx 0.19886$ or about $0.20

Read this information carefully, and calculate the expectation (to the nearest cent) for this contest.

10.5 Frequency Distributions and Graphs

1. Consider the given line graph.

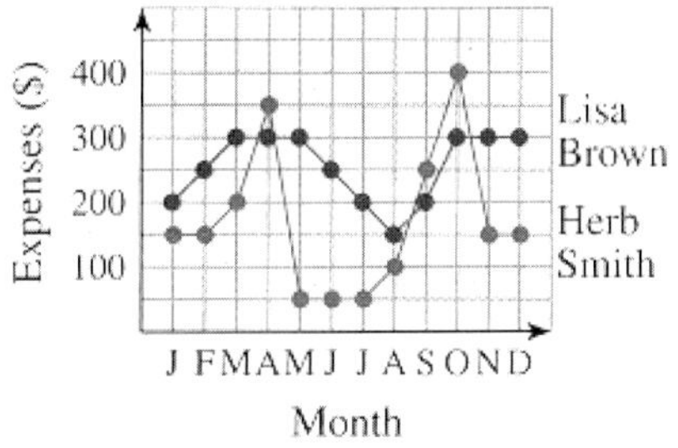

Expenses for two sales people of the Leadwell Pencil Company

a. During which month did Herb incur the most expenses? October

b. During which month did Lisa incur the least expenses? August

2. Consider the given bar graph.

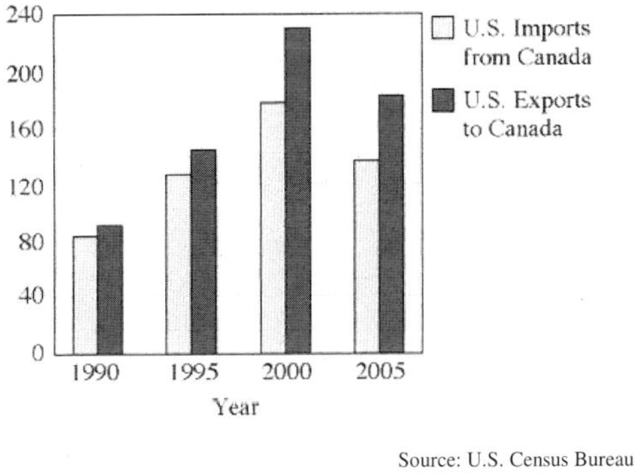

U.S. trade with Canada

a. What is being illustrated in this graph? U.S. trade with Canada for 1990-2005

b. Did the United States have more imports or exports for the years 1990-2005? more imports

3. The amount of electricity used in a typical all-electric home is shown in the given circle graph.

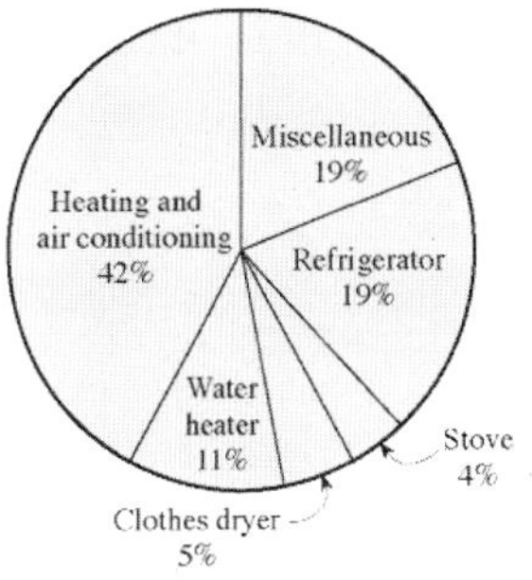

Home electricity usage

If, in a certain month, a home used 1,100 kWh (kilowatt-hours), find the amounts of electricity used from the graph.

a. The amount of electricity used by the water heater 121 kWh

b. The amount of electricity used by the stove 44 kWh

c. The amount of electricity used by the refrigerator 209 kWh

d. The amount of electricity used by the clothes dryer 55 kWh

4. Consider the following data set: The temperatures (°F) at a particular location for 30 days are given.

57	50	58	45	49	50	53	52	43	55
39	53	50	49	57	45	49	40	47	55
52	58	50	44	59	54	51	49	43	54

a. Prepare a frequency distribution.

b. Draw a stem-and-leaf plot.

c. Draw a bar graph.

d. Draw a line graph.

5. The financial report from a small college shows the following expenses:

Salaries	$1,400,000
Academic	$68,000
Plant Operations	$196,000
Student activities	$31,000
Athletic programs	$50,000

TOTAL $1,745,000
Draw a circle graph showing this income.

10.6 Descriptive Statistics

1. Find the three measures of central tendency (the mean, median, and mode), the range, and standard deviation.
0, 1, 1, 2, 3, 4, 16, 21
[6; 2.5; 1] [21; 62.86; 7.93]

EXAMPLE 1 Central tendency and dispersion

1, 4, 9, 16, 25

Solution

$$\overline{x} = \frac{\Sigma x}{n} = \frac{55}{5} = 11$$ The mean is 11.

By inspection, the median is 9 and there is no mode.

Find the range, range $= 25 - 1 = 24$ and the mean, $\overline{x} = \frac{\Sigma x}{n} = \frac{55}{5} = 11$

Find the variance and standard deviation by using a calculator or by constructing a table:

Data values x	*Square of the deviation from the mean* $(x-\overline{x})^2$
1	$(1-11)^2 = (-10)^2 = 100$
4	$(4-11)^2 = (-7)^2 = 49$
9	$(9-11)^2 = (-2)^2 = 4$
16	$(16-11)^2 = 5^2 = 25$
25	$(25-11)^2 = 14^2 = 196$
Sum:	$\Sigma(x-\overline{x})^2 = 374$

Sample variance: $s^2 = \frac{\Sigma(x-\overline{x})^2}{n-1} = \frac{374}{5-1} = 93.5$

Standard deviation: $s = \sqrt{\frac{\Sigma(x-\overline{x})^2}{n-1}} = \sqrt{93.5} \approx 9.67$

□

2. The 2001 monthly cost for health care for an employee and two dependents is given in the following table.

Provider	Cost	Provider	Cost
Maxicare	$415.24	Kaiser	$433.50
Cigna	$424.77	Aetna	$436.11
Health Net	$427.48	Blue Shield	$442.28
Pacific Care	$428.05	Omni Healthcare	$457.86
Redwoods Plan	$431.52	Lifeguard	$457.94

Draw a box plot for the monthly costs of health care (ranked from lowest to highest).

3. The graph shows the distribution of scores on an examination.

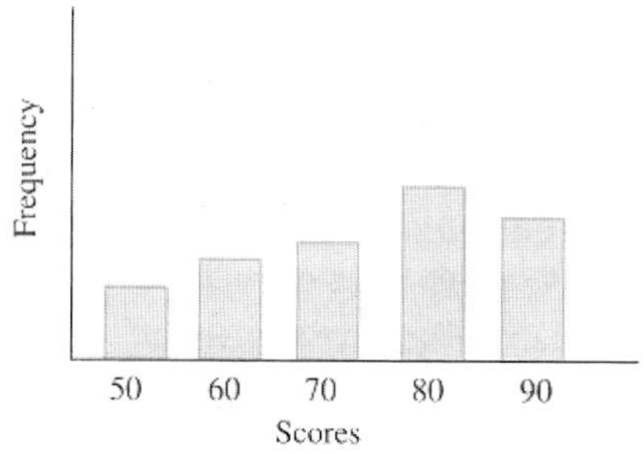

Scores on an examination

Which of the following statements is true about the distribution? [A]

A. The mean is less than the mode.
B. The median is the same as the mode.
C. The median is greater than the mode.
D. The mean is the same as the mode.

EXAMPLE 2 Statistical reasoning

Shoe size for a team of football players ranges from size 10 to 14. The majority of players wear size 12, and the number of players wearing size 11 is the same as the number wearing size 13. It is also true that the number of players wearing size 10 is the same as the number wearing size 14. Which statement is true about the distribution?

A. The median is less than the mode.
B. The mean is less than the mode.
C. The mean is the same as the median.
D. The median is greater than the mean.

Solution Since it is a symmetric distribution, we see the answer is C. □

4. Use the nutritional information about candy bars given in Table 10.1 to answer the questions.

Table 10.1 Nutritional Information about Popular Candy Bars

Company	Serving size (g)	Total size (g)	Calories from fat	Total fat (g)
Almond Joy	36	180	90	10
Baby Ruth	60	280	110	12
Butterfingers	42	200	70	8
Clark Bar	50	240	90	10
5th Avenue	57	280	110	12
Heath Bar	40	210	110	13
Hershey	43	230	120	13
Hershey w/alm.	41	230	120	14
100 Grand	43	200	70	8
Kit Kat	42	220	110	12
Milky Way	61	280	100	11
Mr. Good Bar	49	280	160	18
Nestle milk choc.	41	220	110	13
Nut Rageous	45	250	140	15
Peppermint Patty	42	170	35	4
Reese's Cup	45	240	130	14
Rolo	54	230	110	12
Snickers	59	280	120	14
3 Musketeers	60	260	70	8
Twix	57	280	130	14

a. What is the mean calories from fat? 105.25

b. What is the median (in grams) of total fat? 12

c. What is the mode (in grams) of the serving size? 42

d. Find the three quartiles for serving size. 42; 45; 57

e. Draw a box plot for the calories from fat.

f. What are the mean and standard deviation for total size in Table 10.1? mean = 238; std dev ≈ 35

10.7 It's Normal

Find the cumulative distribution, the mean, median, and mode.

1. The number of bedrooms of homes in a certain community is shown on the table below. Find the cumulative distribution, the mean, median, and mode.

Number of bedrooms	Percent	Cumulative
0	5%	5%
1	11%	16%
2	29%	45%
3	34%	79%
4	15%	94%
5	5%	99%
6 or more	1%	100%

2.62; 3; 3

2. Suppose that people's heights (in centimeters) are normally distributed, with a mean of 170 and a standard deviation of 5. We find the heights of 50 people.

a. How many would you expect to be between 165 and 175 cm tall? 34

b. How many would you expect to be taller than 168 cm? 33

c. What is the probability that a person selected at random is taller than 163 cm? 91.92%

d. What is the cumulative distribution?

3. The breaking strength (in pounds) of a certain new synthetic is normally distributed, with a mean of 165 and a variance of 9. The material is considered defective if the breaking strength is less than 159 pounds. What is the probability that a single, randomly selected piece of material will be defective? 2.28%

4. A package of Toys Galore Cereal is marked "Net Wt. 12 oz." The actual weight is normally distributed, with a mean of 12 oz and a variance of 0.04.
   a. What percent of the packages will weigh less than 12 oz? $\boxed{50\%}$
   b. What weight will be exceeded by 2.3% of the packages? $\boxed{12.4 \text{ oz}}$

11.1 Cartesian Coordinate System

1. *Using the seating chart in Figure 11.3, name the occupant of the seat given by the coordinates.*
   a. (5, 1) $\boxed{\text{Eva Mikalson}}$ **b.** (1, 2) $\boxed{\text{Terry Shell}}$
   c. (1, 5) $\boxed{\text{Hannah Becker}}$ **d.** (2, 1) $\boxed{\text{Beverly Schaap}}$
2. Plot the following coordinates on graph paper, and connect each point with the preceding one: (−2, 2), (−2, 9), (−7, 2), (−2, 2). Start again: (−6, −6), (−6, −8), (6, −8), (10, −8), (10, −6), (6, −6), (6, 0), (10, 0), (10, 2), (6, 2), (6, 16), (−2, 14), (−11, 2), (−9, −1), (−2, −1), (−2, −6), (−6, −6).
3. **a.** How many points lie on a line? $\boxed{\text{infinitely many}}$
   b. How many points do you need to plot in order to determine a line? $\boxed{2}$
4. Plot five points in each of which the second component is 2 less than the first component. Connect the plotted points.

11.2 Functions

1. Which of the sets are functions?
   a. {(1, 4), (2, 5), (4, 7), (9, 12)} $\boxed{\text{function}}$
   b. {(4, 3), (17, 29), (18, 52), (4, 19)} $\boxed{\text{not a function}}$
   c. {(5, 0)} $\boxed{\text{function}}$
   d. {1, 2, 3, 4, 5} $\boxed{\text{not a function}}$

Find the functional values requested in Problems 2-5.

2. $h(x) = 3x - 1$
   a. $h(0)$ $\boxed{-1}$ **b.** $h(-10)$ $\boxed{-31}$
3. $f(x) = x^2 + 1$
   a. $f(-3)$ $\boxed{10}$ **b.** $f(\pi)$ $\boxed{\pi^2 + 1}$
4. $F(x) = x^2 - t^2$
   a. $F(0)$ $\boxed{-t^2}$ **b.** $F(m)$ $\boxed{m^2 - t^2}$
5. $H(m) = 6t + 4m$
   a. $H(t)$ $\boxed{10t}$ **b.** $H(u)$ $\boxed{6t + 4u}$
6. Look at the last frame of the cartoon. What is the velocity when the rock hits the bottom of the well? $\boxed{512 \text{ ft/s}}$

11.3 Lines

1. Find three ordered pairs that satisfy each equation and then draw the line passing through those points.

EXAMPLE 1 Finding and graphing ordered pairs

$y = x + 5$

Solution The ordered pairs may vary.
If $x = 0$, then $y = 0 + 5 = 5$;
$x = 1$, then $y = 1 + 6 = 6$;
$x = 2$, then $y = 2 + 6 = 7$.

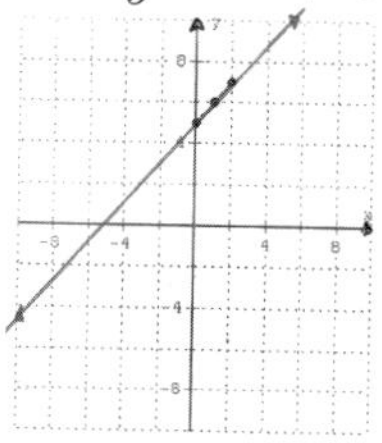

□

a. $y = 2x - 1$ **b.** $y = -3x + 1$
c. $y = 3x = 1$ **d.** $x + 2y = 4$

2. The cost, y, in dollars, for renting a car from a leasing firm is given by $y = 0.2x + 25$, where x is the distance driven, in miles. Graph this equation.

EXAMPLE 2 **Application graph**

If a present value P is invested at the simple interest rate r for t years, then the *future value* after t years is given by the formula $A = P(1 + rt)$. Suppose you invest \$10,000 at 8% simple interest per year. Graph this equation.

Solution

$$\begin{aligned} A &= P(1 + rt) \\ &= 10{,}000(1 + 0.08t) \\ &= 10{,}000 + 800t \end{aligned}$$

If $t = 0$, then $A = 10{,}000 + 800(0) = 10{,}000$;
$t = 2$, then $A = 10{,}000 + 800(2) = 11{,}600$;
$t = 10$, $A = 10{,}000 + 800(10) = 18{,}000$.

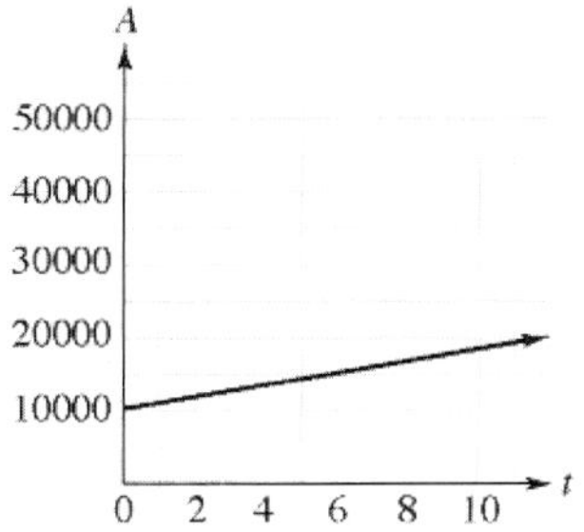

□

3. The water pressure, y, beneath the surface of the ocean is related to the depth, x, by the formula $y = 0.5x + 15$. Graph this equation.
4. The temperature, F, in degrees Fahrenheit, can be approximated by $F = \frac{1}{4}n + 40$ where n is the number of cricket chirps in a minute. Graph this equation for ordered pairs (n, F).

From *Nature* p. 738.

11.4 Systems and Inequalities

Solve the systems in Problems 1-2.

1. $\begin{cases} x + y = 5 \\ x - y = 1 \end{cases}$ $\boxed{(3, 2)}$

EXAMPLE 3 **Solve a system of equations**

$\begin{cases} 2x - y = 6 \\ 4x + y = 6 \end{cases}$

Solution

$\begin{cases} 2x + y = 1 \\ x - y = 5 \end{cases}$

Graph the two lines as shown:

Look for the intersection point; it is $(2, -3)$.

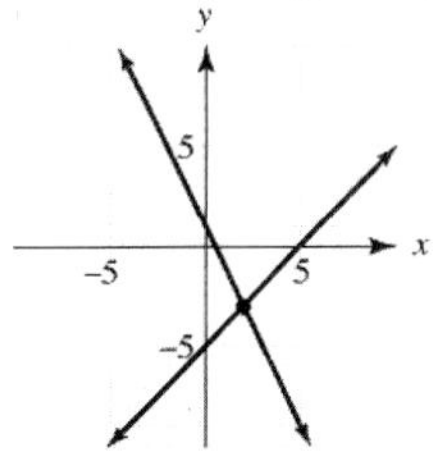

□

2. $\begin{cases} 2x + y = 1 \\ x - y = 5 \end{cases}$ $\boxed{(2, -3)}$

Graph the first-degree inequalities in two unknowns in Problems 3-4.

EXAMPLE 4 **Graphing an linear inequality**

$y > 5x - 3$

Solution

Graph the boundary line: $y = 5x - 3$.
It is dashed because the inequality does not include this boundary line.

Choose a test point, (0, 0), and substitute into the inequality:

$0 > 5(0) - 3$

$0 > -3$ True

Shade in the half plane that includes the test point:

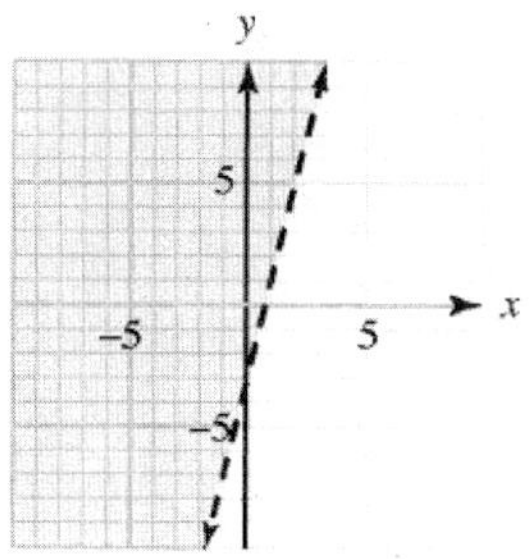

□

3. $y \leq 2x + 1$
4. $3x - 5y < 0$
5. Linda is on a business trip and must rent a car for the day. The car rental agency has the following options on the car she wants to rent: **Option *A***: \$30 plus 25¢ per mile (instead of \$40 and 50¢/mi); **Option *B***: Flat \$50 (instead of \$60) with unlimited mileage. Which option should she chose? [Option *A* if she drives less than 80 miles.]

11.5 Graphing Curves

1. Sketch the graph of each equation.
   a. $y = 3x^2$ **b.** $y = 2x^2 - 3$
2. Sketch the graphs of the equations in for nonnegative values of x.
   a. $y = 3^x$ **b.** $y = -\left(\frac{1}{10}\right)^x$
3. **a.** Graph $h = -\frac{144}{9}(t - 3)^2 + 144$.
   b. Does the parabola in part **a** open upward or downward? [downward]
   c. If we relate the graph in part **a** to the cannonball in Figure 11.18, can t be negative? [no]
   d. Draw the graph of the parabola in part **a** for $0 \leq t \leq 6$.
4. In archeology, carbon-14 dating is a standard method of determining the age of certain artifacts. Decay rate can be measured by half-life, which is the time required for one-half of a substance to decompose. Carbon-14 has a half-life of approximately 5,600 years. If 100 grams of carbon were present originally, then the amount A of carbon present today is given by the formula

$$A = 100\left(\frac{1}{2}\right)^{t/5,600}$$

where t is the time since the artifact was alive until today. Graph this relationship by letting $t = 5,600$, $t = 11,200, \ldots$, and adjust the scale accordingly.

12.1 Voting

1. In voting among three candidates, the outcomes are reported as:

(ABC)	(ACB)	(BAC)	(BCA)	(CAB)	(CBA)
8	4	3	0	2	5

Use this information to answer the questions.
   a. What is the total number of votes? [22]
   b. How many votes would be necessary for a majority? [12]
   c. What does the notation (CAB) mean?
   d. What does the "5" under (CBA) mean?
   e. If a person ranks A as their first choice, B as their second choice, and C last, how would this be written? [(ABC)]
   f. How many voters have this preference? [8]
2. In voting among three candidates, the outcomes are reported as:

(ABC)	(ACB)	(BAC)	(BCA)	(CAB)	(CBA)
8	4	3	0	2	5

Determine the winner, if any, using the indicated voting method.
   a. Majority rule [A]
   b. Plurality method [A]
   c. Borda count method [A]
   d. Hare method [A]
   e. Pairwise comparison method [A]
   f. Tournament method [A]
3. Twelve board members are voting on after-meeting activities, and they are asked to check any that they might like.

The outcome of their choices is shown here:

	1	2	3	4	5	6	7	8	9	10	11	12
Snacks	x	x	x	x	x	x		x	x	x	x	
Drinks	x	x		x	x	x		x		x	x	
Travel talk							x			x	x	
Speaker	x	x		x	x		x	x	x		x	x

What is the outcome using approval voting? [snacks]

4. Twelve people serve on a board and are considering three alternatives: A, B, and C. Here are the choices followed by vote:

(ABC)	(ACB)	(BAC)	(BCA)	(CAB)	(CBA)
2	4	2	1	2	1

Determine the winner, if any, using the indicated voting method.

a. Majority rule [none]
b. Plurality method [A]
c. Borda count method [A]
d. Hare method [A]
e. Pairwise comparison method [A]
f. Tournament method [A]

12.2 Voting Dilemmas

1. Metcalf Faculty Association is using the Hare method to vote for their collective bargaining representative. Their choices are the All Faculty Association (A), American Federation of Teachers (B), and California Teachers Association (C). Here are the results of the voting:

(ABC)	(ACB)	(BAC)	(BCA)	(CAB)	(CBA)
11	1	3	6	3	7

a. Which organization is selected for collective bargaining using the Hare method? [California Teachers Association]
b. Does the choice in part **a** violate the majority criterion? [no]

2. An election with three candidates has the following rankings:

(ABC)	(BCA)	(CBA)
5	4	3

a. Is there a majority? [no] If not, who wins the plurality vote? [A]
b. Who wins using the Borda count method? [B]
c. Does the Borda method violate the majority criterion? [yes]

3. Consider the following voting situation:

(ABC)	(ACB)	(BAC)	(BCA)	(CAB)	(CBA)
2	0	0	2	1	0

Notice that there is no winner using the majority or plurality rules.

a. Who would win in a runoff election by dropping the choice with the fewest first- place votes? [A]
b. Who would win if B withdraws before the election? [C]
c. Does this violate any of the fairness criteria? [yes]

4. The philosophy department is selecting a chairperson, and the candidates are Andersen (A), Bailey (B), and Clark (C). Here are the preferences of the 27 department members:

(ABC)	(BCA)	(BAC)	(CAB)
8	5	8	6

a. Who is the Condorcet candidate, if there is one? [A]
b. Is there a majority winner? [no] If not, who wins the plurality vote? [B] Does this violate the Condorcet criterion? [yes]

5. The Adobe School District is hiring a vice principal and has interviewed four candidates: Andrew (A), Bono (B), Carol (C), and Davy (D). The hiring committee has indicated their preferences:

(ACDB)	(CBAD)	(BCDA)	(DBCA)
7	5	3	2

a. Who is the winner using the plurality method? [A]
b. Suppose that Carol drops out of the running before the vote is taken.

Who is the winner using the plurality method? B

c. Do the results of parts **a** and **b** violate the irrelevant alternatives criterion? yes

12.3 Apportionment

1. Consider the following apportionment problem for College Town:
   North: 8,700
   South: 5,600
   East: 7,200
   West: 3,500

   Suppose each council member is to represent approximately 2,500 citizens. Use the apportionment plan requested assuming there must be 10 representatives.

	N	S	E	W
a. Adams' plan	3	2	3	2
b. Jefferson's plan	4	2	3	1
c. Hamilton's plan	4	2	3	1
d. Webster's plan	4	2	3	1
e. HH plan	4	2	3	1

2. Consider the following apportionment problem:
   North: 18,200
   South: 12,900
   East: 17,600
   West: 13,300

   Use the apportionment plan requested assuming there must be 26 representatives.

	N	S	E	W
a. Adams' plan	8	5	7	6
b. Jefferson's plan	8	5	7	6
c. Hamilton's plan	8	5	7	6
d. Webster's plan	8	5	7	6
e. HH plan	8	5	7	6

3. Consider the following apportionment problem:
   North: 18,200
   South: 12,900
   East: 17,600
   West: 13,300

   Use the apportionment plan requested assuming there must be 16 representatives.

	N	S	E	W
a. Adams' plan	5	3	4	4
b. Jefferson's plan	5	3	5	3
c. Hamilton's plan	5	3	5	3
d. Webster's plan	5	3	4	4
e. HH plan	5	3	5	3

12.4 Apportionment Paradoxes

1. Packard-Hue manufactures testing equipment at four locations, and has just hired 300 new employees. Those employees are to be apportioned using production levels at the four locations according to Jefferson's plan. The locations and production are as follows:

Atlanta:	12,520
Buffalo:	4,555
Carson City:	812
Denver:	947

   a. What is the standard divisor? 62.78
   b. What are the standard quotas?
   c. What are the lower and upper quotas?
   d. Find a modified divisor that will produce appropriate modified quotas totaling the 300 new employees. 62.4
   e. Does this violate the quota rule? no

2. The English enrollments at five high schools in the Santa Rosa Unified School District are as follows:

Elsie Allen:	154
Maria Carillo:	142
Montgomery:	165
Piner:	307
Santa Rosa:	231
TOTAL:	999

   Suppose that 45 copies of an important instructional video are to be allocated to the schools by using Hamilton's plan and the school population.

   a. What is the standard divisor? 22.2

b. What are the standard quotas?
c. What are the lower and upper quotas?
d. What are the allocations for the 45 videos?
e. What are the allocations for 46 videos?
f. Does this illustrate the Alabama paradox? no

3. The township of Bella Rosa is divided into two districts, uptown (pop. 16,980) and downtown (pop. 3,350), and is governed by 100 council members.
a. What is the standard divisor? 203.3
b. What are the standard quotas? up: 83.52; down: 16.48
c. How should the seats be apportioned using Hamilton's plan? up: 84; down: 16
d. Suppose the township annexes a third district (pop. 2,500). Using the standard divisor from part **a**, it was agreed that the new district should add 12 new seats. Carry out this new apportionment for the township using Hamilton's plan. up: 83; down: 17; new: 12
e. Does this example illustrate the new states paradox? yes

4. Suppose the annual salaries of three people are

Employee #1	\$43,100
Employee #2	\$42,150
Employee #3 (half-time)	\$20,000

a. What are their salaries if they are given a 5% raise, and then the result is rounded to the nearest \$1,000 using Hamilton's plan with a cap on the total salaries of \$111,000? #1: \$45,000; #2: \$45,000; #3: \$21,000
b. Suppose the salary increase is to be 6% with a cap of \$111,000. What are the salaries if they are rounded to the nearest \$1,000 using Hamilton's plan? #1: \$46,000; #2: \$44,000; #3: 21,000
c. If you compare parts **a** and **b,** are any of the paradoxes illustrated? Alabama paradox is illustrated.

Index

D

E

F

G

H

I

J

K

L

M

N

O

P

Q

R

S

T

U

V

WHY NOT MATH?

Since we began this book with a post 'em note that asked the question, "Why study math?" it seems appropriate that we end the book with a similar note asking, "Why not study math?" Mathematics is the foundation of all human endeavors. Historically, mathematics has always been at the core of a liberal arts education. I did not write this book to include what you need to "get to the next math course" but rather to those topics you will need for life outside of school and the classroom. I'm not sure which topics you and your instructor chose to investigate, but in retrospect it is appropriate to ask: "Did you find your study using the book worthwhile?" "Is there information that you will be able to use outside the classroom?" I'd appreciate hearing from you. My email address is smithkjs@mathnature.com.

K J Smith

reviewcard CHAPTER 1 THE NATURE OF NUMERATION SYSTEMS

Topic Summaries

1.1 Math Anxiety

If you avoid activities or projects involving math, you may have math anxiety. This book is designed to help math-avoiders succeed and even enjoy math. To improve your chances of success you should commit to attending each class, commit to daily work, read the text carefully, ask questions, and learn to focus on what you know, rather than what you don't.

1.2 What's the Problem?

In mathematics, we focus on sets of numbers. We begin looking at natural numbers and whole numbers. Addition, subtraction, multiplication and division are the basic operations of the whole numbers. The order of operations is parentheses, then multiplication and division, then addition and subtraction, all from left to right. The mathematician George Pólya developed a problem solving method. Remember the steps: 1) Understand the problem, 2) Devise a plan, 3) Carry out the plan, and 4) Look back. Exponential notation gives us a way of writing repeated multiplications of the same number. Exponential notation leads us to scientific notation, which we use to write large or small numbers.

1.3 Early Numeration Systems

Numbers are generally used to count objects. Numeration systems consist of symbols arranged according to basic sets of rules to represent numbers. The two basic types of numeration systems are simple grouping systems and the positional system.

1.4 Hindu-Arabic Numeration Systems

Our modern numeration system, the decimal numeration system, uses the Hindu-Arabic numerals, has ten digits, expresses larger numbers in terms of powers of ten, and is positional. The decimal point in this system is used to separate the whole parts of a number from the fractional parts.

1.5 Different Numeration Systems

The Hindu-Arabic system is a base 10 system. To change a base to base 10, write the numerals in expanded notation, then add them up to get the base 10 number. To change a base from base ten, we devised a plan using repeated divisions, saving the remainders.

1.6 Binary Numeration Systems

The binary numeration system uses only two symbols: zero and one. The relationship between the binary system and electrical systems was critical in the development of computer code.

1.7 History of Calculating Devices

This section provides an overview of how the first calculating devices gave birth to the machines we use today.

Learning Outcomes

Learning Outcomes

After reading chapter 1 you should be able to:

1. Know some of the symptoms and possible cures for math anxiety.
2. Use the order of operations agreement to simplify a numerical expression.
3. Know and use the problem-solving guidelines.
4. Write and use scientific notation.
5. Write a number in expanded notation.
6. Write an expanded number in decimal notation.
7. Convert from base b to base 10.
8. Convert from base 10 to base b.

Key Concepts

Order of Operations
Parentheses, **M**ultiplication and **D**ivision, **A**ddition and **S**ubtraction

Pólya's Method
Understand the problem; Devise a plan; Carry out the plan; Look back.

Decimal System
Ten symbols: 0, 1, 2, 3, 4, 5, 6, 7, 8, 9.

Binary System
Two symbols: 0, 1.

"The availability of low-cost calculators, computers, and related new technology has already dramatically changed the nature of business, industry, government, sciences, and social sciences." – NCTM Standards

Practice Problems

LO1 Know some of the symptoms and possible cures for math anxiety.

Symptoms vary, but may include those shown in Figure 1.1. One possible cure is breaking the cycle. Here are some hints: (1) Make a commitment to attend each class. (2) Make a commitment to daily work. (3) Read the text carefully. (4) Ask questions. (5) Direct your focus to what you can do instead of what you can't do. (6) Keep a mathematics journal.

For more on math anxiety, look back over topic 1.1. If you feel like you have a strong case of math anxiety, you should schedule a meeting with your instructor.

LO2 Use the order of operations agreement to simplify a numerical expression.

$2 \times (15 + 9) \div 3 - 7 \times 2$

$= 2 \times 24 \div 3 - 7 \times 2$	Parentheses first	
$= 48 \div 3 - 7 \times 2$	Multiplication	left to right
$= 16 - 7 \times 2$	Division	left to right
$= 16 - 14$	Multiplication	left to right
$= 2$	Subtraction	

If you have trouble following the order of operations, check out topic 1.2 or work some practice problems at **4ltrpress.cengage.com/math**.

LO3 Know and use the problem-solving guidelines.

Step 1 *Understand the problem.* Ask questions, experiment, or otherwise rephrase the question in your own words.

Step 2 *Devise a plan.* Find the connection between the data and the unknown. Look for patterns, relate to a previously solved problem or a known formula, or simplify the given information to give you an easier problem.

Step 3 *Carry out the plan.* Check the steps as you go.

Step 4 *Look back.* Examine the solution obtained. In other words, check your answer.

To review Pólya's method, check out topic 1.2. You can try out this method on problems at **4ltrpress.cengage.com/math**.

LO4 Write and use scientific notation.

$0.000035 = 3.5 \times 10^{?}$
↑

Step 1 Fix the decimal point.

Step 2 $0.000035 = 0\ 00003.5 \times 10^{?}$
↑ ↓

← 5 places to the left; this is −5

Step 3 $0.000035 = 3.5 \times 10^{-5}$

If you're having trouble following these steps, look over topic 1.2 or work some practice problems at **4ltrpress.cengage.com/math**.

LO5 Write a number in expanded notation.

$52{,}613 = 50{,}000 + 2{,}000 + 600 + 10 + 3$

$= 5 \times 10^4 + 2 \times 10^3 + 6 \times 10^2 + 1 \times 10 + 3$

If you're having trouble understanding this, look over topic 1.4 or try out some practice problems at **4ltrpress.cengage.com/math**.

LO6 Write an expanded number in decimal notation.

$4 \times 10^8 + 9 \times 10^7 + 6 \times 10^4 + 3 \times 10 + 7 = 490{,}060{,}037$

For more on expanded numbers, review topic 1.4 or try out some practice problems at **4ltrpress.cengage.com/math**.

LO7 Convert from base *b* to base 10.

1011.01_{four}

$= 1 \times 4^3 + 0 \times 4^2 + 1 \times 4^1 + 1 \times 4^0 + 0 \times 4^{-1} + 1 \times 4^{-2}$

$= 64 + 0 + 4 + 1 + 0 + 0.0625$

$= 69.0625$

For more on converting to base 10, review topic 1.5, or work problems at **4ltrpress.cengage.com/math**.

LO8 Convert from base 10 to base *b*.

Change 47 to a binary numeral.

0	r.1	There is one thirty-two.
2)1	r.0	There are zero sixteens.
2)2	r.1	There is one eight.
2)5	r.1	There is one four.
2)11	r.1	There is one two.
2)23	r.1	There is one unit.
2)47	← Start here.	

If you read down the remainders, you obtain the binary numeral 101111.

If you're having trouble following base conversions, you might look back over topic 1.5 or work some problems at **4ltrpress.cengage.com/math**.

***remember**

More practice problems are at 4ltrpress.cengage.com/math

reviewcard CHAPTER 2 THE NATURE OF NUMBERS

Topic Summaries

2.1 It's Natural

Chapter 2 begins by discussing the natural numbers. Be familiar with the ideas of a mathematical system and the closure, associative, commutative, and distributive properties.

2.2 Prime Numbers

You can find prime numbers based on their number of divisors—primes have exactly two. The operation of prime factorization is used to find prime factors of a given number; in other words, a list of only prime numbers that can be multiplied together to equal the given number. This can be done by creating a factor tree. When factoring numbers in a set, the greatest common factor (g.c.f.) is the largest number that divides evenly into each of the numbers in that set. The least common multiple (l.c.m.) of a set of numbers is the smallest number that each of the numbers in the set divides into evenly.

2.3 Numbers—Up and Down

With the introduction of the number zero and negative numbers, this topic discusses two new sets of numbers—whole numbers and integers. In examining division of integers, we come across the special case of division by zero. Since division by zero leads to certain absurdities, we determine that you can't divide by zero. We also discover cases of the division of two integers for which no single representative integer exists.

2.4 It's a Long Way from Zero to One

In the search for a closed set for division, we come across the set of rational numbers, which includes fractions. This topic discusses how the basic algebraic operations can be applied to fractions.

2.5 It's Irrational

The Pythagoreans discovered that if they constructed a square on each of the sides of a right triangle, the area of the largest square was equal to the combined areas of the smaller squares, leading to what is known today as the Pythagorean theorem: $a^2 + b^2 = c^2$. Working backwards, we can draw from this the notion of square roots. Not all square roots are rational numbers. The square roots of all numbers that aren't perfect squares are irrational. The irrational number π is the ratio of the circumference of any circle to its diameter.

2.6 Be Real

The set of real numbers is defined as the union of the set of rationals and the set of irrationals. You can use decimals to represent these numbers and use them to carry out the basic algebraic operations. This topic also discusses the creation of a number line and how different number sets can be represented on it. Finally we discuss the identity and inverse properties and their applications to the algebraic operations.

2.7 Mathematical Modeling

Real-world problems can be solved by developing mathematical models, which are mathematical frameworks build based on certain assumptions about the real world. Mathematical modeling involves four steps: abstraction, deriving results, making predictions, and gathering and comparing data. If an existing model does not accurately reflect the real world situation, additional data can be used to revise the model.

Learning Outcomes

Learning Outcomes

After reading chapter 2 you should be able to:

1. Simplify numerical expressions.
2. Find the prime factorization of a number.
3. Find the least common multiple and greatest common factor.
4. Know the definition of subtraction, multiplication, and division. Know why you can't divide by zero.
5. Work with various sets of numbers: natural, integers, rational, irrational, and real.
6. Work with closure, commutative, associative, identity, and inverse properties.
7. Answer questions based on real-world problems.

Key Concepts

Commutative Properties for Addition and Multiplication

$a + b = b + a$; $ab = ba$

Associative Properties for Addition and Multiplication

$(a + b) + c = a + (b + c)$;
$(ab)c = a(bc)$

Distributive Property

$a(b + c) = ab + ac$

Greatest Common Factor

The greatest common factor is the largest number that divides evenly into each of the numbers in a given set.

Least Common Multiple

The least common multiple is the smallest number that each of the numbers in a set divides into evenly.

Absolute Value

$$|x| = \begin{cases} x, & \text{if } x \geq 0 \\ -x & \text{if } x < 0 \end{cases}$$

Fundamental Property of Fractions $\frac{a \cdot x}{b \cdot x} = \frac{x \cdot a}{x \cdot b} = \frac{a}{b}$

Pythagorean Theorem

For a right triangle ABC, with sides of length a, b, and hypotenuse c, $a^2 + b^2 = c^2$.

Practice Problems

LO1 Simplify numerical expressions.

$$\frac{5}{24}+\frac{7}{30}=\frac{53}{120}$$

The denominators are 24 and 30, so we find the l.c.m. of these numbers.

$$24 = 2^3 \cdot 3^1 \cdot 5^0$$
$$30 = 2^1 \cdot 3^1 \cdot 5^1$$
$$\text{l.c.m.} = 2^3 \cdot 3^1 \cdot 5^1 = 120$$

$$\frac{5}{24} = \frac{5}{24}\cdot\frac{5}{5} = \frac{25}{120}$$ We are simply mutiplying each fraction by the identity 1, since $\frac{5}{5}$ and $\frac{4}{4}$ are both equal to 1.

$$+\frac{7}{30} = \frac{7}{30}\cdot\frac{4}{4} = \frac{28}{120}$$

$$\frac{53}{120}$$ The answer is in reduced form, since 53 and 120 are relatively prime.

If you have trouble following this example, you might review topic 2.1 or work some practice problems at **4ltrpress.cengage.com/math**.

LO2 Find the prime factorization of a number.

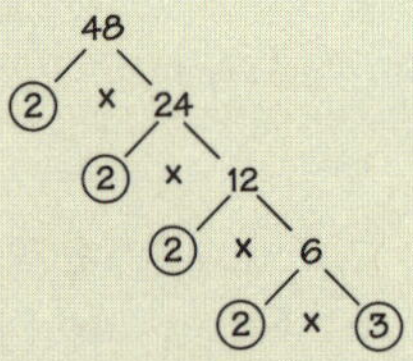

$$48 = 2 \times 2 \times 2 \times 2 \times 3 = 2^4 \times 3$$

If you need help with the prime factorization process, look back at topic 2.2 or find problems at **4ltrpress.cengage.com/math**.

LO3 Find the least common multiple and greatest common factor.

$$300 = 2^2 \cdot 3^1 \cdot \mathbf{5^2}$$
$$144 = \mathbf{2^4} \cdot 3^2 \cdot 5^0$$
$$108 = 2^2 \cdot \mathbf{3^3} \cdot 5^0$$
$$\textbf{l.c.m.} = 2^4 \cdot 3^3 \cdot 5^2 = 16 \cdot 27 \cdot 25 = 10{,}800$$
$$\textbf{g.c.f.} = 2^2 \cdot 3^1 \cdot 5^0 = 4 \cdot 3 \cdot 1 = 12$$

For more practice with these subjects, you can review topic 2.2 or work practice problems at **4ltrpress.cengage.com/math**.

LO4 Know the definition of subtraction, multiplication, and division. Know why you can't divide by zero.

$$a - b = a + (-b)$$
$$a \times b = \underbrace{b + b + \ldots + b}_{a \text{ addends}}$$
$$\frac{a}{b} = m \text{ means } a = bm\ (b \neq 0)$$

If you don't understand these operations, you might review topic 2.3 or work some practice problems at **4ltrpress.cengage.com/math**.

LO5 Work with the various sets of numbers: natural, integers, rational, irrational, and real.

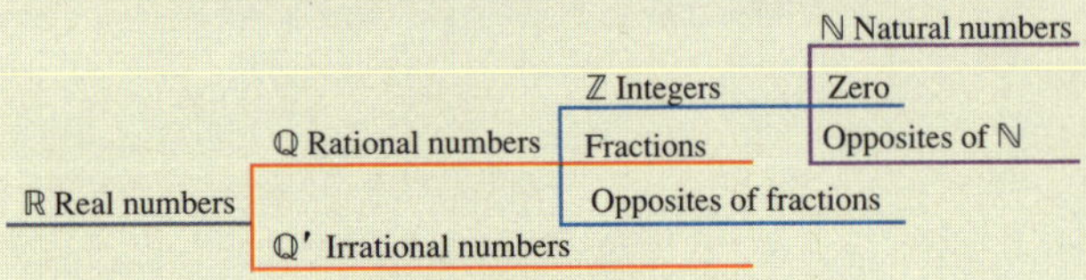

If you need help understanding number sets, you can look back over topics 2.1 and 2.3–2.6 and work practice problems at **4ltrpress.cengage.com/math**.

LO6 Work with the closure, commutative, associative, identitiy, and inverse properties.

Let us partition the set of natural numbers into two sets, E (even) and O (odd). Consider the operations of addition (+) and multiplication (×) in the set $\{E, O\}$. These operations can be summarized in table format:

+	E	O
E	E	O
O	O	E

×	E	O
E	E	E
O	E	O

Property	Addition	Multiplication
1. Closure	Yes	Yes
2. Associative	Yes We prove this by checking all possibilities (there are several).	Yes We prove this by checking all possibilities (there are several).
3. Identity	Yes, it is E.	Yes, it is O.
4. Inverse	Yes Inverse of E is E. Inverse of O is O.	No E does not have an inverse because $E \times ? = O$ has no value for "?".
5. Commutative	Yes The tables are symmetric with respect to the principal diagonal.	Yes The tables are symmetric with respect to the principal diagonal.

LO7 Answer questions based on real world problems.

reviewcard CHAPTER 3 THE NATURE OF ALGEBRA

Topic Summaries

3.1 Polynomials

Understanding the terminology of this algebraic system is essential. The polynomial is a fundamental notion of algebra. Polynomials can be multiplied using the FOIL method.

3.2 Factoring

A polynomial is said to be completely factored if the polynomial is converted to a product with the sum of the terms multiplied by their greatest common factor. The FOIL method and difference of squares provide two factoring strategies.

3.3 Evaluation

Evaluating an expression involves replacing specified variables with given values and then simplifying the resulting expression.

3.4 Equations

To solve an equation containing variables (open), find all replacements for the variable(s) that make the equation true. The two most common types of equations are linear and quadratic equations.

3.5 Inequalities

Based on the comparison property, we can relate two quantities using the inequality symbol. When solving a linear inequality, reverse the order of the inequality symbol when you multiply or divide by a negative number.

3.6 Problem Solving

The procedure for problem solving includes the following steps: 1) Understand the problem, 2) Devise a plan, 3) Carry out the plan, and 4) Look back.

3.7 Ratios and Proportions

Ratios are a way of comparing two numbers or quantities, and proportions are statements of equality between two ratios. When solving for proportions you can think in terms of dividing the cross-product by the number opposite the unknown.

3.8 Percents

The percent is the ratio of a given number to 100. Percents can also be written as decimals by moving the decimal point two places to the left.

3.9 Modeling Uncategorized Problems

Most real-world problems involve several variables and insufficient, superfluous, or inconsistent information. Often additional research might be needed to find an answer, or you might need to identify information that is unnecessary.

Learning Outcomes

Learning Outcomes

After reading chapter 3 you should be able to:

1. **Simplify** a given expression.
2. **Factor** a given expression.
3. **Evaluate** a given expression.
4. **Solve** a given equation or inequality.
5. **Answer** questions based on real-world problems.

Key Concepts

FOIL

First terms + Outer terms + Inner terms + Last terms

Difference of Squares

$a^2 - b^2 = (a - b)(a + b)$

Linear Equations

$ax + b = 0 \ (a \neq 0)$

Quadratic Equations

$ax^2 + bx + c = 0 \ (a \neq 0)$

Quadratic Formula

If $ax^2 + bx + c = 0$, $a \neq 0$, then

$$x = \frac{-b \pm \sqrt{b^2 - 4ac}}{2a}$$

Zero Product Rule

If $A \cdot B = 0$, then $A = 0$ or $B = 0$, or $A = B = 0$.

Property of Proportions

If $\frac{a}{b} = \frac{c}{d}$, then $b \times c = a \times d$.

"Algebra is generous; she often gives more than is asked of her." – D'Alembert

Practice Problems

LO1 Simplify a given expression.

$$(x+2)(x^2+5x-2) = (x+2)(x^2) + (x+2)(5x) + (x+2)(-2)$$
$$= x^3 + 2x^2 + 5x^2 + 10x - 2x - 4$$
$$= x^3 + 7x^2 + 8x - 4$$

If you have trouble following this example, review topic 3.1 or work some practice problems at **4ltrpress.cengage.com/math**.

LO2 Factor a given expression.

$2x^2 + 7x + 6 = (2x \quad)(x \quad)$	First terms Last terms
$= (2x+3)(x+2)$	Check outer and inner terms.

If you have trouble understanding this process, review topic 3.2 or work some practice problems at **4ltrpress.cengage.com/math**.

LO3 Evaluate a given expression.

If $a = 1$, $b = 3$, $c = 2$, and $d = 4$, find T.

$$T = \frac{3a + bc + b}{c}$$
$$= \frac{3(1) + 3(2) + 3}{2}$$
$$= \frac{3 + 6 + 3}{2}$$
$$= \frac{12}{2}$$
$$= 6$$

If you have trouble following this example, review topic 3.3 or work some practice problems at **4ltrpress.cengage.com/math**.

LO4 Solve a given equation or inequality.

Linear equations: $ax + b = 0 \quad (a \neq 0)$

$3(m+4) + 5 = 5(m-1) - 2$	Given equation
$3m + 12 + 5 = 5m - 5 - 2$	Simplify (distributive property).
$3m + 17 = 5m - 7$	Simplify.
$17 = 2m - 7$	Subtract $3m$ from both sides.
$24 = 2m$	Add 7 to both sides.
$12 = m$	Divide both sides by 2.

Quadratic equations: $ax^2 + bx + c = 0$

$5x^2 + 2x - 2 = 0$	Given equation
$= \dfrac{-2 \pm \sqrt{2^2 - 4(5)(-2)}}{2(5)}$	Quadratic formula.
$= \dfrac{-2 \pm \sqrt{44}}{2(5)}$	Simplify.
$= \dfrac{-2 \pm 2\sqrt{11}}{2(5)}$	Fractor and simplify.
$= \dfrac{-1 \pm \sqrt{11}}{5}$	Fractor and simplify.

Linear inequalities: $ax + b < 0$, $ax + b \leq 0$, or $ax + b \geq 0$

$5x - 3 \geq 7$	Given inequality
$5x - 3 + 3 \geq 7 + 3$	Add 3 both sides.
$5x \geq 10$	Simplify.
$\dfrac{5x}{5} \geq \dfrac{10}{5}$	Divide both sides by 5.
$x \geq 2$	Simplify.

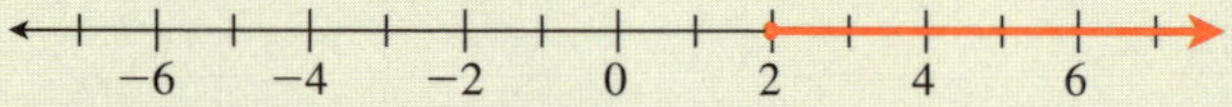

If you have trouble with these examples, look back at topics 3.4, 3.5, 3.7, and 3.8 or work some practice problems at **4ltrpress.cengage.com/math**.

LO5 Answer questions based on real-world problems.

We answer the question posed in the cartoon at the bottom of this page. Let x be the weight of the unpeeled banana. Then $x = \frac{7}{8}x + \frac{7}{8}$. Solve for x.

$x = \dfrac{7}{8}x + \dfrac{7}{8}$	Given equation
$8x = 7x + 7$	Multiply both sides by 8.
$x = 7$	Subtract $7x$ from both sides.

The banana weighs 7 oz.

If you're having a hard time understanding this solution, look back at topics 3.6 and 3.9 or work some practice problems at **4ltrpress.cengage.com/math**.

***remember**

More practice problems are at 4ltrpress.cengage.com/math

reviewcard CHAPTER 4 THE NATURE OF GEOMETRY

Topic Summaries

4.1 Geometry

Geometry can be separated into two categories: traditional (Euclidean) and transformational. Euclidean geometry is based on Euclid's five postulates. Transformational geometry examines the passage from one geometric figure to another by means of reflection, translations, rotations, contractions or dilations. Geometry is also concerned with relationships, such as congruence and similarity, between geometric figures.

4.2 Polygons and Angles

A polygon is a geometric figure with three or more straight sides. Three-sided polygons are called triangles, and four-sided polygons are called quadrilaterals. Angles are composed of two line segments with a common endpoint and are measured using units called degrees. Key relationships between angles include complementary, supplementary, alternate interior, alternate exterior, and corresponding angles.

4.3 Triangles

Every triangle has three sides and three angles. The sum of the angles of every triangle is 180°. Similar triangles occur when two angles of one triangle are congruent to two angles of the other. A right triangle has one angle of 90°.

4.4 Mathematics, Art, and Non-Euclidean Geometries

In a rectangle, the proportion $\frac{h}{w} = \frac{h}{(h + w)}$ is known as the divine proportion yielding a ratio of about 1.618:1—the golden ratio. Many have felt Euclid's fifth postulate is not so intuitively true as the other four and actually needs to be proven. Girolamo Saccheri made one of the earliest attempts, and he found this difficult, producing Saccheri quadrilaterals—rectangles with two right angles and two non-right angles. Nikolai Lobachevski explored this further based on the postulate that these two non-right angles were acute (denying Euclid's fifth postulate). Other geometries besides Euclidean geometry include Hyperbolic geometry (geometry on a pseudosphere) and Elliptical geometry (geometry on a sphere).

4.5 Perimeter and Area

This section discusses the notion of measurement, and when measuring, you must first determine how precise your measurements must be. The two major systems of measurement are the U.S. system and the metric system. The perimeter of a figure is the measure of the length of its outside edge or edges. For circles, the distance around the outside is called the circumference. The area of a figure is a measurement of how many square units will fit within the figure.

4.6 Surface Area, Volume, and Capacity

In this topic we look at measurement in three dimensions. Surface area refers to the sum of the areas of all the exterior faces of an object. Volume is a measure of how many cubic units will fit inside an object. One of the most common applications of volume is determining the amount of liquid a container holds, which we call capacity.

Learning Outcomes

Learning Outcomes

After reading chapter 3 you should be able to:

1. Be able to use the basic terminology of geometry.
2. Classify angles associated with parallel lines cut by a transversal.
3. Find/identify complementary and supplementary angles. Use the angles in a triangle property.
4. State and use the exterior angle property.
5. Understand and use the golden ratio.
6. Describe a Saccheri quadrilateral and its relationship to different geometries.

Key Concepts

Euclid's Fifth Postulate

Given a straight line and any point not on this line, there is one and only one line through that point that is parallel to the given line.

Angles in a Triangle

The sum of the measures of the angles in any triangle is 180°.

The Golden Ratio in Rectangles

$\frac{h}{w} = \frac{h}{(h + w)}$

Perimeter in a Polygon

the sum of the lengths of the sides of the polygon

Circumference of a Circle

$C = 2\pi r$

Area of a Rectangles and Squares

$A = lw, A = s^2$

Area of a Parallelogram

$A = bh$

Area of a Triangle

$A = \frac{1}{2}bh$

Area of a Circle

$A = \pi r^2$

Volume of a Cube and a Box

$V = s^3, V = lwh$

Practice Problems

LO1 Use the basic terminology of geometry.

Characterize the image as illustrating a translation, reflection, rotation, dilation, or a contraction.

© iStockphoto.com

This illustrates a reflection.

For more on the basics of geometry, you can review topic 4.1.

LO2 Classify angles associated with parallel lines cut by a transversal.

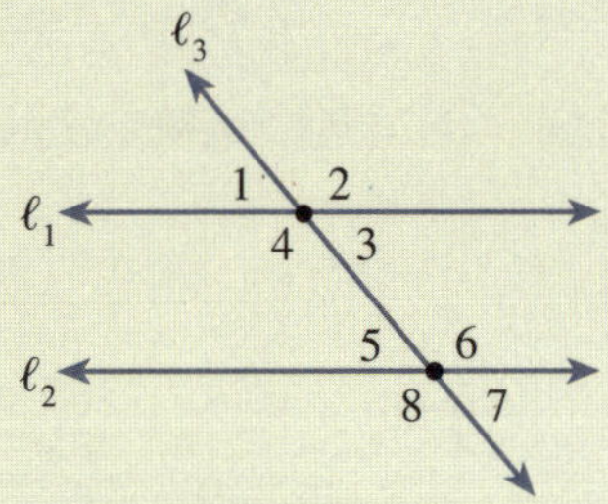

The **verticle angles** are: ∠1 and ∠3; ∠2 and ∠4; ∠5 and ∠7; ∠6 and ∠8.

The **alternate interior angles** are: ∠4 and ∠6; ∠3 and ∠5.

The **corresponding angles** are: ∠1 and ∠5; ∠2 and ∠6; ∠3 and ∠7; ∠4 and ∠8.

The **alternate exterior angles** are: ∠1 and ∠7; ∠2 and ∠8.

If you have problems understanding how these angles are classified, you might look over topic 4.2.

LO3 Find/identify complimentary and supplementary angles. Use the angles in a triangle property.

Find the measures of the angles of a triangle if it is known that the measures are x, $2x - 15$, and $3(x + 17)$ degrees.

$$\begin{aligned} x + (2x - 15) + 3(x + 17) &= 180 \\ x + 2x - 15 + 3x + 51 &= 180 \\ 6x + 36 &= 180 \\ 6x &= 144 \\ x &= 24 \end{aligned}$$

Now find the angle measures:

$x = 24$

$2x - 15 = 2(24) - 15 = 33$

$3(x + 17) = 3(24 + 17) = 123$

The angles have measures of 24°, 33°, and 123°.

For further discussion, review topic 4.3.

LO4 State and use the exterior angle property.

Find x.

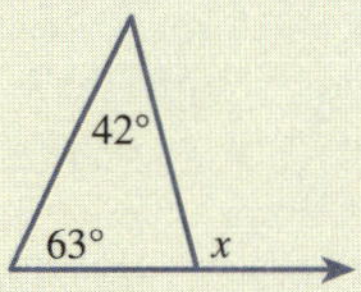

Sum of interior angles: $\overbrace{63 + 42} = x$ (Exterior angle)

$105 = x$

The measure of the exterior angle is 105°.

For more on this property, look back over topic 4.4

LO5 Understand and use the golden ratio.

If the Parthenon is 101 feet wide, what is its height (to the nearest foot) if we assume the dimensions are in a golden ratio?

Understand the Problem. First, understand the problem. Since the Parthenon is built to satisfy the golden ratio, the height h and the width w satisfy the following proportion:

$$\frac{h}{w} = \frac{w}{h + w}$$

Devise a Plan. The width is 101 feet,

$$\frac{h}{101} = \frac{101}{h + 101}$$

We will solve this equation for h.

Carry Out the Plan. There is only one unknown, which is written in variable form, so we now solve the equation for h:

$$h(h + 101) = 101^2$$

$$h^2 + 101h - 101^2 = 0$$

$$\begin{aligned} h &= \frac{-101 \pm \sqrt{101^2 - 4(1)(-101^2)}}{2(1)} \\ &= \frac{-101 \pm 101\sqrt{1 + 4}}{2} \\ &\approx 62.4 \end{aligned}$$

Disregard the negative solution, since distances are nonnegative.

Look Back. The Parthenon is about 62 feet high.

For more on the golden ratio, you might review topic 4.4.

LO6 Describe a Saccheri quadrilateral and its relationship to different geometries.

See topic 4.4 to review different geometries.

reviewcard CHAPTER 5
THE NATURE OF NETWORKS

Topic Summaries

5.1 Euler Circuits and Hamiltonian Cycles

The branch of geometry called graph theory deals with circuits, cycles, and trees. One of the most famous circuit problems was the Königsberg bridge problem, which was solved by the mathematician Leonhard Euler. In an Euler circuit, the goal is to travel on each edge of the network exactly once and then return to the starting vertex. The degree of each vertex is the number of edges that meet at that vertex. Euler's Circuit Theorem states that every vertex on a graph with an Euler circuit has an even degree, and the converse is true as well.

Euler circuits, however, do not address the travelling salesperson problem. For this we use a Hamiltonian cycle, in which we ask if we can visit each vertex only once and return to the original vertex. The sorted-edge method helps us identify an approximate solution to the travelling salesperson problem.

5.2 Trees and Minimum Spanning Trees

Topic 5.2 considers graphs that do not have circuits, which we call trees. One of the most basic examples would be a simple family tree. Another type of tree is a spanning tree, which is created from another graph by removing edges but maintaining a single path to each vertex. A minimum spanning tree is a spanning tree for which the sum of the numbers associated with the edges is a minimum. Kruskal's algorithm presents a procedure for constructing a minimum spanning tree.

5.3 Topology and Fractals

Topology is the study of space conceived as a set of points together with an abstract set of relations between the points. Topologically equivalent figures are figures that can be twisted, stretched, bent, shrunk, or straightened into the same shape. Two dimensional surfaces in a three-dimensional space are classified according to the number of cuts possible without slicing the object in two pieces. The number of such cuts that can be made to an object is called its genus (or more simply, the number of holes it has).

The four-color problem states that any map on a plane or sphere can be colored with at most four colors so that any two countries that share a common boundary are colored differently.

Fractals, invented by Benoit Mandelbrot, allow us to define objects with noninteger dimension (for example, a jagged line which has a fractional dimension between 1 and 2). Tesselations are another interesting mathematical construction which involve repeatedly manipulating basic polygons. The artist M.C. Escher has created many well known tessellations.

Learning Outcomes

Learning Outcomes

After reading chapter 5 you should be able to:

1. Decide if a network is traversable.
2. Examine a network and decide if there is an Euler circuit or a Hamiltonian cycle.
3. Determine if a given graph is a tree. Find a spanning tree and a minimum spanning tree given a graph.
4. Use Kruskal's algorithm.
5. Recognize and describe topologically equivalent figures.
6. Describe the four-color problem.
7. Describe fractal geometry.

Key Concepts

Euler's Circuit Theorem

Every vertex on a graph with an Euler circuit has an even degree, and if every vertex in a connected graph has an even degree, the graph has an Euler circuit.

Hamiltonian Cycle

A cycle which visits each vertex exactly once and returns to the starting vertex.

Tree

A tree is a graph that is connected and has no circuits.

Fractal dimension

$$D = \frac{\log N}{\log \frac{l}{r}}$$

"Mathematics is an aspect of culture as well as a collection of algorithms."
– Carl Boyer

LO1 Decide if a network is traversible.

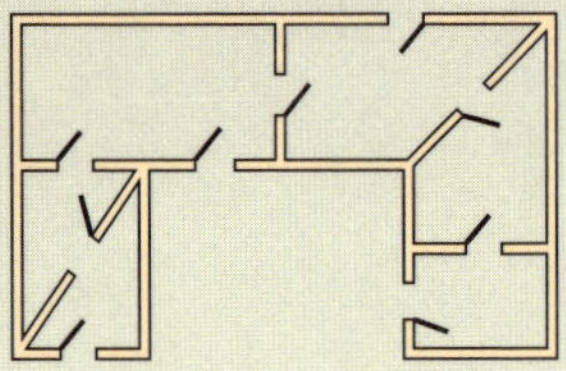

There are 7 rooms, including the exterior. There are two rooms with an odd number of doors, so begin in either of those rooms and end in a room with an even number of doors—it is possible.

Having trouble figuring this out? You might review topic 5.1.

LO2 Examine a network and decide if there is an Euler circuit or a Hamiltonian cycle.

Consider the following network.

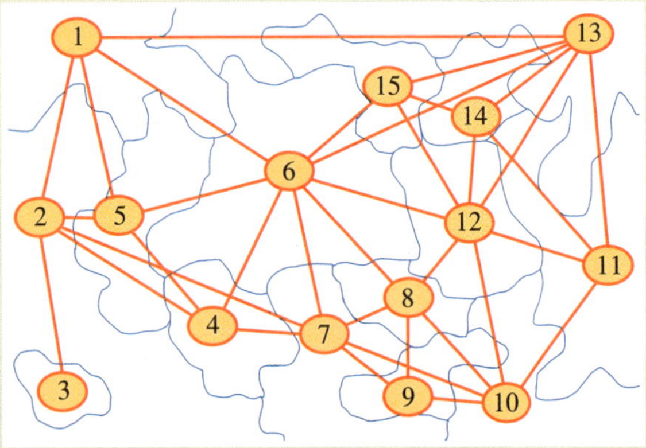

Is there a path that is an Euler circuit? Because the vertex 3 is odd, this cannot be an Euler circuit. Is there a path that is a Hamiltonian cycle? Yes, there is at least one possibility:

$3 \rightarrow 2 \rightarrow 1 \rightarrow 5 \rightarrow 4 \rightarrow 7 \rightarrow 8 \rightarrow 9 \rightarrow 10 \rightarrow 11 \rightarrow 12 \rightarrow 13 \rightarrow 14 \rightarrow 15 \rightarrow 6$

If you're not sure how Euler and Hamiltonian circuits work, look back over topic 5.1.

LO3 Determine if a given graph is a tree. Find a spanning tree and a minimum spanning tree given a graph.

Find two different spanning trees for the given graph.

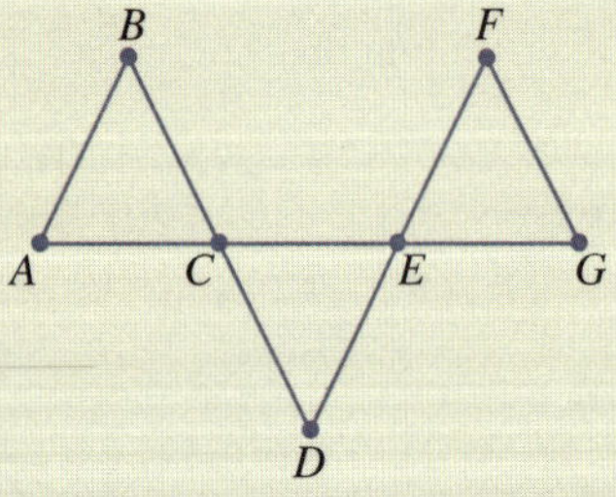

Since a spanning tree must have a path connecting all vertices, but cannot have any circuits, we remove edges (one at a time) without moving any of the vertices and without creating a disconnected graph. We show two different possibilities.

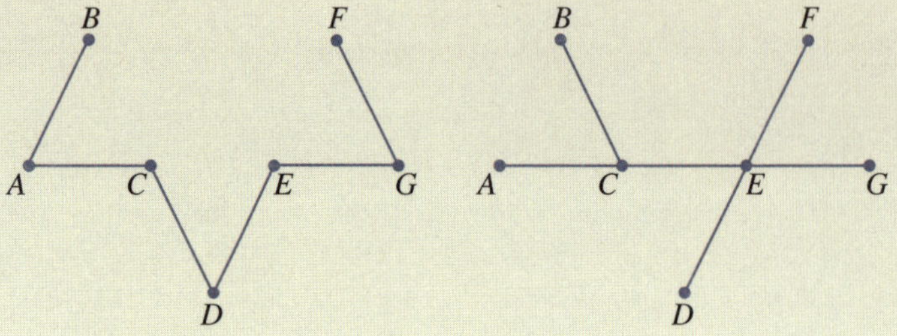

If you have difficulty following this example, review topic 5.2.

LO4 Use Kruskal's algorithm.

Use Kruskal's algorithm to find the minimum spanning tree for the weighted graph. The numbers represent hundreds of dollars.

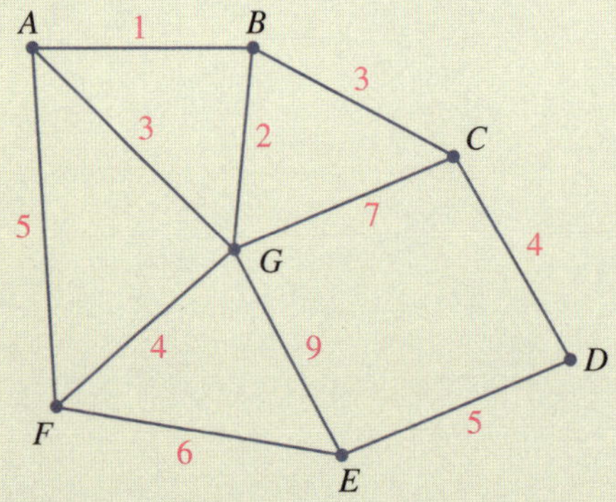

Step 1 Chose the side with weight 1.

Step 2 Chose the side with weight 2.

Step 3 Chose the side with weight 3. Do not connect *AG* because that would form a circuit. Continue with this process to select the two sides with weights of 4.

Step 4 When we connect the side with the next lowest weight, namely, *ED* with weight 5, we know we are finished because we now have a tree with all the vertices connected.

We can now calculate the weight of this tree:

$$1 + 2 + 3 + 4 + 4 + 5 = 19$$

Since those weights are in hundreds of dollars, the weight of the minimum spanning tree is $1,900.

For more on Kruskals' algorithm, check out topic 5.2 or work some practice problems at **4ltrpress.cengage.com/math**.

LO5 Recognize and describe topologically equivalent figures.

You can review the discussion on topology in topic 5.3.

LO6 Describe the four-color problem.

Try working some problems at **4ltrpress.cengage.com/math**.

LO7 Describe fractal geometry.

If you have trouble understanding fractal geometry, you might look back at topic 5.3.

reviewcard CHAPTER 6 THE NATURE OF GROWTH

Topic Summaries

6.1 Exponential Equations

When measuring growth and decay we will often need to use exponential equations and exponential notation. We will also often approximate two irrational numbers: π and e. You should know how to evaluate exponentials with a calculator. A logarithm represents an exponent. The statement $x = \log_b A$ should read as "x is the log (exponent) on a base b that gives the value A." A logarithm with base 10 is called a common logarithm and with base e is called a natural logarithm, denoted by $\ln x$. Evaluating a logarithm means finding a numerical value for the given logarithm. We can use the change of base theorem to evaluate a logarithm to some base other than 10 or e.

There are three types of exponential equations that we can solve: common log, natural log, and arbitrary.

6.2 Logarithmic Equations

The topic of this section is solving logarithmic equations. A logarithmic equation is an equation for which there is a logarithm on one or both sides. The Log of Both Sides Theorem is the key to solving logarithmic equations, and it states that $\log_b A = \log_b B$ is equivalent to $A = B$. There are basically four types of equations you will encounter in this book: 1) the unknown is the logarithm, 2) the unknown is the base, 3) the logarithm of an unknown is equal to a number, and 4) the logarithm of an unknown is equal to the log of a number. Sometimes you will have to do some algebraic simplification to put an equation in one of these forms. The three laws of logarithms (additive, subtractive, and multiplicative) will help you simplify logarithmic expressions.

6.3 Applications of Growth and Decay

We can use the exponential growth and decay formula in situations like populations, bank accounts, and radioactive decay where the rate of change is held constant. Growth implies positive rate and decay implies negative rate. For population examples, we could use this when we know growth rate or when we have population data. Radioactive substances have a negative rate. We often refer to them in terms of their half-life, or the time it takes them to decay to half their original amount.

Logarithmic scales use logarithms to make manage data by expanding small variations and compressing larger ones. One example is the Richter scale, which is used to measure the size of an earthquake. Another example of a logarithmic scale is the decibel rating used for measuring the intensity of sounds.

Learning Outcomes

Learning Outcomes

After reading chapter 6 you should be able to:

1. Use the definition of logarithm to simplify a logarithmic equation without using a calculator or computer.
2. Evaluate logarithmic expressions.
3. Solve an exponential equation.
4. Solve a logarithmic equation.
5. Solve applied growth and decay problems.

Key Concepts

π

irrational number; approximately 3.1416

e

irrational number; approximately 2.7183

Definition of a logarithm

$x = \log_b A$ means $b^x = A$

Common logarithm

$\log x$ means $\log_{10} x$

Natural logarithm

$\ln x$ means $\log_e x$

Change of Base Theorem

$$\log_a x = \frac{\log_b x}{\log_b a}$$

Fundamental Properties of Logarithms

$\log_b b^x = x$, $b^{\log_b x} = x \quad x > 0$

Log of Both Sides Theorem

$\log_b A = \log_b B$ is equivalent to $A = B$

Growth/Decay Formula

$A = A_0 e^{rt}$ where r is the annual growth/decay rate, t is the time (in years), A_0 is the amount present initially and A is the target (future) value.

"Mathematics abounds in bright ideas. No matter how long and hard one pursues her, mathematics never seems to run out of exciting surprises."
– Ross Honsberger

Practice Problems

LO1 Use the definition of logarithm to simplify a logarithmic equation without using a calculator or computer.

$$\log 1{,}000 + \ln e^{-2} - \log_6 36 = 3 + (-2) - 2 = -1$$

Does this example make sense? If not you might review topic 6.1 and look over some sample problems at **4ltrpress.cengage.com/math**.

LO2 Evaluate logarithmic expressions.

$$\log 945 + \ln 4{,}450 - \log_5 169 \approx 2.975 + 8.401 - 3.187 \approx 8.189$$

If you're having trouble evaluating logarithmic expressions, look back over topic 6.1 then work some practice problems at **4ltrpress.cengage.com/math**.

LO3 Solve an exponential equation.

Solve $216^{2x+1} = 36$

$216^{2x+1} = 36$	Given equation
$(6^3)^{2x+1} = 6^2$	
$6^{6x+3} = 6^2$	Properties of exponents
$6x + 3 = 2$	Log of both sides theorem
$6x = -1$	
$x = -\frac{1}{6}$	

Solve $6^{2x+1} = 46$

$6^{2x+1} = 46$	Given equation
$2x + 1 = \log_6 46$	Definition of logarithm
$2x = -1 + \log_6 46$	First, solve for the variable.
$x = \frac{-1 + \log_6 46}{2}$	This is the exact solution.
≈ 0.5684027	This is an approximation solution.

If you have trouble following these examples, you can find more on exponents in topic 6.1 and problems for practice at **4ltrpress.cengage.com/math**.

LO4 Solve a logarithmic equation.

Solve: $\log 15 + 2 = \log(x + 250)$

$\log 15 + 2 = \log(x + 250)$	Given equation
$2 = \log(x + 250) - \log 15$	Subtract log 15 from both sides.
$2 = \log\frac{x + 250}{15}$	Second law of logarithms
$10^2 = \frac{x + 250}{15}$	Definition of logarithm
$1{,}500 = x + 250$	Multiply both sides by 15.
$1{,}250 = x$	Subtract 250 from both sides.

Solve $\log 5 + \log(2x^2) = \log x + \log 15$

$\log 5 + \log(2x^2) = \log x + \log 15$	Given equation
$\log(2x^2) - \log x = \log 15 - \log 5$	Subtract $\log x$ and log 5 from both sides.
$\log\frac{2x^2}{x} = \log\frac{15}{5}$	Second law of logarithms
$\log(2x) = \log 3$	Log of both sides theorem
$2x = 3$	
$x = \frac{3}{2}$	

LO5 Solve applied growth and decay problems.

Phoenix, Arizona, had a population of 983,403 in 1990 and 1,321,045 in 2000. Predict the population in Phoenix in 2003. Compare this calculated number with the actual 2003 population of 1,388,416.

We use the growth/decay formula where $A_0 = 983{,}403$ and $A = 1{,}321{,}045$ for $t = 10$ (years).

$A = A_0e^{rt}$	Growth formula
$1{,}321{,}045 = 983{,}403e^{10r}$	Substitute known values.
$\frac{1{,}321{,}045}{983{,}403} = e^{10r}$	Solve for the exponential.
$10r = \ln\left(\frac{1{,}321{,}045}{983{,}403}\right)$	Definition of logarithm
$r = \frac{1}{10}\ln\left(\frac{1{,}321{,}045}{983{,}403}\right)$	Solve for the unknown, r.
≈ 0.029515936343	Calculator approximation

For 2003, we use the population in 2000 and calculate A using the above value for r:

$$A = A_0e^{rt} = 1{,}321{,}045e^{r(3)} \approx 1{,}443{,}356$$ Round to the nearest unit.

Thus, the predicted 2003 population is 1,443,356. Since the actual population, 1,388,416 is less than the predicted number, we conclude that the growth rate between 2000 and 2003 has decreased a bit from the growth rate in 1990–2000.

If 100.0 mg of neptunium-239 (^{239}Np) decays to 73.36 mg after 24 hours, find the value of r in the growth/decay formula for t expressed in days.

Since $A = 73.36$, $A_0 = 100.0$, and $t = 1$ (day), we have

$A = A_0e^{rt}$	Growth/decay formula
$73.36 = 100e^{r(1)}$	Substitute known values.
$0.7336 = e^r$	Solve for the exponential.
$r = \ln 0.7336$	Definition of logarithm
≈ -0.309791358	Approximate answer by calculator

Thus, the daily decay rate is approximately 31%.

reviewcard CHAPTER 7 THE NATURE OF MONEY

Topic Summaries

7.1 It's Simple

Applying mathematical principles and basic arithmetic skills can help us make intelligent decisions about how we use the money we earn. Interest, simply put, is money paid for the use of money. We earn interest when we let others use our money (such as with a bank deposit) and we pay interest when we use the money of others (for instance, on student loans). The simple interest formula tells us that the interest we owe (I) equals the present value of the loan (P) times the interest rate (r) times the length of time for which the money is borrowed (t).

7.2 Buying on Credit

Two types of consumer credit allow you to make installment payments. The first, called closed-end, is a traditional installment loan. The common method for calculating these types of loans is known as add-on interest, and you should be familiar with the installment loan variables and formulae. Two common applications of installment loans are car and home purchases. The annual percentage rate, or APR, is the rate paid on a loan when that rate is based on the actual amount owed for the length of time that it is owed.

7.3 Credit Card Interest

The second type of installment loan-based consumer credit is called open-end, revolving credit, or more commonly, a credit card loan. For credit cards, the stated interest rate is the APR, but it is often stated as a daily or monthly rate. The three basic methods of calculating these charges are the previous balance, adjusted balance, and average daily balance method.

7.4 Compound Interest

Most banks do not pay interest according to the simple interest formula. Instead they use compound interest, which means, after a period of time, they add your accrued interest to the principal and then calculate interest based on this larger amount. Most banks will compound interest either semiannualy, quarterly, monthly, or daily. We will need new variables for the number of times interest is calculated each year (n), the number of compounding period (N), and the rate per period (i). These are accounted for in the future value formula.

7.5 Buying a Home

Loan contracts for home purchases are called mortgages. If you violate the terms of the contract, the lender can foreclose, or take possession of the house. When you shop for a house, certain rates will be quoted, including the interest rate, the down payment, the origination fee, and discount points. The comparison rate formula can be used to calculate the combined effects of various fees. Monthly payments are calculated based on the length of the loan, the amount of the loan payment, and the APR. Once you know how much you can afford to pay on a monthly basis, you can calculate your Maximum Loan.

Learning Outcomes

Learning Outcomes

After reading chapter 7 you should be able to:

1. Use the formulas $A = P + I$ and $A = P(1 + rt)$ to calculate a missing value.
2. Use the simple interest formula to find principal, rate, or time.
3. Explain what APR means, and find it for a given loan.
4. Calculate the monthly finance charge for credit card transactions, using the previous balance, adjusted balance, and average daily balance methods.
5. Find future value and present value for compound interest.
6. Carry our home purchase calculations: down payment, points, comparable interest rate, monthly payments, maximum loan.
7. Answer questions based on real-world problems.

Key Concepts

Simple Interest Formula

$I = Prt$

Future Value (Simple Interest)

$A = P + I,\ A = P(1 + rt)$

Annual Percentage Rate (APR)

$$APR = \frac{2Nr}{N+1}$$

Future Value (Compound Interest)

$A = P(1 + i)^N$

Present Value Formula

$$P = \frac{A}{(1+i)^N}$$

Comparison Rate

$$\text{APR} + 0.125\left(\text{POINTS} + \frac{\text{ORIGINATION FEE}}{\text{AMOUNT OF LOAN}}\right)$$

Monthly Payment

$$\frac{\text{AMOUNT OF LOAN}}{1{,}000} \times \text{TABLE 7.2 ENTRY}$$

Maximum Loan

$$\frac{\text{MONTHLY PAYMENT YOU CAN AFFORD}}{\text{TABLE 7.2 ENTRY}} \times 1{,}000$$

Practice Problems

LO1 Use the formulas $A = P + I$ and $A = P(1 + rt)$ to calculate a missing value.

If $10,000 is deposited in an account earning 5.75% simple interest, what is the future value in 5 years?

$$\begin{aligned} A &= P(1 + rt) \\ &= 10{,}000(1 + 0.0575 \times 5) \\ &= 10{,}000(1 + 0.2875) \\ &= 10{,}000(1.2875) \\ &= 12{,}875 \end{aligned}$$

The future value in 5 years is $12,875.

LO2 Use the simple interest formula to find principal, rate, or time.

LO3 Explain what APR means, and find it for a given loan.

Consider a 2007 Blazer with a price of $28,505 that is advertised at a monthly payment of $631.00 for 60 months. What is the APR (to the nearest tenth of a percent)?

$$\begin{aligned} I &= Prt \\ 9{,}355 &= 28{,}505(r)(5) \\ 1{,}871 &= 28{,}505r \\ 0.0656376 &\approx r \\ \text{APR} &= \frac{2Nr}{N+1} \\ &= \frac{2(60)(0.065637607437)}{61} \\ &\approx 0.129123 \end{aligned}$$

The APR is 12.9%

LO4 Calculate the monthly finance charge for credit card transactions, using the previous balance, adjusted balance, and average daily balance methods.

Calculate the interest on a $1,000 credit card bill that shows an 18% APR, using the previous balance, adjusted balance, and average daily balance methods. Assume that you sent a payment of $50 on April 1 and that it takes 10 days for this payment to be received and recorded.

Previous:

$$\begin{aligned} I &= Prt \\ &= \$1{,}000\left(\frac{0.18}{12}\right) \\ &= \$15.00 \end{aligned}$$

Adjusted:

$$\begin{aligned} I &= Prt \\ &= \$950\left(\frac{0.18}{12}\right) \\ &= \$14.25 \end{aligned}$$

Average Daily Balance:

$$\begin{aligned} I &= Prt \\ &= \$966.67(0.18)\left(\frac{30}{365}\right) \\ &= \$14.30 \end{aligned}$$

LO5 Find future value and present value for compound interest.

Suppose that you want to take a trip to Tahiti in 5 years and you decide that you will need $5,000. To have that much money set aside in 5 years, how much money should you deposit into a bank account paying 6% compounded quarterly?

$$\begin{aligned} P &= \frac{A}{(1+i)^N} \\ &= \frac{5{,}000}{\left(1 + \frac{0.06}{4}\right)^{20}} \\ &\approx 3{,}712.3521 \end{aligned}$$

You should deposit $3,712.35.

LO6 Carry our home purchase calculations: down payment, points, comparable interest rate, monthly payments, maximum loan.

Suppose that your gross monthly salary is $2,500 and your spouse's gross salary is $2,000 per month. Your monthly bills are $800. The home you wish to purchase costs $178,000, and the loan is a 10% 30-year loan. How much down payment (rounded to the nearest hundred dollars) is necessary for you to be able to afford this home?

First, determine the monthly payment you can afford:

$$\$2{,}500 + \$2{,}000 - \$800 = \$3{,}700$$

You can afford 36% of this for the house payment:

$0.36(\$3{,}700) = \$1{,}332$ This is what you can afford.

Next, determine the Table entry for 10% over 30 years: 8.78.

$$\text{MAXIMUM AMOUNT OF LOAN} = \frac{1{,}332}{8.78} \times 1{,}000 \approx 151{,}708.43$$

DOWN PAYMENT $178,000 − $151,708 = $26,292.

LO7 Answer questions based on real-world problems.

You can find practice problems at **4ltrpress.cengage.com/math**.

*remember

More practice problems are at 4ltrpress.cengage.com/math

reviewcard CHAPTER 8 THE NATURE OF SETS AND LOGIC

Topic Summaries

8.1 Introduction to Sets

Sets are usually specified using either description or the roster method. With description, we describe the set so that we'll know what elements belong in it. With the roster method, we list all the objects (members or elements) in the set. Some common sets of numbers include the natural or counting numbers, whole numbers, integers, and rational numbers. The number of elements in a set is called its cardinality. The universal set is said to contain all elements under consideration in a given discussion. The empty set contains no elements.

8.2 Set Relationships

If every element of a given set is an element of another set, then the first set is called a subset of the second. The number of subsets of a set of size n is 2^n. Sets that have no common elements are disjoint. Sets with some elements in common are overlapping.

8.3 Operations with Sets

There are three common operations with sets: union, intersection, and complementation. The union operation, when applied to two sets, forms a set containing all elements of both those sets. The intersection of two sets is the set consisting of all elements common to both sets. The complement of a given set is the set of all elements in the universal set that are not in the given set.

8.4 Venn Diagrams

Venn diagrams are particularly useful when dealing with combined operations or several sets at the same time. They can also be useful in making general statements about sets. You should be familiar with Cardinality of Union, as it is essential to working with survey problems. Another rule, De Morgan's Law, is very important for use in set theory and logic.

8.5 Survey Problems Using Sets

You should be familiar with working survey problems with both two and three sets. First we will draw the overlapping sets, then label the regions. Then, using what we know about the elements in those sets, we can assign numbers for the elements in each region. Three-set problems are a little more involved and you can find the five step procedure for these on page 176.

8.6 Inductive and Deductive Reasoning

Logic provides us other methods of proving things, similar to our use of Venn diagrams to prove De Morgan's laws. Inductive reasoning is reasoning from the particular to the general. By observing more and more particular examples, you can make a better general statement about them. An example that contradicts your general statement is called a counterexample.

Deductive reasoning is a formal structure based on a set of unproven statements, called premises or axioms, and a set of undefined terms. Logic accepts no conclusions except those that are inescapable, due to its use of strict definition. If the conclusions do not meet this criteria, the reasoning is considered invalid. To avoid invalid forms of reasoning, we look at the form of the argument and not at the independent truth or falsity of each statement. One type of logic is called a syllogism, which provides a conclusion which we form based on two premises.

Learning Outcomes

Learning Outcomes

After reading chapter 8 you should be able to:

1. Distinguish between equal and equivalent sets.
2. Find subsets of a given set.
3. Distinguish among union, intersection, and complement of sets, their English translations, and symbols for denoting.
4. Draw Venn diagrams for unions, intersections, complements, and combinations of these operations.
5. Distinguish between inductive and deductive reasoning.
6. Know what is meant by a syllogism.
7. Answer questions based on real-world problems.

Key Concepts

Number of Subsets

2^n

Union

union of sets A and B is denoted by $A \cup B$

Intersection

intersection of sets A and B is denoted by $A \cap B$

Complement

the complement of set A is denoted by $\overline{A}$

Cardinality of a Union

$|X \cup Y| = |X| + |Y| - |X \cap Y|$

De Morgan's Laws

$\overline{X \cup Y} = \overline{X} \cap \overline{Y}$ and $\overline{X \cap Y} = \overline{X} \cup \overline{Y}$

Practice Problems

LO1 Distinguish between equal and equivalent sets.

Which of the following sets are equivalent? Are any equal?

{○, △, □}, {5, 8, 11}, {1, ⌈, ⊓}, {•, ⊙, ★}, {1, 2, 3}

All of the given sets are equivalent. Notice that no two of them are equal, but they all share the property of "threeness."

LO2 Find subsets of a given set.

Find the proper and improper subsets of $A = \{2, 4, 6, 8\}$. What is the cardinality of A?

The cardinality of A is 4 (because there are 4 elements in A).

There is one improper subset: {2, 4, 6, 8}. The proper subsets are: { }, {2}, {4}, {6}, {8}, {2, 4}, {2, 6}, {2, 8}, {4, 6}, {4, 8}, {6, 8}, {2, 4, 6}, {2, 4, 8}, {2, 6, 8},{4, 6, 8}

LO3 Distinguish among union, intersection, and complement of sets, their English translations, and symbols for denoting.

One question in a survey of 140 students asked the following questions:

☐ I'm enrolled in at least one math class.

☐ I'm enrolled in at least one English class.

a. Draw a Venn diagram showing the possible results of this survey.

b. If 50 students check the first box, what is the percent of the respondents taking math?

c. If 60 students check the second box, what is the percent of the respondents taking English?

d. If 20 check both boxes, what is the percent of respondents taking both math **and** English?

e. If 20 check both boxes, what is the percent of respondents taking math **or** English?

Solution

a. There are two sets, M = {students enrolled in at least one math class} and E = {students enrolled in at least one English class}. These sets are shown in the following figure.

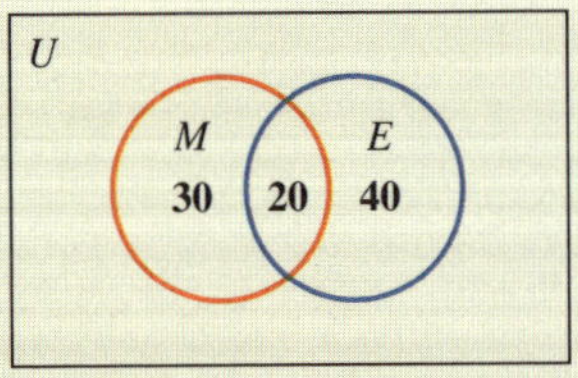

b. $|M| = 50$, so the percent is $\frac{50}{140} \approx 0.357$, or about 36%.

c. $|E| = 60$, so the percent is $\frac{60}{140} \approx 0.429$, or about 43%.

d. The word **and** means those in both sets, so $|M \cap E| = 20$, and the percent is $\frac{20}{140} \approx 0.143$, or about 14%.

e. The word **or** means in either of the sets, so $|M \cup E| = 30 + 20 + 40 = 90$, and the percent is $\frac{90}{140} \approx 0.643$, or about 64%.

LO4 Draw Venn diagrams for unions, intersections, complements, and combinations of these operations.

Illustrate $(A \cup C) \cap \overline{C}$ with a Venn diagram.

Solution First, draw $A \cup C$ (vertical lines). Next, draw $\overline{C}$ (horizontal lines). The result is the intersection of the vertical and horizontal parts, and is the portion shaded in color.

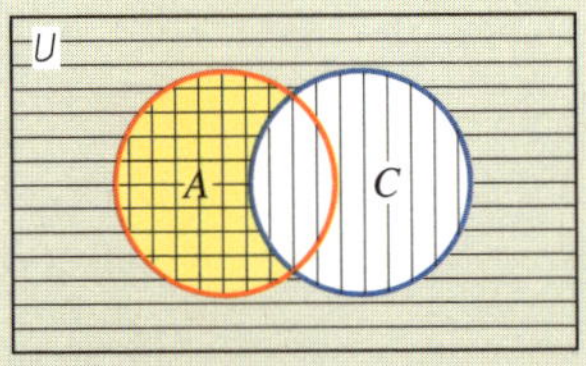

$(A \cup C) \cap \overline{C}$

LO5 Distinguish between inductive and deductive reasoning.

Does the following story illustrate inductive or deductive reasoning?

Q: What has 18 legs and catches flies?

A: I don't know, what?

Q: A baseball team. What has 36 legs and catches flies?

A: I don't know that either.

Q: Two baseball teams. If the United States has 100 senators and 50 states, what does…

A: I know this one!

Q: Good. What does each state have?

A: Three baseball teams!

LO6 Know what is meant by a syllogism.

LO7 Answer questions based on real-world problems.

*remember

More practice problems are at 4ltrpress.cengage.com/math

reviewcard CHAPTER 9 THE NATURE OF COUNTING

Topic Summaries

9.1 Permutations

Sometimes we run into problems for which we need to know "How many?" but can't figure this out by direct counting, like in the election problem, where we need to fill multiple offices in a club. The fundamental counting principle applies here, as it tells us the number of ways of performing two or more consecutive tasks. As we determine the different possibilities, we create ordered pairings of our various possible elements. If the order is important, we call these permutations. If it is not, we call them combinations. Factorial notation is a way of representing the multiplication of consecutive numbers counting down to 1. Some permutations situations involve permutations that are indistinguishable from each other, for which we use the formula for distinguishable permutations.

9.2 Combinations

The committee problem does not distinguish the order of the elements in the arrangement, as the election problem does. These are called combinations, and we have a formula for calculating the number of combinations. Pascal's triangle—Figure 9.3, with which you should be familiar—illustrates an important relationship between n and r in a combination arrangement.

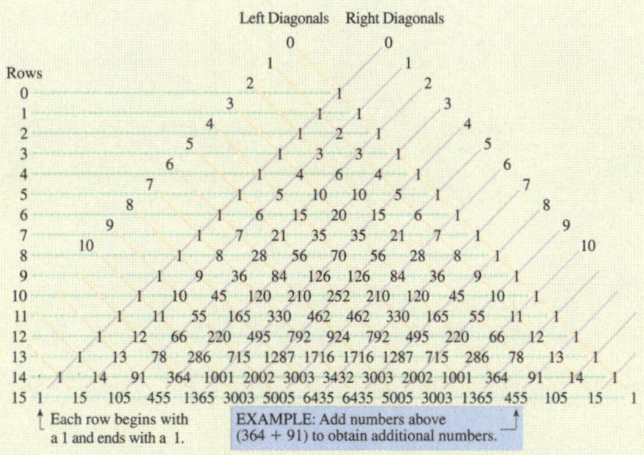

9.3 Counting Without Counting

There are many different ways of counting than just "one, two, three…". Table 9.1 sums up various counting methods. When presented with a counting problem, however, it will usually be up to you to figure out which method best applies to the situation. The principle of counting without counting becomes especially useful the more complicated the results become.

9.4 Rubik's Cube and Instant Insanity

The Rubik's cube and Instant Insanity are two famous puzzles that involve manipulating colored cubes. This topic explains the origins of these puzzles and how they work. It's up to you to go try them for yourself. Do you think you can figure them out?

Learning Outcomes

Learning Outcomes

After reading chapter 9 you should be able to:

1. Simplify expressions involving factorials, permutations, and combinations.
2. Decide if an applied problem is a permutation, combination, distinguishable permutation, or the fundamental counting principle.
3. Be able to carry out operations with a Rubik's cube.
4. Identify solutions to an Instant Insanity puzzle.
5. Answer questions based on real-world problems.

Key Concepts

Fundamental Counting Principle Task A followed by task B can be performed in $m \times n$ ways.

Permutation Notation

permutations of r elements selected from n elements: ${}_nP_r$

Factorials

$n! = n(n-1)(n-2)\cdot \ldots \cdot 3\cdot 2\cdot 1$; also $0! = 1$

Count-Down Property

$n! = n(n-1)!$

Permutation Formula

$${}_nP_r = \frac{n!}{(n-r)!}$$

Formula for Distinguishable Permutations

$$\binom{n}{n_1, n_2, \ldots, n_k} = \frac{n!}{n_1!n_2!\cdot \ldots \cdot n_k!}$$

Combination Formula

$$\binom{n}{r} = \frac{n!}{r!(n-r)!}$$

"There is no problem in all mathematics that cannot be solved by direct counting. But with the present implements of mathematics many operations can be performed in a few minutes which without mathematical methods would take a lifetime." – Ernst Mach

Practice Problems

LO1 Simplify expressions involving factorials, permutations, and combinations.

Evaluate:

a. $6! - 4! = 720 - 24 = 696$

b. $(6 - 4)! = 2! = 2$

Compare order of operations in parts a and b.

c. $\dfrac{100!}{98!} = \dfrac{100 \cdot 99 \cdot 98!}{98!} = 9{,}900$

This example shows that you need the count-down property even if you are using a calculator.

d. $\dbinom{50}{48} = \dfrac{50!}{48!(50 - 48)!} = \dfrac{50 \cdot 49}{2} = 1{,}225$

e. ${}_kP_4 = \dfrac{k!}{(k - 4)!}$

Do these examples make sense? If not, you might review topics 9.1 and 9.2 or work some practice problems at **4ltrpress.cengage.com/math**.

LO2 Decide if an applied problem is a permutation, combination, distinguishable permutation, or the fundamental counting principle.

a. A dispatcher is assigning cars to taxi drivers. There are eight possible cars and five drivers. In how many ways can the assignments be done?

b. How many permutations are there with the word MISSISSIPPI?

c. In how many ways can a full house of three tens and two queens be dealt?

Solutions

a. Five of the eight cars will be assigned to a driver, and since the car one receives could make a difference, the order of selection is important, so this is a permutation problem:

$${}_8P_5 = \frac{8!}{(8 - 5)!} = \frac{8!}{3!} = \frac{8 \cdot 7 \cdot 6 \cdot 5 \cdot 4 \cdot 3!}{3!} = 6{,}720$$

b. $\dbinom{11}{1,4,4,2} = 34{,}650$

c. Begin with the fundamental counting principle:

$$\boxed{\text{Ways of obtaining two queens}} \cdot \boxed{\text{Ways of obtaining three tens}}$$

Each of the numbers in each pigeonhole is a combination (since the order in which the cards are dealt is not important):

$$\overbrace{\binom{4}{2}}^{\text{Queens}} \cdot \overbrace{\binom{4}{3}}^{\text{Tens}} = \frac{4!}{2!2!} \cdot \frac{4!}{3!1!} = \frac{4 \cdot 3 \cdot 4}{2} = 24$$

If you would like to try out some problems like these, go to **4ltrpress.cengage.com/math**. For more on these topics, check out topic 9.3.

LO3 Be able to carry out operations with a Rubik's cube.

Remember that R, F, L, B, T, and U mean rotate 90° clockwise the right, front, left, back, top, and under faces, respectively. Use the standard Rubik's cube shown in Figure 9.5 as your starting point. Consider each clockwise rotation by first turning the cube so that the side you are rotating is facing you.

a. F **b.** B^{-1} **c.** F^2 **d.** RT

Solutions

a.

b.

c.

d.

LO4 Identify solutions to an Instant Insanity puzzle.

Determine whether each of the figures below will be a solution to an Instant Insanity puzzle.

a.

Solution: Yes

b.

Solution: No

LO5 Answer questions based on real-world problems.

reviewcard CHAPTER 10 THE NATURE OF CHANCE

Topic Summaries

10.1 It's Not Certain

The probability of an event is the likelihood that it will occur out of a particular number of mutually exclusive and equally likely ways. Unions and intersections help us find the probabilities of combinations of events.

10.2 Probability Models

If you add probabilities of successful outcomes and unsuccessful outcomes, probabilities whose sum is 1 are called complementary probabilities. The fundamental counting principle can show us the number of ways in which one specific outcome followed by a second specific outcome can be performed.

10.3 Odds and Conditional Probability

The odds of a given event occurring, in contrast to the probability, is calculated using the ratio of successes to failures (odds in favor) or the ratio of failures to successes (odds against). Further, if we know the probability, we can calculate the odds, and if we know the odds, we can calculate the probability. Conditional probability is the probability of an event occurring, given that another particular event has occurred.

10.4 Mathematical Expectation

This section introduces a variety of situations involving gambling and games of chance and how to analyze their value. You can calculate the expected value of a situation by multiplying the amount you could win by the probability of winning. A game is said to be fair if the expected value equals the cost of playing the game—a value of 0. If the expected value of a game is positive, you should play. If the expected value is negative, however, you should not play.

10.5 Frequency Distributions and Graphs

When dealing with large amounts of data, we can organize large batches of them into groups or classes. The number of values within a given class is its frequency. Frequency distribution is a tabulation of the frequencies of all the given classes. There are many different ways of representing data, including a stem-and-leaf plot, bar graphs, line graphs, circle graphs, and pictographs. You should be careful when using graphs, however, as they can easily be used to misrepresent data, depending on how they are constructed.

10.6 Descriptive Statistics

Averages or measures of central tendency include the mean, the median, and the mode. Mean is the quotient of the sum of the data divided by the number of data values. The median is the middle number when the data values are arranged in order by size. Mode is that value that occurs most frequently. When finding the mean of a frequency distribution, you are finding the weighted mean. Range is the difference between the largest and smallest numbers in a data set. The standard deviation is calculated as the square root of the variance of a given data sample.

10.7 It's Normal

Sometimes we represent frequencies cumulatively. A cumulative frequency is the sum of all preceding frequencies in which some order has been established. When we represent frequencies using a curve, two of the most common curves we encounter are bell-shaped curves and normal curves. z-scores can be used to translate normal curves into standard normal curves with a mean of 0 and a standard deviation of 1.

Learning Outcomes

Learning Outcomes

After reading chapter 10 you should be able to:

1. Define and understand the concept of probability.
2. Find probabilities by counting.
3. Find probabilities given the odds and the odds given the probability.
4. Know and use the fundamental counting principle.
5. Find conditional probabilities.
6. Find the mathematical expectation.
7. Use probability to make decisions.
8. Find the mean, median, mode, range, variance, and standard deviation.
9. Read and interpret bar graphs, line graphs, circle graphs, and pictographs. Draw an appropriate graph, given a data set.

Key Concepts

Probability

$$P(E) = \frac{s}{n} = \frac{\text{NUMBER OF OUTCOMES FAVORABLE TO } E}{\text{NUMBER OF ALL POSSIBLE OUTCOMES}}$$

Property of Complements

$P(E) = 1 - P(\overline{E})$ or $P(\overline{E}) = 1 - P(E)$

Fundamental Counting Principle

Task A followed by task B can be performed in $m \times n$ ways.

Mathematical Expectation

$E = a_1p_1 + a_2p_2 + a_3p_3 + \ldots$

Finding Expectation with a Cost of Playing

EXPECTATION $= ap - c$, where a is the amount to win, p is the probability of winning, and c is the cost of playing.

Mean

$$\bar{x} = \frac{\sum x}{n}$$

Weighted Mean

$$\bar{x} = \frac{\sum(w \cdot x)}{\sum w}$$

***z*-score**

$$z = \frac{x - \mu}{\sigma}$$

Practice Problems

LO1 Define and understand the concept of probability.

The formula for finding probability is $P(E) = \frac{s}{n}$, where s is the number of sucesses with n possible outcomes. The outcomes must be mutually exclusive and equally likely.

LO2 Find probabilities by counting.

Suppose that, in a certain study, 46 out of 155 people showed a certain kind of behavior. Assign a probability to this behavior.

$$P(\text{behavior shown}) = \frac{46}{155} \approx 0.30$$

LO3 Find probabilities given the odds and the odds given the probability.

Suppose the probability of an event is 0.45.

a. What are the odds in favor of the event?

b. What are the odds against the event?

Begin by finding $P(E)$ and $P(\bar{E})$ in fraction form.

$$P(E) = 0.45 = \frac{45}{100} = \frac{9}{20} \qquad P(\bar{E}) = 1 - \frac{9}{20} = \frac{11}{20}$$

a. The odds in favor of E are $\frac{P(E)}{P(\bar{E})} = \frac{\frac{9}{20}}{\frac{11}{20}} = \frac{9}{20} \cdot \frac{20}{11} = \frac{9}{11}$

b. The odds against E are $\frac{P(\bar{E})}{P(E)} = \frac{\frac{11}{20}}{\frac{9}{20}} = \frac{11}{20} \cdot \frac{20}{9} = \frac{11}{9}$

LO4 Know and use the fundamental counting principal.

What is a family's probability of having two boys and two girls, if it has four children? The fundamental counting principal tells us the number of possibilities is

$$2 \times 2 \times 2 \times 2 = 16$$

Thus, $n = 16$. To find s, we list the event (by using a tree diagram for four children) that brings success:

{BBGG, BGBG, BGGB, GBGB, GBBG, GGBB}

Since there are 6 elements in this set, we see that $s = 6$. Thus, the desired probability is

$$\frac{6}{16} = \frac{3}{8}$$

LO5 Find conditional probabilities.

Suppose that you draw two cards from a deck of cards. The first card selected is not returned to the deck before the second card is drawn. Let H = {the second card drawn is the heart}. $P(H \mid \text{a heart is drawn on the first draw})$. Since the first card is a heart, the number of remaining cards is $n = 51$, and $s = 12$ (because a heart was drawn on the first draw):

$$P(H \mid \text{a heart is drawn on the first draw}) = \frac{12}{51} \approx 0.235$$

LO6 Find the mathematical expectation.

Consider a game consisting of drawing a card from a deck of cards. If it is a face card, you win \$20. Should you play the game if it costs \$5 to play?

$$E = \overbrace{\$20}^{\text{Amount to win}} \underbrace{\left(\frac{12}{52}\right)}_{\text{Probability of winning}} - \overbrace{\$5}^{\text{Cost of playing}} \approx -\$0.38$$

You should not play this game.

LO7 Use probability to make decisions.

If you were asked to chose between a sure \$10 or a 1% chance of winning \$10,000, you should take the \$10 because it is a sure thing, and the ten thousand dollars will happen only one time out of a hundred.

Game #1: $E = \$10(1) = \$10$

Game #2: $E = \$10{,}000(0.01) = \$100$

Game #2 is better. The stated conclusion is false.

LO8 Find the mean, median, mode, range, variance, and standard deviation.

Suppose that Hannah received the following test scores in a math class: 92, 85, 65, 89, 96, and 71. Find s, the mean, median, mode, and standard deviation, for her test scores.

Mean: $\bar{x} = \frac{92 + 85 + 65 + 89 + 96 + 71}{6} = 83$

Median: The number of scores is even, so we take the mean of the middle entries: $\frac{85 + 89}{2} = 87$.

Mode: The mode is the most frequently occurring score, and since there is none, we say there is no mode.

We find the squares of the deviations from the mean and divide the sum by 5 (one less than the number of scores):

$$\frac{81 + 4 + 324 + 36 + 169 + 144}{6 - 1} = \frac{758}{5} = 151.6$$

We noted that this number, 151.6, is called the variance. We find the standard deviation.

$$s = \sqrt{\frac{758}{5}} \approx 12.31$$

LO9 Read and interpret bar graphs, line graphs, circle graphs, and pictographs. Draw an appropriate graph, given a data set.

reviewcard

CHAPTER 11
THE NATURE OF GRAPHS—THE MARRIAGE OF ALGEBRA AND GEOMETRY

Topic Summaries

11.1 Cartesian Coordinate System

Locating things on a map is a good example of the use of coordinates and coordinate systems. In a coordinate system, the x-axis is the horizontal axis and the y-axis is the vertical axis, separating the graph into four quadrants. We label points in the plane using ordered pairs, the first component giving the horizontal distance, and the second giving the vertical. Plotting points means showing the coordinates of the ordered pair by drawing a dot at the specified location.

11.2 Functions

Ordered pairs provide a useful way of representing relationships between sets of numbers. A function is a set of ordered pairs in which the first component is associated with exactly one second component. We can think of functions in terms of a function machine. If we input one item, the machine will output a single value. If we input 2 in the machine f, we think of the output as $f(2)$, which is called function notation. If the machine squares the input, we would say $f(x) = x^2$.

11.3 Lines

The process of graphing a line requires that you find ordered pairs that make an equation true. To do this, you must choose convenient values for x and use them to solve the given equation for y. There are three steps to graphing a line by plotting points. First, find two ordered pairs that lie on the line. Second, find a third ordered pair to check the line you found with your first two points. Third, draw the line (using a straightedge) passing through your three points. Two special types of lines are horizontal lines, which are parallel to the x-axis, and vertical lines, which are parallel to the y-axis.

11.4 Systems and Inequalities

When two equations are considered together we call them a system of equations. The point where they intersect on the graph is called their simultaneous solution. We can also use graphs to represent linear inequalities. Every line separates a graph into two half-planes and a boundary (which is the line itself). To graph inequalities, first graph the boundary, then choose a test point that is not on the boundary. If the test point makes the inequality true, then shade in that half-plane that contains the test point.

11.5 Graphing Curves

A cannonball, like all projectiles, does not travel in a straight line. It travels in a parabola. Notice that the parabolic curve in Figure 11.18 has a maximum height and is symmetric about a vertical line through that height. You can sketch many different curves by plotting points so long as you plot enough points so that you can draw a smooth curve. An exponential equation is one in which a variable appears as an exponent, and the graph of such an equation is called an exponential curve.

Learning Outcomes

Learning Outcomes

After reading chapter 11 you should be able to:

1. Plot points on a coordinate system.
2. Find the values of a function.
3. Graph a first-degree equation in two unknowns.
4. Solve a system of equations graphically.
5. Graph a first-degree inequality in two unknowns.
6. Sketch the graph of an equation with two variables that is not linear.
7. Sketch the graph of an exponential equation.
8. Answer questions based on real-world problems.

Key Concepts

Cartesian coordinates

(x, y)

Function notation

$f(x)$

"Algebra is but written geometry and geometry is but figured algebra."
— G.B. Halsted

Practice Problems

LO1 Plot points on a coordinate system.

LO2 Find the values of a function.

If you input each of the given values into a function machine named g, which first adds 2 to the input number and then multiplies by 5, what is the resulting output value?

$g(4) = (4 + 2) \times 5 = 30; g(-3) = -5; g(\pi) = 5(\pi + 2)$

LO3 Graph a first-degree equation in two unknowns.

Graph the line $x + 2y = 6$. Write $y = -\frac{1}{2}x + 3$.

If $x = 0$:

$$\begin{aligned} y &= -\frac{1}{2}x + 3 \\ &= -\frac{1}{2}(0) + 3 \\ &= 3 \end{aligned}$$

Plot the point (0, 3).

If $x = 2$:

$$\begin{aligned} y &= -\frac{1}{2}x + 3 \\ &= -\frac{1}{2}(2) + 3 \\ &= 2 \end{aligned}$$

Plot the point (2, 2).

And finally, a third (check) point. Plot the point (−2, 4). Draw the line through the plotted points.

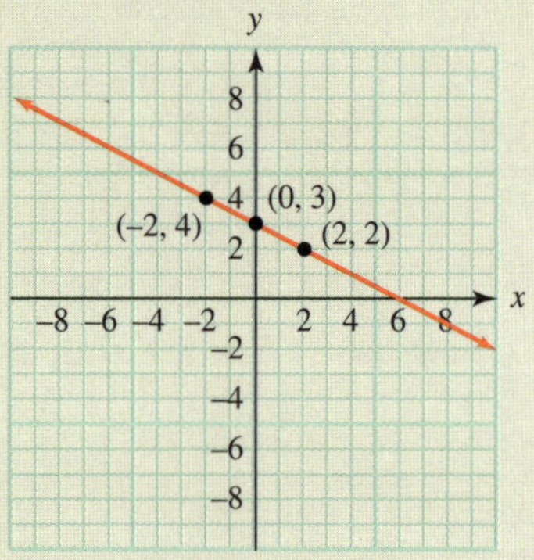

LO4 Solve a system of equations graphically.

Solve: $\begin{cases} x + 2y = 5 \\ 3x - y = 8 \end{cases}$ Graph both lines on the same coordinate axes.

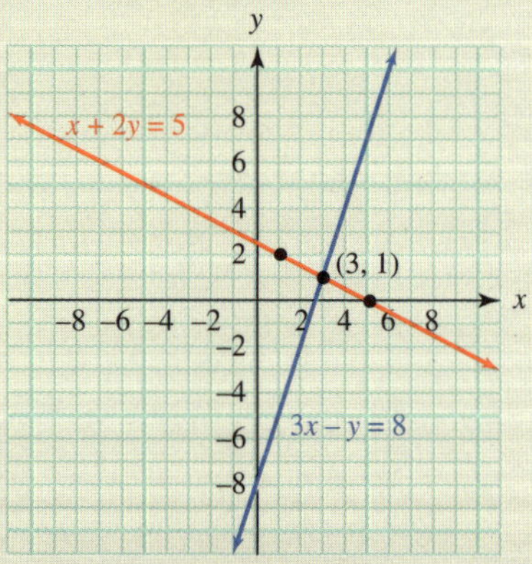

The solution to the system is (3, 1).

LO5 Graph a first-degree inequality in two unknowns.

Graph $y < x$. Note the boundary line is not included.

Step 1 Draw the (dashed) boundary line, $y = x$, as shown.

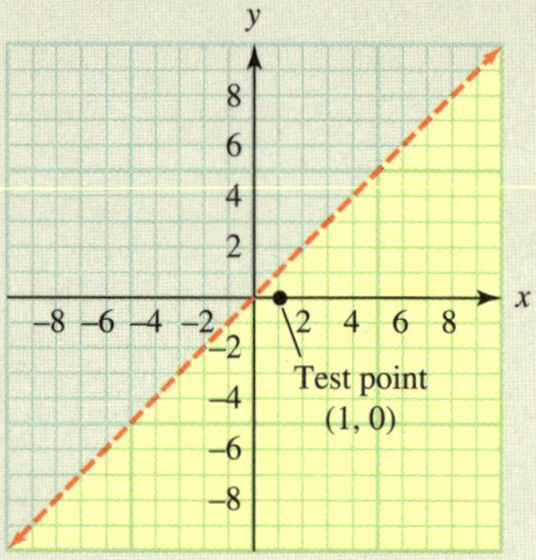

Step 2 Choose a test point. We can't pick (0, 0), because (0, 0) is on the boundary line. Since we must choose some point *not* on the boundary, we choose (1, 0).

$y < x$

$0 < 1$ Substitue coordinates for given point.

The inequality $0 < 1$ is true, so we shade the half-plane that contains the test point, as shown.

LO6 Sketch the graph of an equation with two variables that is not linear.

Sketch $x = y^2 - 6y + 4$. We use the same procedure to find points on the graph, except that in this equation we see that it will be easier to choose y-values and find corresponding x-values.

Let $y = 0$, then $x = (0)^2 - 6 \cdot 0 + 4 = 4$; plot the point (4, 0). Similarly plot (−1, 1), (−4, 2), (−5, 3), (−4, 4), (−1, 5), and (4, 6). Connect the points we have plotted to draw the curve.

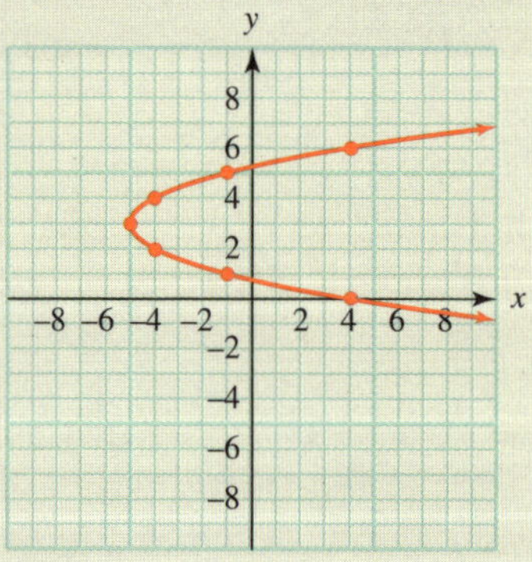

LO7 Sketch the graph of an exponential equation.

LO8 Answer questions based on real-world problems.

reviewcard CHAPTER 12 THE NATURE OF VOTING AND APPORTIONMENT

Topic Summaries

12.1 Voting

Social choice theory is the study of the different methods of selection using a vote. This section discusses different ways of counting a vote to declare a winner. Majority rule means that the winner is the one who receives more than 50% of the vote. The plurality method chooses the candidate with the most votes. In the Borda count, each voter ranks the candidates, and candidates are given a certain number of points based on their rankings. In the Hare method, votes are transferred from eliminated candidates to the remaining candidates. In the pairwise comparison method, voters are paired off two at a time and score points when they are chosen over their counterpart. In the tournament method, candidates face off, with the loser being eliminated and the winners facing new challengers until only one remains. In the approval voting method, voters can cast a single vote for as many candidates as they like.

12.2 Voting Dilemmas

Unlike with correctly formulated principles of mathematics, we often find exceptions to voting principles. This topic presents what we call the fair voting principles: the majority, Condorcet, monotonicity, and irrelevant alternatives criteria. As we demonstrate, each of the voting methods from topic 12.1 fails to follow at least one of these principles. The Borda count can violate the majority criterion. The plurality method violates the Condorcet criterion, as can the Borda count and the Hare method. Both the Hare method and the pairwise method can violate the monotonicity criterion. Finally, all of the voting methods can violate the irrelevant alternative criterion.

STOP *Make sure you understand HOW each of the voting methods does or does not satisfy each criterion.*

12.3 Apportionment

We examine five plans that have been used to apportion, or divide, the number of seats each state receives in the House of Representatives. Those plans are Adams's plan, Jefferson's plan, Hamilton's plan, Webster's plan, and Huntington-Hill's plan. In Adams's plan, any standard quota with a decimal point is rounded up. Jefferson's plan called for any standard quota with a decimal point to be rounded down. Hamilton's plan called for rounding down, but also required each standard quota to be at least 1, to ensure that each district received at least one representative. Webster's plan called for rounding based on comparing the arithmetic mean of the upper and lower quotas. Huntington Hill's plan called for rounding based on comparing the geometric mean of the upper and lower quotas.

12.4 Apportionment Paradoxes

Hamilton's plan can create a paradox when an increase in the total number of seats causes a state to lose seats. This is called the Alabama paradox. Hamilton's plan also creates the population paradox, in which a state with a faster population growth rate might lose seats to a state with a slower growth rate. The final paradox occurs when a new state is added, and an increase in the total number of seats results in a shift in the apportionment to the existing states. Balinski and Young's Impossibility Theorem declares that any plan that does not violate the quota rule will create paradoxes and vice-versa.

Learning Outcomes

Learning Outcomes

After reading chapter 12 you should be able to:

1. Conduct a vote using the majority rule, plurality method, and Borda count method.
2. Conduct a vote using the Hare method.
3. Conduct a vote using the pairwise comparison method.
4. Conduct a vote using the tournament and approval voting methods.
5. Discuss voting dilemmas including the majority criterion, Condorcet criterion, monotonicity criterion, irrelevant alternatives criterion, and Arrow's impossibility theorem.
6. Apportion a population using Adams's plan, Jefferson's plan, Hamilton's plan, Webster's plan, and HH's plan.
7. Discuss apportionment paradoxes including the quota rule, Alabama paradox, population paradox, and the new states paradox.
8. Answer questions based on real-world problems.

Key Concepts

Pareto Principle

If every voter prefers candidate X over candidate Y, then the group should choose X over Y under their voting method.

Standard Divisor

$$\frac{\text{TOTAL POPULATION}}{\text{NUMBER OF SHARES}}$$

Standard Quota

$$\frac{\text{TOTAL POPULATION}}{\text{STANDARD DIVISOR}}$$

Arithmetic Mean (A.M.)

$$\frac{(a+b)}{2}$$

Geometric Mean (G.M.)

$$\sqrt{ab}$$

Practice Problems

LO1 Conduct a vote using the majority rule, plurality method, and Borda count method.

Consider the following voting situation:

Choices:	(ABC)	(ACB)	(BAC)	(BCA)	(CAB)	(CBA)
No. of votes:	3	2	2	0	1	4

Who is the winner using the majority rule and the plurality method? We see the outcome is A: 5 votes $(3 + 2 = 5)$, B: 2 votes $(2 + 0 = 2)$, and C: 5 votes $(1 + 4 = 5)$. There is no majority winner, and there is no winner using the plurality method. The Borda count result for 12 votes is:

$$A: 3 \cdot 3 + 2 \cdot 3 + 2 \cdot 2 + 0 \cdot 1 + 1 \cdot 2 + 4 \cdot 1 = 25$$
$$B: 3 \cdot 2 + 2 \cdot 1 + 2 \cdot 3 + 0 \cdot 3 + 1 \cdot 1 + 4 \cdot 2 = 23$$
$$C: 3 \cdot 1 + 2 \cdot 2 + 2 \cdot 1 + 0 \cdot 2 + 1 \cdot 3 + 4 \cdot 3 = 24$$

A wins the Borda count.

LO2 Conduct a vote using the Hare method.

Consider the following voting situation:

Choices:	(ABC)	(ACB)	(BAC)	(BCA)	(CAB)	(CBA)
No. of votes:	3	2	2	0	1	4

Who is the winner using the Hare method?

We see that A received $5(3 + 2 = 5)$ first-round votes; B received 2 votes; and C received 5 votes. We hold a runoff election by eliminating the alternative with the fewest votes; this is choice B. For convenience, in this book we assume that a voter's order of preference will remain the same for subsequent rounds of voting. Thus, we now have the following possibilities, where we have crossed out candidate B.

Choices:	(A~~B~~C)	(AC~~B~~)	(~~B~~AC)	(~~B~~CA)	(CA~~B~~)	(C~~B~~A)
No. of votes:	3	2	2	0	1	4
	↓	↓	↓	↓	↓	↓

Choices:	(AC)	(CA)
No. of votes:	$3 + 2 + 2 = 7$	$0 + 1 + 4 = 5$

We now declare a second-round winner, A, using the *majority rule.*

LO3 Conduct a vote using the pairwise comparison method.

LO4 Conduct a vote using the tournament and approval voting methods.

LO5 Discuss voting dilemmas including the majority criterion, Condorcet criterion, monotonicity criterion, irrelevant alternatives criterion, and Arrow's impossibility theorem.

In the 2004 vote of the International Olympic Committee to select the site for the 2004 Olympics, there were five cities in the running: Athens (A), Buenos Aires (B), Cape Town (C), Rome (R), and Stockholm (S). Consider the following fictitious preference schedule:

Choices:	(ARSCB)	(BSRCA)	(CBSRA)	(RCSBA)	(SBRCA)	(SCRBA)
No. of votes:	36	24	20	18	8	4

a. Who is the majority/plurality winner?
b. Who wins the Borda count?
c. Who is the winner using the Hare method?
d. Who wins from the pairwise comparison method?
e. Suppose there is a runoff in which the top two contenders of the plurality method face each other. (What, you say . . . we have not previously considered this method! You are right, but we didn't want one of the cities to feel left out.)

Solutions

a. There are 110 votes so a majority is $110/2 + 1 = 56$ votes; there is no majority. The plurality winner is Athens (A) with 36 votes.
b. The Borda count winner is Rome (R).
c. There is no majority winner; the fewest first-place votes are for Stockholm, so the second-round vote eliminates Stockholm and Rome receives the least votes, so Rome is also eliminated. The third-round vote eliminates Buenos Aires. The final round vote eliminates Athens. The Hare method winner is Cape Town (C).
d. For the pairwise comparison method, there are $\frac{(5)(4)}{2} = 10$ matchups. The vote is (the details are left for you) A: 0 points, B: 1 point, C: 2 points, R: 3 points S: 4 points. Stockholm (S) is the winner from the pairwise comparison method.
e. A faces off against B: A: 36; B: $24 + 20 + 18 + 8 + 4 = 74$ Buenos Aires (B) wins the election.

LO6 Apportion a population using Adams's plan, Jefferson's plan, Hamilton's plan, Webster's plan, and HH's plan.

LO7 Discuss apportionment paradoxes including the quota rule, Alabama paradox, population paradox, and the new states paradox.

LO8 Answer questions based on real-world problems.